THE LETTERS AND
PROSE WRITINGS OF

WILLIAM COWPER

1750–1781

William Cowper

from an oil portrait (1792) by L. F. Abbott

THE LETTERS AND PROSE WRITINGS OF William Cowper

VOLUME I

Adelphi and Letters 1750–1781

EDITED BY

JAMES KING

AND

CHARLES RYSKAMP

OXFORD

AT THE CLARENDON PRESS

1979

Oxford University Press, Walton Street, Oxford OX2 6DP

OXFORD LONDON GLASGOW

NEW YORK TORONTO MELBOURNE WELLINGTON

KUALA LUMPUR SINGAPORE JAKARTA HONG KONG TOKYO

DELHI BOMBAY CALCUTTA MADRAS KARACHI

NAIROBI DAR ES SALAAM CAPE TOWN

Published in the United States by
Oxford University Press, New York

British Library Cataloguing in Publication Data

Cowper, William
The letters and prose writings of William Cowper
Vol. 1: on Adelphi and letters 1750–1781
I. Title II. King, James
III. Ryskamp, Charles
821'.6 PR3383.A44 78-40495

ISBN 0-19-811863-5

Printed in Great Britain
at the University Press, Oxford
by Eric Buckley
Printer to the University

PREFACE

AT the beginning of this century the distinguished English critic George Saintsbury wrote that Cowper deserved 'perhaps the highest place among English letter-writers—certainly a place equal to the highest. It is simply that he had the art of letter-writing—the secret of epistolary presentment—as hardly anybody else has had it. His epistles delight because there is in them an infinite virtue of delectation. . . . It is curious, or at any rate noteworthy, that the great tragedy of his life seems hardly to have affected this power in the very slightest degree, except by suspending its exercise. He had it to some extent from the very first, and he kept it and improved it to the very last, whenever he was sufficiently in possession of his faculties to write letters at all . . . the gift of familiar expression was probably in the family. And Cowper, debarred by choice or circumstance from free oral use of it, turned the stream on to paper, writing as nobody else, except Madame de Sévigné, has ever written.'

In the eighteenth century, the golden age of letter-writing in England, Cowper and Walpole stand supreme as the last exponents of what William Henry Irving called 'atticism'—simplicity, elegance, and effortless ease. Cowper, more than any other, reveals himself utterly in his letters; yet no one is less of an egoist. That is because of his gentleness and the modest and artless awareness of his own nature. At the same time, few writers can with such clarity and intimacy reveal not only the writer himself but the personality of the person written to. Other letter-writers are greater than Cowper in the forceful vitality of their prose, in more dashing wit, in wider range of subject. None is more pleasantly amusing; no one can ridicule and criticize and laugh with such unaffected charm. Yet no one has shown more keenly the other extreme of human consciousness. Cowper has given us one of the most terrifying pictures of the suicidal mind. Here is unrelieved and desperate desolation, beyond pathos to the stark heart of total loss and abandonment.

Although Cowper's letters were printed again and again in the nineteenth century and were widely known (Blake said that they were 'Perhaps, or rather Certainly, the very best letters that were

ever published'), they were expurgated and refined by his early editors. William Hayley, the first editor of Cowper's letters, by his own admission, 'suppressed perhaps *even more, than I printed*'. The present edition attempts to print all Cowper's letters that have survived, and in as complete and definitive a form as possible. It will contain approximately 1,300 letters, more than 1,000 of which will be printed from the original manuscripts. About two-thirds of the letters have hitherto unpublished portions, and about one-sixth have not previously been published in any form. This edition also prints a previously unpublished manuscript version from 1772 of Cowper's *Adelphi*, his memoir of his own early life and his biography of his brother, John.

In 1927 Kenneth Povey wrote that the 'text of Cowper's letters is in such an incomplete, corrupt and muddled state that anyone who has occasion to go beyond a popular selection, whether for pleasure or for purposes of study, must soon find how little any of the four collected editions is to be trusted'. It is our aim to 'restore' the texts of 'the very best letters that were ever published' to a high standard of textual accuracy. Above all, we hope to present the texts in a truly readable form to make these celebrated letters available as literature.

* * *

The present edition prints in four volumes the personal letters of Cowper to friends and acquaintances which were intended for transmission by post or messenger. It is hoped that a fifth and concluding volume will contain the remainder of Cowper's writings in prose (including essays and reviews) and a cumulative index.

ACKNOWLEDGEMENTS

THIS edition is dedicated to the memory of two men who gave many years to studying the life and work of William Cowper. First of all, to Professor Neilson Campbell Hannay (1880–1961) of Belmont, Massachusetts, who during the last forty years of his life collected everything he could find relating to Cowper. Hannay's goal was a definitive biography and a scholarly edition of Cowper's letters, but when he died nothing had been written of either work. He did, however, gather thousands of pages of notes and records, most of them of considerable value, and formed the finest collection of Cowperiana in existence: four hundred autograph letters, important poetical manuscripts, among them 'The Norfolk Manuscript' which contains 'The Castaway', miscellaneous manuscripts in Cowper's hand and documents signed by him, extensive collections of manuscripts and letters by John Newton and William Hayley, and dozens of letters by members of the Cowper family, Cowper's circle of friends, and his publisher. This collection is now in the Princeton University Library as the gift of Mr. Robert H. Taylor (the Hannay collection is more fully described in the *Princeton University Library Chronicle*, xxiv (Autumn 1962), 3–38). It is the major source of the letters contained in this edition.

But hundreds of Cowper's autograph letters are in public and private collections all over America and England, and many others are known only from their publication in now obscure journals, miscellanies, biographies, and collections of letters, or from partial publication in auction or dealers' catalogues. Kenneth Povey (1898–1965), after his years as Librarian of the University of Liverpool, was hard at work on a definitive edition of Cowper's poems; but much earlier, in 1929–36, he had published a most important series of articles in the *Review of English Studies* on the provenance and dating of the letters. Throughout his life, Povey kept manuscript notebooks in which he recorded significant information about each of Cowper's letters. Povey was a distinguished Cowperian scholar, and a devoted one, and we are proud to dedicate this edition of Cowper's letters to him also.

The descendants of Cowper's near relations and his close friends have been of great help to us in preparing this text. In particular we should like to thank Miss Mary Barham Johnson, and her late mother, Mrs. Barham Johnson, the late Canon and Mrs. Wilfrid H. Cowper Johnson of Norwich, and their daughters the Misses C. and A. Cowper Johnson, Lady Salmond, Christian, Lady Hesketh, and Miss Catherine M. Bull of Newport Pagnell.

Lady Dalrymple-Champneys (formerly Norma Russell) has provided in her *Bibliography of William Cowper to 1837* (Oxford, 1963) an indispensable tool for all Cowperian scholarship. Professor John D. Baird, who is editing Cowper's verse, has been of enormous help in the annotation of the poetry in these volumes.

The owners of the autograph manuscripts of Cowper's letters are listed separately in the introductions to each volume, but here we should like to record our gratitude to all of them. We are, of course, especially indebted to the Princeton University Library and to Mrs. Wanda Randall and Mr. Alexander Clark, both formerly of its staff, and to Mr. Alfred L. Bush and Mrs. Michael Sherman, who continue to answer our queries concerning the very extensive Princeton archive.

Both Princeton University and McMaster University have been most generous in supporting this edition through various kinds of financial assistance and by providing office space and clerical help. Princeton made Charles Ryskamp a Junior Fellow of the Council of Humanities and later awarded him a Bicentennial Preceptorship; these and a subsequent Bollingen Foundation Fellowship and then a John Simon Guggenheim Memorial Fellowship gave additional time for research on the letters and the poems of William Cowper. He would also like to thank Cambridge University Press and the *Princeton University Library Chronicle* for permission to quote from material he originally published with them. The work of James King has been greatly helped by his research grants and a Leave Fellowship from the Canada Council.

Over the years, many persons at Princeton and McMaster have assisted in preparing this text, on research projects, typing the final manuscript, and preparing the index. At Princeton: Mr. Joseph P. Arnould, Mr. Donald T. Cowles, Mr. David D. Foster, Mr. William G. Whitehead, Mr. Hugh Witemeyer, and Mrs. Helen Wright. At McMaster: Mrs. Audrey G. Alexander, Mr. Gary A. Boire, Mr.

Shawn Conway, Mr. Thomas Corbett, Miss Denise Elley, Miss Lily Fong, Miss Catherine Hall, Mr. Graham Hill, Miss Barbara Jewett, Mr. Ralph Malashevsky, Miss Janice Porter, Miss Sandy Simmons, Mrs. Susan Stencil, Mrs. Charlotte Stewart, and Mr. Randall Toye.

We are also thankful to the following for providing information and assistance: Miss Patricia L. Bell, Professor Alan Bishop, Mrs. Lucy R. Bradbury, the Revd. J. J. Bunting, Mrs. Winifred Burgess, the late Professor James L. Clifford, Professor Joan Coldwell, the Revd. R. Cooling, Professor William F. Cunningham, Mr. E. J. Davis, Mr. Michael Farrar, Mr. R. Hadeley, Professor A. D. Hammond, the Revd. T. C. Hammond, the late Professor F. W. Hilles, Mr. Felix Hull, Mr. Verlyn Klinkenborg, Miss A. Matheson, Professor Richard E. Morton, the Revd. K. C. Newton, Professor Ruth Perry, the Revd. A. K. Pring, Miss Y. Rhymes, Mr. Brian Spiller, Mr. Peter Walne, Professor Richard Wendorf, the Revd. G. M. F. Williams. We are indebted to Mr. Stephen Harvard for redrawing the map of Olney in the time of William Cowper.

The editors are especially indebted to Miss Sandra E. Harris who served as James King's research assistant at McMaster University for this edition from 1975 to 1978. She has worked with great zeal to prepare the typescripts for the printer.

JAMES KING
CHARLES RYSKAMP

CONTENTS

LIST OF PLATES AND MAPS

ABBREVIATIONS AND SHORT TITLES

Standard encyclopedias, biographical dictionaries, peerages, baronetages, knightages, school and university lists, lists of clergy, town and city directories, and road guides have been used but will not be cited unless for a particular reason.

Add. MSS.	Additional Manuscripts, the British Library.
Bailey	*Poems of William Cowper*, ed. J. C. Bailey. London, 1905.
B.L.	British Library.
C	William Cowper.
G.M.	*Gentleman's Magazine*, 1731–1800.
Gray	*Correspondence of Thomas Gray*, ed. Paget Toynbee and Leonard Whibley. 3 vols. Oxford, 1935.
Gregg Commonplace Book	Copies of Cowper's letters transcribed by Charlotte Mayor (d. 1838) from a manuscript book by Judith Madan. These letters were printed in various *Notes and Queries* articles by John E. B. Mayor in 1904. The notebook, which is the basis of our text, was proof-read against the printed texts by N. C. Hannay. The present whereabouts of the manuscript of the commonplace book is unknown.
Hayley	*The Life, and Posthumous Writings, of William Cowper, Esqr.* By William Hayley. 3 vols. Chichester, 1803–4.
Keynes	Geoffrey Keynes, 'The Library of Cowper', *Transactions of the Cambridge Bibliographical Society*, 1959–61.
The Madan Family	Falconer Madan, *The Madan Family*. Oxford, 1933.

Mawe	Thomas Mawe and John Abercrombie, *Universal Gardener and Botanist, or A General Dictionary of Gardening and Botany*. London, 1778.
Milford	William Cowper, *Poetical Works*, ed. H. S. Milford, 4th edition, revised. London, 1967.
Mrs. Cowper's Commonplace Book	Serious Common Place Book, Vol. III of Maria Frances Cecilia Cowper. This volume is at the Cowper and Newton Museum, Olney. The contents of this volume by C or relating to him were first published in *Notes and Queries* by John E. B. Mayor in 1904.
O.E.D.	*The Oxford English Dictionary.*
Olney	The Cowper and Newton Museum, Olney.
Olney Address	Twenty-eight addresses, now at the Cowper and Newton Museum, Olney, cut from letters to Hill, each inscribed by John Johnson on the otherwise blank verso 'This Autograph of the Poet Cowper, was separated from a Letter in the possession of Mrs. Hill, of Wargrave Hill, Berks, by his Relation, John Johnson, December, 1820'. The dates of twenty-three letters, 3 Dec. 1765–9 Mar. 1778, are recorded by Johnson on the respective cuttings. K. Povey, 'Hand-list of Manuscripts in the Cowper and Newton Museum, Olney, Bucks', *Transactions of the Cambridge Bibliographical Society*, iv, 2, 1965.
O.P.R.	*The Register of the Parish of Olney . . . 1665 to 1812.* Transcribed and indexed by Oliver Ratcliff. With introduction by Thomas Wright, etc. Olney, [1907–10].

Princeton (*copy*)	Letters from Cowper to John Newton or Mary Newton transcribed by Mrs. Sophia Ring and others. These letters are described by K. Povey in *The Times* of 25 April 1930.
P.R.O.	Public Record Office, London.
R.E.S.	*Review of English Studies.*
Russell	Norma Russell, *A Bibliography of William Cowper to 1837*. Oxford, 1963.
Ryskamp	Charles Ryskamp, *William Cowper of the Inner Temple, Esq*. Cambridge, 1959.
Southey	*The Works of William Cowper*, ed. Robert Southey. 15 vols. London, 1835–7.
Venn	John Venn, *Alumni Cantabrigienses.* 2 pts. in 10 vols. Cambridge, 1922–54.
Wright	*The Correspondence of William Cowper*, ed. Thomas Wright. 4 vols. London, 1904.
Wright, *Life*	Thomas Wright, *The Life of William Cowper*. London, 1892.
1782	*Poems by William Cowper, of the Inner Temple, Esq*. London, 1782.

CHRONOLOGY OF COWPER'S LIFE

15 November 1731 (O.S.)	William Cowper born in the rectory, Berkhamsted, Hertfordshire; son of the Revd. John Cowper, and of Ann, daughter of Roger Donne of Ludham Hall, Norfolk.
13 November 1737 (O.S.)	Death of Ann Cowper.
c. 1737	At school in Aldbury, Herts., under the Revd. William Davis.
c. 1737–9	At the Revd. Dr. William Pittman's boarding-school at Markyate Street, Herts.
c. 1740–2	A boarder in the house of Mrs. Disney.
April 1742	Enters Westminster School.
29 April 1748 (O.S.)	Admitted to the Middle Temple.
May 1749	Spends nine months at Berkhamsted.
1750–3	Is articled to Chapman, a London solicitor. He spends much time in the company of Theadora and Harriot, the daughters of his uncle, Ashley Cowper.
c. 1753–4	Abandonment of hope of marrying Theadora Cowper.
November 1753	Experiences his first period of depression.
June 1754	Is called to the Bar.
9 July 1756	Death of his father.
1755–63	Association with the 'Geniuses' (Bonnell Thornton, Robert Lloyd, Charles Churchill, George Colman).
15 April 1757	Is admitted to the Inner Temple.
1763	Dispute erupts over the Clerkship of the Journals of the House of Lords; C is summoned to appear at the Bar of the House of Lords. Beginning of his second period of depression. Makes his third suicide attempt on the eve of his examination at the House of Lords. On the urging of his brother, he

	enters Dr. Cotton's 'Collegium Insanorum' at St. Albans.
July 1764	Recovery and beginning of conversion to evangelicalism.
June 1765	Leaves St. Albans and settles in lodgings at Huntingdon.
c. September 1765	First acquaintance with the Unwin family.
11 November 1765	Becomes a boarder with the Unwin family.
2 July 1767	Death of the Revd. Morley Unwin.
14 September 1767	Arrival of C and Mrs. Unwin at Olney, where the Revd. John Newton had offered to find a house for them.
15 February 1768	Move to Orchard Side, Olney.
20 March 1770	Death of C's brother, John.
1771	Begins *Olney Hymns* in collaboration with Newton.
1772	Engaged to Mrs. Unwin.
January–February 1773	Engagement is broken. Third period of severe depression.
April 1773	Moves to Olney vicarage under the care of Newton.
October 1773	Makes another attempt to commit suicide.
23 May 1774	Returns to Orchard Side.
February 1779	*Olney Hymns* published.
December 1780	'The Progress of Error' and 'Truth' begun.
January–March 1781	'Table Talk' and 'Expostulation' written.
Spring 1781	'Charity' written.
July 1781	Meets Lady Austen.
August 1781	'Retirement' begun.
1 March 1782	*Poems by William Cowper, of the Inner Temple, Esq.* published.
October 1782	*John Gilpin* written.
c. October 1783	*The Task* begun.
May 1784	First acquaintance with the Throckmortons.
24 May–12 July 1784	Final breach with Lady Austen.

October 1784	*The Task* completed.
November 1784	'Tirocinium' completed. The translation of the *Iliad* begun.
July 1785	*The Task* published.
October 1785	Resumes his correspondence with Lady Hesketh; receives financial assistance from her and 'Anonymous' (Theadora).
November 1786	Following Lady Hesketh's visit from June to November, C, at the invitation of the Throckmortons, moves to The Lodge, Weston Underwood.
January–June 1787	Fourth period of depression.
September 1788	Translation of the *Odyssey* begun.
January 1790	First acquaintance with his cousin, John Johnson.
July 1791	Translation of Homer published.
September 1791	Translation of Milton's Latin and Italian poems begun.
December 1791	Mrs. Unwin's first paralytic stroke.
May 1792	Mrs. Unwin's second paralytic stroke. First visit from William Hayley.
1 August–17 September 1792	C, Mrs. Unwin, and John Johnson visit Hayley at Eartham, Sussex.
Autumn 1792	Renewed depression.
Autumn 1793	Further deterioration in Mrs. Unwin's health. 'To Mary' written.
November 1793	Lady Hesketh arrives to take charge of C and his household.
January 1794	Beginning of his fifth severe depression, from which he never fully recovers.
April 1794	Granted a yearly pension of £300.
17 May 1794	Mrs. Unwin's third paralytic stroke.
28 July 1795	C and Mrs. Unwin removed by John Johnson to his home in East Dereham, Norfolk.
17 December 1796	Death of Mrs. Unwin.
November 1797	Revision of Homer translation begun.

8 March 1799	Revision of Homer completed.
19 March 1799	'The Cast-away' begun.
31 January 1800	Treated for dropsy.
22 February 1800	Confined to his rooms.
25 April 1800	Death.
2 May 1800	Buried in the parish church of East Dereham.

INTRODUCTION

ADELPHI

TEXTUAL HISTORY

THE narrative of his own life and his affectionate recollection of his brother John's last days are among Cowper's most interesting pieces of writing. They are skilfully conceived, carefully controlled narratives of fearful moments of crisis in the lives of the two brothers. The tormented, self-accusing autobiographical narrative has its foil in the gentle and sensitive rendition of John's conversion to the truths his brother has learned; William, who has been taught God's ways in a harrowing manner, as we learn in his own narrative, becomes, in the second narrative, the patient and gentle interpreter of God's plan to his younger brother.

Cowper's autobiographical narrative was not published in the author's lifetime. In 1816, two rival editions of Cowper's Memoir made their way into print. The Edwards edition claims to be the first publication of the narrative of Cowper's early life. The Cox edition makes the same claim. The best available evidence would suggest simultaneous or near-simultaneous publication.[1]

According to Samuel Greatheed, the Revd. David Simpson published part of Cowper's narrative concerning his brother in *Deathbed Evidences of the Gospel*, although such a work has not been located.[2] The first known printing of Cowper's memoir of his brother, *Adelphi*, as it was known, appeared in 1802, '*Faithfully transcribed from his original Manuscript*, by John Newton', Cowper's close friend.

The whereabouts of Cowper's holograph (or copies of it) of his own life and that of his brother are unknown. Readers of Cowper's Memoir have thus been forced to settle for either the Cox or the

[1] M. J. Quinlan in his edition of the Memoir (*Proceedings of the American Philosophical Society*, xcii, 1953) contends that the Cox edition preceded the Edwards by nearly two months. See, however, *Russell*, pp. 192–5 and Charles Ryskamp, *Modern Philology*, liii, No. 1 (1955) and, especially, ibid. No. 3 (1956).

[2] 'A Collection of Materials towards a Life of Cowper', Cowper and Newton Museum, Olney: 'While Mr C lived at Weston I met with part of it in print, in the late Revd. David Simpson's "Deathbed Evidences of the Gospel". I showed him the book, and having read [it,] he said to the best of his recollection it was accurate, as far as it went.'

Edwards version of 1816. Recently, Mrs. Madan's copy, made from Newton's copy and transcribed in 1772, has become available. This manuscript contains both narratives under the joint title of *Adelphi* (The Brothers). The copyist appears to be Maria Cowper, Mrs. Madan's daughter (a small portion of the copying was perhaps done by Mrs. Madan herself). The manuscript is in 'Common Place Book Vol. 2', once owned by Miss Mary Hog of Edinburgh, and was presented by Mr. Roger Hog in 1967 to the Bodleian Library, Oxford. Despite the fact that the accidentals in spelling and punctuation are obviously not Cowper's, there can be little doubt that the Bodleian manuscript is a much more accurate rendition of Cowper's Memoir than any previously available to the public.

A theory may be advanced concerning the textual history of *Adelphi*. Martin Madan was allowed to read Cowper's holograph copy of his Memoir in 1767 (see Cowper to Mrs. Madan, 26 September 1767). John Newton, Lady Hesketh, and Mrs. Madan were allowed the same privilege in 1768 (see Cowper to Mrs. Madan, 18 June 1768). Cowper lent his manuscript copy of the two narratives to Newton some time after 1770 (either his original Memoir with the narrative concerning John added to it, or a completely new holograph). Newton lent a copy he had made of this manuscript to Mrs. Cowper by 8 August 1772. She then transcribed this copy into Mrs. Madan's Commonplace Book (it would seem by this time that a great number of accidentals not by Cowper were introduced—either by Newton and copied by Mrs. Cowper, or by Mrs. Cowper herself, or a combination thereof). Mrs. Cowper then most probably returned Newton's copy to him after receiving his directions for doing so in his letter of 4 November 1772.[3] Newton published the second part of the narrative in 1802 (Newton took Cowper's title for the entire interlocking narrative and assigned it to the latter, smaller, portion). It is probable that the Cox and Edwards editions of 1816 (as well as the two manuscripts of the Memoir which predate 1816) are derived from an expurgated version of Cowper's holograph. The excisions to the holograph may originate with Newton.

The 'authority' of Mrs. Madan's Commonplace Book over previously available versions of *Adelphi* may be presented by means of

[3] Newton's letters to Mrs. Cowper of 8 Aug. and 4 Nov. 1772 appear on pp. 190–2 of Mrs. Cowper's Serious Common Place Book, vol. iii (Cowper and Newton Museum, Olney).

a tree showing the probable relationship of Cowper's no longer extant holograph to the available versions.

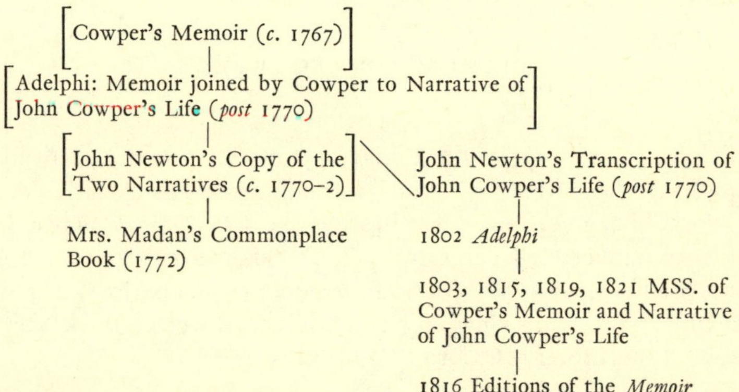

All the manuscript versions (dating from 1803 onwards) and all printed versions of the *Memoir* (two editions, 1816) are probably derived from Newton, either from his copy of the 1767 holograph or from a copy of a possibly new holograph *post* 1770. All these versions are substantively close to each other, and none contains the excised portions found in Mrs. Madan's Commonplace Book. Mrs. Madan's version, which also derives its authority from Newton, is clearly closer to Cowper's holograph than any previously available version. Since Mrs. Madan's version pre-dates all others and since there is no evidence indicating that it was Cowper's intention to 'edit' or 'revise' his original holograph, her version must take precedence over the others now known.

The excisions in the previously available Memoir of Cowper's life are of two kinds. Some of the references to Martin Madan have been omitted. A question of decorum seems to be at issue in the other significant cuts. Cowper's lie about a missing buckle is left out. The vivid evocation that Cowper conjures up of the interior of an imaginary cathedral has been removed. The more ghastly aspects of Cowper's attempts at suicide and his behaviour while in a suicidal frame of mind have also been deleted. The effect of the excisions is to present Cowper's Memoir in a way that was probably considered more readily sympathetic to some of its first readers, and less objectionable to his family.

Adelphi, as Cowper originally conceived it, is a direct and primitive

account of the torments of the suicidal mind. The 'restored' *Adelphi* makes Cowper's interlocking narratives available in a form undoubtedly very close to his holograph narrative.

MANUSCRIPT SOURCES

1772

'Adelphi, an Account of the Conversion of W. C. Esqre., Faithfully transcribed from his own Narrative and likewise His narrative of the memorable Conversion of his Brother the Rev. John Cowper. Late fellow of Bennet Colledge Cambridge.' This is a transcript of Cowper's Memoir, copied by Maria F. Cowper (some perhaps in Judith Madan's hand) from Newton's copy. 'Common Place Book Vol. 2', the Bodleian Library, Oxford.

post 1770

Shorthand transcription of Cowper's Memoir *and* John Newton's transcription of Cowper's Narrative of John Cowper's life. Contemporary marbled boards, 8vo, 46 leaves on paper manufactured by Joseph Portal from 1770 to 1796. Sold as lot 206 at Sotheby's sale, 22 June 1976. Division of Archives and Special Collections, McMaster University.

The shorthand transcription of Cowper's life, similar to that in Mrs. Madan's Common Place Book, is in an unknown hand. Newton's transcription of John's life is very similar to his *Adelphi* (1802). Neither transcript can be accurately dated.

The authority of both transcriptions in the McMaster manuscript is open to serious doubt. John Newton provided Mrs. Madan in 1772 with his copy of the interlocking lives, and there is no evidence of a shorthand version at that time. Furthermore, Mrs. Madan copied what Newton claimed was a literal transcription.

1803

'A Narrative of Cowper's experience by Himself.' The watermark is 1803. It is item 311 in Quaritch catalogue 714. Collection of Mr. Brian Spiller.

1815

'Memoirs of William Cowper, Esqr. 'till the age of 40—Written by himself—.' The half-title page reads, 'Geo. White 1815. Memoirs of

William C'. This copy is written in an old bank book (11·4×18·4×1·2 cm); 1/4 calf, marbled sides, pages unnumbered, but containing 170 including 63 that are blank. Formerly owned by Kenneth Povey. Princeton University Library.

1819

'Life of William Cowper.' This MS. is dated 1819 and once belonged to the late Hiram Corson, Professor of English at Cornell; it probably also belonged to 'Anne White'. Cornell University Library.

1821

'A Narrative of Cowper's Experience, written by Himself.' The paper on which this MS. is written is watermarked 'T. Stains 1812'; there is a frontispiece drawing of Cowper, signed in a hand which is presumably the same as that of the entire MS.: 'A.A. March 10th. 1821.' Pforzheimer Collection, New York.

PRINTED SOURCES

Adelphi

1802

Adelphi. A Sketch of the Character, And An Account of the Last Illness, of the Late Rev. John Cowper, A.M. Fellow of Bennet College, Cambridge. Written by His Brother, the Late William Cowper, Esq. of the Inner Temple. Faithfully Transcribed from His Original Manuscript, by John Newton. London: 1802.

Memoir of the Early Life of William Cowper, Esq.

1816

Memoir of the Early Life of William Cowper, Esq. Written by Himself, And Never Before Published. London: Printed for R. Edwards, Crane Court, Fleet Street; And Sold by All Booksellers. 1816.

Memoirs of the Most Remarkable and Interesting Parts of the Life of William Cowper, Esq. of the Inner Temple. London: Printed for the Editor, and Sold by E. Cox and Son, St. Thomas's Street, Borough; And All Other Booksellers in Town and Country. 1816.

TEXTUAL PRINCIPLES

Although one can be reasonably sure from the statements by Newton and Mrs. Madan that we have an accurate substantive version of Cowper's holograph, there can be little doubt that a variety of accidentals, not of Cowper's making, have crept into the Bodleian manuscript. For example, Cowper is usually careful in the punctuation of his sentences; the Bodleian manuscript is erratic in this respect. Capitalization is also haphazard in the manuscript. It is almost impossible to decide which word Cowper himself would or would not have capitalized. We have, therefore, made no substantive changes in this edition, but have introduced changes in capitalization, punctuation, and spelling so that it may be read without difficulty.

For example, Mrs. Cowper's transcription of the following passage is awkward and difficult to read:

> . . . The morning was clear, and calm, the sun shone bright upon the sea and the country upon the borders of it, was the most beautiful I had ever seen. We sat down upon an eminence at the end of that arm of the sea which runs between Southampton, and the new Forest.
>
> Here it was, that on a sudden, as if another Sun, had been kindled that instant in the Heavens, on purpose to dispel sorrow, and vexation of spirit, I felt the weight of all my Misery taken off. My heart became light, and joyous in a moment, and had I been alone I coud have weept with transport. I must needs beleive that nothing less, than the Almighty Fiat, coud have fill'd me with such inexpressible delight, not by a gradual dawning of peace, but as it were, with one flash, of his Life-giving countenance. I think I remember somewhat of a glow of gratitude to the Father of Merceis for this unexpected blessing, and that I ascribed it to his gracious acceptance of my Prayers . . .

The same passage, changed in accordance with modern punctuation and usage, presents a version which, we trust, is easy to read and yet in all likelihood more faithful to the holograph originally lent to Newton:

> . . . The morning was clear and calm; the sun shone bright upon the sea; and the country upon the borders of it was the most beautiful I had ever seen. We sat down upon an eminence at the end of that arm of the sea which runs between Southampton and the New Forest.
>
> Here it was that on a sudden, as if another sun had been kindled that instant in the heavens on purpose to dispel sorrow and vexation of spirit, I felt the weight of all my misery taken off. My heart became light and joyous

in a moment, and had I been alone, I could have wept with transport. I must needs believe that nothing less than the Almighty Fiat could have filled me with such inexpressible delight, not by a gradual dawning of peace, but, as it were, with one flash of His life-giving countenance. I think I remember somewhat of a glow of gratitude to the Father of Mercies for this unexpected blessing, and that I ascribed it to His gracious acceptance of my prayers. . . .

Although the other manuscript and printed versions of both narratives have been consulted, their authority for substantives and accidentals now seems questionable. It has been decided, therefore, to use Mrs. Madan's Commonplace Book as the basis for what it is hoped is an accurate and readable edition of the *Adelphi*.

LETTERS

IMPORTANT EDITIONS OF COWPER'S LETTERS

1803–4

The Life, and Posthumous Writings, of William Cowper, Esqr. By William Hayley. Three volumes. Chichester: 1803–4.

Four hundred and seventy-three letters by Cowper were published for the first time. Two more were added in the edition of 1809 and four more in 1812.

1817

The Letters of the Late William Cowper, Esq. To His Friends. A New Edition. Revised by His Kinsman, J. Johnson. Three volumes. London: 1817.

The letters, although available as a separate collection, were volumes IV–VI of Johnson's ten-volume collected edition of the works. The 479 Cowper letters collected by Hayley up to 1812 are printed in this edition. These letters were republished in a single volume in 1820 and again in 1827.

1824

Private Correspondence of William Cowper, Esq. with Several oi His Most Intimate Friends. Now First Published from the Originals in the Possession of His Kinsman, John Johnson. Two volumes. London: 1824.

This is a collection of 221 additional letters, of which a few had been published in part by Hayley. The most important of these were

the religious letters addressed to Newton. John Johnson declared in his preface that their deliberate exclusion by Hayley had given a distorted impression of Cowper and that their publication should help to answer the charge that his insanity had been caused by his religion. Johnson also wanted to give a more balanced picture of Cowper by restoring some of the lighter passages of humorous comment on men and events which Hayley had cut out as undignified. There were second and third editions in the year of first publication.

1834

The Miscellaneous Works of William Cowper, Esq. of the Inner Temple. With a Life and Notes, by John S. Memes. Three volumes. Edinburgh, London, and Dublin: 1834.

Memes printed 481 numbered letters by Cowper in his first two volumes, introducing many others, also taken from Hayley, into his *Life*. He also quoted freely from the *Private Correspondence*, although it was still in copyright, sometimes reprinting a whole letter.

1835

The Works of William Cowper His Life and Letters by William Hayley, Esq. Now First Completed by the Introduction of Cowper's Private Correspondence. Edited by the Rev. T. S. Grimshawe. Eight volumes. London: 1835.

Grimshawe's edition of the letters was largely based on Hayley's *Life* which he endeavoured to present and supplement from an evangelical point of view. He printed nearly all the letters published by Hayley and nearly all those in the *Private Correspondence*, adding about a dozen new ones. There was a second edition in 1836.

1835–7

The Works of William Cowper, Esq. Comprising His Poems, Correspondence, and Translations. With a Life of the Author, by the Editor, Robert Southey. Fifteen volumes. London: 1835–7.

Since he had access only to a limited number of originals, Southey was obliged to use Hayley's text. Where he was able to get hold of manuscript letters, he made strenuous efforts to improve upon Hayley's readings. Southey also printed a number of previously unprinted letters from Cowper to Newton, Hill, Bagot, Mrs. King, as well as the collections of letters to Lady Hesketh and William Unwin. He published 753 letters plus parts of a further 128.

1904

The Correspondence of William Cowper. By Thomas Wright. Four volumes. London: 1904.

This edition contains 1,041 letters, 753 being wholly from Southey and 51 from other published sources. Of the remaining 237, 105 were unpublished and 132 had been partly published. Wright had seen the originals of about 400 letters and of these he printed the complete text.

1905

Poems of William Cowper. Edited by J. C. Bailey. London: 1905.

This edition contains 35 new letters to Joseph Hill and John and Catherine Johnson.

1925

The Unpublished and Uncollected Letters of William Cowper. Edited by Thomas Wright. London: 1925.

This adds 31 new letters to various correspondents.

1959

William Cowper of the Inner Temple, Esq. A Study of his Life and Works to the Year 1768. By Charles Ryskamp. Cambridge: 1959.

The appendices add 19 new or substantially new parts of previously known letters. They also include literary essays.

The present edition is indebted to Norma Russell's *A Bibliography of William Cowper to 1837* (Oxford, 1963) for the descriptions of the items analysed in her study. For a list of letters printed separately before 1837, see pp. 205–9 of her book. Since many Cowper letters in print appear only in part, we have not indicated previous publications for any letters which exist as holographs or reliable manuscript copies. For example, Southey printed C's letter to Hill of 10 March 1766, but he omitted the entire second paragraph as well as transcribing 65£ for 15£.

PRINCIPAL COLLECTIONS OF COWPER'S LETTERS

The Hannay Collection, Princeton University Library

It consists of 404 holograph letters and 46 copies of Cowper letters. Assembled by the late Professor Neilson C. Hannay, this is the

largest collection of Cowper letters. Princeton University Library has supplemented the Hannay Collection by purchasing additional letters by Cowper.

Most of the Princeton copies are addressed to John Newton, who lent Cowper's letters to himself to friends, including Dr. and Mrs. Thomas Ring of Reading. Sophia Ring and her friends made copies of the holographs lent them, and the texts of some Cowper to Newton letters are now known only from these transcriptions.

The Cowper Johnson Collection

This is a collection of 176 letters from 10 October 1755 to 10 December 1793 on 472 pages. They were arranged and prepared for binding by John Johnson in 1820. These letters are owned by the Misses C. and A. Cowper Johnson.

The British Library

The British Library owns 118 letters of Cowper to William Unwin from 1770 to 1786 on 244 pages. These were purchased from the Unwin family in 1861; letters to other correspondents have also been acquired.

The Panshanger Collection, Hertford County Record Office

A collection of 72 letters to various correspondents including Joseph Hill, Maria Cowper, William Hayley, Joseph Johnson, and, especially, Lady Hesketh.

The Cowper and Newton Museum, Olney

Approximately fifty Cowper letters are contained in this collection. The holograph letters and copies at Olney are described in K. Povey's 'Hand-list of Manuscripts in the Cowper and Newton Museum, Olney, Bucks', *Transactions of the Cambridge Bibliographical Society*, iv, No. 2 (1965), 107–27.

The Pierpont Morgan Library

In addition to some miscellaneous letters, Morgan MSS. MA 86–7 contain most of the correspondence between Walter Bagot and Cowper (44 letters to Bagot, 9 from Bagot); letters to other correspondents have also been acquired.

TEXTUAL PRINCIPLES

MANUSCRIPT SOURCES

Holograph Letters

Two concerns have governed our printing of holograph letters: the primary authority of a literal transcription and the need for a clear, easily read text. We have retained Cowper's exact spelling, numerals, and use of capital letters; we have preserved the ampersand (which gives one a sense of the immediacy of many letters) and we have transcribed exactly abbreviations of signatures, addresses, endorsements, and dates and places in the headings and conclusions of letters, since conventional usage in this respect has not altered much in two centuries, and so that the reader will be better able to realize the quickness of Cowper's writing. Punctuation is adjusted only when required for smooth reading, with the appropriate stop at the end of each sentence. Several minor changes have been made for the same purpose: other abbreviations in the body of the letters are expanded, raised letters are lowered, capital letters have been added where necessary, and the placement of apostrophes has been rendered consistent with modern practice (they are added for possessives, but deleted in plurals). Square brackets [ ] indicate doubtful readings.

Copies

In the preparation of this edition, we have sometimes employed manuscript copies (mainly in the Hannay Collection, Princeton University Library, and the Cowper and Newton Museum, Olney) as sources for our text. We have done this when a manuscript copy is the only source for a letter. We have also used copies of Cowper's letters in preference to printed versions when the relevant copies seem closer in substantives to Cowper's practice or have better authority than a printed version. In editing these manuscript copies, we have silently changed punctuation and spelling to accord with Cowper's customary usage when the copies are obviously reliable transcripts of holographs (this is true of the copies at Princeton; Mrs. Ring's transcriptions of extant Cowper letters are always faithful to the holographs). In the case of manuscript copies with punctuation, spelling, and syntax that vary significantly from Cowper's practice, we have modernized the texts (this is the case with Mrs. Cowper's transcriptions, now at Olney, of Cowper's letters to herself and to

Mrs. Madan; her transcriptions of extant Cowper holographs are very inexact).

PRINTED SOURCES

Except for silently correcting any misprints, the texts are reprinted literally. In the case of some letters where the punctuation and spelling are obviously not Cowper's, we have changed the letter in accordance with Cowper's practice.

HEADINGS TO LETTERS

The heading to each letter gives the name of the recipient, the day and date of the letter, the address in Cowper's hand (if available), the postmark (if available), and the source of our copy-text. Owners of manuscript letters are identified by name; owners of manuscript copies are identified by name with the addition of the word '*copy*' in parentheses; printed sources are italicized. Information available from franked letters, with the address in the hand of the person providing this service, is also cited. Letters of unknown or questionable dating are placed at the most appropriate point in the text.

ANNOTATION

The introduction to each volume includes biographical sketches of Cowper's correspondents. The emphasis in each biography is on Cowper's relationship to that person during the years covered in the volume.

We have tried to make the footnotes as brief and as informative as possible. In providing documentation on the persons, places, historical and contemporary events, and books mentioned by Cowper, our intention has been to clarify Cowper's references and to present unobtrusively sufficient information for a clear understanding of the context in which Cowper writes.

COWPER'S LETTERS
1750–1781

Cowper is seen in a wide variety of moods in the letters extending from 1750 to 1781. There is first of all the sprightly, energetic man about town revealed in his early letters to such friends as Walter Bagot, John Duncombe, Clotworthy Rowley, and Chase Price. Cowper is cognizant of the latest fashions in dress and literature. He is

anxious to be seen as the earnest lover and the sophisticated raconteur. As might be expected, these letters are youthful attempts at epistle-writing. They are unusually and sometimes precociously self-conscious.

This very real and important side of Cowper's personality disappears almost completely in the sad, weary letters of 1763 (the events leading to this state of mind are chronicled in *Adelphi*). The prosaic and often comfortable life at Huntingdon and Olney (interrupted in his life and in the correspondence from 1772 to 1775 by Cowper's second period of depression) is related in the letters from 1765 to 1772 and from 1775 to 1781. The letters from 1764 to 1770 are strongly evangelical in tone, or they are concerned with his finances, the produce of his garden, requests for fruits and vegetables, meat and fish, his clothes and his tailor in London. His spirit and his writing seem to change mid-way through 1778, and it is only then that the letters which show his particular style, his grace and wit, begin to appear.

Cowper's preparations for his major book of 1782 are clearly seen in the letters of 1780 and 1781. The first volume of letters ends on the eve of the publication of *Poems by William Cowper, of the Inner Temple, Esq.*, the book of verse which contributed significantly in making Cowper one of the best-known English poets.

CORRESPONDENTS

LADY AUSTEN (1738?–1802), born Ann Richardson, the daughter of John Richardson of North End in the parish of Fulham in the county of Middlesex. She married Robert Austen (1708–72) on 23 June 1755; Austen succeeded to the baronetcy in 1760. Sir Robert and Lady Austen probably went to Sancerre in France in 1763 and returned to England in 1767. They were back in Sancerre in 1768, and in Britain in 1771. Sir Robert died on 13 February 1772 and Lady Austen went to Sancerre in 1774; she was not again in England until the autumn of 1778. In 1781, Lady Austen lived at the parsonage, Clifton (Lady Austen's brother-in-law, Thomas Jones, was curate there) and in 1782 at the vicarage of Olney, where Thomas Scott was curate. Cowper met Lady Austen in July 1781, when she first took up residence with the Joneses. Cowper and Lady Austen quarrelled about the end of January 1782. Their reconciliation took place

about the time of her return to Clifton in June–July 1782; the final break happened between 24 May and 12 July 1784. Lady Austen has been immortalized as the muse of *The Task*, and it is evident that Cowper admired much of her charm and wit. It is also clear that Lady Austen had a satirical turn of mind and Mrs. Unwin was offended by her conduct. It seems likely that Mrs. Unwin's influence led Cowper to the two estrangements with Lady Austen. Lady Austen went to Bath in May 1784 and then to Bristol. She married for a second time (probably in 1796) Count Claude Tardiff du Granger. She died at Paris on 12 August 1802.

There is some possibility that Lady Austen made a veiled proposal of marriage to Cowper and that this afforded him the opportunity to renounce her. 'That Cowper rejected her advances as a mere human indiscretion and spoke of her afterwards without bitterness was because his three years' friendship with her had brought him back to the outward habits of a sane and happy life.' (Kenneth Povey, 'The Banishment of Lady Austen', *R.E.S.* xv (1939), 400.)

WALTER BAGOT (1731–1806), of Pipe Hall, Staffs. He was the son of Sir Walter Wagstaff Bagot (1702–68), 5th baronet, and his wife Barbara (d. 1765), eldest daughter of William Legge, first Earl of Dartmouth. The family of Bagot had held property at Blithfield and Bagot's Bromley, Staffs., since the Conquest. Bagot and Cowper were intimate friends at Westminster but drifted apart soon afterwards, and visited each other only twice in the years 1750–81. Bagot was very much like Cowper in his taste and in his simple, amiable, gentle manners, and in a similar relish for humour. He had been a handsome boy and a slovenly dresser; he published poetry in his youth, and throughout his life; while he held the family livings (from 1759) of Blithfield and Leigh in Staffordshire, he spent hours of every day in reading—especially the classics. On 7 September 1773, he married Anne (d. 1786), daughter of William Swinnerton, of Butterton, Staffs. Bagot subsequently married Mary Ward.

MARIA FRANCES CECILIA MADAN, afterwards MRS. COWPER (1726–97), the Major's wife and Martin Madan's sister. An unusually accomplished woman, Mrs. Cowper was sufficiently skilled in French to act in Racine's *Athalie*, and she was so successful in that endeavour that she desired to become an actress. Also a

person of a very devotional cast, she reveals in her letters to Cowper a community of intense religious feelings.

WILLIAM COWPER (1721?–69). William Cowper was the eldest surviving son of William Cowper (1689–1740) of Hertingfordbury, and Cowper's first cousin. He matriculated at Worcester College, Oxford, in 1739 but left without a degree. He was admitted to Lincoln's Inn in 1740 and became a major in the Hertfordshire Militia. As early as 1743, Cowper proposed marriage to Maria Frances Cecilia Madan, his first cousin. Maria's mother, Judith Madan, objected to the marriage of first cousins and also believed that William did not have sufficient means. However, on 5 August 1749, they were married at St. James's, Westminster. The major's profession frequently took him away from Hertingfordbury Park. Cowper bought, late in 1751, Newland Park, near Snaith in the West Riding of Yorkshire, and the family was often in residence there. Major Cowper died at Hertingfordbury on 28 August 1769.

JOHN DUNCOMBE (1729–86). A graduate (B.A. 1749; M.A. 1752) and Fellow (1751–8) of Corpus Christi College, Cambridge. Duncombe probably became acquainted with William Cowper through John Cowper, who must have known Duncombe at Felsted School and Cambridge. At school Duncombe had been the first scholar and captain. He gained the very highest reputation for scholarship, and by his pleasant temperament and manners made strong friendships with his masters and fellow-students. Duncombe, in collaboration with his father, William, published translations of Horace in 1756 and 1759 (*The Works of Horace in English Verse*); in this they were assisted by several friends, including William Cowper. Duncombe also turned very early to studies preparatory to the taking of Holy Orders. His 'inclination, virtuous turn of mind, and unquestionable abilities, concurred to render him peculiarly qualified' for the ministry (Andrew Kippis, *Biographia Britannica*, v (1793), 509). He wrote many original poetical compositions, and was an essayist and reviewer of merit. From 1766 to 1786, he undertook the 'Review of Books' in the *Gentleman's Magazine*, and in this capacity it was he who most probably reviewed Cowper's books for the *Magazine*—the most important reviews to Cowper. In 1757, Duncombe had been presented to the united livings of St. Andrew and St. Mary

Bredman, Canterbury, and he was one of the six preachers at Canterbury Cathedral (from 1766). Duncombe's clerical career also included the following appointments: assistant preacher at St. Anne's, Soho (1758–9); the living of West Thurrock, Essex (1763–9); the masterships of St. John's Hospital, Canterbury, and St. Nicholas, Harbledown (1770); the living of Herne (1773). On 20 April 1761, he married Susanna, daughter of the painter Joseph Highmore of Lincoln's Inn Fields.

HARRIOT COWPER, afterwards LADY HESKETH (1733–1807). Lady Hesketh, the eldest surviving daughter of Ashley Cowper, was Cowper's first cousin and the sister of Theadora Cowper, whom Cowper wished to marry. She was the wife of Thomas Hesketh of Rufford Hall in Lancashire, who was created a baronet in 1761 and died in 1778, leaving Cowper a small legacy. The Hesketh went to Italy after Cowper moved to Olney and lost touch with him. Lady Hesketh resumed correspondence with Cowper after the publication of *The Task* in 1785, and she henceforth devoted a great deal of her time to his welfare. A person of somewhat austere refinement, she sometimes put people off by her manner. Mrs. Thrale in a diary entry of 10 January 1781 provides a description of her: 'Dear Lady Hesketh! and how like a Naples Washball She is: so round, so sweet, so plump, so polished, so red, so white . . . with more Beauty than almost any body, as much Wit as many a body; and six Times the Quantity of polite Literature . . . I never can find out what that Woman does to keep the people from adoring her.' (*Thraliana*, ed. K. Balderston (Oxford, 1942), i. 478.)

JOSEPH HILL (1733–1811). Perhaps Cowper's closest friend during his Temple days, Joe Hill had been born near Chancery Lane, the son of Francis Hill (d. 1741), an attorney who was the nephew and secretary of Sir Joseph Jekyll, Master of the Rolls, and Theodosia Sedgwick (d. 1784). He had been well known to Cowper's Uncle Ashley and his family, and soon after Cowper left Westminster he and young 'Sephus' became friends. Hill had been early bred to the law; he acted as a clerk in Chancery Lane (he served his articles of clerkship under Robert Chester of the Six Clerks' Office in Chancery Lane), later qualified as solicitor and attorney, and became one of the Sixty, or Sworn Clerks in Chancery. He was made Secretary of

Lunatics in 1778. He became a rich man owing to the justified esteem in which so many of his wealthy clients held him. During most of his life Cowper was financially dependent on Hill. Hill not only handled Cowper's small monetary matters—paying his London bills, apportioning his income for expenses in Huntingdon, Olney, etc.—but from his own pocket made it possible for Cowper to live as a gentleman, though still a poor one. Hill married Sarah Mathews (1742–1824) in August 1771.

JOSEPH JOHNSON (1738–1809), publisher and bookseller, was born at Everton, near Liverpool, and arrived in London in 1752. He established himself at St. Paul's Churchyard from 1772 onwards. A man of advanced, firmly held opinions, he published important works on surgery and medicine as well as some of the most innovative works of his time. His authors included Joseph Priestley, Erasmus Darwin, Horne Tooke, Mary Wollstonecraft, Tom Paine, Henry Fuseli, and Maria Edgeworth. Johnson had been one of the booksellers distributing the *Olney Hymns*. Newton, whom Cowper consulted at every stage of the preparation of *Poems* in 1782, found his publisher for him.

JUDITH COWPER, afterwards MRS. MADAN (1702–81), the mother of Martin Madan and Maria Cowper; Cowper's aunt. Mrs. Madan was the only daughter of Judge Spencer Cowper (1669–1728), Cowper's grandfather. A correspondent of Pope's, she was forced to curtail her literary interests when she married Captain Martin Madan, of the King's Own Regiment of Horse, in 1723. She was greatly troubled by the continual separations necessitated by her husband's military life. Though her children were a consolation to her, she found solace primarily in religion after she came to know Lady Huntingdon and John Wesley about 1749. Her letters to Cowper testify to their similar feelings about evangelical religion.

MARTIN MADAN (1725–90). Educated at Westminster (admitted 1736) and Christ Church, Oxford (B.A. 1746), and admitted to the Inner Temple in 1747, Madan was called to the Bar in 1748. He was a member of the Poetical Club from 1748 to 1750. He was very moved by hearing John Wesley preach in 1750 and in this year he obtained Wesley's licence to become an itinerant preacher and was eventually

ordained deacon in the Church of England in 1757. Madan was much involved with the Wesleys, Lady Huntingdon, George Whitefield, and other distinguished Methodists. He was Chaplain at the Locke Hospital from 1762 to 1780 and in 1767 was involved in a simony scandal concerning the parish of Aldwinkle. A man of extraordinary faith and self-confidence, he had published several theological works (among others: *A Collection of Psalms aud Hymns, Extracted from Various Authors*, 1760; *A Scriptural Account of the Doctrine of Perfection*, 1763; *A Scriptural Comment upon the Thirty-nine Articles of the Church of England*, 1771) before the appearance of the infamous *Thelyphthora* in 1781. On 17 December 1751, Martin married Jane (*c.* 1723–91), daughter of Sir Bernard Hale (1677–1729), chief baron of the Irish Exchequer.

JOHN NEWTON (1725–1807) and MARY CATLETT, afterwards MRS. NEWTON (1729–90). Newton, a fervent, extremely dedicated, and sometimes over-zealous man, led a very strange and adventure-filled life before and after his conversion to evangelical Christianity in 1748. His autobiography, *An Authentic Narrative* (1764), tells the story of his life as the master of a slave-ship and of his conversion. Newton had first gone to sea in 1736 and had made six journeys before 1742. After his marriage to Mary Catlett on 12 February 1750, he made three further voyages but in 1754, owing to ill health, he relinquished the sea. When he retired from the sea, Newton became surveyor of tides at Liverpool for five years, using his leisure time for the study of Greek, Hebrew, and theology. He applied for Holy Orders to the Archbishop of York in December 1758 but was refused. He spent three months in charge of an independent congregation at Warwick in 1760. Newton was ultimately ordained deacon (29 April) and priest (17 June) in the Church of England in 1764. He accepted the curacy of Olney in 1764, where he remained until 1780, when he became rector of St. Mary Woolnoth in London. In addition to his contributions to the *Olney Hymns* (1779), Newton was the author of some important theological works, including *Olney Sermons* (1767), *Omicron's Letters* (1774), and *Cardiphonia* (1781). Mrs. Newton was a quiet, unassuming but firm person who suffered from ill health.

CHASE PRICE (1731–77). Price, the 'Toby' of Cowper's early letters, was of Knighton, Radnorshire, Wales, and was in the sixth

form with Cowper at Westminster in 1749, the last boy (twentieth) in the form. He matriculated at Christ Church, Oxford, in the same year. He was admitted to the Inner Temple in 1750 or 1751 and afterwards called to the Bar. Price was a member of parliament for Leominster (1759–67) and for Radnorshire (1768–77) and was constantly embroiled in various schemes involving land grants, mining adventures, and Indian trade. A writer of verse in a very casual way and an enthusiastic patron of the theatre, Price was one of the most ribald and celebrated wits of his time.

CLOTWORTHY ROWLEY (1731–1805). Rowley was the son of Sir William Rowley, K.B., Admiral of the Fleet, of Tendring Hall, Stoke by Nayland, Suffolk. Of a robust and unruly nature, Rowley lived in accordance with the adventurous spirit of his extremely distinguished Admiralty family. Rowley was admitted to Trinity Hall, Cambridge, and then to the Inner Temple in 1750. Rowley and Cowper were neighbours at the Temple. Rowley withdrew from there in 1768, at which time he was called to the Irish Bar, and later became M.P. for Downpatrick (1771–1801).

MARY UNWIN (1724–96), daughter of William Cawthorne, a draper of Ely, and wife of the Revd. Morley Unwin (1703–67), whom she married in 1742. On 11 November 1765, Cowper moved into the house of Mary and Morley Unwin. Of the Unwin family, she in particular made Cowper feel immediately like a near relation, and he found in her what seemed to him a perfect combination of piety with a gentle, cheerful, intelligent character. Mrs. Unwin—it has often been said by Cowper's friends and relatives as well as by himself—was like a mother to him.

WILLIAM CAWTHORNE UNWIN (1744–86), Mrs. Unwin's only son. William had been educated at Charterhouse and at Christ's College, Cambridge. He took his degree, and was awarded the Chancellor's Classical Medal in 1764 (M.A. 1767); was ordained deacon in 1767 and priest in 1769. After a short ministry as curate at Comberton, Cambridgeshire, where his evangelical sermons earned him a substantial reputation, he was instituted rector of Stock with Ramsden Bellhouse in Essex in 1769 (in 1781 he was to become rector of Ramsden Crayes as well). He married Anne Shuttleworth

(d. 1825), by whom he had three children. An ambitious and occasionally over-excitable person, Unwin revered Cowper, and Cowper's letters to him often have the tone of the proud yet cautious parent offering advice to his offspring.

OWNERS OF MANUSCRIPTS

There are 325 letters in this volume, 264 taken from holographs, 1 from facsimile, 38 from manuscript copies, and 24 from printed sources. (The text of one letter—12 July 1765—is derived from both a manuscript copy and a printed source. The letter of 21 December 1780 is a composite made from two manuscript copies.) Manuscripts or manuscript copies of Cowper's letters in this volume are, for the most part, in the collections of The British Library (55), the Misses C. and A. Cowper Johnson (104), The Cowper and Newton Museum, Olney (28), and Princeton University Library (65). In addition, the following own holographs or manuscript copies printed in this volume: The Berkhamsted Historical Society (1), The Boston Public Library (1), The William Andrews Clark Memorial Library (1), Harvard University Library (3), The Historical Society of Pennsylvania (1), Arthur A. Houghton, Jr. (2), The Henry E. Huntington Library and Art Gallery (2), Miss Mary Barham Johnson (3), Professor H. C. Longuet-Higgins (1), The Massachusetts Historical Society (1), The New York Public Library (1), The Panshanger Collection, property of Rosemary, Lady Ravensdale (14), The Pierpont Morgan Library (3), Charles Ryskamp (2), the Marquess of Salisbury (1), Robert H. Taylor (1), Trinity College, Cambridge (1), The Victoria and Albert Museum (1), G. H. H. Wheler (3), Yale University Library (4). The text of four letters is derived from the Gregg Commonplace Book. Mills Memorial Library, McMaster University, owns the holograph of Mrs. Unwin's letter to Mrs. Newton of 7 October 1773.

ADELPHI

ADELPHI

an Account of the

Conversion of W. C. Esquire

Faithfully transcribed from his own Narrative

and likewise

His narrative of the memorable Conversion of his Brother

the Revd. John Cowper. Late fellow of Bene't College

Cambridge.

Isaiah 42 : 16

And I will bring the Blind by a way that they knew not, I will lead them in paths that they have not known. I will make darkness light before them, and crooked things straight. These things will I do unto them, and not forsake them.

I cannot recollect that till the month of December in the thirty-second year of my life, I had ever any serious impressions of the religious kind, or at all bethought myself of the things of my salvation, except in two or three instances.

The first was of so transitory a nature and passed when I was so very young that, did I not intend what follows for a history of my heart so far as religion has been its object, I should hardly mention it. It was as follows.

At six years of age I was taken from the nursery and the immediate care of a most indulgent mother and sent to a considerable school in Bedfordshire.[1] Here I had hardships of various kinds to conflict with, which I felt the more sensibly in proportion to the tenderness with which I had been treated at home. But my chief affliction consisted in being singled out from all the children in the school by a lad about fifteen years of age as a proper subject upon whom he might let loose the cruelty of his temper. I choose to conceal a particular recital of the many acts of barbarity with which he made it his business continually to persecute me. It will be sufficient to say that he had by his savage treatment of me imprinted such a dread of his very figure upon my mind that I well remember being afraid to lift my eyes upon him higher than his knees, and that I knew him by his shoe buckles better than by any other part of his dress.

May the Lord pardon him and may we meet in glory!

One day as I was sitting alone upon a bench in the school, melancholy and almost ready to weep at the recollection of what I had already suffered at his hands and at the apprehension of what was yet to come, expecting at the same time my tormentor every moment, these words of the Psalmist came into my mind, 'I will not fear what man can do unto me.'[2] I applied them to my own use with a degree of trust and confidence in God that would have been no disgrace to a much more experienced Christian.—Instantly, I perceived in myself a briskness of spirits and a cheerfulness which I had never felt before, and took several paces up and down the school with a joyful alacrity, his gift in whom I trusted. Happy had it been for me if this early effort towards a dependence upon the Blessed God had been

[1] Dr. Pittman's School at Markyate Street, near the border of Bedfordshire and Hertfordshire.

[2] Psalm 56: 4.

frequently repeated by me. But alas! it was the first and last instance of the kind between my infancy and manhood.

The cruelty of this boy, which he had long practised in so secret a manner that no creature suspected it, was at length discovered; he was expelled [from] the School, and I was taken from it. From hence at eight years of age I was sent to Mrs. D——,[3] an Oculist, having very weak eyes and being in danger of losing one of them. I continued a year in this family, where Christianity was neither known nor practised, and from thence was dispatched to Westminster.[4]

Whatever seeds of religion I might carry thither with me were all marred and corrupted long before my seven years apprenticeship to the classics were expired. The duty of the schoolboy swallowed up every other; and I acquired Latin and Greek at the expense of a knowledge much more important.

Here occurred the second instance of serious consideration hinted at above. As I was crossing St. Margaret's Churchyard[5] late one evening, I saw a glimmering light in the midst of it which excited my curiosity. Just as I arrived at the spot, a grave digger who was at work there by the light of his lantern threw a skull which struck me upon the leg. This little incident was an alarm to my conscience for that evening, and may be numbered among the best religious documents I received at Westminster. The impression, however, was presently worn off, and I became so forgetful of mortality that, strange as it may seem, surveying my activity and strength and observing the evenness of my pulse, I began to entertain with no small complacence a notion that possibly I might never die. This notion was, however, very short lived, for I was soon after struck with a lowness of spirits uncommon at that age, and had frequent intimations of a consumptive habit. I had skill enough to understand their meaning but never could prevail on myself to disclose them to anyone: for I thought every bodily infirmity a disgrace, especially a consumption. This messenger from the Lord, however, did his errand and perfectly convinced me that I was mortal.

That I may do justice to the place of my education, I must needs recall one mark of religious discipline which in my time was observed at Westminster. I mean the pains which Dr. Nicoll[6] took to prepare

[3] Mrs. Disney. See *Ryskamp*, pp. 8–9.

[4] C entered Westminster School in Apr. 1742.

[5] Beside the Abbey.

[6] Under the quietly pre-eminent leadership of John Nicoll (1683–1765) from 1733 to

us properly for Confirmation. The old man acquitted himself of this duty like one who had a deep sense of its importance, and I believe most of us were struck by his manner, and affected by his exhortation. For my own part, I then for the first time attempted prayer in secret, but being little accustomed to that exercise of the heart and having very childish notions of religion, I found it a difficult and painful task and was even then frightened at my own insensibility. This difficulty, though it did not subdue my good purposes till the ceremony of Confirmation was past, soon after naturally conquered them; and I relapsed into a total forgetfulness of God with the usual disadvantage of being the more hardened for having been softened to no purpose.

At twelve or thirteen years of age, I was seized with the smallpox. I mention it, however, merely in order to show that at so early a period of life my heart was become proof against the ordinary methods which a gracious God employs for our chastisement. Though I was severely handled by the disorder, and at the time of the turn in most imminent danger, yet neither during the course of it nor on my recovery had I any sentiment of contrition, any thought of God, or eternity. On the contrary, I was scarce raised from the bed of sickness before the motions of sin became more violent in me than ever, and the devil seemed to have gained rather than lost an advantage over me on the occasion: so readily did I admit his suggestions and so passive was I under his influences.

By this time I became such an adept in the infernal art of lying that I was seldom guilty of any fault for which I could not at a very short notice invent an apology capable of deceiving the wisest. The following instance may serve for a specimen of my proficiency in the practise of this abominable vice.

My father had given me a pair of silver shoe buckles which I kept till I wanted money and then sold them. The next time I waited on him at home the shoe buckles were missed and enquired after. I told him that being engaged at a match at football, and fearing that my buckles might be broken by kicks, I had put them into my waistcoat pocket, having hung my clothes upon a post; that while I was

1753, Westminster had an extraordinary assemblage of sons of peers and men who would win fame (Rockingham, Portland, Howe, Keppel, Warren Hastings, etc.). In a letter to Samuel Rose of 19 Jan. 1789, C remembered one of Nicoll's comments: 'habit has endued me with that sort of fortitude which I remember my old schoolmaster Dr. Nicol used to call the passive valour of an ass.'

attentive to the sport, a blackguard boy, who had been lurking about us under pretence of looking on, had found an opportunity to steal them and carry them clear off.

These I know are called schoolboy's tricks, but a total depravity of principle, and the work of the father of lies, is universally at the bottom of them.

At the age of eighteen, being tolerably furnished with grammatical knowledge but as ignorant in all points of religion as the satchel at my back, I was taken from Westminster and, having spent about three months at home, was sent to acquire the practice of the law with an attorney.[7] Here I might have lived and died without seeing or hearing anything that might remind me of a single Christian duty, had it not been that I was at liberty to spend my leisure time, which was well nigh all my time, at my uncle's at Southampton Row.[8] By this means I had indeed an opportunity of seeing the inside of a church, whither I went with the family on a Sunday, and which otherwise I should probably never have seen.[9] At the expiration of this time I became in a manner complete master of myself and took possession of a set of chambers in the Temple at the age of twenty-one.[10]

This being a most critical season of my life and upon which much depended, it pleased my all-merciful Father in Christ Jesus to give a check to my rash and ruinous career in wickedness at the very outset. I was struck not long after my settlement in the Temple with such a dejection of spirits as none but they who have felt the same can have the least conception of. Day and night I was upon the rack, lying down in horrors and rising in despair. I presently lost all relish to those studies I had been before closely attached to; the classics had no longer any charm for me; I had need of something more salutary than mere amusement, but had none to direct me where to find it.

[7] C went to the home of Mr. Chapman, a solicitor or attorney, early in 1750. He was sent there by his father to acquire a practical legal knowledge. Chapman's house was in Greville Street, in the heart of the legal district, directly behind Furnivall's Inn. Chapman was a pleasant and fair person, but C found the 'Tricks & illiberal Conduct of his fellow Clerks disgusting, and this association contributed to his dislike of the profession even after he moved to the Temple' (Lady Hesketh to Hayley, 1 July 1801: Add. MS. 30803 A, fol. 142).

[8] No. 30 Southampton Row, at the end of King Street. The houses of the row were new and the area fashionable; they overlooked the gardens and fields of the Bedford estates, and there were no houses opposite them.

[9] Probably the parish church, St. George's, Bloomsbury.

[10] According to the Students' Ledger of the Middle Temple, C took his 'complete set of chambers' there on 15 Nov. 1753.

At length with Herbert's poems, gothic and uncouth as they were, I yet found in them a strain of piety which I could not but admire.[11] This was the only author I had any delight in reading. I pored upon him all day long and though I found not there what I might have found, a cure for my malady, yet it never seemed so much alleviated as while I was reading him. At length I was advised by a very near and dear relation to lay him aside, for he thought such an author was more likely to nourish my melancholy than to remove it. In this state of mind I continued near a twelvemonth when, having experienced the inefficacy of all human means, I at length betook myself to God in prayer. Such is the rank our Redeemer holds in our esteem —never resorted to but in the last instance when all the creatures have failed to succour us.

My hard heart was at length softened and my stubborn knees were taught to bow; I composed a set of prayers adapted to my necessity and made frequent use of them. Weak as my faith was, the Almighty, who 'will not break the bruised reed nor quench the smoking flax',[12] was graciously pleased to hear them. A change of scene having been recommended to me, I embraced an opportunity of going with some friends to Southampton,[13] where I spent several months. Soon after our arrival we walked together to a place called Freemantle[14] about two miles from the town. The morning was clear and calm; the sun shone bright upon the sea; and the country upon the borders of it was the most beautiful I had ever seen. We sat down upon an eminence at the end of that arm of the sea which runs between Southampton and the New Forest.

Here it was that on a sudden, as if another sun had been kindled that instant in the heavens on purpose to dispel sorrow and vexation of spirit, I felt the weight of all my misery taken off. My heart became light and joyous in a moment, and had I been alone, I could have wept with transport. I must needs believe that nothing less than the Almighty Fiat could have filled me with such inexpressible delight, not by a gradual dawning of peace, but, as it were, with one flash of His life-giving countenance. I think I remember somewhat of a glow of gratitude to the Father of Mercies for this unexpected blessing, and

[11] C was not unique in his appreciation of Herbert's poems. For a description of this poet's extensive popularity in the eighteenth century, see K. Williamson, 'Herbert's Reputation in the Eighteenth Century', *Philological Quarterly*, xli (1962).

[12] Isaiah 42 : 3.

[13] C had previously spent happy times at Southampton with Sir Thomas and Lady Hesketh.

[14] A western suburb of Southampton.

that I ascribed it to His gracious acceptance of my prayers. But Satan and my own wicked heart quickly persuaded me that I was indebted for my deliverance to nothing but a change of season and the amusing varieties of this place. By this means he turned the blessing into a poison, teaching me to conclude that nothing but a continual circle of diversion and indulgence of appetite could secure me from a relapse. Upon this hellish principle, as soon as I returned to London, I burnt my prayers and away went all thoughts of devotion and dependence upon God my Saviour.

Surely it was of His mercy that I am not consumed. Glory be to His free grace!

This seems a proper place to take notice of two remarkable deliverances which the Lord vouchsafed me from violent and sudden death. Both are to be about the era of my life, but in what particular year of it is not material.

Having occasion to force my way through a hedge in a walk I was taking with my gun, I uncocked it, and thrust its muzzle foremost as far towards the other side of the hedge as I could reach. Having broke through the bush, I put forth my arm and laid hold of the gun a little above the mouth of it, which was by this means presented directly against my stomach; and then, drawing it towards me in the passage, I heard the trigger click; and having drawn it fairly through the brambles, perceived that it had actually cocked itself against some impediment in the way, and was ready for firing. Had the flint fallen forward upon the steel before it was completely cocked, or had a twig hitched against the finger piece when it was so, in either case I should have received the whole charge in my stomach. I thought I had a lucky escape, and laying my gun on my shoulder walked away.

Another time, as I was running hastily along the street, a large piece of brick fell from the height of three storeys so near to me that had I been a few inches forwarder on my way, it must inevitably [have] crushed me. It dropped close at my foot and covered me with a cloud of dust. Again I thought myself extremely fortunate and having mentioned the circumstance once or twice to others, who thought so too, dismissed it from my mind entirely. Having spent about twelve years in the Temple in an uninterrupted course of sinful indulgences, my associates and companions being either, like myself, pretended Christians or professed infidels,[15] I obtained at

[15] Perhaps a reference to C's association with the Geniuses. See *Ryskamp*, pp. 78–101.

length so complete a victory over my conscience that all remonstrances from that quarter were in a manner silenced. Sometimes, indeed, a question would arise in my mind whether it was safe to proceed any farther in a course so utterly and plainly condemned in the word of God. I saw clearly that if the Gospel was true such a conduct must inevitably end in my destruction, but saw not by what means I should change my Ethiopian complexion[16] or overcome such an inveterate habit of rebelling against God. The next thing that occurred to me at such a time was a doubt whether the Gospel was true or false. To this succeeded many an anxious wish for the decision of this important question, for I foolishly thought that obedience would presently follow were I but convinced that it was worthwhile to attempt it. Having no reason to expect a miracle, nor hoping to be satisfied by anything less, I acquiesced at length in the force of that devilish conclusion that, therefore, the only course I could take to secure my present peace was to wink hard against the prospect of future misery and to resolve to banish all thought upon a subject upon which I thought to so little purpose. Nevertheless, when in company with Deists I have heard the Gospel blasphemed, I never failed to assert the truth of it with much vehemence of disputation, for which I was the better qualified having always been an industrious and diligent inquirer into the evidences by which it was externally supported. I think I once went so far in a controversy of this kind as to assert that I would gladly submit to have my right hand cut off, so I might but be enabled to live according to the Gospel. Thus have I been employed when half intoxicated in vindicating the truth of Scripture [while] in the very act of rebellion against its dictates. Lamentable inconsistency of a convinced judgment with an unsanctified heart! An inconsistence, evident to others as well as to myself, insomuch that a deistical friend of mine with whom I was disputing upon the subject cut short the matter by alleging that if what I urged was true, I was certainly damned by my own scheme.

Towards the middle of this period which I spent in the Temple, it pleased the great Shepherd of the sheep to call upon me in a most extraordinary manner by exhibiting to me an emblematical representation of my great danger. Such at least I have always esteemed it, and such I believe the reader will think it when he compares it with the subsequent narrative, however it may appear to him in a

[16] See Jeremiah 13: 23.

different light at present. Far be it from me through a spirit of vain-glory to arrogate to myself a larger share of the Divine attention (if I may so express myself) than has actually been bestowed upon me. The grace and mercy of God are His own, and He dispenses them in what measure and manner He pleases, not regarding the merit of the object (which is infinitely less than nothing in the best of us) but His own glory. It is of the same nature with some facts which follow, and which, though they may expose me to the suspicion of enthusiasm, I dare not omit. For who am I that I should be too wise to relate what God has thought proper to perform? I confess they are not according to the ordinary methods of His dealings, but who shall set bounds to His power, 'or being his counsellor hath taught him?'[17] While I believe them to have been the works of the Lord, which in my soul I do, I must needs revere the deed for the sake of the hand that wrought it, and adore that amazing grace which was pleased to seek and to find me in a way so extraordinary and unusual. I was at this time spending the latter part of the summer at Brighthelmston,[18] where I lived as everywhere else forgetful of God, an alien from the commonwealth of Israel. One day as I walked about by the cliffside about a mile from the town, having my eye towards the downs, I saw a shepherd driving his sheep to pasture. He and his flock were distant from me about a quarter of a mile. Suddenly his dog seized one of the flock by the wool of his neck and galloped with him at full speed directly down to me; nor did they slacken their pace till the dog had brought the sheep close to the very edge of the cliff, from whence if he had fallen, he must have been dashed to pieces. At the edge of the precipice they stopped. The sheep immediately faced about looking wistfully at the flock he had left, and trembling as conscious of his danger. The dog laid down before him, so near that their noses met. In this position they remained to the best of my remembrance two minutes when the sheep began to creep forward a little. The dog raised himself upon his feet but followed him no further. They took different ways, the sheep stealing by degrees into a quicker pace after having taken a large circle, joined the flock close by the shepherd; and the dog trotted up towards the headmost sheep, behaving himself after this incident quietly enough.

The subsequent matter of these pages will furnish the best comment upon the foregoing occurrence. If the reader will carry it in his

[17] Isaiah 40: 13. [18] Brighton.

memory as he proceeds, he will find that the interpretation I have given it, so far from being constrained or unnatural, applies itself to the fact, as the only solution of so singular a transaction. For it is not to be conceived that a shepherd would teach his dog a trick which would answer no purpose but to endanger the lives of his flock, and that the dog should do it without instruction cannot I think be accounted for otherwise than by supposing a supernatural agency. It may be alleged possibly that had it been for a warning to me, it would have had its effect, but this is no necessary consequence. There are many instances in Holy Writ of express warnings given, and by the mouth of a prophet too, yet not taken by those to whom they were directed. Besides which, it is reasonable to suppose that these annunciations may be given with a more remote intention, and that their principal design may be to give testimony to God's watchful care of His people when such tokens of it receive their full explanation from a comparison of what has followed with the prefiguring type of it.

This, having reached my lodging, I related to my companions there, who, I well remember, thought it a most strange occurrence. They, I suppose, having wondered at it sufficiently, forgot it; and as to myself, I no otherwise remembered it than as a matter of curiosity.

By this time, my patrimony being well nigh spent and there being no appearance that I should ever repair the damage by a fortune of my own getting, I began to be a little apprehensive of approaching want. It was, I imagine, under some impressions of this kind that I one day said to a friend of mine, if the Clerk of the Journals in the House of Lords[19] should die I had some hopes that my kinsman[20] who had the place in his disposal would appoint me to succeed him. We both agreed that the business of that place, being transacted in private, would exactly suit me, and both expressed an earnest wish for his death that I might be provided for. Thus did I covet what God had commanded me not to covet, and involved myself in still deeper guilt by doing it in the spirit of a murderer. It pleased the Lord to give me my heart's desire and in it, and with it, an immediate punishment of my crime.

The poor man died. By his death not only the Clerkship of the Journals became vacant, but it became necessary to appoint a new

19 Francis Macklay, the Clerk of the Journals, died in Apr. 1763.

20 Ashley Cowper. See *Ryskamp*, pp. 148–50.

officer to two other places which he had served jointly as deputy to Mr. De Grey,[21] who at this time resigned. These were the Office of Reading Clerk and the Clerkship of the Committees—of much greater value than that of the Journals.[22] The patentee of these appointments (whom I pray God to bless for his benevolent intention to serve me) called on me at my chambers and having invited me to take a turn with him in the garden there made me an offer of the two most profitable places, intending the other for his friend Mr. Arnott.[23]

Dazzled by so splendid a proposal and not immediately reflecting upon my incapacity to execute a business of so public a nature, I at once accepted it, but at the same time (such was the will of Him whose hand was in the whole matter) seemed to myself to receive a dagger in my heart. The word [*sic*] was given, and every moment added to the smart of it.

All the considerations by which I endeavoured to compose my mind to its former tranquility did but torment me the more, proving miserable comforters and counsellors of no value. I returned to my chambers thoughtful and unhappy; my countenance fell, and my friend was astonished, instead of that additional cheerfulness he might so reasonably expect, to find an air of deep melancholy in all I said or did. Having been harassed in this manner day and night for the space of a week, perplexed between a sense of the apparent folly of casting away the only visible chance I had of being well provided for and the impossibility of keeping it, I determined at length to write a letter to my friend, though he lodged, in a manner, at the next door and we generally spent the day together. I did so and therein begged him to accept my resignation: to appoint Mr. Arnott to the place he had given me, and permit me to succeed Mr. Arnott. I was well aware of the disproportion between the value of his appointment and mine, but my peace was gone; pecuniary advantages were no equivalent to what I had lost, and I flattered myself that the Clerkship of the Journals would fall fairly and easily within the scope of my abilities. Like a man in a fever, I thought a change of posture would relieve my pain, and, as the event will show, was equally disappointed.

[21] William de Grey (1719–81), who was married to C's cousin, Mary Cowper (1719–1800).

[22] Macklay had purchased the office of the Clerk of Journals from Ashley Cowper in 1736 for £300 and had collected annually £50 from the Royal Bounty.

[23] Mathew Robert Arnott (d. 1800), the family friend, who was to take C's place as Clerk of the Committees.

At length I carried my point, my friend in this instance preferring the gratification of my desires to his own interest, for nothing could be so likely to bring a suspicion of bargain and sale upon his nomination, which the Lords would not have endured, as his appointment of so near a relation to the least profitable office while the most valuable was allotted to a person not at all related to him.

The matter being thus settled, something like a calm took place in my mind. I was indeed not a little concerned about my character, being aware that it must needs suffer by the strange appearance of my proceedings. This, however, being but a small part of the anxiety I had laboured under, was hardly felt when the rest was taken off, and [I] thought my path towards an easy maintenance was now smooth and open, and for a day or two was tolerably cheerful.

But behold the storm was gathering all the while, and the fury of it was not the less violent for this little gleam of sunshine in the beginning. A strange opposition to my friend's right of nomination began to manifest itself.[24] A powerful party among the Lords was formed to thwart it in favour of an old enemy of the family, though much indebted to their bounty; and it appeared plain that if we succeeded at last it would only be after fighting our ground by inches. Every advantage I was told would be sought for and eagerly seized to disconcert us. I was bid to expect an examination at the Bar of the House touching my sufficiency for the post I had undertaken. Being necessarily ignorant of the nature of that business, it became expedient that I should visit the office daily in order to qualify myself for the narrowest scrutiny. All the horrors of my fears and perplexity returned. A thunderbolt would have been as welcome to me as this intelligence. I knew to a demonstration that upon these terms the Clerkship of the Journals was no place for me. To require my attendance at the Bar of the House that I might there publicly entitle myself to the office was in effect to exclude me from it. In the mean time the interest of my friend, the honour of his choice, my own reputation and circumstances all urged me forward; all pressed me to undertake that which I saw to be impracticable. They whose spirits are formed like mine, to whom a public exhibition of themselves on any occasion is mortal poison, may have some idea of the horror of my situation; others can have none.

[24] The pressures came from William Macklay, Francis's son. The younger Macklay had been brought into the Office of Clerk of the Journals by his father.

My continual misery at length brought on a nervous fever. Quiet forsook me by day and sleep by night. A finger raised against me was now more than I could stand against. In this posture of mind I attended regularly at the office, where, instead of a soul upon the rack, the most active spirits were essentially necessary to my purpose. I expected no assistance from anybody there, all the inferior clerks being under the influence of our opponent. Accordingly I received none. The journal books were indeed thrown open to me—a thing which could not be refused, and from which perhaps a man in health and with a head turned to business might have gained all the information he had wanted. But it was not so with me. I read without perception and was so distressed that had every clerk in the office been my friend it would have availed me little, for I was not in a condition to receive instruction, much less to elicit it out of a number of manuscripts, some without direction. Many months went over me thus employed—constant in the use of the means, despairing as to the issue. The feelings of a man when he arrives at the place of execution are probably much like what I experienced every time I set my foot in the office, which was almost every day, near half a year together. At length the vacation being pretty far advanced, I made shift to get into the country and repaired to Margate.

There by the help of cheerful company, a new scene, and the intermission of my painful employment, I presently began to recover my spirits, though even here for some time after my arrival (notwithstanding the preceeding day had been spent agreeably and without any disturbing recollection of my circumstances) my first reflections when I awakened in a morning were horrible and full of wretchedness. I looked forward to the approaching winter and regretted the flight of every moment that brought it nearer, like a man borne away by a rapid torrent into a stormy sea from which he sees no possibility of returning, and where he knows he cannot subsist. At length, indeed, I acquired such a facility of turning away my thoughts from the ensuing crisis that for weeks together I hardly adverted to it [at] all. But the stress of the tempest was yet to come and was not to be avoided by any resolution of mine to look another way.

How wonderful are the works of the Lord and His ways past finding out! Thus was He preparing me gradually for an event which I least of all expected—even for the reception of His Blessed Gospel. Working by means which in all human contemplation must needs

seem directly opposite to that purpose, but which in His wise and gracious disposal have, I trust, effectually accomplished it.

About the beginning of October 1763 I was again required to attend the office and to prepare for the push. This no sooner took place than all my misery returned. Again I visited the scene of my ineffectual labours; again I felt myself pressed by necessity on either side with nothing but despair in prospect.

To this dilemma I was reduced: either to keep possession of the office to the last extremity and by so doing expose myself to a public rejection for insufficiency (for the little knowledge I had would have quite forsaken me at the Bar of the House); or else to fling it up at once and, by that means, run the hazard of ruining my benefactor's right of appointment by bringing his discretion in the use of it into question. In this situation such a fit of passion has sometimes seized me when alone in my chambers that I have cried out aloud and cursed the very hour of my birth, lifting up my eyes to heaven at the same time not as a suppliant but in the hellish spirit of rancorous reproach and blasphemy against my Maker. A thought would sometimes come across me that my sins had perhaps brought this distress upon me, that the hand of divine vengeance was in it, but in the pride of my heart I presently acquitted myself and thereby implicitly charged God with injustice, saying, 'What sins have I committed to deserve this misery?' I saw plainly that God alone could deliver me, but was firmly persuaded He would not and therefore omitted to ask it.

Ask it at His hands I would not, but as Saul sought to the witch,[25] so did I to the physician, and was so diligent in the use of drugs as if they would have healed my wounded spirit or have made 'the rough places plain'[26] before me. I made indeed one effort of a devotional kind, for having found a prayer or two in that repository of self-righteous and pharisaical lumber, The Whole Duty of Man,[27] I said them a few nights but with so little expectation of prevailing that way, that I soon laid aside the book and with it all thoughts of God and all hope of a remedy.

I now began to look upon madness as the only chance remaining, I had a strong kind of foreboding that it would fare so with me, and

25 The encounter between Saul and the witch of Endor is described in 1 Samuel 28 : 8–25.

26 Isaiah 40 : 4.

27 An extremely popular statement of traditional church doctrine and Christian ethics since its publication in 1658, this tract, generally ascribed to Richard Allestree (1619–81), also found disfavour with men like Whitefield.

I wished for it earnestly and looked forward to it with impatient expectation. My chief fear was that my senses would not fail me time enough to excuse my appearance in the House, which was the only purpose I wanted it to answer.

Accordingly the day of decision drew near and I was still in my senses, though in my heart I had formed many wishes and by word of mouth expressed many expectations to the contrary.

Now came the great temptation, the point to which Satan had all the while been drawing me, the dark and hellish purpose of self-murder. I grew more sullen and reserved, fled from all society, even of the most intimate friends, and shut myself up in my chambers. The ruin of my fortune, the contempt of my relations and acquaintance, the prejudice I should do my patron, were all urged upon me with irresistible energy. Being reconciled to the apprehension of madness, I began to be reconciled to the apprehension of death. Though formerly in my happiest hours I had never been able to glance a single thought that way without shuddering at the idea of dissolution, I now wished for it and found myself but little shocked at the thought of procuring it for myself. Perhaps, thought I, there is no God; or if there be, the Scripture may be false, and if so then God has nowhere forbid suicide. I considered life as my property and therefore at my own disposal. Men of great name, I observed, had destroyed themselves, and the world still entertained the profoundest respect for their memory. But above all I was persuaded to believe that if the fact was ever so unlawful and even supposing Christianity to be true, my misery even in hell itself would be more supportable.

I recollected too that when I was about twenty years of age my father desired me to read a vindication of self-murder in the Persian Letters,[28] written I think by Montesquieu, and to give him my sentiment upon the question. I did so and argued against it. My father heard my reasons and was silent, neither approving nor disapproving, from whence I inferred that he sided with the author against me, though at this time, I believe, the true motive of his conduct was that he wanted to think favourably of the state of a departed friend who had some years before destroyed himself and whose death had struck him with the deepest affliction.[29] But this

[28] C is referring to Letter 76 of *Lettres persanes* (1721).

[29] This friend has not been identified.

solution of the matter never once occurred to me, and the circumstance weighed mightily with me. At this time I fell in with company at a chop-house with an elderly well-looking gentleman whom I had often seen before there, but never till then spoken to. He began the discourse and talked much of the miseries he had suffered. This opened my heart to him, and I freely and readily took part of the conversation. At length self-murder became the topic, and in the result we agreed that the only reason why some men were content to drag their sorrows with them to the grave and others not was that some men were endued with a certain indignant fortitude of spirit teaching them to despise life which others wanted. Another person whom I met at a tavern told me he had made up his mind about that matter and had no doubt of his liberty to die as he saw convenient, though, by the way, the same person has suffered many and great afflictions since and is alive. Thus were the emissaries of the Prince of Darkness let loose upon me. Blessed be the Lord for it who has brought much good out of all this evil. This concurrence of sentiment in men of sense unknown to each other I considered as a satisfactory decision of the question and determined to proceed accordingly.

One evening in the month of November 1763, as soon as it was dark, affecting as cheerful and unconstrained an air as I could, I went to an apothecary's shop and asked for an half ounce phial of liquid laudanum. The man seemed to observe me narrowly, but if he did I managed my voice and countenance so as to deceive him. The day that required my attendance at the Bar of the House being not yet come (I think it was about a week distant), I kept my bottle close in my side-pocket, resolved to use it when I should be convinced there was no other way of escaping. This indeed seemed evident already, but I was willing to allow myself every possible chance of that sort and to protract the execution of my horrid purpose till the last moment.

But Satan was impatient of delay. The day before the period above mentioned arrived, being at Richard's Coffee-house[30] at breakfast, I read the newspaper and in it a letter which the farther I proceeded in it the more closely [it] engaged my attention. I cannot now recollect the purport of it, but before I had finished it, it appeared

30 This establishment, at No. 8 Fleet Street (south side, near Temple Bar), was named after Richard Torner, or Turner, to whom the house was let in 1680. See Bryant Lillywhite, *London Coffee Houses* (1963), pp. 190–3.

demonstrably true to me that it was a libel or satire upon me. The author seemed to be acquainted with my purpose of self-murder and to have written that letter to secure and hasten the execution of it. My mind at this time possibly began to be disordered; however it was, I was certainly given up to a strong delusion. I said within myself, 'your cruelty shall be gratified; you shall have your revenge,' and flinging down the paper in a fit of strong passion, rushed hastily out of the room, directing my way towards the fields where I intended to find some house to die in, or, if not, determined to poison myself in a ditch when I should meet with one sufficiently retired.

Before I had walked half a mile in the fields a thought struck me that I might yet spare my life: that I had nothing to do but to sell what I had in the Funds[31] (which might be done in an hour), to go on board a ship, and transport myself to France. There, when every other way of maintenance should fail, I promised myself a comfortable asylum in some monastery, an acquisition easily made by changing my religion. Not a little pleased with this new expedient, I returned to my chambers to pack up all that I could at so short a notice. But while I was looking over my portmanteau my mind changed again, and self-murder was recommended to me once more in all its advantages. Not knowing where to poison myself, for I was liable to continual interruption in my chambers from my laundress and her husband, I laid aside that intention and resolved upon drowning. For this purpose I immediately took coach and ordered the man to drive to Tower Wharf, intending to throw myself into the river from the Custom House quay.

It would be strange should I omit to observe here how I was continually hurried away from such places as were most favourable to my design to others where it was almost impossible to execute it—from the fields, where it was improbable that anything should happen to prevent me, to the Custom House, where everything of that kind was to be expected; and this by a sudden impulse which lasted just long enough to call me back again to my chambers, and then immediately withdrawn. Nothing ever appeared more feasible to me than the project of going to France till it had served its purpose, and then in an instant it appeared to me impracticable and absurd even to a degree of ridicule. My life which I had called my own and proudly claimed a right to dispose of as my own was kept from me by Him

[31] The stock of the national debt, considered as a mode of investment (*O.E.D.*).

whose property indeed it was and who alone had a right to dispose [of] it. This is not the only occasion on which it is proper to make this remark; others will offer themselves in the course of this narrative so fairly that the reader cannot overlook them.

I left the coach upon Tower Wharf intending never to return to it, but upon coming to the quay I found the water low and a porter or two seated upon some goods there, as if placed on purpose to prevent me. This passage to the bottomless pit being mercifully shut against me, I returned to the coach and ordered the man back to the Temple. I drew up the shutters, once more had recourse to the laudanum, and determined to drink it off directly. But God had otherwise ordained. A conflict that shook me to pieces almost suddenly took place: not properly a trembling but a convulsive kind of agitation which deprived me in a manner of the use of my limbs. My mind was as much shaken as my body, distracted betwixt the desire of death and the dread of it. Twenty times I had the phial at my mouth and as often received an irresistible check, and even at the time it seemed to me that an invisible hand swayed the bottle downwards as often as I set it against my lips. I well remember that I took notice of this circumstance with some surprise, though it affected no change in my purpose. Panting for breath and in a terrible agony, I flung myself back into the corner of the coach. A few drops of the laudanum which had touched my lips, besides the fumes of it, began to have a stupefying effect upon me. Regretting the loss of so fair an opportunity, yet utterly unable to avail myself of it; determined not to live, and already half dead with anguish of spirit, I once more returned to the Temple. I instantly repaired to my room and having shut both the outer and inner door prepared myself for the last scene of the tragedy. I poured the laudanum into a small basin, and set it in a chair by the bed-side, half undressed myself, and laid down between the blankets, shuddering with horror at the thought of what I was now about to perpetrate. I reproached myself bitterly with folly and rank cowardice for having suffered the fear of death to influence me as it had done and was filled with disdain at my own pitiful timidity, but still something seemed sensibly to overrule me; something seemed to say, 'Think what you are doing; consider, and live.'

At length, however, with a most confirmed resolution, I reached forth my hand towards the basin, when behold, the fingers of both my hands were so closely contracted, and so forcibly drawn together

as if bound with a cord, that they became entirely useless. Still, indeed, I could have made shift with both hands (dead and stiff as they were) to have raised the basin to my mouth, for my arms were not at all affected. But this new difficulty struck me with wonder. It had the air of a divine interposition. I lay down in bed again to muse upon it and while thus employed heard the key turn in the outer door and my laundress's husband come in. By this time the use of my fingers was restored to me. I started up, hastily dressed myself again, hid the basin, and, affecting as composed an air as I could, went out into the dining-room. In a few minutes I was left alone, and now unless God had evidently interposed again for my preservation, should certainly have done execution upon myself, having a whole afternoon before me, both the man and his wife being gone to dinner.

Outward obstructions were no sooner removed than new ones arose within. The man had just shut the door behind him when the convincing spirit came upon me and a total alteration in my sentiments took place. The horror of the crime was immediately exhibited to me in so strong a light that, being seized with a kind of furious indignation, I snatched up the basin, poured away the laudanum into a pail of foul water, and, not content with that, flung the phial out at the window with such violence as dashed it in pieces.

This impulse having served the present purpose was withdrawn. I spent the remainder of the day in a stupid kind of insensibility, undetermined as to the manner of dying but still bent upon self-murder as the only possible deliverance. That sense of the enormity of the crime which I had just experienced had left me entirely, and unless my Eternal Father in Christ Jesus had decreed that my covenant with death and my agreement with Hell should vanish before His covenant of mercy, I had by this time been a companion of devils and the just object of His boundless vengeance.

In the evening a most intimate friend[32] called on me and felicitated me on a happy resolution he heard I had taken to stand the brunt and to keep the office. I knew not whence this intelligence arose but did not contradict it. We conversed a while with a real cheerfulness on his part and an affected one on mine, and when he left me I said in my heart, 'I shall see thee no more.'

Behold to what extremity a good sort of a man may fall. Such was I in the estimation of those who knew me best; a decent outside is all

[32] This friend has not been identified.

the good-natured world requires. Thus equipped, though all within be rank atheism, rottenness of heart, and rebellion against the blessed God, we are said to be good enough; and if we are damned, alas, who shall be saved? Invert this charitable reflection and say, if a good sort of man be saved, who then shall perish? and the reverse of it comes much nearer to the truth. But this is a hard saying and the world cannot bear it. See Matthew 21: 31.[33]

I went to bed to take, as I thought, my last sleep in this world. The next morning was to place me at the Bar of the House of Lords, and I determined not to see it. I slept as usual and awoke about three o'clock. Immediately I arose and by the help of a rush light found my penknife, took it into bed with me, and lay for some hours with it pointed directly against my heart. Twice or three times I placed it upright under my left breast, bearing with my weight upon it, but the point was broken off square and it would not penetrate. In this manner the time passed till day began to break. I heard the clock strike seven. Instantly it occurred to me that there was no time to be lost; the chambers would soon be open and my friend call upon me to take me with him to Westminster. 'Now is the time,' thought I, 'This is the crisis; no more dallying with the love of life. I have not a moment to spare.' I arose and bolted, as I verily thought, the inner door of the chamber but was mistaken; my touch deceived me and I left it as I found it. My preservation, indeed, as will appear, did not turn upon that incident, but I mention it because it looks as if the good Providence that watched over me kept every way open for my deliverance that nothing might seem to be left to hazard.

Now let the reader revert a moment to the dog and sheep above mentioned, and I think he must necessarily admit the propriety of the application. Surely I was brought to the very edge of the precipice. Not one hesitating thought remained, but I fell greedily to the execution of my purpose. My garter was made of a broad scarlet binding with a sliding buckle being sewn together at the ends; by the help of the buckle I formed a noose and fixing it about my neck, strained it so tight that I hardly left a passage for breath or the blood to circulate. The tongue of the buckle held it fast. At each corner of the bed was placed a wreath of carved work fastened by an iron pin which passed up through the midst of it. The other part of the garter

[33] 'Jesus said to them, "Truly, I say to you, the tax collectors and the harlots go into the kingdom of God before you." '

therefore which made a loop I slipped over one of these and hung by it some seconds, drawing up my feet under me that they might not touch the floor. But the iron bent, the carved work slipped off, and the garter with it. I then fastened the garter to the frame of the tester, winding it round and tying it in a strong knot. The frame broke short and let me down again. The third effort was more likely to succeed. I set the bed chamber door open, which reached within a foot of the ceiling. By the help of a chair I could command the top of it, which being rough and ragged, the garter hitched upon it, and the loop, being wide enough to admit a large angle of the door, was easily fixed so as not to slip off again. I pushed away the chair with my foot and hung at my whole length. While I hung I heard a voice say distinctly three times, ' 'Tis over, 'tis over, 'tis over.' Though I am sure of the fact, and was so at the time, yet it did not at all alarm me or affect my resolution. I hung so long that I lost all sense, all consciousness of existence. When I came to myself again I thought myself in Hell. The sound of my own dreadful groans was all that I heard, and a feeling like that of flashes, just beginning to seize upon me, passed upon my whole body. In a few seconds I found myself fallen with my face to the floor. In about half a minute I made a shift to recover my feet, and reeling and staggering, tumbled into bed again.

By the blessed Providence of my God the garter which had held me till the bitterness of temporal death was past broke just before eternal death would have taken place upon me. A stagnation of the blood under one eye in a broad crimson spot and a red circle about my neck showed plainly that I had been upon the brink of eternity; the latter, indeed, might have been occasioned by the pressure of the garter, but the former was certainly the effect of strangulation, for it was not attended with the sensation of a bruise, as it must have been had I in the fall received one upon so tender a part. And I rather think the circle round my neck was owing to the same cause, for the part was not excoriated nor at all in pain where the skin was red, and I have heard that a death of this sort is attended with both these symptoms.

Soon after I was got into bed I was surprised to hear a noise in the dining-room, where the laundress was lighting the fire; she had found the door unbolted, notwithstanding my design to fasten it, and must have passed by the bed chamber door, for it opened into the passage,

while I was hanging upon it and yet never perceived me. She heard me fall, however, and presently came to ask me if I was well, adding that she feared I had been in a fit. I sent her to a friend of mine to whom I related what I had done, and dispatched him to my kinsman at the coffee-house. As soon as the latter arrived I pointed to the broken garter, which lay in the middle of the room, and apprised him also of the attempt I had been making. His words were, 'My dear Mr. C——, you terrify me to death. To be sure you cannot hold the office at this rate. Where is the deputation?' I gave him the key of the drawer where it was deposited, and his business requiring his immediate attendance, he took it away with him. And thus ended all my connection with the Parliament Office.

To this moment I had felt no concern of a spiritual kind. Ignorant of Original Sin, insensible of the guilt of actual transgression, I understood neither the Law nor the Gospel—the condemning nature of the one or the restoring and reconciling mercies of the other. I was as much unacquainted with Christ and all His saving offices as if His Blessed Name had never reached me. Now, therefore, a new scene opened upon me. Conviction of sin took place, especially of the sin I had just committed; the meanness of it, as well as its atrocious nature, was exhibited to me in colours so inconceivably strong that I despised myself with a contempt not to be imagined or expressed for having attempted it. This sense of it secured me from the repetition of a crime which I could not now reflect upon without the greatest abhorrence. Before I rose from bed it was suggested to me that there wanted nothing but murder to fill up the measure of my iniquity, and that though I had failed in my design, yet I had all the guilt of that crime to answer for. A sense of God's wrath and a deep despair of escaping it instantly succeeded. The fear of death became much more prevalent in me now than ever the desire of it had been. A frequent flashing like that of fire before my eyes and an excessive pressure upon my brain made me apprehensive of an apoplexy—an event which I thought the more probable as an extravasation[34] in that part seemed likely enough to happen in so violent a struggle. By the advice of my dear friend and benefactor, who called upon me again at noon, I sent for a physician [and] told him the fact and the stroke I apprehended. He assured me there was no danger of it and advised me by all means to retire into the country. Being easy in

[34] The escape of blood from its proper vessels into the surrounding tissues (*O.E.D.*).

that particular and not knowing whither to betake myself, I continued in my chambers, where the solitude of my situation left me at full liberty to attend to my spiritual state, a matter I had never till this day sufficiently thought of.

At this time I wrote to my brother at Cambridge to inform him of the distress I had been in and the dreadful method I had taken to deliver myself from it, assuring him (as I faithfully might) that I had laid aside all such horrid intentions and was desirous to live as long as it would please the Almighty to permit me. My sins were now set in array against me; I began to see and to feel that I had lived without God in the world. As I walked to and fro in my chamber I said within myself, 'There never was so abandoned a wretch, so great a sinner.' All my worldly sorrows seemed as if they had never been. The terrors which succeeded them seemed so much greater and more afflicting. One moment I saw myself, as I thought, shut out from mercy by one chapter, and the next by another. The sword of the Spirit seemed to guard the tree of life from my touch and to flame against me in every avenue by which I attempted to approach it. I particularly remember the barren fig tree was to me a theme of inconceivable misery, and I applied it to myself with a strong persuasion upon my mind that when Our Saviour pronounced a curse upon it He had me in His eye and pointed that curse directly at me. I turned over all Archbishop Tillotson's sermons[35] in hopes of finding one upon that subject and consulted my brother upon the true meaning of it, desirous if possible to arrive at a gentler interpretation of the passage than my evil conscience would suffer me to fasten upon it. 'O Lord Thou didst vex me with all Thy storms, all Thy billows went over me. In the day time Thou didst run upon me like a giant; and in the night season Thou didst scare me with visions.'[36]

In every book I opened I found something that struck me to the heart. I remember taking up a volume of Beaumont and Fletcher which lay upon the table in my kinsman's lodging and the first sentence I saw was this, 'The justice of the gods is in it.'[37] My heart immediately answered, 'So it is of a truth,' and I cannot but observe that as I found something in every author to condemn me, so it was

[35] The belief that he had committed the unpardonable sin may have been suggested to C's distraught mind by reading Archbishop Tillotson's sermon, 'Of the Unpardonable Sin against the Holy Ghost'.

[36] C is conflating various passages from Job.

[37] *Philaster*, I. ii. 105–6. 'In that the secret justice of the gods / Is mingled with it . . .'

generally the first sentence I pitched upon. Everything preached to me, and everything preached the curse of the Law.

I was now strongly tempted to use laudanum, not as a poison, but as an opiate to compose my spirits—to stupefy my awakened and feeling mind, harassed with sleepless nights and days of uninterrupted misery. But God forbad it, Who would have nothing interfere with the quickening work He had begun in me. And neither want of rest nor continual agony of soul could bring me to the use of it. I hated and abhorred the very smell of laudanum.

I never went into the street but I thought the people stared and laughed at me and held me in contempt, and could hardly persuade myself but the voice of my conscience was loud enough for everybody to hear it. They who knew me seemed to avoid me, and if they spoke to me they seemed to do it in scorn. I bought a ballad of a hawker who was singing it in the street because I thought it was written upon me. I either dined alone at the tavern, whither I went in the dark, or at the chop-house, when I always took care to hide myself in the darkest corner of the room. I slept generally an hour in the evening upon the bed, but it was only to be terrified in dreams, and when I awakened again it was some time before I could walk steadily. And through the passage into the dining-room I reeled and staggered like a drunken man. The eyes of men I could not bear, but to think that the eye of God was upon me (which I was now well assured of) gave me the most intolerable anguish. If for a moment either a book or a companion stole away my attention from myself, a flash from Hell seemed to be thrown into my mind immediately, and I said within myself, 'What are these things to me who am damned?' In a word, I saw myself a sinner altogether, and every way a sinner, but as yet I saw not a glimpse of the mercy of God in Jesus.

The capital engine in all the artillery of Satan had not yet been employed against me; already overwhelmed with despair, I was not yet quite sunk to the bottom of the gulf. This was a fit season for the use of it. Accordingly I was set to inquire whether I had not been guilty of the unpardonable sin, and was presently persuaded that I had. A neglect to improve the mercies of God vouchsafed to me at Southampton on the occasion above mentioned was represented to me as the sin against the Holy Ghost. No favourable construction of my conduct in that instance, no argument of my brother's, who was now come to town to comfort me, nothing he could suggest in

extenuation of my offence could gain a moment's admission. Satan furnished me so readily with weapons against myself that neither scripture nor reason could undeceive me.

Life appeared now more eligible than death only because it was a barrier between me and everlasting burnings. My thoughts in the day became still more gloomy and the visions of the night more dreadful. One morning as I lay between sleeping and awake, I seemed to myself to be walking in Westminster Abbey, walking till prayers should begin; presently I thought I heard the minister's voice and hastened towards the Choir; just as I was upon the point of entering, the iron gate under the organ was flung in my face with a jar that made the Abbey ring.

The noise awakened me. A sentence of excommunication from all the churches upon earth would not have been so dreadful to me as the interpretation I could not avoid putting upon this dream.

Another time while I was musing, I seemed to myself to pronounce those words from Milton, 'Evil be thou my Good.'[38] I verily thought that I had adopted that hellish sentiment, it seemed to come so directly from my heart. I arose from bed to look for my prayer book, and having found it endeavoured to pray, but immediately experienced the impossibility of drawing nigh to God unless He first draws nigh to us. I made many passionate attempts towards prayer, but failed in all. Having an obscure notion about the efficacy of faith, I resolved upon an experiment to prove whether I had faith or not. For this purpose I began to repeat the Creed. When I came to the second period of it, which professes a belief in Christ, all traces of the form were struck out of my memory, nor could I recollect one syllable of the matter. While I endeavoured to recover it, and just when I thought myself upon the point of doing so, I perceived a sensation in my brain like a tremulous vibration in all the fibres of it. By this means I lost the words in the very instant when I thought to have laid hold on them. This threw me into an agony, but growing a little calmer I made an attempt upon the third member of the Creed, professing a belief in the Holy Ghost. Here again I failed in the same manner and by the same means as before.

The extraordinary sensation in my brain, just in the very article of recollection, I considered as a supernatural interposition to inform me that, having sinned against the Holy Ghost, I had no longer any

[38] *Paradise Lost*, iv. 110.

interest in Christ or in the gifts of the Spirit. Being therefore assured of this with the most riveted conviction, I delivered myself over to absolute despair. I felt besides a sense of burning in my heart like that of real fire, and concluded it an earnest of those eternal flames which should soon receive me. I laid myself down in bed, howling with horror, while my knees smote against each other. In this condition my brother found me; the first word I spoke to him (and I remember the very expression) was, 'Oh brother, I am damned—damned. Think of eternity, and then think what it is to be damned.' I had indeed a sense of eternity impressed upon my mind which seemed almost to amount to a full comprehension of it. My poor brother, pierced to the heart at the sight of my misery, endeavoured to comfort me, but all to no purpose. I refused to be comforted, and my ruin appeared to me in such colours, and with such demonstration attending it, that to administer consolation to me was only to exasperate and mock my fears. At length I remembered my friend Martin Madan and resolved to send for him. I had been used to think him an enthusiast, but it now seemed that if there was any 'balm in Gilead'[39] for me his hand must administer it. My brother undertook to be the messenger and spent almost the whole evening in seeking him.

On former occasions when my spiritual concerns had at any time occurred to me I thought likewise on the necessity of repentance. I knew that many persons had spoken of shedding tears for sins, but when I asked myself whether the time would ever come when I should weep for mine, it seemed to me that a stone might sooner do it. Not knowing that 'Christ was exalted to give repentance,'[40] I despaired of ever attaining it.

My friend, Mr. Madan, came to me; we sat on the bedside together and he began to declare to me the Gospel. While he spoke of original sin and the corruption of every man born into the world, whereby we are all the children of wrath, without any difference, I perceived something like a glimpse of hope dawning in my heart. This doctrine set me more upon a level with the rest of mankind and made my condition appear to me less desperate. Next he insisted on the all-atoning efficacy of the Blood of Jesus and His infinitely perfect righteousness for our justification. While I heard this part of his discourse, and while he opened and expounded to me the scriptures

[39] See Jeremiah 8: 22 and 46: 11. [40] Acts 5: 31.

on which he supported it, my heart began to burn within me; my soul was pierced with a sense of my bitter ingratitude to so merciful a Saviour, and those tears which I had thought it so impossible for me to shed burst forth abundantly. I saw clearly that my case required such a remedy and I had not the least doubt within me but that this was the Gospel of Salvation. Lastly he urged the necessity of a lively faith in Jesus, not an assent only of the understanding, but a faith of application; not merely an acquiescence in the Gospel as a truth, but an actual laying hold upon and embracing it as a salvation wrought out for and offered to me personally and particularly. Here I failed and deplored my want of such a faith. He told me it was the free gift of God which he trusted He would bestow upon me. I could only reply, 'I wish He would; I wish He would,' a very irreverent petition but a very sincere one and such as the Blessed God in His due time was pleased to answer.

Convinced of my ignorance in the way of salvation and deeply sensible of the necessity of being instructed in so important a matter, I could not rest at a distance from him whom I had found so capable of pointing out to me my disorder and its only remedy. I therefore desired my friend Madan to take a lodging for me in his neighbourhood and he immediately hired one for me in a house adjoining to his own.[41] My brother, finding I had received some consolation from the discourse he had with me, was extremely anxious that I should take the earliest opportunity of conversing with him again and for this purpose pressed me with great earnestness to go immediately to Knightsbridge. I was at first for putting it off till the next day, but my brother seemed impatient of delay and at length prevailed upon me to set out. I mention this circumstance as much to the honour of his candour and humanity, which were such as would suffer no difference of sentiment or persuasion to interfere with them. My welfare seemed to be his only object, and all prejudices to be put to flight and vanish before his zeal to procure it. May he receive for his recompense all that happiness which the Gospel I then first became acquainted with is alone calculated to impart. I went to my new lodging in the evening, my brother accompanying me and rejoicing to see me so much easier than I was in the morning.

Easier, indeed I was, but far from easy. The wounded spirit within

[41] Martin Madan moved to Knightsbridge in 1761, where he remained until at least 1772. See *The Madan Family*, p. 112.

me was less in pain but by no means healed. The application of these truths to my heart by the Spirit of the Lord was not yet made. Nor did His infinite wisdom see fit to make it, till near eight months after. What I had hitherto experienced was but the beginning of sorrows, and a long train of still greater terrors was at hand.

That night after some discourse with Mr. Madan and Mr. Haweis[42] upon the subject of faith I went to bed full of resolutions that I would believe in Jesus, though they had taken every possible precaution to prevent my trusting in my own strength in this material article by telling me it was a task which nothing less than Sovereign Grace could enable me to perform. I slept my usual three hours well and then awakened with ten times a stronger sense of my alienation from God than ever. Satan plied me close with horrible visions and more horrible voices. My ears rang with the sound of the torments that seemed to await me and inevitable damnation was denounced upon me in such strains of malice impatient to be gratified that the united world could not have assured me of being reprieved from Hell one hour longer. Thus did the pains of Hell get hold upon me and before daybreak the very sorrows of death itself encompassed me. A numbness seized upon the extremities of my body, and life seemed to retreat before it. My hands and feet became cold and stiff; a cold sweat stood upon my forehead; my heart seemed at every pulse to beat its last and my soul to cling to my lips as if upon the very point of departure.

No convicted criminal ever feared death more or was more assured of dying. At seven in the morning I sent the servant, who came to light the fire, to entreat Mr. Madan to come to me. Every moment seemed an hour till he came, so persuaded was I that I should die before he reached me. The instant he entered the room, I asked him what dreams he had the preceding night, having been so terrified myself that I thought every one else must have dreamt about me. I could hardly believe him when he answered, 'None at all my dear friend. Why do you ask me such a question?' He treated me with a truly Christian tenderness, and the comfortable things he spoke to me out of the Gospel of Jesus once more prevailed with me to hope a little for mercy. I arose and dressed myself, and again contrary to my expectation I saw the light of the sun. But now the pangs

[42] Revd. Thomas Haweis (1734–1820), at this time Madan's assistant, who obtained the rectorship of Aldwinckle in 1764. See *The Madan Family*, pp. 282–4, 295.

of death, which had been intermitted with a short cessation, again took hold of me. When I sat down I seemed to be in the very article of expiring, so that I walked to and fro till I was ready to drop in order to keep life in me. At eleven o'clock my brother called on me, and in about an hour after his arrival that distemper of mind which I had before so ardently wished for actually seized me.

While I traversed the room in the most terrible dismay of soul, expecting every moment the earth would open her mouth and swallow me, my conscience scaring me, the avenger of blood pursuing me, and the city of refuge out of reach and out of sight, suddenly a strange and horrible darkness fell upon me. If it were possible that a heavy blow could light upon the brain immediately without touching the skull, such was the sensation I felt. I clapped my hand to my forehead and cried aloud through the pain it gave me.

At every stroke my thoughts and expressions became more wild and incoherent. When they ceased, they left nothing but disorder and a confused imagination behind them; all that remained clear was the sense of sin and the expectation of punishment. These kept undisturbed possession all the way through my illness without interruption or abatement. My brother instantly perceived this change and went to consult with friends at next door in what manner it would be best to dispose of me. It was agreed among them that I should be carried to St. Albans, where Dr. Cotton[43] kept a house for the reception of such patients, with whom I was known to have some slight acquaintance. Not only his skill as a physician recommended him to their choice, but his well known humanity and sweetness of temper. My brother returned and proposed the journey to me. At first I rejected the proposal with disdain; asked if he thought me mad—what business I had with Dr. Cotton, or he with me? At length, however, beginning to yield a little to his persuasion, I said: 'Do you think it will be for my good?' He replied, 'I am sure it will.' The words were no sooner out of his lips than I was unaccountably transported with such a sudden ecstasy of joy and struck at once with such an

[43] Nathaniel Cotton (1705–88) had received his medical training at Leyden. At Dunstable, Bedfordshire, and at St. Albans he had acquired considerable fame for his humanitarian attention to the insane. His hospital for their care in St. Albans had first been on a small scale, but before C came to him he had moved to a spacious place called 'The College' or the 'Collegium Insanorum'. It was on Dagnall Street, not far from the great abbey. The doctor lived with his family in St. Peter's Street, where he quietly passed most of his life, visiting his patients, and writing poetry and prose.

eager desire to go to St. Albans that nothing but main force could have detained me. I fell on my knees to thank God for the joy I felt. I waited with the utmost impatience for the chaise that was to carry me. —I mention this sudden, and extraordinary change because I believe it was affected on purpose to incline me to go willingly to a physician who would treat me with skill and tenderness, who was himself a pious man and able to converse with me on the subject which lay so near my heart. We set forward on our journey, my brother terrified at his situation, as he might well be, and I overwhelmed with joy. Neither did this joy forsake me, till I was introduced to the doctor in his study.

It is proper to record it as an instance of God's providence over me in this journey that when we arrived at Barnet,[44] where we changed horses, the people of the inn advised us to proceed no farther that night because a gentleman had been just before attacked by a highwayman within a mile or two of the town. I was too impatient to see the end of my journey to listen to any precaution of that kind, and got hastily into the chaise again, laughing at the danger and encouraging my brother to do the same. Accordingly we passed on without molestation from the highwayman. The night was come on, and there was the greatest apparent probability that we should meet him.

We arrived at the doctor's house. He had no sooner taken me by the hand than my spirits sunk, and all my jealousy returned. His dwelling house is at some distance from that where he keeps his patients; thither his own chaise was to carry me. But perceiving now that I had trepanned myself into danger of close confinement, I refused to go into it, and made such resistance that three or four persons were employed to compel me, and as many to take me out again, when I arrived at the place of my destination.

It will be proper to draw a veil over 'the secrets of my prison house'.[45] Let it suffice to say that the low state both of body and mind to which I was here reduced was perfectly well calculated to humble the natural pride and vainglory of my heart and to lay them in the dust. These were the efficacious means which infinite wisdom thought meet to make use of for these purposes. A vein of self-loathing and

[44] Barnet is ten miles south of St. Albans and would have been a convenient stopping point on the journey.

[45] Isaiah 42: 7.

abhorrence ran through all my insanity. Conviction of sin and expectation of instant judgment never left me from the seventh December 1763 till the middle of July following. The accuser of the Brethren was busy with me day and night, bringing to my recollection, even in dreams, the commission of forgotten sins, and charging upon my conscience things of an indifferent nature as the most atrocious crimes. At length I thought every motion of my body a sin, and could not find out the posture in which I could sit or stand without offending. This was heaping one mountain upon another and by these means my guilt was made to appear to me of such an enormous size that I was once more tempted to destroy myself. He even persuaded me that it would be an act of duty to rid the world of such a sinner, and I thought that the sooner I did it, the more tolerable would be my damnation. The chief difficulty now lay in finding opportunity for the purpose. I was narrowly watched, and the more narrowly as my design became continually more and more apparent. At length, however, I flattered myself that I had carried my point. As I sat by the fireside, I saw something glister in the cinders, and picking it up unobserved by the servant, I found it to be a large stocking-needle. The better to conceal it, I thrust it into the paper hangings by the bedside where the curtains covered it and where I could easily reach it in the night. I went to bed and slept some hours. Waking, I recollected my purpose, felt for the needle and found it. With my finger, as I lay on my left side, I explored the pulse of my heart, thrust in the needle, nearly to the head. Failing in the first attempt, I repeated it, and did so ten or a dozen times, till at length having broke the point of it in a rib, I was obliged to give over. These repeated stabs were attended with no subsequent mischief at all. I lost indeed about half an ounce of blood, which being found upon my shirt in the morning, betrayed the attempt I had been making and occasioned my being more closely watched than ever. Thus did the Almighty convert an ineffectual endeavour upon my life into the means of preserving it for the future, and Satan was made to defeat his own purpose.

All that passed in this long interval of eight months may be classed under the two general heads—conviction of sin and despair of mercy. But blessed be the God of my Salvation for every sigh I drew, for every tear I shed, since thus it pleased Him to judge me here that I might not be judged hereafter.

Two remarkable occurrences I shall mention which happened, the one in the beginning, the other towards the latter end of my malady. So remarkable, indeed, that I should fear to relate them was it not that I think it my duty to conceal none of God's dealings with me, however uncommon they may have been, and with whatever suspicious colours they may appear to others.

They befell me indeed while in a state of insanity, but recollecting them now and weighing them in my cooler judgment, which I thank God was never more its own master, I am forced to admit the solidity and reality of the facts and think myself in conscience bound to relate them accordingly. God knows, I have frequently prayed for His direction, whether to record them or not, being as ready to suppress them, if such be His Holy Will, as to perpetuate the memory of them; and He knows too that I make the recital as in His presence, and I call His Holy Spirit to witness that I lie not.

One evening as I was walking to and fro in my chamber, the day being now shut in, I saw myself suddenly enclosed in a temple as large as a cathedral. It had two cupolas, one at each end, and the roof was supported by tall and straight columns in rows parallel to each other. One of these cupolas was vertically over my head and formed the most radiant appearance. The whole edifice was built with beams of the purest light, mild and soft indeed, but bright as those of an unclouded sun. I cannot conceive a more regular piece of architecture or imagine to myself a more delightful object. It lasted so long that I had time to consider it attentively. At length I cried aloud, 'Bless me; I see a glory all around me.' At the first word I spoke, the whole disappeared. The servant who attended me laughed at the exclamation but had not the curiosity to ask any questions about the cause of it. At first I was willing to draw some favourable inferences to myself from so extraordinary an exhibition. But Satan quickly persuaded me that it had been made with no other view than to increase my regret for the loss of that glory which I had just seen a glimpse of, but which was now irrecoverably lost and gone.

The other was still more remarkable, and capable of being authenticated more to the satisfaction of the reader because I had the testimony not only of my own but of another's eyes for the truth of it.

The servants who attended me had been conversing together upon the subject of thunder and lightning. At length one of them asserted that he had seen several thunderbolts, supposing them to be

round smooth stones which are often found in brick walls and which are pretty generally understood to be so by the common people. The other, not believing that they were such in reality, contradicted him and appealed to me to decide the question. I answered: No; that it was vulgar error, and that there was no such thing as a thunderbolt. This happened in the former part of the summer of the year 1764.

Either the next day, or two days after at the most, there came a violent tempest. I was in the garden when the rain began and took shelter in an arbour, but the shower, soon penetrating it, drove me to the house. Before I quitted the arbour, a clap of thunder came, just over the yew-tree in which it was made, so deep and awful in the sound of it that neither before or since have I heard any like it. Having gained the house, I planted myself at the chamber window, which stood open, and one of the servants above mentioned (the most hardened sinner I ever knew) stood close to my elbow. The storm gathered thick over a wood nearly opposite to us about a mile's distance from us. While we were remarking the uncommon blackness of the cloud, there appeared suddenly in the midst of it the form of a fiery hand clenching a bolt or arrow of lightning. I kept my eye steadily fixed upon it, having been so long acquainted with despair that I was afraid of nothing, and watched it with a most undisturbed attention. Instantly the hand was lifted up towards the meridian and let fall again towards the earth till it seemed to reach the top of the opposite wood—as if in the very act of transfixing an enemy. This was six or seven times repeated, till at length it was caught upward into the zenith and the cloud, as it were, closing over it, it disappeared.

I asked the servant (one of the profanest wretches in the world) if he had seen it. He forced a kind of smile, and answered, 'Yes, but I was afraid to look at it,' and seemed to wonder that I was not as much affrighted as himself. Nothing more passed between us. I gave him not the least intimation of what I understood it to be, but found presently after that as soon as he left me he declared to the servants below that he had seen a thunderbolt.

My chief surprise was that I had only seen it without suffering the wrath which I believed had kindled it. I looked upon it, however, as a rebuke to me for denying the existence of what the Scripture asserted, and as a divine threatening of what would speedily be fulfilled upon me.

After five months thus spent in continual expectation of the fatal moment when Divine Vengeance should plunge me into the bottomless abyss, I became at length so familiar with despair as to have contracted a kind of hardiness and indifference to the event. I began to persuade myself that while the execution of the evil sentence was suspended it would be for my interest to indulge a less horrible train of ideas than I had been accustomed to muse upon. 'Eat and drink today for tomorrow you shall be in Hell'[46] was the maxim on which I proceeded. By this means I became capable of entering with some small degree of cheerfulness into conversation with the doctor. I laughed at his stories, which were all well calculated to amuse me, and perhaps matched them with some of my own—still, however, carrying a sentence of irrecoverable doom in my heart. He observed this seeming alteration with pleasure. Believing as he well might that my smiles were sincere, he thought my recovery well nigh completed, though they were in reality like the green surface of a morass—pleasant indeed to the eye but a cover for nothing but rottenness and filth. The only thing that could promote and effectuate my cure was yet wanting—an experimental knowledge of the Redemption that is in Christ Jesus. I remember about this time a diabolical species of regret that found harbour in my wicked heart. I was sincerely sorry that I had not seized every opportunity of giving a full scope to my wicked appetites and even envied those who, being departed to their own place before me, had the consolation to reflect that they had well earned their miserable inheritance by indulging their sensuality without restraint or limitation. O merciful Lord God! What a tophet[47] of pollution is the human soul? and wherein do we differ from devils, unless Thy grace prevents us!

In about three months more, viz. on 25 July 1764, my brother came from Cambridge to visit me. Dr. Cotton having told him that he thought me greatly amended, he was rather disappointed at finding me almost as silent and reserved as ever, for the sight of him struck me with so many painful sensations, both of sorrow for my own remediless condition, as I thought it, and envy of his present and future happiness, so that I was in no humour to do justice to the doctor's representation.

As soon as we were left alone he asked me how I found myself;

[46] See Isaiah 22: 13; 1 Corinthians 15: 32.

[47] 'A place, state, condition, or company likened to hell' (*O.E.D.*).

I answered (which was true), 'As much better as despair can make me.' We went together into the garden. There upon expressing that settled assurance I had of sudden judgment, he protested to me that it was all a delusion, and protested it too with so much earnestness, that I could not help giving some attention to him. I burst into tears and cried out, 'If it be a delusion then am I the happiest of beings.' Something like a ray of hope was shot into my heart, though still I was afraid to indulge it. We dined together, and spent the afternoon in more cheerful conversation than I had before been capable of. Something seemed to whisper to me every moment, 'Still there is mercy.'

Even after he left me, which he did in the evening, this change of sentiment gathered ground continually. Yet my mind was in a state of such fluctuation that I can only call it a vague kind of presage of better things at hand without being able to assign a reason for it. The servants observed a sudden alteration in me for the better, and the man[48] whom I have since retained in my service expressed in particular great joy on the occasion.

I went to bed and slept well. In the morning I dreamt that the sweetest boy I ever saw came dancing up to my bedside. He seemed just out of leading strings, yet I took particular notice of the firmness and steadiness of his tread. The sight affected me with pleasure and served at least to harmonize my spirits upon waking, so that I arose for the first time with a sense of delight upon my mind. Still, however, I knew not where to look for any establishment of the comfort I felt, and my joy was as much a mystery to myself as to those about me. The Blessed God was preparing me for the clearer light of His countenance by this first dawning of that light upon me. Within a few days of my first arrival at St. Albans I had thrown aside the word of God as a book in which I had no longer any interest, at least no beneficial interest, or portion. The only instance in which I can recollect reading a single chapter was about two months before my recovery. Having found the Bible upon a bench in the garden, I opened it upon the eleventh of St. John's Gospel, where Lazarus is raised from the dead. I saw so much benevolence and mercy, so much goodness and sympathy with miserable mankind in our Saviour's conduct as melted my heart, and I almost shed tears over the relation. Little did I think that it was an exact type of the mercy which Jesus

[48] Samuel Roberts (d. 1832), who remained with C over thirty years.

was upon the point of extending towards myself. I sighed and said, 'Oh that I had not rejected so good a Redeemer! that I had not forfeited all His favour!' Thus was my heart softened, though not as yet enlightened, and I closed the book without any intention ever to open it again.

Having risen from my bed, as I said, with somewhat of a more cheerful frame of spirit than I had experienced for eight months before, I repaired to the room where breakfast waited for me. While I sat at the table I perceived that the cloud of horror which had so long hung over me was every moment passing away; every moment came fraught with hope. And I was continually more and more persuaded that I was not devoted to destruction.

The way of salvation was, however, still hid from my eyes; nor did I see it at all more clearly than before I was afflicted. I only thought that if it pleased God to spare me I would lead a better life, and that I would yet escape hell if a religious observance of my duty could secure me from it. Thus may the terrors of the Lord make a Pharisee. But the sweet voice of mercy in the Gospel can only make a Christian.

Having breakfasted I continued some time full of musing upon this unexpected relief, yet still trembling with apprehensions lest my new-born hopes should prove a dream, and doubtful whether I had most reason to expect deliverance or an eternal dungeon.

But the happy period that was to strike off my fetters and to afford me a clear opening into the free mercy of the Blessed God in Jesus was now arrived. I flung myself into a chair near the window seat and, seeing a Bible there, ventured once more to apply to it for comfort and instruction. The first verse I saw was the twenty-fifth of the third chapter to the Romans where Jesus is set forth as the propitiation for our sins.

Immediately I received strength to believe it. Immediately the full beams of the sun of righteousness shone upon me. I saw the sufficiency of the atonement He had made, my pardon sealed in His blood, and all the fullness and completeness of my justification. In a moment I believed and received the Gospel. Whatsoever my friend Madan had said to me so long before recurred to me with the clearest evidence of its truth, 'with demonstration of the Spirit and with power'.[49] Unless the Almighty Arm had been under me I think

[49] 1 Corinthians 2 : 4.

I now should have died with gratitude and joy. My eyes filled with tears and my voice was choked with transport. I could only look up to Heaven in silence, overwhelmed with love and wonder! But the work of the Holy Ghost is best described in His own words. It was 'joy unspeakable and full of glory'.[50] Thus was my Heavenly Father in Christ Jesus pleased to give me the full assurance of faith at once, and out of a stony and unbelieving heart to raise up a child unto Abraham.

How glad should I have been to have spent every moment of this day in praise and thanksgiving! I lost no opportunity of repairing to the throne of grace, but flew to it with an earnestness irresistible and never to be satisfied. Could I help doing it? Could I do otherwise than love and rejoice and triumph in the presence of my reconciled Father in Christ Jesus? 'The Lord had enlarged my heart, and I ran in the ways of His commandments.'[51] For many succeeding weeks tears were ready to flow if I did but speak of the Gospel or mention the name of Jesus. To rejoice day and night was all my employment. Too happy to sleep much, yet I rose refreshed as after long rest; I thought it all lost time that was spent in slumber. Oh that this ardour of my first love had continued! But I have known many a lifeless and unhallowed hour since—long intervals of darkness interrupted by short returns of joy, and peace in believing.

My physician, ever watchful and attentive to my welfare, was now alarmed with contrary apprehensions, and began to fear lest the sudden transition from despair to joy should terminate in a fatal frenzy. But 'the Lord was my strength and my song and was become my salvation; the voice of rejoicing and salvation was in my dwelling, for the right hand of the Lord was exalted. I said, I shall not die but live and declare the works of the Lord; for the Lord has chastized me sore, but He has not given me over unto death. O give thanks to the Lord, for He is good, and His mercy endureth forever.'[52]

In a short time Dr. Cotton became satisfied and acquiesced in the soundness of the cure, and much sweet communion I had with him concerning the things of our salvation. He visited me every morning while I stayed with him, which was near twelve months after my recovery, and the Gospel was always the delightful theme of our conversation. A sweet calm and serenity of mind succeeded this

[50] 1 Peter 1 : 8.
[51] Psalm 119 : 32.
[52] Psalm 118 : 14–18, 29.

season of triumph. The Lord said, 'Peace, be still,'[53] and it was so. Blessed be the God of my Salvation. No trial has befallen me since, nor any temptation assailed me, greater than must needs be expected in a state of warfare. Satan, indeed, has changed his battery: before my conversion my appetite for sensual gratification was the weapon by which he sought to destroy me; being naturally of an easy, quiet disposition, I was seldom tempted to anger; yet that passion is at present, of all others, that with which I have the sharpest conflict, and which gives me the most disturbance. But Jesus being my strength I fight against it, and if I am not conqueror, yet I am not overcome. Glory be to His great name! I know that He will get Himself the victory over all my enemies.

I now employed my brother to seek an abode for me in the neighbourhood of Cambridge, being determined by the Lord's leave to see London (the scene of my former abominations and misery) no more. I had still one piece of preferment left which seemed to bind me under a necessity of returning thither again. But I resolved to break the band, and chiefly because my peace of conscience was in question. I had for some years held the office of Commissioner of Bankrupts worth about £60 per annum. Conscious of my ignorance in the law I could now no longer be contented to swear that I would do my duty faithfully in every commission, according to my ability, while I knew that I had no ability to perform it at all. I resigned it therefore and by so doing released myself from an occasion of great sin, and from every obligation to return to London. By this means, indeed, I reduced myself to an income scarcely sufficient for my maintenance, but I would rather have been starved in reality than have deliberately offended against my Saviour. In His great mercy to me the Lord has since raised me up such friends as have enabled me to enjoy all the comforts and conveniences of life and I am well assured that while I live, by means which the Almighty best knows, He will so dispose and order my circumstances that bread shall be given me and my waters shall be sure, according to His gracious promise.[54]

After my brother had made many unsuccessful attempts to find me a dwelling near him, and it began to seem doubtful whether he would ever be able to compass it, I one day poured out my heart in prayer before the Lord beseeching Him that wherever He should

[53] See Mark 4: 39. [54] Isaiah 33: 16.

be pleased in His fatherly mercy to lead me, it might be into the society of those that feared His name and loved the Lord Jesus in sincerity—a prayer of which I have substantial reason to acknowledge His favourable and kind acceptance.

In the beginning of June 1765, I received a letter from my brother informing me that he had seen a lodging at Huntingdon which he believed would suit me.[55] Though it was sixteen miles from Cambridge I resolved to take it, for I had now been ten months in perfect health, and my circumstances required a less expensive way of life than what I had been obliged to at St. Albans. To say the truth, however, it was with great reluctance that I thought of leaving the place of my second nativity; my time there was so much at my own disposal; I had so much leisure to study the blessed word of salvation; I had enjoyed so much happiness there that I dreaded a change of place, being so unmindful of the Gracious Hand which had led me thither and on which I ought to have placed more confidence as everywhere equally able and ready to protect me. But God had ordered everything for me like an indulgent father, and had prepared me a more comfortable place of rest than I could have chosen for myself.

On the 7th June 1765,[56] having spent more than eighteen months at St. Albans, partly in bondage and partly in the liberty wherewith Christ had made me free, I took leave of the place at four in the morning and set out for Cambridge. The servant whom I lately mentioned as rejoicing in my recovery attended me. He had maintained such an affectionate watchfulness over me during my whole illness and waited on me with so much patience and gentleness that I could not bear to leave him behind, though it was with some difficulty that the doctor was prevailed on to part with him.

The strongest argument of all, indeed, was the earnest desire he expressed to follow me. He seems to have been providentially thrown in my way, having entered into Dr. Cotton's service just time enough to be appointed to attend me. And I have strong grounds to hope that God will make me of use as an instrument in His hands of bringing him to the knowledge of Jesus.

[55] John Cowper succeeded in obtaining rooms for his brother at Huntingdon, in a sixteenth-century house on the west side of High Street, north of the George Hotel. (*The Victoria History of the Counties of England*, *Huntingdon* (1932), ii. 128.)

[56] C actually left St. Albans on Monday, 17 June 1765, arriving in Huntingdon on Saturday, 22 June. See C to Hill, 24 June 1765.

It is impossible to say with how delightful a sense of His protection and fatherly care of me it pleased the Almighty to favour me during the whole journey. I remembered the pollution that is in the world and the sad share I had had in it myself. I remembered these things and was troubled, and my very heart ached at the thought of returning to it again after having been so long sequestered from it. The Blessed God had endued me with some concern for His Glory, and I was fearful of hearing it traduced by oaths and blasphemies—the common language of this highly favoured but ungrateful country. But 'fear not, I am with thee'[57] was my comfort. I passed the whole time of my journey in silent communion with God, and those hours were among the happiest I have known. I repaired to Huntingdon to take possession of my new lodgings the Saturday after my arrival at Cambridge. My brother who attended me hither had no sooner left me than, finding myself surrounded by strangers in a place with which I was utterly unacquainted, my spirits began to sink and I felt (such was my backsliding and unfaithful heart) like a traveller in the midst of an inhospitable desert, without a friend to comfort or a guide to direct him. I walked forth towards the close of the day in this melancholy frame of mind, and having wandered about a mile from the town I found my heart at length so powerfully drawn towards the Lord that, having gained a retired and secret nook in the corner of the field, I knelt under a bank and poured out my complaints before Him. It pleased my Saviour to hear me, so that the oppression under which I had laboured was entirely taken off. I was enabled to trust in Him, 'who careth for the stranger, to roll all my burden upon Him',[58] and to rest assured that wherever He might cast my lot, the 'God of all consolation'[59] would still be near me.

But this was not all. He did for me more than I had either asked or thought. The next morning I went to church for the first time after my recovery. Throughout the whole service I had much ado to restrain my emotions, so plainly did I see the fair beauty and glory of the Lord so as I had never before seen it in the sanctuary. My heart was full of love to all the congregation, especially to them in whom I observed an air of serious attention. A grave and sober person[60] sat in the pew with me; him I have since visited and often conversed with, and have found him a pious man and a true servant of the

[57] Isaiah 41 : 10. [58] See Psalm 55 : 22.
[59] Romans 15 : 5. [60] Unidentified.

Blessed Redeemer. While he was singing the psalm I looked at him, and observing him intent upon his holy employment I could not help saying in my heart with much emotion, 'bless you for praising Him whom my soul loveth'. Such was the goodness of the Lord to me that 'He gave me the oil of joy instead of mourning, and the garment of praise for the spirit of heaviness.'[61] And though my voice was silent, being stopped by the intenseness of what I felt, yet my soul sung within me and even leaped for joy.

When the Gospel for the day was read, the sound of it was more than I could well support. O what a word is the Word of God when the Spirit quickens us to receive it! And gives us the hearing ear and the understanding heart to taste it. The harmony and sweetness of Heaven is in it, and discovers the Author. The parable of the repenting prodigal[62] was the portion appointed for the day, and I saw myself in that glass so clearly, and the loving kindness of my slighted and forgotten Lord, that the whole scene was realized to me and acted over in my heart. I went immediately after church to the place where I had prayed the day before and found that the relief I had then received was but the earnest of a richer blessing.

How shall I express what the Lord did for me except by saying that He made all His goodness pass before me. I seemed to speak to Him, 'face to face, as a man converseth with his friend',[63] except that my speech was only in tears of joy and 'groanings that cannot be uttered'.[64] I could say with Jacob, not, indeed, 'how dreadful', but, 'how lovely is this place. This is none other than the House of God.'[65]

Four months I continued in my lodging. Some few of the neighbours came to see me, but their visits were not very frequent, and in general I had but little intercourse except with my God in Christ Jesus. It was He who made my solitude sweet and the 'wilderness to bloom and blossom as the rose',[66] and my meditation of Him was so delightful that if I had few other comforts, neither did I want any. One day, however, towards the expiration of this period, I found myself in a state of desertion. That communion I had so long been enabled to maintain with the Lord was suddenly interrupted. I began to dislike my solitary situation and to fear that I should never be able

[61] Isaiah 61 : 3.
[62] Luke 15 : 11–32.
[63] Exodus 33 : 11.
[64] Romans 8 : 26.
[65] Genesis 28 : 17.
[66] Isaiah 35 : 1.

to weather out the winter in so lonely a dwelling. Suddenly a thought struck me which I shall not fear to call a suggestion of the good Providence which had brought me to Huntingdon.

About two months before I had formed an acquaintance with the Revd. Mr. Unwin's family. His son, though he had heard that I rather declined society than sought it, and though Mrs. Unwin herself dissuaded him from visiting me on that account, was yet so strongly inclined to it that, notwithstanding all objections and arguments to the contrary, he one day engaged himself as we were coming out of Church after morning prayers to drink tea with me that afternoon. To my inexpressible joy I found him one whose notions of religion were spiritual and lively, one whom the Lord had been training from his infancy for the service of the temple. We opened our hearts to each other at the first interview, and when we parted I immediately retired to my chamber and prayed the Lord who had been the Author to be the Guardian of our friendship, to grant to it fervency and perpetuity even unto death, and I doubt not but my gracious Father has heard this prayer also.

The Sunday following I dined with him. That afternoon, when the rest of the company was withdrawn, I had much discourse with Mrs. Unwin. I am not at liberty to describe the pleasure I had in conversing with her because she will be one of the first who will have the perusal of this narrative. Let it suffice to say I found we had one Faith, one Lord, and had been baptized with one baptism of the Spirit. When I returned to my lodging I gave thanks to God, who had so graciously answered the prayer I had preferred to Him at St. Albans, by bringing me into the society of Christians. She has since been a means in the hand of God of supporting, strengthening, and quickening me in my walk with Him who has called me by His Gospel, and she must be contented to see recorded here those blessings I have received from her hands, which gratitude to the Author will not suffer me to suppress.

It was long before I thought of any other connection with this family than merely as a friend and a neighbour. On the day, however, above mentioned, while I was revolving in my mind with much anxiety the nature of my situation, and beginning for the first time to find an irksomeness in such retirement, suddenly, I cannot say how, suddenly it occurred to me that I might possibly find a place in Mr. Unwin's family as a boarder. A young gentleman who had lived with

him as his pupil was the day before gone to settle at Cambridge, and it appeared to me possible at least that I might be allowed to succeed him. From the moment this thought struck me such a tumult of anxious thoughts seized me that for two or three days I could not divert my mind to any other subject. I blamed and condemned myself for want of submission to the Lord's will. But still the language of my mutinous and disobedient heart was, give me this blessing or I die. About the third evening, after I had determined upon this measure, I at length made a shift to fasten my thoughts upon a theme which had no manner of connection with it. While I was pursuing my meditation—Mr. Unwin and his family being quite out of sight—my attention was suddenly called home again by these words, which had been continually playing upon my mind and were at length repeated with such importunity that I could not help regarding them: the Lord God of truth will do this. I was effectually convinced that they were not of my own production, and accordingly received from them some degree of assurance of success. But my unbelief and fearfulness robbed me of much of the comfort they were intended to convey, though I have since had many and blessed experiences of the same kind for which I can never be sufficiently thankful.

I immediately began to negotiate the affair and in a few days it was entirely concluded. I took possession of my new abode on November 11, 1765. I have found it a place of rest prepared for me by God's own hand, where He has blessed me with a thousand mercies, a thousand instances of His fatherly protection, where He has given me abundant means of furtherance in the knowledge of our Lord Jesus Christ, both by the study of His word and by communion with His dear disciples. May nothing but death interrupt our union!

If the Lord gives me life, I shall not in this place make an end of my testimony to His goodness; at some future time I shall resume the story, and I have lately received a blessing from His hand which shines as bright as most of the foregoing favours, having the evident stamp of His love upon it, and well deserving to be remembered by me with all gratitude and thanksgiving.

Peace be with thee, reader, through faith in the Lord Jesus Christ. Amen.

Huntingdon, 14 February 1767.

N.B. I have added two hymns, which I composed at St. Albans, not for the composition, but because they are specimens of my first Christian thoughts, being written very shortly after my conversion, and I am glad to present them, because I cannot read them even now without feeling that joy of heart which the Lord gave me, freshening as it were upon my mind at the perusal of them.[67]

Hymn I

Behold I make all things new:

How blest Thy creature is, O God!
When with a single eye,
He views the lustre of Thy Word,
The day spring from on high.

Thro' all the storms that veil the skies
And frown on earthly things;
The Sun of Righteousness he eyes
With healing on His wings.

Struck by that light, the human heart,
A barren soil no more,
Sends the sweet smell of Grace abroad,
Where serpents lurk'd before.

The soul a dreary province once,
Of Satan's dark domain;
Feels a new empire form'd within,
And owns an heav'nly reign.

The glorious orb whose silver beams
The fruitful year control
Since first obedient to Thy word,
He started from the goal;

[67] These are Olney hymns XLVI and XLVII, first published in 1779.

Has cheer'd the nations with the joys
His orient rays impart,
But Jesus, 'tis Thy light alone,
Can shine upon the heart.

Hymn II

Far from the world, O Lord, I flee,
From strife and tumult far,
From scenes, where Satan wages still
His most successful war.

The calm retreat, the silent shade,
With prayer and praise agree;
And seem by Thy sweet bounty made,
For those who follow Thee.

There, if Thy Spirit touch the Soul,
And grace her mean abode;
O with what peace, and joy, and love,
She communes with her God!

There, like the nightingale she pours
Her solitary lays;
Nor asks a witness of her song,
Nor thirsts for human praise.

Author, and Guardian of my life,
Sweet fount of light divine!
And all endearing names in one,
My Saviour——I am Thine!

What thanks I owe Thee, and what love,
A boundless, endless store;
Shall echo thro' the realms above,
When time shall be no more.

A Narrative

Of the memorable conversion of the Revd. John Cowper, M.A.

Late Fellow of Bene't College, Cambridge.[68]

Philippians 3: 7

But what things were gain to me, those I counted loss for Christ.

As soon as it had pleased God, after a long and sharp season of conviction, to visit me with the consolations of His Grace, it became one of my chief concerns that my relations might be partakers of the same mercy. In the first letter I wrote to my brother,[69] I took occasion to declare what God had done for my soul and am not conscious that from that period down to his last illness, I wilfully neglected any opportunity of engaging him (if it were possible) in conversation of a spiritual kind. When I left St. Albans, and went to visit him at Cambridge, my heart being full of the subject, I poured it out before him without reserve and in all my subsequent dealings with him, so far as I was enabled, took care to show that I had received not only a set of notions, but a real impression of the truths of the Gospel.

At first I found him ready enough to talk with me upon these subjects: sometimes he would dispute but always without heat or animosity, and sometimes he would endeavour to reconcile the difference of our sentiments by supposing that at the bottom we were both of a mind and meant the same thing.

[68] The college is officially known as Corpus Christi College, but took its common name, Bene't College, from the church adjoining it, since Corpus Christi holds 'in mortmain the appropriations of the tythes of St. Benedict'. See E. Dyer, *History of the University and Colleges of Cambridge*, ii (1814), 119.

[69] This letter has not survived.

He was a man of a most candid and ingenuous spirit, his temper remarkably sweet, and in his behaviour to me he had always manifested an uncommon affection. His outward conduct, so far as it fell under my notice or I could learn it by others, was perfectly decent and unblameable. There was nothing vicious in any part of his practice, but being of a studious, thoughtful turn, he placed his chief delight in the acquisition of learning and made such acquisitions in it that he had but few rivals in that of a classical kind. He was entirely skilled in the Latin, Greek, and Hebrew languages, was beginning to make himself master of the Syriac, and perfectly understood the French and Italian, the latter of which he could speak fluently. These attainments, however, and many others in the literary way, he lived heartily to despise, not as useless when sanctified and employed in the service of God, but when sought after for their own sake and with a view to the praise of men. Learned, however, as he was, he was easy and cheerful in his conversation, and entirely free from that stiffness which is generally contracted by men devoted to such pursuits.

Thus we spent about two years conversing as occasion offered (and we generally visited each other once a week as long as I continued at Huntingdon) upon the leading truths of the Gospel. By this time, however, he began to be more reserved; he would hear me patiently but never reply, and this I found upon his own confession afterwards was the effect of a resolution he had taken in order to avoid disputes and to secure the continuance of that peace which had always subsisted between us. When our family removed to Olney, our visits became less frequent: we exchanged an annual visit. And whenever he came amongst us, he observed the same conduct, conformed to our customs, attended the meetings with us, and heard the preaching, received civilly whatever passed in conversation upon the subject but adhered strictly to the rule he had prescribed to himself, never remarking upon or objecting to any thing he heard or saw. This through the goodness of his natural temper he was enabled to carry so far that though some things unavoidably happened which we feared would give him offence, he never took any: for it was not possible to offer him the pulpit. Nor when Mr. Newton was with us once at the time of family prayer could we ask my brother to officiate, though being himself a minister and one of our family, the office seemed naturally to fall into his hands.

In September 1769 I learned by letters from Cambridge that he

was dangerously ill. I set out for that place the day after I received them and found him as ill as I expected. He had taken cold on his return from a journey into Wales and lest he should be laid up at a distance from home, he pushed forward as fast as he could from Bath, with a fever upon him. Soon after his arrival at Cambridge, he discharged (unknown to himself) such a prodigious quantity of blood that the physician ascribed it only to the strength of his constitution that he was still alive and assured me that if the discharge should be repeated, he must inevitably die upon the spot. In this state of imminent danger he seemed to have no more concern about his spiritual interests than when in perfect health. His couch was strewn with volumes of plays to which he had frequent recourse for amusement. I learned afterward, indeed, that even at this time the thoughts of God and Eternity would often force themselves upon his mind, but not apprehending his life to be in danger and trusting in the morality of his past conduct, he found it no difficult matter to thrust them out again.

As it pleased God, he had no relapse. He presently began to recover strength and in ten days' time I left him so far restored that he could ride many miles without fatigue and had every symptom of recovering health. It is probable, however, that though his recovery seemed perfect, this illness was the means which God had appointed to bring down his strength in the midst of his journey and to hasten on the malady which proved his last.

On the 16th February 1770, I was again summoned to attend him by letters which represented him as so ill that the physicians entertained little hopes of his recovery. I found him afflicted with an asthma and dropsy, supposed to be the effect of an imposthume in his liver. He was, however, very cheerful when I first arrived, expressing great joy at seeing me. [He] thought himself much better than he had been and seemed to flatter himself with hopes that he should soon be well again. My situation at this time was truly distressful. I learned from the physician that, in this instance, as in the last, he was in much greater danger than he suspected. He did not seem to lay his illness at all to heart, nor could I find by his conversation that he had one serious thought. As often as a suitable occasion offered when we were free from company and interruption, I endeavoured to give a spiritual turn to the discourse and, the day after my arrival, asked his permission to pray with him, to which he readily consented. I renewed

my attempts in this way as often as I could, though without any apparent success. He seemed as careless and unconcerned as ever, yet I could not but consider his willingness in this instance as a token for good and observed with pleasure that though at other times he discovered no mark of seriousness, yet, when I spoke to him of the Lord's dealings with myself, he received what I said with affection, would, pressing my hand, look kindly on me and seemed to love me the better for it.

On the 21st of the same month, he had a violent fit of the asthma which seized him when he arose about an hour before noon, and lasted all the day. His agony was dreadful. Having never seen any person afflicted in the same way, I could not help fearing that he would be suffocated, nor was the physician without fears of the same kind. This day the Lord was very present with me and enabled me, as I sat by the poor sufferer's side, to wrestle for a blessing upon him. I observed to him that though it had pleased God to visit him with great afflictions, yet mercy was mingled with the dispensation. I said, 'You have many friends who love you and are willing to do all they can to serve you. And so perhaps have others in like circumstances, but it is not the lot of every sick man, how much so ever he may be loved, to have a friend that can pray for him.' He replied, 'That is true and [I] hope God will have mercy upon me.' His love to me from this time became very remarkable—there was a tenderness in it more than was merely natural, and he generally expressed it by calling for blessings on me in the most affectionate terms and with a look and manner not to be described.

At night when he was quite worn out with the fatigue of labouring for breath and could get no rest, his asthma still continuing, he turned to me and said with a melancholy air, 'Brother, I seem marked out for misery, you know some people are so—.' That moment I felt my heart enlarged and such persuasion of the Love of God to him was wrought in my soul that I replied with confidence, and as if I had authority given me to say it, 'But that is not your case, you are marked out for mercy.'

Through the whole of this most painful dispensation, he was blest with a degree of patience and resignation to the will of God not always seen in the behaviour of established Christians under sufferings so great as his. I never heard a murmuring word escape from him; on the contrary, he would often say when his pains were most acute,

'I only wish it may please God to enable me to suffer without complaining; I have no right to complain.' Once he said with a loud voice, 'Thy rod and thy staff support and comfort me.'[70] And, 'Oh that it were with me as in times past when the candle of the Lord shone upon my tabernacle.'[71] One evening when I had been expressing my hope that the Lord would show him mercy, he replied, 'I hope He will. I am sure I pretend to nothing.' Many times he spoke of himself in terms of the greatest self-abasement, which I cannot now particularly remember. I thought I could discern in these expressions the glimpse of approaching day and have no doubt at present but that the Spirit of God was gradually preparing him in a way of true humiliation for that bright display of Gospel Grace, which He was afterward pleased to afford him.

On Saturday the 10[th of] March, about three in the afternoon, he suddenly burst into tears and said with a loud cry, 'Oh forsake me not!'[72] I went to his bedside. When he grasped my hands and presently by his eyes and countenance, I found that he was in prayer. Then turning to me, he said, 'O brother, I am full of what——I could say to you.' The nurse asked him if he would have any hartshorn or lavender.[73] He replied, 'None of these things will serve my purpose.' I said, 'But I know what would, my dear, don't I?' He answered, 'You do, brother.'

Having continued some time silent, he said, 'Behold, I create new heavens and a new earth'[74]—then after a pause, 'Ay, and He is able to do it too.'

I left him for about an hour, fearing lest he should fatigue himself with talking and because my surprise and joy were so great that I could hardly bear them.

When I returned, he threw his arm about my neck and leaning his head against mine, he said, 'Brother, if I live, you and I shall be more like one another than we have been, but whether I live or live not, all is well and will be so. I know it will. I have felt that which I never felt before and am sure that God has visited me with this sickness to teach me what I was too proud to learn in health. I never had satisfaction till now. The doctrines I had been used to referred me to myself for the foundation of my hopes and then I could find nothing

70 Psalm 23: 4. 71 See Job 29: 3–4. 72 See Psalms 119: 8.
73 Smelling salts. See n. 2, C to Newton, 11 Mar. 1770.
74 Isaiah 65: 17.

to rest upon: the sheet anchor of the soul was wanting.[75] I thought you wrong yet wished to believe as you did. I found myself unable to believe yet always thought I should one day be brought to do so. You suffered more than I have done before you believed these truths, but our sufferings, though different in their kind and measure, were directed to the same end. I hope He has taught me that which He teaches none but His own. I hope so. These things were foolishness to me once, but now I have a firm foundation and am satisfied.'

In the evening when I went to bid him good night, he looked steadfastly in my face, and with great solemnity in his air and manner, resumed the discourse in these very words——'As empty and yet full, as having nothing and yet possessing all things, I see the rock upon which I once split, and I see the rock of my salvation. I have peace in myself, and, if I live, I hope it will be that I may be made a messenger of peace unto others. I have learned that in a moment, which I could not have learned by reading many books for many years. I have often studied these points and have studied them with great attention but was blinded by prejudice and unless He 'who alone is worthy to unloose the seals'[76] had opened the book to me, I had been blinded still. Now they appear so plain, that though I'm convinced no comment could ever have made me understand them, I wonder I did not see them before. Yet great as my doubts and difficulties were, they have only served to pave the way and being solved they make it plainer. The light I have received comes late, but it is a comfort to me that I never made the Gospel truths a subject of ridicule. Though I dissented from the persuasion and the ways of God's people, I ever thought them respectable and therefore not proper to be made a jest of. The evil I suffer is a consequence of my descent from the corrupt original stock and of my own personal transgressions. The good I enjoy comes to me as the overflowing of His bounty; but the crown of all His mercies is this, that He has given me a Saviour, and not only the Saviour of mankind, but my Saviour!

'I should delight to see the people at Olney but am not worthy to appear amongst them.' (He wept at speaking these words and repeated them with emphasis). 'I should rejoice in an hour's conversation with Mr. Newton, and, if I live, shall have much discourse with him upon these subjects but am so weak in body that at present I

[75] See Hebrews 6: 19. [76] Revelation 5: 9.

could not bear it.' At the same time, he gave me to understand that he had been five years enquiring after the truth. That is, from the time of my first visit to him after I left St. Albans. And that from the very day of his ordination, which was ten years before, he had been dissatisfied with his own views of the Gospel and sensible of their defect and obscurity. That he had always had a sense of the importance of the ministerial charge and had used to consider himself accountable for his doctrine no less than his practice. That he could appeal to the Lord for his sincerity in all that time and had never wilfully erred but always been desirous of coming to the knowledge of the truth. He added that the moment when he sent forth that cry was the moment when light was darted into his soul. That he thought much about these things in the course of his illness but never, till that instant was able to understand them.

It was remarkable that from the very instant when he was first enlightened, he was also wonderfully strengthened in body, so that from the 10th to the 14th (March) we all entertained hopes of his recovery. He was himself very sanguine in his expectations of it but frequently said that his desire of recovery extended no farther than his hope of usefulness. Adding, 'Unless I may live to be an instrument of good to others, it were better for me to die now.'

As his assurance was clear and unshaken, so he was very sensible of the goodness of the Lord to him in that respect. On the day when his eyes were opened, he turned to me and in a low voice said, 'What a mercy is it to a man in my condition to know His acceptance. I am completely satisfied of mine.' On another occasion, speaking to the same purpose, he said,'This bed would be a bed of misery and it is so, but it is likewise a bed of joy and a bed of discipline. Was I to die this night, I know I should be happy. This assurance, I hope, is quite consistent with the word of God. It is built upon a sense of my own utter insufficiency and the all sufficiency of Christ.'

At the same time he said, 'Brother, I have been building my glory upon a sandy foundation. I have laboured night and day to perfect myself in things of no profit, I have sacrificed my health to these pursuits and am now suffering the consequences of my misspent labour. But how contemptible do the writers I once highly valued now appear to me. 'Yea doubtless, I count all things loss and dung for the excellency of the knowledge of Christ Jesus my Lord.'[77]

[77] Philippians 3: 8.

'I must now go to a new school. I have many things to learn. I succeeded in my former pursuits. I wanted to be highly applauded and I was so. I was flattered up to the height of my wishes. Now I must learn a new lesson.'

On the evening of the 13th, he said, 'What comfort have I in this bed, miserable as I seem to be? Brother, I love to look at you. I see now who was right and who was mistaken, but it seems wonderful that such a dispensation should be necessary to enforce what seems so very plain. I wish myself at Olney. You have a good river there, better than all [the] rivers of Damascus. What a scene is passing before me! Ideas upon these subjects crowd upon me faster than I can give them utterance. How plain do many texts appear to which after consulting all the commentators I could hardly affix a meaning! And now I have their true meaning without any comment at all. There is but one key to the New Testament. I cannot describe to you, nor shall ever be able to describe, what I felt in the moment when it was given to me. May I make a good use of it. How I shudder when I think of the danger I have just escaped! I had made up my mind upon these subjects and was determined to hazard all upon the justness of my own opinions.'

Speaking of his illness, he said he had been followed night and day from the beginning of it with that text, 'I shall not die but live and declare the works of the Lord.'[78] This notice was fulfilled to him, though not in such a sense as my desires of his recovery prompted me to put upon it. His remarkable amendment soon appeared to be no more than a present supply of strength and spirits that he might be able to speak of the better life which God had given him, which was no sooner done than he relapsed as suddenly as he had revived.

About this time he had formed a purpose of receiving the Sacrament, induced to it principally by desires of setting his seal to the truth in presence of those who were strangers to the change which had taken place in his sentiments. It must have been administered to him by the Master of the College to whom he designed to have made this short declaration. 'If I die, I die in the belief of the doctrine of the Reformation and of the Church of England as it was at the time of the Reformation.' But his strength declining apace and his pains becoming more severe, he could never find a proper opportunity of doing it. His experience was rather peace than joy, if a distinction

[78] Psalm 118: 17.

may be made between joy and that heart-felt peace, which he often spoke of in the most comfortable terms and which he expressed by a heavenly smile upon his countenance under the most bitter bodily distress. His words upon this subject were these:

'How wonderful is it that God should look upon man! Especially that He should look upon me: yet He sees me and takes notice of all I suffer. I see Him too. He is present before me, and I hear Him say, "Come unto me all you that are weary and heavy laden, and I will give you rest." '[79]

On the 14th in the afternoon, I perceived that the strength and spirits which had been afforded him were suddenly withdrawn; so that by the next day, his mind became weak and his speech roving and faltering. But still at intervals, he was enabled to speak of divine things with great freedom and clearness.

On the evening of the 15th, he said, ' "There is more joy in Heaven over one sinner that repenteth than over ninety and nine just persons that need no repentance."[80] That text had been sadly misunderstood, and by me as well as by others. Where is that just person to be found? Alas! What must have become of me if I had died this day se'nnight? What should I have had to plead? My own righteousness?—That would have been of great service to me to be sure. Well—Whither then? Why, to the mercy of God: but I had no right to hope for that, except upon scriptural grounds. Well, whither next? Why, to the mountains to fall on us, and to the hills to cover us.[81] I am not duly thankful for the mercy I have received. Perhaps I may ascribe some part of my insensibility to my great weakness of body. I hope so at least that if I was better in health, it would be better with me in that respect also.'

The next day, perceiving that his understanding began to suffer by the extreme weakness of his body, he said, 'I have been vain of my understanding and of my acquirements in this place, and now God has made me little better than an idiot as much as to say: "Now be proud if you can." Well, while I have any senses left, my thoughts will be poured out in the praise of God! I have an interest in Christ, in His blood and sufferings, and my sins are forgiven me. Have I not cause to praise Him? When my understanding fails me, as I think it will soon, then He will pity my weakness!'

Though the Lord intended that his warfare should be but short,

[79] Matthew 11 : 28. [80] Luke 15 : 7. [81] See Revelation 6 : 16.

yet a warfare he was to have and to be exposed to a measure of conflict with his own corruptions. His pain being extreme, his powers of recollection much impaired, and the Comforter withholding for a season His sensible support, he was betrayed into an impatience and fretfulness of spirit which had never been permitted to show itself before. This appearance alarmed me and having an opportunity afforded me by everybody's absence, I said to him, 'You was happier last Saturday than you are today. Are you entirely destitute of the consolations you then spoke of, and do you not sometimes feel comfort flowing into your heart from a sense of your acceptance with God?' He replied, 'Sometimes I do, but sometimes I am left to desperation.' The same day he said, 'Brother, I believe you are often uneasy lest what lately passed should come to nothing.' I replied by asking him whether when he found his patience and his temper fail, he endeavoured to pray for power against his corruptions? He answered, 'Yes, a thousand times in a day. But I see myself odiously vile and wicked. If I die of this illness, I beg you will place no other inscription over me than such as may just mention my name and the parish where I was minister.[82] For that I ever had a being and what sort of being I had cannot be too soon forgot. I was just beginning to be a Deist and had long desired to be so, and I will own to you what I never confessed before, that my function and the duties of it were a weariness to me which I could not bear. Yet, wretched creature and beast as I was, I was esteemed religious though I lived without God in the world.'

About this time, I reminded him of the account of Janeway's death which he once read at my desire.[83] He said, '[I] had laughed at it in [my] own mind and accounted it mere madness and folly. Yet base as I am,' (said he), 'I have no doubt now but God has accepted me also and forgiven me all my sins.'

I then asked him what he thought of my narrative? He replied, 'I thought it strange and ascribed much of it to the state of mind in which you had been. When I came to visit you in London and found you in that deep distress—I would have given the universe to have administered some comfort to you. You may remember that I tried

[82] John had been vicar of Foxton, seven miles from Cambridge.

[83] C is referring to James Janeway's biography of his brother, *Invisible Realities, Demonstrated in the Holy Life and Triumphant Death of Mr. John Janeway, Fellow of King's-Colledge in Cambridge* (1673). James Janeway (1636?–1674) describes the painful death from consumption of his brother John (1633–57) in the concluding seventeenth chapter.

every method of doing it. When I found that all my attempts were vain, I was shocked to the greatest degree. I began to consider your sufferings as a judgment upon you, and my inability to alleviate them as a judgment upon myself. When Mr. Madan came, he succeeded in a moment. This surprised me, but it does not surprise me now. He had the key to your heart which I had not. That which filled me with disgust against my office as a minister was the same ill success in my own parish. Then I endeavoured to soothe the afflicted and to reform the unruly by warning and reproof, but all that I could say in either case was spoken to the wind and attended with no effect.'

There is that in the nature of salvation by grace when it is truly and experimentally known which prompts every person to think himself the most extraordinary instance of its power. Accordingly, my brother insisted upon the precedence in this respect, and upon comparing his case with mine would by no means allow my deliverance to have been so wonderful as his own. He observed that from the beginning both his manner of life and his connections had been such as had a natural tendency to blind his eyes and to confirm and rivet his prejudices against the truth. Blameless in his outward conduct and having no open immorality to charge himself with, his acquaintance had been with men of the same stamp, 'who trusted in themselves that they were righteous',[84] and despised the doctrines of the Cross. Such were all who from his earliest days he had been used to propose to himself as patterns for his imitation—Not to go farther back, such was [the] clergyman under whom he received the first rudiments of his education. Such was the schoolmaster under whom he was prepared for the University, and such were all the most admired characters there with whom he was most ambitious of being connected.[85] He lamented the dark and Christless condition of the place where learning and morality were all in all, and where, if a man were possessed of these qualifications, he neither doubted himself nor did anybody else question the safety of his state. He concluded, therefore, that to show the fallacy of such appearances and to root out the prejudices which a long familiarity with them had fastened in his mind required a more than ordinary exertion of Divine power, and that the Grace of God was more clearly manifested in such a work

[84] Luke 18 : 9.

[85] Clergyman and schoolmaster unidentified.

than in the conversion of one like me, who had no outside righteousness to boast of and who, if I was ignorant of the truth, was not, however, so desperately prejudiced against it.

His thoughts, I suppose, had been led to the subject when in the afternoon, while I was sitting by the fireside, he thus addressed himself to the nurse, who sat by his bolster. 'Nurse, I have lived three and thirty years, and I will tell you how I have spent them. When I was a boy, they taught me Latin and, because I was the son of a gentleman, they taught me Greek. These I learned under a sort of private tutor. At the age of fourteen or thereabouts, they sent me to a public school where I learned more Latin and more Greek, and last of all to this place where I have been learning more Latin and Greek still. Now, has not this been a blessed life and much to the glory of God?' Then directing his speech to me, he said, 'Brother, I was born in such a year, but I correct myself. I would rather say, "In such a year I came into the world." You know when I was born.'

As long as he expected to recover, the souls committed to his care were much upon his mind. One day, when none was present but myself, he prayed thus. 'O Lord, Thou art good, goodness in the very essence, and Thou art the fountain of wisdom; I am a poor worm, weak and foolish as a child. Thou hast entrusted many souls unto me. And I have not been able to teach them because I knew Thee not myself. Grant me liberty, O Lord, for I can do nothing without Thee! And give me grace to be faithful.'

In a time of severe and continual pain, he smiled and said, 'Brother, I am as happy as a king.' And the day before he died, when I asked him what sort of a night he had, he replied, 'a sad night, not a wink of sleep.' I said, 'Perhaps though your mind has been composed to pray?' 'Yes', said he, 'I have endeavoured to spend the hours in thoughts of God and in prayer. I have been much comforted and all the comfort I get comes to me in this way.'

The next morning I was called up to be a witness of his last moments. I found him in a deep sleep, lying perfectly still, and seemingly free from pain. I stayed with him till they pressed me to quit the room and in about five minutes after I had left him, he died. Sooner, indeed, then I expected, though for some days we had no hope of his recovery. His death at that time was rather extraordinary, at least I thought it so, for when I took leave of him the night before, he did not seem worse or weaker than he had been and for aught that

appeared might have lived many days. But the Lord, in Whose sight the death of His saints is precious, cut short his sufferings and gave him a speedy and peaceful departure.

He died at seven in the morning on the 20th March 1770.[86]

[86] The following statements are added to the text:

These narratives were faithfully, and, to the best of my care, literally transcribed by John Newton.

Transcribed from the Reverend Mr. Newton's Copy, September 1772.

J. Madan.

LETTERS

Greville Street March 12th 1749

Dear Watty

In order to Vindicate Mr Morgans Veracity & my own honour, I send you this. Does not this Sound well? I think there is something Theatrical in it; & the same Spirit kept up through a Tragedy might make a great Figure upon ye English Stage.

Odd Enough! two Friends corresponding by letter at the Distance of a Mile & a half. An Indifferent person would think we were afraid of seeing each other. No rivers to interpose their Streams impassable; the Distance so inconsiderable; ye weather fine, and both desirous of a Meeting: Why then says that Indifferent person, what a Devil should hinder you? why don't you meet? why thou Leaden-headed Puppy, says I, I'll tell thee why. This same Mr Bagot is confined within ye musty walls of a nasty, stinking abominable Prison; and I myself am an humble Servant to old Father Antick the Law; and Consequently have but very little time to myself. But methinks, says he, you might find an hour or two some Evening, and that would be a little Satisfaction — well thought on, faith Sir says I — & now Watty what say you to this honest Fellows proposal? will you appoint a time? I'll meet you at any place you shall name? Can you impose upon old Argus? Or is ye Dog more watchfull with 2 Eyes than his Grandfather was with a Hundred?

Morgan wanted me to come & shake Hands with you through the Door; but that was so like Pyramus & Thisbe that I could not bear ye Thoughts of it.

Let me know in your Answer where Toby is, when you heared from him & how I may direct to him. I writ to him at Oxford & I hear he is in Whales; & though I have writ to him twice, would you think it? I have not heared from him once since I have been at Chapmans.

I am Dear Watty, thinking this long Enough for ye Penny post, yours sincerely

William Cowper

Direct to me at Mr Chapmans in Greville Street near Holborn

The earliest extant Cowper Letter

to Walter Bagot, 12 March 1749/50

WALTER BAGOT Monday, 12 March 1749/50[1]

Address: To / Walter Bagot Esqr / at the College in Little Deans Yard / Westminster
Postmark: PENY POST PAYD T[EMPLE] MO[NDAY]
Morgan Library

Grevile Street March 12th. 1749

Dear Watty

In order to Vindicate Mr. Morgan's[2] Veracity & my own honour, I send you this. Does not this Sound well? I think there is something Theatrical in it; & the same Spirit kept up through a Tragedy might make a great Figure upon the English Stage.

Odd Enough! Two Friends corresponding by Letter at the Distance of a Mile & a half. An Indifferent person, would think we were afraid of seeing each other. No Rivers to interpose their Streams impassable; the Distance so Inconsiderable; the Weather fine, and both desirous of a Meeting: Why then says that Indifferent person, what a Devil should hinder you? Why don't you meet? Why thou Leaden-headed Puppy, says I, I'll tell thee why. This same Mr. Bagot[3] is confined within the musty Walls of a nasty, stinking, abominable Prison;[4] and I myself am an humble Servant to old Father Antick the Law;[5] and Consequently have but very little time to myself. But Methinks, says he, you might find an hour or two some Evening, and that would be a little Satisfaction—Well thought on, faith Sir says I—& now Watty what say you to this honest Fellow's proposal? Will you appoint a time, I'll meet you at any place you shall name?

1 C has used Julian or Old Style dating for this letter, since the Gregorian, or New Style, was not accepted in England until 2 Sept. 1752. For further information on the dating of the letter, see *Ryskamp*, pp. 177–8.

2 Almost surely, Charles Morgan (b. *c.* 1733), from Llandovery, Carmarthenshire (now Dyfed), who was admitted to Westminster in 1746 and left in 1750. He matriculated at Christ Church, Oxford, in the same year (B.A. 1754, M.A. 1757). When subscribing to Smart's *Poems on Several Occasions* (1752) and Robert Lloyd's *Poems* (1762), he styled himself the 'Rev. Mr. Morgan, Stud. of Christ Church, Oxon.' C had probably seen him and had told him that he planned to write to Bagot.

3 See C to Lady Hesketh, 30 Nov. 1785: 'In the course, as I suppose of more than twenty years after we left school, I saw him but twice;—once when I called on him at Oxford, and once when he called on me in the Temple.'

4 Bagot is still a student at Westminster at this time.

5 *1 Henry IV*, I. ii. 59.

Can you impose upon old Argus?[6] Or is the Dog more watchfull with 2 Eyes than his Grandfather was with a Hundred?

Morgan wanted me to come & shake Hands with you through the Door; but that was so like Pyramus & Thisbe that I could not bear the Thoughts of it.

Let me know in your Answer where Toby[7] is, when you heared from him & how I may direct to him. I writ to him at Oxford & I hear he is in Whales; & though I have writ to him twice, would you think it! I have not heared from him once since I have been at Chapman's.

I am Dear Watty, (thinking this long Enough for the Penny post) yours sincerely

William Cowper

Direct to me at Mr Chapman's in Grevile Street near Holbourn.

CHASE PRICE *c.* June 1750

Marquess of Salisbury (*copy*) [1]

Dear Toby

I am heartily sorry for poor Arthington.[2] Remember him ay or my Memory must be very Treacherous Indeed. But however no more upon this melancholy Subject.

No rather in the silent Tomb[3]
Deaths dismal dark Capacious Womb

[6] 'Argus' was probably the Second or Under Master, at this time Pierson Lloyd. In the eighteenth century Westminster does not appear to have had a school porter, other than one of the King's Scholars during the day. See *Ryskamp*, p. 181.

[7] Chase Price.

[1] The transcription of this letter occupies pp. 38–40 in the first Chase Price Commonplace Book at Hatfield House. For a description of the Commonplace Book, see Charles Ryskamp, 'New Poems by William Cowper,' *The Book Collector*, vol. xxii, No. 4 (Winter 1973), 443–78. Since the transcriptions in the Commonplace Book may represent C's practice at that time in transcribing his poetry, we have not, contrary to our principles in presenting material from manuscript copies, introduced any punctuation in printing the four poems which occupy most of this letter.

[2] Cyril Arthington (1730–50), who was admitted to Westminster in June 1745, and matriculated at University College, Oxford, on 16 Feb. 1748/9. He had died on 28 May.

[3] These lines derive in part from Cowley's pindaric ode, 'Life'.

Be the Remembrance with the Body laid
  Than let vain Sorrow discompose
  Our Minds with unavailing Woes
Perhaps our Tears but persecute the Dead
Tears against Heav'n's Decrees Impertinently Shed

If I my Friend should drop before you
  Think the Joyful Prize is mine
A whole Eternity of Glory
  While poor Mortality is thine
Then if one silent Tear should fall
One Sigh escape let that be all
  Lest bitter Envy claim a part
  In thy Friendly faithfull Heart
Death's the best Blessing Heaven can give
  We live to Dye but dye to Live

Well said, good Mrs. Clio. I ask your pardon for Invoking you at the wrong End of a Poem but better so than not at all.

Come Heavenly Muse who Cowleys Bosom fired
His Judgment Strengthen'd and his Wit inspired
Explore the Secrets of my Mind. Expell
All Sin-born Counsels, all the just reveal
  Hail Happy Freedom of the Mind.
  Guiltless Generous Union find
  Wisdoms Sister Bane of Lust
  Sweet Companion of the Just
  Scorning Censures keenest Edge
  Virtues Choicest Privilege
  Virtue the plant so seldom found
  In British or in Foreign Ground
  Buds in the Morning blows at Noon
  And Ripens with the Setting Sun
  Gracefull alike in Every Stage
  Of Life Youth Manhood and Old Age
  Intended e'er Mankind began
  The lasting Ornament of Man
  Cherish the Plant and it shall be
  A Lasting Ornament to thee

If you must botch, my Friend, let your botches be your own. Clio is good natur'd. Give her good Words and She is always ready to assist, Especially in the Country—

The Muses are Romantick Jades
And only Frisk it in the Shades
Love-Tinkling Rills and Cooling Streams
Harmonious Groves And airy Dreams
But fly the City with Disdain
Where ceaseless Hubbub stuns the Brain
Thus sung old Horace[4] and thus sings
Each Bard that mounts on Fancys Wings
You then may safely dare to rise
Stride Pegasus and reach the Skys
Whether you climb the threatning Steep
Or in the lowly Valley creep
The Hill whence many a Rood between
Fair Oxfords Glittering Spires are Seen
The Vale where Simple Shepherds dwell
In Cottage clean or Mossy Cell
Or if within the Dusky Grove
All pensive you delight to rove
Where Woodbine creeps the Trees among
All aid the Gentle Poet's Song
Sing Gentle Poet then with Chyme
Of Jingling Ear-bewitching Rhyme

Just what you please; any thing you know by way of Botch. Now Methinks I hear you Cry—

Curse Curse the[e]
On the Prose and Verse
This Jingling is worse
Than the Noise of a Herse
Or another Mans Purse
Neither here nor there
Like a Sow with one Ear
Or a Pie-bald Mare
Or a Baited Bear

[4] Cf. *Epistles*, II. ii. 77.

Who has lost half his Hair
At a Wake or a Fair
In a Damnable War
With Killbuck and Star[5]
Ding Dong
For an end to the Song
Of this Villain e'er long
Or we'll cut out his Tongue
Or give him a Dose
A Hogshead of Physick
Some Kicks and some Blows
For having made me Sick

I am Dear Toby yours Sincerely

William Cowper

CHASE PRICE — Wednesday, 1 April 1752

Address: To / Chace Price Esqr. / at Knighton near Presteign, / Radnorshire. / By the Presteign Bag.
Postmarks: 2/AP *and* II
Robert H. Taylor

Grevile Street April 1st. 1752

Dear Toby

In return for your very agreeable favour I shall only present you with a few Lines which enter'd into my Pate as I was walking in the fields this Morning before Breakfast, and thinking what Compliment I should coin that might be worthy your Acceptance. In which you are to understand that with the Politeness of most Criticks I bestow much greater Commendation upon my own Judgment, than upon your Performance—However tho' I have Impudence enough to commend myself, I know you too well to shock your Modesty with an Encomium which tho' you really deserve, it would require more Eloquence than I am Master of, to make you think so. Ah! que Je suis bien poli—

Trust me, the Meed of Praise dealt thriftily
From the Nice Scale of Judgment, Honours more,

[5] Perhaps familiar names of dogs on a bear-baiting team. *O.E.D.* defines a killbuck as a fierce-looking person.

Than does the lavish and o'erbearing Tide
Of profuse Courtesy—& not all the Gems
Of India's richest Soil at random spread
O'er the gay Vesture of some glittering Dame,
Give such bewitching Graces to the person,
As the scant Lustre of a few, with choice
And Comely guise of Ornament bestow'd.[1]

I shall only observe how artfully you have ensur'd my Approbation by paying a Compliment to Celia at the same time that you flatter my Vanity no less, by shewing that you think my Nonsense worth a place in your Memory, & even in your Performance. But I Question whether if you look in your Common Place Book you will not find all this under Title, *Flummery*[2] according to the Modern Expression, so it were best to have done.

The very thing you say of Happiness I said t'other Day of Content, which is only another Name for the same thing. It will help to fill up this side so I will send it you.

O! ask not where Contentment may abide
  In whose still Mansion those true Joys abound
  That pour sweet Balm o'er Fortune's fest'ring Wound,
Whether she chuse sequester'd to reside
In the lone Hamlet on some Mountain wide,
  Whose rough top with brown Oaks or Pine Trees crown'd,
  Casts a dim Shade a settled gloom around:—
Or whether She amidst the glittering Tide
  Of Courtiers, pouring from the thick-throng'd Gate
Of Majesty, be seen: She nor assumes
  The high-swol'n Pomp of haughty-miened State,
Nor constant to the low-roof'd Cottage comes:
  On Honest Minds alone she deigns to wait.
There closes still her downy-feather'd Plumes;
  Nor wand'ring thence shifts her serene abode,
Pleas'd to possess the Noblest Work of God[3]

[1] This poem is Item XIV in the first Chase Price Commonplace Book at Hatfield House, and it was first published in *Poems, The Early Productions of William Cowper*, ed. James Croft (1825).

[2] Mere flattery or empty compliment (*O.E.D.*).

[3] These lines were, to the best of our knowledge, first published in the Sotheby catalogue of 29 Apr. 1897 (lot 283).

N:B: Pope says—

An Honest Man's the Noblest Work of God.[4]

I am sorry to find my Surmise was but too well grounded, I hope the Rheumatism will not prevent your coming to Town soon, 'till when I shall defer looking out for Chambers, for I shall be more likely to chose right and to my own Satisfaction when you are here to *help chose*.[5]

I hear from a good person that Watty Bagot is surpriz'd that he hears not from me, I could tell him that I am no less *surpriz'd at his surprize*, than he can be at my Silence. And so you may tell him when you write to him next.

An Admirable thing is just publish'd by Mason of Cambridge, which you shall read when you come to Town. He calls it Elfrida a Dramatick Poem:[6] It is written upon the Greek Plan, like Samson Agonistes, & Comus—I do [not][7] find that it is much known in the World as yet, I pick[ed it] up accidentally at Brown's Coffee House,[8] & having read it there, recommended it to 2 or 3 who may be call'd sound & staunch Judges of all works of Genius. I need not tell you how they approved of it, *after having told you that it met with my Sov'reign Approbation.*

I am Dear Toby
Your in & Sincere Friend
W Cowper.

Do prithee learn to write with your Mouth or your Toes, for your hands may probably be so often disabled for writing, that you may burst for want of communicating your Thoughts.

[4] *An Essay on Man*, iv. 248.

[5] According to the Students' Ledger of the Middle Temple, C did not take up his 'complete set of chambers' until 15 Nov. 1753.

[6] *Elfrida*, published the previous March, was the work of William Mason (1724–97), the friend, literary executor, and biographer of Thomas Gray. Gray commended this poetic drama to Walpole in a letter of [20 Feb.] 1751 (*Gray*, i. 343): 'The story is Saxon, and the language has a tang of Shakespeare, that suits an old-fashioned fable very well.'

[7] The MS. is torn at the seal.

[8] Located in 'Mitre court, leading to the temple. Chiefly frequented by gentlemen of the law. Tea, coffee, and other refreshments': [JohnFeltham], *The Picture of London for 1803* (1803), p. 353.

CHASE PRICE Thursday, 21 February 1754

Arthur A. Houghton, Jr.

Temple Feb: 21:1754.

Dear Toby

I was just going to bestow the highest Encomiums upon you for having been so very punctual, when casting my Eyes upon your Postscript, it occurr'd to me, that you was not entirely disinterested in the Affair; yet I must in Justice to my *own Merit* allow it to be a very Laudable Motive, and wonder not that you who have been bless'd with a Specimen of my *Excellent Taste* in Poetry, are Impatient 'till you are in full Possession of all my Works. A certain Person who is not at all Dear to me to speak of, has given herself the Air of calling me a *Coxcomb* often before now; I am willing to allow *her* the Privilege of *calling* me so, because I know she cannot in reality think me one, and Love me as she does.[1] Now think not that because I have a *small Regard* for you, that therefore I shal dispense with your taking the same Liberty, for you may still Entertain a Friendship for me and nevertheless be really & truly convinced that I am a Coxcomb, nay, you may like me the better for that Reason, Because—Simile agit in Simile.[2]

And are you not a Coxcomb? Can you deny it? Is not your last Letter a Proof of it? Don't you there Brag of being better Qualified to entertain the Fair Sex than my Worship? And don't you undervalue me as being Deficient in the most Essential point perhaps of good Breeding? Whatever Merit you are willing to ascribe to yourself from a more frequent Communication with the vicious part of the Sex, I am very ready to allow you—Only at the same time you must acknowledge that all the Advantages which arise from a Decent Familiarity with the worthiest part of it, are on my Side. The *Honest Impudence* (as Ranger calls it)[3] of a Libertine, will hardly defend him from Bashfullness in the Company of a Modest Woman; nay the very means he has made use of, whereby he has Acquir'd this Honest

[1] Probably a reference to Theadora.

[2] Like leads on like.

[3] C's reference is probably to Benjamin Hoadly's *The Suspicious Husband* (1747). Although C's quotation does not appear in the text of the play, he may be referring to the claim of the hero, Ranger, who says he retains his honesty even though he admits to acts of impudence. C cites Hoadly's play in a very similar context in his letter to Walter Bagot of 2 Aug. 1791.

Impudence, disqualify him for the Entertainment of any, except those Women to whom he owes it. If this be the case, which is likely to make the best Figure in the best Company, He who cannot say a Rude thing, or he, who in order to avoid saying a Rude thing, must take care not to open his Lips! Come then, *Honest*, *Impudent* Toby, own for once, that it is not so wonderfull that I should have won the Affections of a Virtuous Woman, who saw that my Behaviour, various as it was, had no Mixture of Affectation in it: as it would have been; had you prevail'd in the same manner, who could not do it by appearing in your own undisguis'd Character, nor have affected to put on a Sedate Sober Appearance, without being discover'd for an Impostor. I beleive I have said rather more in my own Favour than there is Foundation for, and have somewhat Extenuated, or rather been Silent upon the Subject of the good Qualitys you are really Master of—But all this you must Impute to my *Modest assurance*. It is plain from your Letter, that you have a Heart susceptible of those sublime Enjoyments which you seem almost to Envy me. There is also some Appearance of Contrition towards the latter End of it; for which reason, if the Maxim be true that when a Man of Sense perceives & confesses his Error he is in a fair way to Amend it, I know not any Reason you have to Despair of succeeding in your Addresses to a Virtuous Woman. I wish you was once fairly taken in, for an affair of that sort would undoubtedly complete your Reformation; nothing else can—However I would advise you to wait 'till you are deeply smitten before you accost her as a Lover; your Reformation must be the Effect of your Regard for her, and of your *very Sincere* Regard for her, otherwise it can never last. I think I know enough of you to pronounce, that any good Resolution you can make merely from a *Conviction* that it is Right, will be of no long Continuance; Your *Passions* must be strongly affected, so that what you Resolve upon, it shall become Delightfull to you to perform, or you are as far from the Performance of it as before you resolved.

I will answer your Question in your own Words—You must Amend, or Despair of finding in Honest Matrimony a sure Content-ment. —Whatever means you think likely to work such a Reformation I would advise you to pursue; Neither the Single nor the Marry'd State afford any sure Contentment But to the Virtuous. A Vicious man in the Single State may perhaps find his Existence at the latter end of his Days barely tolerable, while he is young it may

possibly be Agreeable rather than not, but this is very Hazardous: In the marry'd State his Case is Desperate, whether Young or Old he must be miserable. —For *Vicious* please to Read *Libertine* and you may apply all I have said to Yourself.[4] I look upon you as one of the very best Species of Libertines otherwise I should not Subscribe myself your Affectionate Friend W Cowper.

PS:

You may remember that there was some small Difference between me and the Person I hinted at in the Beginning of my Letter; the Enclosed[5] was wrote upon that Subject since I saw you last. All is Comfortable & Happy between us at presant and I doubt not will continue so for ever. Indeed we had neither of us any great reason to be Dissatisfied, & perhaps Quarrel'd merely for the sake of the Reconciliation—which you may be sure made Ample Amends. Adieu!

CHASE PRICE *c.* 1754

Clark Library

Great Berkhamstead I don't know when.

Dear Toby

I am in such a hurry, I hardly know how to set one Leg—before t'other to get to the End of my Letter; and God knows if I shall be able to do it to Night.

Dancing all last Night; In bed one half of the Day & Shooting all the other half, and now am going to—what? To kill a boding Screech

[4] In *Connoisseur*, No. 111 (11 Mar. 1756), 54–5, C very playfully and elegantly proceeds to debunk the 'delicate *Billy Suckling*' who has little appetite for love-making: 'If he escapes a nervous fever a month, he is quite a Buck: if he walks home after it is dark, without his mamma's maid to attend him, he is quite a Buck: if he sits up an hour later than his usual time, or drinks a glass or two of wine without water, he calls it a debauch; and because his head does not ache the next morning, he is quite a Buck. In short, a woman of the least spirit within the precincts of St. *James*'s would demolish him in a week, should he pretend to keep pace with her in her irregularities; and yet he is ever dignifying himself with the appellation of a Buck.' C clearly saw himself at this time as having found a *via media* between Billy and Toby.

[5] Perhaps 'Written in a Quarrel'. See *Milford*, pp. 274–6.

Owl perch'd upon a—Walnut Tree just by my Window, have at you old Wise Acre![1]—

What an Irishman am I? I went to Destroy one of Dame Pallas's Poultry, and she to defend her Songster cast a cloud before my Eyes, and Behold! I could not see to the End of my Gun.

I have had no time Toby to Versify for you except what I stole under a Hedge to day, while I was—Shooting; so there I sat me down with my Pencil in my Hand, and my Gun by my side, in utrumque paratus.[2] A Piece of a rare Song[3] Toby I heard t'other Day follows here (as it deserves the first place) and then my own.

I

Young Gentlemen listen awhile
  And unto you I will declare,
Oh! how the *King's Fisher* did serve
  Those Rogues that belong to Algier.

Captain Wheeler he did us Command
  And no Man shall force me to lye,
And the cheifest of his whole delight,
  Was in chasing of the Enemy.

The Turks swam as thick by her Side
  As e'er you saw Fish in the Sea,
But we spared as many as we could
  And that was out of Christianity.
                    Da Capo.

I have twisted the Sense of the Words to your present Condition as much as possible; not taking it in Horace's Meaning, which I suppose you would chuse.[4]

[1] C has added a note in the margin: 'By the Way I kill'd one today.'

[2] Prepared in either way.

[3] The author or source of the 'rare song' has not been traced. Sir Francis Wheler (1656?–1694), a captain in the Navy in 1680, was responsible for capturing the Algerine corsairs in 1681.

[4] C's poem begins by alluding to *Epistles*, II. i. 1: 'Cum tot sustineas et tanta negotia solus' ('While you alone sustain the important responsibility'), but it quickly moves away from direct borrowing from Horace.

Cum tot sustineant Reges et tanta, neque ulla
  Parte, Voluptati Deliciisque Vacent:
Cum varios Capiti affigat Diadema Dolores,
  Bellorumque premant Sollicitentque Minæ:
Cur queritur Populus? Cur cæco Murmure mussat?
  Inque suum Insane Vim meditatur Herum?
Qui Vigil Excubias agit usque, et sustinet usque
  Imperii, Populus ne quà Laboret, Onus.
Hoc Satanæ scelus est, nec Dæmone dignius ul[lum]
  Nam primum in Satanæ pectore, Crime[n erat]
Præmia quin date digna Viro, verusque sequatur
  Collata in gentem, commoda, gentis Amor.
Illum Iure colant Populi, tueantur, Amente[s]
  Ille colit Populos, ille tuetur, Amat.
Tu vero (si talis erit) quicunque verendum
  Execrære caput Principis, Eia! Tacé;
Necquia rara, fides Regi fert præmia, Demens
  Immeritum Regem quem Venerere, putes;
Ipse tibi plaudas, quæ Laus est Optima, Laudem
  Externam Ingenuis est meruisse Satis—[5]

Though kings sustain so many and such great things, yet they have no part of their time for pleasures and delights. Though the royal crown brands the head with many sorrows, [yet] threats of wars agitate and pursue closely. Why should the common people complain? Why does the [nation] murmur with a blind humming? Tell me, does he madly exercise his heroic power who, keeping a watchful guard (lest the people be oppressed), continuously performs and everywhere sustains the burden of rule?

This infamy is Satan's and nothing is more fitting to this Demon, for this sin first dwelt in the breast of Satan. Nay, rather, give noble rewards to a man [of character], and true and agreeable love of the people, drawn together into a nation, will follow.

Let nations rightly foster this [fealty]; let a loving nation guard [it]; this [loyalty] honours nations, protects them and cherishes them.

You, in truth, such as you are (if such there be) that would curse the venerable head of the Prince, ah! be silent; because loyalty to the king bears no extraordinary rewards, foolish one, you think the king whom you honour, unworthy. You would have self approval, which is the best glory; it is honour enough for a freeman to have won foreign fame.

This poem was first published by Thomas Wright in *The Life of Cowper*, *Evendale Biographical Series no. 4* (1895).

[5] The remainder of the letter is missing.

JOSEPH HILL — Friday, 10 October 1755

Address: To / Joseph Hill Esqr. / at No. 17: in / Gloucester Street, / Queen Square, / London.
Postmark: 13/OC
Cowper Johnson

Mr. Hill—

If I write not to you
As I gladly would do
To a Man of your Mettle & Sense,
'Tis a Fault I must own
For which I'll attone
When I take my Departure from hence

To tell you the Truth,
I'm a queer kind of Youth
And I care not if all the World knows it;
Whether Sloven, or Beau,
In Square, Alley, or Row,
At Whitehall, in the Court, or the Closet.

Having written thus much
In Honest high Dutch,
I must now take a Nobler Stile up:
Give my Fancy, a prick,
My Invention, a Kick,
And my Genius a pretty smart Fillip

For the Bus'ness in hand
You are to understand,
Is indeed neither trifling nor small:
But which you may transact
If your Scull is not crackt
As well as the best of them all.

And so may your *Dear Wife*
Be the Joy of your Life,
And of all our brave Troops the Commandress,
As you shall convey
What herein I say
To the very fair Lady, my Laundress.

That to Town I shall Trot
(No I Lie, I shall not,
For to Town I shall Jog in the Stage)
On October the Twentieth,
For my Father consenteth
To make me the Flower of the Age.[1]

So bid her prepare
Every Table & Chair,
And warm well my Bed by the Fire,
And if this be not done
I shall break her Back bone
As sure as I ever come nigh her.

I am Jovial & Merry,
Have writ till I'm weary.
And become, with a great deal of Talking, horse
So farewell—Sweet Lad!
Is all I shall add,
Except——

your obedient *Stalking Horse*[2]
W Cowper.

G Berk:
Octbr. 10th. 1755.

JOHN DUNCOMBE — Thursday, 16 June 1757

Princeton

My Dear Jacky,

I wish you had a more comfortable place to end your days in, than that which I have so lately taken my leave of.[1] For my own part,

[1] C is commissioning Hill to have C's chambers at the Middle Temple readied for his return from a visit to his father at Berkhamsted.

[2] 'A person whose agency or participation in a proceeding is made use of to prevent its real design from being suspected' (*O.E.D.*). This verse letter was first published in *Milford*, pp. 624–5.

---

[1] Berkhamsted. This comment should be compared with C's remarks ten years later in his letter to Mrs. Madan of 15 Oct. 1767.

I believe no man ever quitted his Native place with less Regrett than myself, and were it not for the sake of a Friend or two that I have left behind me, one of which small Number you will doubtless reckon yourself, I should never wish to see either the place or any thing that belongs to it again.[2] Notwithstanding this Jack, you & I have spent many merry hours together in the Parsonage, my poor Father has often been the better for your Drollery, for you had the Knack, or the *Natural* Gift of making him Laugh, when no Creature else could have done it.

For this single reason, I should always have a regard, & a very Sincere one, for old Cicero, had I no other, and by the same rule, I shall continue to despise some certain persons, who treated him in a manner which did not indeed disgrace him, so much as it did themselves. It was hard upon him who did nothing to create him an Enemy, that he should find so few Friends; but it is the Lot of many others, and I hope as to myself, that the sort of men who professed themselves his Enemys, will everlastingly be mine.[3]

God bless you Jack, I can write no more at present, let me hear from you again & believe me in the mean time

Yours Wm Cowper.

PS.
I have desired my Mother to send you the Gold Sleeve buttons, which were my Father's, & imagine they will not be the less acceptable because they were his.
June 16.
1757.

[2] Perhaps C would have included Jones Redman (1695?–1763), the physician, as one of the friends in Berkhamsted (see *Ryskamp*, pp. 11, 265). He is also probably referring to Richard Bard Harcourt (see C to Duncombe, 31 Dec. 1757) and Mary Essington (see C to Duncombe, 21 Nov. 1758).

[3] 'He made himself envied and misliked of many men, not for any ill act he did, or meant to do: but only because he did too much boast of himself. . . . Now to use these fine taunts and girds to his enemies, it was a part of a good orator: but so commonly to gird every man to make the people laugh, that won him great ill-will of many. . . .' (Plutarch's *Life of Cicero*, North's translation.)

JOHN DUNCOMBE Saturday, 31 December 1757

Address: To / Mr. Jno. Duncombe at the / Post House / Great Berkhamsted / Harts
Postmark: 31/DE
Princeton

Dear John,

You are an honest old Whore, and he that says more of you, will be in danger of saying more than is true. As to your long Story of Gingerbread and Faggots,[1] I understand but half of it. I know I promised you some Gingerbread with Sweetmeats, which promise I have not yet perform'd, but are you sure therefore that I will never perform it? You are too hasty in reproaching me with Breach of promise; I would rather marry a Pastry Cook's Daughter, on purpose to supply you with Gingerbread, than you should want it. Indeed Jack I will send you some, I do not say when, but if I ever send it you know, I am as good as my word.

You have split my Brain with your confounded Faggot-sticks, & I can make neither Head nor Tail of the whole Story; But it is like the rest of your Narrations, the chief Perfection of which is that they are absolutely unintelligible. I am glad to find you read, and observe upon what you read; a Man without Learning says Grotius, let his Birth and Extraction be what it will, is no better than one of the Vulgar.[2] I would recommend it to you, now you have made yourself almost a Master of the Paradise lost, to read the Iliad & the Odyssey in their Original Languages. You are a pretty adept in Latin, and as to Greek, you will understand it tolerably well by the time you have read Homer with attention.

Let me hear no more of your Faggots, but tell me what is become of Dick Harcourt,[3] I never hear from him or of him, & he is almost the only Man in your part of the World, that I want to hear of. —God

[1] See Richard Bradley, *Dictionaire Oeconomique: or, The Family Dictionary* (1725), i, s.v. *Faggots of Oranges*: 'Orange-Peels turn'd or par'd very thin, in order to be preserv'd, more especially those of sweet *Oranges* . . . commonly call'd *Faggots.*' This meaning of 'Faggots' is suggested by the parallel word 'Sweetmeats', often preserved or candied fruit. C may be using 'Faggots' in the more obvious meaning of the word, as he does later in the letter with his reference to 'Faggot-sticks'.

[2] C's legal studies would have made him familiar with *De Jure Belli ac Pacis* (1625), a treatise on international law, by Hugo Grotius (1583–1645), the Dutch jurist and humanist.

[3] A boyhood friend of C's, Richard Bard Harcourt (1724?–1815) of Pendley, Herts., attended Eton and entered Caius College, Cambridge, in 1742 and Lincoln's Inn two years later.

bless you Old Boy—take care you don't burst yourself this Christmas & believe me

Yours Affectionately
Wm Cowper.

Dec. 31.
1757.

I am sorry to have no Frank, but you may charge the Postage to one of your Clients.

JOHN DUNCOMBE — Saturday, 22 July 1758

Sotheby, Wilkinson and Hodge Catalogue, 8–9 July 1878, lot 65.

You are descended from Job, as you are plagued with more than half his sufferings.[1]

CLOTWORTHY ROWLEY — August 1758

Southey, i. 323–4

Lond. Aug. 1758.

Deliciæ et Lepores mei![1]

Qui Gallicé scripsisti, responsum habes Latinum; non quia Linguam hanc satis calleo, sed istam quia nimis ignoro. Literas Anglicanas

[1] This is the only excerpt given. The letter, from the collection of George Manners, is described as a 3-page A.L.S. (4to) and was sold to Naylor for £2. 10*s*.

---

[1] Translation (*Wright*, i. 15–17):

My Delightfully-Funny Friend,—You wrote in French and are now to receive an answer in Latin, not because I am sufficiently versed in this language, but because I know very little about the other. I knew, for certain, that you would despise a letter in English.

While you are following your Rhadamanthus with more pains, as you tell me, than profit, I, who neither take pains nor hope for profit, am leading an idle, and therefore what is to me a most agreeable life: nor do I envy you the country, dirty as it now is, and daily deluged with unseasonable rain. Sometimes, indeed, I go into the adjacent parts of the country, to visit a friend or a lady; but it is a short journey, and such as may easily be performed on foot, or in a hired carriage, for never, unless compelled to do it, do I mount a horse, because I have a tender skin, which with little exercise of that kind suffers sorely. I lately passed three days at Greenwich; a blessed three days, and if they had been three years I should not have envied the gods their immortality. There I found that lovely and beloved little girl, of whom I

te contempturum certò scivi. Dum tu Rhadamanthum tuum,[2] quicunque is est, per villas atque oppida sectaris, majori, ut ais, opere quam lucro; ego, neque laborans, neque lucrum sperans, otiosam, ideoque mihi jucundissimam vitam ago; neque rus tibi invideo, lutulentum scilicet, et intempestivo diluvio quotidie obrutum. Aliquando autem et ego in suburbana rura, amicum vel amicam visurus, proficiscor: breve est iter, quod vel pedes, vel currû conducto facile perficias; perrarò enim, et nunquam nisi coactus, in caballum ascendo, quippe qui nates teneras habeo, quas exiguus usus contundit et dilacerat. Triduum nuper, Villæ quam dicunt Greenwich, commoratus sum. O beatum Triduum, quod si Triennium fuisset, immortalitatem Superis minime invidissem. Puellulam ibi amabilem et amatam, de quâ sæpius tibi locutus sum, inveni.[3] Eâ Virgo est ætate (annos nata sedecim) ut dies singuli novum aliquod decus ad formam afferant. Modestiâ, et (quod mirum videtur in Fæminâ) taciturnitate est maximâ; quando autem loquitur, crederes Musam loqui. Hei mihi, quod Sidus tam clarum aliô spectet! Indiâ Occidentali oriundum, illuc rediturum est; mihique nihil præter suspiria et lacrymas relicturum. Tu me amore sentes torqueri,—ego te lasciviâ.—

Paucis abhinc diebus ad Hortos Bonæ Mariæ[4] sum profectus; delicias ejus loci nequeo satis laudare. Ludi Scenici qui ibi exhibentur, more Italorum, nostrâ vero linguâ, sunt constituti. Partes quas

have often talked to you; she is at that age, sixteen, at which every day brings with it some new beauty to her form. No one can be more modest, nor (which seems wonderful in a woman) more silent; but when she speaks, you might believe that a Muse was speaking. Woe is me that so bright a star looks to another region; having risen in the West Indies, thither it is about to return, and will leave me nothing but sighs and tears.

You see me tortured with love, I you with lasciviousness.

A few days ago I set off for Marylebone gardens, to the delights of which place it is impossible to do justice. Theatrical plays have been organised, which they perform there in the Italian fashion, only in our language. The portions styled recitatives are absurd beyond measure, but the songs are most sweet. There is this one thing, however, to be feared, namely, that, sitting in the open air, one may catch a cold, if not a fever.

As to our friend Alston, he has not written to me, nor is he likely to write; for I have long understood the sluggish and forgetful nature of the man. Should you see him, give him a sound rating for me. Farewell.

[2] Rowley was probably going on circuit as a judge's marshal. Rhadamanthus, in Greek mythology, is one of the judges in the underworld, and the term refers to an inflexible judge.

[3] The young lady has not been traced.

[4] Located at the back of a tavern called 'The Rose of Normandy' on the east side of High Street, Marylebone, these gardens, originally constructed in the seventeenth century, were a celebrated place of entertainment. In 1758 an adaptation of Pergolesi's *La Serva Padrona* enjoyed great popularity.

Recitativas vocant, ridiculæ sunt ultrà modum; cantilenæ autem suavissimæ. Unum hoc timendum, ne sub Dio sedentem, tussis occupet vel febris.

Quod ad amicum nostrum Alston[5] attinet, neque Epistolam mihi misit quamlibet, neque missurum reor; scio enim jamdudum ignavam hominis naturum, et obliviosam. Si videris, objurgationes aliquos a me in eum confer, Culumque meum osculetur, jube.

Vale.

JOHN DUNCOMBE Tuesday, 21 November 1758

Address: To / Mr. John Duncombe at / the Post house / Great Berkhamsted / Hartfordshire.
Postmark: 21/NO
Historical Society of Pennsylvania

My Dear John,

The Old Proverb You mention may hold good with respect to most people but has nothing to do with You, who are not to be forgot by any man that has seen half so much of you as I have. And for This you are not more obliged to my Memory, than to your own Extraordinary Qualitys, which exist only in yourself.

My Brother told me that you entertained him sumptuously; I wish I could have partaken of the Treat, both because it is a singular Honour to be Entertained by You, who seldom make any Entertainments, and because I know no man at whose Table I should be more welcome. 'Tis true enough that I am not fond of the Law, but I am very fond of the Money that it produces, and have much too great a Value for my own Interest to be Remiss in my Application to it. I heartily wish I had an Opportunity of seeing you, because I believe you are Sincere when you say it would give you Pleasure to find yourself once more in my Company. It is long since our last Meeting Old Jack, and may be long before we meet again, but never Imagine, whether you hear from me or not, that I have so treacherous a Memory as to forget you. My Oldest Friends have the highest place in my Esteem, & you know very well that you are not a New one.

[5] William Alston (1728–99) of Bramford, Suffolk, who had come to the Middle Temple in 1751 from Pembroke College, Cambridge. Alston and C had read through Homer together as well as Pope's translation. See C to Rowley, 21 Feb. 1788.

Make my Compliments to Mrs. Essington,[1] and light your Pipe with This Epistle, unless you have immediate Occasion to make a different Use of it—

Yours Old Friend Wm Cowper.

Temple
Nov: 21. 1758.

JOHN DUNCOMBE? Thursday, 11 January 1759

Huntington Library

My Dear Jack

I am glad you can prevail with yourself now & then to Stick a Pen in your Old Claw, and tell me you are in the Land of the Living. If your Face and Person are as little Altered as your Stile, you must needs be as well worth seeing as ever, and I heartily wish I could have Ocular Proof of it. Dick[1] says you never could write or Speak good English in your Life, which is so true, that it were vain to denie it, but your Language has always been more Entertaining than the best English I ever met with. I shall be sorry to recieve a Letter from you in more Elegant Phrase than usual, and immediately conclude that being too much Indisposed to write yourself, you have made Roley Poley,[2] or your Clerk or some such Scholar, your Amanuensis. I met Dick Harcourt in Hyde Park yesterday, he looked well & was in high Spirits, so perhaps he has swallowed the Grape shot you speak of with Success.[3] Martin Madan's Wife is just brought to bed of another Son, his Family now consists of 2 Sons and as many Daugh-

[1] Mary Essington, probably the widow of either Thomas or John Essington: see N. Salmon, *The History of Hertfordshire* (1728), p. 125; the Church Accounts, St. Peter's, Berkhamsted [1584–1748]: Add. MS. 18773, fo. 304. She was in 'A List of Owners of Land in Berkhamsted, Herts, 1755' (B. L. Lansdowne MS. 656, fo. 6), as the owner of 'Broadoak ffarm, Meadow by Ravens Lane, Land at ffriday street, Land by Cross of the oak'.

---

[1] Richard Bard Harcourt.

[2] Unidentified. A generic term for rascal (*O.E.D.*).

[3] The reference to 'grape shot', that is, small cast-iron balls, strongly connected together so as to form a charge for a cannon, probably had a personal or contemporary significance which cannot be traced. Kenneth Povey suggested that it might be a humorous name for one of those remedies with numerous constituents, aimed at everything in the hope of hitting something.

ters—[4] The Girls are both likely to be handsome; I have never seen the Boys, but they say That which is just born, has a Foot much longer than yours already, so he is likely to be a Proper Man.—I am going to spend 2 or 3 days at the Park,[5] if the Bankrupts will give me leave;[6] Will Cowper always enquires after you, when he has an Opportunity, and so does every Will Cowper I know. They are Whimsical Fellows, or they would not do it.

I had been Informed before your Letter told me so that Mrs. Essington had been out of Order, & was sorry to hear it.[7] Upon your Account as well as her own I heartily wish she may recover, for I look upon her as one of the few Comforts you have, and as a Friend you can't well afford to part with. Though you don't mention Madam Harcourt, I will—How should I know whether she is well or Ill unless you tell me?[8]—Farewell Old Boy! Shall I never see your Belly peeping from under your Waistcoat again, and your left Foot shaking itself upon your right Knee? You Date your Letter the 9th. of May, no doubt intending to persuade me that April is past, that so I may forget to make a Fool of you—But look well to yourself, for I have a Cap & Bells that will just fit you.

Yours Dear Jack, with the Old Wish of a Happy New Year

Wm Cowper

Temple
Jan. 11. 1759.

[4] Their children living at this date were (1) Martin (1756–1809), (2) Ann Judith (d. 1829), (3) Maria (d. 1829), and (4) William (1759–69), the son just born to Mrs. Madan at the time of this letter.

[5] The residence at Hertingfordbury, Herts., of William Cowper who married Maria Frances Cecilia Madan.

[6] C was a Commissioner of Bankrupts, which brought him £60 a year: Wright, *Life*, p. 86. He probably began work in this office shortly after the death of his father, who was the patentee for making out commissions of bankruptcy. C's name appears in the list of sixty Commissioners of Bankruptcy appointed by the Lord Keeper of the Great Seal (Lord Chancellor), from 1758 to 1765 (*Court and City Register*).

[7] See C to Duncombe, 21 Nov. 1758, n. 1.

[8] Sarah Frances Bard Harcourt (d. 1764), widow of Henry (d. 1743) and mother of Dick Harcourt. In 1755 she owned the house occupied by 'Mrs. Duncombe' in Berkhamsted and herself lived in Egerton House (B. L. Lansdowne MS. 656, fos. 10, 12). On 17 Dec. 1737 O.S. she had been godmother to William Cowper's brother John (Cowper family Bible).

JOHN DUNCOMBE Tuesday, 12 June 1759

Huntington Library

Dear Jack,

I have a great respect for your Virtues, notwithstanding that in your Letter to my Brother you talk Bawdy like an Old Midwife. You wonder I am not a more Punctual Correspondent; how the Devil should I be so, or what Subject can I possibly find to Entertain you upon? If I had a share in the Cabinet Councils of every Court in Europe, you would have no Pleasure in a Political Epistle; if I was a greater Philosopher than Sir Isaac Newton, you would think me a Fool if I should write to you upon the Subject of the Centripetal & Centrifugal Powers, the Solar System, and the Eccentrick Orbits of the Comets; And as great a Lawyer as I am, I dare not Indulge myself in the Pedantry of my Profession, lest you should not understand me, or I should not understand myself—In short I am afraid to tell you anything but that I am your most Obedient & Affectionate humble Servant

Wm C.

June 12.
1759.

JOSEPH HILL Thursday, 18 October 1759

Cowper Johnson

Dear Joe,

I recieved a Letter from your Clerk yesterday containing an Account of a Treaty he has had with Mr. Fry a Limner[1] about the House in R: L: S.[2] I shall be obliged to [*sic*] if you will desire him to

[1] Perhaps the 'Limner' is Thomas Frye (1710–62), portrait painter and engraver in mezzotint. He may have been looking for a house, because he had given up his position as manager of the china factory at Bow, moved to Wales, and then taken a house in Hatton Garden, London, about this time. Frye apparently did not rent the house (see below) since the Rate Books indicate that Miles Baxter took over the occupation of the house in 1756 and was still there in 1757. Dr. Monro is listed as the occupant in the Rate Books from 1759 to 1776.

[2] C and his brother must have inherited the house in Red Lion Square through the death of their father in 1756. According to the Rate Books, the Revd. John Cowpoer (*sic*) was

acquaint that Gentleman that we shall be glad to come to an Agreement with him. That we do not intend to Let the House however, without the Stables; and that for both together we cannot possibly take a less Rent than 60£ per Annum. As to the Roof I imagine it cannot want a great deal of Repair, as it was made entirely new not much more than Ten Years ago, but if it is any where defective shall have no sort of Objection to making it good, upon the Terms Mr. Fry proposes. As to the Stables, I should imagine it would be rather beneficial to Mr. Fry to take them, even though he makes no use of them himself, as there are many people in the Neighbourhood, who would be glad of them, & would hire them at a rent of 10£ or 12£ per Annum. There are some Goods in the House such as Kitchen grate, Marble Tables, Bottle Rack, Looking glasses, Lamp at the Door &c, which we intend to dispose of, and should imagine Mr. Fry would find it convenient to be the Purchasor; but they will be sold at all Events. I shall be in Town probably to-morrow, that is Friday Sen'night, and at any time after, shall be glad to treat with Mr. Fry about these matters in person.

I wish you Joy of our Successes in America,[3] and shall Jump at a Letter from you.

Your affectionate Friend & Servant
Wm Cowper.

Gt Berkhamstead
Thurs: Oct. 18. 1759.

If Mr. Fry is not satisfied with these Terms, or should have any thing further to propose, I shall be glad if your Clerk will be so good as to acquaint me with it, while I am here.

one of the occupants of No. 7 on the Square from 1750 to 1756. No. 7 was the second house on the south side after Fisher Street. See Hugh Phillips, *Mid-Georgian London* (1964), pp. 287, 292.

Further evidence of John Cowper's ownership of such a piece of property is contained in a letter of Martin Madan to his wife Judith, 4 June 1741 (Bodleian): '. . . the Honest Doctor [John Cowper] wrote to me this Morning to "desire I woud [*sic*] Come to his House in Red Lyon Square". . . .'

[3] A reference to the celebrated victory of the English led by Wolfe over the French at Quebec on 13 Sept. 1759. The news of Wolfe's victory had reached England on the evening of 16 Oct.

NONSENSE CLUB[1] c. 1760

John Johnson, *Private Correspondence of William Cowper, Esq.* (1824), vol. i, pp. xxi–iv.

Letter from an owl to a bird of paradise.

Sir,

I have lately been under some uneasiness at your silence, and began to fear that our friends in Paradise were not so well as I could wish; but I was told yesterday that the pigeon you employed as a carrier, after having been long pursued by a hawk, found it necessary to drop your letter, in order to facilitate her escape. I send you this by the claws of a distant relation of mine, an eagle, who lives on the top of a neighbouring mountain. The nights being short at this time of the year, my epistle will probably be so too; and it strains my eyes not a little to write, when it is not as dark as pitch. I am likewise much distressed for ink: the blackberry juice which I had bottled up having been all exhausted, I am forced to dip my beak in the blood of a mouse, which I have just caught; and it is so very savoury, that I think in my heart I swallow more than I expend in writing. A monkey who lately arrived in these parts, is teaching me and my eldest daughter to dance. The motion was a little uneasy to us at first, as he taught us to stretch our wings wide, and to turn out our toes; but it is easier now. I, in particular, am a tolerable proficient in a horn-pipe, and can foot it very nimbly with a switch tucked under my left wing, considering my years and infirmities. As you are constantly gazing at the sun, it is no wonder that you complain of a weakness in your eyes; how should it be otherwise, when mine are none of the strongest, though I always draw the curtains over them as soon as he rises, in order to shut out as much of his light as possible? We have had a miserable dry season, and my ivy-bush is sadly out of repair. I shall be obliged to you if you will favour me with a shower or two, which you can easily do, by driving a few clouds together over the wood, and beating them about with your wings till they fall to pieces. I send you some of the largest berries the bush has produced, for your children to play withal. A neighbouring physician, who is a goat of great experience, says they will cure the

[1] The Nonsense Club was a group of seven Old Westminsters who dined together every Thursday. Among the members were James Bensley, Robert Lloyd, George Colman the Elder, Bonnell Thornton, and C. See *Ryskamp*, pp. 82–3.

worms; so if they should chance to swallow them, you need not be frightened. I have lately had a violent fit of the pip,[2] which festered my rump to a prodigious degree. I have shed almost every feather in my tail, and must not hope for a new pair of breeches till next spring; so shall think myself happy if I escape the chincough,[3] which is generally very rife in moulting season.

I am, dear Sir, &c. &c.

Madge.[4]

P.S.—I hear my character as first minister[5] is a good deal censured; but 'Let them censure; what care I?'

LADY HESKETH *post* Saturday, 31 July 1762

Olney (*copy*)[1]

You may now dearest Coz: congratulate me on being an Independent man—if indeed a man may properly be said to be *Independent*, who has *nothing* to depend upon: my Mother:in:law is dead and has left her fortune to be divided equally between my brother & myself—a division not very unlike Splitting a hair, and which must be very agreeable to my brother, who is a Cambridge man & a Logician, and to me no less who have the honor to be Call'd a Lawyer. But pity me

[2] Probably diarrhoea. Pip is usually considered to be a disease in poultry occurring in the mouth and throat, often causing a scale on the tip of the tongue; C uses the word in this way in 'Conversation', l. 356: 'Faint as a chicken's note that has the pip' (*Milford*, p. 97). The *O.E.D.* gives no authority for making it a disease affecting the rump, but there is a tradition of applying the word to various diseases in human beings, usually humorously, and often suggesting venereal disease.

[3] Chincough, now more commonly called whooping cough. The word was also used in connection with animals for a humorous effect by Addison (*Tatler*, No. 121): '. . . Cupid, her lady's lap-dog, was dangerously ill . . . "[he] has always been phthisical, and as he lies under something like a chin-cough, we are afraid it will end in a consumption." '

[4] According to *O.E.D.*, a madge is a barn-owl. It may have been the practice in the Nonsense Club or among C's friends to take names of birds or animals. This letter from Madge may have been addressed to Hill. Hill had the MS. in 1802, when it was sent to Hayley. Hill to Hayley, 19 Feb. 1802: copy owned by the Misses Cowper Johnson.

[5] In the latter part of the eighteenth century, the common designation for the Premier or Prime Minister (see *O.E.D.*, s.v. 'Prime Minister'). The sentence suggests that C may have been president of the Nonsense Club at the time.

[1] This letter, which concerns the death of Rebecca Cowper at Bath on 31 July 1762, survives only in this fragment quoted by Lady Hesketh to William Hayley in a letter of 17 Sept. [1805], Cowper and Newton Museum, Olney.

not dear Coz: the comforts of life lie so near the Ground, that we poor folks are sure to find them, while rich Rogues Jump over them & *know nothing of the* MATTER.[2]

CLOTWORTHY ROWLEY Thursday, 2 September 1762

Address: To / Clotworthy Rowley Esqr. / at Tendring Hall / near Ipswich / Suffolk.
Postmark: 3/SE
Princeton

Dear Rowley,

Your Letter has taken me just in the Crisis, to:morrow I set off for Brighthelmston,[1] and there I stay 'till the Winter brings us all to Town again. This World is a shabby Fellow & uses us ill, but a few years hence there will be no difference between Us and our Fathers of the Tenth Generation upwards. I could be as splenetick as you & with more reason if I thought proper to indulge that Humour, but my Resolution is, & I would advise you to adopt it, never to be melancholy while I have a hundred pounds in the world to keep up my Spirits. God knows how long that will be, but in the mean time, Iö Triumphe.[2]—If a great Man struggling with Misfortunes is a Noble Object, a little Man that despises them is no contemptible one; And this is all the Philosophy I have in the World at present; it savours pretty much of the Ancient Stoic, but 'till the Stoics became Coxcombs they were in my Opinion a very sensible Sect. If my Resolution to be a Great Man was half so strong as it is to despise the Shame of being a little one, I should not despair of a House in Lincoln's Inn Fields with all its Appurtenances, for there is nothing more certain, & I could prove it by a thousand Instances, than that every man may be Rich if he will. What is the Industry of half the Industrious Men in the World but Avarice, and call it by which name you will, it almost always succeeds. But this provokes me, that a Covetous Dog who will work by Candle:light in a Winter Morning

[2] Lady Hesketh told Hayley that the concluding words of the letter may have read '*know not they exist*' rather than '*know nothing of the* MATTER.'

[1] Brighton.

[2] A Latin and Greek expression of exaltation.

to get what he does not want, shall be praised for his thriftiness, while a Gentleman shall be abused for submitting to his Wants, rather than work like an Ass to relieve them. Did you ever in your Life know a man that was guided in the general Course of his Actions by any thing but his natural Temper? And yet we blame each other's Conduct as freely as if that Temper was the most tractable Beast in the World, and we had nothing to do but to twitch the Rein to the Right or the Left, and go just as we are directed by others. All this is Nonsense, & nothing better. There are some sensible Folks who having great Estates have Wisdom enough too to spend them properly; there are others who are not less Wise perhaps in knowing how to shift without 'em. Between these two degrees are they who spend their Money dirtily, or get it so. If you ask me where they are to be placed who amass much Wealth in an honest way, you mu[st][3] be so good as to find them first and then I'll Answer [the] Question. Upon the whole my dear Rowley, there is a degree of Poverty that has no Disgrace belonging to [it, th]at degree of it I mean in which a man enjoys clean Linnen and good Company, & if I never sink below this degree of it, I care not if I never rise above it. This is a strange Epistle nor can I imagine how the Devil I came to write it, but here it is such as it is & much good may [do you] with it. I have no Estate [as it] happens, so if it should fall into bad hands I shall be in no danger of a Commission of Lunacy. Adieu! Carr[4] is well & gives his Love to you.

Yours ever Wm Cowper.

Sep. 2. 1762.

[3] MS. is torn on the right-hand side of the third folio.

[4] Arthur Carr (b. 1727), son of the Bishop of Killaloe, had attended Trinity College, Dublin, before being admitted to the Middle Temple on 3 Feb. 1746/7 (*Register of Admissions to the . . . Middle Temple*, ed. H. A. C. Sturgess (1949), i. 337). Although Carr and C were close friends during C's time at the Middle Temple, they drifted apart during C's Inner Temple years.

Carr was extremely kind to C at the time of the writing of this letter, in the midst of his last difficult year at the Inner Temple. It is to this generosity that C refers in his letter to Rowley of 22 Oct. 1791: 'I often think of Carr, and shall always think of him with affection. Should I never see him more, I shall never, I trust, be capable of forgetting his indefatigable attention to me during the last year I spent in London.'

JOSEPH HILL Friday, 18 February 1763

Cowper Johnson

Dear Joe,

If the Wise acre had offer'd me 800£ for the House, I have a Conscience that would have fitted it exactly. As to Mr. Hawkins[1] he may hang himself upon the Sign Post whenever he pleases, but if he thinks I will wait to Chaffer and Haggle with such a Fusty Old: Cloathsmonger as He, he is mistaken. I shall write to him by this Post to hasten his Resolution. He may know as well in 10 Minutes as in a Month, whether he will pay that Price for it or no.

Hawkins's Lease did Lie upon the black Leathern Table when I left the Chambers, & there I dare say you will find it. There are but 8 Years to come, & I am as certain that he has no right to renew.

God bless you, & thank you for your Intelligence. We heard by another Wind this Morning that she[2] had begun to drink Tar Water & that it agreed with her. Dii Vortant bené![3]

Feb: 18. 1763

Yours ever
Wm Cowper.

Shall I trouble you to put the Letter to Hawkins into the Penny Post?

JOSEPH HILL Friday, 1 April 1763

Cowper Johnson

Dear Joe,

This Dawson[1] is a sly Fellow; he has waited thus long in hopes that I would send for him, and sell him the House for less than its real Value. He now offers more than it is worth, yet seeing that he is a Scoundrel, I will take his Money.

Yours Affectionately
Wm Cowper.

April 1st. 1763.

[1] Unidentified. [2] Unidentified.

[3] Terence, *Hecyra*, I. ii. 121: 'Good luck!'

[1] Unidentified.

LADY HESKETH Tuesday, 9 August 1763

Hayley, iii. 373–5

The Temple, August 9, 1763.

My Dear Cousin,

Having promised to write to you, I make haste to be as good as my word. I have a pleasure in writeing to you at any time, but especially at the present, when my days are spent in reading the Journals, and my nights in dreaming of them.[1] An employment not very agreeable to a head that has long been habituated to the luxury of chusing its subject, and has been as little employed upon business, as if it had grown upon the shoulders of a much wealthier gentleman. But the numscull pays for it now, and will not presently forget the discipline it has undergone lately. If I succeed in this doubtful piece of promotion, I shall have at least this satisfaction to reflect upon, that the volumes I write will be treasured up with the utmost care for ages, and will last as long as the English Constitution. A duration which ought to satisfy the vanity of any author who has a spark of love for his country. Oh, my good Cousin! If I was to open my heart to you, I could shew you strange sights; nothing I flatter myself that would shock you, but a great deal that would make you wonder. I am of a very singular temper, and very unlike all the men that I have ever conversed with. Certainly I am not an absolute fool; but I have more weaknesses than the greatest of all the fools I can recollect at present. In short, if I was as fit for the next world, as I am unfit for this, and God forbid I should speak it in vanity, I would not change conditions with any Saint in Christendom.

My destination is settled at last, and I have obtained a furlough. Margate[2] is the word, and what do you think will ensue, Cousin? I know what you expect, but ever since I was born, I have been good at disappointing the most natural expectations. Many years ago, Cousin, there was a possibility that I might prove a very different thing from what I am at present. My character is now fixt, and rivetted fast upon me, and, between friends, is not a very splendid one, or likely to be guilty of much fascination.

[1] C was preparing to qualify for the position of Clerk of the Journals in the House of Lords.

[2] Thomas Gray characterized Margate as 'Bartholomew-Fair by the seaside' (Gray to Wharton, 26 Aug. 1766: *Gray*, iii. 930).

Adieu, my dear Cousin! So much as I love you, I wonder how the Deuce it has happened I was never in love with you. Thank Heaven that I never was, for at this time I have had a pleasure in writing to you, which in that case I should have forfeited. Let me hear from you, or I shall reap but half the reward that is due to my noble indifference.

Yours ever, and ever more,

W.C.

JOSEPH HILL Monday, 24 June 1765[1]

Address: To Joseph Hill / Cooke's Court / Carey Street / London
Cowper Johnson

Huntingdon June 24. 1765.

Dear Joe,

The only Recompense I can make you for your friendly Attention to my Affairs, during my Illness, is to tell you that by the Mercy of God I am restored to perfect Health both of Mind and Body. This I beleive will give you Pleasure, and I would gladly do any thing from which you may receive it.

I left St. Albans on the 17th., arrived that day at Cambridge, spent some time there with my Brother, and came hither on the 22d. I have a Lodging that puts me continually in mind of our Summer Excursions; we have had many worse, and except the Size of it which however is sufficient for a single Man, but few better. I am not quite alone, having brought a Servant[2] with me from St. Albans, who is the very Mirrour of Fidelity and Affection for his Master. And whereas the Turkish Spy[3] says he kept no Servant because he would not have an Enemy in his House, I hired mine because I would have a Friend. Men do not usually bestow these Encomiums upon their Lacqueys, nor do they usually deserve them, but I have had Experience of mine both in Sickness and Health and never saw his Fellow.

[1] The hiatus in the correspondence between this letter and the previous one (9 Aug. 1763) is due to C's second period of depression.

[2] Samuel Roberts (d. 1832).

[3] The first volume of *Letters Writ by a Turkish Spy*, attributed to Giovanni Paolo Marana (1642–93), appeared in France in 1684 and was translated into English in 1687. The remaining seven volumes, of unknown authorship, were apparently first published in English between 1691 and 1694. C's citation is to Book I, Letter I: 'And because I will have no enemy near me, I will therefore admit of no servant.'

The River Ouze, I forget how they spell it, is the most agreeable Circumstance in this part of the World. At This Town it is I beleive as wide as the Thames at Windsor; nor does the Silver Thames better deserve that Epithet, nor has it more Flowers upon its Banks, these being Attributes which in strict Truth belong to neither. Fluellin[5] would say they are as like as my Fingers to my Fingers, and there is Salmons in both. It is a noble Stream to bath in, and I shall make that use of it three times a Week, having introduced myself to it for the first time this Morning.

I beg you will remember me to all my Friends, which is a Task it will cost you no great Pains to execute. Particularly remember me to those of your own House, and beleive me your very Affectionate

Wm Cowper.

Direct to me at Mr. Martin's Grocer
at Huntingdon.

MARTIN MADAN — Monday, 24 June 1765

Gregg Commonplace Book (*copy*)

Huntingdon June 24. 1765

My Dear Martin,

I have long had a desire to write to you, indeed ever since it pleased God to restore to me the perfect health both of my mind and body; and have with difficulty prevailed upon myself to defer it 'till I had left St. Albans. I have suppressed my impatience to do it hitherto in the full persuasion that a letter from me in a state of *enlargement* would be more acceptable to you, than anything I could send from that *suspected* quarter. Blessed be God! I am indeed *enlarged*, and you, who know so well the Spiritual as well as ordinary import of *that* word, will easily apprehend how much I mean to crowd into it.

Martin, I have never forgot, nor ever shall forget, the instruction you gave me at our Interview in my chambers.[1] It was the first lesson of the kind I had ever heard with attention, perhaps I may say, the first I ever had heard at all—And notwithstanding the terrible disorder of mind I fell into soon after, not all the thousand deliriums that

[5] *Henry V*, IV. vii. 30.

[1] See pp. 29–31.

afflicted me have been able to efface it. My heavenly Father intended it should be to me an earnest of His love, which is the reason I have not lost it, but by His blessing upon it, it has been a key to me, together with the assistance of His grace, to right understanding of the Scriptures ever since. I bless His holy name for every sigh, and every groan, and every tear I have shed in my illness. He woundeth and His hands make whole—they heal the wounds which He Himself hath made for our chastizement, and those deeper wounds which by our sins we have inflicted upon ourselves.

You remember the poor wretch[2] whose illness so much resembled mine, and you remember too how he was seen 'Clothed, and in his right mind, and sitting at the feet of Jesus'—I thank God I resemble him in my recovery, and in the blessed effects of it, as well as in my distemper. Pray for me, Martin, that I ever may, and believe me that I suppress much lest I should alarm even you by the warmth of my expressions; but you might read it in my eyes.

Give my love to all your family, and to your mother.

Yours Martin very thankfully
and very affectionately
W. C.

LADY HESKETH — Monday, 1 July 1765

Hayley, iii. 375–7

Huntingdon, July 1, 1765.

My Dear Lady Hesketh,

Since the visit you were so kind as to pay me in the Temple (the only time I ever saw you without pleasure), what have I not suffered? And since it has pleased God to restore me to the use of my reason, what have I not enjoyed? You know by experience, how pleasant it is to feel the first approaches of health after a fever; but, Oh the fever of the brain! To feel the quenching of that fire is indeed a blessing which I think it impossible to receive without the most consummate gratitude. Terrible as this chastizement is, I acknowledge in it the hand of an infinite justice; nor is it at all more difficult for me to perceive in it the hand of an infinite mercy likewise, when

[2] C is probably referring to the incident described in Luke 8 : 26–39, in which Jesus casts out the demons from a young man.

I consider the effect it has had upon me. I am exceedingly thankful for it, and, without hypocrisy, esteem it the greatest blessing, next to life itself, I ever received from the divine bounty. I pray God that I may ever retain this sense of it, and then I am sure I shall continue to be as I am at present, really happy.

I write thus to you that you may not think me a forlorn and wretched creature; which you might be apt to do, considering my very distant removal from every friend I have in the world—a circumstance which, before this event befel me, would undoubtedly have made me so; but my affliction has taught me a road to happiness which without it I should never have found; and I know, and have experience of it every day, that the mercy of God, to him who believes himself the object of it, is more than sufficient to compensate for the loss of every other blessing.

You may now inform all those whom you think really interested in my welfare, that they have no need to be apprehensive on the score of my happiness at present. And you yourself will believe that my happiness is no dream, because I have told you the foundation on which it is built. What I have written would appear like enthusiasm to many, for we are apt to give that name to every warm affection of the mind in others, which we have not experienced in ourselves; but to you, who have so much to be thankful for, and a temper inclined to gratitude, it will not appear so.

I beg you will give my love to Sir Thomas, and believe that I am much obliged to you both, for enquiring after me at St. Albans.

Yours ever,
W.C.

JOSEPH HILL — Wednesday, 3 July 1765

Address: To / Mr Hill / Cook's Court / Carey Street / London.
Postmarks: 4/IY *and* HUNTING/DON
Cowper Johnson

Dear Joe,

Whatever you may think of the Matter it is no such easy thing to keep House for two People. A Man cannot always live upon Sheeps' Heads and Liver & Lights[1] like the Lions in the Tower,[2] and a Joint

[1] Lungs of sheep, pigs, bullocks, etc., used as food especially for cats and dogs (*O.E.D.*).

[2] C is referring to the lions kept at the Tower of London.

of Meat in so small a Family is an endless Incumbrance. My Butcher's Bill for last Week amounted to four Shillings & Ten pence—I set off with a Leg of Lamb, & was forced to give part of it away to my Washer woman; then I made an Experiment upon a Sheep's Heart, and that was too little; next, I put three pounds of Beef into a Pye, and This had like to have been too much, for it lasted three days tho' my Landlord was admitted to a Share in it. Then as to Small Beer, I am puzzled to pieces about it. I have bought as much for a Shilling as will serve us at least a Month, and it is grown sower already. In short I never knew how to pity poor Housekeepers before, but now I cease to wonder at that Politic Cast which their Occupation usually gives to their Countenance, for it is really a Matter full of Perplexity.

I have received but one Visit since I came—I don't mean that I have refused any, but that only one has been offered. This was from my Woollen Drapier,[3] a very Healthy Wealthy Sensible Sponsible Man, and extremely Civil. He has a Cold Bath, and has promised me a Key of it, which I shall probably make use of in the Winter. He has undertaken too to get me the St. James's Chronicle[4] 3 times a Week, & to shew me Hinchinbrook House,[5] and to do every Service for me in his Power; so that I did not exceed the Truth you see when I spoke of his Civility.

Here is a Card Assembly and a Dancing Assembly, and a Horse Race, and a Club and a Bowling Green, so that I am well off you perceive in point of Diversions, especially as I shall go to 'em just as much as I should if I lived a Thousand Miles off. But no Matter for that; the Spectator at a Play is more entertain'd than the Actor, and in real Life it's much the same. You will say perhaps that if I never frequent these Places, I shall not come within the Description of a Spectator; and you will say right; I have made a Blunder which shall be corrected in the next Edition.

3 Reade Peacock. See C to Hill, 4 Jan., 16 Aug., and 27 Oct. 1766.

4 Henry Baldwin, the printer, had brought this paper of wit and literature 'to a height of eminence unknown to any preceding Journal, nor exceeded by any of its successors' (John Nichols, *Literary Anecdotes of the Eighteenth Century* (1812–16), viii. 479), with the help of Thornton, Colman, Lloyd, Garrick, Steevens, and Wilkes. C had been an 'occasional contributor' to the *Chronicle*, but his letters and essays in that periodical have not been identified (*Southey*, i. 49). See *Russell*, p. 5.

5 Hinchinbrooke, Lord Sandwich's seat near Huntingdon, had been sold by Sir Oliver Cromwell, the Protector's uncle, in 1627.

You are old Dog at a bad Tenant.[6] Witness all my Uncle's and your Mother's Geese and Gridirons. There is something so extremely Impertinent in entering upon a Man's Premisses, and using them without paying for 'em, that I could easily resent it if I would, but I rather chuse to entertain myself with thinking how you will scower the Man about, and worry him to Death if once you begin with him. Poor Toad! I leave him entirely to your Mercy.

My dear Joe, you desire me to write long Letters—I have neither Matter enough nor Perseverance enough for the purpose. However if you can but contrive to be tired of Reading as soon as I am tired of Writing, we shall find that short ones Answer just as well; And in my Opinion this is a very practicable Measure.

My Friend Colman[7] has had good Fortune. I wish him [better] Fortune still, which is that he may make a right use of it. The Tragedies of Loyd[8] & Bensley[9] are both very deep. If they are not of use to the surviving part of the Society, it is their own Fault.

I was Debtor to Bensley Seven pounds or Nine I forget which, the Remaining part of a Hundred I had borrowed of him. If you can find out his Brother,[10] you will do me a great Favour if you will pay him for me. But do it at your Leisure.

Yours and Theirs[11]
Wm Cowper.

Huntn.
July 3. 65.

[6] Perhaps the Morgan who rented C's chambers at the Inner Temple. See C to Hill, 27 May 1777 and n. 1.

[7] George Colman the Elder (1732–94) and C had been intimate friends during the Temple years. Colman's edition of the comedies of Terence ('translated into familiar blank verse') appeared in 1765. See also C to Hill, 10 Mar. 1766.

[8] The late Robert Lloyd (1733–64) had been captain of the 'School' at Westminster in 1750 and was elected 'Head' to Cambridge in 1751. C had known Lloyd at Westminster, and he saw him later during the time of his involvement with 'the Geniuses' (see *Ryskamp*, pp. 78–101).

[9] James Bensley (1733?–65), a graduate of Trinity College, Cambridge (B.A. 1755; M.A. 1758; Fellow, 1756), entered the Inner Temple in 1752 and Lincoln's Inn in 1756. Robert Lloyd's three epistles 'to J. B. Esq.' (two of them in 1757) were probably written to Bensley: *Works* (1774), i. 96–100, 101–3; ii. 37–50.

[10] Bensley's brother Robert (1738?–1817?) was admitted to Westminster in Sept. 1748; he became one of the most acclaimed actors of his time.

[11] There is an asterisk and a note added to the MS. in C's hand: 'The Author is supposed to mean Mrs. Hill & her 2 Daugthers. The Word *Theirs* cannot so well refer to the last Antecedents, the persons who stand in That Relation with it being both Dead at the time he wrote, as is evident from the Context. Lipsius—'

LADY HESKETH Thursday, 4 July 1765

Hayley, iii. 377–80

Huntingdon, July 4, 1765.

Being just emerged from the Ouze, I sit down to thank you, my dear Cousin, for your friendly and comfortable Letter. What could you think of my unaccountable behaviour to you in that visit I mentioned in my last? I remember I neither spoke to you, nor looked at you. The solution of the mystery indeed followed soon after, but at the same time it must have been inexplicable. The uproar within was even then begun, and my silence was only the sulkiness of a thunder-storm before it opens. I am glad however, that the only instance in which I knew not how to value your company was, when I was not in my senses. It was the first of the kind, and I trust in God it will be the last.

How naturally does affliction make us Christians! and how impossible is it when all human help is vain, and the whole earth too poor and trifling to furnish us with one moment's peace, how impossible is it then to avoid looking at the Gospel! It gives me some concern, though at the same time it increases my gratitude, to reflect that a convert made in Bedlam is more likely to be a stumbling-block to others, than to advance their faith. But if it has that effect upon any, it is owing to their reasoning amiss, and drawing their conclusions from false premises. He who can ascribe an amendment of life and manners, and a reformation of the heart itself, to madness, is guilty of an absurdity that in any other case would fasten the imputation of madness upon himself; for by so doing, he ascribes a reasonable effect to an unreasonable cause, and a positive effect to a negative. But when Christianity only is to be sacrificed, he that stabs deepest is always the wisest man. You, my dear Cousin, yourself, will be apt to think I carry the matter too far, and that in the present warmth of my heart, I make too ample a concession in saying that I am *only now* a convert. You think I always believed, and I thought so too, but you were deceived, and so was I. I called myself indeed a Christian, but he who knows my heart knows that I never did a right thing, nor abstained from a wrong one, because I was so. But if I did either, it was under the influence of some other motive. And it is such seeming Christians, such pretending believers, that do most mischief

to the cause, and furnish the strongest arguments to support the infidelity of its enemies: unless profession and conduct go together, the man's life is a lie, and the validity of what he professes itself is called in question. The difference between a Christian and an Unbeliever would be so striking, if the treacherous allies of the Church would go over at once to the other side, that I am satisfied religion would be no loser by the bargain.

I reckon it one instance of the Providence that has attended me throughout this whole event, that instead of being delivered into the hands of one of the London physicians, who were so much nearer that I wonder I was not, I was carried to Doctor Cotton.[1] I was not only treated by him with the greatest tenderness, while I was ill, and attended with the utmost diligence, but when my reason was restored to me, and I had so much need of a religious friend to converse with, to whom I could open my mind upon the subject without reserve, I could hardly have found a fitter person for the purpose. My eagerness and anxiety to settle my opinions upon that long neglected point, made it necessary that while my mind was yet weak, and my spirits uncertain, I should have some assistance. The Doctor was as ready to administer relief to me in this article likewise, and as well qualified to do it as in that which was more immediately his province. How many physicians would have thought this an irregular appetite, and a symptom of remaining madness! But if it were so, my friend was as mad as myself, and it is well for me that he was so.

My dear Cousin, you know not half the deliverances I have received; my Brother is the only one in the family who does. My recovery is indeed a signal one, but a greater if possible went before it. My future life must express my thankfulness, for by words I cannot do it.

I pray God bless you and my friend Sir Thomas.

Yours ever,

W.C.

[1] See n. 43, *Adelphi.*

LADY HESKETH Friday, 5 July 1765

Hayley, iii. 380–2

Huntingdon, July 5, 1765.

My Dear Lady Hesketh,

My pen runs so fast you will begin to wish you had not put it in motion, but you must consider we have not met even by Letter almost these two years, which will account in some measure for my pestering you in this manner; besides, my last was no answer to yours, and therefore I consider myself as still in your debt. To say truth, I have this long time promised myself a correspondence with you as one of my principal pleasures.

I should have written to you from St. Albans long since, but was willing to perform quarantine first, both for my own sake, and because I thought my Letters would be more satisfactory to you from any other quarter. You will perceive I allowed myself a very sufficient time for the purpose, for I date my recovery from the twenty-fifth of last July, having been ill seven months, and well a twelve-month. It was on that day my Brother came to see me; I was far from well when he came in. Yet, though he only staid one day with me, his company served to put to flight a thousand deliriums and delusions, which I still laboured under, and the next morning found myself a new creature. But to the present purpose.

As far as I am acquainted with this place, I like it extremely. Mr. Hodgson,[1] the minister of the parish, made me a visit the day before yesterday. He is very sensible, a good preacher, and conscientious in the discharge of his duty. He is very well known to Doctor Newton,[2] bishop of Bristol, the author of the treatise on the Prophecies, one of our best bishops, and who has written the most demonstrative proof of the truth of Christianity in my mind, that ever was published.

There is a village called Hertford, about a mile and a half from hence. The church there is very prettily situated, upon a rising ground, so close to the river, that it washes the wall of the churchyard. I found an epitaph there the other morning, the two first lines of which,

[1] Robert Hodson (*sic*) (1744–1803), who was admitted to Clare College, Cambridge, in 1744 and received his M.A. in 1762, was rector of Huntingdon St. Mary from 1757 until his death; he was also rector of All Saints from 1762 and of Offord Cluny from 1765.

[2] Thomas Newton (1704–82): his *Dissertation on the Prophecies* was published in three volumes (1754–8).

being better than any thing else I saw there, I made shift to remember. It is by a widow on her husband.

'Thou was too good to live on earth with me,
And I not good enough to die with thee!'[3]

The distance of this place from Cambridge is the worst circumstance belonging to it. My Brother and I are fifteen miles asunder, which considering that I came hither for the sake of being near him, is rather too much. I wish that young man was better known in the family. He has as many good qualities as his nearest kindred could wish to find in him.

As Mr. Quin[4] very roundly expressed himself upon some such occasion, 'here is very plentiful accommodation, and great happiness of provision.' So that if I starve, it must be through forgetfulness, rather than scarcity.

Fare thee well my good and dear Cousin.

Ever yours,
W.C.

LADY HESKETH — Friday, 12 July 1765

Gregg Commonplace Book (*copy*) *and Hayley*, iii. 385[1]

July 12, 1765.

My Dear Cousin,

You are very good to me, and if you will only continue to write at such intervals as you find convenient, I shall receive all that pleasure I proposed to myself from our correspondence. I desire no more than that you would never drop me for any great length of time together, for I shall then think you only write because something happened to put you in mind of me, or from some other reason equally mortifying. I am not however so unreasonable as to expect you should perform this act of friendship so frequently as myself, for you live in a world swarming with engagements, and my hours are almost all my own.

[3] This tombstone cannot now be found (information from Mr. A. Beaton).
[4] James Quin (1693–1766), the wit and actor.

[1] The text of this letter is from the Gregg Commonplace Book; the postscript is from *Hayley*.

You must every day be employed in doing what is expected from you by a thousand others, and I have nothing to do but what is most agreeable to myself.

Our mentioning Newton's Treatise on the Prophecies[2] brings to my mind an anecdote of Dr. Young,[3] who you know died lately at Welwyn. Dr. Cotton who was intimate with him, paid him a visit about a fortnight before he was seized with his last illness. The old man was then in perfect health. The antiquity of his person—the gravity of his utterance, and the earnestness with which he discoursed about religion, gave him, in the doctor's eye, the appearance of a prophet. They had been delivering their sentiments upon this book of Newton, when Young closed up the Conference thus:—'My friend, there are three considerations on which my faith in Christ is built as upon a rock. The Fall of Man—The Redemption of Man—and the Resurrection of Man—these cardinal articles of our religion are such as human ingenuity could never have invented. Therefore they must be divine. The other argument is this—If the Prophecies have been fulfilled, (of which there is abundant demonstration) the Scripture must be the Word of God, and if the Scripture is the Word of God, Christianity must be true.'

This Treatise on the Prophecies serves a double purpose. It not only proves the truth of our religion in a manner that never has been, nor ever can be controverted, but it proves likewise that the Roman Catholic is the apostate and antichristian church so frequently foretold both in the old and new Testament. Indeed so fatally connected is the refutation of popery with the truth of Christianity, when the latter is evinced by the completion of the Prophecies, that in proportion as light is thrown upon the one, the deformities and errors of the other are more plainly exhibited. But I leave you to the book itself. There are parts of it which may possibly afford you less entertainment than the rest because you have never been a school-boy, but in the main it is so interesting, and you are so fond of what is so, that I am sure you will like it.

My dear Cousin, how happy am I for having a friend to whom I can open my mind on these subjects! I have many intimates in the

[2] See n. 2, C to Lady Hesketh, 5 July 1765.

[3] Edward Young (1683–1765) had died on 5 Apr. Further evidence of a friendship between Young and Cotton is contained in a letter of John Jones to Thomas Birch of 2 Apr. 1765, as printed in *The Correspondence of Edward Young*, ed. H. Pettit (Oxford, 1971), p. 591. Cotton cared for Young in his last illness.

world, and have had many more than I shall have hereafter, to whom a long letter upon these most important articles would appear tiresome at least, if not impertinent, but I am not afraid of meeting with that reception from you who have never made it your interest that there should be no truth in the Word of God. How often have I wished either that I could believe it in such a manner as to make it the animating principle of all my conduct, or that I could clearly and roundly get rid of it all, even to the last scruple, and the least bias in its favour.—But as I despaired of ever compassing the former, so the severe strokes that I felt upon my conscience at particular intervals, when I reflected ever so slightly on the arguments it is built upon, have given me very sensible proofs that I never should compass the latter. Three and thirty years of my life did I spend in this manner, balancing between faith and infidelity, and leaving the upshot of all, and the final destination of a being built for eternity, to be cleared up at the universal judgment, which yet I hoped would never happen. What a terrible reference of my everlasting interests to a period decisive and without appeal! and at which every stain of unpardoned guilt must be pronounced a stain for ever. In this dreadful condition, while I was growing every day more insensible to my duty, though at the same time not less convinced of the truth of the Gospel, it pleased my All-Merciful Maker to visit me with a chastisement for which I will be ever thankful, and when the hour of discipline was past, and the scourge had done its work, He was likewise pleased to visit me with such clear apprehensions of the truth of His Divine Revelation, and such delightful assurances that all should be forgiven, and forgot, if I would but return to Him, as I trust will never forsake me. Nor let this appear strange to you, my dear Cousin, as it does to many, that my Faith should be increased without any additional arguments to persuade me. It is called enthusiasm by many, but they forget this passage in St. Paul, 'We are saved by grace through faith, and that not of ourselves, it is the Gift of God.'[4] The arguments indeed in favour of this glorious cause are more than sufficient to prove the truth of it to any man, but the heart is so often engaged to vote on the other side that they fail to produce conviction till it pleases God to strike upon the rock, and melt it into a sense of its own corruption, and the necessity there is for an atonement.

My dear Cousin, may these everlasting truths be your happiness

[4] Ephesians 2: 8.

while you live, and attend you with peace and joy in your last moments! I love you too well not to make this a part of my prayers, and while I remember my friends on these occasions there is no likelihood you should be forgot.

Yours ever
W.C.

Cambridge. July 12. 1765.

P.S.—Cambridge.—I add this postscript at my Brother's rooms. He desires to be affectionately remembered to you, and if you are in Town about a fortnight hence, when he proposes to be there himself, will take a breakfast with you.

MARTIN MADAN — Friday, 19 July 1765

Gregg Commonplace Book (*copy*)

My Dear Martin,

I am exceedingly obliged to you for the letter with which you was so kind to favour me. I know your continual employments, and how difficult it must be for you to find opportunities of writing, but when you happen to meet with one which you can bestow upon me without prejudice to any body else, you will contribute much to my happiness by making that use of it. I have more than once been witness to your indefatigable labour with those who receive not the truth, and I flatter myself you will not think a small share of your pains thrown away on one, who, blessed be God! has already received it. A line from one whom I know to be a real Christian, in the sterling sense of that appellation, is of more value to me now than all the eloquence of all the orators that ever spoke. Indeed I have much to be thankful for, so much that I am continually apt to suspect myself of ingratitude, and how is it possible for a human heart to be sufficiently grateful for the blessings I have received? Blessings which I have forfeited all possible pretensions to as many times as I have hairs upon my head. A life of three and thirty years spent without God in the world, passing upon others, and upon myself too, for a Christian, with immoralities enough to stain me as black, and sink me as deep as ever sinner fell, were circumstances which might well drive me to that despair in which you saw me when once it had pleased God to let loose my

conscience upon me, and to make me sensible of my wickedness. Eight months did I continue in that terrible condition, expecting day and night when the thunderbolt should fall that was to be my last and final visitation from the Almighty. And whatever mixture of insanity there might be in these apprehensions (and doubtless there was much of that,) still there was this mixture of reason in them that I certainly apprehended no more than my soundest judgments must acknowledge I had deserved. At the end of that period it pleased God, at once, and as it were by a touch, to restore me to the use of my reason—and to accompany that blessing with two others of inestimable value, and which I trust in His great mercy He will not suffer me to forfeit hereafter. Even faith in His Dear Son, and a most intimate and comfortable assurance of complete forgiveness. Oh, who can express my joy at this happy time! That harmony, and peace of heart, which a perfect reconciliation with our Heavenly Father alone can give, dissolved me into tears of joy, and the delightful sense of it still dwells with me!

I have thought myself happy often in the gratification of my wretched passions and affections, but I now felt how much I had been mistaken, and that I had disgraced the name of happiness by such a foolish misapplication of it; nor would I exchange one hour of my personal comfort for ten thousand years of the utmost felicity I ever enjoyed before.—The book you recommend to me I read at St. Albans, and with great pleasure, and with great conviction.[1] I plead guilty to the Doctrine of original Corruption, derived to me from my great progenitor, for in my heart I feel the evidences of it that will not be disputed. I rejoice in the Doctrine of Imputed Righteousness for without it how should I be justified? My own righteousness is a rag, a feeble defective attempt insufficient of itself to obtain the pardon of the least of my offences, much more my justification from them all. My dear Martin, 'tis pride that makes these truths unpalatable, but pride has no business in the heart of a Christian. I borrowed the book at St. Albans but intend to buy it—I read there likewise Doddridge's Sermons on Regeneration, and his Rise and Progress of Religion in the Soul, and was highly delighted with them both.[2] I love these subjects; next to the Word itself they are my daily bread,

[1] Unidentified.

[2] Philip Doddridge (1702–51), the nonconformist divine, was one of the most popular writers of hymns and spiritual tracts in the eighteenth century. His *Practical Discourses on Regeneration* appeared in 1741–2 and *The Rise and Progress of Religion in the Soul* followed in 1745.

and I beg you would mention to me any other books of that kind you think may be of use to me. I always loved reading, but I never loved it so much, for these topics had no charms for me once—and now all others are insipid.

Yours my dear Martin
with my affectionate respects to Mrs. M.
W.C.

July 19. 1765. Huntingdon.

LADY HESKETH Thursday, 1 August 1765

Hayley, iii. 385–8

Huntingdon, August 1, 1765.

My Dear Cousin,

If I was to measure your obligation to write, by my own desire to hear from you, I should call you an idle correspondent if a post went by without bringing a Letter, but I am not so unreasonable; on the contrary, I think myself very happy in hearing from you upon your own terms, as you find most convenient. Your short history of my family is a very acceptable part of your Letter; if they really interest themselves in my welfare, it is a mark of their great charity for one who has been a disappointment and a vexation to them ever since he has been of consequence enough to be either. My friend the Major's behaviour[1] to me, after all he suffered by my abandoning his interest and my own, in so miserable a manner, is a noble instance of generosity and true greatness of mind: and indeed, I know no man in whom those qualities are more conspicuous; one need only furnish him with an opportunity to display them, and they are always ready to show themselves in his words and actions, and even in his countenance at a moment's warning. I have great reason to be thankful—I have lost none of my acquaintance, but those whom I determined not to keep. I am sorry this class is so numerous. What would I not give that every friend I have in the world, were not almost but altogether Christians. My dear Cousin, I am half afraid to talk in this style, lest I should seem to indulge a censorious humour, instead of hoping, as I ought, the best for all men. But what can be said against ocular

[1] For C's relations with the Major at this time, see his letter to him of 18 Oct. 1765. For the Major's role as patentee of the office of Clerk of the Parliaments, see *Ryskamp*, pp. 148–9.

proof, and what is hope when it is built upon presumption? To use the most holy name in the universe for no purpose, or a bad one, contrary to his own express commandment; to pass the day, and the succeeding days, weeks, and months, and years, without one act of private devotion, one confession of our sins, or one thanksgiving for the numberless blessings we enjoy: To hear the word of God in public, with a distracted attention, or with none at all; to absent ourselves voluntarily from the blessed communion, and to live in the total neglect of it, though our Saviour has charged it upon us with an express injunction, are the common and ordinary liberties which the generality of professors allow themselves: and what is this but to live without God in the world? Many causes may be assigned for this Anti-christian spirit, so prevalent among Christians, but one of the principal I take to be their utter forgetfulness that they have the word of God in their possession.

My friend Sir William Russell[2] was distantly related to a very accomplished man, who, though he never believed the Gospel, admired the Scriptures, as the sublimest compositions in the world, and read them often. I have been intimate myself with a man of fine taste, who has confessed to me, that though he could not subscribe to the truth of Christianity itself, yet he never could read St. Luke's account of our Saviour's appearance to the two Disciples going to Emmaus[3] without being wonderfully affected by it, and he thought that if the stamp of divinity was any where to be found in Scripture, it was strongly marked and visibly impressed upon that passage. If these men, whose hearts were chilled with the darkness of infidelity, could find such charms in the mere style of the Scripture, what must they find there, whose eye penetrates deeper than the letter, and who firmly believe themselves interested in all the invaluable privileges of the Gospel? 'He that believeth on me, is passed from death unto life,'[4] though it be as plain a sentence as words can form, has more beauties in it for such a person than all the labours of antiquity can boast of. If my poor man of taste whom I just mentioned, had searched a little further, he might have found other parts of the sacred history as strongly marked with the characters of divinity, as

[2] Sir William Russell (1736–57), son of Sir Francis Russell of Chippenham, Cambridgeshire, was admitted to Westminster School on 7 Feb. 1742/3. He was drowned while bathing in the Thames. Henry Cromwell (1628–74), fourth son of the Protector, had married into the Russell family on 10 May 1653.

[3] Luke 24: 13.

[4] See John 6: 47.

that he mentioned. The parable of the prodigal son,[5] the most beautiful fiction that ever was invented; our Saviour's speech to his Disciples,[6] with which he closes his earthly ministration, full of the sublimest dignity, and the tenderest affection, surpass every thing that I ever read, and like the spirit by which they were dictated, fly directly to the heart. If the Scripture did not disdain all affectation of ornament, one should call these, and such as these, the ornamental parts of it, but the matter of it is that, upon which it principally stakes its credit with us, and the style, however excellent and peculiar to itself, is only one of those many external evidences by which it recommends itself to our belief.

I shall be very much obliged to you for the book[7] you mention; you could not have sent me any thing that would have been more welcome, unless you had sent me your own meditations instead of them.

Yours,
W.C.

JOSEPH HILL — Wednesday, 14 August 1765

Cowper Johnson

Dear Joe,

Both Lady Hesketh and my Brother had apprized me of your Intention to give me a Call, and herein I find they were not mistaken, but they both informed me likewise that you was already set out for Warwickshire; in consequence of which latter Intelligence I have lived in continual Expectation of seeing you any time this Fortnight. Now how these two Ingenious Personages, (for such they are both) should mistake an Expedition to French Flanders for a Journey to Warwickshire, is more than I with all my Ingenuity can imagine. I am glad however that I have still a chance for seeing you, and shall treasure it up amongst my agreeable Expectations. In the mean time you are welcome to the British Shore as the Song has it,[1] and I thank

5 Luke 15: 11–32.

6 John 14: 23–16: 16.

7 Unidentified.

1 This song has not been identified, but C may be referring to one of the nine welcome-songs composed by Purcell to commemorate the return to London of Charles II and James II. See *Grove's Dictionary of Music and Musicians*, ed. E. Blom, ix (1954), 250.

you for your Epitome of your Travels. You don't tell me how you escaped the Vigilance of the Custom House Officers, tho' I dare say you was Knuckle-deep in Contrabands, and had your Boots stuffed with all and all manner of unlawfull Wares and Merchandizes.

You know Joe I am very deep in Debt to my little Physician at St. Albans, and that the handsomest thing I can do will be to pay him le plutôt qu'il sera possible (this is vile French I beleive, but you can now correct it). My Brother Informs me that you have such a Quantity of Cash in your Hands on my Account, that I may venture to send him £40 immediately. This therefore I shall be glad if you will manage for me, and when you receive the £100 which my Brother likewise brags you are shortly to receive, I shall be glad if you will discharge the Remainder of that Debt, without waiting for any further Advice from your Humble Servant.

I am become a professed Horseman, and do hereby assume to myself the Stile and Title of the Knight of the Bloody Spur. It has cost me as much Ass's Skin as would make a reasonable Pocket Book to bring this Point to bear, but I think I have at last accomplished it.

The Snuff arrived safe.

My Love to all your Family—
Yours ever Wm Cowper

Hunt:n.
August 14. 1765.

If you see Lady Hesketh, give my Love to her, & thank her much for the little Book which I received after having given it over.

LADY HESKETH — Saturday, 17 August 1765

Hayley, iii. 388–90

Huntingdon, August 17, 1765.

You told me, my dear Cousin, that I need not fear writing too often, and you perceive I take you at your word. At present however, I shall do little more than thank you for the Meditations,[1] which I admire exceedingly; the Author of them manifestly loved the truth with an undissembled affection, had made a great progress in the knowledge of it, and experienced all the happiness that naturally

[1] Unidentified.

results from that noblest of all attainments. There is one circumstance which he gives us frequent occasion to observe in him, which I believe will ever be found in the philosophy of every true Christian, I mean the eminent rank which he assigns to faith among the virtues, as the source and parent of them all. There is nothing more infallibly true than this, and doubtless it is with a view to the purifying and sanctifying nature of a true faith, that our Saviour says, 'He that believeth in me hath everlasting life,'[2] with many other expressions to the same purpose. Considered in this light, no wonder it has the power of salvation ascribed to it! Considered in any other, we must suppose it to operate like an oriental talisman, if it obtains for us the least advantage; which is an affront to him who insists upon our having it, and will on no other terms admit us to his favour. I mention this distinguishing article in his Reflections, the rather because it serves for a solid foundation to the distinction I made in my last, between the specious professor, and the true believer, between him whose faith is his Sunday-suit, and him who never puts it off at all—a distinction I am a little fearful sometimes of making, because it is a heavy stroke upon the practice of more than half the Christians in the world.

My dear Cousin, I told you I read the book with great pleasure, which may be accounted for from its own merit, but perhaps it pleased me the more, because you had travelled the same road before me. You know there is such a pleasure as this, which would want great explanation to some folks, being perhaps a mystery to those, whose hearts are a mere muscle, and serve only for the purposes of an even circulation.

W.C.

LADY HESKETH Wednesday, 4 September 1765

Hayley, iii. 390–3

Sept. 4, 1765.

Though I have some very agreeable acquaintance at Huntingdon, my dear Cousin, none of their visits are so agreeable as the arrival of your Letters. I thank you for that, which I have just received from

[2] John 6: 47.

Droxford,[1] and particularly for that part of it where you give me an unlimited liberty upon the subject I have already so often written upon. Whatever interests us deeply as naturally flows into the pen as it does from the lips, when every restraint is taken away, and we meet with a friend indulgent enough to attend to us. How many, in all that variety of characters, with whom I am acquainted, could I find after the strictest search, to whom I could write as I do to you? I hope the number will encrease, I am sure it cannot easily be diminished. Poor——![2] I have heard the whole of his history, and can only lament what I am sure I can make no apology for. Two of my friends have been cut off during my illness, in the midst of such a life, as it is frightful to reflect upon, and here am I, in better health and spirits than I can almost remember to have enjoyed before, after having spent months in the apprehension of instant death.[3] How mysterious are the ways of Providence! Why did I receive grace and mercy? Why was I preserved, afflicted for my good, received as I trust into favour, and blessed with the greatest happiness I can ever know or hope for in this life, while these were overtaken by the great arrest, unawakened, unrepenting, and every way unprepared for it? His infinite wisdom, to whose infinite mercy alone I owe it all, can solve these questions, and none beside him. If a free-thinker, as many a man miscalls himself, could be brought to give a serious answer to them, he would certainly say—'Without doubt, Sir, you was in great danger, you had a narrow escape, a most fortunate one indeed.' How excessively foolish, as well as shocking! As if life depended upon luck, and all that we are or can be, all that we have or hope for, could possibly be referred to accident. Yet to this freedom of thought, it is owing that he, who, as our Saviour tells us, is thoroughly apprized of the death of the meanest of his creatures, is supposed to leave those whom he has made in his own image, to the mercy of chance, and to this therefore it is likewise owing that the correction which our heavenly Father bestows upon us, that we may be fitted to receive his blessing, is so often disappointed of its benevolent intention, and that men despise the chastening of the Almighty. Fevers and all diseases are accidents, and long life, recovery at least from sickness,

[1] A village 12 miles north-east of Southampton. Lady Hesketh would have had direct access to Droxford from Southampton, and she may have gone there on a visit to a friend, a Miss Morley. See also C to Lady Hesketh, 18 Oct. 1765.

[2] Unidentified.

[3] See C to Hill of 3 July 1765 concerning the deaths of Lloyd and Bensley.

is the gift of the physician. No man can be a greater friend to the use of means upon these occasions than myself, for it were presumption and enthusiasm to neglect them. God has endued them with salutary properties on purpose that we might avail ourselves of them, otherwise that part of his creation were in vain. But to impute our recovery to the medicine, and to carry our views no further, is to rob God of his honour, and is saying in effect, that he has parted with the keys of life and death, and, by giving to a drug the power to heal us, has placed our lives out of his own reach. He that thinks thus, may as well fall upon his knees at once and return thanks to the medicine that cured him, for it was certainly more immediately instrumental in his recovery than either the apothecary or the doctor. My dear Cousin, a firm persuasion of the superintendence of Providence over all our concerns, is absolutely necessary to our happiness. Without it we cannot be said to believe in the Scripture, or practise any thing like resignation to his will. If I am convinced that no affliction can befall me without the permission of God, I am convinced likewise, that he sees and knows that I am afflicted; believing this, I must in the same degree believe that if I pray to him for deliverance, he hears me; I must needs know likewise, with equal assurance, that, if he hears, he will also deliver me, if that will upon the whole be most conducive to my happiness; and if he does not deliver me, I may be well assured that he has none but the most benevolent intention in declining it. He made us, not because we could add to his happiness, which was always perfect, but that we might be happy ourselves; and will he not in all his dispensations towards us, even the minutest, consult that end for which he made us? To suppose the contrary, is (which we are not always aware of) affronting every one of his attributes, and at the same time the certain consequence of disbelieving his care for us, is that we renounce utterly our dependence upon him. In this view it will appear plainly, that the line of duty is not stretched too tight, when we are told, that we ought to accept every thing at his hands as a blessing, and to be thankful even while we smart under the rod of iron with which he sometimes rules us. Without this persuasion, every blessing, however we may think ourselves happy in it, loses its greatest recommendation, and every affliction is intolerable. Death itself must be welcome to him who has this faith, and he who has it not, must aim at it if he is not a madman. You cannot think how glad I am to hear you are going to commence lady and

mistress of Freemantle.[4] I know it well, and could go to it from Southampton blind-fold. You are kind to invite me to it, and I shall be so kind to myself as to accept the invitation, though I should not for a slight consideration be prevailed upon to quit my beloved retirement at Huntingdon.[5]

Yours ever,
W.C.

LADY HESKETH Saturday, 14 September 1765

Hayley, iii. 394–6

Huntingdon, Sept. 14, 1765.

My Dear Cousin,

The longer I live here, the better I like the place, and the people who belong to it. I am upon very good terms with no less than five families, besides two or three odd, scrambling fellows like myself. The last acquaintance I made here is with the race of the Unwins, consisting of father[1] and mother, son and daughter,[2] the most comfortable social folks you ever knew. The son is about twenty-one years of age, one of the most unreserved and amiable young men I ever conversed with. He is not yet arrived at that time of life, when suspicion recommends itself to us in the form of wisdom, and sets every thing but our own dear selves at an immeasurable distance from our esteem and confidence. Consequently he is known almost as soon as seen, and having nothing in his heart that makes it necessary for him to keep it barred and bolted, opens it to the perusal even of a stranger. The father is a clergyman, and the son is designed for orders. The design however is quite his own, proceeding merely from his being and having always been sincere in his belief and love of the Gospel.

[4] Southampton had become a popular spa resort in the 1740s, and Freemantle House, in the east part of the city, was one of those 'wooded estates which gave the town a rural setting that contributed much to its attractions': A. Temple Patterson, *A History of Southampton, 1700–1914* (Southampton, 1966), i. 40.

[5] Owing to a change in Lady Hesketh's plans, this visit was never made. *Southey*, i. 170.

---

1 Morley Unwin was 'lecturer' (a preacher chosen and supported by the parish—or in this case, the Mason's Company— to give afternoon or evening lectures) from 1734 to 1767 at Huntingdon. He had been from 1746 to 1762 master of the Huntingdon school. See *Ryskamp*, p. 167.

2 Susanna Unwin (1746–1835), later Mrs. Powley.

Another acquaintance I have lately made is with a Mr. Nicholson,[3] a North-country divine, very poor, but very good, and very happy. He reads prayers here twice a day, all the year round, and travels on foot to serve two churches every Sunday through the year, his journey out and home again being sixteen miles. I supped with him last night. He gave me bread and cheese, and a black jug of ale of his own brewing, and doubtless brewed by his own hands. Another of my acquaintance is Mr. ——,[4] a thin, tall, old man, and as good as he is thin. He drinks nothing but water, and eats no flesh, partly (I believe) from a religious scruple (for he is very religious) and partly in the spirit of a valetudinarian. He is to be met with every morning of his life, at about six o'clock, at a fountain of very fine water, about a mile from the town, which is reckoned extremely like the Bristol spring.[5] Being both early risers, and the only early walkers in the place, we soon became acquainted. His great piety can be equalled by nothing but his great regularity, for he is the most perfect time-piece in the world. I have received a visit likewise from Mr. ——.[6] He is very much a gentleman, well-read, and sensible. I am persuaded in short, that if I had had the choice of all England, where to fix my abode, I could not have chosen better for myself, and most likely I should not have chosen so well.

You say you hope it is not necessary for salvation to undergo the same afflictions, that I have undergone. No! my dear Cousin. God deals with his children, as a merciful father; he does not, as he himself tells us, afflict willingly the sons of men. Doubtless there are many, who having been placed by his good providence out of the reach of any great evil and the influence of bad example, have from their very infancy been partakers of the graces of his Holy Spirit, in such a manner as never to have allowed themselves in any grievous offence against him. May you love him more and more day by day, as every day while you think upon him, you will find him more worthy of your love, and may you be finally accepted with him for his sake, whose intercession for all his faithful servants cannot but prevail!

Yours ever,

W.C.

[3] Revd. Isaac Nicholson (b. 1730). The curacies to which he walked were Papworth St. Agnes in Cambridgeshire and Yelling in Huntingdonshire.

[4] Unidentified.

[5] C is referring to the medicinal qualities of the warm springs at Clifton near Bristol.

[6] Unidentified.

Mary Unwin

from the engraving (1823) by Richard Cooper after the Arthur Devis painting (c. 1750)

LADY HESKETH Thursday, 10 October 1765

Hayley, iii. 396–7

Huntingdon, Oct. 10, 1765.

My Dear Cousin,

I should grumble at your long silence, if I did not know, that one may love one's friends very well, though one is not always in a humour to write to them. Besides I have the satisfaction of being perfectly sure, that you have at least twenty times recollected the debt you owe me, and as often resolved to pay it: and perhaps, while you remain indebted to me, you think of me twice as often as you would do, if the account was clear. These are the reflections with which I comfort myself under the affliction of not hearing from you; my temper does not incline me to jealousy, and if it did, I should set all right by having recourse to what I have already received from you.

I thank God for your friendship, and for every friend I have, for all the pleasing circumstances of my situation here, for my health of body, and perfect serenity of mind. To recollect the past, and compare it with the present, is all I have need of to fill me with gratitude; and to be grateful is to be happy. Not that I think myself sufficiently thankful, or that I ever shall be so in this life. The warmest heart perhaps only feels by fits, and is often as insensible as the coldest. This, at least, is frequently the case with mine, and oftener than it should be. But the mercy that can forgive iniquity, will never be severe to mark our frailties; to that mercy, my dear Cousin, I commend you, with earnest wishes for your welfare, and remain your ever affectionate

W.C.

LADY HESKETH Friday, 18 October 1765

Hayley, iii. 397–400

Huntingdon, Oct. 18, 1765.

I wish you joy, my dear Cousin, of being safely arrived in port from the storms of Southampton. For my own part, who am but as a

Thames-wherry,[1] in a world full of tempest and commotion, I know so well the value of the creek I have put into, and the snugness it affords me, that I have a sensible sympathy with you in the pleasure you find in being once more blown to Droxford. I know enough of Miss Morley to send her my compliments, to which, if I had never seen her, her affection for you would sufficiently entitle her. If I neglected to do it sooner, it is only because I am naturally apt to neglect what I ought to do: and if I was as genteel as I am negligent, I should be the most delightful creature in the universe. I am glad you think so favourably of my Huntingdon acquaintance, they are indeed a nice set of folks, and suit me exactly. I should have been more particular in my account of Miss Unwin, if I had had materials for a minute description. She is about eighteen years of age, rather handsome and genteel. In her Mother's company she says little, not because her Mother requires it of her, but because she seems glad of that excuse for not talking, being somewhat inclined to bashfulness. There is the most remarkable cordiality between all the parts of the family, and the Mother and Daughter seem to doat upon each other. The first time I went to the house, I was introduced to the Daughter alone; and sat with her near half an hour, before her Brother came in, who had appointed me to call upon him. Talking is necessary in a *tête-à-tête*, to distinguish the persons of the drama from the chairs they sit on: accordingly she talked a great deal, and extremely well; and, like the rest of the family, behaved with as much ease of address as if we had been old acquaintance. She resembles her Mother in her great piety, who is one of the most remarkable instances of it I have ever seen. They are altogether the cheerfulest and most engaging family-piece it is possible to conceive.—Since I wrote the above, I met Mrs. Unwin in the street, and went home with her. She and I walked together near two hours in the garden, and had a conversation which did me more good than I should have received from an audience of the first prince in Europe. That woman is a blessing to me, and I never see her without being the better for her company. I am treated in the family as if I was a near relation, and have been repeatedly invited to call upon them at all times. You know what a shy fellow I am; I cannot prevail with myself to make so much use of this privilege as I am sure they intend I should, but perhaps this aukwardness will wear off hereafter. It was

[1] A light rowing-boat used to carry passengers and goods (*O.E.D.*).

my earnest request before I left St. Albans, that wherever it might please Providence to dispose of me, I might meet with such an acquaintance as I find in Mrs. Unwin. How happy it is to believe with a steadfast assurance, that our petitions are heard even while we are making them—and how delightful to meet with a proof of it in the effectual and actual grant of them! Surely it is a gracious finishing given to those means, which the Almighty has been pleased to make use of for my conversion—after having been deservedly rendered unfit for any society, to be again qualified for it, and admitted at once into the fellowship of those, whom God regards as the excellent of the earth, and whom, in the emphatical language of Scripture, he preserves as the apple of his eye,[2] is a blessing, which carries with it the stamp and visible superscription of divine bounty—a grace unlimited as undeserved; and, like its glorious Author, free in its course, and blessed in its operation!

My dear Cousin! Health and happiness, and above all, the favour of our great and gracious Lord attend you! While we seek it in spirit and in truth, we are infinitely more secure of it than of the next breath we expect to draw. Heaven and earth have their destined periods, ten thousand worlds will vanish at the consummation of all things, but the word of God standeth fast, and they who trust in him shall never be confounded.

My love to all who enquire after me.

Yours affectionately,

W.C.

MAJOR COWPER — Friday, 18 October 1765

Address: To / Major Cowper at the / Park House near / Hartford / Hartfordshire
Postmarks: 19/OC *and* HUNTING/DON
Panshanger Collection

My dear Major,

I have neither lost the Use of my Fingers nor my Memory, though my unaccountable Silence might incline you to suspect that I had lost both. The History of those things which have from time to time

[2] Among other places, this expression occurs in Psalm 17: 8.

prevented my scribbling, would be not only insipid but extremely voluminous, for which reasons they will not make their Appearance at present, nor probably at [any time][1] hereafter. If my Neglecting to write to you were a [Proof] that I had never Thought of you, and that had b[een] really the case, five Shillings a piece would have been much too little to give for the Sight of such a Monster; but I am no such Monster, nor do I perceive in myself the least Tendency to such a Transformation.

You may recollect that I had but very uncomfortable Expectations of the Accommodation I should meet with at Huntingdon. How much better is it to take our Lot where it shall please Providence to cast it, without Anxiety.—Had I chosen for myself, it is impossible I could have fixt upon a Place so agreeable to me in all respects. I so much dreaded the Thought of having a New Acquaintance to make, with no other Recommendation than that of being a perfect Stranger, that I heartily wished no Creature here might take the least Notice of me. Instead of which, in about 2 Months after my Arrival, I became known to all the Visitable People here, and do verily think it the most agreeable Neighbourhood I ever saw.

Here are three Families who have received me with the utmost Civility; and two in particular have treated me with as much Cordiality as if their Pedigree and [mi]ne had grown upon the same Sheepskin. Besides [thes]e there are three or four Single Men, who suit my Temper to a Hair. The Town is one of the neatest in England, the Country is fine for several Miles about it, and the Roads which are all Turnpike and strike out four or five different ways, are perfectly good all the Year round. I mention this latter Circumstance chiefly because my Distance from Cambridge has made a Horseman of me at last, or at least is likely to do so. My Brother and I meet every Week, by an alternate Reciprocation of Intercourse, as Sam: Johnson would express it. Sometimes I get a Lift in a Neighbour's Chaise, but generally Ride.

As to my own personal Condition, I am much happier than the Day is long, and Sunshine and Candle light alike see me perfectly contented. I get Books in Abundance, as much Company as I chuse, a deal of *comfortable Leisure*, and enjoy better Health, I think, than for many Years past. What is there wanting to make me Happy? Nothing, if I can but be as thankfull as I ought, and I trust that He

[1] The MS. is torn slightly.

who has bestowed so many Blessings upon me, will give me Gratitude to crown them All.

I beg you will give my Love to my Dear Cousin Maria, and to every body at the Park. If Mrs. Maitland[2] is with you, as I suspect by a Passage in Lady Hesketh's Letter to me, pray remember me to her very affectionately,

and beleive me my Dear Friend
Ever yours
Wm Cowper.

Huntingdon
Octr. 18. 1765

JOSEPH HILL — Friday, 25 October 1765

Address: To / Mr. Joseph Hill / at the Chancery Office / London
Postmarks: 28/OC *and* HUNTING/DON
Cowper Johnson

Dear Joe,

I am afraid the Month of October has proved rather unfavourable to the belle Assemblée at Southampton; High Winds and continual Rains being bitter Enemies to that agreeable Lounge which you and I are equally fond of,[1] I have very cordially betaken myself to my Book and my Fireside, and seldom leave them unless merely for Exercise. I have added another Family to the Number of those I was acquainted with when you was here. Their Name is Unwin—the most agreeable People imaginable; quite Sociable, and as free from the ceremonious Civility of Country Gentlefolks as any I ever met with. They treat me more like a near Relation than a Stranger, and their House is always open to me. The Old Gentleman carries me to Cambridge in his Chaise. He is a Man of Learning and good Sense,

[2] Penelope Maitland (1730–1805), 2nd daughter of Mrs. Madan and sister of Martin Madan and Maria Cowper. 'Penny' and Lady Hesketh had been close friends in youth, but her great beauty seems to have made Lady Hesketh jealous. In 1754 she had married the Hon. Alexander Maitland (d. 1820). She was 'converted' to evangelical beliefs in 1757 and composed a great many poems of a devotional cast. See *The Madan Family*, pp. 124–5.

[1] *The Daily Register of Commerce and Intelligence* for Saturday, 26 Oct. (vol. vi, no. 1813) carries the following notice: 'The late heavy rains have caused the river Thames above Chertsey, and other parts of the west country, to overflow its banks; and great damage has been sustained in the meadow lanes contiguous, and many sheep, &c. drowned.'

and as simple as Parson Adams.[2] His Wife, who is Young compared with her Husband, has a very uncommon Understanding, has read much to excellent purpose, and is more polite than a Dutchess. The Son, who belongs to Cambridge, is a most aimable Young Man, and the Daughter quite of a piece with the rest of the Family. They see but little Company which suits me exactly. Go when I will, I find a House full of Peace and Cordiality in all its parts, and am sure to hear no Scandal, but such Discourse instead of it, as we are all the better for. You remember Rousseau's Description of an English Morning;[3] such are the Mornings I spend with these Good People, and the Evenings differ from them in nothing, except that they are still more Snug and quieter. Now I know them, I wonder that I liked Huntingdon so well before I knew them, and am apt to think I should find every place disagreeable that had not an Unwin belonging to it.

This Incident convinces me of the Truth of an Observation I have often made, that when we circumscribe our Estimate of all that is clever within the Limits of our own Acquaintance, (which I at least have been always apt to do) we are guilty of a very uncharitable Censure upon the rest of the World, and of a Narrowness of Thinking disgracefull to ourselves. Wapping and Redriff[4] may contain some of the most Aimable Persons living, and such as one would go even to Wapping or Redriff to make an Acquaintance with. You remember Mr. Grey's Stanza

> Full many a Gem of purest Ray Serene
> The deep unfathom'd Caves of Ocean bear,
> Full many a Rose is born to blush unseen,
> And waste its Fragrance on the Desart Air.[5]

I have wrote to Eamonson,[6] and, as I expected have received no Answer. My Letter went the Day after You left Cambridge. I am afraid the Ten pounds you spoke of will grow mouldy if they lie at

[2] Fielding's comical parson in *Joseph Andrews.*

[3] *La Nouvelle Héloise*, v, letter III: '. . . nous avons passé aujourd'hui une matinée à l'angloise, réunis et dans le silence, goûtant à la fois le plaisir d'être ensemble et la douceur du recueillement. Que les délices de cet état sont connues de peu de gens!'

[4] Districts in the Stepney and Southwark regions respectively of London which were notorious for robberies.

[5] C is slightly misquoting lines 53–6 of the *Elegy Written in a Country Churchyard.*

[6] Possibly a reference to the Eamonson of Eamonson & Butterworth, Oilmen, 76 Cannon Street, London, who are listed in various trade directories for 1766, 1768, and 1775. In his letter to Hill of 10 Mar. 1766, C mentions his 'Mother's [a reference probably to his step-mother] Fondness for Him and his quondam Partner'.

Child's[7] any longer. Shall be obliged to you therefore if you will remit them to Huntingdon.

My Love to all your Family,

Yours Dear Joe,
Wm Cowper.

Oct. 25. 1765

JOSEPH HILL — Tuesday, 5 November 1765

Cowper Johnson

Dear Joe,

I wrote to you about 10 days ago

Solliciting a quick Return of Gold,
To purchase certain Horse that like me well.

Either my Letter or your Answer to it I fear has miscarried; the former I hope, because a Miscarriage of the latter might be attended with bad Consequences. I shall want more Cash however than I wrote for at that time, having totally changed my Scheme of Operations. Upon taking a deliberate View of my Outgoings and Incomeings, I find it impossible to proceed any longer in my present Course without Danger of Bankruptcy. I have therefore enter'd into an Agreement with the Revd. Mr. Unwin to Lodge and Board with him, by which means I shall save 50 or 60 pounds per Annum. The Family are the most agreeable in the World. They live in a special good House, and in a very genteel Way. I know nobody so like Mrs. Unwin as my Aunt Madan. I don't mean in Person for she is a much younger Woman, but in Character. They are all exactly what I would wish them to be, and I know I shall be as Happy with them as I can be on this side of the Sun. You may remember perhaps that as we walked on the Morning of your Arrival here towards the Bridge End of the Town, we heard a Harpsichord from a Parlour Window on the Right Hand. That is the House. I was not acquainted with them at that Time, nor did I dream of this Matter 'till about 5 Days ago. But now the whole is settled.

[7] Child's, the first banking house established in London and one of its most distinguished merchant banks, was at this time located at the Temple Bar Within: Henry Benjamin Wheatley, *London, Past and Present* (1891), i. 390–1.

I shall transfer myself thither as soon as I have satisfied all Demands upon me here, for which purpose I shall want Thirty pounds instead of Ten which I wrote for before, being engaged here you know for a year certain, and having a few odd Bills to pay besides.

My Love to your Mother & Sisters.

Yours ever Wm Cowper.

Huntn.
Nov 5. 1765

If the Ten Pounds should arrive in the Interim, you will be pleased to add 20 in a Twinkling.

JOSEPH HILL — Friday, 8 November 1765

Address: To / Mr. Joseph Hill / at the Chancery Office / London.
Postmarks: 11/NO *and* HUNTING/DON
Cowper Johnson

Dear Sephus,

I am much obliged to you for the Notes, which I found safe arrived upon my Return from Cambridge, where I have been since Wednesday Morning.

Notwithstanding it is so agreeable a thing to Read[1] Law Lectures to the Students of Lyon's Inn,[2] especially to the Reader himself, I must beg leave to waive it. Danby Pickering[3] must be the Happy Man, and I heartily wish him Joy of his Deputyship. As to the Treat,[4] I think if it goes before the Lecture, it will be apt to blunt the Apprehension of the Students, and if it comes after, it may erase from their Memories Impressions so newly made. I could wish therefore

[1] Read is used in the sense of deliver. As a member of the Inner Temple, C still had obligations to meet.

[2] Lyon's Inn, Newcastle Street, Strand, an Inn of Chancery belonging to the Inner Temple.

[3] Danby Pickering (*fl.* 1737–69), legal writer, was admitted to Gray's Inn on 28 June 1737 and called to the Bar in May 1741. His most important work, an abridgement of the Statute Book, is *The Statutes at Large* (1762–9).

[4] Another of C's obligations to the Inner Temple. The ceremony referred to here is similar to the Candle Exercise in the Middle Temple: 'when there were Supper Commons, it was performed after supper, consequently by candle light. . . . The performance of which is enforced by the penalty of forty shillings each'. *Master Worsley's Book on the History and Constitution of the Honourable Society of the Middle Temple*, ed. A. R. Ingpen (1910), p. 131.

that for their Benefit and Behoof, this Circumstance were omitted. But if it be absolutely necessary, I hope Mr. Salt[5] or whoever takes the Conduct of it, will see that it be managed with the Frugality and Temperance becoming so Learned a Body. I shall be obliged to you if you will present my Respects to Mr. Treasurer Salt, and express my Concern at the same time that he has had the Trouble of sending me two Letters upon this Occasion. The first of them never came to hand.

I think the Welshman[6] must Morris,[7] what think You? If he withdraws to his native Mountains, we shall never catch him, so the best way is to let him run in Debt no longer.

As to Eamonson, if he will Listen to any thing it must be to a Remonstrance from You. A Letter has no more Effect upon him than a Messenger sent up to a Paper Kite, and he will make me pay the Postage of all my Epistles into the Bargain.

I shall be obliged to you if you will tell me whether my Exchequer is full or empty, and whether the Revenue of last Year is yet come in, that I may proportion my Payments to Cotton to the Exigencies of my Affairs.

My dear Sephus give my Love to your Family, and beleive me much obliged to you for your Invitation. At present I am in such an unsettled Condition, that I can think of nothing but laying the Foundations of my future Abode at Unwin's. My being admitted there is the Effect of the great Good Nature and friendly Turn of that Family, who, I have great Reason to beleive, are as desirous to do me Service, as they could be after a much longer Acquaintance. Let your next, if it comes a Week hence, be directed to me there.

My Brother thinks the Books[8] are not pack'd seperate, but the Lawyers and the rest of them all in a Medley. He will be in Town at Christmas when I will get him to set that matter Right. The greatest part of the Law Books are those which Lord Cowper gave me. Those, and the very few which I bought myself, are all at the Major's Service.

[5] Samuel Salt (d. 1792), lawyer and benefactor of Charles Lamb, was admitted to the Middle Temple in 1741, the Inner Temple in 1745, and was called to the Bar in 1753.

[6] Perhaps the Morgan who rented C's chambers at the Inner Temple. See C to Hill, 27 May 1777 and n. 1.

[7] A slang expression meaning to decamp (*O.E.D.*).

[8] For a list of many of the legal texts current at this time, see *Master Worsley's Book*, p. 46 n. 2. C, presumably, would have owned many of these books, including editions of Coke, Crompton, and Staunford.

Earlier, *c.* 1757, C had acquired Martin Madan's manuscript legal case books, and these give evidence of careful reading. See *Ryskamp*, p. 68 n. 2.

Stroak Puss's Back the wrong way, and it will put her in mind of her Master.[9]

Yours ever Wm Cowper.

Friday Night.
Nove. 8. 1765.

JOSEPH HILL — Tuesday, 3 December 1765

Address: Mr. Hill in Cook's Court / near Lincolns Inn Fields / London[1]
Cowper Johnson

Huntingdon
Decr. 3. 1765

Dear Sephus,

That I may return as particular an Answer to your Letter as possible, I will take it Item by Item.

First then I rejoice with you in the Victory you have obtained over the Welshman's Pocket; the Reluctance with which he pays, and promises to pay, gives me but little Concern, further than as it seems to threaten You with the Trouble of many fruitless Applications hereafter in the Receipt of my Lordship's Rents.

Secondly I am glad that you have received 40£ on my Account, and am still more pleased that you have in Bank after the Remittances already made, the Sum of £55.11.0, but that which encreases my Joy to the highest Pitch of possible Augmentation, is that you expect to receive more shortly.

Thirdly, I should be quite in Raptures with the fair Promises of Mr. Eamonson, if I beleived he was in earnest. But the Propensity of that Gentlemen to indulge himself in a Jocular Humour upon these serious Occasions, tho' it is very entertaining, is not quite so good a Joke as the Performance of those Promises would be. But Men of Wit are apt to be a little Whimsical.

Fourthly, I do recollect that I myself was a little guilty of what I blame so much in Mr. Eamonson, in the last Letter I wrote you; having returned you so facetious an Answer to your serious Enquiry

9 Hill had perhaps taken in a pet cat which C had left behind when he went to St. Albans.

1 Olney Address. See Abbreviations and Short Titles, p. xvi.

concerning the Entertainment[2] to be given, or not to be given to the Gentlemen of New Inn,[3] that you must needs have been at a Loss to collect from it my real Intentions. My sincere Desire however in this respect is that they may Fast; and being supported in this Resolution not only by an Assurance that I can, and therefore ought to make a better Use of my Money, but also by the Examples of my Predecessors in the same Business, Mr. Barrington and Mr. Schutz,[4] I have no longer any doubt concerning the Propriety of condemning them to Abstinence upon this Occasion; and cannot but Wish That Point may be carried, if it can be done without engaging You in the Trouble of any disagreeable Haggling and Higgling, and twisting and Wriggling to Save my Money.

Lastly I shall be much obliged to you if you will Remitt to Dr. Cotton the Sum of 30£ which, I think, will leave 25 unpaid. If I am not mistaken I owe Thurlow five Guineas. Be so kind as to pay him when he happens to fall in your Way.

Yours my Dear Joe,
Wm Cowper

The Fire of the General Election begins to Smoke here already.[5]

JOSEPH HILL — Saturday, 4 January 1766

Address: To / Mr. Joseph Hill / Cook's Court Carey Street / near Lincolns Inn Fields / London
Postmarks: 6/IA *and* HUNTING/DON
Panshanger Collection

My dear Sephus,

E'er many Suns have risen and set You will receive a Draught of mine payable to Mr. Reade Peacock, for the Sum of 13.12.0.—For aught I know I may have drawn for more than I am worth, and if I have, I must refer you to your next Receipts to set that Matter right.

[2] See n. 4, C to Hill, 8 Nov. 1765.

[3] '*New Inn*, since the destruction of *Strand Inn*, which anciently belonged to the Middle Temple, is the only law seminary remaining in the possession of that society': W. Herbert, *Antiquities of the Inns of Court and Chancery* . . . (1804), p. 281.

[4] Schutz is unidentified, but C's other reference is probably to Daines Barrington (1727–1800), author of *Observations on the Statutes* (1776).

[5] The Marquis of Rockingham, who had taken office on 13 July 1765, was not succeeded by the Duke of Grafton until 2 Aug. 1766, but the election campaign was already in motion as C notes.

In the mean time if my Affairs here continue to proceed in the same even Course as at present, I comfort myself with the Thoughts of drawing no more this half Year, and then only for the Payment of Mr. Unwin.

Unwin the Younger is now in Town, and if you should happen to be at Ashley's[1] when he calls there, you will see one of the most Aimable Young Men I ever met with. I hope my Uncle will make much of him, for if he sees two more such before he dies, he will have better Fortune than falls to the Share of most men.

If I had built this House and chosen my Company, I could not have been better fitted, and so perhaps my Brother has told you; if he has not, I remember I told you so before, and it will be well if I don't repeat it in my next. I strike Root here every day deeper and deeper, as Vegetables are apt to do in a Soil which suits them. Not that I lead the Life of a Vegetable, Mr. Animal! for I assure you I never conversed with any body that kept my Mind in better Training or more constant Exercise than Mrs. Unwin does, but I make the Comparison by way of humble Acquiescence in the Imputation which you Londoners are apt to fasten upon us Rustics.

That I may not overload the Post Horse this slippery Weather, I conclude myself my dear Joe with my Love to all your Family and my own,

Your ever Affectionate Wm Cowper.

Huntn.
Jan 4. 1766.

MARTIN MADAN — Monday, 10 February 1766

Gregg Commonplace Book (*copy*)[1]

—Unwin has furnished me with your Collection of Hymns,[2] and bespoke the music for them. Mrs. Unwin plays well on the harpsi-

[1] Unwin probably went to introduce himself to Ashley in the same manner as he was to present himself to Maria Cowper on 20 Mar. 1767. See C to Mrs. Cowper, 14 Mar. 1767.

[1] The following inscription precedes the copy of the letter in the commonplace book: 'Part of a letter from Wm. Cowper to my Son M. Madan. Febry 10th. 1766.'

[2] Martin Madan's *A Collection of Psalms and Hymns*, which first appeared in 1760, had gone into a fourth edition by 1765.

chord, and I doubt not those Songs of Sion will sound sweetly in the ears of one so lately escaped from the thunders of Sinai.—The time past suffices me to have lived the life of the Gentiles; I can lay my hand on my heart and say, with the Apostle, 'The life I live, I live by the faith of the Son of God';[3] thought, word, and deed, devoted to His Service, and may they be so forever. I mention not this in the spirit of boasting, God forbid! but that you, together with me, may give praise to the glory of His Grace who has interposed, by such wonderful means, for the salvation of so vile a sinner. Perhaps I have many friends who pity me, ruined in my profession—stript of my preferment—and banished from all my old acquaintance. They wonder I can sustain myself under these evils, and expect that I should die broken hearted—and if myself were all I had to trust to, so perhaps I might, nay I believe, certainly should, but the Disciples of Christ have bread to eat which the world knows not of—The hope of Israel fainteth not, neither is weary, and peace, and joy in the Holy Spirit are effectual preservatives against worldly sorrow.[4] I have lost indeed a good deal of that dung the Apostle speaks of,[5] but the treasure hid in the field[6] is an Infinite Compensation for such losses — — —

JOSEPH HILL — Tuesday, 11 February 1766

Address: To / Mr. Joseph Hill /at the Chancery Office / London
Postmarks: 12/FE *and* HUNTING/DON
H. C. Longuet-Higgins

Feb. 11. 1766.

Dear Joe,

My Brother did, as you suppose upon his Return from Town, submit the proper Estimates to my Lordly & Gentlemanlike Consideration; the Result of which is, that I am inclined to think myself in a Condition to fadge[1] through the Year without increasing my Debts, or derogating from the Splendor of my Birth. It is my fixt purpose to Live upon my Income; in which Resolution I am supported by reflecting, that I have nothing else to Live upon. Their

[3] Galatians 2 : 20.
[4] See Isaiah 40 : 28.
[5] Philippians 3 : 8.
[6] Matthew 13 : 44.

[1] Trudge (*O.E.D.*).

proper Income is the least part of the Maintenance of some Men, but then they are successful either in Gambling or robbing on the High-way; Resources to which my natural Indolence has so many Objections that I despair of ever surmounting 'em. In the mean time I am happy in my Situation; I Love the People I am with, and they Love Me, and there is not a Family in England that could afford me such, or greater Comfort however, during the Interruption and Suspension of almost every Connexion besides. I hear from you and Lady Hesketh—there are others to whom I have written, but a Wintry kind of Indifference seems to have frozen up their Ink:bottles. I wish them a gentle Thaw, and wait for it with Patience.

The. Snow keeps us close Prisoners; the Ladies work while I read to 'em. We have invented a new kind of Battledore[2] & Shuttlecock at which Mrs. Unwin & myself are excellent. It consists of keeping up two Shuttlecocks at a time; Mr. Unwin's Stud is always at my Service, and I use the Privilege with a very discreet Moderation, Walking much, but hardly ever Riding, except to Cambridge.

I have taken care to thank Schutz[3] for his Services in the Lecture matter—Adieu Sephus! Yours ever

Wm Cowper

My Love To your Family.[4]

LADY HESKETH — Thursday, 6 March 1766

Hayley, iii. 400–2[1]

Huntingdon, March 6, 1766.

My Dear Cousin,

I have for some time past imputed your silence to the cause which you yourself assign for it, viz. to my change of situation; and was even sagacious enough to account for the frequency of your Letters

[2] An instrument like a small racket used in playing with a shuttlecock. The persons playing use the battledore to strike the shuttlecock back and forth (*O.E.D.*).

[3] See C to Hill, 3 Dec. 1765.

[4] The following note in Hill's hand is written on the address portion of the letter: 'I always have wish'd that Mr. Unwin had not died and that they had all continued at Huntingdon—while there he seem'd comfortable and happy and his Religious Notions seem'd to produce that Peace and Content which it is their Nature to inspire when Genuine and Sincere.'

[1] The MS. of this letter was offered for sale by Sotheby, Wilkinson, and Hodge in their catalogue of 20–2 May 1878, lot 111 (A.L.S. 3-page 4to).

to me, while I lived alone, from your attention to me in a state of such solitude as seemed to make it an act of particular charity to write to me. I bless God for it, I was happy even then; solitude has nothing gloomy in it if the soul points upwards. St. Paul tells his Hebrew converts, 'Ye are come (already come) to Mount Sion, to an innumerable company of angels, to the general assembly of the first-born, which are written in Heaven, and to Jesus the mediator of the new convenant.'[2] When this is the case, as surely it was with them, or the Spirit of Truth had never spoken it, there is an end of the melancholy and dulness of a solitary life at once. You will not suspect me, my dear Cousin, of a design to understand this passage literally. But this however it certainly means, that a lively faith is able to anticipate in some measure, the joys of that heavenly society, which the soul shall actually possess hereafter.

Since I have changed my situation, I have found still greater cause of thanksgiving to the Father of all Mercies. The family with whom I live are Christians, and it has pleased the Almighty to bring me to the knowledge of them, that I may want no means of improvement in that temper, and conduct, which he is pleased to require in all his servants.

My dear Cousin! one half of the Christian world would call this madness, fanaticism, and folly: but are not these things warranted by the word of God, not only in the passages I have cited, but in many others? If we have no communion with God here, surely we can expect none hereafter. A faith that does not place our conversation in Heaven; that does not warm the heart and purify it too; that does not in short, govern our thought, word, and deed, is no faith, nor will it obtain for us any spiritual blessing here, or hereafter. Let us see, therefore, my dear Cousin, that we do not deceive ourselves in a matter of such infinite moment. The world will be ever telling us, that we are good enough, and the same world will vilify us behind our backs. But it is not the world which tries the heart, that is the prerogative of God alone. My dear Cousin! I have often prayed for you behind your back, and now I pray for you to your face. There are many who would not forgive me this wrong, but I have known you so long, and so well, that I am not afraid of telling you how sincerely I wish for your growth in every Christian grace, in every thing that may promote and secure your everlasting welfare.

[2] Hebrews 12: 22–4.

I am obliged to Mrs. Cowper for the book,[3] which you perceive, arrived safe. I am willing to consider it as an intimation on her part that she would wish me to write to her, and shall do it accordingly. My circumstances are rather particular, such as call upon my friends, those I mean who are truly such, to take some little notice of me; and will naturally make those who are not such in sincerity, rather shy of doing it. To this I impute the silence of many with regard to me, who before the affliction that befel me, were ready enough to converse with me.

Yours ever,
W.C.

JOSEPH HILL — Monday, 10 March 1766

Cowper Johnson

My dear Sephus—

I think the Remainder of Dr Cotton's Account is 15£. I should have advised the Payment of it before this time, but the time of general Payment advances apace, and I have been afraid of wanting Money for other purposes. In the pleasant Month of May I intend to discharge a half Year's Reckoning with Mr. Unwin; soon after that I shall have Servants' Wages to pay, and half a Year's Maintenance of a small Youth whom I brought with me by way of Pensioner from St. Albans.[1] The Whole Amount of these three Articles will be about 60£.—If *in these Circumstances & in this Situation* you think I can afford to quit Scores with the little Doctor, I shall be obliged to you if you will do it forthwith. You may contrive when you send him the Cash to ask him whether he is fully paid or no, and if not, how much remains due and unsatisfied.—More Debts than Money has been my Distress this many a day, & is likely to continue so.

Eamonson has the Game in his own hands so much, and it is so much out of my Power to check him in his charges, that I fully expect he will make good what he threatens; and doubtless if he

[3] Richard Pearsall, *Reliquia Sacrae: or, Meditations on Select Passages of Scripture, and Sacred Dialogues between a Father and his Children* (1765).

[1] See C to Hill, 12 Nov. 1766 for a description of Dick Coleman, who was 8 or 9 at this time.

claims to be paid for receiving the Jointure at the usual Rate, he may easily do it. But I think he ought not, for it never cost him 10 Minute's Trouble, the Tenants having always waited on him at the very day of Payment, and there were but two of them. 'Tis fit however that it should be settled. My Mother's Fondness for Him and his quondam Partner inclined her to think that they were equally fond of Her, but I doubt we shall find, tho' she never did, that herein her Prudence failed her.

I have not seen the New Play, nor is my Curiosity so much agog as one would have expected. We live much out of the Theatrical Sphere, my Connection with Colman is probably at an end, & it would give me therefore more Pain than Pleasure to read his Productions. I have seen the Epilogue and think it wonderfully Silly. I ask Fanny's Pardon, for I recollect it is Garrick's.[2]—My Love to your Family—Yours my dear Sephus

Huntn. Mar 10. 1766. Wm Cowper.

Remember me to my Uncle when you see him.

MRS. COWPER Tuesday, 11 March 1766

Address: To / Mrs. Cowper / at the Park House / near Hartford / Hartfordshire
Postmarks: 12/MR *and* illegible
British Library

My dear Cousin,

I am much obliged to you for Pearsall's Meditations, especially as it furnishes me with an Occasion of writing to you which is all I have waited for. My Friends must excuse me if I write to none but those who lay it fairly in my way to do so. The Inference I am apt to draw from *their* Silence is that they wish *me* to be Silent too, and my Circumstances are such as not only Justify that Apprehension in point of Prudence, but even make it Natural.

I have great Reason, my dear Cousin, to be thankfull to the

[2] One of C's closest friends among the Geniuses, George Colman the Elder (1732–1794), had established himself as a successful practising dramatist in 1761 with *The Jealous Wife*. *The Clandestine Marriage*, a collaboration between Colman and David Garrick, opened at Drury Lane on 20 Feb. 1766. C had evidently seen a report which had correctly attributed the epilogue, which takes place at the quadrille table at a fashionable assembly, to Garrick. Fanny is Hill's sister, Frances (*fl. c.* 1733–1800).

gracious Providence that conducted me to this Place. The Lady in whose House I live is so excellent a Person, and regards me with a Friendship so truly Christian, that I could almost fancy my own Mother restored to Life again, to compensate to me for all the Friends I have lost and all my Connections broken. She has a Son at Cambridge in all respects worthy of such a Mother, the most Aimable Young Man I ever knew. His natural and acquired Endowments are very considerable, and as to his Virtues I need only say that he is a Christian. It ought to be matter of daily Thanksgiving to me that I am admitted into the Society of such Persons, and I pray God to make me and keep me worthy of them.

My dear Cousin! I am much altered since you saw me Last. I have both suffered much, and received great Consolation. I was not then a Christian, whatever my partial Friends might think me, but now I trust by the Grace of God, I am one. I know what it is to assent with the Head, and what it is to beleive with the Heart. Blessed be the God of all Mercy that I have experienced both, and may he enable me to hold fast to that which is best.—I doubt not there are many who having heard it surmised that I am become mighty Religious, and perhaps that I am turned Methodist, say, ay! no great wonder—Distempers of that kind are apt to take such a turn; well, it may wear off in time perhaps, and if it should not, it's better than being confined.—So reason they—but you, my dear Cousin, well know that a Religious Turn is the Gift of God. There is no true Faith but what is of his Operation, and they in whom by his Holy Spirit he has wrought it, understand this, tho' the World cannot understand them when they say so.

Your Brother Martin has been very kind to me, having wrote to me twice (since my Enlargement), in a stile which though it once was irksome to me to say the least, I now know how to value. I pray God to forgive me the many light things I have both said and thought of Him and his Labours. Hereafter I shall consider him as a burning and a shining Light, and as one of those who having turned many to Righteousness, shall shine hereafter as the Stars for ever and ever.

So much for the State of my Heart. As to my Spirits I am cheerfull and happy, and having Peace with God have Peace within myself. For the Continuance of this Blessing. It is Him who gives it, and they who trust in Him shall ne[ver][1] be confounded.

1 The MS. is torn at the seal.

My Love to the Major and to All your Family. Beleive me my Dear Cousin,

Yours affectionately
Wm Cowper.

Huntn.
At the Revd. Mr. Unwin's.
Mar. 11. 1766.

JOSEPH HILL Thursday, 3 April 1766

Address: To / Mr. Joseph Hill / at the Chancery Office / London.
Postmarks: 4/AP *and* illegible
Morgan Library

My dear Sephus,

I return you many Thanks for the final Settlement of my Accounts with the little Medical Man of St. Albans. We have contrived between us to turn the Tables upon him, and instead of a Creditor he is become my Debtor, not indeed in the Money Way but the Epistolary; having owed me a Letter a long time. I Correspond with the little Man because I Love him and have great Reason to do so. I should be glad if my Uncle can find Leisure, and it be not contrary to Act of Parliament, if he will be so good as to furnish me with half a Dozen Franks to Dr. Cotton and as many to yourself. Pray remember me to him very affectionately.—

In my last I threatened you with Draughts for the Sum of 60£. I shall draw for 20 of 'em in a day or two, and for the rest in May. A Long Cessation I hope will follow, and such as will be sufficient for the Replenishment of my exhausted Treasury.

I read a great deal though I have neither read Colman nor Sterne.[1] I agree with you entirely in your Judgment of the Works of the latter considered as Moral Performances, for the two first Volumes of his Sermons I read in London. He is a great Master of the Pathetic, and if that or any other Species of Rhetoric could renew the Human Heart and turn it from the Power of Satan unto God, I know no Writer better qualified to make Proselytes to the Cause of Virtue than Sterne. But alas! my Dear Joe the Evil of a corrupt nature is too

[1] The first two volumes of *The Sermons of Mr. Yorick* had appeared in May 1760; volumes 3 and 4 appeared on 22 Jan. 1766.

deeply rooted in us all to be extirpated by the puny Efforts of Wit or Genius. The Way which God has appointed must be the true and the only Way to Virtue, and that is, Faith in Christ. He who has received that inestimable Blessing deep into his Heart, has received a Principle of Virtue that will never fail him. *This is the Victory that overcometh the World, even our Faith*,[2] and there is no other.—The World by *Wisdom* knew not God, it therefore pleased Him by the *Foolishness* of Preaching to *save* them that *beleive*. To save them from their Sinfull Nature here and from his Wrath hereafter, by that plain but despised and rejected Remedy, Faith in Christ. Therefore it is that though I admire Sterne as a Man of Genius, I can never admire him as a Preacher. For to say the least of him he mistakes the Weapon of his Warfare, and fights not with the Sword of the Spirit for which only he was ordained a Minister of the Gospel, but with that Wisdom which shone with as effectual a Light before our Saviour came as since, and which therefore cannot be the Wisdom which he came to Reveal to us.

My dear Joe! I Love you heartily, and frequently since the Discourse I had with you at Mr. Martin's, have wish[ed wi]th[3] much Fervency of true Friendship for you, that yo[u may th]ink daily and daily deeper of this only Source of Happiness either present or future. It is the warmest Prayer I can form for any of my Friends, and I form it for them all, that they may arrive at the Knowledge and Love of God through Faith in his blessed Son. God is Witness, that upon this Foundation is built all the Happiness I enjoy, and that I never enjoyed any thing that deserved the Name of Happiness 'till it pleased him to bestow that inestimable gift upon me.—Pardon my Preaching to you, but the Hint you dropt in your Letter seemed to require it.

My Love to your Family

Yours ever Wm Cowper.

April 3. 1766.

[2] 1 John 5: 4.

[3] The MS. of this letter is slightly torn.

MRS. COWPER — Friday, 4 April 1766

Address: To / Mrs. Cowper / at the Park House / near Hartford / Hartfordshire
Postmarks: 5/AP *and* HUNTING/DON
Panshanger Collection

My dear Cousin,

I agree with you that Letters are not essential to Friendship, but they seem to be a natural Fruit of it, when they are the only Intercourse that can be had. And a Friendship producing no sensible Effects is so like Indifference, that the Appearance may easily deceive even an Acute Discerner. I retract however All that I said in my last upon this Subject, having reason to suspect that it proceeded from a Principle which I would discourage in myself upon all Occasions, even a Pride that felt itself hurt upon a mere Suspicion of Neglect. I have so much Cause for Humility, and so much need of it too, and every little sneaking Resentment is such an Enemy to it, that I hope I shall never give Quarter to any thing that appears in the Shape of Sullenness or Self Consequence hereafter. Alas! If my best Friend, who laid down his Life for me, were to remember all the Instances in which I have neglected Him, and to plead them against me in Judgment, where should I hide my guilty Head in the Day of Recompense? I will pray therefore for Blessings upon my Friends even though they cease to be so, and upon my Enemies though they continue such.

The deceitfullness of the natural Heart, the Mystery of Iniquity that works there, is inconceivable. I know well that I passed upon my Friends for a person at least religiously inclined, if not actually religious, and what is more wonderfull, I even thought Myself a Christian. Thought myself a Christian when I had no Faith in Christ, when I saw no Beauty in him that I should desire him, in short when I had neither Faith, nor Love nor any Christian Grace whatever, but a thousand Seeds of Rebellion instead, evermore springing up in Enmity against him. Thus qualified for the Christian Life, and by the additional Help of a little Hypocritical Attendance upon Ordinances, I thought myself as well off in point of Security as most, and though my Iniquities had set me on fire round about, I knew it not, and though they burned me, yet I laid it not to heart. But Blessed be God, even the God who is become my Salvation! The hail of Affliction and Rebuke for Sin, has swept away the Refuge of Lies. It pleased the Almighty in great Mercy to me, to set all my Misdeeds before me, and to thunder into my very Heart with the Curses of

his broken Law in such manner that for near a Twelvemonth I beleived myself Sealed up under eternal Wrath and the Sentence of unquenchable Vengeance. Then all my Christian Seeming, all my fair & specious Professions which had been my Support and Confidence before, became the Objects of my Horror and Detestation. At length the Storm being past, and having answered all the gracious purposes of Him who sent it forth to convince me of Sin, of Righteousness, and of Judgment, a quiet and peacefull Serenity of Soul succeeded, such as ever attends the Gift of a lively Faith in the allsufficient Attonement, and the sweet Sense of Mercy and Pardon purchased by the Blood of Christ. Thus did he break me and bind me up, thus did he wound me and his Hands made whole.

My dear Cousin! I make no Apology for entertaining you with the History of my Conversion, because I know you to be a Christian in the Sterling Import of the Appellation. This is however but a very summary Account of the Matter, neither would a Letter contain the astonishing Particulars of it. If we ever meet again in this World I will relate them to you by Word of Mouth, if not they will serve for the Subject of a Conference in the next, where I doubt not I shall remember and record them with a Gratitude better suited to the Subject.

It will give me great Pleasure to hear from you; and though I know you are not fond of Writing, and do well remember the Complaints you used to make of the Necessity that obliged you to it, yet I shall hope that considering the much nearer Relation in which we now stand to each other than when we were only Cousins, being at length Members of the same Mystical Body, I shall hope I say that your Love for a Brother will over come what your Affection for an ordinary Connection would probably yield to, & that you will find in your Heart to write to one who will remember you in his Prayers and hopes for a Place in yours.

How I shall rejoice to see the Major & Mr. Cleator![1] My Love to 'em both and to all your Family.

Yours my dear Cousin! affectionately

Wm Cowper.

April 4. 1766.

[1] A friend of Maria Cowper's, John Cleator (1739–*post* 1792), B.A. Cambridge, 1762, was ordained in 1764 and became rector of Wroot, Lincs. (near Doncaster) in 1769, a post he retained until 1792. John Peile, *Biographical Register of Christ's College* (Cambridge, 1913), ii. 266. According to Frederick Madan, Cleator was Martin Madan's curate in 1764 (Bodleian MS. Eng. Misc. d. 636, vol. ii, fo. 12).

MRS. COWPER   Thursday, 17 April 1766

Address: To / Mrs. Cowper at the Park House / near Hartford / Hartfordshire
Postmarks: 18/AP *and* HUNTING/DON
Panshanger Collection

My dear Cousin,

As in Matters unattainable by Reason, and unrevealed in the Scripture, it is impossible to Argue at all; so in Matters concerning which Reason can only give a probable Guess, and the Scripture has made no explicit Discovery, it is, though not impossible to Argue at all, yet impossible to Argue to any certain Conclusion. This seems to me [to] be the very Case with the Point in Question. Reason is able to form many plausible Conjectures concerning the Possibility of our knowing each other in a future State, and the Scripture has here & there favoured us with an Expression that looks at least like a slight Intimation of it, but because a Conjecture can never amount to a Proof, and a slight Intimation cannot be construed into a positive Assertion; therefore I think we can never come to any absolute Conclusion upon the Subject. We may indeed Reason about the Plausibility of our Conjectures, and we may discuss with great Industry and Shrewdness of Argument those Passages in the Scripture which seem to favour the Opinion, but still no certain Means having been afforded us, no certain End can be attained, and after all that can be said it will still be doubtfull whether we shall know each other or not.

As to Arguments founded upon Human Reason only, it would be easy to muster up a much greater Number on the Affirmative Side of the Question than it would be worth my while to write, or yours to Read. Let us see therefore what the Scripture says, or seems to say towards the Proof of it; and of this kind of Arguments also I shall insert but a few of those which seem to me to be the fairest & clearest for the purpose. For after all, a Disputant on either side of this Question, is in Danger of that Censure of our Blessed Lord's 'Ye do err not knowing the Scripture, nor the Power of God.'[1]

As to Parables, I know it has been said in the Dispute concerning the intermediate State, that they are not Argumentative; but this having been controverted by very Wise and good Men, and the Parable of Dives and Lazarus[2] having been used as an Argument by

[1] Matthew 22: 29. [2] Luke 16: 19–31.

such to prove an intermediate State, I see not why it may not be as fairly used for the Proof of any other matter which it seems equally to imply. In this Parable we see that Dives is represented as knowing Lazarus, and Abraham as knowing them both, and the Discourse between them is entirely concerning their respective Characters & Circumstances upon Earth.—Here therefore our Saviour seems to Countenance the Notion of a mutual Knowledge & Recollection, and if a Soul that has perished shall know the Soul that is saved, surely the Heirs of Salvation shall know & recollect each other.

In the 1st. Epistle to the Thessalonians the 2d. Chapter & 19 Verse—St. Paul says, 'What is our Hope, or Joy, or Crown of Rejoicing, are not even Ye, in the Presence of our Lord Jesus Christ at his Coming? For Ye are our "Glory and our Joy." '

As to the Hope which the Apostle had formed concerning them, he Himself refers the Accomplishment of it to the Coming of Christ, meaning that then he should receive the Recompense of his Labours in their behalf; his Joy and Glory he refers likewise to the same Period, both which would result from the Sight of such Numbers redeemed by the Blessing of God upon his Ministration, when he should present them before the great Judge, and say in the Words of a greater than Himself, Lo! I, and the Children whom thou hast given me.[3] This seems to imply that the Apostle should know the Converts, and the Converts the Apostle, at least in the Day of Judgment, and if then, why not afterwards?

See also the 4th Chapter of the same Epistle 13. & 14.[4] which I have not room to transcribe. Here the Apostle comforts them under their Affliction for their deceased Brethren, exhorting them not to Sorrow as without Hope. And what is the Hope by which he teaches them to support their Spirits? Even This—that Them which Sleep in Jesus shall God bring with him. In other Words and by a fair Paraphrase surely, telling them that They were only taken from them for a Season, and that they should receive them again at the Resurrection.

If you can take off the Force of these Texts my Dear Cousin, you will go a great way towards shaking my Opinion, if not, I think they must go a great way towards shaking yours.

The Reason why I did not send you my Opinion of Pearshall was

[3] C has paraphrased Isaiah 8: 18 and Hebrews 2: 13.

[4] 1 Thessalonians 4: 13–14.

because I had not then read him. I have read him since and like him much, especially the latter part of him. But you have whetted my Curiosity to see the last Letter by tearing it out; unless therefore you can give me a good Reason why I should not see it, I shall enquire for the Book the next time I go to Cambridge.[5] Perhaps I am partial to Hervey[6] for the sake of his other Writings (you know I hated him once) but I cannot give Pearshall the Preference to him now, for I think him one of the most Spiritual & truly Scriptural Writers in the World.

Yours ever Wm Cowper.

April 17. 1766.

MRS. COWPER Friday, 18 April 1766

Address: To / Mrs. Cowper at the Park House / near Hartford / Hartfordshire
Postmarks: 21/A[P] *and* HUNTING/DON
Harvard

My dear Cousin,

Having gone as far as I thought needfull to Justify the Opinion of our meeting and knowing each other hereafter, I find upon Reflection that I have done but half my Business, and that one of the Questions you proposed remains entirely unconsidered; viz. whether the Things of our present State will not be of too low and mean a Nature to engage our Thoughts or make a part of our Communications in Heaven.

The common and ordinary Occurrences of Life no doubt, and even the Ties of Kindred and of all Temporal Interests will be entirely discarded from amongst that happy Society, and possibly even the Remembrance of them done away. But it does not therefore follow that our Spiritual Concerns even in this Life will be forgotten, neither do I think that They can ever appear trifling to us in any [of] the most distant Period of Eternity. God, as you say in reference to the Scripture, will be All in All. But does not that Expression mean

5 Pearsall's *Reliquiae Sacrae: or, Meditations on Select Passages . . .* is divided into dialogues, not letters. The final, eleventh dialogue is concerned with the immortality of the human soul, on which issue Pearsall takes a stance very similar to C's in this letter.

6 Revd. James Hervey (1714–58), author of such works as *Meditations among the Tombs, in a Letter to a Lady* (1746) and *Theron and Aspasio: or a Series of Dialogues and Letters upon the Most Important and Interesting Subjects* (3 vols., 1755, 1755, 1767).

that being admitted to so near an Approach to our heavenly Father and Redeemer, our whole Nature the Soul and all its Faculties will be employed in Praising and adoring him? Doubtless however this will be the case, and if so, will it not furnish out a glorious Theme of Thanksgiving to recollect the Rock whence we were hewn and the Hole of the Pit whence we were digged? To recollect the time when our Faith, which under the Tuition and Nurture of the Holy Spirit has produced such a plentifull Harvest of immortal Bliss, was but as a Grain of Mustard Seed, small in itself, promising but little Fruit, and producing less? To recollect the various Attempts that were made upon it by the World, the Flesh, and the Devil, and its various Triumphs over all by the Assistance of God through our Lord Jesus Christ? At present, whatever our Convictions may be of the Sinfullness and Corruption of our Nature, we can make but a very imperfect Estimate either of our Weakness or our Guilt. Then, no doubt, we shall understand the full Value of the wonderfull Salvation wrought out for us: And it seems reasonable to suppose that in order to our forming a just Idea of our Redemption, we shall be enabled to form a just one of the Danger we have escaped; when we know how weak and frail we were, surely we shall be more able to render due Praise & Honour to his Strength who fought for us; when we know completely the Hatefullness of Sin in the Sight of God and how deeply we were tainted by it, we shall know how to value the Blood by which we are cleansed, as we ought. The twenty four Elders in the 5th. of the Revelation give Glory to God for their Redemption out of every kindred, and Tongue, and People, & Nation. This surely implies a Retrospect to their respective Conditions upon Earth, and that each remember'd out of what particular kindred & Nation he had been redeemed, and if so, then surely the minutest Circumstances of their Redemption did not escape their memory.—They who Triumph over the Beast in the 15th. Chapter, sing the Song of Moses the Servant of God; and what was that Song? A sublime Record of Israel's Deliverance, and the Destruction of her Enemies in the Red Sea, Typical no doubt of the Song which the Redeemed in Sion shall sing to celebrate their own Salvation and the Defeat of their Spiritual Enemies. This again implies a Recollection of the Dangers they had before encountered, and the Supplies of strength and Ardour they had in every Emergency received from the great Deliverer out of All. These Quotations do not indeed prove that their Warfare upon Earth

makes a part of their Converse with each other, but they prove that it is a Theme not unworthy to be heard even before the Throne of God, and therefore it cannot be unfit for reciprocal Communication.

But you doubt whether there is *any* Communication between the Blessed at all, neither do I recollect any Scripture that proves it, or that bears any Relation to the Subject. But Reason seems to require it so peremptorily, that a Society without Social Intercourse seems to be a Solecism and a Contradiction in Terms, and the Inhabitants of those Regions are called you know in Scripture an innumerable *Company* & an *Assembly*, which seem to convey the Idea of Society as clearly as the Word itself. Human Testimony weighs but little in matters of this sort, but let it have all the Weight it can. I know no greater Names in Divinity than Watts[1] and Doddridge.[2] They were both of this Opinion, and I send you the very Words of the latter. 'Our *Companions in glory* may probably assist us by their wise and good Observations, when we come to make the *Providence of God here upon Earth*, under the Guidance and Direction of our Lord Jesus Christ, *the Subject of our mutual Converse*.'

Thus, my dear Cousin, I have spread out my Reasons before you for an Opinion which whether admitted or denied, affects not the State or Interest of the Soul. May our Creator, Redeemer, and Sanctifier conduct us into his own Jerusalem where there shall be no Night neither any Darkness at all, where we shall be free even from innocent Error, and perfect in the Light of the Knowledge of the Glory of God in the Face of Jesus Christ!

Yours faithfully
Wm Cowper.

April 18. 1766.

1 Isaac Watts (1674–1748), the eminent dissenting divine and hymn-writer.

2 Philip Doddridge (1702–51). C is quoting from 'Christ's Mysterious Conduct to be Unfolded Hereafter', a funeral sermon occasioned by the death of the Revd. James Shepherd (1722–46). Although the sermon was first preached at Northampton on 25 May 1746, it was not published until 1748 when it appeared as the end piece in a collection of nine of Shepherd's own sermons.

JOSEPH HILL — Saturday, 3 May 1766

Cowper Johnson

My dear Sephus,

Excuse the Trouble I give you. An Old Friend[1] of Mr. Unwin's died this Morning, and Mr. Unwin has occasion to send an Express to his Executor at Bath. The Post-Master here says he can send it to London, but cannot get it through the General Post Office unless there be somebody to pay the Freight of it there. Mr. Unwin is not sure that any of his London Friends or Kindred are now in Town, and the thing requiring immediate Dispatch, for the Old Gentleman can't be buried 'till the Express returns, I take the Liberty to trouble You with it. Mr. Unwin will account with Me, and I must account with You for the Payment at the Post Office.

Your Wm. Cowper.

Huntn. May 3. 1766

JOSEPH HILL — Friday, 9 May 1766

Address: To / Mr. Joseph Hill / Cookes Court / Carey Street / London.
Postmarks: 12/MA *and* HUNTING/DON
Harvard

My dear Sephus!

Faith was never yet the Fruit of Controversy; I have therefore no more than You, an Appetite to it, both because I have not Talents for such a Task, and because I should despair of any good Effect of it. I shall therefore content myself with supporting my Opinion of Faith in Christ by a Text or two from Scripture, and there leave, and take leave of the Argument.

We both beleive that our Saviour was the Messiah or the Sent of God. His Words upon the Subject are, He that beleiveth shall be Saved, He that beleiveth not shall be Damned.[1] You think I ascribe too much to Faith—Our Saviour ascribes All to it. No need of a Commentator upon Words so very explicit as these. But how is it possible say you that Faith can be of such high Estimation in the Sight

[1] Unidentified.

---

[1] Mark 16: 16.

of God—Again our Saviour Answers—If ye Beleive not that I am He, Ye shall Die in your Sins.[2] But what does he mean when he says to us, Ye must beleive that *I am He*?[3] Doubtless that We must beleive him to have taken away the Sins of the World by the Sacrifice of himself. But can this Persuasion Justifie us?—The Scripture says, in Him, they who *beleive* are *freely* Justified from all things.[4] And even the Just themselves shall live—how? By Works? Nay but by Faith.[5] What then becomes of Works? Say you. The Scripture says, that Faith *Worketh* by Love. And every Man that merits the Appellation he received in Baptism, can bear Testimony to this Truth from the Bottom of his Heart. So then the Word of the Almighty assures us that we are Justified *freely* by Faith *working* by Love, and this in the plainest Language, in Terms the most express and certain.[6]

But you think at this rate few shall be saved. Our Saviour says, narrow is the way and few there be that find it.[7] You see therefore that your Opinion in this Articl[e][8] coincides exactly with the Scripture.

My dear Joe! Variety Of Opinions in these things matters not. There is the same Variety in Matters of Science and Philosophy, but a Number of false Notions can never prove that there is not a true one. Let us humble our Hearts before God, and beseech him to *reveal his Son in us*,[9] according to the Scripture Expression, and we shall soon see the Excellence of the Salvation which Christ has purchased for us, and our own utter Insufficiency to be our own Redeemers.

I shall only add that admitting Christ to be the Son of God, and that He has himself annexed Salvation to Faith, which he has certainly done, it is quite impossible to suppose that he has left no Account of that Faith behind him to which he has annext so great & precious a Recompense. We must take our Saviour's Counsel to the Jews therefore, & *Search the Scriptures*,[10] for in them we beleive that we have Eternal Life.

I shall be obliged to you if you will give my Love to Colman when you see him next, & thank him for his Enquiries after me. The Poem he wants is in a black Pocket Book or Letter Case amongst my

[2] John 8 : 24.
[3] See John 13 : 19.
[4] Acts 13 : 39; Romans 3 : 22–4.
[5] Habakkuk 2 : 4; Romans 1 : 17; Galatians 3 : 11; Hebrews 10 : 38.
[6] Galatians 5 : 6.
[7] Matthew 7 : 14.
[8] MS. torn.
[9] Galatians 1 : 16.
[10] John 5 : 39.

Lumber in Town.[11] If it can possibly be extricated from that Farrago of Stuff in which it is at present dead & Buried, I shall be [glad to] have it restored to him according to his Request.

I shall draw on you the 11th. Instant for Mr. Unwin's h[alf-yearly ren]t viz. 42£.[12]

I have little to say concerning myself, except that I am in good Health, and Happy; Neither have I known one uneasy Hour since into this House I came. My Brother also is well, and would send his Respects if he knew I was writing to you. My Love to All your Family and to the little Woman[13] in Grosvenor Street &c.

Yours ever
Wm Cowper.

Huntn.
May 9. 1766.

Pray let me know in your next the Name of the Ship[14] to which Sir Thomas has consigned his Person.

JOSEPH HILL — Saturday, 16 August 1766

Address: To / Mr. Joseph Hill at the Chancery / Office London, or in Cooke's Court Carey Street / Lincolns Inn Fields. / If not at either of the above Places, to be / forwarded to him immediately.
Cowper Johnson

Dear Sephus,

Uncertain whether or no this will ever reach your Hands, I shall lay an Embargo upon all that Wit & Humour which generally pours itself into my Epistles, and only write the needful.

I have a Bill to pay here and immediate Occasion for Cash besides. £20 will answer both these Emergencies. I should be glad therefore if my Finnances will stretch so far, of a Bank Note by the first Opportunity, to that Amount.

[11] See C to Hill, 4 May 1767.

[12] This was C's first payment to the Unwins. He had moved into their home on 11 Nov. 1765. The payments were continued at half-yearly intervals (see C to Hill, 4 May 1767).

[13] This is presumably *not* the woman who in 1771 became Hill's wife, Sarah Mathews (1742–1824), who lived at Wargrave. (*Notes and Queries*, 12th ser., v (1919), 259.)

[14] Sir Thomas Hesketh was a born sailor and kept at Southampton a yacht (the good sloop the *Harriet*). See C to Newton, 24 Sept. 1785.

I am much concerned to hear of Ashley's Illness.[1] You will oblige me by sending me some Account of him.

Yours Dear Joe,
Wm Cowper.

Augt. 16. 1766.

JOSEPH HILL   Saturday, 16 August 1766[1]

Cowper Johnson

Dear Sephus,

I sent you a Scrap this Morning, but the Post not being yet gone out I shall trouble you with another Scrap upon the Subject of yours which I have just received.

I am sorry my Finnances are not only exhausted, but overdrawn. This being the Case, I shall chuse to let the Drapier's Bill at this place remain unpaid a while longer 'till Cash comes in. I shall lower my Demands therefore, and instead of 20£ must beg of you to convey to me 5 Guineas for immediate Use. My Brother is gone into the North with no more Money than he wants, & will return, I suppose, wanting more than he has. I thought he had made out our Account with Eamonson, for I charged him by Letter just before he set out for London not to forget it.

These Deficiencies of Money frighten me, lest I should not be able to continue in this comfortable Retreat, for I shall never, I doubt, find such another. Another half year will be due to Mr. Unwin in November, which must be paid him at the time, if I sell the only Hundred I have for the purpose. I was always good at Selling.—It has, as you say, been an expensive Year, & I shall hope better things of the next.

[1] Lady Hesketh told Hayley that 'tho' nobody had in general finer Spirits, or more Animation' than her father, yet he was subject to 'a degree of low Spirits, which would sometimes hang upon him for months together, and which were almost as affecting to see as those which you and I Sir have witness'd with so much Pain! My dear Fathers were different indeed in some respects, as he was always perfectly quiet and Composed, avoided Company, and never Join'd in any Conversation, but he was not apparently actuated by those horrors, which were permitted so cruelly to distress his Invaluable Nephew!' 25 Oct. 1801: Add. MS. 30803 A, fo. 174.

---

[1] This longer letter accompanied the 'Scrap this morning' of 16 Aug. 1766.

I rejoice with you in the Snugness of your Situation, & if you continue to like it, wish you may always have the same, or just such another.

My Love attends your Family,

Yours dear Joe
Wm Cowper.

JOSEPH HILL — Saturday, 23 August 1766

Address: To / Mr. Joseph Hill at / Taplow Common near / Maidenhead / Bucks.
Postmarks: 25/AV *and* illegible
Massachusetts Historical Society

Dear Sephus,

I return you my Thanks for the 10£ Note which came yesterday safe to hand. I am willing to think upon recollecting the extraordinary Expences of the last Year, that I shall not find my Income so deficient hereafter. My necessary Charges upon leaving St. Albans, such as Fees to Servants, Journey hither &c, my very expensive Housekeeping at the first Lodging I went to, where it cost me in 4 Months almost as much as it does here in a Twelvemonth, and my Remittances to Dr. Cotton; amount in the whole to the best part if not the whole of an 100£, and readily enough account for the Defects that so much alarmed me. My personal Expences at this House hardly ever come to more than a Guinea a Month, including Washing, so that the Taylor, the Drapier, the Servant's Wages, and the little Boy's Board, are the only material Articles of Expence I am exposed to after payment of Mr. Unwin, and for these I think the remaining 80£ must be, nay half of it must be sufficient.

The People of this House have contracted such a Friendship for me, and behave to me with so much Affection and Tenderness, that it would cut me to the Heart to be obliged to leave them. If that however should be the case, which I don't much apprehend, I will retire far North, or far West, into a Country where I may be sure not to exceed my Income; for if I can't live here the South will always be too hot to hold me. Besides it is so painfull a thing to me, to be forced to break Connections as fast as I make them, that as far as I can, I will endeavour with Submission to Providence, to secure myself from any

future Sorrows of that kind. In the mean time I hope better things, and am easy.

Yours my Dear Joe
Wm Cowper

Pray inform Lady Hesketh that my Servant having travelled as far as High:Gate in his way to London, with the Book[1] she was so kind as to lend me, stopt there without reaching Town, and brought it back again. She may depend however on its being safely restored to her.

Augt. 23. 1766.

MRS. COWPER — Wednesday, 3 September 1766

Hayley, i. 51–4[1]

Huntingdon, Sept. 3, 1766.

My Dear Cousin,

It is reckoned, you know, a great achievement to silence an opponent in disputation, and your silence was of so long continuance, that I might well begin to please myself with the apprehension of having accomplished so arduous a matter. To be serious, however, I am not sorry, that what I have said, concerning our knowledge of each other, in a future state, has a little inclined you to the affirmative. For though the redeemed of the Lord shall be sure of being as happy in that state as infinite power, employed by infinite goodness, can make them, and therefore it may seem immaterial whether we shall, or shall not, recollect each other hereafter; yet our present happiness at least is a little interested in the question. A parent, a friend, a wife must needs, I think, feel a little heart ache at the thought of an eternal separation from the objects of her regard: and not to know them, when she meets them in another life, or never to meet them at all, amounts, though not altogether, yet nearly to the same thing. Remember them, I think, she needs must. To hear that they are happy, will indeed be no small addition to her own felicity: but

[1] Probably the unidentified book first mentioned by C in his letter to Lady Hesketh of 1 Aug. 1765.

[1] The MS. of this letter was listed in a Sotheby catalogue of 22 July 1909; it was sold to Meylen.

to see them so, will surely be a greater. Thus at least it appears to our present human apprehension; consequently, therefore, to think that when we leave them, we lose them for ever, that we must remain eternally ignorant whether they, that were flesh of our flesh, and bone of our bone,[2] partake with us of celestial glory, or are disinherited of their heavenly portion, must shed a dismal gloom over all our present connexions. For my own part, this life is such a momentary thing, and all its interests have so shrunk in my estimation, since by the Grace of our Lord Jesus Christ I became attentive to the things of another; that like a worm in the bud of all my friendships and affections, this very thought would eat out the heart of them all, had I a thousand; and were their date to terminate with this life, I think I should have no inclination to cultivate, and improve such a fugitive business. Yet friendship is necessary to our happiness here, and built upon Christian principles, upon which only it can stand, is a thing even of religious sanction—for what is that love, which the Holy Spirit, speaking by St. John, so much inculcates, but friendship? The only love, which deserves the name; a love which can toil, and watch, and deny itself, and go to death for its brother. Worldly friendships are a poor weed compared with this, and even this union of spirit in the bond of peace, would suffer in my mind at least, could I think it were only coeval with our earthly mansions.—It may possibly argue great weakness in me, in this instance, to stand so much in need of future hopes to support me in the discharge of present duty. But so it is—I am far, I know, very far, from being perfect in Christian love, or any other divine attainment, and am therefore unwilling to forego whatever may help me in my progress.

You are so kind as to inquire after my health, for which reason I must tell you, what otherwise would not be worth mentioning, that I have lately been just enough indisposed to convince me, that not only human life in general, but mine in particular, hangs by a slender thread. I am stout enough in appearance, yet a little illness demolishes me. I have had a severe shake, and the building is not so firm as it was. But I bless God for it with all my heart. If the inner man be but strengthened day by day, as I hope under the renewing influences of the Holy Ghost, it will be, no matter how soon the outward is dissolved. He who has in a manner raised me from the dead, in a

[2] See Genesis 2 : 23.

literal sense, has given me the grace I trust to be ready at the shortest notice, to surrender up to him that life, which I have twice received from him. Whether I live or die, I desire it may be to His Glory, and it must be to my happiness—I thank God that I have those amongst my kindred to whom I can write without reserve of sentiments upon this subject, as I do to you. A letter upon any other subject is more insipid to me than ever my task was, when a schoolboy, and I say not this in vain glory, God forbid! But to shew you what the Almighty, whose Name I am unworthy to mention, has done for me, the chief of sinners. Once he was a terror to me, and his service, Oh what a weariness it was! Now I can say I love him, and his Holy Name, and am never so happy as when I speak of his Mercies to me.

Yours, dear Cousin,
Wm. Cowper.

JOSEPH HILL — Thursday, 9 October 1766

Cowper Johnson

Dear Joe,

It would be rather an unreasonable Proceeding methinks, to trouble you so frequently as I do with my paultry Affairs, and by way of Recompense to make use of your Money without rememb'ring to restore it. That I may Act therefore more in Character as a Reasonable Being, I desire you will be so kind as to send me a Letter of Attorney to impower you to sell as much of the 100£, as my Arrears with you amount to. Mr. Unwin's 40 Guineas will be due on the Eleventh of November; if my Treasury has been sufficiently replenished to answer that Demand, or is likely to be so before the time mentioned, well and good. If not, I must beg you to dispatch the whole 100£, that the Money may be forth coming. My Drapier's Bill amounting to about 14£, I shall endeavour to discharge out of my Right Breeches Pocket, which I hope will be rich enough for the purpose.

My Brother is returned from Yorkshire, and will send you a Copy of our Account with Eamonson. He thought he had given you one when he saw you in Town, having written it out for the purpose,

but certainly forgot it, as he did his great Coat which he has left at an Inn upon the North Road; besides having with the same noble Contempt of Wealth and Self Interest, accepted half a Moidore[1] from an Inkeeper, made of Tin and not worth a penny. I Laugh at his Carelessness, and so does He; whether Laughing at it be the way to cure it, Time will shew.

I direct this to your Office, lest it should not find you at Taplow.[2] My Love to your Family and beleive me ever Yours

Wm Cowper.

Oct 9. 1766.

MRS. COWPER — Monday, 20 October 1766

Address: To / Mrs. Cowper / at the Park House / near Hartford / Hartfordshire
Postmarks: 21/OC *and* HUNTING/DON
Panshanger Collection

Huntinn. Oct. 20. 1766.

My dear Cousin,

I am sorry for poor George's Illness,[1] and hope you will soon have Cause to thank God for his complete Recovery. We have an Epidemical Fever in this Country likewise, which leaves behind it a continual Sighing almost to suffocation; not that I have seen any Instance of it, for Blessed be God our Family have hitherto escaped it, but such was the Account I heard of it this Morning.

I am obliged to you for the Interest you take in my Welfare, and for your enquiring so particularly after the manner in which my time passes here. As to Amusements, I mean what the World calls such, we have none: the Place indeed swarms with them, and Cards and Dancing are the professed Business of almost all the *Gentle* Inhabitants of Huntingdon. We refuse to take part in them, or to be Accessories to this way of Murthering our Time, and by so doing have acquired the Name of Methodists. Having told you how we *do not* spend our time, I will next say how we *do*. We Breakfast commonly

[1] The moidore, valued at 27 shillings, was a gold coin of Portugal acceptable as currency in Britain.

[2] See C to Lady Hesketh, 30 Jan. 1767 aud n.1.

[1] There is an asterisk in the text of the manuscript at this point accompanied by the legend in the margin: 'he meant Charles's'.

between 8 and 9, 'till 11, we read either the Scripture, or the Sermons of some faithfull Preacher of those holy Mysteries: at 11 we attend divine Service which is performed here twice every day, and from 12 to 3 we separate and amuse ourselves as we please. During that Interval I either Read in my own Apartment, or Walk or Ride, or work in the Garden. We seldom sit an hour after Dinner, but if the Weather permits adjourn to the Garden, where with Mrs. Unwin and her Son I have generally the Pleasure of Religious Conversation 'till Tea time; if it Rains or is too windy for Walking, we either Converse within Doors, or sing some Hymns of Martin's Collection,[2] and by the Help of Mrs. Unwin's Harpsichord make up a tolerable Concert, in which however our Hearts I hope are the best and most musical Performers. After Tea we sally forth to walk in good earnest. Mrs. Unwin is a good Walker, and we have generally travel'd about 4 Miles before we see Home again. When the Days are short we make this Excursion in the former part of the Day, between Church time and Dinner. At Night we read and Converse as before 'till Supper, and commonly finish the Evening either with Hymns or a Sermon, and last of all the Family are called in to Prayers.—I need not tell *you* that such a Life as this is consistent with the utmost cheerfullness, accordingly we are all happy, and dwell together in Unity as Brethren. Mrs. Unwin has almost a maternal Affection for me, and I have something very like a filial one for her, and her Son and I are Brothers. Blessed be the God of m[y Sal]vation[3] for such Companions, and for such a Life [above] all, for an Heart to like it.

I have had many anxious Thoughts about taking Orders: and I beleive every new Convert is apt to think himself called upon for that purpose; but it has pleased God, by means which there is no need to particularize, to give me full Satisfaction as to the Propriety of declining it. Indeed, they who have the least Idea of what I have suffered from the Dread of public Exhibitions, will readily excuse my never attempting them hereafter. In the mean time, if it please the Almighty, I may be an Instrument of turning many to the Truth, in a private way, & hope that my Endeavours in this Way have not been entirely unsuccessfull. Had I the Zeal of Moses, I should want

C thought George Cowper (1754–87) was the son of Mrs. Cowper suffering from 'Epidemical Fever'. Evidently the son in question was Charles (b. 1765), still an infant.

[2] As early as 1760 Martin Madan had brought out a little volume of 171 selected *Psalms and Hymns*, chiefly from Charles Wesley and Isaac Watts.

[3] The MS. is torn slightly here.

an Aaron to be my Spokesman.—Yours ever my Dear Cousin—Wm Cowper.

I beg you will give my affectionate Respects to Mrs. Maitland when you write to her, & to my Aunt Madan, whom now I *cannot* see her, I know how to value.—

JOSEPH HILL — Monday, 27 October 1766

Address: To / Mr. Joseph Hill / at Taplow Common / near Maidenhead / Bucks.
Postmarks: 28/OC *and* HUNTING/DON
Cowper Johnson

Huntn. Oct. 27. 1766.

Dear Sephus,

If every Dealer and Chapman was connected with Creditors like You, the poor Commissioners of Bankrupts would be ruined. I can only wonder at you, considering my Knack at running in Debt, and my slender Ability to pay. After all I am afraid that the poor Stock must suffer. When I wrote my last, the Payment of my Boy's Board[1] was farther distant, therefore I suppose it was that I did not mention it. Mr. Peacock's Bill too being a growing Evil, though at that time I thought of paying it out of my Pocket, must I find receive its Satisfaction from another Quarter. The former of these Demands amounts to about 6£, and the latter to about 16£, and has waited so long for Payment, that in a little time my Credit and Interest in that Gentleman will begin to totter. My Financies will never be able to satisfy these craving Necessities, without leaving my Debt to you entirely unsatisfied; and though I know you are sincere in what you say, and as willing to wait for your Money as Heart can wish, yet Query whether the next half year, which will bring its Expences with it, will be more propitious to you than the present? The succeeding half years may bear a close Resemblance to their insolvent Predecessors continually, and unless we break Bank some time or other, your Prospect of Payment may be always what it is at present. What matters it therefore to Reprieve the Stock, which must come to Execution at last?

I am heartily glad my Uncle has recovered his Spirits, and desire

[1] Richard Coleman. See C to Hill, 12 Nov. 1766.

you will remember me to all your Associates at Taplow. I sympathize with you upon the fugitive Nature of the longest Vacation; and wish for your sake that the Chancellor would pack up his great Seal and hold his Court in your Neighbourhood.

Yours ever Wm Cowper.

Our Account with Eamonson stands thus.

Drawn by Me,

1763.

June 25. .... 30. 0. 0.

August 16. .... 30. 0. 0.

By my Brother

1764.

January 30. 0. 0

[I][2] think I have omitted something, but hardly m[ore than] 30 or 40£. The Sum in his Hands, was to the best of my Remembrance, 360.

JOSEPH HILL — Wednesday, 12 November 1766

Address: To / Mr. Joseph Hill / at the Chancery Office / London
Postmarks: 13/NO *and* HUNTING/DON
Cowper Johnson

Dear Sephus,

I drew yesterday for Mr. Unwin's Money; and when I have drawn about 6£ more for the Young Gentleman's Maintenance whose Birth and Parentage you inquire after, I shall have drawn my last for the present.

He is the Son of a drunken Cobler at St. Albans, who would probably have starved him to death by this time or have poisoned him with Gin, if Providence had not thrown it in my way to rescue him. I was glad of an Opportunity to shew some Mercy in a place where I had received so much, and hope God will give a Blessing to my Endeavours to preserve him. He is a fine Boy, of a good Temper and Understanding, and if the Notice that is taken of him by the

[2] MS. torn.

Neighbours here don't spoil him, will probably turn out well. His Name is Richard Colman; for further particulars enquire of Dr. Cotton.[1]

At present I have thoughts of dealing with him much after the same Manner when he is a Year or two Older, as I do with my present Servant. He will be about Nine Years of Age when my Man leaves me, at which time I think of taking him into my Service, for he will be old enough to do all the Business for which I shall want him, and of a right Age to be taught the Trade and Mystery of a Breeches' Maker. This though not so cheap a way as keeping no Servant, will yet be a considerable Saving to me, for I shall have but one to maintain instead of two, and in the mean time an Advantage will result from it not to be overlooked, the Securing him I mean from ill Example and bad Company, which if I turn him quite loose into another Family, cannot be so easily done. But after all, my Measures in this Instance and in all others, are precarious things, because my Income is so, but God will order All for the best.

I am sorry my Uncle's Disorder still hangs about him, the Grief of a wounded Spirit is of all the most dreadfull. Give my sincere Love to your Family and all my Friends and beleive me Dear Joe

Your very Affectionate
Wm Cowper.

Huntingdon
Novr. 12. 1766.

LADY HESKETH — Friday, 30 January 1767

Olney

Jan: 30. 1767.

My dear Lady Hesketh,

I am glad you spent your Summer in a Place so agreeable to you. As to me, my Lot is cast in a Country where we have neither Woods nor Commons nor pleasant Prospects. All Flat and insipid; in the Summer adorned only with blue Willows, and in the Winter covered with a Flood. Such it is at present; Our Bridges shaken almost in pieces, our poor Willows torn away by the Roots, and our Haycocks almost afloat. Yet even here we are happy, at least I am so; and if I have no

[1] For C's later opinion of Richard Coleman, see his letter to Joseph Johnson of 8 July 1792.

Groves with Benches conveniently disposed, nor Commons overgrown with Thyme to regale me, neither do I want them. You thought to make my Mouth water at the Charms of Taplow,[1] but you see you are disappointed. My dear Cousin! I am a living Man. —And I can never reflect that I am so, without recollecting at the same time that I have infinite Cause of Thanksgiving and Joy. This makes every Place delightfull to me, where I can have leisure to meditate upon those Mercies by which I live, and indulge a Vein of Gratitude to that gracious God who has snatched me like a Brand out of the Burning. Where had I been but for his Forbearance and long Suffering? Even with those who shall never see his Face in Hope, to whom the Name of Jesus by the just Judgment of God, is become a Torment instead of a Remedy. Thoughtless and inconsiderate Wretch that I was! I lived as if I had been my own Creator, and could continue my Existence to what Length and in what State I pleased. As if Dissipation was the narrow way which leads to Life, and a Neglect of the blessed God would certainly end in the Enjoyment of him. But it pleased the Almighty to convince me of my fatal Error, before it indeed became such; to convince me that in Communion with Him we may find that Happiness for which we were created, and that a Life without God in the World, is a Life of Trash and the most miserable Delusion. Oh how had my own Corruption and Satan together, blinded and befooled me. I thought the Service of my Maker and Redeemer a tedious and unnecessary Labour, I despised those who thought otherwise, and if they spoke of the Love of God, I pronounced them Madmen. As if it were possible to Serve and to Love that Almighty Being too much, with whom we must dwell for ever, or be for ever miserable without him. Would I were the only one that had ever Dream'd this Dream of Folly and Wickedness! But the World is filled with such, who furnish a continual Proof of God's almost unprovokeable Mercy, who set up for themselves in a Spirit of Independence upon Him who made them, and yet enjoy that Life by his Bounty which they abuse to his Dishonour.—You remember Me, my dear Cousin, one of this trifling and deluded Multitude. Great and grievous Afflictions were applied to awaken me out of this deep Sleep, and under the Influences of divine Grace have, I trust, produced the Effect for

[1] Taplow, one of the fashionable towns C had visited as a young man, is in southern Buckinghamshire near the Berkshire border; it is a short distance from Slough and Eton.

which they were intended. If the Way in which I had till that time proceeded had been according to the Word and Will of God, God had never interposed to change it. That he did is certain; though others may not be so sensible of that Interposition, yet I am sure of it. To think as I once did therefore must be wrong. Whether to think as I do now be Right or not, is a Question that can only be decided by the Word of God; at least it is capable of no other Decision 'till the great Day determine it finally. I see and see plainly in every Page and Period of that Word my former Heedlessness and Forgetfullness of God condemned; I see a Life of Union and Communion with him inculcated and injoined as an essential Requisite. To this therefore, it must be the Business of our Lives to attain, and happy is He who makes the greatest Progress in it. This is no Fable, but it is our Life. If we stand at the Left Hand of Christ while we live, we shall stand there too in the Judgment—The Seperation must be begun in this World, which in that Day shall be made for ever. My dear Cousin! may the Son of God who shall then assign to each his everlasting Station, direct and settle All your Thoughts upon this important Subject. Whether you must think as I do or not, is not the Question; but it is indeed an awfull Question, whether the Word of God be the Rule of our Actions, and his Spirit the Principle by which we Act. Search the Scriptures for in them ye beleive ye have Eternal Life. This Letter will be Mr. Howe's[2] Companion to London; I wish his Company were more worthy of him, but it is not fit it should be less. I pray God to Bless you, and Remember you where I never forget those I Love.

Yours and Sir Thomas's affectionate Friend Wm Cowper.

MRS. COWPER — Wednesday, 11 March 1767

Address: To / Mrs. Cowper at the Park House / near Hartford / Hartfordshire
Postmarks: 12/MR *and* HUNTING/DON
Panshanger Collection

My dear Cousin,

To find those whom I love, clearly and strongly persuaded of Evangelical Truth, gives me a Pleasure superior to any that this World can afford me. Judge then, whether your Letter in which the

[2] Perhaps a work by the Revd. John Howe (1630–1705).

Body and Substance of a saving Faith is so evidently set forth, could meet with a lukewarm Reception at my Hands, or be entertained with Indifference. Would you know the true Reason of my long Silence?[1] Conscious that my Religious Principles are generally excepted against, and that the Conduct they produce wherever they are heartily maintained, is still more the Object of Disapprobation than those Principles themselves, and rememb'ring that I had made both the one and the other known to you, without having any clear Assurance that our Faith in Jesus was of the same Stamp & Character, I could not help thinking it possible that you might disapprove both my Sentiments and Practise, that you might think the One unsupported by Scripture, and the Other, whimsical and unnecessarily strict & rigorous, and consequently would be rather pleased with the Suspension of a Correspondence, which a different way of thinking upon so momentous a Subject as that we wrote upon, was likely to render tedious and irksome to you. I have told you the Truth from my Heart; forgive me these injurious Suspicions, and never imagine that I shall hear from you upon this delightfull Theme without a real Joy, or without Prayer to God to prosper you in the way of his Truth, his sanctifying and saving Truth.

The Book you mention lies now upon my Table. Marshal[2] is an Old Acquaintance of mine; I have both read him and heard him read with Pleasure and Edification. The Doctrines he maintains are under the Influence of the Spirit of Christ, the very Life of my Soul, and the Soul of all my Happiness. That Jesus is a *present* Saviour, from the Guilt of Sin by his most precious Blood, and from the Power of it by his Spirit, that corrupt and wretched in ourselves, in Him, and in *Him only* we are complete, that being united to Jesus by a lively Faith, we have a solid and Eternal Interest in his Obedience & Sufferings, to Justify us before the Face of our Heavenly Father, and that All this inestimable Treasure, the Earnest of which is in Grace, and its Consummation in Glory, is *Given*, *freely Given* to us of God, without

[1] Mrs. Cowper to C, 5 Mar. 1767 (Olney): 'I never took you for a Man of Ceremony, but I find you a [*sic*] are strictly so! not a line, not a dash of your Pen, since you ansd. my last, I acknowledge the omission chiefly to be on my Side, but considering the difference of our Situations in regard to Leisure, dear Cousin who is realy to blame, that So long an Interval has happen'd in our correspondence?' The previous surviving letter to Mrs. Cowper is of 20 Oct. 1766.

[2] Walter Marshall (1628–80), a Presbyterian divine whose *Gospel-Mystery of Sanctification* appeared first in 1692 and which had reached a seventh edition by 1764.

Regard to our Sins on the one hand, to hold it back, or to our imperfect Services on the other to bring it forward, in short that he hath opened the Kingdom of Heaven to *All Beleivers*, these are the Truths which by the Grace of God, shall ever be dearer to me than Life itself, shall ever be placed next my Heart as the Throne whereon the Saviour himself shall sit, to sway all its Motions, and reduce that World of Iniquity and Rebellion to a State of Filial and Affectionate Obedience to the Will of the most Holy.

These, my dear Cousin, are the Truths to which by Nature we are Enemies, they abase the Sinner and exalt the Saviour to a degree which the Pride of our Hearts, 'till Almighty Grace subdue them, is determined never to allow. For the Reception of these Truths, of this *only Gospel*, it pleased the Lord to prepare me by many and great Afflictions, by Temporal Distress, by a Conscience full of the Terrors of Eternal Death, by the Fire of his Law. Thus humbled, I was glad to receive the Lord Jesus in his own appointed way; the Self righteous, Self justifying Spirit of Pride was laid low, and was no longer a Barrier, to shut in Destruction and Misery, and to keep out the Saviour. May the Almighty reveal his Son in our Hearts continually more and more, and teach us to increase in Love towards him continually for having *given* us the unspeakable Riches of Christ.

My Love to my dear Friend the Major, & to all my little Cousins.[3] May the Lord Bless them & make them all true M[embe]rs[4] of his Mystical Body.

Y[ours fai]thfully Wm Cowper.

Mar: 11. 1767.

MRS. COWPER — Saturday, 14 March 1767

Address: To / Mrs. Cowper at the Park House / Hartingfordbury / near Hartford.
Postmarks: 16/MR *and* HUNTING/DON
Panshanger Collection

My dear Cousin,

I just add a Line by way of Postscript to my last, to apprize you of the Arrival of a very dear Friend of mine at the Park on Friday

[3] Maria's children: William (1750–98), Maria Judith (1752–1815), George (1754–87), Frances Cecilia (1764–1849), and Charles (b. 1765). Another child, Spencer, had died in his eighth year in 1759. *The Madan Family*, p. 243.

[4] Part of MS. torn away at seal.

next, the Son of Mr. Unwin, whom I have desired to call on you in his way from London to Huntingdon. If you knew him as well as I do you would love him as much. But I leave the Young Man to speak for himself, which he is very able to do. He is ready possessed of an Answer to every Question you can possibly ask concerning me, and knows my *whole Story* from first to last. I gave you this previous Notice, because I know you are not fond of strange Faces, and because I thought it would in some degree save Him the Pain of announcing himself.

I am become a great Florist and Shrub Doctor. If the Major can make up a small Pacquet of Seeds that will make a Figure in a garden where we have little else besides Jessamine and Honey Suckle, such a Pacquet I mean as may be put in one's Fob, I will promise to take great Care of them, to give them a good Education, and to value them as I ought to value Natives of the Park. They must not be such however as require great Skill in the Management, for at present I have no Skill to spare.

Give my Love to the Major

and beleive me my Dear Cousin

Yours affectionately

Wm Cowper.

Sat: Mar 14. 1767.

I think Marshal one of the best Writers and the most Spiritual Expositor of Scripture I ever read. I admire the Strength of his Argument and the clearness of his Reasonings upon those parts of our most Holy Religion, which are generally least understood even by real Christians, as Masterpieces of the kind. His Section upon the Union of the Soul with Christ is an Instance of what I mean, in which he has spoken of a most Mysterious Truth with admirable Perspicuity, and with great Good Sense, making it all the while subservient to his main purpose of proving Holiness to be the Fruit and Effect of Faith.

I subjoin thus much upon that Author, because though you desired my Opinion of him, I remember that in my last, I rather left you to find it out by Inference, than expressed it as I ought to have done. I never met with a Man who understood the Plan of Salvation better, or was more happy in explaining it.

MRS. COWPER Friday, 3 April 1767

Address: To / Mrs. Cowper / at the Park House / Hartingfordbury near / Hartford
Postmark: 4/AP *and* HUNTING/DON
Panshanger Collection

My dear Cousin,

You sent my Friend Unwin home to us, charm'd with your kind Reception of him, and with every thing he saw at the Park. Shall I once more give you a Peep into my vile and deceitfull Heart? What Motive do you think lay at the Bottom of my Conduct when I desired him to call upon you? I did not suspect at first that Pride and Vain:Glory had any share in it, but quickly after I had recommended the Visit to him, I discovered in that fruitfull Soil the very Root of the Matter. You know I am a Stranger here; all such are suspected Characters, unless they bring their Credentials with them. To this Moment I beleive it is matter of Speculation in the Place, whence I came, and to whom I belong. My Story is of such a Nature that I cannot satisfy this Curiosity by relating it, and to be close and reserved as I am obliged to be, is in a manner to plead Guilty to any Charge their Jealousy may bring against me. Though My Friend You may suppose, before I was admitted an Inmate here, was satisfied that I was not a mere Vagabond, and has since that time received more convincing Proof of my *Sponsibility*, yet I could not resist the Opportunity of furnishing him with Ocular Demonstration of it, by introducing him to one of my most splendid Connections; that when he hears me called *that Fellow Cowper*, which has happened heretofore, he may be able upon unquestionable Evidence, to assert my Gentlemanhood, and releive me from the Weight of that opprobrious Appellation. Oh Pride, Pride! It deceives with the Subtlety of a Serpent, and seems to walk erect, though it crawls upon the Earth. How will it twist and twine itself about, to get from under the Cross, which it is the Glory of our Christian Calling to be able to bear with Patience and Good Will. They who can guess at the Heart of a Stranger, and you especially who are of a compassionate Temper, will be more ready perhaps to excuse me in this Instance, than I can be to excuse myself. But in good Truth it was abominable Pride of Heart, Indignation & Vanity, and deserves no better Name. How should such a Creature be admitted into those pure and sinless Mansions where nothing shall enter that defileth, did not the

Blood of Christ applied by the Hand of Faith, take away the Guilt of Sin, and leave no Spot or Stain behind it? Oh what continual Need have I of an Almighty, All sufficient Saviour!

I am glad you are acquainted so *particularly* with *all* the Circumstances of my Story, for I know that your Secresy and Discretion may be trusted with any thing. A Thread of Mercy ran through all the [in]t[ric]ate[1] Maze of those afflictive Providences, so [mysteri]ous to myself at the time, and which must ever remain so to all who will not see what was the great Design of them, 'till at the Judgment Seat of Christ the whole shall be laid open. How is the Rod of Iron changed into a Sceptre of Love!

I thank you for the Seeds. I have committed some of each sort to the Ground, whence they will soon spring up like so many Mementos to remind me of my Friends at the Park. My Love attends Mr. Cowper and all my Cousins.

Yours ever Wm Cowper.

April 3. 1767.

MRS. COWPER — Monday, 4 May 1767

Address: To / Mrs. Cowper at the Park House / Hartingfordbury / near Hartford / Hartfordshire
Postmarks: 5/MA *and* HUNTING/DON
Olney

My dear Cousin,

Having no Memorial by me, from whence to collect the particulars of the Charity you mention, I can't take upon me to set forth with any Certainty the Nature of it or the Terms on which it is bestowed. To the best of my Remembrance the Sum is five Guineas, to be given to the Widow of One Husband, upwards of 60 Years of Age, having no Children, or none able to maintain her, and incapable of maintaining Herself, who also, while she was in a Capacity to work, behaved herself like a discreet and Industrious Person. I am not sure of all these Requisites, but such in general was the Description of the Object of this Benefaction.

[1] The MS. was torn in removing the seal; missing words supplied from *Southey*, iii. 289.

Mr. Thurlow[1] was the Person from whom I used to receive it. He was at that time a Trustee under the Will of Bishop Williams,[2] who I think was the Founder of the Exhibition.[3] I was then very intimate with Mr. Thurlow, and it was at his Request that I endeavoured to find persons properly qualified to receive the Bounty. But my Connection with him having entirely ceased, (for I have never had the least Correspondence with him since my Journey to St. Albans,) it would be extremely painfull to me to deal with him as if upon the Terms of a Friendship which I look upon as absolutely extinct. The Extinction of it has been owing I imagine on His part, to a Variety of much more important Subjects and Pursuits, and on mine to a total Difference from what I know to be his Principles and Practise. I think Mr. Cowper must know him well enough to apply to him in such a Case as this, which is rather doing a Favour, than Asking one, for unless his Stock of Old Pensioners is encreased, he will be glad of a new Recommendation.[4]

My dear Cousin, may the Blessed God who has given it you, continually build you up & establish you in that most Holy Faith you entertain so warmly. To know that we are lost, and that the Son of God has alone wrought out our Redemption, is to know the Only true God, and Jesus Christ whom he hath sent, & this Knowledge is eternal Life.

I dare say you condole with me upon Poor A——'s Publication.[5]

[1] Edward Thurlow, later 1st Baron Thurlow (1731–1806), had first become acquainted with C in the summer of 1751 when they were both clerks at Mr. Chapman's. Thurlow was sent down from Cambridge in 1751 without a degree and was called to the Bar in 1754; he was an energetic and tireless man who busied himself with his profession. He was appointed Solicitor-General in 1770 and Attorney-General in 1771. His support for George III's North American policies was to help him greatly in becoming Lord Chancellor in 1778.

[2] Probably a reference to John Williams (1582–1650), archbishop of York and a noted philanthropist.

[3] A pension (*O.E.D.*).

[4] Ashley Cowper, in his capacity as Clerk of the Parliaments, would have been in charge of the administration of such pensions.

[5] Ashley Cowper's *Poems and Translations* appeared in 1767. Such lines as these from 'To a Young Lady, from the Country, desiring her to buy some Muslin for the Author', on pp. 163–4, would have struck C as indecorous:

> Now, Miss, in terms so neat and spruce,
> Were I to do as others use,
> I shou'd conclude this hubble-bubble,
> With asking pardon for this trouble,
> And (for God knows there's nothing in it)
> *Repent*—to *sin* again next minute—.

Surely the wrong Side of the grand Climacteric is no Season for Rhiming. And that Holy and Blessed Name too, at which he bows the Head upon a Sabbath, is treated with as little Reverence as that of Mahomet; he has indeed packed them & jumbled them together in a manner very shocking to a Christian Reader. May God give him to stand in Awe of that Name which is exalted above every Name whether in Earth or Heaven, & which is fragrant and refreshing as Ointment poured forth to them that beleive in it.

I answer for Unwin, though he is not at home, that he will be very happy in an Acquaintance with my Friend William at Cambridge.[6]

My Love to Mr Cowper &c

Beleive me ever Yours[7]

May 4. 1767.

JOSEPH HILL — Monday, 4 May 1767

Cowper Johnson

Dear Joe,

The Day of Reckoning draws nigh. I shall draw upon you the Eleventh Instant for the Sum of Forty two pounds payable to Mr. Unwin or Order, and soon after, for Payment of a Middle-sized Bill due to Mr. Peacock the Draper. If these Draughts are inconsistent with the Discharge of my Arrears to You, I shall insist upon satisfying them out of the Bank.

I have a Red Leather Trunk somewhere. If it is at your House, I shall be obliged to you for the Dispatch of it hither by the first convenient Opportunity; if Colman's Poem is any where to be found, I shall find it there, nor is that the only Valuable, or invaluable Trinket it contains. But the things I want most, are a pair of Gold Sleeve Buttons which were my Father's.[1]

6 Unidentified.

7 The signature has been removed from this letter and the following is written in the margin: 'NB The signature cut off to form part of a Collection of Autographs of Eminent Authors. CC. [Charles Cowper] Mar. 1814.'

1 See postscript of C to John Duncombe, 16 June 1757.

I beg you will give my Love to your Family, and believe me

Yours faithfully

Wm Cowper.

May 4. 1767.

JOSEPH HILL Thursday, 14 May 1767

Cowper Johnson

Dear Joe,

I only know that I was once the happy Owner of a red Leather Trunk, and that my Brother, when I first saw him at Cambridge, upon my enquiring after my Papers &c, told me that in a red Leather Trunk they were all safely deposited. The whole Contents of it, except the Buttons, are little worth, and if I never see them more, shall be but very moderately afflicted by the Loss, tho' I fancy the Trunk upon the Road will prove to be the very Trunk in question.

Together with your Letter came a Bill from my quondam Hosier in Fleetstreet, Mr Reynolds:[1] for the Sum of 2.10.0, with a Note at the Bottom desiring present Payment, Cash being scarce. I send him an Order for the Money by this day's Post. My future Expences in the Hosiery way will be small, for Mrs. Unwin knits all my Stockings, and would knit my Hats too, if that were possible.

I imagine my Brother will be in Town about Midsummer, when he will be able to confer with you upon the Subject of the inexorable Mr. Eamonson, more to the purpose than I can by Letter.

Having commenced Gardiner, I study the Arts of pruning, sowing, and Planting, and enterprize every thing in that way from Melons down to Cabbages. I have a large Garden to display my Abilities in, and were we 20 Miles nearer London, might turn Higgler,[2] and serve your Honour with Cauliflowers and Brocoli at the best hand. I shall possibly now and then desire you to call for me at the Seed Shop in your way to Westminster, though sparingly; should I

[1] Thomas Reynolds, Hosier & Hatter, Fleet-Street. *Kent's London Directory* (1766).

[2] An itinerant dealer (*O.E.D.*).

do it often, you would begin to think you had a Mother in Law at Berkhamsted.[3]

Yours dear Joe
Wm Cowper.

Hunt:n
May 14. 1767.

MRS. MADAN — Thursday, 4 June 1767

Address: To / Mrs. Madan / in Stafford Row / near the Queen's House / Westminster.
Postmarks: 5/O'CLOCK/W, 4 JV, *and* HUNTING/DON
Arthur A. Houghton, Jr.

My dear Aunt,

When I might have enjoyed your Company as often as I pleased, not being fit for it I declined it, and now that I should rejoice to see you, my heavenly Father having in his great Mercy in some measure qualified me for the Society of them that beleive, I have it not in my Power to converse with you in Person. This which I dare not call my Misfortune, because it is the Dispensation of his Will who hath called me; I must make my Excuse for writing to you, and doubt not you will admit it as a sufficient one: for I know you will not be sorry to hear from a person, not only nearly allied to you by Blood, for that is little, but now more closely united to you I trust, by the unspeakable Gift of God, in the same Spirit. I never recollect the Kindness of your Behaviour to me whenever we met, notwithstanding all my apparent Neglect of you, without seeing in it an Instance of that meek and forgiving Temper which the Lord is pleased to work in all those who beleive in the Name of Jesus. I beg your Pardon of my strange Behavior my dear Aunt, and can venture to assure you without Danger of Dissimulation, that were it in my Power to give Proof of the Change I have undergone in this respect also, that Proof should not be wanting. Alas! How could I truly love a Disciple of the Lord, while I was at Enmity with her Master? How was it possible that one of the dear Children of God should find a place in my unrenewed unsanctified Heart? I would not, neither need I represent myself worse than I was: I always respected you, but it was with a Respect painfull to myself. I had Eyes to see the Holiness & Beauty

[3] A facetious reference to C's late stepmother, Rebecca.

of a Christian Character, but neither a Will to imitate it, nor a Heart to be pleased with it. The Light of the Father of Lights shining in his Elect People, is too much for the feeble Sight of a Child of Wrath whose Delight is to walk in Darkness. Blessed be the God of my Salvation, who in his due time, and in his own appointed way, has enabled me to love the Brethren, & hereby given me Evidence of my Adoption into his Blessed Family. I doubt not you know the particulars of my Story, how it pleased the Lord to lead me through the Waters and they did not overwhelm me, through the Fire, but it did not consume me. And why not? Because the Blood of the Lamb was mercifully interposed between me and that Wrath from which the whole Creation of God could not have screened me for a Moment. Oh that I retained my first Love, that it were with me as when I first came forth from the Furnace: when the Name of Jesus was like Honey and Milk upon my Tongue, and the very Sound of it was sufficient to quicken and comfort me. But I am still what I ever was, a chief Sinner, and shall be so while I inhabit a Body of Death; an ungratefull, unthankfull, wrath:provoking Sinner. But there is abundance of grace and of the Gift of Righteousness for all who are content to be saved as such, therefore I pray that I may be saved as the worst of the Lord's People, as indeed I beleive I am.

My dear Aunt, may the Spirit of Christ dwelling in your Heart, continually testify his Residence there by his comforting and peacefull Influences, 'till at length he shall fill you for ever with Joy unspeakable & full of Glory.

Yours ever Wm Cowper.

Huntingdon
June 4. 1767.

JOSEPH HILL — Tuesday, 16 June 1767

Address: To / Mr. Joseph Hill / Chancery Office / London.
Postmarks: 17/IV *and* HUNTING/DON
Cowper Johnson

Dear Joe,

Instead of Mr. Peacock's Bill, which upon Enquiry I find there is no need to discharge immediately, I send you by this Post a Draft

for Payment of my Taylor's, Mr. Williams of Arundel Street; the Sum, £8.16.0. due this Twelvemonth.

This part of the World is not productive of much News, unless the Coldness of the Weather be so, which is excessive for the Season. We expect, or rather experience a warm Contest between the Candidates for the County, the preliminary Movements of Bribing Threat'ning and Drunkenness being already taken. The Sandwich Interest seems to shake, tho' both Partys are very sanguine. Lord Carysfort is supposed to be in great Jeopardy, tho' as yet I imagine a clear Judgment cannot be formed, for a Man may have all the Noise on his Side, and yet lose his Election.[1] You know me to be an uninterested Person, and I am sure I am a very ignorant one in things of this kind; I only wish it was over, for it occasions the most detestable Scene of Profligacy & Riot that can be imagined.

Yours ever Wm Cowper.

June 16, 1767.

MRS. MADAN — Friday, 10 July 1767

Address: To / Mrs. Madan / Stafford Row / near the Queens House / Westminster.
Postmarks: 5/O'CLOCK/W, 11/IY, *and* HUNTING/DON
Olney

My dear Aunt Madan,

We have lost Mr. Unwin by a very awfull and afflictive Dispensation. As he was riding to his Cure last Sunday sev'night[1] in the Morning, his Horse took Fright, ran away with him homeward, and in a Village about a Mile off he was flung to the Ground with such Violence, that his Scull was fractured in the most desperate manner. He lived about 4 days, contrary to the Expectation of the Surgeons, who pronounced him within a few Hours of Death at the first Sight of him. But we trust there was Hope in his latter End. His Senses seemed to be restored to him at short Intervals, not only for his own Benefit, but for the Comfort and Satisfaction of his Friends. For at

[1] John Proby, 1st Baron Carysfort (1720–72), was Member of Parliament for Huntingdonshire from May 1754 until the dissolution of Parliament in Mar. 1768. John Montagu, 4th Earl of Sandwich (1718–92), was at this time opposing Carysfort because the latter had taken a stand against some of Sandwich's policy decisions at the Admiralty.

[1] The accident had occurred on 29 June, and Morley Unwin had died on 2 July 1767.

those times he was enabled to utter Truths, which before, he could never be brought to the Beleif of. He was one of those many poor deluded Persons, whom Dr. Clark[2] has infected with his Antichristian Errors, and consequently denied the Divinity of our Lord and the infinite Merit of his Sufferings. But upon his Death Bed he was heard to say, 'Jesus Christ is God, and therefore he can save me.' Those Words were frequently in his Mouth—Very God of Very God—And, Jesus Christ died for us. So that he seemed to be pleading these Foundation Truths against the Charges of the Adversary, and an accusing Conscience. Surely then we do not vainly flatter ourselves, when we Hope that the Lord, though he was pleased to take a dread-full course with him, yet sealed him effectually for his own. By this means a Door is opened to us to seek an Abode under the Sound of the Gospel. Mrs. Unwin has determined to do so, thinking it her indispensible Duty. Accordingly we have employed Dr. Conyers,[3] Mr. Newton of Olney, and our Friend Haweis[4] who lay here last Night, to enquire for us. Pray for us, my dear Aunt, that it may please the Good Shepherd, to lead us by the Footsteps of the Flock, and to feed us in his own Pasture; for my Soul within me is Sick of the Spiritless unedifying Ministry at Huntingdon. It is a Matter of the utmost Indifference to us where we settle, provided it be within the Sound of the Glad Tidings of Salvation. I shall be much obliged to you, if you will beg my Friend Martin to assist us, whose extensive Knowledge of those Places where the Gospel is ministered, may perhaps enable him under God, to direct us.

I am a sort of adopted Son in this Family, where Mrs. Unwin has always treated me with Parental Tenderness: Therefore by the Lord's leave, I shall still continue a Member of it. Our Aim and End are the same, the Means of Grace & the Hopes of Glory; so that there seems to be no Reason why we should be parted.

When I said that all Places are alike to us, I should have excepted London, to which we have both Objections that cannot easily be removed.

[2] Perhaps Samuel Clarke (1675–1729), the metaphysician, whose work deduced the moral law from logical necessity.

[3] Richard Conyers (1724–86), vicar of Helmsley (1756–76) and Kirby Misperton, Yorkshire (1763–8). While taking an LL.D. at Cambridge in 1767, Conyers had met William Unwin, whom he later introduced to Newton.

[4] The Revd. Thomas Haweis (1734–1820) had been assistant chaplain at the Lock Hospital, London, under Martin Madan, and was now rector of Aldwinkle, Northants.

I beg my affectionate Respects to all my Friends of the Name of Madan, and am

my Dear Aunt, Yours I trust in the only Savior.

Wm Cowper.

Huntn.
July 10. 1767.

MRS. COWPER Monday, 13 July 1767

Address: To / Mrs. Cowper at the Park House / near Hartford / Hartfordshire
Postmarks: 15/IY *and* HUNTING/DON
British Library

My dear Cousin,

The Newspaper[1] has told you the Truth. Poor Mr. Unwin being flung from his Horse as he was going to his Cure on Sunday Morning, received a dreadfull Fracture on the back part of his Scull, under which he languished 'till Thursday Evening and then died. This awfull Dispensation has left an Impression upon our Spirits which will not presently be worn off. He died in a poor Cottage to which he was carried immediately after his Fall, about a Mile from home, and his Body could not be brought to his House, till the Spirit was gone to Him who gave it. May it be a Lesson to us to Watch, since we know not the Day nor the Hour when our Lord cometh.[2]

The Effect of it upon my Circumstances will only be a Change of the Place of my abode, for I shall still, by God's leave, continue with Mrs. Unwin, whose Behaviour to me has always been that of a Mother to a Son. By this afflictive Providence, it has pleased God, who always drops Comfort into the bitterest Cup, to open a Door for us out of an unevangelical Pasture, such as this is, into some better Ministry where we may hear the glad Tidings of Salvation, and be nourished by the Sincere Milk of the Word. We know not yet where we shall settle, but we trust that the Lord whom we seek, will go before us, and prepare a Rest for us. We have employed our Friend Haweis, Dr. Conyers of Helmsley in Yorkshire, and Mr. Newton of Olney to look out for us, but at present are entirely

[1] Mrs. Cowper could have seen the notice of Morley Unwin's death in such newspapers as the *Public Advertiser* (6 July) and *Saint James's Chronicle* (4–7 July).

[2] Matthew 24 : 42.

ignorant under which of the three we shall settle, or whether under either. I have wrote too to my Aunt Madan, to desire Martin to assist us with his Inquiries. It is probable we shall stay here 'till Michaelmas.

I beg my affectionate Respects to Mr. Cowper & all your Family, & am my Dear Cousin

Your Affectionate Friend & Servant
Wm Cowper.

July 13. 1767.

JOSEPH HILL — Thursday, 16 July 1767

Address: To / Mr. Joseph Hill / at the Chancery Office / London.
Postmarks: 17/IY *and* HUNTING/DON
Cowper Johnson

Dear Joe,

Your Wishes that the Newspaper may have misinformed you are in vain. Mr. Unwin is dead, and died in the manner there mentioned. At Nine o'clock on Sunday Morning he was in perfect Health and as likely to live 20 Years as either of us, and before 10 was stretched speechless and senseless upon a Flock Bed[1] in a poor Cottage, where, (it being impossible to remove him) he died on Thursday Evening. I heard his dying Groans, the Effect of great Agony, for he was a strong Man, and much convulsed in his last Moments. The few short Intervals of Sense that were indulged him, he spent in earnest Prayer, and in Expressions of a firm Trust & Confidence in the only Saviour. To that strong Hold we must all resort at last if we would have Hope in our Death; when every other Refuge fails, we are glad to fly to the only Shelter to which we can repair to any purpose: And happy it is for us, when the false Ground we have chosen for ourselves being broken under us, we find ourselves obliged to have Recourse to the Rock which can never be shaken. When this is our Lot, we receive great and undeserved Mercy.

Our Society will not break up, but we shall settle in some other Place; where, is at present uncertain.

[1] A material consisting of the coarse tufts and refuse of wool or cotton, or of cloth torn to pieces by machinery, used for quilting garments and stuffing beds, cushions, mattresses (*O.E.D.*).

I found Colman's Poem in the Trunk, and have committed it to my Brother's Care who will probably soon deliver it into your Hands. I shall acquaint him with the agreeable News of the 2.12.0., perhaps to day, for I expect him to Dine with us.

You don't say whether you are of the Brecknock Party,[2] I remember it used to be a favourite Project of ours. My poor Aunt always brings up the Rear, and now more lamely than ever.—Give me your Opinion about selling my Chambers, do you think upon the whole it would be the most advantageous Course. They cost me 230£.

Yours affectionately
Wm Cowper.

July 16. 1767.

My Servant will call upon you for five Guineas, part of his Wages; the rest I have paid him here.

MRS. MADAN — Saturday, 18 July 1767

Address: To / Mrs. Madan / Stafford Row near the / Queens House / Westminster.
Postmarks: 20/IY *and* HUNTING/DON
Olney

I wish, my dear Aunt, that any of my Letters may be made as effectual to your Consolation, as your last was to mine. I had for many days stood in great need of some spiritual Refreshment, having walked in Darkness, and found it a Trial of my utmost Strength to trust ever so little in the Lord, and stay upon my God. But his Mercy is ever watchfull over us, to pour Oil and Wine into our Wounds either with his own Hand, or by the Ministry of his faithfull Servants. I know he will recompense you for it, for though my Prayers are wretched things, and seem to myself generally to be little more than Lip:labour; yet he hears them graciously in my own behalf, and will not therefore turn away from them when they are preferred in yours. I may say safely that I *know* he hears them, because I know by the Gift of his free Mercy, that I have an allprevailing High: Priest and Intercessor at his Right Hand for ever, Jesus Christ the

[2] Brecknock, or Brecon, a large town in South Wales. Ashley Cowper evidently spent part of his summers there.

Righteous. Therefore though I am nothing and less than nothing & Vanity, yet the mighty God, the everlasting Lord, the Creator of the Ends of the Earth, will hear me. Oh! To what Privileges are Worms advanced, and how do the Extremes of Power & Weakness, Purity & Sinfullness meet together, by the Mediation of the Man Christ Jesus! The Lord give me some little Sense of his Goodness in this wonderfull Reconciliation!

I am afraid at present to put a Stop to the Enquiries of my Friends after a House for us, though I think I shall soon be able to do it with Security. Mr. Newton has sent us an Account of one, which seems by his Description to be the very thing we want, at a Village called Emberton, within about a Mile of his Church at Olney. He is in Treaty for us with the Owner of it, who lives it seems at a great Distance, so that we cannot have his definitive Answer in less than 10 days or a Fortnight. But there seems to be no Probability of any Objection to us on his part, nor are any Difficulties likely to arise on ours. It will be empty at Michaelmass.[1] Its Situation in this part of the World, recommends it to Mrs. Unwin, who would wish to be near her Son, and to me who would wish to be not altogether seperated from my Brother. The Lord will dispose of us according to his Goodness. Mr. Newton seems to have conceived a great Desire to have us for Neighbours, and I am sure we shall think ourselves highly favoured to be committed to the care of such a Pastor. May we be enabled to hold him in double Honour for his Work's sake, according to the Will of the great Shepherd of us All!

I have a great Regard for Lady Hesketh, a sincere Affection; and am therefore glad of Opportunities to lead her thoughts, as far as the Lord shall enable me, to the Things that belong to her Peace, so that I never write to her without attempting it. But there are wide Gaps in our Correspondence, which nevertheless proceeds after a Fashion.

[1] Newton's letter to C of 14 July (Princeton) contains information on the house in Emberton which ultimately was not rented: 'I am afraid you have thought me negligent, but I could not obtain a definitive answer till today, I am now to inform you that the person from whom I hold my present habitation chooses to return to it, when we quit which I hope will be at Michaelmas. The house in which he at present lives will then be vacant—but by the articles of the Case he is not at liberty to let it without the consent of the owner, tho he may live in it himself; he holds it together with a large parcel of land. . . . It is a much better house than that which we live in & I believe may pass for a very good one—modern built, & sufficiently large I suppose for a family of ten people, with stables & outhouses for a carriage, if needed . . . It is pleasantly situated upon a rising ground, in a decent village, & stands about a measured mile from Olney Church.'

John Newton

from the engraving (1808) by Joseph Collyer after John Russell

I received from her very lately a kind Invitation to Ealing, but Necessity is laid upon me, and I cannot accept those Offers. Though she is every thing that's Aimiable among men, yet I fear the Vail is upon her Heart, for I have never heard her speak Shibboleth plainly, nor does the Abundance of her poor Heart seem to be what it should be. Yet the Lord may have purposes of Grace toward her, which I beseech him to manifest in his own time. She sent me some time since the Stanzas[2] you mention, which I think are exceeding good. My dear Aunt! How lovely must be the Spirits of just men made perfect, since Creatures so lovely in our Eyes, may yet have the Wrath of God abiding on them. The Lord avert it from Her, and number her with the glorious Assembly before his Throne for ever.

Your Affectionate Nephew Wm Cowper.

July 18. 1767.

MRS. MADAN — Monday, 10 August 1767

Address: To / Mrs. Madan in Stafford Row / near the Queen's Gate / Westminster.
Postmarks: 5/O'CLOCK/W, 11/AV, *and* HUNTING/DON
Olney

My dear Aunt,

On Monday last we went to see our Friend Newton at Olney, and to take a View of the Place where we trust the Lord has fix'd the Bounds of our Habitation. One House is fairly and clearly open to us, but it is a Mile distant from Olney Church, and the Walk rough & Stony and liable to Floods, which is a very unfavourable Circum: stance to Mrs. & Miss Unwin, though it would seldom be an Impediment to Me.—Beside this, we hope we have a Chance to succeed Mr. Newton in his present Dwelling, which in every respect will exactly suit us—If we fail there, there is another House in the Town which the Owner of it offers to repair for us.[1] Either of the latter

[2] Unidentified.

[1] This house, which was on 'the Parade . . . on the south side of the Market Place' (Newton to the Earl of Dartmouth, *Historical Manuscript Commission 15th Report*, Appendix, Pt. 1 (Dartmouth MSS.), pp. 183–6) was not ready until 15 Feb. 1768. From Sept. 1767 until 15 Feb. 1768, C and Mrs. Unwin were in two residences: from September until 23 Oct. 1767 they were at the residence the Newtons occupied until the Vicarage was refurbished; they were then at the Vicarage from October until February.

would be preferred by *Us*, but if *the Lord* have appointed the former, it will be our Business to take Possession of it & be thankfull. Indeed I am weary of this Place, more so perhaps than I ought to be: but I want to be with the Lord's People, having great Need of quickening Intercourse and the Communion of his Saints. Possibly, the black and shocking Aspersions which our Neighbours here amuse themselves with casting upon our Names & Conduct, may add to my Impatience to be gone. Things which our Soul abhorrs are imputed to us, and by those who never meet us but with Smiles. This ought not, I know, to disturb us, nor does it much, but it is a Trial, and Trials are seldom agreeable to our Weak & feeble Spirits. On the other Hand, the Lord seems to have filled the Hearts of Mr. & Mrs. Newton with Christian Tenderness & Affection towards us, the Number of the Flock there is considerable, and they all dwell together as becomes Brethren, in Unity. So that the Lord seems to be drawing us out of this Wilderness with one Hand, & driving us out with the other. So be it, O thou God of our Salvation, only let thy Presence go along with us, for men & means are Nothing without Thee!

I send you an Extract of a Letter from Unwin at Bristol, giving an Account of the Death of a Child at Clifton about a Mile from Bristol, the Son of the Clerk of that Parish. I think it will please you.—He died aged 8 Years & 8 Months. About 2 Months before his Death, he was for some time in the Church Yard with his Father, a day or two after he said to his Mother. 'Mother I was so happy t'other day in the Church Yard that I did not know what to do, or how to Account for it. I was forced to say, Praised be God!'—On Sunday Morning about One o'clock he was suddenly taken ill with a violent Pain in his Bowels; his Sufferings were extremely Acute during his whole Illness, which lasted little more than 48 Hours, During which time at Intervals he would pray with great Fervency. To his Nurse on Monday morning early, he said, 'Nanny, I have nothing more to do with Books and Learning now—I have laid 'em all aside.' Even in his Rovings which were frequent, he was either talking of his Books, or praying earnestly & Singing Hymns. On Monday he desir'd his Mother to read to him the 21st. Psalm, or rather, said He, let Me read it. He took the Book in hand, but his Eyes were already dim—He then desired his Mother again to read it, & afterwards to Pray with him. She did so, & he Joined with Fervor. At One time he lay quite still & calm. My dear, said his Mother, how do you do?

Are you in Pain? Oh no, said he, I am very easy and very well. On Tuesday Night about 2 Hours before he died, his Mother was for applying fresh warm Flannels to his Bowels; upo[n][2] to[uc]hing him, he said, Oh you disturb me in my Journey. [About] 2 Hours after he died, without a Struggle or a [Groa]n, in the Midst of a Hymn.—The Death of this Child made me take particular Notice of 2 Stanzas of a H[ymn in] Dodderidge's Collection, which I met with Yesterday.

Thy Saints in earlier Life remov'd
  In sweeter Accents sing,
And bless the Swiftness of their Flight,
  That bore them to their King.
The Burthens of a lengthen'd Day
  With Patience we would bear,
'Till Ev'ning's welcome Hour shall shew
  We were our Master's Care.[3]

Our Friends here define a Methodist to be—One who committs every Sin he can think of and invents New Ones every Day,—That he may be saved by Faith.

How truly pitiable is their Blindness & Enmity to the Truth!

Yours my Dear Aunt, in a Way they little dream of
Wm Cowper.

Augt. 10. 1767.

N:B: I had always rather have double Letters than single ones[4] from my Christian Friends, whether frank'd or not.

[2] MS. torn at the seal.

[3] The extract is from Hymn 'CCXXXIV. CHRIST's mysterious Conduct to be unfolded hereafter. John xiii. 7.' in Philip Doddridge's *Hymns Founded on Various Texts in the Holy Scriptures* (3rd ed. 1766), pp. 206–7.

[4] A single letter would have been written on one sheet of paper sealed; a double letter consisted of two sheets of paper, the outer one sealed. Since the charge for a single letter not exceeding one post stage would have been 1*d.*, a double letter would have cost 2*d.* Postage was collected from the recipient unless the letter had been franked.

JOSEPH HILL — Saturday, 12 September 1767

Address: Mr. Joseph Hill / at the Chancery Office / London.[1]
Cowper Johnson

Dear Sephus,

A Man possessed of Lands in right of his Wife, dies, leaving his Son Executor.[2] Do the Arrears of Rent down to the time of his Death belong to the Widow or the Son?

I am so important a Character in the present Circumstances of our Drama,[3] that I can't possibly be spared, and should undoubtedly turn the Tables upon you by inviting You to Olney, had we any Accommodation for you, but we are obliged to the Hospitality of a Friend[4] for our own, & probably shall be so till Christmas.

You will oblige me by a speedy Answer to the above Question, & by delivering my Affectionate Respects to your Mother & Sisters.

Yours my dear Sephus
Wm Cowper.

Sepr 12. /67.

JOSEPH HILL — Monday, 21 September 1767

Cowper Johnson

My dear Joe,

I return you Thanks for your Information in the Law Matter, & shall be obliged to you for further assurance when you can consult your Authorities.

Many more Thanks are due to you for the tender and friendly manner in which you bring me acquainted with the Distress that attends my circumstances. I beg my Friend, that you will no longer make any Objections to the Sale of the 100£. I cannot be easy 'till that is done; My Peace of Mind is concerned in it. Not because I suspect you of the least Anxiety about Payment, but because I

1 Olney Address.

2 The man in question is Morley Unwin, and the reference is to his will (P.R.O. PROB. 11/931) by which he names his son William sole executor.

3 The removal to Olney, 14 Sept.

4 John Newton. See n. 1, C to Mrs. Madan, 10 Aug. 1767.

abhor the Thought of trespassing upon the Goodness of a faithfull Friend.—My Brother has a Letter of Attorney already to impower him to receive the Interest; but I beleive it extends no farther. Send me one therefore to impower You to sell the Principal and I shall be easy; As to any future Exigences, I am entirely so. My Expences hereafter will be so much reduced in some capital Articles that I have not the least remaining Doubt, but that the Income of my future Years will be much more than sufficient for the Demands of them. I might say something of this sort before perhaps unadvisedly, and the Event proves it to have been so, but Now I say it upon good Warrant & can not be mistaken. I should wish if it can be so managed that the Sale of the Stock might be kept Secret from my Family, because it would probably alarm their Fears upon my Account, and possibly once more awaken their Resentment—But the Lord's Will be done, whatever it be—If they must know it, you will do me the Kindness to assure them from me, that I have taken such Order about my Circumstances that there can be no Danger of Exceding them hereafter; Only I beg to be excused descending to particulars. Once more I entreat it as a Favour, (and shall consider it as a New Proof of your Attention to my Happiness) that you will consent to the Sale of the Stock, and take measures for that purpose immediately. It cannot possibly be an Inconvenience to me, nor can I possibly in any Emergency whatever, make a better Use of it.

My Love to your Mother & Sisters.

Yours ever Wm Cowper.

Olney Sepr. 21. 1767.

MRS. MADAN — Saturday, 26 September 1767

Address: To / Mrs. Madan in Stafford Row / near the Queen's House / Westminster.
Postmarks: 5/O'CLOCK/W, 28/SE, *and* OULNEY
Olney

My dear Aunt,

It is fit I should acknowledge the Goodness of the Lord in bringing me to this Place, abounding with Palm Trees and Wells of living Water.[1] The Lord put it into my Heart to desire to partake of his

[1] Song of Songs 4: 15.

Ordinances and to dwell with his People, and has graciously given me my Heart's Desire: Nothing can exceed the Kindness and Hospitality with which we are received here by his dear Servant Newton: and to be brought under the Ministry of so Wise and faithfull a Steward of his Holy Mysteries is a Blessing for which I can never be sufficiently thankfull. May our heavenly Father grant that our Souls may thrive and flourish in some Proportion to the Abundant Means of Grace we enjoy: for the whole Day is but one continued Opportunity either of seeking him, or conversing about the things of his Kingdom. I find it a difficult matter when surrounded with the Blessings of Providence, to remember that I seek a Country, and that this is not the Place of my Rest. God glorifies himself by bringing Good out of Evil, but it is the Reproach of Man that he is able and always inclined to produce Evil out of the greatest Blessings. The Lord has dealt graciously with me since I came, and I trust I have in two Instances had much delightfull Communion with him: Yet this Liberty of Access was indulged to me in such a way, as to teach me at the same time his great Care that I might not turn it to my Prejudice. I expected that in some Sermon or Exposition I should find him, and that the Lips of this excellent Minister would be the Instrument by which the Lord would work upon & soften my obdurate Heart. But he saw my proneness to idolize the Means, and to praise the Creature more than the Creator, & therefore though he gave me the thing I hoped for, yet he conveyed it to me in a way which I did not look to. On the last Sabbath Morning at a Prayer Meeting before Service, while the poor Folks were singing a Hymn and my Vile Thoughts were rambling to the Ends of the Earth, a single Sentence (And is there no Pity in Jesus's Breast?)[2] seized my Attention at once, and my Heart within me seemed to return Answer, Yes, or I had never been here. The Sweetness of this Visit lasted almost thro' the Day, and I was once more enabled to weep under a Sense of the Mercies of a God in Jesus.—On Thursday Morning I attended a Meeting of Children, and found that Passage 'Out of the Mouth of Babes & Sucklings thou hast ordained Praise'[3] Verified in a Sense I little thought of. For at almost every Word they spoke in answer to the several Questions proposed to them, my Heart burned within me, and melted into Tears of Gratitude and Love.

[2] We have not been able to locate this hymn.

[3] Matthew 21 : 16.

I thought the Singularity of this Dispensation worth your Notice, and having communicated it, am in a manner obliged to break off rather abruptly. Mr. Newton has just brought me one of Martin's Pamphlets,[4] which makes it impossible for me to write any longer. Pray tell him he is a bit of a Traytor for not sending my Narrative[5] at the same time with his own, for I want much to shew it to Mr. and Mrs. Newton.

Yours my dear Aunt affectionately
Wm Cowper.

Olney
Sepe. 26. 1767.
Mrs. Newton begs to be remember'd to you.

JOSEPH HILL — Saturday, 10 October 1767

Address: To / Mr. Joseph Hill / at Wargrave / near Twyford / Berks.
Postmarks: 12/OC *and* OULNEY
Cowper Johnson

Olney Oct: 10. 67.

Dear Joe,

I am obliged to you for complying with my Request, and shall be glad to have the Matter expedited as fast as may be.—One more Law Question and I beleive the last.—A man holds Lands in right of his Wife, the rents payable half yearly, viz at Lady Day and Michaelmas, dies in July. Are not the rising Rents the Property of the Widow?[1] I mean the Rent of the whole last half Year. You are a better Counsellor than I was, but I think you have much such a Client in me, as I had in Dick Harcourt.[2] Much good may do you with me.

Neither have I any Map to consult at present, but by what Remembrance I have of the Situation of this Place in the last I saw, it lies at the Northernmost Point of the County. We are just five Miles

[4] Probably *An Answer to . . . A Faithful Narrative of Facts, Relative to the Late Presentation of Mr. H - - - - - - s To the Rectory of Al - - - - - - le, In Northamptonshire . . .* (1767). This cannot have been issued before the beginning of September since a letter of 29 Aug. 1767 is printed on p. 31.

[5] Martin Madan had been entrusted with C's Memoir.

[1] Another legal question arising out of Morley Unwin's death.

[2] See n. 3, C to Duncombe, 31 Dec. 1757.

beyond Newport Pagnel. I am willing to suspect that you make this Enquiry with a *View* to an *Interview* when Time shall serve. We may possibly be settled in our Own House in about a Month, where so good a Friend of mine will be extremely welcome to Mrs. Unwin; We shall have a Bed and a warm Fire Side at your Service if you can come before next Summer, and if not, a Parlour that looks the North Wind full in the Face, where you may be as cool as in the Groves of Valombrosa.[3]

Yours my Dear Sephus affectionately ever

Wm Cowper.

The Stock is in the three per Cent Consolidated. You may send the Letter of Attorney by the Wagon from the George in Smithfield. It sets out on Tuesday Morning Early. But upon Recollection it had better come by the Post.

MRS. MADAN — Thursday, 15 October 1767

Address: To / Mrs. Madan Stafford Row / near the Queens House / Westminster
Postmarks: 16/OC *and* OULNEY
Olney

My dear Aunt,

I should sooner have acknowledg'd your last Favour, had not many Circumstances concurred to put by my Intention to do it from time to time. We are many of us pack'd together in a small House, our own not being yet ready for us, and though every thing that is not in a manner impracticable, is done to accomodate us, yet Convenience and Opportunity for writing are the scarcer upon that Account. I have taken a Journey too since I received it with Mr. Newton, to a Place called Dunton about 25 Miles from hence, and within about 12 of Berkhamsted. Our Visit was to the Revd. Mr. Moody,[1] an old Gospel Minister, whom Mr. Newton assists annually with a Sermon. From his Orchard I could see some Hills within a small Distance of my Native Place, which formerly I have often Visited. The Sight

[3] A village in Tuscany beautifully situated in the Apennine forest at an altitude of 4,000 feet.

[1] The Revd. James Moody (*c.* 1694–1772) of Simpson, Bucks., matriculated from Christ's College, Cambridge, on 17 Dec. 1711 and received his Bachelor's degree in 1715. He was rector of Dunton from 1717 until his death.

of them affected me much, and awakened in me a lively Recollection of the Goodness of the Lord in caring for and Protecting me in those dark and dangerous Days of Ignorance and Enmity against him, and his own Blessed Word teaches me to draw an Inference from these Premises of more Worth than Millions of Gold and Silver; If while I was an Enemy he Loved Me, much more reason have I to rest assured of his Love, being reconciled by the Blood of his Son. I found myself at this Place not entirely among Strangers as I had expected to be. The Old Gentleman was formerly acquainted with my Father, both at the University and at Berkhamsted, and his Wife travelled with me from thence to London in the Stage Coach above 20 Years since. It pleased the Lord to take Occasion by these seemingly trivial Circumstances, to make my Childhood and Youth in their most affecting Colours pass in review before me, and these were followed by such a tender Recollection of my dear Father and all his Kindness to me, the Aimiableness and Sweetness of his Temper & Character, that I went out into the Orchard and burst forth into Praise and Thanksgiving to God for having made me the Son of a Parent whose Remembrance was so sweet to me. I have frequently thought (and expressed myself with more Anxiety than perhaps was right) upon the Subject of his State towards God, at the Time of his Dissolution. I was not with him, and they who were, were not likely to be very observant of any Evangelical Words that might possibly fall from his Lips in his last moments. He was every thing that is excellent and Praiseworthy towards Man, but to One who has been enabled to see Jesus as the *Alone* Saviour, this is no Evidence of the Acceptance of any Man. I am willing to hope, that the Lord who pities all our Infirmities, and knows all our Desires, was pleased to fill my Heart and my Mouth with Thanksgivings on his behalf, that I might have a comfortable Expectation of meeting him before the Throne hereafter. I could hardly help giving Thanks to Jesus that he had numbered him with his redeemed People, though Fearfullness to offend, and a Consciousness that I had no right to pry into the Secrets of the Almighty, or to expect Satisfaction upon such a Subject, restrained me.—I would not build Hay or Stubble[2] upon this or any other Experience, nor lay more upon it than it will

[2] Although we have not located this expression in any dictionary of proverbs, *O.E.D.* cites Richardson in *Clarissa* using a similar expression ('. . . one day you will be convinced, that what you call friendship, is chaff and stubble.') in what seems a proverbial context.

bear, but I am willing to Hope the best concerning him, to wait patiently for greater Certai[nty in][3] a Life to come, and in the mean while to rest satis[fied] that the Judge of All the Earth will do right.

I shall very gladly write to Mrs. Maitland as soon as we are settled, and if possible before. Pray give my Love to her, and assure her that I will take the earliest Opportunity of doing it. My Cousin Maria, will think I have quite forgot her, but I only wait to get into our own House, when I shall be more at large and less liable to Interruptions.—Mrs. Unwin presents her Respects to you, and thinks herself much obliged to you for the Passage relating to her in your last.—I am, my Dear Aunt,

Your Affectionate Nephew
Wm Cowper.

Olney
Oct. 15.—67.

MRS. MADAN *c.* November 1767

Olney (*copy*)[1]

. . . I thank you for the history of the two minikin saints of ——.[2] What numbers are there, who steal out of this life into glory, who do but just touch the cup of affliction with their lips, and go immediately to the rivers of pleasure, which are at God's right hand forevermore! I think they are two of the most remarkable instances I have heard of, and younger than any of Janeway's Collection.[3] They gave me not a little pleasure, but Mrs. U—— much more, whose heart was in a livelier frame than mine, and better disposed to rejoice at the sound of such wonderful salvation.

Ingratitude to the Author of all my mercies is my continual

[3] MS. torn at the seal.

---

[1] The MS. copy, which is undated, is No. 7 in Mrs. Cowper's Commonplace Book, and it is placed between her copies of C's letters to Mrs. Madan of 15 Oct. and 10 Dec. 1767. We have therefore assigned this letter to Nov. 1767.

[2] Not identified.

[3] *A Token for Children; being an Exact Account of the Conversion, Holy and Exemplary Lives and Joyful Deaths, of several Young Children* (2 vols., 1671, 1672), was frequently reprinted in the eighteenth century.

burthen, yet I do not groan under it as I ought, and wish to do. My spirit is dull and heavy in prayer, slow in meditation, and I have but little sensible communion with my Almighty Redeemer. Yet I am supported secretly, and my enemy doth not triumph over me; a firm belief that none can perish that have an all-powerful Saviour on their side, though it is not always attended with sensible consequences, is yet always a rock that neither wind nor flood can overturn. Lord increase in me this precious faith!

Worst of all things that has breath,
Bondsman born to sin and death,
Lo! I come to Glory brought,
By the mercies Thou hast wrought.

Snatch'd from never-ending doom,
Freed from Death and Hell I come,
Antient of eternal days,
God and Man! be Thine the praise.

Alas! My dear aunt, there is more of the head than heart in all I write; and in all I do towards God, but I shall be sincere in praising Him, when I shall see Him as He is. The Lord bless you continually!

&c. &c.

JOSEPH HILL — Tuesday, 10 November 1767

Cowper Johnson

Dear Joe,

Inclosed you have the Letter of Attorney. I shall be glad if you will find an Opportunity of sending me Six Guineas in a Parcel by the Olney Wagon which sets out from the George in Smithfield early on Tuesday Morning, therefore it must be sent to the Inn on Monday Night.

It seems to me, (though it did not occurr to me at first) that you may be drawn into Circumstances disagreeable to your Delicacy by being laid under the Restraint of Secrecy with respect to the Sale of this Money. I desire therefore that if any Questions are asked about the Manner in which my Arrears to you have been discharged, you will declare it at once.

Think a little my dear Friend! of a Subject we corresponded upon about 2 Years since. We are apt to let Years pass over us without attending to it, though it is of the last Importance. It was not without many dreadfull Afflictions and a deep Sense of the Wrath of God against Sin, that I was brought to a Serious Hearing of the Word of God. Depend upon it, it is well worth your while to enquire into these things with diligence and earnest Prayer for the Assistance of that Spirit which is promised to those who Ask it. You may escape much Anguish even in this Life by so doing, and get a lively and Animating Hope of future Mercies and Blessings in a Life to come, which will make you happy in every Circumstance. What I tell you is no Fable—I tell it you because I know that your everlasting Interests are at Stake, and because I have an Affection for you. Remember that Morality has two parts, Our Duty towards God, as well as towards our Neighbour. When these are rightly performed they constitute true Scriptural Holiness, without which no Man shall see the Lord. Either without the Other, is but a Pretence, a Broken Reed which will pierce the Hand that leans upon it.[1]—Excuse my Freedom, the Weight and Value of these things is infinite, and must be my Apology, and perhaps I am the only Friend you have in the World that will write thus to you, or give you the least Hint of their Importance.[2]

Yours with my Love to your Family

Wm Cowper.

Olney
Nove. 10. 67.

MRS. MADAN — Thursday, 10 December 1767

Address: To / Mrs. Madan / Stafford Row / near the Queens House / Westminster
Postmarks: 11/DE *and* OULNEY
Charles Ryskamp

Dear Aunt,

I should not have suffered your last kind Letter to have laid by me so long unanswer'd, had it not been for many Hindrances and

[1] Isaiah 36: 6.

[2] There is a note in Lady Hesketh's hand at the top of the letter: 'This is a charming letter full of good Sense Piety & Truth, without any of the methodistical Cant wch. I dislike extremely—'.

especially One, which has engaged much of my Attention. My dear Friend Mrs. Unwin, whom the Lord gave me to be a Comfort to me in that Wilderness from which he has just delivered me, has been for many Weeks past in so declining a way, and has suffered so many Attacks of the most excruciating Pain, that I have hardly been able to keep alive the faintest Hope of her Recovery. I know that our God heareth Prayer, and I know that he hath opened mine and many Hearts amongst this People to pray for her. Here lies my chief Support, without which I should look upon myself as already deprived of her. Again when I consider the great Meetness to which the Lord has wrought her for the Inheritance in Light, her most exemplary Patience under the sharpest Sufferings, her truly Christian Humility and Resignation, I am more than ever inclined to beleive that her Hour is come. Let me engage your Prayers for Her, and for Me. You know what I have most need of upon an Occasion like this: Pray that I may receive it at His Hands from whom every good and perfect Gift proceeds. She is the chief Blessing I have met with in my Journey since the Lord was pleased to call me, and I hope the Influence of her edifying and Excellent Example will never leave me. Her Illness has been a sharp Trial to me—Oh that it may have a sanctified Effect, that I may rejoice to Surrender up to the Lord my dearest Comforts the Moment he shall require them. Oh! for no Will but the Will of my Heavenly Father! Doctor Cotton for whose advice we went together to St. Albans about a Month since, seemed to have so little Expectation that Medicine could help her, that he might be said to give her over. He prescribed however, but she has hardly been able to take his Medicines. Her Disorder is a Nervous Atrophy attended with violent Spasms of the Chest and Throat, and This is a bad Day with her; worse than common.

I return you many Thanks for the Verses you favor'd me with, which speak sweetly the Language of a Christian Soul. I wish I could pay you in kind, but must be contented to pay you in the best kind I can. I began to compose them Yesterday Morning before Daybreak, but fell asleep at the End of the two first Lines, when I awaked again the third and fourth were whisper'd to my Heart in a way which I have often experienced.

> Oh for a closer Walk with God,
>   A calm & heav'nly Frame,

A Light to shine upon the Road
That leads me to the Lamb!

Where is the Blessedness I knew
When first I saw the Lord?
Where is the Soul:refreshing View
Of Jesus in his Word?

What peacefull Hours I then enjoy'd,
How sweet their Mem'ry still!
But they have left an Aching Void
The World can never fill.

Return, O Holy Dove, Return,
Sweet Messenger of Rest,
I hate the Sins that made thee mourn
And drove thee from my Breast.

The dearest Idol I have known,
Whate'er that Idol be,
Help me to tear it from Thy Throne,
And worship Only Thee.

Then shall my Walk be close with God,
Calm and serene my Frame,
Then purer Light shall mark the Road
That leads me to the Lamb.[1]

Yours my dear Aunt in the Bands of that Love which cannot be quenched

Wm Cowper.

Olney. Dece. 10. 67.

1 'Walking with God', based upon Genesis 5 : 24, appeared as No. 3 in the *Olney Hymns* Book I.

MRS. MADAN — Friday, 15 January 1768

Olney (*copy*)[1]

My dear Aunt

I put off writing to you from day to day in hopes, that I shall find a subject in my own experience that may make it worth your while to hear from me. I would not always be complaining of barrenness and deadness, yet alas! I have little else to write about. The Lord has given me so many blessings in possession, and enabled me to hope assuredly for such unspeakable things when the great work of redemption shall be effectually completed in me that wheresoever I look, I see something that reminds me of ingratitude. If I look behind me, I see dangers, and precipices, and the bottomless pit, from whence He has plucked me with an outstretched arm, made bare for my deliverance. If I look forward, I see the sure portion of His people, an everlasting inheritance in light, and the covenant that secures it, sealed with the blood of Jesus. My present condition too is full of tokens of His love: the things which others may reckon in the number of their common mercies are not so to me, at least ought not to be such in my esteem. The breath I draw, and the free excercise of my senses, He has not only given to me, but restored them when I had deservedly forfeited both; and not only restored them to me, but accompanied them with such additional mercies, as can alone make them true and real blessings, faith in the Lord Jesus Christ as the only Saviour, and a desire to employ them, and every gift I receive from Him to the glory of His name. In the day of my first love I could not have enumerated those instances of His goodness without tears, but now, my reflections upon them serve rather to convince me of the dreadful obduracy of my nature, and afford me even a sensible proof that nothing less than the breath of the Almighty Spirit can soften it. But blessed be the Lord. Our anchor of hope is fastened on good ground, not in our own righteousness, but in that of Jesus: and every view of our own unworthiness is sanctified to us, and becomes a solid blessing if it drives us closer to our only refuge. Since I wrote the above, I have been taking a walk, and from my going out, to my coming in, I have been mourning over (I am afraid I ought to say repining at) my great insensibility. I began with

[1] Mrs. Cowper's Commonplace Book, 53–5: 'Lett. 9. dated Ol—y Jan. 15. 1768.'

these reflections soon after I rose this morning, and my attempt to write to you has furnished me with additional evidences of it. I profess myself a servant of God, I am writing to a servant of God, and about the things of God, and yet can hardly get forward so as to fill my paper. I can only tell you my dear Aunt that I love you, and I hope too for the Lord's sake; but I cannot *speak* any more than I can *do* the things that I would. I shall only add at this time that I am

dear aunt
Your Affectionate
&c. &c

JOSEPH HILL — Thursday, 21 January 1768

Address: Mr. Joseph Hill / at the Chancery Office / London.[1]
Cowper Johnson

Olney Jan:21. 68.

Dear Sephus,

The Notes arrived safe last Night. We rejoice that the Venison proved good. Pray send me Word in your next whether Grainger the Taylor[2] is dead or alive. So much for the needfull. You are always busy, and I am just going to be so, which will make Brevity and Conciseness convenient to us both.

Yours faithfully & truly
Wm Cowper.

MRS. MADAN — Tuesday, 1 March 1768

Address: To / Mrs. Madan / Stafford Row near the / Queen's House, / Westminster
Postmarks: 5/O'CLOCK/W, NEWPORT / PAGNELL, *and* illegible
Olney

My dear Aunt,

Your Silence makes me fear for your Health. If it be owing to Illness, may the Lord sanctify it to you, and abundantly compensate to you all your bodily Sufferings by the Manifestation of his Gracious Presence.

[1] Olney Address. [2] Unidentified.

1 March 1768

We are at last settled in our own Mansion. The Lord provided it for us, and we hope has said concerning it—Peace be to this House. He has called both our Servants, and brought them I trust to an effectual Acquaintance with the Savior and themselves since we came to Olney. The Man Servant you may remember is the same that attended me at St. Albans. What various Methods does the good Shepherd use, and how wonderfull is he in many of those Dispensations by which he brings his People within the Sound of the Gospel.

We had no sooner taken Possession of our own House, than I found myself called to lead the Pray'rs of the Family. A formidable Undertaking you may imagine to a Temper & Spirit like mine. I trembled at the Apprehension of it, and was so dreadfully harrass'd in the Conflict I sustain'd upon this Occasion in the first Week, that my Health was not a little affected by it. But there was no Remedy, and I hope the Lord brought me to that point, to chuse Death rather than a Retreat from Duty. In my first Attempt he was sensibly present with me, and has since favour'd me with very perceptible Assistance. My Fears begin to wear off, I get rather more Liberty of Speech at least, if not of Spirit, and have some Hope that having open'd my Mouth he will never suffer it to be closed again, but rather give Increase of Utterance and Zeal to serve him. How much of that Monster Self has He taken Occasion to shew me by this Incident. Pride, Ostentation and Vain Glory have always been my Hindrance in these Attempts. These lie at the Root of that Evil Tree which the world Good natur'dly calls Bashfullness. Evil indeed, in the Character of a Disciple of Christ. May our gracious Teacher, Mortify them all to Death, and never leave me 'till he has made the Dumb to speak, and the Stammering Tongue like the Pen of a ready Writer!

My dear Friend Mrs. Unwin is wonderfully restor'd. Her Recovery, of which there seems to be no doubt, is as extraordinary and as evident an Answer to Pray'r, as any that has fallen within my Experience. The Lord make me thankfull to him for the Continuance of this and all his Mercies, which I deserve every day to be deprived of, but he is an unchangeable God, & delights in shewing Mercy.

I am ashamed of my Behavior to Maria, whose kind Enquirys after Mrs. U: I have never yet Answer'd. I shall write to her soon in all Probability, and beg that if you have an Opportunity in the mean time, you will present my Love to her & tell her so.

Remember me to Mrs. Maitland & beleive me my dear Aunt, Yours Affectionately

Wm Cowper.

Olney. Mar: 1.—68.

MRS. COWPER Friday, 15 April 1768

Address: To / Mrs. Cowper.
Olney

Dear Cousin,

Your Letter brought me the first News of Mr Cowper's Success at Hartford.[1] I heartily wish that All the Members of a certain August Assembly, were equally worthy of their Office and the Confidence reposed in them: which will be the case when they are all nominated and chosen in the same disinterested manner, out of mere respect to their Honour and Integrity, and never before.—I was never much skilled in Politics, and am now less versed in them than ever, the Olney Folks are all mere Ignoramuses upon this Subject, and the Wind seldom blows any body this way, that knows more of the matter than themselves. But this I know: that when I see a great Building full of Cracks, weather beaten and mouldering apace, and much declined from the Perpendicular, the Downfall of that House is not far distant, unless it be set right again by an extraordinary Repair. This is too much the case, I am afraid, with our poor Country. I am neither a Prophet nor the Son of a Prophet, but I know that the natural Tendency of Iniquity is to Ruin, and every Kingdom that has fallen in pieces in the past Ages of the World, gives Testimony to the Truth of the Assertion. May God raise up many to intercede with him in behalf of a Sinfull Land, for I am sure if the Pray'rs of his own People, those that Love and Fear him, do not prevail for a Blessing, not all the Contrivances of the Wisest Heads amongst us will be able to divert the Storm that threatens us.

My dear Cousin! How happy are they who have been taught of God that this is not their Rest, that here they have no continuing

[1] Major William Cowper. He was returned unopposed for Hertford borough in 1768. In the House, he voted with the Administration on Wilkes's expulsion and on the Middlesex election. There is no record of his having spoken in the House. See Namier and Brooke, *House of Commons, 1754–1790* (1964), ii. 266.

City![2] Who can look from this Mass of perishing things to a City which hath Foundations, whose Builder and Maker is God.[3] Whose Hearts glow with a comfortable Hope, that amongst those many Mansions which Jesus tells us are in his Father's House,[4] there is One reserved for them: where no Fear of Dissolution and Ruin shall ever find them out, where nothing shall enter that can defile them, consequently nothing that can grieve them, and of which Jesus himself, the unchangeable and everlasting Savior, is the chief Corner Stone. Blessed are we indeed, if God has given us this precious Hope through Faith in his Son's Name, this Hope that purifies the Soul even as He is pure, makes All Sin hatefull, and All that is Holy and according to the Will of God, lovely and desireable in our Eyes, and is day by day bringing us to a greater Meetness for an Inheritance among the Saints in Light. May You and I and all dear to us be made intimately acquainted here with the things that belong to our Peace, have more and more Experience of the transforming Power of the Grace of Christ, and follow him through this poor fleeting World, that we may rejoice with him for ever and reign with him in his own heavenly Kingdom.

I beg you will give my Love to my Friend the new Member, and to all my Cousins great and small—& beleive me Affectionately Yours[5]
Olney April 15.—68.

JOSEPH HILL — Tuesday, 3 May 1768

Address: Mr. Joseph Hill / at the / Chancery Office / London.[1]
Cowper Johnson

Dear Joe,

I shall be obliged to you if you will send me a Ten pound Note by the first Opportunity, and at the same time I shall be glad to be informed of the State of my Finances. The last time I wrote, I beg'd you would be so good as to tell me whether Grainger is to be

[2] Hebrews 13 : 14. [3] Hebrews 11 : 10. [4] John 14 : 2.

[5] The signature is cut away, and the following note is added: 'NB The Signature cut off to form part of a Collection of autographs of Emminent Authors. Charles Cowper Mar. 1814.—'.

[1] Olney Address.

found above Ground or no, if he is, whether he lives where he did or has changed his Dwelling, and if not, where his Executors, Administrators or Assigns[2] are to be met with. You will oblige me too, and so will your little tiney Mother, if you will favour me with Mrs. Rebecca Cowper's[3] Receipt to Pickle Cabbage.—My Respects await on *Her* (viz your Mother, not mine.)[4] and your Sisters—You will ascribe my Dryness and Conciseness in the Epistolary way, to almost a total Disuse of my Pen; My Youth and my Scribbling Vein are gone together, and unless they had been better employed, it is fit they should.

Yours affectionately
Wm Cowper.

May. 3.—68

JOSEPH HILL Saturday, 7 May 1768

Cowper Johnson

Dear Joe,

Thanks for the Receipt and for the Note. When you come this way next, I hope your Business will not be so impatient. We can shew you a beautifull Country, tho' not much celebrated in Song, and a fine long Town, pretty clean in Summertime and full of poor Folks. My Love to Mrs. Doe,[1] and thanks for the Exercise of her transcribing Abilities, not forgetting the rest of your Houshold.

I shall want to draw for 20£ next Month, and intend to leave the Remainder by way of Nest Egg.

Yours affectionately
Wm Cowper.

Olney
May 7.—68.

[2] Assigns are 'Assignees; those to whom property shall have been transferred. Now seldom used except in the phrase in deeds, "heirs, administrators, and assigns." ': *Black's Law Dictionary* (St. Paul, 1968), p. 154.

[3] C's stepmother, who had died in 1762.

[4] The last five words were inserted by C beneath 'on Her'.

[1] Probably Hill's mother, with his thanks for transcribing the 'Receipt to Pickle Cabbage'. Hill did not marry until 1771.

MRS. MADAN Saturday, 11 June 1768

Address: To / Mrs. Madan / Stafford Row near the / Queen's House / Westminster
Postmarks: 5/O'CLOCK/W, *and* 13/IV
Olney

My dear Aunt,

After so long a Silence to write only because I have need of your Assistance, is very Selfish and like Myself: But so it is—If I remember right, I wrote you word some time since that we thought ourselves happy that the Lord had been pleased to call both our Servants to the Knowledge of himself, upon our first Settlement at Olney. The Man Servant stands fast, and his Case has been from the Beginning I trust clearly a Gracious one. The Maid, whose Experiences were at the best of a mixt Nature, has since fallen away so dreadfully as to occasion much doubt whether she ever had any grace at all, and we have been forced to dismiss her at the shortest Notice. The poor Town of Olney furnishes nothing like a Servant to supply her Place. If you know or should hear of any one that is fit to be Cook in a small Family, and that will accept of a Place where there is no other Maid Servant kept, we shall be exceedingly obliged to you if you will direct her hither. Her Work will be very easy, as we have no Dining or Supping Company, and wash nothing at home but Table and Kitchen Linen. In case of Illness or any other Hindrance she will always be sure of Occasional Help. In short, she must be, as Mrs. Unwin tells me the Term is, a Maid of all Work. There will be no Difficulties made about Wages, and she will be paid for her Journey down. Only she must expect no Vales.[1]

I had a Letter from Lady Hesketh by the last Post to inform me that she had just read my Narrative. She seems to have been much Affected by it, and I should have been very happy if she had been enabled to learn from it the only Lesson it is intended to teach, the Sovereignty of God's free Grace in the deliverance of a Sinfull Soul from the nethermost Hell. But the Lord has not seen fit to bless it to that Effect, for she says she cannot see how such a Life as mine had been could *Merit* such bitter Sufferings at the Hand of a Mercifull God, and bestows all the Honour of the Repentance that follow'd them entirely upon Myself. How is the Work of the Redeemer

[1] Possibly C is referring to a settlement given to an employee leaving service. *O.E.D.* defines vale as a farewell.

conceal'd from the Natural [eyes][2] so that though his Grace be as evidently display'd in the Salvation of a lost Sinner, as his Power is in the Works of Creation, not a Beam breaks through to enlighten it, 'till his own Hand takes away the Veil!

My dear Aunt, beleive me your

very Affectionate Nephew
Wm Cowper.

Olney
June 11.—68.

MRS. MADAN Saturday, 18 June [1768]

Address: To / Mrs. Madan / Stafford Row near / the Queen's House / Westminster
Postmarks: 5/O'CLOCK/W, 20/IV, *and* OULNEY
Olney

Thank you my dear Aunt, for the trouble you are so kind as to take to furnish us with a Servant.[1] Mrs. Unwin begs I would present her Respects to you, and assure you of the Sense she has of your Kindness upon the Occasion.—I forgot in my last to mention one Qualification in the Servant Mrs. Unwin wants, viz. that she must be able to get up small Linen. As to Wages, Mrs. Unwin would be willing to give 8£ a Year, but not more, as that far exceeds the Wages of any Servant in this Place. We would rather leave it to the Lord to send us whom he pleases, than insist upon having a converted Person. Who knows but he may take Occasion by this Opportunity to bring a stray Sheep Home to the Fold, and add One to the Number of his People.

She must come to Newport by the Northampton Stage which puts up at the George in Smithfield. Newport is 5 Miles from Olney. If we know of her Coming beforehand Mrs. Unwin will send a person to meet her.[2]

I know not by what means Lady Hesketh heard that there was such a thing in the World as my Narrative; but the News of it having reached her, she wrote to me to beg a Sight of it. At first I was very

[2] MS. torn at the seal.

---

[1] Mary Powel, who was to prove unsatisfactory (see C to Mrs. Madan, 9 July 1768).
[2] This travel information was added by C at the side of the first paragraph.

unwilling to shew it to her, but having consulted with Mr. Newton about the Propriety of doing so, and finding Him of Opinion that it might be done safely, I consented; but restrained it absolutely to her own Perusal, and she assures me no Eye has seen it but her own. I have always thought it unfit to be trusted in the Hands of an unenlighten'd Person, the Lord having dealt with me in a way so much out of the common Course of his Proceeding, nor do I intend that any such shall hereafter read it. However, if she has got no Light from it, I do not perceive that she has been Stumbled by it, and it may possibly at some future time be made usefull to her. Temporal Trouble is often the Forerunner of Spiritual; and I pray the Lord to sanctify her Sufferings to her, that it may be so with her.

We have had a Holiday Week at Olney. The Association of Baptist Ministers[3] met here on Wednesday. We had three Sermons from them that day, and One on Thursday, besides Mr. Newton's in the Evening. One of the Preachers was Mr. Booth,[4] who has lately published an excellent Work called the Reign of Grace. He was bred a Weaver, and has been forced to work with his Hands hitherto for the Maintenance of himself and a large Family. But the Lord who has given him excellent Endowments, has now called him from the small Congregation he minister'd to in Nottinghamshire, to supply Mr. Burford's[5] Place in London. It was a comfortable Sight to see thirteen Gospel Ministers together. Most of them either Preach'd or Pray'd a[nd][6] All that did so approved themselves sound in the Word and Doctrine, whence a good Presumption arises in favour of the rest. I should be glad if the Partition Wall between Christians of different Denominations would every where fall down flat as it has done at Olney. The Dissenters here, most of them at least who are serious,

[3] The Particular or Calvinistic Baptists 'except for their insistence on believers' Baptism, are doctrinally and liturgically indistinguishable from the Independents (or Congregationalists) of the period': Horton Davies, *Worship and Theology in England, From Watts and Wesley to Maurice, 1690–1850* (Princeton, 1961), p. 43.

[4] Abraham Booth (1734–1806) was superintendent of the Kirby-Woodhouse Congregation of Baptists in 1760 but declined to become their pastor. He became a Particular Baptist soon after this and, as one of this sect, he preached at Sutton-in-Ashfield, Chesterfield. Soon after the appearance of *The Reign of Grace* in 1768, he was invited by the Particular Baptist Church of Little Prescot Street, Goodman's Fields, to be their pastor. He was ordained on 16 Feb. 1769.

[5] Samuel Burford (d. 1768) of the Sabbatarian congregation of Particular Baptists which met at Curriers' Hall, Cripplegate. See W. Wilson's *Dissenting Churches* (1808–14), ii. 607.

[6] MS. torn.

forget that our Meeting House has a Steeple to it, and we that theirs has none. This shall be the Case universally, may the Lord hasten it in his time!

I am my dear Aunt
your very affectionate Nephew
Wm Cowper.

June 18.
I am sorry for poor ——.[7] Thoughtless as a Child he stands upon the Shore of Eternity, and laughs in Circumstances that are frightfull to those that understand them. Indeed my Heart was troubled when I read that part of your Letter which relates to him.

JOSEPH HILL — Saturday, 18 June 1768

Address: Mr. Joseph Hill / at the Chancery Office / London.[1]
Cowper Johnson

Dear Joe,

I thank you for so full an Answer to so empty an Epistle. If Olney furnished any thing for your Amusement you should receive it in return, but Occurrences here are as scarce as Cucumbers at Christmas. —I visited St. Albans[2] about a Fortnight since in person, and I visit it every day in thought. The Recollection of what passed there and the Consequences that followed it, fill my Mind continually, and make the Circumstances of a poor transient half spent Life, so insipid and unaffecting, that I have no Heart to think or write much about them. Whether the Nation are worshipping Mr. Wilkes[3] or any other Idol, is of little Moment to one who hopes and beleives that he shall shortly stand in the Presence of the great and Blessed God.

[7] The word 'Ashley' in C's hand has been crossed out.

[1] Olney Address.

[2] To see Dr. Cotton.

[3] John Wilkes (1727–97) had attacked Lord Bute's foreign policy in the *North Briton* (1762–3). With imprisonment impending, he fled to Paris in 1764 and during his absence was convicted of seditious libel. Having returned to England in 1768, he was now successfully contending for a seat in Parliament as the Member for Middlesex. C would have known Wilkes from his time with the Geniuses (see *Ryskamp*, pp. 78–101).

I thank him that he has given me such a deep impress'd Persuasion of this awfull Truth as a thousand Worlds would not purchase from me. It gives a Relish to every Blessing, and makes every Trouble light.

Yours affectionately
Wm Cowper.

Olney
June 18.—68

MRS. MADAN — Tuesday, 28 June 1768

Address: To / Mrs. Madan / Stafford Row / near the Queen's House / Westminster.
Postmarks: 5/ O'CLOCK/W, 29/IV, *and* OULNEY
Olney

My dear Aunt,

I write once more to thank you on my own behalf and Mrs. Unwin's for negotiating this Affair for us. John[1] will be sent over to meet the Maid at Newport on Saturday, and will bring her hither behind him.

I think I write to you with an Aching Heart upon my poor Brother's Account. He is with us. And his Presence necessarily gives a Turn to the Conversation that we have not been much used to. So much said about nothing, and so little about Jesus, is very painfull to us, but what can be done? May the good Lord make me thankfull that he has given me, I trust, an understanding to know him that is true, and may he in his due time afford me an Occasion of thanking him for the same unspeakable Mercy bestowed upon my Brother. He is going with us this Evening to a Prayer:Meeting at the Vicarage, and we shall have two Sermons preach'd here in the course of the Week. Oh that his Ears may be unstopped, and his Eyes opened to the Things that concern his Peace.

My dear Aunt, Praise the Redeemer upon my Account, for teaching me, and breaking the Snares of the Enemy, and chastening me for my Good. I have been much afflicted of late, and have been enabled to say with a burning Heart, It is good for me that I was afflicted. I see

[1] C's brother.

plainly that the Good Shepherd watches over me & keeps me every Moment.

Yours ever in a kind & gracious
Redeemer
Wm Cowper.

Olney
June 28.—68.

MRS. MADAN — Saturday, 9 July 1768

Address: To / Mrs. Madan / Stafford Row / near the Queens House / Westminster.
Postmarks: 5/O'CLOCK/W, 11/IY, *and* OULNEY
Olney

My dear Aunt,

You and We and poor Mary Powel have All lost our Labour: After a Week's Trial Mrs. Unwin found her absolutely unqualified in every Respect both as Cook & Housemaid, and unable to do the least thing aright. She has accordingly paid her for the Time and the Expence of her Journey back again, and she has taken her leave of Olney this Morning. What Improvements she may make hereafter is uncertain, but 40 shillings a Year is as high as her Pretensions can reasonably soar at present. She was blamed for nothing but deceiving You, as she must needs have known that the Wages agreed for were more than she could possibly earn by her Services. This Reproof together with some pious Advice which Mrs. Unwin gave her at Parting she took very quietly, and seemed rather glad of her Dismission, finding no doubt that she had undertaken what she was not fit for. We are both sorry you have had so much Trouble to so little purpose, but we trust the Hand of the Lord was in it, for her Place is now supplied by a very gracious Young Woman,[1] one of our own People, whom Mrs. Unwin would have taken at first, only she fear'd that her Health & Strength would not be sufficient for the Work. But if the Lord has design'd her for it, he will give her Strength equal to it: she has a great Affection for us which is no small Recommendation, and is every way qualified for her Place.

[1] Probably Mary Coles, referred to by C as Molly, who was buried on 28 Feb. 1771 (*O.P.R.*, p. 362).

It is well for Us my dear Aunt, that having a Gracious Master who has no need of our Services, he does not dismiss us for Insufficiency. Though our very best Performances fall so far short of what he is entitled to yet he accepts them, and does not rebuke us even for the worst. The Little we are enabled sometimes to render to him, we first receive from Himself, the Desire and the Power are derived from Him; Yet he continues us in his Family, treats us as Children rather than as Servants, satisfies us with the Fullness of his House, and clothes us with his own Raiment, the Righteousness of Jesus. Blessed and happy are They that belong to this Family, they shall never hear even of their willfull Faults except in a Way of Fatherly Chastisement, and in his own time, their Master & Lord will make them Heirs with his own most beloved Son, of an Inheritance incorruptible and undefiled and that fadeth not away.

I hope my Friend Martin[2] is restored to Health; it was a great Disappointment to us all that he could not come with Lord Dartmouth[3] as he intended. Pray give my Love to him, & accept of the same yourself together with Mrs. Unwin's best Respects. Yours, my Dear Aunt,

with true Affection
Wm Cowper.

Olney
July 9. —68.

JOSEPH HILL Thursday, 20 October 1768

Cowper Johnson

Olney Oct: 20. —68.

Dear Joe,

By this time I presume you are return'd to the Precincts of the Law; the latter end of October I know generally puts an End to your

[2] Martin Madan had taken the waters at Cheltenham in 1756 and 1757, and he had been severely ill in the autumn of 1760.

[3] William Legge (1731–1801), 2nd Earl of Dartmouth, knew C from their days at Westminster School. Dartmouth succeeded to the earldom in 1750 and attended Trinity College, Oxford (M.A. 1751). Among the distinguished posts held by Dartmouth were those of president of the board of trade and foreign plantations (1765–6), colonial secretary (1772–5), and lord privy seal (1775–82). A patron of John Newton, he centred his life on the Evangelical movement rather than the House of Lords. He was, according to C, 'one who wears a coronet, and prays' ('Truth', l. 378). In 1776 Lord Dartmouth attempted to gain an Irish bishopric for Madan.

Relaxations, such as reading upon Sunshiny Banks; and contemplating the Clouds as you lie upon your Back. Permit it to be one of the Aliena Negotia centum,[1] which are now beginning to Buzz in your Ears, to send me a 20£ Note by the first Opportunity. I beg my Affectionate Respects to my Friends in Cooke's Court, & am

Dear Sephus

Yours Sincerely

Wm Cowper.

JOSEPH HILL [Sunday, 26 October 1768][1]

Cowper Johnson

Dear Joe,

I send you the Welshman's[2] Mittimus.[3] I have just time to tell you that if you hear nothing to the contrary by Tuesday's Post, you may conclude the Note comes safe. I am obliged to write before the Post comes in, because the Letters for London set out first.

Yours ever Wm Cowper.

Sun: P: M:

MRS. COWPER [December 1768][1]

Address: To / Mrs. Cowper.
Morgan Library

My dear Cousin,

I have not been behind hand in reproaching myself with Neglect, but desire to take Shame to myself for my Unprofitableness in this as

[1] Horace, *Satires*, II. vi. 33: 'hundred foreign matters'.

[1] Dated '31st Octr 68', presumably by Hill. This must have been the day Hill received the letter, which would have been written on Sunday, 26 Oct.

[2] Unidentified, but perhaps the Mr. Morgan of C's letter to Hill of 27 May 1777.

[3] A dismissal from office (*O.E.D.*). In this case, probably an eviction notice from C's chambers.

[1] There is a copy of this letter at Olney in Mrs. Cowper's hand with the note: 'No date, but wrote to me in Decr. 1768'.

well as in all other respects. I take the next immediate Opportunity however of thanking you for yours, and of assuring you that instead of being surprized at your Silence, I rather wonder that You or any of my Friends have any Room left for so careless & negligent a Correspondent in your Memories. I am obliged to you for the Intelligence you send me of my Kindred, and rejoice to hear of their Welfare. He who settles the Bounds of our Habitations has at length cast our Lot at a great Distance from each other, but I do not therefore forget their former Kindness to me, or cease to be interested in their Well:being. You live in the Center of a World which I know you do not delight in. Happy are you my dear Friend in being able to discern the Insufficiency of all that it can afford to fill & satisfy the Desires of an immortal Soul. That God who created us for the Enjoyment of himself, has determined in Mercy that it shall fail us here, in order that the blessed Result of all our misguided Enquiries after Happiness in the Creature, may be a warm Persuit and a close Attachment to our true Interest, in Fellowship & Communion with him, thro' the Name & Mediation of a dear Redeemer. I bless his Goodness and grace that I have any Reason to hope I am a Partaker with you in the Desire after better things than are to be found in a World polluted with Sin, and therefore, devoted to Destruction. May he enable us both to consider our present Life in its only true Light, as an Opportunity put into our Hands to glorify him amongst Men by a Conduct suited to his Word and Will. I am miserably defective in this Holy and blessed Art, but I hope there is at the Bottom of all my Sinfull Infirmities a sincere Desire to Live just so long as I may be enabled in some poor Measure to answer the End of my Existence in this respect, and then to obey the Summons, and attend him in a World where they who are his Servants here, shall pay him an unsinn[ing][2] Obedience for ever.

Your dear Mother is too good to me, and puts a more charitable Construction upon my Silence than the Fact will warrant. I am not better employed than I should be in corresponding with her. I have That within which hinders me wretchedly in every thing that I ought to do, but is prone to trifle and let Time & every good thing run to waste. I hope however to write to her soon.

My Love & best Wishes attend Mr. Cowper & all that Enquire after me. May God be with you to Bless you, and do you Good by all

[2] MS. torn.

his Dispensations. Don't forget me when you are speaking t[o our] best Friend before his Mercy-Seat.—Yours ever

Wm Cowper.

N:B: I am not Married.[3]

MRS. MADAN Saturday, 24 December 1768[1]

Olney (*copy*)

My dear Aunt,

My Cousin Maria tells me you long to hear from me, and I assure you I have for a long time desired to write to you. My barrenness in spiritual things has been the cause of my silence; when I can declare what God hath done for my soul with some sense of His goodness, then writing is a pleasant employment, but to mention the blessed name of my Lord and Master with dryness and hardness of heart is painful and irksome to me! He knows however that I desire nothing so much as to glorify Him, and that my chief burden is that I cannot speak more to His praise. In the worst times, blessed be His name! I can bear testimony to His faithfulness, and truth; He has never left me since He first found me, no, not for a moment. I know that the Everlasting Arm is underneath me, and the Eternal God my refuge. O blessed state of a believing soul who trusteth in the Lord, and whose hope the Lord is; the Almighty hath graven him upon the palms of his hands, and all his interests and concerns are continually before him. What a blessed peace belongs to this sweet persuasion! A persuasion not founded in fancy, as the world profanely dreams, but built upon the sure promise of an unchanging God. Did not the remainder of sin, and unbelief deprive us of much of our enjoyments, what a delightful portion should we possess even here below. How much of Heaven does a believing view of Jesus as our all-sufficient Good bring down into the soul! We seem to breathe the pure air of that better country where all the inhabitants are holy, and more than seem to converse with God, for our fellowship is with the Father and with his Son Jesus Christ. Truly the Lord is gracious. Blessed are all

[3] The Olney copy has a note at this point in Mrs. Cowper's hand: 'It was reported he was.'

[1] Mrs. Cowper's Commonplace Book, 73–5: 'Lett. 15. dated O——y Decr. 24. 1768.'

they that wait for Him! To as many as receive Him, gives He power to become the Sons of God. May we always be enabled to receive Him with our whole heart! May we charge our souls continually to lift up their everlasting gates and admit this King of Glory, the Christ of God, in all the fulness of His free salvation. So shall we be the children of the most High. He that is in us will prove Himself greater than he that is in the world by giving us more than victory over all our enemies. The warfare seems often difficult to us because we are weak, and the Lord keeps us sensible of our weakness for wise and gracious ends. But how easy is it in His hand, who hath on His vesture and on His thigh a name written,—King of Kings and Lord of Lords![2] before Whom the powers of darkness are as nothing, and less than nothing, and the legions of Hell, with all their devices and subtleties, are as naked in His sight. Then let us not fear because of them—but be very courageous, for the Lord God is with us. He it is that fights for us—who can be against us?

Yours my dear Aunt in the
best bonds &c. &c.

JOSEPH HILL — Saturday, 21 January 1769

Address: Mr. Joseph Hill / Cook's Court / Carey Street / Lincolns Inn Fields London.[1]
Cowper Johnson

Dear Joe,

I rejoice with you in your Recovery, and that you have escaped from the Hands of One from whose Hands you will not always escape. Death is either the most formidable or the most comfortable thing we have in Prospect on this Side of Eternity. To be brought near to him and to discern neither of these Features in his Face, would argue a Degree of Insensibility of which I will not suspect my Friend whom I know to be a thinking Man. You have been brought down to the Sides of the Grave, and you have been raised again by Him who has the Keys of the invisible World, who opens and none can shut, who shuts and none can open. I do not forget to return Thanks to him

[2] Revelation 19: 16.

[1] Olney Address.

on your behalf, and to pray that your Life which he has spared may be devoted to his Service. *Behold! I stand at the Door and knock*,[2] is the Word of Him on whom both our Mortal and immortal Life depend, and blessed be his Name, it is the Word of One who wounds only that he may heal, and who waits to be Gracious. The Language of every such Dispensation is, Prepare to Meet Thy God.[3] It speaks with the Voice of Mercy and Goodness, for without such Notices whatever Preparation we might make for other Events, we should make none for This. My dear Friend, I desire and pray that when this last Enemy shall come to execute an *Unlimited* Commission[4] upon us, we may be found ready, being established and rooted in a well grounded Faith in his Name, who conquer'd and triumph'd over him upon his Cross.

Yours ever
Wm Cowper.

Olney. Jan 21.
1769.

JOSEPH HILL — Sunday, 29 January 1769[1]

Address: Mr. Joseph Hill / Chancery Office / London.[2]
Cowper Johnson

My dear Joe,

I have drawn upon you by this Post for the Sum of Ten pounds Seven Shillings payable to Mr. Alexander Clunie or Order.[3]

I have just a Moment to spare 'till the Tea Kettle boils to tell you that your Letter is just come to hand, and to thank you for it. I do assure you, the Gentleness and Candour of your manner, engages

[2] Revelation 3 : 20.

[3] Amos 4 : 12.

[4] As he sometimes does in his letters to Hill, C uses legal terminology to make a religious or personal point to a fellow lawyer: 'Commission, Is taken for the warrant or letters patent, which all men exercising jurisdiction either ordinary or extraordinary, have to authorise them to hear or determine any cause or action: as the *commission* of the judges, *&c.*', Giles Jacob, *A New Law-Dictionary* (10th ed. 1783).

---

[1] Hill dated this letter 'Jan. 29, 1769'.

[2] Olney Address.

[3] Princeton owns two bank drafts from C to Alexander Clunie, whose address in 1767 was 77 Lower Thames Street, London. C's reference is to the note for £10. 7*s*. 0*d*. dated 'Jan. 28. 1769'. The other note, for £11. 18*s*. 0*d*., is dated 'Dece. 30.1769'. According to Bernard Martin, *John Newton* (1950), pp. 145–7 and *passim*, Captain Alexander Clunie(*fl*. 1755–75), a devout Congregationalist, was a close friend of Newton's.

my Affections to you very much. You answer with Mildness to an Admonition which would have provoked many to Anger. I have not time to add more, except just to hint that if I am ever enabled to look forward to Death with Comfort, which I thank God, is some times the case with me, I do not take my View of it from the Top of my own Works & deservings, though God is Witness that the Labour of my Life is to keep a Conscience void of Offence towards him. He is always formidable to me, but when I see him disarmed of his Sting by having sheath'd it in the Body of Christ Jesus.

Yours my dear Friend
Wm Cowper.

Olney.
Sun: Eve:

JOSEPH HILL — Saturday, 5 August 1769

Address: Mr. Joseph Hill / at Wargrove / near Twyford / Berks.[1]
Cowper Johnson

Olney Augt. 5. 69.

Dear Joe,

The Note came safe.

My Brother left us last Saturday, and is now I suppose refreshing his Lungs with the pure Air which blows upon the Welsh Mountains: if indeed his Lungs which have been so long used to the Fogs of Alma Mater, can be refresh'd by the thin Atmosphere of Snowdon or Plinlimmon.

I find that the Vacancy I left at St. Albans is filled up by a near Relation.[2] May the same Hand which struck off *my* Fetters, deliver *Her* also out of the House of Bondage: and may she say when she comes forth, what I hope to be able to say from my Heart, while I have Breath to utter it,—It is good for me that I was afflicted.[3]

Yours my Dear Joe, with my Love to all who enquire after me
Wm Cowper.

[1] Olney Address.

[2] Probably Theadora. 'She is still living, single, but has many years been melancholy': [Samuel Greatheed], 'Memoranda respecting Cowper the Poet': John Rylands Library, Eng. MS. 352/55, fo. 3 (n.d.; watermark 1802; written in 1803, or shortly thereafter). See *Ryskamp*, pp. 124–5.

[3] Psalm 119: 71.

MRS. COWPER — Thursday, 31 August 1769

Address: To / Mrs. Cowper / at the Park House / near Hartford / Hartfordshire
Postmarks: 1/SE *and* OULNEY
Panshanger Collection

Olney Augt. 31. 1769.

My dear Cousin;

A Letter from your Brother Frederic[1] brought me yesterday the most afflictive Intelligence[2] that has reached me these many Years. I pray God to comfort you, and to enable you to sustain this heavy Stroke with that Resignation to his Will, which none but Himself can give, and which he gives to none but his own Children. How blessed and happy is your Lot, my dear Friend! beyond the common Lot of the greater Part of Mankind, that you know what it is to draw near to God in Prayer, and are acquainted with a Throne of Grace! You have Resources in the infinite Love of a dear Redeemer, which are witheld from Millions: And the Promises of God, which are Yea and Amen in Jesus are sufficient to answer All your Necessities, and to sweeten the bitterest Cup which your Heavenly Father will ever put into your Hand. May He now give you Liberty to drink at these Wells of Salvation, 'till you are filled with Consolation and Peace in the midst of Trouble. He has said, when thou passest through the Fire I will be with thee, and when thro' the Floods, they shall not overflow thee.[3] You have need of such a Word as this, and he knows your Need of it, and the time of Necessity is the time when he will be sure to appear in behalf of those who trust him. I bear you and yours upon my Heart before him Night and Day, for I never expect to hear of a Distress which shall call upon me with a louder Voice to pray for the Sufferer. I know the Lord hears me for myself, vile and sinfull as I am, and beleive and am sure, that he will hear me for you also. He is the Friend of the Widow, and the Father of the fatherless,[4] even God in his Holy Habitation; in all our Afflictions he

[1] Frederick Madan (1742–80), the 7th son and youngest child of Mrs. Madan. A handsome and high-spirited young man, Frederick was constantly in debt between 1763 and 1775. A Grenadier Guard, he became lieutenant and captain in 1765, and in 1776 he obtained the rank of lieutenant-colonel, a short time before his departure to North America. See C to Mrs. Cowper, 10 May 1780.

[2] C's correspondent, Major William Cowper, M.P. and a major in the Hertfordshire Militia (see n. 1, C to Mrs. Cowper, 15 Apr. 1768), had died on 28 Aug.

[3] Isaiah 43 : 2.

[4] Psalm 68 : 5.

is afflicted, and chastens us in Mercy. Surely he will sanctify this Dispensation to you, do you great and everlasting Good by it, make the World appear like Dust and Vanity in your Sight, as it truly is, and open to your View the Glories of a better Country, where there shall be no more Death, neither Sorrow nor Pain, but God shall wipe away all Tears from your Eyes for ever.[5] Oh that comfortable Word! I have chosen thee in the Furnace of Affliction,[6] so that our very Sorrows are Evidences of our Calling, and he chastens us because we are Children.

My dear Cousin, I commit you to the Word of his Grace, and to the Comforts of his Holy Spirit. Your Life is needfull for your Family, may God in Mercy to Them prolong it, and may he preserv[e you][7] from the dangerous Effects which a Stroke like This, might have upon a Frame so tender as yours. I grieve with you, I pray for you; could I do more, I would, but God must Comfort you.

Yours in our dear Lord Jesus
Wm Cowper.

JOSEPH HILL — November 1769[1]

Cowper Johnson

Dear Joe,

I received the Notes for Thirty pounds.

Sir Thomas crosses the Alps,[2] and Sir Cowper, (for that is his Title at Olney) prefers his Home to any other Spot of Earth in the World. Horace observing this Difference of Temper in different Persons, cried out a good many Years ago, in the true Spirit of Poetry, How much one man differs from another![3] This does not seem a very

[5] Revelation 21 : 4.

[6] Isaiah 48 : 10.

[7] A small part of this MS. is torn away at the seal.

[1] MS. is dated 'Novr. 69/' in pencil.

[2] The Hesketh had settled in Italy. '. . . During the Poet's long retirement his fair Cousin had passed some years with her Husband abroad . . . .' *Hayley*, i.143. Sir Thomas appears in the Rate Books for Grosvenor Street from 1762 to 1769; his name does not recur until 1775 when he is listed at Charles Street, Berkeley Square.

[3] The allusion may be to the *Epistles*, I. xiv. 10–11 : 'Rure ego viventem tu dicis in urbe, beautum : cui placet alterius, sua nimirum est odio sors.' (I call a country life happy, you live in the town; and no doubt he who likes another man's life must dislike his own.)

sublime Exclamation in English, but I remember at Westminster, we were taught to admire it in the Original.

My dear Friend I am obliged to you for your kind Invitation: but being long accustom'd to Retirement, which I was always fond of, I am now more than ever unwilling to revisit those noisy & crowded Scenes which I never loved, & which I now abhorr. I remember you with all the Friendship I ever professed, which is as much as I ever entertained for any man. But the strange and uncommon Incidents of my Life, have given an entire new Turn to my whole Character and Conduct, and render'd me incapable of receiving Pleasure from the same Employments & Amusements of which I could readily partake in former days.

I Love you, & yours; I thank you for your continued Remembrance of me, & shall not cease to be their & your Affectionate Friend & Servant.

Wm Cowper.

I am glad to hear of
my Uncle's Recovery.[4]

JOSEPH HILL — Saturday, 20 January 1770

Cowper Johnson

Dear Joseph,

The News:paper informed me last Week that the Society of the Middle Temple were come to a Resolution that no more Chambers should be sold with a Power of Assignment, & that this Resolution would speedily become a Law.[1]—If this be the case, it were better that mine were sold immediately, for it will never be worth my while

[4] Ashley, on his part, frequently asked Hill about C. 'If you shou'd have any further Intercourse with the fair Recluses before they remove from their *Hermitage*, please to give our Love to them . . .' (8 Sept. 1771. Princeton). Earlier in the same letter, Ashley cannot resist a slightly antagonistic reference to his nephew: 'Bless'd however as *W.C.* is with supernatural Aids & assistances, we may allow Him to have a nearer Insight into these Matters than we must pretend to —— as to Myself, I am contented to jogon [*sic*] in the plain, beaten Road of *Common Sense*. . . .'

[1] We have not been able to find this resolution in any of the contemporary newspapers. 'An *Assignment* is the Transferring and Setting over to another some Right, Title, or Interest in Things, in which a third Person, not a Party to the *Assignment*, has a Concern and Interest.': *A New Abridgement of the Law by a Gentleman of the Middle Temple* (1736), i. 157.

to keep them 'till they shall want considerable Repairs, which they must before many years are pass'd, and to sell them after this Alteration takes place, upon Terms so much less valuable than those upon which I bought them, will be to lose half my Money, unless the Inn is disposed to make up the Difference.

I have been in Treaty with Colonel Cowper[2] about the Sale of my Law Books, and desired him to pay the Purchase Money into your Hands. If it is done, should be glad to receive it.

Yours Dear Joe Affectionately Wm Cowper.

Olney
Jan. 20. 1770.

JOSEPH HILL — Saturday, 10 February 1770

Address: Mr. Joseph Hill / Chancery Office / London.[1]
Cowper Johnson

Dear Joe,

I wrote to you above a Fortnight since about my Chambers, and desiring you if I have any Money in Town to send it. The last Post brings me word from Cambridge that my Brother is very ill, and it may be absolutely necessary for me to go over to him next Week; His Disorder is supposed to be owing to an inward Decay, the Consequence of a Violent Hæmorrhage he had in the Autumn. Nothing is so likely to prevent my Journey at present, as the Want of Money to defray the Expences of it. I shall be glad of an immediate Answer, whether I have any Money in your Hands or not, that if I have none, I may furnish myself with it as I can.

Yours, Dear Joe, with much
Affection
Wm Cowper.

Olney.
Feb:10:1770.

2 Spencer Cowper (1723 or 4–97), the younger brother of William, the M.P. who had died in Aug. 1769. A graduate of Westminster, Spencer had attended Worcester College, Oxford, and the Inner Temple. He was at this time lieutenant-colonel in the Foot-guards; he became a major-general on 19 Feb. 1779.

1 Olney Address.

JOSEPH HILL — Thursday, 15 February 1770

Cowper Johnson

Dear Joseph,

I thank you for the Notes which I received yesterday, 10£. and 15£. If there should be the same Deficiency next Winter, I shall be obliged to you if without waiting to hear farther from me, you will be so good as to sell my Chambers.

I had a Letter yesterday from a Friend[1] of my Brother's at Ben'et. I do not find that there is any immediate Occasion for my going over to Cambridge, especially as I have wrote to desire that my Brother will come to Olney. He is not at present in a Condition to undertake the Journey, but Dr. Glynn[2] approves of his coming and will send him as soon as it shall be expedient. The Account I have of him, is, that he has a great Shortness of Breath attended with a troublesome Cough, and that within this Week his Legs are very much swelled: but when his Friend wrote, he had had a good Night, was pretty cheerfull, and upon the whole not worse than when he wrote before.

I should be glad if my Uncle Ashley would be so good as to get an Answer from Colonel Cowper with respect to the Books, that if he does not chuse to be the Purchaser, they may be sold to another, for I imagine Time and Cobwebs will not much encrease their Value.

Yours my dear Friend
Wm Cowper.

Olney
Feb:15. 1770.

[1] Perhaps Luke Heslop. See n. 1, C to Unwin, 31 Mar. 1770.

[2] The winner of the Seatonian prize in 1757, Robert Glynn, afterwards Cloberry (1719–1800), had been a scholar of King's College, Cambridge, where he had taken the degrees of B.A., M.A., and M.D. (1752). A noted bibliophile, Glynn defended the authenticity of Chatterton's *Rowley Poems*.

MRS. UNWIN Monday, 26 February 1770

Address: To / Mrs. Unwin / Olney / Bucks.
Postmarks: 27/FE *and* CAMBRIDGE
British Library

My dear Friend,

The Blank which Mr. Newton left at the Bottom of his Letter, came, a Blank, to Me.[1] And why so? Do you imagine that a Line from you, tho' it were but a Line, would not be welcome to me, especially in my present distressfull Circumstances? This is my fourth Letter to you since I came hither, and I have received but One from You: perhaps to:morrow's Post will bring me another, at least I shall be much disappointed if it does not, and shall begin to suspect that I have done something wrong. Though wherever I fail, I am very sure I never *intentionally* fail in any point where your Peace & Happiness are concern'd.

My poor Brother continues much as he was, only worse in this respect, that the longer the Imposthume[2] remains unbroken, the greater Danger there is of a confirm'd Dropsy. Within these 2 Days his Hands have begun to swell, and having lately been obliged to keep his Bed, he is grown much weaker. If at any time I find Liberty to speak to him, it is when his Sufferings are greatest, for when his Pains are abated, he is cheerfull in his Spirits, and exactly the Man he always was. I have found at last however that he is not destitute of Notions about the Truth. He told me Yesterday that he had read Mr. Newton's Sermons,[3] and that the Thought upon which they were built was not New, but borrowed from Witsius.[4] He has read Witsius, and I suppose understands him as far as he is intelligible without Spiritual Light, for he observed that those Doctrines had been mixt & interwoven with others 'till at last they had been quite lost; I told him they were the Truth, and that there was no other Gospel, that we were not to look for Novelty in such things, & that neither Witsius nor Mr. Newton were the Inventors of them, but

[1] Newton to C, 22 Feb. 1770 (Princeton): 'I shall . . . leave a little bit blank, in case Mrs. Unwin should have anything to add.'

[2] An abscess.

[3] Newton's *Sermons Preached in the Parish Church in Olney* had appeared in 1767.

[4] Herman Wits (d. 1708), professor of theology at Utrecht and Leyden. In 1761 Martin Madan published *A Treatise on Christian Faith*, a paraphrase of the section 'De Fide' which forms chapter 7 of Book III of Wits's *Œconomia Fœderum Dei cum Hominibus*.

they were evidently to be seen in St. Paul's Epistles. I found I had a fair Opportunity to make a Confession of my own Faith, which I did as well as I was able, illustrating it by my own Experience. At present however I see no Effect of all that I have said. I have a trembling Hope however, that when the Lord has made it sufficiently evident that the Excellency of the Power is his own, he will take the Matter into his own Hand, and plead the Cause of Gospel Grace himself. He alone can do it effectually, and I desire that He may have all the Glory.

In the mean while I am toss'd upon the Waves of Hope and Fear, I see my Brother asleep upon the very Brink of Ruin, and the only Hand that can pluck him thence is not yet stretch'd out for his Deliverance. Every Day brings him sensibly nearer to the great Decision, my Thoughts are interested in his Condition all day long, and at Night I pray for him in my Dreams. I go to Sleep in a Storm, imagining that I hear his Cries, and wake in Terrour lest he should be just departing. The Enemy I doubt not has a share in this, [and whispers][5] in the Ears of my Fancy in order to make my Situation more distr[essing. But] sometimes I see the Lord, and can pour out my Heart before him. [I awoke] yesterday Morning with these Words, which are plainly an Imitation of [Herbe]rt, some of whose Poems I have been reading to my Brother.

> But what, my lovely One? and meek
> Tho' maim'd, who liv'st, with Bruises dying—

I thought of them while at Dinner, and made a comfortable Meal upon them, while the Lord was pleased to spread my Table in the Wilderness.[6] He knows I am maim'd and Bruised, but still he maintains my Life, and frequently makes the Bones he has broken to rejoice.[7]

By a Letter from Colonel Cowper I understand that Worral[8] values my Books at no more than 20.10.0. Hill has by this time received the money; if you chuse it, I will order it down to You directly.

[5] Parts of the MS. are torn away.

[6] Psalm 78 : 19.

[7] Psalm 51 : 8.

[8] Most likely John Worrall, bookseller and publisher, who was located at the Bible and Dove in Bell Yard near Lincoln's Inn from 1736 to 1763. Interested chiefly in books relating to the law, he was the compiler of two catalogues published in 1763: *Bibliotheca Legum Angliæ* and *Bibliotheca Topographica Anglicana*. See H. R. Plomer *et al.*, *A Dictionary of the Printers and Booksellers . . . in England . . . from 1726 to 1775* (Oxford, 1932), p. 272.

Let nothing that I have said distress you, your Peace is as dear to me as my own, and I cannot grieve You, without suffering myself. I will now take my Revenge by leaving a Blank too, and then I shall be satisfied.

Yours ever, in the best Bonds.
Wm Cowper.

Camb:
Feb: 26. 1770.

JOSEPH HILL — Sunday, 4 March 1770

Address: To / Mr. Joseph Hill / Chancery Office / London[1]
Cowper Johnson

Dear Joe,

I wish I could tell you that my Brother is better than I found him upon my Arrival here: he is much in the same State as when I wrote to my Uncle, only weaker, as might be expected. The Imposthume is not broke, consequently the other Disorders which are the Effect of it, continue. I do not indeed perceive that the Dropsy encreases; and I think his Asthma rather less troublesome than it was. Thus far it is well for the present, but the great Event remains undecided, & must do so 'till the Imposthume is discharged.

I can't afford to pay you the Money you have advanced out of what has arisen from the Sale of the Books. You will receive a Draft payable to Mr. Standert[2] for 10£ 13s. od. & another payable to Mr. Clunie for 9£ 3s od.—You will hear no more from me upon Money matters, 'till you tell me you are pay'd, and Money over. My respects to all Friends,

Yours ever
Wm Cowper.

Camb:
Mar 4. 1770.

[1] Olney Address.

[2] Perhaps Thomas Standert who in 1767 was a broker with offices at 43 Mark Lane, Tower-street.

MRS. COWPER Monday, 5 March 1770

Address: To / Mrs. Cowper at the Revd. Dr. Madan's / in the / Minster Yard / York / By Caxton Bag.[1]
Postmark: CAMBRIDGE
Panshanger Collection

Dear Cousin,

My Brother continues much as he was. His Case is a very dangerous one. An Imposthume of the Liver, attended by an Asthma & Dropsy. The Physician has little Hope of his Recovery. I beleive I might say none at all, only, being a Friend, he does not formally give him over by ceasing to Visit him, lest it should sink his Spirits. For my own part I have no Expectation of his Recovery except by a signal Interposition of Providence in Answer to Prayer. His Case is clearly out of the Reach of Medicine, but I have seen many a Sickness heal'd where the Danger has been equally threatening, by the only Physician of Value. I doubt not he will have an Interest in your Prayers, as he has in the Prayers of many—may the Lord incline his Ear, and give an Answer of Peace!

I am much to be blamed for having so long neglected to write to you—I have as long neglected to write to my Aunt, but I hope that a fair Confession of my Fault, with a purpose of Amendment, will plead my Pardon with you both.

I know it is good to be afflicted—I trust that you have found it so, and that under the Teaching of God's own Spirit we shall both be purified by the many Furnaces into which he is pleased to cast us. The World is a Wilderness to Me, and I desire to find it such, 'till it shall please the Lord to release me from it. It is the Desire of my Soul to seek a better Country, where God shall wipe away all Tears from the Eyes of his People, and where, looking back upon the Ways by which he has led us, we shall be filled with everlasting Wonder, Love, & Praise.

My present Affliction is as great as most I have experienced: but

When I can hear my Saviour say,
Strength shall be equal to thy Day,
Then I rejoice in deep Distress,
Leaning on All:sufficient Grace.[2]

1 Mrs. Cowper was staying with her brother Spencer Madan (1729–1813) and his family.

2 These lines are probably not by C, but we have been unable to locate them in any collection of hymns.

I beg you will present my affectionate Respects to the Family you are with. I often think of them, and when I do so, I think we shall meet no more 'till the great Trumpet brings us together. May we all appear at the Right Hand of that Blessed Emanuel, who has loved poor Sinners, & washed them from their Sins in his own most precious Blood.

My poor Brother is continually talking in a delirious way, which makes it difficult for me to know what I write. I must add no more therefore, but that I am

my dear Cousin

Yours ever, with sincere Affection,

Wm Cowper.

Mar. 5. 1770.

JOHN NEWTON — Sunday, 11 March 1770

G. H. H. Wheler (*copy*)[1]

Cambridge, 11 Mar: 1770

My dear Friend

I am in haste to make you a partaker of my Joy. Oh praise the Lord with me, and let us exalt his name together. My lamb that was lost is found, my child that was dead is alive again—The Lord has done it, he has given me the desire of my heart, my Brother is born of God.—My joy will not suffer me to sleep, and I have peace which cannot be expressed.

Yesterday in the afternoon he suddenly burst into tears, and said with a loud cry, 'O forsake me not!' I went to the bed-side when he grasped my hand, and I presently by his eyes and countenance found he was in prayer. Then turning to me, he said, 'Brother, I am full of what I could say to *You*.' The Nurse asked him if he would have any hartshorn or lavender.[2] He replied, 'none of these things will

[1] The whereabouts of the holograph of this letter, as well as C's letters to Newton of 14 and 17 Mar., is unknown. Copies of these three letters exist in two places: Mrs. Cowper's Commonplace Book (pp. 112–19) at Olney, and Mr. G. H. H. Wheler's packet entitled, 'Mr. Cowpers Letters to Mr. Newton giving an account of his Brothers Illness & happy Death'. Although we have not been able to identify the hand of the copyist of Mr. Wheler's manuscript, we feel that the version offered there is substantially closer to C's usual practice in punctuation, spelling, paragraphing, and usage than Mrs. Cowper's, and we have used it as our copy-text.

[2] In his *Medical Pocket-Book* (3rd ed. 1791), John Elliot states that burnt hartshorn is

serve my purpose.' But I said, 'I know what would my dear, don't I?' He answered, 'you do, Brother.'

I left him for about an hour because I was afraid lest he should fatigue himself by too much talking, and because I wanted to praise the Lord for what I understood to be clear evidence of a work begun. When I returned he said, 'Brother, if I live you and I shall be more like one another than we have been; whether I live or not all is well and will be so, I know it will, for I have felt that which I never felt before, and I am sure that God has visited me with this sickness to teach me what I was too proud to learn in health. I never had satisfaction 'till now. The doctrines I had been used to referred me to myself for the foundation of my hope, and then I could find nothing to rest upon. The sheet anchor of the soul was wanting. I thought you wrong, yet wanted to believe as you did. I found myself unable to believe, yet always thought that one day I should be brought to do so. You suffered more than I have done before you believed these truths, but our sufferings though different in their kind & measure were directed to the same end. I hope he has taught me *that* which he teaches none but his own. I hope so. These things were foolishness to me once, I could not understand them, but now I have a solid foundation, and am satisfied.'

He spoke this with his arm about my neck, leaning his head against mine in the most composed manner.—When I went to bid him good night, he took hold of my hand, and resumed his discourse as follows.

'As empty and yet full, as having nothing and yet possessing all things. I see the rock upon which I once split, and I see the rock of my salvation. I have peace myself, and if I live I hope it will be that I may be made a messenger of the same peace to others. I have learned *that* in a moment which I could not have learned by reading many books in many years. I have often studied these points, and studied them with great attention, but was blinded by prejudice; and unless he who alone is worthy to unloose the seals,[3] had opened the book to

used as both an astringent and an absorbent (p. 81). R. James makes the following observation on lavender: 'That Lavender is far more potent and penetrating, and of greater Efficacy, in Cephalic, Uterine, and Nervous Disorders . . . appears from the Oil of it distilled, and from the Salivation excited by the Leaves and Flowers in chewing; which it is much commended in soporific and catarrhous Disorders. Lavender given in a Phrensy, proceeding from an Inflammation, infallibly destroys the Patient; but it is good for vertiginous old Persons, and Distempers owing to Dulness and Want of Spirits.' (*Pharmacopœia Universalis: or, A New English Dispensatory* . . . (2nd ed. 1752), p. 228.)

[3] Revelation 5: 9.

me, I had been blinded still. Now they appear so plain, that though I am convinced no comment could ever have made me understand them, I wonder I did not see them before—Yet my doubts and difficulties have only served to pave the way, and now they are solved, they make it plainer. The light I have received comes late, but it is a comfort to me that I never made the Gospel truths a subject of ridicule. Though I was averse to the persuasion and ways of God's people, I ever thought them respectable, and therefore not proper to be made a jest of.—I should delight to see the people of Olney, but am not worthy to appear amongst them. I should rejoice in an hour's conversation with Mr. Newton, but I am so weak in body that at present I could not bear it.'

I bid him good night, having talked with him so long as I thought it was safe to do so—and he tells me this morning, that the moment when he sent forth that cry, was the moment when light was darted into his soul.—He had thought much about these things in the course of his illness, but never 'till that instant was able to understand them.

It seems he has been in pursuit of the truth these five years, and tells me he believes he has read every author of note upon the subject. He has been long used to consider himself as appointed to instruct the people committed to his care in the most important concerns, and therefore accountable for his doctrine as well as his practice. He thinks he can say he never wilfully erred, but can make his appeal to the Lord, that in all that time, he was sincerely desirous of coming to the knowledge of the truth. I should be glad to fill my paper, but want of sleep and fatigue of spirits through the great emotions I have felt upon this occasion, oblige me to conclude. I will only add what he said to me this evening, as a wonderful proof of the power of God to build up a Soul and establish it in the truth in a few hours. His words were these: 'The evil I suffer is the consequence of my descent from the corrupt original stock and of my own transgressions. The Good I enjoy comes to me as the overflowing of his bounty; but the crown of all his mercies is this, that he has given me a Saviour, and not only the Saviour of Mankind, but my Saviour.'

Yours my dear friend, you may imagine in much joy & peace & in the bonds of Gospel love

Wm. Cowper

MRS. MADAN — Tuesday, 13 March 1770

Olney (*copy*)[1]

My dear Aunt

I am asham'd of my long, and very blameable silence, I make the best amends I can by sending you the best news I have had to communicate this many a day! You have heard of my brother's most dangerous sickness; he seems to be recovering very fast, and the most delightful circumstance of the dispensation is, that our gracious Lord hath taken occasion by this affliction to open his eyes and his heart—to bring him to the acknowledgement of the truth as it is in Jesus, and to heal him with the holy spirit of promise. I have not time to add more: I hope what I have written, may be a comfort to you—may it fill your heart with praise.

Yours ever in the Lord
&c. &c.

JOHN NEWTON — Wednesday, 14 March 1770

G. H. H. Wheler (*copy*)[1]

In the evening he said, 'This bed would be a bed of misery and it is so, but it is likewise a bed of Joy, and it is a bed of discipline. Were I to die tonight I know I should be happy. This assurance, I trust, is quite consistent with the word of God; it is built upon a sense of my own utter insufficiency, and the all-sufficiency of Christ. Brother, I have been building my glory upon a sandy Foundation. I have laboured night & day to perfect myself in things of no profit. I have sacrificed my health to these pursuits, and am now feeling the consequences. But how contemptible do the writers I once highly valued, appear to me now, yea, doubtless and I count all things but loss and dung for the excellency of the knowledge of Christ Jesus my Lord. I must now go to a new school. I have many things to learn—I succeeded in my former pursuits. I wanted to be highly

[1] Mrs. Cowper's Commonplace Book, 80: 'Lettr. 16th. date March, 13, 1770. Bennet C.'

[1] See n. 1, C to Newton, 11 Mar. 1770.

applauded and I was so; I was flattered up to the height of my wishes; now I must learn a new lesson.'

The next day in the morning he said, 'God is very good to me, I have had a charming night, and I hope and believe I shall recover; but my desire of recovery extends no farther than my hope of usefulness. Unless I live to be an instrument of good to others, it were better for me to die now.'

In the evening, 'What comfort I have in this bed, miserable as I seem to be. Brother, I love to look at you. I see now who was right and who was mistaken, but it seems wonderful that almost a miracle should be necessary to enforce that which appears so very plain. What a scene is passing before me! Ideas upon these subjects crowd upon me faster than I can give them utterance. How plain do many texts appear, to which I could once hardly affix a meaning after consulting all the Commentators, and now they are as clear as the day without any comment at all. There is but one key to the New Testament, there is but one Interpreter; I cannot describe to you, nor shall ever be able to describe what I felt in the moment he gave it to me. I hope I shall make a good use of it. I shudder when I think of the danger I have just escaped—I had made up my mind on these subjects, and was determined to hazard all upon the justness of my own opinions.'

JOHN NEWTON — Saturday, 17 March 1770

G. H. H. Wheler (*copy*)[1]

The sweats which at first seemed so favourable to my Brother's recovery have at last greatly lowered him both in strength & spirits. He is so weak, he can hardly move a limb, and for the most part rather delirious. His difficulty of breathing returns, and the swelling in his legs is much as it was. The Lord has not yet made me willing to resign him. I cannot help being concerned for his recovery, and very anxious about it.

That which I thought would make me willing to part with him, is become the strongest argument with me to desire his stay. Now he knows the truth, I want to have him sent forth to preach it. Nor am I yet without hopes that it will be so. I send the underwritten

[1] See n. 1, C to Newton, 11 Mar. 1770.

to show the clearness of his views, even in his present disordered and almost delirious state.

'There is more joy in heaven over one sinner that repenteth than over ninety & nine just persons that need no repentance.[2] That text has been sadly Misunderstood. Where is that just Person to be found? Alas! What must have become of me if I had died this day sevennight? What should I have had to plead? My own Righteousness? That would have been of great service to be sure. Well, whither then? Why to the mercy of God: but I had no reason to hope for that except upon Scriptural grounds. Well, whither next? Why to the Mountains to cover us & to the rocks to fall on us.[3] I am not duly thankful for the mercy I have received.

Perhaps I may ascribe some part of my insensibility to my great weakness of body. I hope at least that if I was better in health, it would be better with me in these respects also. I have been proud. I have been vain of my Understanding & of my Acquirements in this place. Now God has made me little better than an Idiot, as much as to say, "Now be proud if you can." While I have my senses left, my thoughts will be poured out in the praises of God. I have an interest in Christ, in his blood & sufferings, and my sins are forgiven me; have I not cause to praise him? When my understanding fails me quite, as I think it will soon, then he will pity my weakness.'

He continues extremely ill, but to God belong the issues from death.[4]

MRS. UNWIN — Sunday, 11 March–Sunday, 18 March 1770

Barham Johnson (*copy*)[1]

Camb: March 11. 1770.

I am in haste to make you a partaker of my joy. Oh praise the Lord with me, and let us exalt his Name together. Yesterday, in the after-

[2] Luke 15: 7. [3] See Revelation 6: 16.

[4] This concluding sentence is found only in Mrs. Cowper's transcription (p. 119).

[1] This journal-letter, copied by John Johnson, is headed 'To Mrs. Unwin', and it is similar in content to C's letters to Newton of 11, 14, and 17 Mar. 1770. According to notes by N. C. Hannay in his copy of *Wright*, there are letters of C to Mrs. Unwin of 13 and 18 Mar. 1770. Hannay's reference is most likely to this letter which has entries for 11, 12, 13, and 18 March.

noon, my Brother suddenly burst into tears, and said with a loud cry, 'Oh! forsake me not!' I went to his bed-side, when he grasped my hand, and I presently by his eyes and countenance found that he was in prayer. Then, turning to me, he said, 'Brother, I am full of what I could say to *you*.' I left him for about an hour, lest he should fatigue himself by too much talking, and because I wanted to praise the Lord for what I understood to be a clear evidence of a work begun. When I returned, he said, 'Brother, if I live, you and I shall be more like one another than we have been. Whether I live or not live, all is well and will be so. I know it will, for I have felt that which I never felt before; and I am sure that God has visited me with this sickness, in order to teach me what I was too proud to learn in health. I never had satisfaction till now. The doctrines I had been used to referred me to myself for the foundation of my hope, and there I could find nothing to rest upon. The sheet anchor of the soul was wanting. I thought you wrong, yet wanted to believe as you did. I found myself unable to believe, yet always thought that I should one day be brought to do so. You suffered more than I have done, before you believed these truths, but our sufferings, though different in their kind and measure, were directed to the same end. I hope he has taught me *that* which he teaches none but his own. I hope so. These things were foolishness to me once, I could not understand them, but now I have a solid foundation and am satisfied.'

When I went to bid him good night, he resumed his discourse as follows—'As empty, yet full, as having nothing, and yet possessing all things. I see the rock upon which I once split, and I see the Rock of my salvation. I have peace, myself, and if I live, I hope it will be that I may be made a messenger of the same peace to others. I have learnt that in a moment, which I could not have learnt by reading many books for many years. I have often studied these points, and studied them with great attention, but was blinded by prejudice, and unless He who alone is worthy to unloose the seals,[2] had opened the book to me, I had been blinded still. Now they appear so plain, that though I am convinced no comment could ever have made me understand them, I wonder I did not see them before. Yet my doubts and difficulties have only served to pave the way, and now they are solved, they make it plainer. The light I have received comes late, but it is a comfort to me, that I never made the Gospel truths a

[2] Revelation 5 : 9.

subject of ridicule. Though I was averse to the persuasion and the ways of God's people, I ever thought them respectable, and therefore not proper to be made a jest of. The evil I suffer, is the consequence of my descent from the corrupt original stock, and of my own transgressions. The good I enjoy, comes to me as the overflowing of his bounty. But the crown of all his mercies is this, that he has given me a Saviour, and not only the Saviour of mankind, but *my* Saviour.'

He said that the moment when he sent forth that cry was the moment when light was darted into his soul.

March 12. In the evening, he said, 'This bed would be a bed of misery, and it is so; but it is likewise a bed of joy, and it is a bed of discipline. Were I to die this night, I know I should be happy. This assurance, I trust, is quite consistent with the word of God. It is built upon a sense of my own utter insufficiency, and the all-sufficiency of Christ.—Brother, I have been building my glory upon a sandy foundation. I have laboured night and day to perfect myself in things of no profit. I have sacrificed my health to these pursuits, and am now suffering the consequences. But how contemptible do the writers I once so highly valued appear to me now. Yea, doubtless, and I account all things loss and dung for the excellency of the knowledge of Christ Jesus my Lord. I must now go to a new school. I have many things to learn. I succeeded in my former pursuits. I wanted to be highly applauded, and I was so. I was flattered up to the height of my wishes. Now I must learn a new lesson.'

March 13. In the morning—'God is very good to me. I have had a charming night. I hope I shall recover. These sweats have been my cure. They are not the effect of medicine; they are the finger of God. I see it, and hope I am thankful for it. But my desire of recovery extends no further than my hope of usefulness. Unless I live to be an instrument of good to others, it were better for me to die now. What comfort I have in this bed! miserable as I seem to be. Brother! I love to look at you. I see now who was right, and who was mistaken. But it seems wonderful that almost a miracle should be necessary to inforce that which appears so very plain. I wish myself at Olney. You have a good river there, better than all the rivers of Damascus. What a scene is passing before me! Ideas upon these subjects, crowd faster upon me than I can give them utterance. How plain do many texts appear, to which I could hardly once affix a meaning, after consulting all the commentators, and now they are as clear as the day,

without any comment at all. There is but one key to the New Testament. There is but one Interpreter. I cannot describe to you, nor shall ever be able to describe what I felt in the moment He gave it to me. I shudder to think of the danger I have just escaped. I had made up my mind on these subjects, and was determined to hazard all upon the justness of my own opinions.'

March 18. The sweats which seemed so favourable at first to my brother's recovery, have at last greatly lowered him both in strength and spirits, so that it is found necessary to check them. He is so weak, he can hardly move a limb. His difficulty of breathing is returned; yet the clearness of his views remain, even though he is delirious at times. Last night, he spoke as follows—'There is more joy over one sinner that repenteth, than over ninety and nine just persons that need no repentance.[3] That text has been sadly misunderstood—Where is that just person to be found? Alas! what must have become of me, if I had died this day sennight! What should I have had to plead? My own righteousness? That would have been of great service to me, to be sure. Well, whither then? Why to the mercy of God—but I had no reason to hope for that, except upon scriptural grounds. Well, whither next? Why, to the mountains, to cover us, and to the rocks to fall upon us![4] I am not duly thankful for the mercy I have received. Perhaps I may ascribe some part of my insensibility to my great weakness of body. I hope, at least, that if I was better in health, it would be better with me in these respects also.'

He is indeed exceedingly weak, and complains a little that his understanding fails him. His speech is like that of an infant, and it is not possible that he should be laid much lower than he is.

He said just now—'I have been proud—I have been vain of my understanding, and of my acquirements in this place; and now God has made me little better than an idiot, as much as to say, Now be proud if you can.' And again he said, 'While I have any senses left, my thoughts will be poured out in the praise of God. I have an interest in Christ, in his blood and sufferings, and my sins are forgiven me. Have I not cause to praise him? When my understanding fails me quite, as I think it will soon, then he will consider my weakness.'

W. C.

[3] Luke 15: 7. [4] Luke 23: 30.

MRS. MADAN Saturday, 24 March 1770

Address: To / Mrs. Madan / Stafford Row / Westminster
Trinity College, Cambridge (*copy*)[1]

Dear Aunt,

You may possibly by this time have heard of the Death of my dear Brother. I should not have left you to learn of it from any but myself, had I either spirits or opportunity to write sooner. He died on Tuesday last, the 20th. It was not judged proper that I should attend the Funeral. I therefore took leave of the melancholy scene as soon as possible, and returned to Olney on Thursday. He has left me to sing of Mercy and Judgment. Greater sufferings than he underwent are seldom seen, Greater Mercy than he received, I believe never. His views of Gospel Grace were as clear, and his sense of his Interest in Christ, as strong, as if he had been exercised in the Christian walk and warfare many years. This is my consolation, and strong consolation I find it, that he is gone to his Father and my Father, to his God and my God.

He is to be buried at his Living[2] about seven miles from Cambridge, by his own desire, this day. The Master[3] and Fellows attend the Funeral.

I am, Dear Aunt,

Yours affectionately in the Lord
Wm Cowper

Olney
March 24th 1770

I shall be obliged to you, my Dear Aunt, if the next time you write to dear Mrs Cowper at York, you will be so good as to inform her of this event.

[1] Typescript copy of letter, in the possession on 20 Mar. 1919 of Alexander M. Carstairs, Albany Chambers, Charing Cross, Glasgow; sent to Sir James Frazer.

[2] John Cowper had been appointed rector of Foxton in Cambridgeshire in 1765; Foxton is south-west of Cambridge.

[3] The Master of Bene't (Corpus Christi College) at this time was the Revd. John Barnardiston (d. 17 June 1778) who had been elected to the post on 7 July 1764.

WILLIAM UNWIN Saturday, 31 March 1770

Address: To / The Revd. Mr. Unwin / at Stock / near Ingatestone / Essex.
Postmarks: 2/AP *and* OULNEY
British Library

My dear Friend,

I am glad that the Lord made you a Fellow Labourer with us in Praying my dear Brother out of Darkness into marvellous Light. It was a Blessed Work, and when it shall be your turn to die in the Lord, and to rest from your Labours, that Work shall follow you.

I once entertained Hopes of his Recovery; from the Moment when it pleased God to give him Light in his Soul, there was for four days such a visible amendment in his Body, as surprized us all. Dr. Glynn himself was puzzled, and began to think that all his threat'ning Conjectures would fail of their Accomplishment. I am well satisfied that it was thus order'd, not for his own sake, but for the sake of Us who had been so deeply concern'd for his Spiritual Welfare; that he might be able to give such evident Proof of the Work of God upon his Soul, as should leave no doubt behind it. As to his Friends at Cambridge, they knew nothing of the Matter. He never spoke of these things but to myself, nor to me when others were within Hearing, except that sometimes he would speak in the Presence of the Nurse. He knew well to make the Distinction between those who could understand him, & those who could not, and that he was not in Circumstances to maintain such a Contraversy as a Declaration of his New Sentiments & Views would have exposed him to. Just after his Death, I spoke of this Change, to a dear Friend[1] of his, a Fellow of the College, who had attended him thro' all his Sickness with the greatest Assiduity and Tenderness, but he did not understand me.

I now proceed to mention such particulars as I can recollect, and which I had not Opportunity to insert in my Letters to Olney, for I left Cambridge suddenly and sooner than I expected.

[1] Perhaps the Revd. Luke Heslop (1738–1825), later archdeacon of Buckingham, who was elected a Fellow of Corpus Christi College in 1769 (B.A. 1764; M.A. 1767; B.D. 1775). According to the following note in a manuscript, now at Olney, entitled 'A Collection of Materials towards a Life of Cowper' (probably the work of Greatheed), 'Mr. Cooper sent one copy [of his *Memoir*] to Mr Newton and another to Archdeacon Hister [Heslop] of Bucks, who had I think known his Brother intimately.' C later had unpleasant dealings with Heslop concerning John Cowper's mare and her upkeep (see C to Lady Hesketh, 25 Feb. 1789, 6 and 17 June 1790).

He was deeply impress'd with a Sense of the Difficulties he should have to encounter, if it should please God to raise him again. He saw the Necessity of being faithfull, and the Opposition he should expose himself to by being so. Under the Weight of these Thoughts he one day broke out in the following Prayer when only myself was with him. —O Lord, Thou art Light, and in Thee is no Darkness at all,[2] Thou art the Fountain of All Wisdom, and it is essential to Thee to be Good & Gracious. I am a Child O Lord, I am a Fool, teach me how I shall conduct myself, give me the Wisdom of the Serpent with the Harmlessness of the Dove.[3] Bless the Souls thou hast committed to the Care of thy helpless miserable Creature, who has no Wisdom or Knowledge of his own, and make me faithfull to them for thy Mercie's sake.

Another time he said, How wonderful it is that God should look upon Man, and how much more wonderfull that he should look upon such a Worm as I am. Yet he does look upon me—and takes the exactest Notice of all my sufferings. He is present, and I see him, I mean by Faith—and he stretches out his Arms toward me (and then he stretched out his own) and He says, Come unto me, All Ye that are weary & heavy:laden, and I will give you rest.[4]—He smiled & wept when he spoke these Words.

Again he said to the Nurse who sat by his Bedside, while I was writing at the other end of the Room.—Nurse! I will tell you my History. Oh what an unprofitable worthless Creature I have been!—When I was a Child, they put a Hornbook into my Hand, and taught me the Alphabet. In a few Years they sent me to learn Latin, and because I was the Son of a Gentleman, I learn'd Greek too. Then I came to this Place, and here I learn'd more Latin, and more Greek. And thus I have spent my three & thirty Years. Then addressing himself to Me, he said—Brother, I was going to say, in such a Year I was born, but I correct myself—I would rather say, in such a Year I came into the World—*You* know when I was born.

When he express'd himself upon these Subjects, there was a Weight and a Dignity in his Manner, such as I never saw before. He spoke with the greatest Del[ibera]tion,[5] making a Pause at the end of every Senten[ce, &] there was something in his Air & in the Tone of his Voice, inexpressibly solemn, unlike Himself, & indeed unlike what I had ever seen in another.

[2] 1 John 1: 5. [3] Matthew 10: 16. [4] Matthew 11: 28. [5] MS. torn.

This hath God wrought—I have praised him for his marvellous Act, and have felt a Joy of Heart upon the Subject of my Brother's Death, such as I never felt but in my own Conversion. He is now before the Throne, and yet a little while & we shall meet never more to be divided.

Mrs. Unwin sends her Love to Yourself & Mrs. & Miss Unwin.[6] The Objections to our visiting you this Year, remain as they were. We shall have Occasion for all our Money and All our Management.

Yours my dear Friend, with my Affectionate Respects to Yourself & Yours—

Wm Cowper.

Mar. 31. 1770.

A day or two before his Death he grew so weak & was so very ill, that he required continual Attendance, so that he had neither Strength or Opportunity to say much to me. Only the Day before, he said he had had a Sleepless, but a composed & quiet Night. I ask'd him if he had been able to collect his Thoughts. He replied, All Night long I have endeavour'd to think upon God, & to continue in Prayer. I had great Peace & Comfort, & what Comfort I had, came in that Way.

When I saw him the next Morning at 7 o'clock, he was dying, fast asleep, & exempted in all Appearance, from the Sense of those Pangs which accompany Dissolution.

I shall be glad to hear from you, my dear Friend, when you can find time to write, & are so inclined. The Death of my beloved Brother, teems with many usefull Lessons. May God seal the Instruction upon our Hearts.

[6] Mary Unwin (d. 3 Sept. 1833), William's cousin, was the daughter of Henry Unwin, who had been a stationer in Pater Noster Row, London. At his death, Unwin became one of her two trustees. Mary, who was heiress to a large fortune, lived with William and his family until she married John Hiley Aldington (1759–1818) on 25 Oct. 1785 at a ceremony performed by William.

JOSEPH HILL Saturday, 21 April 1770

Cowper Johnson

Dear Joe,

You will oblige me by enquiring at the Bank the next time your Business calls you that way, what Stock my Brother left, and by what means it is to be transferred to me; when the next Dividend is payable, and whether it will be convenient to you to receive it for me by Letter of Attorney. You may be sure it will give me great pleasure to find myself now enabled to purchase such an Annuity as may enable me to subsist comfortably without being any longer chargeable to my Friends. You are the best Judge of these matters, & I shall be glad of your Advice. I know not what is in the Bank, but should hope there may be as much as with the Sale of my Brother's Effects at Cambridge, and my own Chambers, may enable me to compass this very desireable Point.—I mention this in Confidence.

Yours dear Joe
with my Affectionate Remembrances
to Mrs. Hill & your Sisters

Olney
April 21.1770. Wm Cowper.

JOSEPH HILL Tuesday, 8 May 1770

Address: To Mr. Joseph Hill / Chancery Office / London.
Postmarks: 9/MA *and* OULNEY
Cowper Johnson

Dear Joe,

Your Letter did not reach me 'till the last Post, when I had not time to Answer it. I left Cambridge immediately after my Brother's Death.

I am much obliged to you for the particular Account you have sent me of the expended and remaining Stock. I could wish that more had been left, and begun to flatter myself with the Prospect of a Sufficiency which I might call my own: but He to whom I have surrender'd myself and all my Concerns, has otherwise appointed, and let his Will be done. He gives me much which he witholds from others,

and if he was pleased to withold All that makes an outward Difference between me and the poor Mendicant in the Street, it would still become me to say, Let His Will be done.

I fancy my Brother's Bursarship[1] was something like my Inrollership,[2] an Office more expensive than profitable. However That was, he consider'd himself as on the point of being handsomely settled, being morally secure of a good Living in Essex if he had lived a Year or two longer. But it pleased God to cut short his Connections and Expectations here, yet not without giving him lively and glorious Views of a better Happiness than any he could propose to himself in such a World as this. Notwithstanding his great Learning, (for he was one of the chief Men in the University in that respect) he was candid and sincere in his Enquiries after Truth. Tho' he could not come into my Sentiments when I first acquainted him with them, nor in the many Conversations which I afterward had with him upon the Subject, could be brought to acquiesce in them as Scriptural and true, yet I had no sooner left St. Albans than he began to study with the deepest Attention those Points in which we differ'd, and to furnish himself with the best Writers upon them. His Mind was kept open to Conviction for five years, during all which time he labour'd in this Pursuit with unwearied Diligence, as Leisure and Opportunity were afforded. Amongst his dying Words were these—'Brother, I thought you wrong, yet wanted to Beleive as you did—I found myself unable to beleive, yet always thought that I should One Day be brought to do so.' From the Study of Books he was brought upon his Death Bed to the Study of himself, and there learn'd to renounce his Righteousness and his own most Aimable Character, and to submit himself to the Righteousness which is of God by Faith. With these Views, he was desirous of Death, satisfied of his Interest in the Blessings purchased by the Blood of Christ, he prayed for Death with Earnestness, felt the Approaches of it with Joy, & died in Peace.

A Gentleman at Cambridge, an intimate Friend of my Brother's,[3] has undertaken to manage all my little Concerns in that place. When the Books and Furniture are sold, I shall remit the Money to you, and

[1] John Cowper was Bursar of Corpus Christi from 1767 until his death.

[2] C is referring to his office as Clerk of the Journals, where his function was to 'enter information among the rolls of the court'.

[3] Luke Heslop's later financial argument with C concerning John Cowper's mare might suggest that he may have been the person who offered to help C manage his Cambridge business affairs. See C to Unwin, 31 Mar. 1770, n. 1.

then be obliged to you for your Help in disposing of it to the best Advantage. I think my Chambers should by all means be sold to encrease the Purchase Money, for when the chief part of my Property is converted into an Annuity, the Expence of Occasional Repairs would be attended with great Inconvenience. I shall not be able to send a Discharge in full to my Friends who have hitherto supplied me, but shall certainly [soon be in][4] need of less Help than in time past, and shall [beg] the Favour of You to tell them so.

Yours my dear Friend
Wm Cowper.

P.S.

Our Clergyman's Name here is John Newton.

Olney May 8th. 1770.

The Bursarship Account was settled for the last year just before my Brother's Death, but will be carried on in his Name to the End of the present.

His Debts are paid; I am not yet informed of their Amount, but beleive they were not considerable.

MRS. COWPER — Thursday, 7 June 1770

Address: To / Mrs. Cowper / Holles Street / Cavendish Square / London.
Postmarks: 8/IV *and* OULNEY
Panshanger Collection

Olney June 7. 1770.

Dear Cousin,

I am obliged to you for sometimes thinking of an unseen Friend, and bestowing a Letter upon me. It gives me Pleasure to hear from you, especially to find that our gracious Lord enables you to weather out the Storms you meet with, and to cast Anchor within the Veil.

You judge rightly of the manner in which I have been affected by the Lord's late Dispensation towards my Brother. I found in it cause of Sorrow that I lost so near a Relation, and one so deservedly dear to me, and that he left me just when our Sentiments upon the most interesting Subject became the same: But much more Cause of Joy

[4] MS. torn.

that it pleased God to give me clear & evident Proof that he had changed his Heart, and adopted him into the Number of his Children. For this I hold myself peculiarly bound to thank him, because he might have done All that he was pleased to do for him, and yet have afforded him neither Strength nor Opportunity to declare it. I doubt not that he enlightens the Understandings and works a gracious Change in the Hearts of many in their last moments, whose surrounding Friends are not made acquainted with it.

He told me that from the time when he was first ordained, he began to be dissatisfied with his Religious Opinions, and to suspect that there were greater things concealed in the Bible than were generally beleived or allowed to be there. From the time when I first visited him after my Release from St. Albans, he began to read upon the Subject. It was at that time I informed him of the Views of divine Truth which I had received in that School of Affliction. He laid what I said to Heart, and began to furnish himself with the best Writers upon the contraverted Points, whose Works he read with great Diligence and Attention, comparing them all the while with the Scripture. None ever truly and ingenuously sought the Truth, but they found it; a Spirit of earnest Inquiry is the Gift of God, who never says to any, seek ye my Face in vain. Accordingly in the time of great Need, about 10 days before his Death, it pleased the Lord to dispell all his Doubts, to reveal in his Heart the Knowledge of the Savior, and to give him firm & unshaken Peace in the Belief of his Ability and Willingness to save.

As to the Affair of the Fortune:teller,[1] he never mention'd it to me, nor was there any such Paper found as you mention. I looked over All his Papers before I left the Place, and had there been such a one, must have discover'd it. I have heard the Report from other Quarters, but no other Particulars than that the Woman foretold him when he should die. I suppose there may be some Truth in the matter, but

[1] Southey (vii. 258) quotes a letter to himself of 24 March 1836 by an anonymous person who claims his father, a friend of John Cowper, witnessed the incident with the fortune-teller: 'John Cowper and my father were both, when children, at a preparatory school, then much frequented, at Felstead, in (I think) Essex. They both together enquired their future fortunes from a traveling gipsy tinker, or pedler, who came to beg at the school, and in an old soldier's red coat. (He was a man, and *not an "old woman,"* as it seems the poet Cowper had been told).' John Cowper attended Felsted School from *c.* 1751 to 1754. The friend of John Cowper was John Sawrey Morritt (1738?–1791); his son, John Bacon Sawrey Morritt (1772?–1843), a friend of Southey, was the source for this story. The elder Morritt purchased Rokeby Park, Yorks. in 1769.

whatever he might think of it before his Knowledge of the Truth, and however extraordinary her Predictions might really be, I am satisfied that he had then received far other Views of the Wisdom and Majesty of God, than to suppose that he would intrust his Secret Counsels to a Vagrant, who did not mean I suppose, to be understood to have received her Intelligence from the Fountain of Light, but thought herself sufficiently honour'd by any who would give her Credit for a secret Intercourse of this kind with the Prince of Darkness.

Mrs. Unwin is much obliged to you for your kind Enquiries after her. She is well I thank God, as usual, and sends her respects to you. Her Son is in the Ministry, and has the Living of Stock in Essex. We were last Week alarm'd with an Account of his being dangerously ill—Mrs. Unwin went to see him, and in a few days left him out of Danger.

My Love to my Aunt & to all who enquire after me—

Yours my Dear Cousin Wm Cowper.

JOSEPH HILL Monday, 3 September 1770

Address: Mr. Joseph Hill[1]
Cowper Johnson

Dear Joseph,

At length you receive the Letters of Administration.[2] The Difficulty of meeting with a Clergyman to whom I chose to apply, for we have not the least Connexion with any of the Neighbouring ones, and of being able to bring two Suretys[3] & a Witness together, at the same time, in a place where the Generality are poor and where All work for their Living, has occasioned this long Delay.

My affairs at Cambridge are not yet finally adjusted, nor can they

[1] Olney Address.

[2] A short form of probate in which the maker of the will simply assigns all power of attorney to one or more persons. In this letter, C is probably referring to the legal work he wishes Hill to do on his behalf regarding his chambers and his brother's estate (as mentioned in his letter to Hill of 8 May).

[3] A person who undertakes some specific responsibility on behalf of another who remains primarily liable (*O.E.D.*).

be 'till the Close of the year. Then you shall hear farther from me. I beg you will mention me affectionately to your own Family, and to all who enquire after

Yours
Wm Cowper.

Olney.
Sepr. 3. 1770.

JOSEPH HILL Tuesday, 25 September 1770

Cowper Johnson

Dear Joe,

Upon farther Consideration, I am partly come to a change of Purpose with respect to the Purchase of an Annuity. At least I do not design to make that Disposition of my Finnances at present. In my own Judgment, it will be more suitable to the Nature of my Circumstances, as soon as I have *amassed* the whole Bulk of my Treasure, to place it out in private Hands at 4 per cent Interest. I have thought of Mr. John Unwin[1] for this purpose, unless it will be Agreeable to Yourself, who for many reasons deserve my first Attentions in preference to every one else.

I have not done conversing with terrestrial Objects, though I should be happy were I able to hold more continual Converse with a Friend above the Skies. He has my Heart—but he allows a Corner in it for all who shew me Kindness, and therefore one for You. The Storm of 63 made a Wreck of all the Friendships I had contracted in the Course of many Years, Yours excepted, which has survived the Tempest, and I am not without Hopes, & I am sure not without many wishes, that I may Live to see the Day when a Similarity of Sentiments in the most important Concerns, shall unite us to each other in closer Bonds than ever. An Event which I leave in *His* Hands who alone can bring it to pass.

I thank you for your repeated Invitation; singular Thanks are due to you for so *singular* an Instance of your Regard. I could not leave

[1] Mary Unwin's brother-in-law John (d. 21 Sept. 1789) was of Doctors Commons and was employed as an agent in the buying and selling of livings: *G.M.* lx, pt. 1 (1790), 83.

Olney, unless in a case of Absolute Necessity, without much Inconvenience to myself & others.

I have corrected the Letters of Administration according to Advice from your Amanuensis.

My Love & best Wishes attend yourself, Mother & Sisters—Beleive me Ever Yours

Wm Cowper.

Olney.
Sep. 25. 1770.

JOSEPH HILL — Between Sunday, 30 September & Sunday, 11 November 1770[1]

Cowper Johnson

Dear Joe,

I thank you for the Notes for Fifty pounds which are just arrived, and shall be obliged to you if you will make my Acknowledgments when & where they may be made with Propriety. The Kindness of my Friends demands my Gratitude, and if an Opportunity should ever happen, which according to present Appearances is not very likely, I flatter myself I should not be backward to express it.

I leave the Welshman to your Mercy.

Remember me affectionately to my Uncle. It always gives me Pleasure to hear of his Welfare. I am not conscious that I forget any One of my Friends, tho' long absent from them, & likely to be so, notwithstanding I seldom mention them by Name.

Beleive me Yours faithfully
Wm Cowper.

Olney.
Sun: Eve.

[1] This letter is placed in the volume of letters to Hill in the Cowper Johnson collection between those of 25 Sept. and 17 Nov. 1770.

JOSEPH HILL Saturday, 17 November 1770

Address: Mr. Joseph Hill / Chancery Office / London.[1]
Cowper Johnson

Dear Joe,

Your Letter, intercepted all Night by the Floods, was heartily welcom'd here this Morning. My Debt to Grainger the Taylor has long been a Burthen upon my Mind. After several Applications I at length obtain'd a Letter from him, some time last Summer, by which he agreed the Sum to be as I had stated it, 40£ 9s. 0. but desired Interest from the time of the last Payment. I shall be extremely glad to have this tedious affair adjusted, & beg that when you have Leisure you will settle it with him. The Matter of Interest I leave entirely with yourself; whatever you think reasonable will satisfy me.

I am likewise indebted for a Suit or two, to Thomas Williams, Taylor in Arundel Street. If after Payment of Grainger's Account there should be a Surplus sufficient, as I imagine there will, you will oblige me by paying Williams.

I wait for an Opportunity, which will offer soon to send the Letter of Attorney by a private Hand. When you receive it, I hope you will pay yourself.

Yours Dear Joe
Wm Cowper.

Olney.
Nov: 17. 1770.

I shall be obliged to you for the earliest Notice of Mr. Thomas de Grey's Arrival from his Travels, together with his Address.[2]

[1] Olney Address.

[2] Thomas de Grey, later 2nd Baron Walsingham, of Merton, Norfolk (1748–1818), who was the second but only surviving son of Willaim de Grey (1719–81) and C's cousin Mary Cowper (1719–1800).

JOSEPH HILL — Tuesday, 1 January 1771

Address: Mr. Joseph Hill / Chancery Office / London.[1]
Cowper Johnson

Dear Joseph,

You will receive two parcels of Venison, a Haunch and a Shoulder. The first was intended for you, the other comes to you by Mistake. Some hours after the Basket was sent to the Waggon, we discover'd that the Shoulder had been pack'd up instead of the Haunch. All imaginable Endeavours were used to recover it, but without Success; the Waggon could not be unloaded again, and it was impossible otherwise to get at it. You may therefore thank a blundering Servant for a Venison Pasty, which if she had minded her Business better, would have been eaten at Olney.

I sent you some time since the Letter of Attorney by a private Hand.

Yours my dear Friend
Wm Cowper.

Jan: 1. 1771.

JOSEPH HILL — Saturday, 12 January 1771

Cowper Johnson

My dear Friend,

I thank you for executing all my troublesome Commissions, and am glad to find that after Payment of my two Taylors, there is a Surplus left. I should be glad to have ten pounds sent hither in a Note. The Remainder I purpose to dispose of in the Purchase of a dozen and half, red & white, small pattern Handkerchiefs at half a Crown apiece, and a yard & half narrow striped Muslin for Gentleman's Ruffles. If either of your Sisters[1] should chuse a Walk, now the Streets

[1] Olney Address.

---

[1] Frances and Theodosia (both *fl. c.* 1733–1800). They are the 'Modern Antiques' in Mary Russell Mitford's *Our Village* (First Series, 1819).

are clean & frozen, I shall be glad of her Assistance to procure them for me. My affectionate respects attend them & your Mother.

Yours dear Joe, Wm Cowper.

The Parcel must be sent on a Wednesday to the Windmill in St. John Street Smithfield.[2]

Jan: 12. 1771

JOSEPH HILL — Tuesday, 22 January 1771

Address: To / Mr. Joseph Hill / Chancery Office / London
Postmark: 23/IA
Princeton

My dear Friend,

I should have sent you Advice of the safe Arrival of the Note, by the Return of the Post, but had not a convenient Opportunity. Thanks for the Muslin and the Handkerchiefs.

Yours Wm Cowper.

Olney
Jan. 22 1771.

MRS. COWPER — Saturday, 2 March 1771

Olney (*copy*)[1]

My dear Cousin

I was unwilling to let the post go by without my earnest congratulations on the subject of your last. I doubt not all your friends rejoice with you. But none has so much cause as myself from whom sprang all the danger there was of a disappointment. I consider myself as bound to acknowledge the goodness of the Lord in this instance

[2] The parcel would have to be at St. John Street on Wednesday because the Olney carriage left at 4 a.m. on Thursdays.

[1] Mrs. Cowper's Commonplace Book, 160–1: 'Lettr. 17. dated O——y March 2d. 1771.'

equally with those who seem more immediately concerned. It was not His pleasure that I should succeed in the business, but at the same time, having all events, and all hearts in His hand, he provided that others should not suffer by my miscarriage.—I have reason to praise Him with my latest breath for this and every other affliction and disappointment I have met with: I knew not then, but I know now that He designed me a blessing, and that He only brought a cloud over my earthly prospect in order to turn my eyes towards a heavenly one. It gives me true pleasure to learn by all your letters that you are looking the same way: we may possibly meet no more on earth (for our thread of time is winding off apace) but we shall surely meet in glory. Jesus has, I trust, purchased us to be a part of His crown in the day of His appearing. How we shall bless Him then for all our sorrows below, which he was pleased to make effectual to wean us from a world of sin and vanity that we might place our affections on things above. There is a blessing in every bitter cup, not always perceptible to the taste but sure to have its effect in keeping the soul which knows Him dependent upon His power and grace, and obedient to His holy will.

I am obliged to be short, being rather straitened for time. We have been driven from our house this week by the sickness and death of a maid servant,[2] whose body putrefied before she died, and are just returned to it again. Such a spectacle I never saw! But the Lord filled her with the spirit of gladness, enabled her to sing the praises of redeeming love, and gave her an abundant entrance into His kingdom.

I beg you will give my love to my aunt: Mr. Newton designs to call upon her. He is not as yet (as you imagine) prepared with a second volume.[3] Writing is slow work, when the charge of a numerous people so often interferes with it.

Believe me Sincerely Yours &c.

[2] Molly. See n. 1, C to Mrs. Madan, 9 July 1768.

[3] *Letters, Sermons, and a Review of Ecclesiastical History* did not appear until 1780.

JOHN NEWTON — Thursday, 14 March 1771

Address: To / The Revd. Mr. Newton[1] at Dr. Fords[2] N– 25 / Old Jury / London
Postmarks: 15/MR *and* Penny Post
Princeton

My Dear Friend,

The Post is welcome that brings your Letters, for we are always glad to hear of yours and Mrs. Newton's Welfare. I would be thankfull to the gracious Providence that has hitherto preserved you both in your several Removals, and hope I am so at the Bottom, for to the Bottom I am forced to go for the Discovery of every grace I wish to be in Possession of.—If you find yourself hinder'd by an Outside Bustle, I am equally hinder'd by a Bustle within; the Lord I trust will give Peace in his own time, but I can truly say that for the most part my Soul is among Lions. Last Sunday at the Morning Meeting, the Lord favour'd me with leave to Complain, and gave me such a use of the 51st. Psalm in the Morning Service, that it seemed to have been penn'd on Purpose for me. So indeed it was, as well as the rest of his precious Word, for myself, and for all his People; but how often does a hard and unbelieving Heart deprive me of its proper Effect! I had a measure of the same Liberty again on Tuesday Night at the Meeting, but yet, neither then, nor on the Sabbath was my Burthen removed. I got Paul's Answer I trust, 'My grace shall be sufficient for thee,'[3] but was not like Him, content with it.

We beg you will present our Compliments to Mrs. Wilberforce,[4] and Mrs. Unwin's Thanks for the Trouble she has taken about the Maid.[5] We take it for granted, not having heard to the contrary, that she has had the Small Pox, for the upper part of our House, the Maid's Room at least, will probably be an infected Place for a long

1 C had originally addressed this letter: 'at William Wilberforces Esqr./St. James Place/ St. James' Street/Westminster.' Wilberforce presumably re-addressed the letter.

2 Probably Dr. James Ford (1752–99), who was physician to St. George's Hospital, London, from 1786 to 1793. Newton was a close friend of the Revd. Dr. Thomas Ford (1743–1824), James's brother, who had attended Christ Church, Oxford (B.A. 1762; M.A. 1765; D.C.L. 1770), and who was vicar of Melton Mowbray from 1773 to 1820.

3 2 Corinthians 12: 9.

4 Hannah Wilberforce (d. 1788), the sister of John Thornton of Clapham and the wife of William Wilberforce (d. *pre* 1776) of Wimbledon and St. James's Place. Mrs. Wilberforce's famous abolitionist nephew William (1759–1833) spent a large part of his boyhood with his aunt and uncle, and it was partially through them that Newton met Wilberforce in 1781.

5 Ruth Sales was recommended by Mrs. Wilberforce in a letter to C of 12 Mar. 1771 (Princeton).

time.—The Lord's Hand is still stretch'd out amongst us, nor does the Distemper seem to abate. Our People indeed are spared, but several in the Town are ill. Nanny Whitney[6] has had it, and is getting up again.

The Lord has dealt awfully with an Old Woman at the Bridge End whose Name I forget.[7] She had 400£ left her 2 or 3 years ago, and having been given to Drunkenness before, upon this Accession of Wealth, became doubly addicted to it. She went to Bed drunk, was taken with a Bleeding at the Nose in the Night, and was found dead in the Morning. Her last Words were, give me some more Stuff for I am dying. Accordingly they gave her a glass of gin in the Dark, not knowing that she had been bleeding to Death, and soon after she expired. How different from the glorious Dismission of our poor Molly.[8]

The Nephew of this Woman is the Person to whom Bet Ping designs to give her Hand in Matrimony, if he will deign to accept it. He is Executor to his Aunt, and may now possibly look out for a better Bargain. By what I hear of this unhappy Girl, she has cast off even her Profession, and it is well for the Profession in general that she has.

Blessed be God we have so many who have learn'd Christ to better purpose—may the Lord increase the chosen number!

You will find at Lord Dartmouth's[9] a letter from Mr. Bowman,[10] as the Post Mark informs me. Pray remember me affectionately to his Lordship, my Thoughts about him are not so few as my Letters, but I grow worse & worse as a Correspondent.

You will *both* believe that we *both* Love You, and shall be glad of your Return.

Yours Wm Cowper

[6] C mentions Mrs. Whitney's spiritual distresses in his letter to Newton of 21 Aug. 1780.

[7] As C's next paragraph makes clear, she is the aunt of Thomas Stanley who married Elizabeth Ping (1744–80) on 28 Apr. 1771 (*O.P.R.*, p. 364).

[8] Molly's death is related by C in his letter to Mrs. Cowper of 2 Mar.

[9] See n. 3, C to Mrs. Madan, 9 July 1768.

[10] The Revd. Thomas Bowman (*c.* 1728–92) was vicar of Martham in Norfolk from 1758 until his death. Bowman was the author of several tracts, including *A Review of the Doctrines of the Reformation* (1768).

In a letter to C of 16–18 Apr. 1768 (Princeton), Newton, on a speaking tour away from Olney, mentions being met at Norwich 'by Mr. Bowman, & another Gospel minister in the neighbourhood'. Later in the letter, Newton remarks on Bowman's isolation among his parishioners: 'Poor Mr. Bowman has as yet few or none to pray for him, or strengthen his hands—how glad would he be to be encompassed as I am— !'

Olney.
Mar: 14. 1771.

My Respects to Mr. Wilberforce.

Next Wednesday will do as well as any day. If you will send word in your next when you think you shall be at Wooburn,[11] we will endeavour to meet you there.

JOSEPH HILL — Saturday, 6 April 1771

Cowper Johnson

My dear Friend—

My Brother's Accounts as Bursar of Bene't College are at length settled. His Effects at Cambridge are not sufficient to answer the Demands of the Society upon them. There is a Deficiency of 300£.— This Money must be raised immediately by the Sale of Stock. The New Bursar is appointed, and will be in Town before this Letter reaches you. He will probably call upon you soon after his Arrival, for he is gone on purpose to place the College Money in the Funds.[1]— I should have sent you earlier Notice, but by some Accident the Letter which brought me this Intelligence was delay'd upon the Road, and did not reach me 'till Yesterday.

I knew that my Brother had lodged some of the College Stock in the Bank, but did not know that it made a part of the 700£.[2] I am afraid however that it does.

My Love to your Family & all Friends

Beleive me yours affectionately
Wm Cowper.

Olney
April 6. 1771.

[11] Woburn is 16½ miles south-east of Olney on the London road and would have been a convenient place for C and Newton to meet.

---

[1] On 17 Apr. the Revd. James Nasmith (1740–1808) wrote in his capacity of Bursar to Hill concerning 'the Sum of three hundred pounds in part of the balance due from the late Mr John Cowper . . . to the Master & fellows of ye society' (Princeton).

[2] The £700 is explained below in C to Hill, 5 Nov. 1772.

JOSEPH HILL — Tuesday, 27 August 1771

Address (at Princeton): Mr. Joseph Hill / Chancery Office / London.
Cowper Johnson

Dear Joe,

I take a Friend's share in all your Concerns, so far as they come to my Knowledge, and consequently did not receive the News of your Marriage[1] with Indifference. I wish You and your Bride all the Happiness that belongs to the State, and the still greater Felicity of that State which Marriage is only a Type of. All these Connections shall be dissolved; but there is an indissoluble Bond between Christ and his Church, the Subject of Derision to an unthinking World, but the Glory and Happiness of All his People.

I hope my Uncle has by this time received the Bond from Cambridge. The Master's Absence from College almost the whole Summer has occasion'd the Delay; but One of the Fellows was here lately, who undertook to remitt it to you in a few days.

My Brother expended about Eight Pounds for a Mr. Pierse,[2] an Eaton Boy, a Relation of Mr. Morritt of York.[3] He wrote me Word that he would Order Mr. Butter (Mr. Pierse's Agent) to pay the Money to You, if upon Enquiry he found that it had not been paid already. Have you received it?—I expected to have received the Ballance of my Cambridge Account a Year ago, but it is still in Arrear; this Disappointment has made me and kept me Poor. You will oblige me by disposing of Fifty pounds Consolidated,[4] and sending me the Money by the first Opportunity, for I suppose I have nothing considerable in your Hands.

I join with your Mother and Sisters in their Joy upon the present Occasion, and beg my affectionate Respects to them, and to Mrs. Hill unknown.

Yours ever
Wm Cowper.

Olney.
Augt. 27. 1771.

[1] Hill married Sarah (1742–1824), the daughter of John Mathews of Wargrave, during this month. See *Notes and Queries*, 12th ser. v (1919), 259.

[2] Henry Peirse (1754–1824), of Bedale, Yorks, entered Eton in 1764 and left there in 1770. He was admitted as a fellow-commoner at Pembroke College, Cambridge, in 1771 and served as M.P. for Northallerton, 1774–1824. *The Eton College Register, 1753–1790*, ed. R. A. Austen Leigh (Eton, 1921), p. 411.

[3] See n. 1, C to Mrs. Cowper, 7 June 1770.

[4] Consolidated annuities.

JOSEPH HILL Saturday, 2 November 1771

Cowper Johnson

My dear Friend,

Such Paper Currency as the inclosed is good for nothing at Olney; you will oblige me if you will get it changed for Mrs. Unwin, into two 20£. Notes,[1] and send them down by the first Opportunity. I would not trouble a Man of your many Concerns with such a matter, but Necessity swallows up all my Scruples. My Respects wait on yours whether in Cooke's Court or elsewhere.

Beleive me your Affectionate
Wm Cowper.

Olney
Nov: 2. 1771.

JOSEPH HILL Sunday, 17 November 1771

Cowper Johnson

My dear Friend,

We cannot bear that after your Kindness to us, there should be a Door left open for the least Suspicion of Neglect on our part. I just send you therefore a hasty Line to tell you that either by some Accident, or the Negligence of Mrs. Unwin's Agent at Ely the Bill which we have expected by the two last Posts, is not yet return'd. You may depend upon hearing again, as soon as we can either send you That, or another.

Yours ever
Wm Cowper.

Nov: 17. 1771.

[1] There was no paper currency issued at this time by the government, but promissory notes were assignable in law. Hill's £40 note was probably an engraved promissory note issued by Child's. See R. D. Richards, *The Early History of Banking in England* (1965), pp. 41–2, 192–3.

JOSEPH HILL — Thursday, 21 November 1771

Cowper Johnson

My dear Friend

Behold the Note!

We shall be obliged to you for a Line to inform us of its safe Arrival.

Yours ever
Wm Cowper.

Olney
Nov: 21. 1771.

JOSEPH HILL — Tuesday, 31 December 1771

Princeton

My dear Friend,

My Cambridge Business, still unsettled, occasions me many Difficulties. If you have received the 20£ you expected I shall be glad to have it remitted immediately.

Yours Wm Cowper.

Decb. 31.
1771.

JOSEPH HILL — Thursday, 9 January 1772

Princeton

My dear Friend,

Thanks for the Note for 20£ which reached me last Night. I wish we had it in our Power to send you a Summer Haunch as well as a Winter one, but am afraid that for the future we shall be able to send

you neither; Lord Northampton[1] has inclosed my Chace and converted it into a Park.

My Respects attend your Family,
Beleive me ever yours
Wm Cowper

Olney
Jan: 9 1772.

JOSEPH HILL — Thursday, 30 January 1772

Cowper Johnson

Dear Joe,

An Article in the last General Evening, compar'd with an Advertisement in the same Paper, has affected me with the deepest Concern upon my Uncle Ashley's Account.[1] In the present Uncertainty of my Mind I am left to imagine the worst. It would have been kind in some of my many Relations, if they had not left me to learn such melancholy Intelligence from the Public Prints. I shall be obliged to you for such Particulars as you can favour me with, they will at least serve to releive me from the Variety of restless Conjectures which cannot but employ my Mind upon such an Occasion.

Yours my Dear Friend
Wm Cowper.

Olney.
Jan: 30. 1772.

[1] Spencer Compton, 8th Earl of Northampton (1738–96), was educated at Westminster and served as Lord Lieutenant of Northamptonshire from 1771 until his death. Northampton had evidently ordered the enclosure of the chase or hunting ground from which C procured his venison.

---

1 *The General Evening Post* of 25 to 28 Jan. (No. 5975) carries a brief note in its London section: 'Mr. C—r, Clerk to the House of L—ds, has been missing for some days.' It also carries the following advertisement: 'Whereas a gentleman went out on a Monday afternoon last, the 20th inst. and has not since been heard of, and there is the greatest reason to apprehend some fatal accident has befallen him. . . .'

C evidently learned quite soon (possibly from Hill) that the missing Cowper was his namesake, William Cowper (1750–98), Maria's eldest son, and not his uncle Ashley, who was Clerk of the Parliaments. Maria's son may have held the patent of this office and thus the confusion on the part of the newspaper. See *Ryskamp*, pp. 148–9. C speaks to Hill (4 Feb. 1772) of 'the poor Young Man'. See also n. 2, C to Mrs. Cowper, 4 Apr. 1772.

JOSEPH HILL Tuesday, 4 February 1772

Cowper Johnson

My dear Friend,

I am much indebted to you for your Goodness in releiving me, by the first Opportunity, from the Fears I had upon my Uncle's Account. The Newspaper led me into the Mistake, where the Person was described as the Clerk of the House of Lords, without the Addition of his proper Distinction. But I feel much for Mrs. Cowper & the poor Young Man, and love him better than he is aware of, tho' I have not seen him many Years, & he was but a Child when I saw him last. So sudden a Stroke must fall very heavy upon her, but I know her Principles to be such as will afford her Support under the heaviest that can befall her.—The Dress, the Circumstance of his having no Baggage, & the Time, all seem to concurr in giving us a good Hope that he was the Person seen at Dover. You will make me happy by sending me the first Intelligence you hear of him, for I could hardly be more interested in any case, not immediately my own, than I am in this. I am, with my best Respects to Mrs. Hill, & Thanks for her Kindness,

Yours ever
Wm Cowper.

Feb: 4. 1772

MRS. COWPER Tuesday, 25 February 1772

Olney (*copy*)[1]

My dear Cousin—

It never grieved me that I did not hear from you or my Aunt upon this most melancholy occasion. Great sorrows are best spoken of to Him who alone can relieve us from them, but do not easily express themselves either in conversation or by letter. Your writing to me at all upon this subject strikes me as a most valuable and convincing proof of your friendship for me, who am so unworthy of it. Not but

[1] Mrs. Cowper's Commonplace Book, 172–5: 'The Answer dated Feb. 25. 1772. Letter 18.'

that I may truly say, I have a share in your sorrows, and that you and my poor kinsman are upon my heart all the day long, and night and day my subject at the throne of Grace.[2]

> Whether on the rolling wave,
> Or in distant lands he stray,
> Lord, I cry, be near to save,
> Guard him and direct his way.[3]

How true is that word of the prophet, 'God has his way in the whirlwind, and the clouds are the dust of His feet!'[4] But He has told us for our comfort that He will not contend forever,[5] for the spirit should fail before Him, and the souls which he has made. The support He has graciously afforded you, my dear cousin, in your most trying circumstances, is an amazing proof of His compassion, faithfulness, and power. He is glorified by the faith and patience of His saints; and how great is the honour He has done you by enabling you to praise Him in such a furnace of affliction! I thank Him on your behalf, and I could praise Him too—but it is a time of great darkness and trouble in my soul so that I am hardly able to lift up a thought towards Him. It is with the utmost difficulty I write a short answer to your kind letter, but assure yourself that while I have power to pray at all, I shall not cease to do it that you may still be supported, that He would still place beneath you the Everlasting Arm and make your strength equal to your day. May He watch over our dear ——[6] with a father's eye, preserve the poor wandering bird cast out of its nest, and restore him to you in peace and safety. God does know that if I could pray with all the fervency of all the saints that ever lived, I would beg with constant importunity that he might return, if not to be enriched with the treasures of this spiritual Egypt, yet filled with all the fullness of the blessings of the Gospel of Christ. Then perhaps I should be enabled to praise Him too—for of a truth I had rather see him at the foot of a Redeemer's Cross, as I had rather be there myself, than placed upon the very pinnacle of all earthly grandeur and prosperity.

I beg my love to my dear aunt. I have more need to apologize for my silence than she for hers, but am not so able to do it. I am very

[2] Three lines of the letter are blotted out.

[3] We have not been able to locate the source of these lines.

[4] Nahum 1 : 3.

[5] Isaiah 57 : 16.

[6] William Cowper, Maria Cowper's son. See n. 1, C to Hill, 30 Jan. 1772.

sorry that she has so good an excuse. May the Lord heal her or grant her His presence which is better than health.

I remember my cousin,——[7] the Less, with much affection. May God bless her, and my friend ——[8] with each of yours, known and unknown.

I shall rejoice to hear that you have received good and comfortable tidings, and remain my dear Cousin,

Your truly affectionate
&c.

MRS. COWPER — Saturday, 4 April 1772

Olney (*copy*)[1]

My dear Cousin,

Your letter was a welcome messenger of glad tidings; I truly rejoice with you, and desire to join you in praising a gracious and merciful God, who though he chastens us sore, does not give us over unto death. I have been constantly mindful of you in my prayers, and shall continue to be so; by God's help, still hoping in His mercy that He will crown the dispensation with His goodness, and finish it in love.—The last sacramental opportunity we had, the Lord was pleased to favour me with much liberty in pleading and wrestling with Him for my dear kinsman, and his afflicted mother. I can truly say my soul travailed in birth with his soul, and that I never desired my own salvation more feelingly than I was then strengthened to agonize for his. I could plead with Him for that precious body and blood which I then saw exhibited before me that he might be admitted into a saving participation of that glorious mystery. Washed, sanctified, justified in the name of the Lord Jesus and by the spirit of our God. Nor did I leave the throne till I received a comfortable and sweet assurance that the Lord would answer us in peace, and in the truth of His salvation.

The times and the seasons are in His own hand. The ways and

[7] There is an erasure here and then a dash over it. 'Maria' seems to be the word eradicated. C was probably referring to Maria Judith (1752–1815), Mrs. Cowper's oldest daughter.

[8] Probably George Cowper. See n. 3, C to Mrs. Cowper, 14 July 1772.

[1] Mrs. Cowper's Commonplace Book, 177–9: 'Lett: 19'.

means entirely under His disposal, but I mention this experience in hopes that it may be made a comfort to you. I remember it was comfortable news to me, when I was at Cambridge attending my brother in his last illness, to hear from Olney that the Lord was pleased to pour out a spirit of prayer for him, and the event answered and exceeded my highest expectations. I am not the only one whom a gracious God is employing upon the occasion to plead your cause in this place. My dear friend Mrs. U— lays it much to heart, and I can answer for Mr. & Mrs. N. that they both feel for you; and pray continually that an abundant blessing may spring up for you and yours out of this affliction.

I pray God, who has preserved him hitherto,[2] still to preserve him[3] and bring him home in peace. How I shall long to see him! Surely I should embrace him as a brother, and more than a brother, could I but see him at O—y devoted to that Jesus who gave Himself, I trust, for him and for me. May he come home in the best sense, home to God, and home to the Mediator of the new covenant: then, after having been tossed, as the Lord says, like a ball into a far country,[4] he shall find in the smiles of a reconciled God and Father what Dr. Watts calls—

A young heaven on earthly ground.
And glory in the bud.[5]

Mrs. Unwin desires me to present her Christian respects to you. She has mourned with you. She begins to rejoice with you, and will accompany you step by step through all the dispensation. Mr. N. speaks of calling upon you when he goes next to London for he takes a deep interest in your concerns upon this occasion. My dear cousin, may He who makes the widow's heart to sing for joy, bless you and yours and shine upon you! Let the men of this world carve it out amongst themselves. We will not envy them, though we will pity and pray for them. But may we and ours have our portion in God. The pearl of great price is a possession which makes us rich indeed.[6]

[2] News of William's safety had evidently reached Mrs. Cowper, and she had passed the word along to C.

[3] Note in Mrs. Cowper's hand appended to the margin: 'this came to Pass, 4 Years after!! viz: his Return.'

[4] Isaiah 22: 18.

[5] This is from Hymn LIX, 'Paradise on Earth', from Book II of *Hymns and Spiritua Songs* (1707).

[6] Matthew 13: 46

But as to the earth and the glory of it, the sound of the last trumpet shall soon shatter it all to pieces.[7] Then happy they, and only they, who when they see the Lord coming in the heavens with power and great glory shall be able to say, 'Lo! this is our God, and we have waited for Him.'[8]

Yours my dear Cousin, ever &c.

O—ny Ap. 4. 1772.

JOSEPH HILL — Tuesday, 7 April 1772

Address: Mr. Joseph Hill / Chancery Office / London.[1]
Cowper Johnson

My dear Friend,

I am very much obliged to you that in the Hurry of so much Business, you could yet find time to fulfill your Promise, & send me the earliest Intelligence of my poor Cousin. But as Mrs. Cowper is so kind as to write to me herself upon the Occasion, I will discharge you from any farther Trouble about it. We have seen the dark Side of the Dispensation, and I yet hope it has a bright one. This I know, that if he reap the same Fruit of his Sorrows, as thousands have found springing up from the deepest Afflictions, he will rejoice in the Remembrance of them, as I do, and shall do while I Live in the Recollection of mine.

Yours my Dear Friend, with my
Respects to Mrs. Hill & all your Family

Wm Cowper.

Olney.
April 7. 1772.

7 1 Corinthians 15 : 52.
8 Isaiah 25 : 9.

1 Olney Address.

MRS. MADAN Tuesday, 9 June 1772

Olney (*copy*)[1]

My dear Aunt

I thank you for your kind note and for the papers you was so good as to send me by Mr. N. The last words of a dying saint, and some of the first lispings of, I trust, a living one![2] May the Lord accomplish the work He seems to have begun and sanctify to my dear kinsman all his disappointments, and the great affliction with which He has seen good to visit him. This has been my prayer for him every day since I was acquainted with his troubles; except at sometimes when my own soul has seemed to be almost swallowed up in spiritual distress. At such times, I am forced to account it a great matter if I can groan out something a little like a prayer for myself. I bless God I can say, 'I know in Whom I have believed!' and am persuaded He will keep me. But together with this persuasion which one would think would smooth the roughest road of life and make a paradise of a desert, I have temptations that are almost ever present with me and shed a thick gloom upon all my prospect. Sin is my burthen—a sure token that I shall be delivered from its remaining power. But while it remains, it will oppress me. The Lord who chose me in the furnace of affliction is pleased to afford the tempter a large permission to try me: I think I may say, 'I am tried to the utmost, or nearly to the utmost that spiritual trials can amount to.' And when I think of the more even path in which some are led to glory, I am ready to sigh and say, 'Oh that the lines were fallen unto me in such pleasant places!'[3] In my judgement I approve of all I meet with, see the necessity there is that I should be in heaviness, and how good it is to bear the yoke of adversity. But in my experience there is a sad swerving aside, a spirit that would prescribe to the only wise God, and teach Him how He shall deal with me: I weary myself with ineffectual struggles against His will, and then sink into an idle despondence equally unbecoming a soldier of Christ Jesus. A seaman terrified at a storm who creeps down into the hold, when he should be busy amongst the tackling

[1] Mrs. Cowper's Commonplace Book, 184–6: 'Letter 17. to my Mother from W.C. dated Olney June 9. 1772.'

[2] A reference to the missing William Cowper, Mrs. Madan's grandson, mentioned in C's letter of 30 Jan. to Hill.

[3] Psalm 16: 6.

aloft, is just my picture. But let me not conceal my Master's goodness. I have other days in my calendar—days that would be foolishly exchanged for all the monarchies of the earth! That part of the wilderness I walk through is a romantic scene. There is but little level ground in it, but mountains hard to ascend, deep and dark valleys, wild forests, caves, and dens in abundance—but when I can hear my Lord invite me from afar, and say, 'Come to me, my spouse, come from the Lebanon, from the top of Amana, from the lions' dens, from the mountains and the leopards,'[4] then I can reply with cheerfulness, 'Behold, I come unto thee for thou art the Lord my God.'

I beg my love to Mrs. Cowper and do not cease to pray for her. Remember me affectionately to Mrs. Maitland, and to Martin[5] &c when you see them. Believe me my dear Aunt

Affectionately Yours in the Lord

&c.

JOSEPH HILL — Saturday, 27 June 1772

Cowper Johnson

My dear Friend,

I only write to return you Thanks for your kind Offer—Agnosco veteris Vestigia Flammæ[1]—But I will endeavour to go on without troubling you. Excuse an Expression that dishonours your Friendship; I should rather say it would be a Trouble to myself, and I know you will be generous enough to give me Credit for the Assertion. I had rather want many things, any thing indeed that this World could afford me, than Abuse the Affection of a Friend. I suppose you are sometimes troubled upon my Account, but you need not. I have no doubt it will be seen when my Days are closed, that I served a Master who would not suffer me to want any thing that was good for me. He said to Jacob, I will surely do thee Good[2]—And This he said, not

[4] Song of Songs 4: 8.

[5] Probably 'Maitland' and 'Martin' respectively, but the eradicated words cannot be completely deciphered.

[1] *Aeneid*, iv. 23: 'I discern the remains of the long-standing flame.'

[2] Genesis 32: 9.

for His sake only, but for Ours also if we trust in him. This thought releives me from the greatest part of the Distress I should else suffer in my present Circumstances, and enables me to sit down peacefully upon the Wreck of my Fortune.

Yours ever my dear Friend, with my Respects and Compliments as before

Wm Cowper.

June 27.
1772.

JOSEPH HILL — Thursday, 2 July 1772

Cowper Johnson

My dear Friend

My obligations to You sit easy upon me, because I am sure you confer them in the Spirit of a Friend. 'Tis pleasant to some Minds to confer obligations, and it is not unpleasant to others to be properly sensible of them. I hope I have this Pleasure—and can with a true Sense of your Kindness subscribe myself

Yours
Wm Cowper.

July 2. 1772.

MRS. COWPER — Tuesday, 14 July 1772

Olney (*copy*)[1]

My Dear Cousin

I return you many thanks for the papers Mr. N. brought with him. I am acquainted with those deeps through which your son has passed, and can therefore sympathize with him. A spirit of conviction breathes in the prayers he left behind him;[2] they are the language of a soul in anguish on the account of sin, that finds itself a guilty creature, helpless as it is miserable, and under a necessity of seeking pardon and peace from God: while it was thus with me, the world, which till

[1] Mrs. Cowper's Commonplace Book, 186–9: 'Lettr. 20 dated July 14. 1772.'

then had satisfied me, could satisfy me no longer; I found it was a mere wilderness, a dark, uncomfortable scene. The face of man became terrible to me, and I could not bear to meet the eye of a fellow-creature. The distress of my poor friend seems to be of this kind. 'Tis true he has always been virtuous, and of a religious cast, but the Lord in order to show that persons of all characters have equal need of mercy, and that all are amenable to His holy law, having sinned and come short of His glory, deals sometimes more sharply with such an one than with the most profligate and abandoned. The latter perhaps shall be drawn gently towards Him with the cords of love, whilst the sweet and amiable amongst the children of men shall be made a terror to themselves. The self-righteous spirit (which such are in peculiar danger of) must be humbled in the dust, and these as well as others become guilty before God! I pity him therefore, for it is sad indeed when the arrows of the Almighty stick fast in the conscience and His hand presseth us sore. I know well for my own part (and my conduct proved it) that rather than stand at the bar of the house in that condition, I should have been glad of a retreat in the bowels of the earth, and to have hid myself in the center of it. God knows how gladly I would have laid down my existence, had that been possible, and that I should have shouted for joy at the thought of annihilation—but God had better things in store for me, and so I doubt not He has for my dear namesake. 'Twas a rough way by which He brought me out of Egypt, but He did it with an outstretched arm; if He sees that affliction is good for us, we shall find it—He will not be turned aside from His purpose. He does not grieve us willingly, but we must drink the cup He has mixt for us, and when we have done so, and our trouble has had its due effect, He will reveal His compassion to us, and convince us that He pitied us all the while, and made our burthen heavy only because He had a favor towards us. Thus He dealt with me; and thus I trust He will deal with B—.[2] In the mean time, my dear cousin, we have much to praise Him for—how kindly did the Lord provide for him the most hospitable reception even in a strange land, and how did He watch over him in all his way, preserving him from those many dangers to which, unattended as he was, he was continually exposed! I don't write to remind you of these things, for I dare say you have no need of such a monitor, but I mention them as affording a ground of much

[2] 'Bill' or 'Billy', i.e. the missing William Cowper.

encouragement to hope that grace, mercy and peace to you and yours shall close the dispensation.

You may depend upon my taking the utmost care of the papers, and that they shall be returned by the first safe opportunity. I congratulate you upon G——'s[3] safe arrival, give my love to him, and to M—a[4] and believe me

Affectionately yours
&c.

JOSEPH HILL — Thursday, 29 October 1772

Cowper Johnson

My dear Friend,

If my Revenues for the present Year should not exceed those of the last, I imagine the whole will be sunk in discharging my Arrears to You (which I desire may be done in the first place) and in the Payment of my Taylor's Bill. Should this be the case, I must beg the Favour of you to supply me from the Bank, and that as soon as possible. You expected no doubt to have heard from me upon this Subject sooner, but a small Reinforcement, which I received from Cambridge upon the final Settlement of my Accounts there, has made it unnecessary for me to trouble you 'till now.[1] I forget whether the Letter of Attorney You have from Me, impowers you to Sell or not. If it be only for the Receipt of Dividend, you will be so good as to send me another which I will execute and remitt to you immediately.

My Affectionate Respects attend upon yourself and your whole Family, as well as my own Relations who are so good as to enquire after me.

Yours Wm Cowper.

Olney, Octr. 29.
1772.

[3] George Cowper (1754–87), Maria's third son.
[4] Maria's daughter, Maria Judith.

[1] See C to Hill, 21 Apr. 1770.

JOSEPH HILL — Thursday, 5 November 1772

Address: Mr. Joseph Hill / Chancery Office / London.[1]
Cowper Johnson

My dear Friend—

You will certainly find the Mistake on your side. When, on the Occasion of my Brother's Death, you was so good as to make Enquiry for me at the Bank, you found 700£ there. 350 were sold as you say to pay the College 300, consequently 350 remain. As you had forgot the Principal, doubtless you have not received the Interest for the last 2 years; I would have it reserved if you please for Payment of my Taylor's Bill. You say you expect farther Remittances on my Account, out of these you will be so good as to pay yourself. I thank you for the Money you sent me by the Post, but 20£ will not serve my present Exigences. This is the Season of the Year when my Wants are always most importunate. I shall be glad therefore if you will sell the odd 50, and remitt me the Money by the first Opportunity.

Beleive me my dear Friend truly sensible of your kind Invitation, tho' I do not accept it. My Peace of Mind is of so delicate a Constitution, that the Air of London will not agree with it. You have my Prayers, the only Return I can make you, for your many Acts of still continued Friendship.

If You should Smile, or even Laugh at my Conclusion, & I were near enough to see it, I should not be angry, tho' I should be grieved. It is not long since I should have Laugh'd at such a Recompense myself. But Glory be to the Name of Jesus, those days are past, & I trust never to return.

I am Yours & Mrs. Hill's, with much Sincerity

Wm Cowper.

Nove. 5.
1772.

[1] Olney Address.

JOSEPH HILL Saturday, 14 November 1772

Address: Mr. Joseph Hill / Chancery Office / London.[1]
Cowper Johnson

My dear Friend,

I received last Night the two Notes for 30£ & 10£. I will not trouble you at present with my Taylor's Bill; I shall have Occasion to employ him in the Spring, by which time it is possible there may be enough in my Bank to answer his Demand, & you may expect to see him about March or April with a Draft in his Hand. I do not design to break into the Stock unless it should be unavoidably necessary, but you know well that I have been a considerable Loser in point of Income by my Brother's Death, and that the Price of every thing is continually advancing, so that it is become much more difficult to bring the Year about Now, than when I first left St. Albans. I am guilty of no Extravagance or Inattention to what is call'd the Main chance, nor would be on any Account. My Situation in Life is comfortable; my Friends would wish it to be so, nor is there a Place in the Kingdom where I should enjoy so many Advantages as here. And yet, as I say, there may possibly arise a Necessity of having recourse to the Funds, tho' nothing less than Necessity shall compell me to it. In that case, I should hope not to be censured for the Reasons abovemention'd, and in the mean time, shall do my best to prevent the Necessity of such a Measure.

Beleive me my dear Friend,

Affectionately yours Wm Cowper.

Olney. Nove. 14. 1772.

There are no extant letters by Cowper from 14 November 1772 until 18 May 1776. The absence of any correspondence in these years is partly due to the derangement Cowper suffered in early 1773 and which lasted until about the middle of 1774. It was in late February 1773 that Cowper experienced the dream 'before the recollection of which, all consolation vanishes' (Cowper to Newton, 16 Oct. 1785). In this dream, Cowper heard the dreadful words: 'Actum est de te, periisti' ('It is all over with thee, thou hast perished'). Cowper's engagement to Mrs. Unwin was broken off during this period, and he moved to Olney Vicarage, under the care of the Newtons, in April. He did not return to Orchard Side until 23 May 1774. The following letter of

[1] Olney Address.

7 October 1773 from Mrs. Unwin to Mrs. Cowper is concerned, in part, with Cowper's condition.

FROM MRS. UNWIN TO MRS. NEWTON

Thursday, 7 October 1773

Address: Mrs. Newton / at Mr. Trinder's / Northampton / Turn at Newport
Postmarks: OULNEY *and* NEWPORT/PAGNEL
McMaster

I hope my Dear Madam this will meet you well & safely returned thus far on your Journey. Though it will be a sincere pleasure to me to see you & Dear Mr. Newton again, yet I beg you will not put yourselves to the least ilconvenience or hurry to reach home till the most fit & agreable time. The Lord is very gracious to us; for though the cloud of affliction still hangs heavy on Mr. Cowper yet he is quite calm & persuadable in every respect. He has been for these few days past more open & communicative than heretofore. It is amazing how subtilly the cruel adversary has worked upon him. & wonderfull to see how the Lord has frustrated his wicked machinations; for though He has not seen good to prevent the most violent temptations & distressing delusions, yet He has prevented the Mischeivous effects the enemy designed by them. A most Marvellous story will this Dear Child of God have to relate when by His Almighty power he is set at liberty. As nothing short of Omnipotence could have supported him through this sharp Affliction so nothing less can set him free from it. I allow that means are in general not only lawfull but also expedient, but in the present case we must I am convinced advert to our first Sentiment, that this is a peculiar & exempt one, & that the Lord Jehovah will be alone Exalted when the day of deliverance comes.

I must beg the favour of you to buy for me two pounds of Chocolate, half a pound or ten Ounces of white sixpenny Worsted, half a Dozen Lemons, & two Sets of Knitting Needles, Six in a Set, one the finest that can be got of Iron or Steel, the other a Size Coarser. Sally Nor Judy know of my writing else I am sure they would desire me to insert their Duty.

Pray present my Affectionate remembrance to Mr. Newton, & my Sincere Respects to Mr. & Mrs. Trinder & Miss Smith & believe me to be My Dearest Madam your truly

Affectionate & hig[hly]
indebted friend
M: Unwin

Ocbr: 7—73

JOSEPH HILL — Saturday, 18 May 1776

Address: Mr. Joseph Hill / Chancery Office / London.[1]
Cowper Johnson

Dear Joseph,

You have my Thanks for the very fine Mackarel you sent, and for your kind Invitation to Wargrove;[2] I was a little mortified to find that I had not got the Start of your Gardener so much as I hoped to have done, but let him be upon his guard, or I shall be too nimble for him another year.

I want Money—not to lend, nor to give, but for my own personal and particular Use, and want it so much, that I can't go on without it. You will oblige me if you will give yourself the Trouble to sell 50£ and remit me the Produce immediately. I beg you will do this without making any sad Reflections upon it, for, assure yourself, neither you nor I shall ever have any reason to regret the doing it.

Yours affectionately Wm Cowper.

Olney May 18. 1776.

JOSEPH HILL — Sunday, 26 May 1776

Address: Mr. Joseph Hill / Wargrove near / Twyford / Berks.[1]
Cowper Johnson

My dear Friend,

More thanks for more Mackarel, and many more for the 50£ which I receiv'd Yesterday. It gave me the greater Pleasure, as it afforded a convincing Proof that in your former Refusal you was guided by nothing but an Attention to my Interest.

The Winter having swallow'd up the Spring this Year, has thrown me so backward in some of my nicer Productions, that I shall not be able to send you any Melons 'till late in the Season, but if you raise none yourself they shall wait upon you as soon as they are ripe.

Yours affectionately Wm Cowper.

Olney
May 26.—76.

[1] Olney Address. [2] Hill's country residence, seven miles north-east of Reading.

[1] Olney Address.

JOSEPH HILL Saturday, 6 July 1776

Cowper Johnson

My dear Friend,

As you have an extensive Acquaintance you may possibly be able to serve me in a Design I have lately form'd, of taking two, three or four Boys under my Tuition, to instruct them in the Greek & Latin Languages. I should persue, with some few Exceptions the Westminster Method of Instruction,[1] being That which I am best acquainted with myself, and the best upon the Whole that I have had an Opportunity of observing. They would Lodge & Board under our Roof, and be in all respects accommodated & attended in a manner that would well warrant the Demand of a 100 Guineas per Annum.

You have often wish'd me an Employment, and I know none but this for which I am qualified; if I can engage in it, it will probably be serviceable to me in more respects than one, but as it will afford me some sort of Establishment, at least for a time, it cannot but be desireable to one in my Circumstances. If you are acquainted therefore with any Person who has a Son or Sons between 8 and 10 years of Age, for whom he would wish to find a Tutour who will not make a Property of them, nor neglect any means in his Power to inform them thoroughly in what he undertakes to teach, you will oblige me by recommending *Me*. Doubtless there are many such, and it is not an easy matter to find a Family where the two grand Points of Education, Literature and Sobriety, would be more closely attended to than in This.

We return you many Thanks for the fine Turbot you was so kind as to send.

Beleive me Yours &c. Wm Cowper.

July 6. 1776.

[1] C is referring to the emphasis on Latin and Greek at Westminster during his days there, but he may very well be recalling the equal importance placed on 'living manners' by his headmaster John Nicoll who made it policy 'to cherish every spark of genius, which he could discover in his scholars': Richard Cumberland, *Memoirs* (1806), pp. 52–4.

JOSEPH HILL — Thursday, 1 August 1776

Cowper Johnson

My dear Friend,

I am obliged to you for the Bank Note for 25£ which I receiv'd by Yesterday's Post.

The Coldness of the past Season would be forgotten in the Heat of the present, if the Effects of it were not still visible in the Garden. My Melons which ought to have been eaten or at least Eatable by this time, are not yet ripe, and as you are taking your Repose at Wargrove, you will agree with me I imagine that it would hardly be worth while to trundle them so far. Else as I flatter myself they will be better flavour'd than such as are raised for Sale, which are generally flashy, and indebted to the Watering Pot for their Size, I should have been glad to have sent you half my Crop.

If it were to Rain Pupils, perhaps I might catch a Tub full, but till it does, the Fruitlessness of my Enquiries makes me think I must keep my Greek & Latin to Myself.

Yours Affectionately Wm Cowper.

Augt. 1. —76.

JOHN NEWTON[1] — Tuesday, 15 October 1776

Address: Reverend Mr. Newton / at Doctr: Fords / No: 25 / Old Jewry / London
Postmark: 16/OC
Olney

I rejoice greatly my Dear Sir that the Lord carried you safely & honourably through the late operation.[2] May He Now & ever be your stay & support! His strength is made perfect in Our Weakness. Had He endow'd you with great Natural resolution, you would not so plainly have perceived His everlasting Arm underneath you. I am sincerely glad at His provident Mercies toward you, for the good

[1] This letter is in Mrs. Unwin's hand but signed by C as well as Mrs. Unwin.

[2] According to Josiah Bull (*John Newton* [*c.* 1868], p. 222), Newton 'underwent an operation for a tumour in his thigh. He was mercifully brought through it, and was very soon able to resume his ordinary duties.' Bull mistakenly places this incident in November 1776.

accommodations, the kind friends & in short for all the mercies His bountifull hand supplies you with. What a blessing the serenity of mind you enjoy! Many share with you in outward things, but a gloominess or anxiety of mind prevents their enjoyment of them. I hope Mrs Newton is reconciled to the dispensation. She was so overwhelm'd with fear & sorrow when she so kindly came to take leave of me that I was quite Concern'd for her. May the Joy of the Lord be her strength! I sent your Welcome Letter to Mr. Catlett[3] & Sally Johnson,[4] the latter's sincere love for you Created many fears & Misgivings on your account. Mr Cowper & I did what we Could to persuade her to believe that every Circumstance seemed to bear a favourable Aspect. By her desire she kept the letter till yesterday Afternoon, by her frequent reading of it, As she was obliged to do to all the Mollys & Bettys & Sallys & Nannys that came to enquire after you, she Almost got it by heart, & believes now that she may indulge a hope that you are in a fair way of recovery.

For several Weeks past I have had very little respite from Sore Conflicts. The Lord blessed be his Name has Now & then given me the Cordial of a promise; but is pleased to keep me waiting for the fulfilment. How often have I experienced that Word: 'Hope deferred maketh the heart Sick'.[5] I know that in due Season I shall reap if I faint not. O Thou who givest power to the faint, & to them who have no might encreasest Strength, Undertake for me!

I thank God Mr Cowper is well. I am Middling. That you May be speedily restored & brought back in safety & peace is the desire of your affectionate &

Obliged friends & Servants
Wm Cowper.
M. Unwin

Our affectionate respects wait on Mrs. Newton
Ocbr: 15 —76

My Sally was so affected by your remembrance of her that she Could testify her gratitude no other way than by tears, & a wish that she could pray for you as she Ought.

[3] Mrs. Newton's father, George Catlett (d. 1778), spent the last year and a half of his life at the Vicarage. Bernard Martin, *John Newton* (1950), p. 256.

[4] Mrs. Newton's maid. See C to Newton, 6 Feb. 1780.

[5] Proverbs 13: 12.

JOSEPH HILL Tuesday, 12 November 1776

Cowper Johnson

Dear Friend,

The very agreeable Contents of your last came safe to hand in the Shape of two Notes for 30£.—I am to thank you likewise for a Barrel of very good Oysters received about a Fortnight ago.

One to whom Fish is so welcome as it is to me, can have no great Occasion to distinguish the Sorts. In general therefore whatever Fish are likely to think a Jaunt into the Country agreeable, will be sure to find me ready to receive them; Butts, Plaice, Flounder or any other. If Herrings are yet to be had, as they cannot be bought at Olney 'till they are good for nothing, they will be welcome too. We have seen none this year except a Parcel that Mrs. Unwin sent for, & the Fishmonger sent Stale ones, a Trick they are apt to put upon their Customers at a Distance.

Having suffer'd so much by Nervous Fevers myself, I know how to congratulate Ashley upon his Recovery. Other Distempers only Batter the Walls, but They creep silently into the Citadel & put the Garrison to the Sword.

You perceive I have not made a Squeamish Use of your obliging Offer. The Remembrance of past Years, & of the Sentiment formerly exchanged in our Evening Walks convinces me still that an unreserved Acceptance of what is generously offer'd, is the Handsomest way of dealing with one of your Character.

Beleive me Yours

Wm Cowper.

Nove. 12. 76.

The Willingborough Diligence passes our Door ev'ry Tuesday, Thursday & Saturday, & Inns at the Cross Keys St. John Street Smithfield.

As to the Frequency which you leave to my Choice too, you have no need to exceed the Number of your former Remittances.

JOSEPH HILL — Tuesday, 10 December 1776

Address: Mr. Joseph Hill / Chancery Office / London.[1]
Cowper Johnson

Dear Joe,

Received 2 Notes for 25£.

This day Fortnight came 2 dozen Herrings, remarkably fine; if you order'd any other Fish to follow them, they swam another way.

Dr. Madan's Preferment[2] was in the Paper, but I overlook'd it, so I know neither the Name nor the Value of it, but being a Sine Cure, & as you say a very valuable one, it has every Requisite to raise the Spirits.

Yours affectionately Wm Cowper.

Olney.
Dece. 10. 1776.

JOSEPH HILL — Sunday, 5 January 1777

Address: Mr. Joseph Hill / Chancery Office / London.[1]
Cowper Johnson

Dear Joseph,

I am much obliged to you for a Tub of very fine Spiced Salmon which arrived yesterday: it cost us some Debate, & a Wager into the Bargain, one asserting it to be Sturgeon, & the other what it proved to be—But the Lady was in the right, as she should be upon all such Occasions.

My respects wait upon your Family—the Cold is excessive, but I have a little Greenhouse, which by the Help of a little Fire is as blooming & as Green as May.

Yours affectionately Wm Cowper.

Jan 5. —77.

[1] Olney Address.

[2] Martin's brother, Dr. Spencer Madan, prebendary of Peterborough, became rector of Ashbury in Berkshire in 1776.

---

[1] Olney Address.

JOSEPH HILL — Sunday, 30 March 1777

Address: Mr. Joseph Hill / Chancery Office / London.[1]
Cowper Johnson

My Dear Friend,

Tho' you are by this time in Berkshire at least, if not in Warwickshire, I thought it would be best to acknowledge the Receipt of the Draft upon Child for 20£, by the Return of the Post.

I sent you two Brace of Cucumbers by the Diligence on Friday, that is to say critically at the time when they were sure to miss you. If yours are as forward you have outstripp'd all our Nobility & Squires in this Country—neither the Duke of Bedford nor Lord Sussex have cut yet:[2] But you must not be angry with your Gardiner, for we have more Sunshine in 2 Months at some Seasons, than we have had this half Year.

Yours ever Wm Cowper.

Mar. 30. —77.

JOSEPH HILL — Saturday, 5 April 1777

Address: Mr. Joseph Hill / Chancery Office / London[1]
Cowper Johnson

Dear Joe,

If you can invent an Excuse for my Negligence in forgetting to thank you for your Opinion upon the Will[2] I sent you, you will oblige me much, for it is more than I am able to do for myself.—My Vines are coming into full bearing, if Cucumbers are worth sending, & will be acceptable to you, just send me a Line to tell me so, & I will take care to supply you weekly, if your own are not yet in Fruit.—

[1] Olney Address.

[2] C is referring to the gardens at Woburn Abbey in Bedfordshire and at Easton Maudit in Northamptonshire of, respectively, Francis Russell (1765–1802), 5th Duke of Bedford, and Henry Yelverton (1728–99), 3rd Earl of Sussex.

---

[1] Olney Address.

[2] C often asked Hill's advice in legal matters (see C to Hill, 12 Sept. 1767), but the context of this letter does not make clear whose will was sent to Hill.

Have you Brydone's Tour[3]—if you can lend it to me, or borrow it for me, I will use it well & return it soon.

Yours affectionately Wm Cowper.

April 5. —77.

Thank you for some sliced Cod.

JOSEPH HILL Sunday, 20 April [1777]

Cowper Johnson

My dear Friend,

Thanks for a Turbot, a Lobster and Capt. Brydone: a Gentleman who relates his Travels so agreeably that he deserves always to Travel with an agreeable Companion. I have been reading Grey's Works,[1] and think him the only Poet since Shakespear entitled to the Character of Sublime. Perhaps you will remember that I once had a different Opinion of him: I was prejudiced; he did not belong to our Thursday Society[2] & was an Eaton[3] man, which lower'd him prodigiously in our Esteem. I once thought Swift's Letters[4] the best that could be written, but I like Grey's better; his Humour or his Wit, or whatever it is to be called is never illnatur'd or offensive, & yet I think equally poignant with the Dean's.

I am Yours affectionately Wm Cowper.

April—I fancy the 20th.[5]

[3] *A Tour through Sicily and Malta. In a Series of Letters to William Beckford* (1773) by Patrick Brydone (1736–1818). Brydone's book had reached a fourth edition by 1776.

---

[1] C owned a copy of William Mason's *The Poems of Mr. Gray, with Memoirs Prefixed* (York, 1775). See Norma H. Russell, 'Addenda to "The Library of William Cowper"', *Transactions of the Cambridge Bibliographical Society*, iii (1961), 225. Mason's memoirs are largely composed of quotations from Gray's correspondence.

[2] The Nonsense Club. See *Ryskamp*, pp. 82–7.

[3] Gray was at Eton *c.* 1725–34.

[4] Various editions of Swift's letters, edited by John Hawkesworth (1715?–73), had appeared during the years 1766 to 1769.

[5] In another hand: 'This date ought undoubtedly to be 1777.'

JOSEPH HILL — Sunday, 25 May 1777

Cowper Johnson

My dear Friend,

You will receive soon after this reaches you the first ripe Melon I have cut that was worth sending. It is called the Crimson Melon; the seed was sent by Sir Joseph York to Lord Hardwick's Gardener,[1] and is reckon'd the very best Fruit of the kind. I wish it may answer the Character I have heard of it; I have never tasted it myself.

We differ not much in our Opinion of Mr. Gray. When I wrote last I was in the Middle of the Book. His later Epistles I think are worth little *as such*, but might be turn'd to excellent Account by a Young Student of Taste & Judgement. As to Mr. West's[2] Letters I think I could easily bring your Opinion of them to square with mine. They are elegant & Sensible, but have nothing in them that is Characteristic, or that discriminates them from the Letters of any other young Man of Taste and Learning.—As to the Book[3] you mention I am in Doubt whether to read it or not. I should like the Philosophical part of it, but the Political, which I suppose is a Detail of Intrigues carried on by the Company & their Servants, a History of rising & falling Nabobs, I should have no appetite to at all.—I will not therefore give you the Trouble of sending it at present.

Yours affectionately Wm Cowper.

May 25. —77.

Obliged to you for the Mackarell.

[1] Sir Joseph Yorke (1724–92), the diplomat, had sent the melons to his elder brother Philip (1720–90), 2nd Earl of Hardwicke, whose estate, Wimpole, was in Cambridgeshire.

[2] Gray's friend, Richard West (1716–42).

[3] *A Philosophical and Political History of the Settlements and Trade of the Europeans in the East and West Indies. Translated from the French* (*of G. T. F. Raynal*) *by J. Justamond* (1776). A third revised edition in five volumes appeared in 1777. See C to Hill, 1 Mar. 1778.

JOSEPH HILL — Tuesday, 27 May 1777

Address: Mr. Joseph Hill / Chancery Office / London.
Postmarks: 28/MA *and* OULNEY
New York Public Library

My dear Friend,

I am afraid Mr. Morgan[1] has not yet paid his Rent, but if you will advance me the money & add as much as will make up the Sum of Thirty pounds you will serve me materially; and then I shall be glad if you will pay yourself out of the first Monies of mine that may come to your Hands.

I always write upon this Subject under the disagreeable Apprehension of raising an Alarum, as if I begun to be less attentive to the Measure of my Income than formerly. But that is not the case, neither will the Anticipation of this Sum have any ill Effect upon my Circumstances the Succeeding Year.

I should be glad to receive it by the Return of the Post, & am Yours affectionately

May 27 — 1777. Wm Cowper.

JOSEPH HILL — Saturday, 31 May 1777

Cowper Johnson

My dear Friend,

I received Yesterday Mr. Child's Note for Thirty pounds, and return my best Thanks for it.

I wish it had been possible to have sent you a riper Fruit, but it is necessary to gather Melons a day or two too soon when they are to be sent to a Distance, else they would be as Yellow as a Gourd before they could be brought to Table. Three days after I cut yours I sent

[1] Perhaps one of the Morgans admitted with C to the Middle Temple, either Samuel Morgan, 2nd son of William Morgan, Alderman of the City of Watford, Ireland, or Brunton Morgan, 3rd son of Richard Morgan of the City of Dublin, Merchant.

A Calendar of the Inner Temple Records, ed. R. A. Roberts (1936), v. 663, contains evidence that a Mr. Morgan rented C's chambers from at least 1764 till C's death. The accounts record for the period 15 Nov. 1799–14 Nov. 1800 reads in part: 'Rents belonging to the Society, including:—Mr. Morgan, for his Chamber, follow to the House by the Death of William Cowper. . . .'

the Fellow to it to a Neighbouring Clergyman who gives me all my Litter,[1] and That was so ripe that it parted from the Stalk. We have eat part of one to day, of a different sort, (the Early Cantaleup) as high flavor'd a Fruit as ever I tasted. I have a third sort to produce by & by, call'd the Black Rock,[2] which I design you shall partake of, & for Experiment sake I will let it hang 'till it cracks.

If you can furnish me, (I mean if Mrs. Hill can) at Michaelmas with any Embellishments for my Borders, I shall be obliged to her; a Crocus in Spring, a Pink in Summer, & a Sun Flower in Autumn, is almost the Ne plus of our Gardens in this Neighbourhood.

Yours affectionately Wm Cowper. May 31. —77.

JOSEPH HILL — Sunday, 13 July 1777

Cowper Johnson

My dear Friend,

I send you a Melon of my Second Crop, riper I beleive than the last, tho' not much indebted to Sunshine for its Maturity. It ought to be of a different kind from the last I sent, but by the Roughness of the Rind I suspect it to be of the same, and that thro' a Mistake of the Seedsman neither of them is the Crimson Cantaleup, but Both, the Black Rock.

You need not give yourself any farther Trouble to procure me the South Sea Voyages; Lord Dartmouth who was here about a Month since, & was so kind as to pay me two Visits, has furnish'd me with both Cook's[1] & Forster's.[2] 'Tis well for the poor Natives of those distant Countries, that our National Expences cannot be supplied

[1] Material for mulching.

[2] 'Large Black Carbuncled or Black rock Cantaleupe Melon, being of a blackish green colour, having the surface covered with high, rugged, faxtile protuberances' (*Mawe*).

---

[1] The particular narrative being mentioned here is *A Voyage Towards the South Pole, and Round the World. Performed in His Majesty's Ships the Resolution and Adventure, in the Years 1772, 1773, 1774, and 1775 . . . In Which is Included Captain Furneaux's Narrative of His Proceedings in the Adventure . . .* (2 vols., 1777). See C to Hill, 28 Oct. 1777.

[2] *A Voyage Round the World, in His Britannic Majesty's Sloop Resolution, Commanded by Captain J. Cook, during the Years 1772, 3, 4 and 5* (1777) by Johann Georg Forster (1754–94).

by Cargoes of Yams & Bananas. Curiosity therefore being once satisfied, they may possibly be permitted for the future to enjoy their Riches of that kind in Peace.

If when you are most at leisure you can find out Baker upon the Microscope,[3] or Vincent Bourne's Latin Poems the last Edition,[4] and send them, I shall be obliged to you. Either, or Both if they can be easily found.

Accept my Thanks for the two last Parcels of Mackarell, which came hither perfectly fresh & in their Beauty.

I am Yours affectionately
Wm Cowper.

July 13. 1777.

JOSEPH HILL — Thursday, 23 October 1777

Cowper Johnson

My dear Friend,

If a Melon in the Spring is a Rarity, a Melon in the beginning of Winter, perhaps may be so too, especially after so sharp a Frost as we have lately had, & still more agreeable if it should happen to be a Frost when you eat it. This & the Fellow to it grew upon one Joint; the Vine was never water'd since it was a Seed. We ate part of one of them to day, & thought it good; the other which is better ripen'd we supposed might be even worthy of a Place at your Table, & have sent it accordingly.

[3] A fifth edition of *The Microscope Made Easy* . . . by Henry Baker (1698–1774) appeared in 1769.

[4] The *last* edition of Bourne in 1777 was the sixth, published in 1772; a greatly augmented quarto volume, it was entitled *Miscellaneous Poems, Consisting of Originals and Translations*. It was a subscription edition and contains no editor's name, preface, or advertisement. C is known to have possessed at one time or another two of the earlier editions: his copy of the 1750 edition, signed and dated 'June 5, 1758', is now in the Clark Library; a copy of the 1743 edition was in his library when he died (*Keynes*, 47, 53).

Vincent Bourne (1695–1747), who had been educated at Westminster and Trinity College, Cambridge (M.A. 1721), was C's master at Westminster when he entered the fifth form. C recalled Bourne's ever generous and genial nature in his letter to Unwin of 23 May 1781. C, as well as Charles Lamb at a later date, translated portions from *Poematia, Latine Partim Reddita, Partim Scripta* (1734).

I am obliged to you for 3 Parcels of Herrings—the Melon is a Crimson Cantalupe.

Beleive me affectionately Yours
Wm Cowper.

Octr. 23.—77.
The Basket contains besides Bourne's Poems and Baker on the Microscope with Thanks.

JOSEPH HILL Tuesday, 28 October 1777

Cowper Johnson

My dear Friend,

As Lord Dartmouth was so kind as to furnish me with Captain Cook's *last* Tour round the Globe, & with Mr. Forster's Account of the same Voyage, I am unwilling to be further troublesome to him, and as I can venture to take a little Liberty with you, which I could not handsomely take with his Lordship, I will beg the favour of you, when you can do it conveniently to send me either Commodore Byron's Voyage round the World[1] or Captain Cook's *first* Voyage,[2] or both, if they are both to be had, which, as the Public Curiosity is pretty well satisfied by this time, may possibly be the Case.—There was an Account publish'd by some of the People of the long Boat, who parted from Captain Cheap upon the Coast of Patagonia.[3] Their Seperation is all that is mention'd in Mr. Byron's first publication;[4]

[1] *A Journal of a Voyage Round the World, In His Maejsty's Ship The Dolphin, Commanded by the Honourable Commodore Byron* (1767).

[2] The narrative of Cook's first voyage to which C is referring is probably that which occupies volumes 2 and 3 of John Hawkesworth's *An Account of the Voyages Undertaken by the Order of His Present Majesty for Making Discoveries in the Southern Hemisphere, and Successively Performed by Commodore Byron, Captain Wallis, Captain Carteret, and Captain Cook* (1773).

[3] [John Bulkeley and John Cummins], *A Voyage to the South-Seas, By His Majesty's Ship Wager* (1743). 'Whereas captain David C—p, our commander in his majesty's ship the Wager, never consulted any of his officers for the safety and preservation of the said ship . . . he is now a prisoner. . . .' (p. 73).

[4] *The Narrative of the Honourable John Byron . . . Containing an Account of the Great Distress Suffered by Himself and his Companions on the Coast of Patagonia, From the Year 1740, till Their Arrival in England, 1746* (1748).

if this can be procured I shall be glad of it. And pray do not scruple to tell me if I am too troublesome in pestering you with these Commissions, for I had rather never see the Books than extort from you one single *Pish.*

Yours affectionately
Wm Cowper.

Olney
Octr. 28. —77.

JOSEPH HILL Thursday, 11 December 1777

Cowper Johnson

My dear Friend,

If I begin with thank you I must end with it too, unless I manage it thus—I am obliged to you & Thank you for the Books, for the Fish, for the 30£ which I hope I shall be able to negociate here; and Mrs. Hill for the Seeds she is so kind as to send me, is entitled to the same Return; besides which when I return the Books, I will inclose with them some Seed of the plant called the Broallia,[1] a new Flower in this Country—a few Seeds were given me last Year, which have produced a Quantity. Gordon[2] I am told sells it 2 Guineas an Ounce. We account it the most Elegant Flower we have seen, & when Lord Dartmouth was here he did it the Honour to think with us.—I will send with it Directions for the Management of it.

I am with Compliments to Mrs. Hill

Yours affectionately Wm Cowper.

Dece. 11 —77.

[1] The browallia was named after John Browall (1707–55), bishop of Abo, Sweden, who in 1739 had written a defence of Linnaeus.

[2] *The New Complete Guide* (1777): 'Gordon and Dermer, seedmen, 25 Fenchurch street'. James Gordon (1708?–80) had served as gardener to Lord Petre at Thorndon Hall in Essex, and from 1742 kept various seed shops and nurseries. See Blanche Henrey, *British Botanical and Horticultural Literature before 1800* (Oxford, 1975), II, 350–3.

JOSEPH HILL — Thursday, 1 January 1778

Cowper Johnson

My dear Friend,

Your last Pacquet was doubly welcome, and Mrs. Hill's Kindness gives me peculiar Pleasure, not as coming from a Stranger to me, for I do not account her so tho I never saw her, but as coming from One so nearly connected with yourself. I shall take care to acknowledge the Receipt of her obliging Letter, when I return the Books. Assure yourself in the mean time that I Read as if the Librarian was at my Elbow, continually Jogging it, and growling out, Make Haste—But as I read aloud, I shall not have finish'd before the End of the Week, & will return them by the Diligence next Monday.

I shall be glad if you will let me know whether I am to understand by the Sorrow you express, that any part of my former Supplies is actually cut off, or whether they are only more tardy in coming in than usual. It is usefull even to the Rich to know as nearly as may be, the exact Amount of their Income—but how much more so to a Man of my Small Dimensions? If the former should be the Case, I shall have less Reason to be surprized, than I have to wonder at the Continuance of them so long. Favors, are Favors indeed when laid out upon so barren a Soil, where the Expence of Sowing is never accompanied by the smallest Hope of a Return. What Pain there is in Gratitude I have often felt, but the Pleasure of requiting an Obligation has always been out of my Reach.

On the other Side I write a Receipt for the Money,[1] and am

Affectionately Yours

Wm Cowper.

Jan. 1.

—78.

[1] There is no receipt on the other side of this letter.

JOSEPH HILL

Sunday, 1 March 1778

Cowper Johnson

My dear Friend,

Mrs. Unwin has an Estate in the Isle of Ely,[1] which pays a Drainage Tax of about 5£ per Annum. The Collector has neglected to Demand it these Six Years, and now expects Payment for the whole Interval. Is there any Remedy? The Inconvenience of Disbursing the whole Sum at once, is so great that one would Hope there is. If he is Justifiable in such Neglect, the same sort of Reason would Justify an Omission for a much longer time, so that he might run away with several years' Rent at once.

The History of the Indies[2] shall be return'd on Monday. It found me engaged in reading Robertson's America,[3] which I was obliged to finish & return, else you should have received it sooner. My Respects wait on Mrs. Hill &c.

Yours affectionately Wm Cowper.

Feb. 28. —78.

Many Thanks for a fine Cod & Shrimps.

P.S.

I have just recover'd my Letter from the Office to tell you that I have this Minute received your Draft for 17£. 11s. 3d.

Mar. 1. 1778.

I am much pleas'd with the Abbé,[4] & found no fault at all with his Calculations—You know why.

[1] The land owned by Mary Unwin lay in the parish of Ely St. Mary. She paid eight shillings land tax on property described as 'late Cawthorne' in 1778 and 1779. In the 1780 land tax assessment the proprietor is given as '—Unwin', the occupier being Philip Cawthorne. We are grateful to J. M. Farrar, County Archivist, Cambridgeshire and Isle of Ely County Council, for this information.

[2] See n. 3, C to Hill, 25 May 1777.

[3] *The History of America* by William Robertson (1721–93) appeared in two volumes in 1777.

[4] A reference to Abbé Guillaume Thomas François Raynal (1713–96), the author of the history of the Indies cited above. A renegade priest turned *philosophe*, his history was condemned by the Parlement of Paris in 1781 because of its impiety and its insistence on the right of a nation to revolt and to give or withhold consent to taxation.

JOSEPH HILL — Sunday, 8 March 1778

Cowper Johnson

My dear Friend,

The last Paper made mention of the Death of Sir Thomas Hesketh.[1] I cannot upon Occasion of so interesting an Event be contented to receive no other Account than what that uncertain Vehicle convey'd to me. As he was said to have died at his House in Berkley Square, & I never heard of his Removal from Grosvenor Street, a Hope is left that it may be a false Report. You will oblige me by a speedy Answer, as on several Accounts I cannot but be anxious for further Information.

I am Yours Affectionately
Wm Cowper.

Many Thanks to Mrs. Hill for the Seeds—& many for the Fish & the Books.
Mar. 8. 1778.

JOSEPH HILL — Monday, 9 March 1778

Address: Mr. Joseph Hill / Chancery Office / London.[1]
Cowper Johnson

My best Thanks wait on my good Friend for the Fish he has been so kind as to send since I heard from him last. As the Remittances of last Year fell rather short, amounting only to 65£, I am willing to hope I have a little Money in your Hands, & shall be obliged to you for it.

I shall just add, and confess at the same time that I do it to gratify myself, that Mr. Nicholl's[2] Affair has turn'd out as I expected. He brought two Actions—under the first he has recover'd 100£ Damages & Costs of Suit. The other, at the pressing Instances of the Defendants and their Intercessors, he agreed to compromise for 40 Guineas

[1] Sir Thomas died on 4 Mar. 1778. *The Gazetteer and New Daily Advertiser* of 5 Mar. and the *Morning Post* of 6 Mar. carried the news.

---

[1] Olney Address.

[2] For C's opinion of James Nichols, 'a sort of pedlar and hawker' in religious matters, see C to Newton, 19 July 1784. Nichols was a 'mason's labourer at Ostend' in 1784.

and the Costs. An Instance of Moderation that does him great Honour, for there was little reason to doubt that the Jury would have given him much larger Damages under this than the former, the whole Court, and the Judge especially, being uncommonly full of Indignation at the Cruelty with which he had been treated. He did not seek Revenge, but Security. He has now obtain'd it, together with the Reestablishment of his Credit, & is going on quietly in his Business as before.

Yours Wm C.

Mar. 9.[3]

JOSEPH HILL Saturday, 11 April 1778

Cowper Johnson

My dear Friend,

I am obliged to you for the Contents of your last. Money is sure to be acceptable come when it will, and I had no small Pleasure in the Pacquet of Seeds Mrs. Hill was so kind as to send me. I shall begin the Cultivation of them immediately. Pray don't forget to inform her, that I have raised 4 Plants of the Flower Fence, which are now 6 Inches high and in a most flourishing State.

Poor Sir Thomas! I knew that I had a Place in his Affections, and from his own Information many Years ago, a Place in his Will. But little thought that after the Lapse of so many Years without Intercourse, I should still retain it.[1] His Remembrance of me after so long a Season of seperation has done me much Honour, and leaves me the more Reason to regret his Decease. I depend upon your Kindness to inform me more particularly upon this Subject when you are at Liberty to do it.

I am reading the Abbé[2] with great Satisfaction, and think him the most Intelligent Writer upon so extensive a Subject I ever met with: in every Respect Superior to the Abbé in Scotland.[3] You may depend

[3] After the date is inscribed in pencil: '78—', presumably by Hill.

---

[1] According to the abstract of his will of 7 May 1776 (Hesketh Papers: Lancashire Record Office MS. DDF. 413/2), Sir Thomas bequeathed £100 to C.

[2] Abbé Raynal. See C to Hill, 1 Mar. 1778.

[3] Most probably a reference to William Robertson. See n. 3, C to Hill, 1 Mar. 1778 for

upon his Return as soon as I can get through him & that I shall proceed with him as fast as I can.

Yours affectionately

Wm Cowper.

Many Thanks for the intended Fish.

Sunday Morning

Which is just come, & should have been here last Night; we shall Bumble[4] my Landlady at Newport.

April 11. 1778.

Received of Mr. Hill by Draft on Child the Sum of Twenty Pounds

£20. 0. 0 Wm Cowper

JOSEPH HILL Thursday, 7 May 1778

Address: Mr. Joseph Hill / Chancery Office / London.
Postmarks: 11/MA *and* OULNEY
Cowper Johnson

My dear Friend,

I have been in continual Fear lest every Post should bring a Summons for the Abbé Raynal, and am glad that I have finish'd him before my Fears were realized. I have kept him long, but not through Neglect or Idleness. I read the 5 Volumes to Mrs. Unwin, & my Voice will seldom serve me with more than an Hour's Reading at a time. I am indebted to him for much Information upon Subjects which, however Interesting, are so remote from those with which Country Folks in general are conversant, that had not his Work reached me at Olney, I should have been for ever Ignorant of them. I admire him as a Philosopher, as a Writer, as a Man of extraordinary Intelligence, and no less extraordinary Abilities to digest it. He is a true Patriot, but then the World is his Country. The Frauds &

C's interest in Robertson's *History of America*. Robertson was a licensed minister of the Church of Scotland. In 1763, after he had been appointed Principal of Edinburgh University, Robertson was elected Moderator of the General Assembly of the Church of Scotland and until 1780 he was popularly regarded as leader of the moderate party in church politics. William Robertson's *History* was a work which could well be compared with Raynal's from the point of assessing their respective success as early histories of America.

[4] Blame (*O.E.D.*).

Tricks of the Cabinet & the Counter, seem to be equally the Objects of his Aversion. And if he had not found that Religion too had undergone a Mixture of Artifice in its turn, perhaps he would have been a Christian.

I beg you will present my Respects to Mrs. Hill, I had great Hope that I should have been able to have sent her a Basket of Peas by the Middle of this Month, but a Killing Frost, having destroy'd all the first Bloom, has robb'd me of that Pleasure. Such of the Barbadoes Seeds as have vegetated are in a thriving way, but whether I sow'd them too early, or the cloudiness of the Season has hurt them, I know not, but several have failed. If She *can* favor me with half a dozen Seeds of Scarlet Convolvulus,[1] I should be much obliged to her. I raised 3 Plants, but they outgrew my Frames & the Green house was not warm enough to carry them on.

Yours affectionately Wm Cowper. —May 7. —78.

One Trouble more, and then I hope to allow you a Respite for some time. My stock of Eyewater is spent, & I have lately more than once had Occasion for some. I shall be obliged to you if you can procure me a Phial of it at your Leisure.

JOSEPH HILL — Tuesday, 26 May 1778

Address: Mr. Joseph Hill / Chancery Office / London
Postmarks: 27/MA *and* OULNEY
Princeton

My dear Friend,

I am much obliged to you for all your Attentions, not forgetting a Nice Turbot and a Lobster its Companion, as fresh as when first taken. You trod so close upon my Heels last year in the Articles of Cucumbers that I thought it would be superfluous to send any, but I hope it will not be long before my Beds will produce you a Melon or two.

It is strange that I cannot write without having Occasion to charge you with some Commission or other. Will you be so kind as to receive my Legacy for me? I suppose you know the Executor,[1] and

1 C is probably referring to an annual which has ivy leaves and small, scarlet flowers. Philip Miller, *The Gardeners Dictionary* (2nd edn. 1733), fos. Ss–Tt.

1 The abstract of Sir Thomas Hesketh's will reads in part: 'Appoints Mr Thomas Hunt

that this Letter may be his sufficient Warrant for Paying it to You, if not, I can send any other. I hope it will not be thought unreasonable if I desire to have it remitted to me. There are Seasons in the Affairs of every man when a little ready Money, rather than the Interest of it, is particularly desireable. Some things are absolutely necessary to me, which without some such Occasional Help are hardly within my Reach. One of these Articles is Wine. I have all my Life been used to drink 2 or 3 Glasses after Eating, and when I have attempted to leave it off as Too Expensive for me, I have suffer'd so much in my Health by the Omission, that I have been obliged to return to it again.[2] A Hogshead serves me two years, & I am the only Person in the Family that ever tastes it. I imagine it is not necessary to enter into a more minute Detail of my present Exigences, which would be tedious to the Reader, and not very agreeable to the Compiler. My Respects attend Mrs. Hill. My Garden puts me in Mind of her every Day.

Yours affectionately Wm Cowper.

May 26.—78.

I shall be glad of an Answer as soon as convenient, that I may order the Wine in. I have it from Lynn[3] & upon the best Footing.

JOSEPH HILL — Saturday, 6 June 1778[1]

Cowper Johnson

My dear Friend,

I am much obliged to you for your Offer to advance the necessary Sum upon this important Occasion, but it is now Summer time, and

Sole Executor and gives him £100 for his Trouble'. *Browne's General Law-list for the Year 1779* (p. 41) includes Thomas Hunt of Bread Street, Cheapside.

[2] For C's interest in wine, see his to Lady Hesketh of 17 Nov. 1785.

[3] 'Among the out-ports, King's Lynn was one of those which had held out against the competition of London in the early part of the century and had preserved a sizable wine trade for the East Anglian squirearchy . . . In the second half of the century the out-ports caught up on London and even surpassed the capital in their aggregate trade. King's Lynn, though no longer the biggest importer of wine after London, still took nearly 500 tuns. No doubt this was where much of the better wine went, and the high-class trade flourished in the rich agricultural districts where noblemen and gentlemen had their finest seats.' A. D. Francis, *The Wine Trade* (1972), pp. 233–4.

[1] Dated in pencil, presumably by Hill: 'June 6. 78.'

I should fear lest the Wine might suffer by a Journey in Hot Weather. My Stock is not exhausted & I can wait till Michaelmas. Nevertheless as you gave me Reason not long since to hope that you would receive near 20£ more on my Account, in the course of the Summer, I shall be glad, should that be the case, to have it remitted to me; otherwise I shall be in Danger of being straitened.

Thurlow's Advancement to the Seals I imagine, surprizes Nobody.[2] I should formerly have conceived great Pleasure from such an Event, in which Self would have had its Share. A certain Provision for Me would have been the Consequence of his Promotion. But Damnosa quid non imminuit Dies?[3]—It has worn out the Traces of our former Intimacy, and the Sinecure he promised me must fill a happier Pocket than mine.

Pray tell Mrs. Hill my Mimulus ringens,[4] my Flower Fence, my Wild Olive and Silk Cotton are all well and thriving. As to the rest, the Day of their Sowing was the Day of their Burial; and there they Lie to this Hour. If she is fond of Carnations, I have some very good ones, & if she chuses any and my Layers[5] succeed, I will send her some at the proper Season. But they are Stage Flowers[6] & must be framed in Winter.

Yours affectionately Wm Cowper.

It is impossible to say too much in Praise of the Mackarel.

[2] See n. 1, C to Mrs. Cowper, 4 May 1767. In his letter to Lady Hesketh of 11 Feb. 1786, C mentions that Thurlow agreed in 1762 that if he became Lord Chancellor, he would provide for C.

C finally obtained his pension in Apr. 1794. According to Hayley ('Two Memorials of Hayleys Endeavours to serve his Freind Cowper': Add. MS. 38887, fos. 25–6), Thurlow was called to C's chambers at the Temple during one of C's periods of 'darkest Despondency'. The long breach between C and Thurlow may have been caused by Thurlow's embarrassment at having been present in C's rooms at that time.

[3] Horace, *Odes*, III. vi. 45: 'Time corrupts all. What has it not corrupted?'

[4] An 'oblong-leav'd Monkey-flower', a native of 'Virginia and Canada', which was first cultivated in Britain in 1759. See William Aiton, *Hortus Kewensis; or, A Catalogue of the Plants Cultivated in the Royal Botanic Garden at Kew* (1789), ii. 361.

[5] 'A shoot or twig of a plant fastened down and partly covered with earth, in order that it may strike root while still attached to the parent stock and so propagate the plant' (*O.E.D.*).

[6] 'A tier of shelves or platform for plants, especially in a greenhouse; hence, a display of flowers on such a stage' (*O.E.D.*).

JOSEPH HILL Thursday, 18 June 1778

Cowper Johnson

My dear Friend,

I truly rejoice that the Chancellor has made you such a Present,[1] that he has given an Additional Lustre to it by his Manner of conferring it, and that all this happen'd before you went to Wargrave, because it made your Retirement there the more agreeable. This is just according to the Character of the Man; He will give grudgingly in Answer to Sollicitation, but delight in surprizing those he Esteems with his Bounty. May you live to receive still further Proofs that I am not mistaken in my Opinion of him.

My Carnations abound with Layers but they are dismally given to Spindling; I hope however I shall be able to catch some of them before they run away, and shall rejoice to send Mrs. Hill the best of them. I have a Stage which will hold about 40 Pots, & is at present about half furnish'd. But I sow the Seed of my own Flowers, & hope to raise some Capital ones every Year.

My Melons are large & take a deal of ripening, especially as the Vines are in full Vigour. But I hope shortly to have a Brace at your Service.

The Eye Water came safe, by the Help of which & the Ointment I have perfectly cured a Disorder which troubled me at least a Month.

Yours affectionately

June 18. Wm Cowper.

78.

WILLIAM UNWIN Thursday, 18 June 1778

British Library

Dear Unwin,

I feel myself much obliged to you for your kind Intimation, and have given the Subject of it all my best Attention, both before I

[1] Hill was made Secretary of Lunatics, a position he held until 1788. See Thomas Duffus Hardy, *A Catalogue of Lord Chancellors, Keepers of the Great Seal, Masters of the Rolls, and Principal Officers of the High Court of Chancery* (1843), pp. 30–1.

received your Lettter, and since. The Result is that I am persuaded it will be better not to write.[1] I know the Man & his Disposition well; he is very Liberal in his Way of thinking, Generous, and discerning. He is well aware of the Tricks that are played upon such Occasions, and after 15 years' Interruption of all Intercourse between us, would translate my Letter into this Language—Pray remember the Poor—This would disgust him, because he would think our former [intimacy disgrac]ed[2] by such an Oblique [applica]tion. He has not forgot me, and if [he had,] there are those about him, who cannot come into his Presence without reminding him of me, and he is also perfectly acquainted with my Circumstances. It would perhaps give him Pleasure to Surprize me with a Benefit, and if he means me such a Favor, I should disappoint him by Asking it. Thus he dealt with my Friend Mr. Hill (to whom by the way I introduced him, and to All my Family Connections in Town). He sent for him the Week before last, and without any Sollicitation freely gave him one of his Secretaryships. I know not the Income, but as Mr. Hill is in good Circumstances, and the Gift was unasked, I dare say it is no Trifle. I repeat my Thanks for your Suggestion; you see a Part of my Reasons for thus conducting myself, if we were together I could give you more.

Mrs. Unwin sends her best Love to you and to all at Stock, my Affectionate Respects accompany it.—[ ] the Gout does not sweeten [ ] the Gravel[3] is apt to Sour i[ ]

Yours affectionately [ ]

June 18.—78

JOSEPH HILL — Tuesday, 23 June 1778

Cowper Johnson

My dear Friend,

I just send you a Line to announce the Approach of two Persian Melons[1] which I hope you will receive soon after this reaches you.

[1] Unwin had evidently urged C to apply to Thurlow for some sort of preferment.

[2] Parts of the MS. have been cut away.

[3] A term applied to aggregations of urinary crystals and figuratively used to describe difficulty in passing urine (*O.E.D.*).

[1] This melon 'is an exotic from the hot parts of the world, supposed principally of Persia,

The Season having been remarkably favorable, I imagine you will find them perfectly ripe. They are not the first I have cut, but they are the best.

Yours affectionately
Wm Cowper

June 23.—78.

WILLIAM UNWIN Saturday, 18 July 1778

Address: Revd. William Unwin / at Stock near / Ingatestone / Essex.
Postmark: Illegible
British Library

My dear Friend,

I hurry you into the Midst of things at once, which if it be not much in the Epistolary Stile, is acknowledg'd however to be very Sublime.—Mr. Morley, Videlicet the grocer, is guilty of such Neglect and Carelessness, and has lately so much disappointed your Mother, that she is at last obliged to leave him, and begs you will send her Mr. Rawlinson's Address, that she may transfer her Custom to Him.[1]—She adds moreover, that she was well aware of the Unseasonableness of Salmon at this time, & did not mean that you should order any to Olney till the Spring.

We are indebted to you for your Political Intelligence, but have it not in our Power to pay you in kind. Proceed however to give us such Information as cannot be learn'd from the Newspaper, and when any thing arises at Olney that is not in the threadbare Stile of daily Occurrences, you shall hear of it in Return. Nothing of this sort has happen'd lately, except that a Lion was imported here at the Fair,[2] Seventy Years of Age, & as tame as a Goose. Your Mother and I saw him embrace his Keeper with his Paws, and lick his Face. Others saw

from which country, however, it was first introduced into the different parts of Europe; and consequently its culture in every part of Britain can be effected only by artificial heat, and constant shelter of glass, &c. till July, as at an early season they require a temperature of heat almost equal to that of our pineapple stoves' (*Mawe*).

---

[1] *London Directory for the Year 1778*: 'Francis Morley, *grocer*, 155, Cheapside' (p. 116); 'William Rawlinson, *Mer.*, 94, Cornhill' (p. 135). Morley may have been a friend at one time to the Unwin family; he witnessed Morley Unwin's will, which is dated 30 Apr. 1767.

[2] Cherry Fair, celebrated on 29 June.

him receive his Head in his Mouth, and restore it to him again unhurt. A Sight we chose not to be favor'd with, but rather advised the Honest Man to discontinue the Practise. A Practise hardly reconcileable to Prudence, unless he had had a Head to spare. The Beast however was a very Magnificent one, and much more Royal in his Appearance, than those I have seen in the Tower.

The Paper tells us that the Chancellor is frequently at the Register Office, having conceived a Design to shorten the Pro[ceedings][3] in his court.[4] If he has indeed such a Purpose in View, he is so Industrious and so Resolute, that he will never let it drop unaccomplish'd. Perhaps the Practitioners will have no reason to regret it, as they may gain in such an Event, more by the Multiplicity of Suits, than they do at present by the Length of them.

Your Mother joins me in affectionate Respects, I should have said, in Love, to yourself, Mrs. Unwin, Miss Shuttleworth[5] and little John.[6] If you will accept this for a Letter, perhaps I may be able to furnish more such upon Oc[casio]n.

Yours with Thanks for your last
Wm Cowper.—

July 18.—78.

JOSEPH HILL — Thursday, 10 September 1778

Address: Mr. Joseph Hill / Wargrove near / Twyford / Berkshire.
Postmark: 11/SE
Boston Public Library

My dear Friend,

Mrs. Collett's[1] Note is come to Olney by Mistake and mine I suppose is gone to Her. If I had not cut your Letter out, I could have return'd it wrong Side outward, and not have put you to the charge

3 MS. torn.

4 *The Morning Chronicle, and London Advertiser* (Tuesday, 14 July 1778, No. 2854): 'The Lord Chancellor is taking some pains to endeavour to shorten the proceedings in Chancery suits, for which purpose his Lordship has been these two days at the Registry-office in Chancery-lane, for several hours examining the books and entries.'

5 Elizabeth Shuttleworth, Mrs. Unwin's sister.

6 John Unwin was three at this time.

1 Unidentified.

of double Postage. But that is past Remedy.—I am obliged to Mrs. Hill for her kind Intentions; every thing in the Garden way is heartily welcome here.—Six fine Mackarel came yesterday, for which tho' I knew not the Hand Writing of the Direction, I doubt not that my Thanks are due at Wargrove.

Yours affectionately
Wm Cowper.

Sepr. 10.—78.

JOSEPH HILL Tuesday, 20 October 1778

Address: Mr. Joseph Hill / Chancery Office / London.
Postmarks: 21/OC *and* OULNEY
Yale

My dear Friend,

According to the Liberty you was so kind as to allow me, I have drawn upon you for the Sum of £22.1.6. in Payment for a Hogshead of Port and 2 Dozen of Brown Port. The Draft is dated the 19th and made payable to Mr. Thomas Steward[1] or Order.

Yours affectionately Wm Cowper.

Octe. 20th. 1778.

[1] Not identified in any London directory.

JOSEPH HILL Tuesday, 3 November 1778

Cowper Johnson

Dear Joe,

I shall be obliged to you if you will send me a Letter of Attorney by which I may impower you to receive what is due to me at the Bank, and what Stagg[1] has in his Hands: and shall be glad to have it remitted to me by the first Opportunity. I know I am in your Debt,

[1] Kent's *London Directory* (1766): 'William Stagg, Stock-broker, Castle-alley, Cornhill' (p. 126). John Cowper to Hill, 2 May 1765 (Princeton): 'I have one more favour to beg of you, which is, that you wd. be so good as to send a Line to Stagg the Broker, informing him that I would be glad of an Answer to a Letter. . . .'

but as this is the Month in which you say my Purse is generally replenish'd, hope you will be able to pay yourself, and if when You have done so, there should be a Ballance coming to me, the sooner it comes the better.

Yours, with my Respects to all Friends

Wm Cowper.

Olney

Nov: 3. 1778.

WILLIAM UNWIN Thursday, 3 December 1778

Address: Revd. William Unwin / Stock / near Ingatestone / Essex.
Postmarks: 4/IA *and* OULNEY
British Library

My dear Friend,

I was last Night agreeably surprized by the Arrival of Mr. Dodsley;[1] His own Merit is his sufficient Recommendation, but his Appearance without having been expected or even thought of, made him still more Welcome. You have done a kind thing in sending him, & I wish we could recompense it by a Pine Apple for every Volume.

I made Mr. Wright's[2] Gardener a Present of 50 Sorts of Stove Plant Seeds,[3] in Return he has presented me with Six Fruiting Pines, which I have put into a Bark Bed,[4] where they thrive at present as well as I could wish. If they produce good Fruit, you will stand some little Chance to partake of them. But you must not expect Giants, for

[1] C is referring to the volumes of the *Annual Register*, which Dodsley had founded, with the aid of Edmund Burke, in 1759. Hardly a magazine in the usual sense, the annual volume contained a retrospective account of the year, including reviews of selected books and pieces of poetry. C's contributions to the *Register* have never been identified satisfactorily (see *Russell*, pp. 5–6).

[2] Gayhourst or Gotehurst, *c.* 5 miles from Olney, was at that time the seat of George Wrighte, a retired judge. Wrighte (d. 1804) was a great-grandson of Sir Nathan Wrighte, the Lord Keeper in Queen Anne's reign; the family had owned Gayhurst only since 1704. Mrs. Wrighte was the former Anne Jekyll, granddaughter and co-heiress of George, Earl of Halifax. Mr. Wrighte was one of the subscribers to the Homer.

[3] 'Such tender exotics from the hot parts of the world, that require the aid of a Stove to preserve them in this country' (*Mawe*).

[4] 'Hot-beds, formed of tanner's-bark, and such that support the most uniform and durable temperature of heat, and the best calculated hot-beds yet known, for the cultivation of all sorts of tender exotics from the warm parts of America, Asia, and Africa, that require the continual aid of artificial heat to maintain them in this country' (*Mawe*).

being transplanted in December will certainly give them a Check, and probably diminish their Size. He has promised to supply me with still better Plants in October, which is the proper Season for Moving them, and with a Reinforcement every Succeeding year.—Mrs. Hill sent me the Seeds, which perhaps could not have been purchased for less than three Guineas.—'Tis thus we Great Gardeners establish a beneficial Intercourse with each other, & furnish ourselves with valuable things that therefore, cost us Nothing.

How did you escape the Storm? It did us no Damage except keeping us awake, and giving your Mother the Head ache and except, what can hardly be called a Damage, Lifting a long and heavy Palisade from the Top of our Garden Wall, & setting it so gently down upon two old Hot Beds that it was not at all broken or impaired.

Your Mother is well at present, & sends her Love, Joining with me at the same time in affectionate Remembrances to all the Family.

Yours Wm Cowper.

Dece. 3. 1778.

WILLIAM UNWIN *c.* Sunday, 7 February 1779[1]

Address: Revd. William Unwin at / Mrs. Ords,[2] Leman Street / No. 20 / Goodmans Fields / London.
Postmarks: 8/FE *and* OULNEY
British Library

My dear Friend,

The Fish happening to swim uppermost in my Mind, I give it the Precedence, and begin with returning our Thanks for it, not forgetting the Circumstance of Free Carriage. Upon the Whole, I think this a Handsomer way of acknowledging a Present, than to tuck it into a Postscript.

I find the Register in all respects an Entertaining Medley, but especially in This, that it has brought to my View, some long forgotten Pieces of my own Production. I mean by the way 2 or 3. These

[1] Kenneth Povey, in his article 'Some Notes on Cowper's Letters and Poems', *R.E.S.* v (Apr. 1929), 18 dates this letter 6–7 Feb. 1779 from an examination of the postmark and the contents of the letter.

[2] Unidentified, but perhaps a relation of Anne Dillingham Ord (d. 1808), the celebrated London hostess and patroness of the arts. Anne Ord was a subscriber to C's Homer.

I have mark'd with my own Initials, & you may be sure I found them peculiarly agreeable, as they had not only the Grace of being Mine but that of Novelty likewise to recommend them; it is at least 20 Years since I saw them.—You, I think, was never a Dabbler in Rhime; I have been one ever since I was 14 years of Age, when I begun with translating an Elegy of Tibullus.[3] I have no more Right to the Name of a Poet, than a Maker of Mousetraps has to That of an Engineer, but my little Exploits in this way have at times amused me so much, that I have often wish'd myself a good one. Such a Talent in Verse as mine, is like a Child's Rattle, very entertaining to the Trifler that uses it, and very disagreeable to all beside. But it has served to rid me of some melancholy Moments, for I only take it up as a gentleman Performer does his Fiddle. I have this Peculiarity belonging to me as a Rhimist, that though I am charmed to a great Degree with my own Work while it is on the Anvil, I can seldom bear to Look at it when it is once finish'd. The more I contemplate it, the more it loses of its Value, 'till I am at last quite disgusted with it. I then throw it by, take it up again perhaps Ten Years after, and am as much delighted with it as at first.

Few People have the Art of being agreeable when they Talk of themselves, if you are not weary therefore by this time, you pay me a high Compliment.

I dare say Miss Shuttleworth was much diverted with the Conjecture of her Friends. The true Key to the Pleasure she found at Olney was plain enough to be seen, but they chose to overlook it. She brought with her a Disposition to be pleas'd, which whoever does, is sure to find a Visit agreeable, because they make it so.

Your Mother Joins me in Affectionate Remembrances to all your Family.

Yours W:C.

We are obliged to little John for his P.S. We think his Observation very Just, but are a little doubtful about the Exactness of his Calculation.

[3] This translation has never been found.

JOSEPH HILL Sunday, 11 April 1779

Cowper Johnson

My dear Friend—

When you favor'd me with the last Remittance of 20£, you was so kind as to say I might draw for more if I had Occasion for it. The Occasion is now come, & I shall be obliged to you for a further Advance. I know I am in your Debt, which sits the easier upon me because I am almost always so. Long Habit & Custom are able to familiarize to us things much more disagreeable than this. A Debt of this kind I am, at present at least, able to Discharge.—But I owe you upon other Accounts what I can never pay, except by continuing Affectionately Yours

Wm Cowper.

My Respects attend Mrs. Hill.
April 11. 79.

WILLIAM UNWIN Saturday, 1 May 1779[1]

Address: Revd. William Unwin / Stock near / Ingatestone / Essex
Postmark: 3/MA
British Library

My dear Friend,

You are my Mahogany Box with a Slit in the Lid of it, to which I Committ my Productions of the Lyric kind, in perfect Confidence that there they are safe, & will go no furthur. All who are attach'd to the Jingling Art have this Peculiarity, that they would find no Pleasure in the Exercise, had they not one Friend at least to whom they might Publish what they have composed. If you approve my Latin, & your Wife and Sister my English, this, together with the Approbation of your Mother, is Fame enough for me.

1 The text of this letter and its poem are not bound together in the collection of C to Unwin letters at the British Library; in fact, 'You are my Mahogany Box' is bound with the MS. of 'Translation of Verses in Memory of Dr. Lloyd'. This cannot be right, since C is presenting verses which would have made an acceptable school exercise thirty years before. A translation from Prior would have been acceptable, and the likelihood is that the fragment dated 'May 1.—79' and headed 'Translation of Prior's Poem' belongs to the undated letter fragment, and both can thus be dated 1 May 1779 with some certainty.

1 May 1779

He who cannot Look forward with Comfort, must find what Comfort he can in Looking backward. Upon this Principle I t'other Day sent my Imagination upon a Trip, thirty Years behind me. She was very Obedient and very swift of foot, presently perform'd the Journey, and at last set me down in the Sixth Form at Westminster. I fancied myself once more a School Boy, a Period of Life in which if I had never tasted true Happiness, I was at least equally unacquainted with its contrary. No Manufacturer of waking Dreams ever succeeded better in his Employment than I do, I can weave such a Piece of Tapestry in a few Minutes, as not only has all the Charms of a Reality, but is Embellish'd also with a Variety of Beauties, which tho' they never existed, are more captivating than any that ever did. Accordingly I was a School Boy in high Favour with the Master, receiv'd a Silver Groat for my Exercise, & had the Pleasure of seeing it sent from Form to Form for the Admiration of all who were able to understand it. Do you wish to see this highly applauded Performance? It follows on the other Side.

Translation of Prior's Poem beginning
The Merchant to conceal his Treasures.

Not having the Poem, & not having seen it these 20 Years, I had much ado to recollect it, which has obliged me to tear off the first Copy, & write another.

Mercator vigiles Oculos ut fallere possit,
  Nomine sub ficto trans Mare mittit Opes.
Lene sonat liquidumque meis Euphelia Chordis,
  At solam exoptant Te, mea Vota, Chlöe.

2

Ad speculum ornabat Nitidos Euphelia Crines,
  Cum dixit mea Lux, Heus, Cane, Sume Lyram.
Namque Lyram juxtá positam cum Carmine vidit,
  Suave quidem Carmen, dulcisonamque Lyram.

3

Fila Lyræ Vocemque paro. Suspiria surgunt
  Et miscent Numeris Murmura mæsta meis,

Dumque tuæ memoro Laudes Euphelia Formæ,
Tota anima intereá pendet ab ore Chlöes.

4

Subrubet illa Pudore, et contrahit altera Frontem,
Me torquet mea Mens conscia, Psallo, Tremo.
Atque Cupidineâ dixit Dea cincta Coronâ,
Heu! Fallendi Artem quàm didicere parùm.[2]

Your Mother Joins me in all you can wish us to say to yourself & all your Family, by no means forgetting Great John and Little Marianne.[3] May 1.—79.

[2] *The Literary Works of Matthew Prior*, ed. H. Bunker Wright and Monroe K. Spears (Oxford, 1959), i. 259:

An Ode.

I.

The Merchant, to secure his Treasure,
Conveys it in a borrow'd Name:
Euphelia serves to grace my Measure;
But Cloe is my real Flame.

II.

My softest Verse, my darling Lyre
Upon Euphelia's Toylet lay;
When Cloe noted her Desire,
That I should sing, that I should play.

III.

My Lyre I tune, my Voice I raise;
But with my Numbers mix my Sighs:
And whilst I sing Euphelia's Praise,
I fix my Soul on Cloe's Eyes.

IV.

Fair Cloe blush'd: Euphelia frown'd:
I sung and gaz'd: I play'd and trembl'd:
And Venus to the Loves around
Remark'd, how ill We all dissembl'd.

[3] Mary Anne (1779–99); John would be Four on 9 May.

MRS. COWPER — Saturday, 8 May 1779

Address: [ ] Grosvenor Sq[uare] / London.[1]
Postmark: OULNEY
Olney

My dear Cousin,

I wish the Post would have allowed me to acknowledge the Receipt of the Bank Bills sooner, which arrived safe this Afternoon. But it is impossible that a Letter written in answer to one received at Olney on Friday, should reach the place of its Destination before Monday. I mention this, lest you should think I had neglected to send you the earliest Advice, which, on such an Occasion, would be unpardonable. The Executor's[2] inscrutable Objections to Negotiating this Business himself, have occasion'd You & Lady Hesketh a great deal of Trouble, for which I am much concern'd. I am much obliged to You for the Part you have taken in it, & must beg you to make for me the same Acknowledgment to Her, and to tell her how sensible I am of her Kindness in taking it up when Mr. Hunt had dropp'd it. My Aunt will accept of my affectionate Respects, which join'd with Mrs. Unwin's to Her and to Yourself, concludes me Your Obliged & Affectionate Kinsman

Wm Cowper.

Olney.
May 8.—79.

WILLIAM UNWIN — Wednesday, 26 May 1779

Address: Revd. William Unwin / Stock near / Ingatestone / Essex.
Postmark: 28/MA
Princeton

My dear Friend,

I must beg your Assistance in a Design I have formed to cheat the Glazier. Government has laid a Tax upon Glass,[1] and He has trebled

[1] One-half of the address sheet has been torn away.
[2] See n. 1, C to Hill, 26 May 1778.

[1] According to 17 Geo. III, c. 39, s. 26, the duties on glass were imposed at double the

it; I want as much as will serve for a large Frame, but am unwilling to pay an exorbitant Price for it. I shall be obliged to you therefore if you will enquire at a Glass Manufacturer's, how he sells his Newcastle Glass,[2] such as is used for Frames & Hot Houses. If you will be so good as to send me this Information, & at the same time, the Manufacturer's Address, I will execute the rest of the Business myself, without giving you any further Trouble.

I am obliged to you for the Poets, & though I little thought that I was Translating so much Money out of your Pocket into the Booksellers' when I turn'd Prior's Poem into Latin,[3] yet I must needs say that if you think it worth while to purchase the English Classics at all, you cannot possess yourself of them upon better Terms. I have look'd into some of the Volumes, but not having yet finish'd the Register, have *merely* look'd into them. A few things I have met with, which if they had been burnt the Moment they were written, it would have been better for the Author & at least as well for his Readers. There is not much of This, but a little is too much. I think it a Pity he admitted Any; the English Muse would have lost no Credit by the Omission of such Trash. Some of them again, seem to me to have but a very disputable Right to a Place among the Classics, & I am quite at a Loss, when I see them in such Company, to conjecture what is Dr. Johnson's Idea or Definition of Classical Merit. But if he inserts the Poems of some who can hardly be said to deserve such an Honor, the Purchaser may Comfort himself with the Hope that he will Exclude none that do.

Your Mother sends her Love & affectionate Remembrances to all at Stock from the Tallest to the Shortest there, in which she is accompanied by Yours

Wm Cowper.

May 26. —79.

previous rate (on garden glass it would have been 3*s*. 6*d*. per cwt.). North's increase in excise duties in 1779 would have pushed the tax up slightly more.

2 [John Baillie], *An Impartial History of the Town and Country Of Newcastle upon Tyne . . .* (1801), pp. 512–13: 'The glass works, next to the coal-trade, are the richest branch of the trade of Newcastle; as the duty to government, from glass alone, is reckoned at 140,000 l. per annum.'

3 C's translation of Prior (see C to Unwin, 1 May 1779) had stimulated Unwin to purchase the first four volumes, which appeared in 1779, of Johnson's *Prefaces, Biographical and Critical, to the Works of the English Poets.*

WILLIAM UNWIN — July 1779[1]

British Library

My dear Friend,

If you please you may give my Service to Mr. James Martin, Glazier,[2] & tell him that I have furnish'd myself with Glass from Bedford for just half the Money.

When I was at Margate it was an Excursion of Pleasure to go to see Ramsgate.[3] The Pier, I remember, was accounted a most excellent Piece of Stonework, and such I found it. By this time I suppose it is finish'd, and surely it is no small advantage that you have an Opportunity of Observing how nicely those great Stones are put together, as often as you please, without either Trouble or Expence. But you think Margate more lively—So is a Cheshire Cheese full of Mites more Lively than a Sound one, but that very Liveliness only proves its Rottenness. I remember too that Margate tho' full of Company, was generally fill'd with such Company, as People who were Nice in the choice of their Company, were rather fearfull of keeping Company with. The Hoy[4] went to London every Week Loaded with Mackarel & Herrings, and return'd Loaded with Company. The Cheapness of the Conveyance made it equally commodious for Dead Fish and Lively Company. So Perhaps your Solitude at Ramsgate may turn out another Advantage, at least I should think it One.

There was not at that Time, much to be seen in the Isle of Thanet besides the Beauty of the Country & the fine Prospects of the Sea: which are no where surpass'd except in the Isle of Wight, & upon some Parts of the Coast of Hampshire. One Sight however, I remember engaged my Curiosity & I went to See it. A Fine Piece of Ruins, built by the late Lord Holland at a great Expence, which the Day after I saw it, Tumbled down for Nothing.[5] Perhaps therefore it is

[1] This date is supplied by Unwin on the MS.

[2] Unidentified.

[3] Thomas Gray had written to William Mason, 15 Feb. 1767 (*Gray*, iii. 952): '. . . my idea therefore is, that you might go at present to Ramsgate, wch is shelter'd from the North, & opening only to S: & S:E:, with a very fine pier to walk on. it is a neat Town, seemingly with very clean houses to lodge in, & one end of it only running down to the shore. it is at no season much pester'd with company, & at present I suppose there is no body there'. For C's earlier reflections on Margate, see his to Lady Hesketh of 9 Aug. 1763.

[4] 'A small vessel, usually rigged as a sloop, and employed in carrying passengers and goods, particularly in short distances on the sea-coast' (*O.E.D.*).

[5] Henry Fox (1705–74) was created Baron Holland of Foxley in 1763. After his career in

still a Ruin, and if it is I would advise you by all Means to Visit it, as it must have been much improved by this fortunate Incident. It is hardly possible to put Stones together with that Air of Wild & Magnificent Disorder which they are sure to acquire by falling of their own Accord.

We heartily wish that Mrs. Unwin may receive the utmost Benefit of Bathing. At the same time we caution *You* against the use of it, however the Heat of the Weather may seem to recommend it. It is not safe for thin Habits, Hectically inclin'd.

I remember (the fourth & last thing I mean to Remember upon this Occasion) that Sam: Cox the Council,[6] walking by the Sea Side as if absorb'd in deep Contemplation, was question'd about what He was Musing on. He replied, I was wondering that such an almost infinite and unwieldly Element, should produce a Sprat.

Our Love attends the Whole Party.

Yours Affectionately Wm Cowper.

You are desired to Purchase 3 Pounds of Sixpenny White Worsted, at a Shop well recommended for that Commodity. The Isle of Thanet is famous for it beyond any other Place in the Kingdom.

WILLIAM UNWIN — Saturday, 17 July 1779

Address: Revd. William Unwin / Ramsgate / Kent.
Postmark: 19/[I]Y
British Library

My dear Friend,

We envy you your Sea Breezes. In the Garden we feel nothing but the Reflection of the Heat from the Walls, and in the Parlour, from

politics ended in 1763 (he had been Secretary of State in the Newcastle ministry), he travelled on the Continent and constructed the strange residence at Kingsgate, near Margate, which C visited. According to James Dallaway, *Anecdotes of the Arts in England* (1800), p. 385, the house itself was 'a correct imitation of Cicero's Formian villa, at Baiae'; and another account (*Letters from Mrs. Carter to Mrs. Montagu*, ed. M. Pennington (1817), iii. 89) states that 'scattered around it [were] many fanciful representations of antique and ruined buildings'. Gray immortalized the place in his poem, 'On Lord Holland's Seat near Margate, Kent'.

6 Sam Cox (1720–76), one of the builders of the residences in Dean's Yard for Westminsters and often the protector of Westminsters who went on to the Inner Temple, used to take vacations with C and his friends at such places as Ramsgate and Margate. See *Ryskamp*, p. 53.

the Opposite Houses. I fancy Virgil was so situated when he wrote those 2 Beautifull Lines—

——Oh quis me gelidis in Vallibus Hæmi
Sistat, et ingenti Ramorum protegat Umbrâ![1]

The worst of it is, that tho' the Sun beams strike as forcibly upon my Harp Strings as they did upon His, they elicit no such Sounds, but rather produce such Groans as they are said to have drawn from those of the Statue of Memnon.[2]

As you have ventured to make the Experiment, your own Experience will be your best Guide in the Article of Bathing. An Inference will hardly follow, tho' one should pull at it with all one's Might, from Smollett's Case to yours.[3] He was Corpulent, Muscular, & Strong—Whereas if you were either Stolen or Stray'd, Such a Description of you in an Advertizement, would hardly direct an Enquirer, with sufficient Accuracy & Exactness. But If Bathing does not make your Head Ach, or prevent your Sleeping at Night, I should imagine it could not Hurt you.

I remember taking a Walk upon the Strand at Margate where the Cliff is high & perpendicular. At long Intervals there are Cartways cut thro' the Rock down to the Beach, and there is no other way of Access to it, or of Return from it. I walk'd near a Mile upon the Water Edge, without observing that the Tide was rising fast upon me. When I *did* Observe it, it was almost too late. I ran every Step back again, and had much ado to save my Distance. I mention this as a Caution, lest you should happen at any time to be surprized as I was. It would be very unpleasant to be forced to cling like a Cat to the Side of a Precipice, & perhaps hardly possible to do it for 4 Hours without any Respite.

It seems a Trifle, but it is a real Disadvantage to have no better Name to pass by than the Gentleman you mention. Whether we suppose him settled and promoted in the Army, the Church or the

[1] *Georgics*, ii. 488–9: 'O for one to place me in Hæmus' cool glen, and shield me under the branches' mighty shade.'

[2] In the Trojan War, Memnon, King of Ethiopia, fought against the Greeks and was ultimately killed by Achilles. Memnon was supposed to have lived in Egypt, and the Greeks gave his name to the great statue of Amenhotep III (*c.* 1370 B.C.). This statue was said to make a musical sound at daybreak, at which time Memnon greeted his mother, Eos.

[3] Probably a reference to Smollett's *An Essay on the External Use of Water* (1752) in which Smollett exposed the unhygienic conditions which endangered those who sought health at Bath.

Law, how uncouth the Sound—Captain Twopenny! Bishop Twopenny! Judge Twopenny! The abilities of Lord Mansfield[4] would hardly impart a Dignity to such a Name. Should he perform Deeds worthy of Poetical Panegyric, how difficult would it be to ennoble the Sound of Twopenny.

Muse! Place him upon the Lists of Fame,
The wond'rous Man, & Twopenny his Name.

But to be Serious, if the French should Land in the Isle of Thanet, & Mr. Twopenny should fall into their Hands, he will have a fair Opportunity to Frenchify his Name, & may call himself Monsieur Deux Sous, which when he comes to be exchanged by Cartel, will easily resume an English Form, & Slide naturally into Two Shoes, in my Mind a considerable Improvement.

We hope Mrs. Unwin receives Benefit, tho' you have not said so, & that the rest of the Party are all in good Health. Our Love attends yourself and them.

Your Mother purposes to write next Week.

Yours affectionately Wm Cowper.

July 17. 79.

JOSEPH HILL — Sunday, 8 August 1779

Address: Mr. Joseph Hill / Wargrove near Twyford / Berks.
Harvard

My dear Friend,

As a School Boy longs for fine Fruit, but feels himself too poor to purchase it, so have I longed for Millar's Dictionary.[1] And as the same Boy is the happiest of all imaginable Beings upon Earth, when a Friend passing by & observing him Slips half a Crown into his Hand, so was I at the Receipt of your Present. At least Poetically so,

[4] William Murray, 1st Earl of Mansfield (1705–93), the jurist. He would have been well known to C as codifier of English law regarding rules of procedure.

[1] Philip Miller (1691–1771) was the author of several gardening books of wide circulation which appeared in a number of editions, including *The Gardeners Dictionary* (1731) and *The Gardeners Kalendar* (1732). Hill had presented C with a copy of the 1763 edition of the *Dictionary*. See *Keynes*, 61.

for in all Similes there is some Allowance to be made for the Want of Resemblance. I rejoice in it however, and Thank you for it.

A Lady who was here about a Fortnight ago, and about a Week since at Kew, sent me a considerable Number of Slips from the King's Conservatory. But so Bumbled in the Journey!—they were all of one Hue, viz.—Black as Ink. They came in a Box, the Bottom of which was Ramm'd & Cramm'd with a Black Loam, & in this they were Stuck fast as one would have thought: but the contrary proved the Case; for They broke loose, & the Loam broke loose, & by the Jolts of the Carriage was gradually formed into Bullets of about a Pound Weight and about Thirty in Number, which rolling backward & forward in the Box & round about it, & in all Sorts of Directions, did so assimilate the said plants to itself that it was no easy Matter to find them. With this Distress came another by the same Opportunity. My Benefactress forgot to send me their Names, & the Gardener did not think it worth his while. So that unless I can invent Names for them, they are likely to be Nameless for ever. She wrote me Word that one was an American Plant, & that 2 or 3 of them were from Otaheité,[2] but which, she said not. Oh for Dr. Solander,[3] for I don't like Dr. Forster,[4] to help me out.

I beg you will remember me affectionately to Mrs. Hill—she is a Gardener & will know how to Sympathize with me.

Yours Wm Cowper.

Two fine Salmon Trout & a Lobster demand my Acknowledgements. The same are due for the Hopes Mrs. Hill gives me of a fresh Cargo from the West Indies.

Augt. 8. —79.

[2] Tahiti.

[3] Probably a reference to the edition of Linnaeus's *Elementa Botanica* which Daniel Charles Solander (1736–82) had translated in 1756.

[4] Probably *Characteres Generum Plantarum, Quas in Itinere ad Insulas Maris Australis, Collegerunt, Discripserunt, Delinearunt, Annis MDCCLXXII–MDCCLXXV. Joannes Reinoldus Forster, LL.D. . . . et Georgius Forster* (1776). This quarto volume met with some ridicule owing to the minute scale on which the plants were drawn as compared with the size of the paper. C was familiar with the elder Forster from having read his *A Voyage Round the World* (see n. 2, C to Hill, 13 July 1777). More significant than any allusions to works of a botanical nature is the fact that C is probably well aware of Solander's great popularity at this time with Cook and the rest of the scientific world, whereas Forster was generally despised. See J. C. Beaglehole, *Life of Captain James Cook* (Stanford, 1974).

WILLIAM UNWIN Tuesday, 17 August 1779

Address: Revd. William Unwin / Stock near / Ingatestone / Essex.
Postmark: 18/AV
British Library.

My dear Friend,

You will not Expect Line for Line, or that I should measure your two last Letters by a Foot Rule, and send you so many Feet so many Inches in Return. I like very well to write, but then I am fond of Gardening too, and can find but little Leisure for the Pen, except when the Weather forbids me to employ myself amongst my Plants. Such is the Case this Morning, the almost Tropical Heat of the day, has driven me into the House, where not knowing how to Employ myself better, I am doing as you see.

You thought you had said too much about the Doctor, & I fear'd I had said too much, or with too much Freedom about Mr. Twopenny. Tho' I stood quite clear of any Design to undervalue the Man, at the same time that I made Merry with his Name, I used it as a Play thing, imagining I should hardly find a cheaper.

Respecting the Doctor you Judge exactly as I had Judged before I received your last, and so I had told your Mother. It would be wrong to Court him—non est tanti[1]—You held him by the Hand while he was Sinking, & if upon his first beginning to Emerge, he is capable of putting an intended Slight upon you, your best Course is to suffer it patiently, & to take care that it be the last.

As to your Kentish Petitioners,[2] they mean well, but the Case is hopeless, & consequently the Attempt (may I venture to say it?) idle. When Henry 8th reformed the Church, he had twice as much Power as George 3rd, both Houses of Parliament were on his Side, & the Clergy themselves in Convocation, being both ashamed & afraid to

[1] 'It is of no account.'

[2] We have not been able to locate any such Petition presented in 1779; Mrs. Winifred Bergess, County Reference Librarian, County Library, Springfield, Maidstone, Kent, has suggested that the passage could refer to the preparation or agitation preceding a petition which was actually drawn up in a later year. The *London Evening Post* of Thursday, 9 Mar. to Saturday, 11 Mar. 1780 (No. 9037) mentions a Kent Petition, 'without Committee, or Association' addressed to 'the Honourable the Commons in Great Britain assembled' which calls for frugality in government spending.

Unwin was obviously thinking of forming a movement in Essex to present a similar petition to Parliament.

do otherwise, concurred heartily in the Work. But when the Parliament itself is to be reformed, itself must Effect the Reformation. And do you think you have Eloquence enough in all your County to persuade them to Relinquish what they have so earnestly Labor'd to obtain? Will Pensioners when they have read your Harrangue, resign their Emoluments, Placemen quit their Offices, and Candidates for Preferment abandon all their blooming Hopes, & say, these Gentlemen are in the right, the Nation will be ruined, we will retire & be content? I am afraid not. Luxury makes Men Necessitous, Necessity exposes them to Corruption, Corruption inclines them still more to Profusion, & Profusion continually encreasing, begets new Necessities—These again Engender Corruption & Profligacy of Principle, & as Poor Robin says, So the World goes round.[3] The King, in the mean time, is a Sorrowfull Spectator of the Scene, but a Helpless one. No Measure of Government can proceed without a Majority on its Side, a Majority cannot be had unless it be bought, then what Answer can his Majesty possibly return to the Petition? If it is conceived in Loyal & Obedient Terms, it is teizing him, if otherwise, Insulting. So you see I differ from your Neighbors upon the Subject. A longer Arm & a Stronger Hand is requisite to this Business. Man never was Reform'd by Man, nor ever can be. Your Petition therefore should be carried elsewhere, or it will be in Vain. Dixi.[4]

We Rejoice that you are All Safe at Stock again. Your Mother is well & sends her best Love. You will be pleased to Remember me affectionately to All under your roof, & to beleive me Yours

Wm Cowper.

Augt. 17. 79.

[3] 'Poor Robin' was the pseudonym adopted by William Winstanley (1628?–98) for a series of almanacs and chap-books he issued from *c.* 1661. The almanac, in various guises, survived until 1827.

[4] 'I have spoken.'

WILLIAM UNWIN Tuesday, 21 September 1779

Address: Reverend William Unwin / at Mr. Longman's / No. 39 Pater Noster Row / London
Postmark: 22/SE
British Library

Amico Mio!

Be pleased to Buy me a Glazier's Diamond Pencil; I have Glazed the two Frames designed to receive my Pine Plants,[1] but I cannot mend the Kitchen Windows 'till by the Help of that Implement I can reduce the Glass to its proper Dimensions. If I were a Plumber I should be a complete Glazier, and possibly the happy time may come when I shall be seen trudging away to the Neighbouring Towns with a Shelf of Glass hanging at my Back. If Government should impose another Tax upon that Commodity, I hardly know a Business in which a Gentleman might more successfully employ himself.[2] A Chinese of ten times my Fortune would avail himself of such an Opportunity without Scruple, & why should not I, who want Money as much as any Mandarin in China. Rousseau would have been charmed to have seen me so occupied, & would have exclaimed with Rapture, that he had found the Emilius who he supposed had subsisted only in his own Idea.[3] I would recommend it to you to follow my Example, you will presently qualify yourself for the Task, and may not only amuse yourself at Home, but may even exercise your Skill in mending the Church Windows, which as it would save Money to the Parish, would conduce together with your other Ministerial Accomplishments to make you extremely popular in the Place.

I have 8 Pair of tame Pigeons—when I first Enter the Garden in a Morning, I find them Perched upon the Wall, waiting for their Breakfast, for I feed them always upon the Gravel Walk. If your Wish should be accomplished, & you should find yourself furnish'd with the Wings of a Dove, I shall undoubtedly find you amongst them. Only be so good, if that should be the Case, as to announce yourself by some means or other, for I imagine, your Crop will require something better than Tares to fill it.

1 Pineapples. See C to Hill, 2 Oct. 1779.

2 The tax on window glass specifically was increased in 1778. For C's concern with the tax on glass, see his letter to Unwin of 26 May 1779.

3 In *Émile* (1762), Rousseau's imaginary pupil was sent to learn a trade.

Your Mother and I, last Week made a Trip in a Post Chaise to Gayhurst, the Seat of Mr. Wright, about 4 Miles off. He understood that I did not much affect Strange Faces, and sent over his Servant on purpose to inform me that he was going into Leicestershire, & that if I chose to see the Gardens, I might gratify myself without Danger of seeing the Proprietor. I accepted the Invitation & was delighted with all I found there; the Situation is happy, the Gardens elegantly disposed, the Hot House in the most flourishing State, & the Orange Trees the most captivating Creatures of the kind I ever saw. A Man in short had need have the Talents of Cox or Langford the Auctioneers,[4] to do the whole Scene Justice.

Our Love attends you all.

Yours Wm Cowper.

Sepr. 21, 79.

The Snuff Shop is Arnold's in Newgate Street.[5]

JOSEPH HILL — Saturday, 2 October 1779

Address: Mr. Joseph Hill at / Wargrove near / Twyford / Berkshire
Postmarks: 4/OC *and* OULNEY
Cowper Johnson

My dear Friend,

You begin to Count the remaining Days of the Vacation, not with Impatience, but through unwillingness to see the End of it: For the Mind of Man, at least of most Men, is equally Busy in Anticipating the Evil and the Good. That WordAnticipation puts me in Remembrance of the Pamphlet of that Name, which if you purchased I should be glad to Borrow. I have seen only an Extract from it in the Review, which made me Laugh heartily & wish to peruse the Whole.[1]

[4] Christopher Cock (d. 10 Nov. 1748) and Abraham Langford (1711–74). In 1748 Langford succeeded Cock at the latter's establishment at Covent Garden. At the time of his death, Langford was the foremost auctioneer in England.

[5] *The London Directory for the Year 1780*, p. 5: 'Arnold & Pearkes, tobacconists, 6 Newgate-Street.'

[1] A review of *Anticipation: containing the Substance of his M—y's most gracious Speech to both Houses of P—l—t . . . together with a full and authentic Account of the Debate which will take Place in the H— of C—s . . .*, which had been published on 23 Nov. 1778, appeared in the *Monthly Review* (lix. 390–1) for that month.

The reviewer also was amused by the pamphlet's deft attack on the Opposition speakers

The News Paper informs me of the Arrival of the Jamaica Fleet.[2] I hope it imports some Pine Apple Plants for Me. I have a good Frame & a Good Bed prepared to receive them. I send you annex'd, a Fable in which the Pine Apple makes a Figure, & shall be glad if you Like the Taste of it.—2 Pair of Soals with Shrimps which arrived last Night, demand my Acknowledgments. You have heard that when Arion performed upon the Harp the Fish followed him.[3] I really have no Design to Fiddle you out of more Fish, but if you should Esteem my Verses worthy of such a Price, though I shall never be so renown'd as he was, I shall think myself equally indebted to the Muse that helps me.

The Pine Apple & the Bee.[4]

The Pine Apples in triple Row
Were basking hot, & all in Blow,
A Bee of most discerning Taste
Perceived the Fragrance as he pass'd,
On Eager Wing the Spoiler came
And searched for Crannies in the Frame,
Push'd his Attempt on every Side,
To ev'ry Pane his Trunk applied,
But all in Vain, the Frame was tight,
And pervious only to the Light.
Thus having wasted half the Day,
He trimm'd his Flight another way.—
Methinks, I said, in thee I find
The Sin and Madness of Mankind.
To Joys forbidden, Man aspires,
Consumes his Soul with Vain Desires,
Folly the Spring of his Pursuit,
And Disappointment all the Fruit.
While Cynthio Ogles, as she passes,

and claimed that 'their several and general modes of declamation against ministerial measures are *hit off*, with a considerable degree of humour'. The author of *Anticipation* was probably Richard Tickell (1751–93).

[2] The *Gazetteer* of 29 and 30 Sept. and the *Morning Post* of 30 Sept. tell of the arrival of various ships from Jamaica at such ports as Cork, Liverpool, Lancaster, and Portsmouth.

[3] C is referring to the music-loving dolphins who were attracted by Arion's singing and who guided him to safety when he was forced to jump from the ship returning him to Corinth.

[4] Published in *1782*.

The Nymph between two Chariot Glasses,
She is the Pine Apple, and He
The Silly unsuccessfull Bee.
The Maid who views with pensive Air
The Show Glass fraught with glitt'ring Ware,
Sees Watches, Bracelets, Rings & Lockets,
But Sighs at Thoughts of Empty Pockets,
Like thine, her Appetite is keen,
But Ah! the cruel Glass between.

Our dear Delights are often such,
Exposed to View but not to Touch,
The Sight our foolish Heart inflames,
We Long for Pine Apples in Frames,
With hopeless Wish *One* Looks & Lingers,
One breaks the Glass & Cuts his Fingers,
But they whom Truth & Wisdom lead,
Can gather Honey from a Weed.

My affectionate Respects attend Mrs. Hill. She has put Mr. Wright to the Expence of Building a New Hot house. The Plants produced by the Seeds she gave me, being grown so large as to require an Apartment to themselves.

Yours Wm Cowper.

Octr. 2. 79.

WILLIAM UNWIN — Sunday, 31 October 1779

Address: Revd. William Unwin at / Stock near / Ingatestone / Essex.
Postmark: 1/NO
British Library

My dear Friend,

I wrote my last Letter merely to inform you that I had nothing to say, in Answer to which you have said Nothing. I admire the Propriety of your Conduct, tho' I am a Loser by it. I will endeavour to Say something now, and shall hope for Something in return.

I have been well entertain'd with Johnson's Biography, for which

I thank you.[1] With One Exception, and that a Swingeing one, I think he has acquitted himself with his usual Good Sense & Sufficiency. His Treatment of Milton is unmercifull to the last Degree. A Pensioner is not likely to Spare a Republican, and the Doctor, in order I suppose, to convince his Royal Patron of the Sincerity of his Monarchical Principles, has belabor'd that great Poet's Character with the most Industrious Cruelty. As a Man, he has hardly left him the shadow of one good Quality. Churlishness in his private Life, and a rancorous Hatred of every thing Royal in his Public, are the two Colours with which he has smear'd all the Canvass. If he had any Virtues, they are not to be found in the Doctor's Picture of him, and it is Well for Milton that some Sourness in his Temper is the only Vice with which his Memory has been charged. It is evident enough that if his Biographer could have discover'd more, he would not have spared him. As a Poet, he has treated him with Severity enough, and has pluck'd one or two of the most beautifull Feathers out of his Muse's Wing, & trampled them under his Great Foot. He has passed Sentence of Condemnation upon Lycidas; & has taken Occasion from that charming Poem, to expose to Ridicule (what is indeed Ridiculous Enough) the childish Prattlement of Pastoral Compositions, as if Lycidas was the Prototype & Pattern of them all.[2] The Liveliness of the Description, the Sweetness of the Numbers, the Classical Spirit of Antiquity that prevails in it, go for nothing. I am convinced by the way that he has no Ear for Poetical Numbers, or that it was stopp'd by Prejudice against the Harmony of Milton's. Was there ever any thing so delightfull as the Music of the Paradise Lost? It is like that of a fine Organ; has the fullest & the deepest Tones of Majesty, with all the Softness & Elegance of the Dorian Flute. Variety without End! & never equal'd unless perhaps by Virgil. Yet the Doctor has little or nothing to say upon this copious Theme, but talks something about the unfitness of the English Language for Blank Verse, & how apt it is, in the

[1] Unwin evidently sent the four volumes of Johnson's *Prefaces* to C. See n. 3, C to Unwin, 26 May 1779.

[2] *Prefaces*, ii. 153–4. 'One of the poems on which much praise has been bestowed is *Lycidas*; of which the diction is harsh, the rhymes uncertain, and the numbers unpleasing . . . In this poem there is no nature, for there is no truth; there is no art, for there is nothing new. Its form is that of a pastoral, easy, vulgar, and therefore disgusting: whatever images it can supply, are long ago exhausted; and its inherent improbability always forces dissatisfaction on the mind.'

Mouth of some Readers to degenerate into Declamation.[3] Oh! I could thresh his old Jacket 'till I made his Pension Jingle in his Pocket.

I could talk a good while longer but I have no Room. Our Love attends yourself, Mrs. Unwin, & Miss Shuttleworth, not forgetting the two Miniature Pictures at your Elbow.

Yours affectionately
Wm Cowper.

Octr. 31. 79.

JOSEPH HILL — Sunday, 14 November 1779

Address: Mr. Joseph Hill / Chancery Office / London.
Postmarks: 15/NO *and* OULNEY
Cowper Johnson

Nov. 14. 79

My dear Friend,

You did not send me a Draft, though you are welcome to send as many as you please, and as soon as you please.

I thank you for the Idea of a Basket of Fish, and while I wait in Hopes that it will be realized, am in some Pain, lest it should have miscarried, and the Parcel of Seeds with it. This would be a Loss indeed, which would be felt from hence to Goathurst,[1] & which would vex me for half a Year to come. I beg you will inform me whether this is indeed the Case, or whether as I much Wish, they have only been delayed by Accident.

Your Approbation of my last Heliconian Present,[2] encourages me to send you another. I wrote it indeed on purpose for you, for my Subjects are not always such as I could hope would prove agreeable to You. My Mind has always a melancholy Cast, and is like some Pools I have seen, which though filled with a Black and putrid

[3] *Prefaces*, ii. 220–1: 'Blank verse makes some approach to that which is called the *lapidary stile*; has neither the easiness of prose, nor the melody of numbers, and therefore tires by long continuance.'

[1] See n. 2, C to Unwin, 3 Dec. 1778.
[2] 'The Pine Apple & the Bee' in C's letter of 2 Oct.

Water, will nevertheless in a bright Day, reflect the Sunbeams from their Surface.

On the Promotion of
Edward Thurlow Esq
To the Lord Chancellorship of
England.[3]

Round Thurlow's Head in Early Youth,
And in his Sportive Days,
Fair Science pour'd the Light of Truth,
And Genius shed his Rays.

2.

See! with united Wonder cried
Th' Experienced & the Sage,
Ambition in a Boy supplied
With all the Skill of Age.

[3.]

Discernment, Eloquence & Grace
Proclaim him born to Sway
The Balance in the Highest Place,
And Bear the Palm away.

4.

The Praise bestow'd was Just & Wise,
He sprung impetuous forth,
Secure of Conquest, where the Prize
Attends Superior Worth.

5.

So the best Courser on the Plain
E'er yet he Starts, is known,
And does but at the Goal obtain
What all had deem'd his Own.

---

[3] Published in *1782*.

My Respects attend Mrs. Hill, with many Thanks to her for Remembering my Suit for Seeds from One End of the year to the other.

Yours & Hers Affectionately
Wm Cowper.

The Fish are come since this was written, for which—Thanks—as no Seeds are come with 'em—Alas! Alas! I find that I misunderstood what you said about them in your last. The Herrings are remarkably fine.

WILLIAM UNWIN Thursday, 2 December 1779

Address: Revd. William Unwin / Stock near / Ingatestone / Essex
Postmarks: 3/DE *and* OULNEY
British Library

My dear Friend—

How quick is the Succession of Human Events! The Cares of to:day are seldom the Cares of to:morrow, and when we lie down at Night we may safely Say to most of our Troubles—Ye have done your worst & we shall Meet no more. This Observation was suggested to me by reading your last Letter, which, though I have written since I received it, I have never answer'd. When that Epistle passed under your Pen, you was miserable about your Tythes, & your Imagination was hung round with Pictures that terrified you to such a Degree, as made even the Receipt of Money burthensome. But it is all over now—You sent away your Farmers in good Humour, for you can make People merry whenever you please, & now you have nothing to do but to chink your Purse, & laugh at what is past. Your Delicacy makes you groan under that which other Men never Feel, or Feel but Slightly. A Fly that settles upon the Tip of the Nose is troublesome, and this is a Comparison adequate to the most that Mankind in General are sensible of upon such tiney Occasions. But the Flies that Pester You, always get between your Eyelids, where the Annoyance is almost insupportable.

I would follow your Advice, and endeavour to furnish Lord North[1] with a Scheme of Supplies for the ensueing Year, if the Difficulty I

[1] Frederick North, 2nd Earl of Guilford and 8th Baron North (1732–92), was Prime Minister at this time.

find in answering the Call of my own Emergencies, did not make me Despair of satisfying those of the Nation. I can say but This—If I had Ten Acres of Land in the World, whereas I have not one, and in those 10 Acres should discover a Gold Mine richer than all Mexico & Peru, when I had reserved a few Ounces for my own Annual Supply, I would willingly give the Rest to Government. My Ambition would be more gratified by annihilating the National Incumbrances, than by going daily down to the Bottom of a Mine to wallow in my own Emolument. This is Patriotism you will allow—but alas! this Virtue is for the most part in the Hands of those who can do no good with it. He that has but a Single Handfull of it, catches so greedily at the first Opportunity of growing Rich, that his Patriotism drops to the Ground, & he grasps the Gold instead of it. He that never meets with such an Opportunity, holds it fast in his clench'd Fist, & says oh how much Good I would do if I could.—I thank you for your Interest employ'd to procure me a Place in the Paper, perhaps I may use it; but I am not always in a Humour to appear in Print. What follows is for Private Use.

Human Frailty.[2]

Weak & Irresolute is Man,
The Purpose of to:Day,
Woven with Pains into his Plan:
To:Morrow rends away.

2.

The Bow well bent & Smart the Spring
Vice seems already Slain,
But Passion rudely Snaps the String,
And it revives again.

3.

Some Foe to his Upright Intent
Finds out his weaker Part,
Virtue engages his Assent,
But Pleasure wins his Heart.

[2] Published in *1782*.

4.

'Tis here the Folly of the Wise
  Thro' all his Art we View,
And while his Tongue the Charge denies
  His Conscience owns it true.

5.

Bound on a Voy'ge of awfull Length
  And Dangers Little known,
A Stranger to Superior Strength
  Man vainly trusts his own:

6.

But Oars alas could ne'er prevail
  To reach the distant Coast,
The Breath of Heav'n must Swell the Sail,
  Or all the Toil is lost.

Your Mother says Pray send my Dear Love. There is hardly Room to add mine, but you will Suppose it—Yours Wm Cowper.
Dece. 2. —79.

JOHN NEWTON — Sunday, 6 February 1780

Princeton (*copy*)

I write merely to tell you that your Account of Mrs. Newton's safe arrival gave us real & sincere pleasure. She could not but be fatigued, she was so before she set out, but where that is the worst consequence of a Journey, the Traveller is soon set right again. We hope she will find her situation as favourable to her health as when she was in Town before, & that Sally Johnston, whose imagination told her that she would be happier in a hollow Tree or under a Hedge at Olney than in a Palace in London will soon be reconciled to the life of a Citizen.

I do not know how long Mr. Jones[1] may continue to officiate in

[1] Revd. Thomas Jones, who had been expelled in 1768 from St. Edmund's Hall, Oxford, for holding Methodist views, was curate at Clifton from 1772 to 1792. Five of the letters in Newton's *Cardiphonia* (1781) are addressed to Jones.

this place, but if you should write to him before his Ministry closes, perhaps it would be worth your while to caution him against assuming the Politician's character in the Pulpit. I suppose he is but indifferently qualified for a statesman, & his hearers on such subjects may be nearly as wise as he can make them. I am obliged to you for the Title Page[2] you sent me, & think that the hard name the Author has baptized his Book with is rather unfortunately chosen. I have no Lexicon, & now you are gone, no friend to supply the place of one, but I suppose it might be properly render'd *Woman debauched*; to which I would add in the Dramatic stile,

Or a bold stroke for a Wife![3]

I know not how many wise & good Men may have approved the Manuscript, few good Women I believe will think themselves much indebted to the Writer. However he may dote upon his Offspring & think it likely to bring a blessing with it into society, no arguments would ever lead me to expect a beneficial effect from it, while it remains true, as it will for ever, that happiness cannot be found within the walls of a Seraglio. Time has indeed buried many things in oblivion, but such a privilege as this, (if it deserved to be called a privilege) could never have become obsolete while insatiable Lust & Appetence continued to infest Mankind. In vain therefore does he flatter himself that he has made a great discovery, he has found nothing but a new way to expose himself to the censure of those who Think, & the laughter of those who do not.

Mrs. U. desires me to add her best love

I am Dear Sir
Yours affectionately
W. Cowper.

Febry 6th
80.

[2] Martin Madan's *Thelyphthora or, a Treatise on Female Ruin, Considered on the Basis of the Divine Law* appeared anonymously on 31 May 1780. Basing his argument on a literal interpretation of the Pentateuch, Madan advocated a return to polygamy as a solution to the evils of prostitution. Newton had attempted to dissuade Madan from publishing the book. Title-pages of books were sometimes printed in advance of publication to act as advertisements.

[3] *A Bold Stroke for a Wife* by Susanna Centlivre (*c.* 1670–1723) was first published in 1718.

WILLIAM UNWIN Sunday, 13 February 1780

Address: The Revd. William Unwin at / Mrs. Ords No. 20 Leman Street / Goodmans Fields / London.
Postmarks: 14/FE *and* OULNEY
British Library

My dear Friend,

The last of your Mother's two reasons for not writing sooner, must serve as an Apology for me. Uncertain when you would go to Town, I chose to stay 'till that Affair was decided. I am to thank you for your Pourtraits taken from the Life in the House of Commons, not forgetting the Chancellor, the Duke of Richmond[1] & the Bishops' Wigs. Mr. Burke's Mispronunciation of the Word Vectigal,[2] brings to my Remembrance a Jocular Altercation that passed when I was once in the Gallery, between Mr. Rigby[3] & the late Alderman Beckford.[4] The latter was a very incorrect Speaker, & the former I imagine not a very accurate Scholar. He ventured however upon a Quotation from Terence, & deliver'd it thus, sine *Scelere* et Baccho friget Venus—the Alderman interrupted him, was very severe upon his Mistake, & restored Ceres to her place in the Sentence.[5] Mr. Rigby replied that he was obliged to his worthy Friend for teaching him Latin, & would take the first Opportunity to return the Favor by teaching Him English.

You are not alone I beleive in thinking that you see a striking Resemblance between the Reign of his present Majesty & that of Charles the first. The undue Extension of the Influence of the Crown, the Discountenancing and Displacing of Men obnoxious to the Court, though otherwise men of unexceptionable Conduct & Character, the Waste of the Public Money, & especially the Suspicion that obtains of a fixt Design in Government to favor the Cause of Popery

[1] Charles Lennox, 3rd Duke of Richmond and Lennox (1735–1806) was admitted to Westminster in Apr. 1746, and C had known him there.

[2] Payment of a tax (*O.E.D.*). This may have been the session of 11 Feb. 1780 at which Edmund Burke introduced his bill for the strict regulation of spending on various bureaucratic establishments within the government. See *G.M.* l (1780), 353 ff.

[3] A notoriously unscrupulous politician and the butt of some of Junius' bitterest attacks, Richard Rigby (1722–88) was M.P. for Tavistock from 1754 to 1788.

[4] William Beckford (1709–70), who was M.P. for London from 1754 to 1770. Gray in a letter to Wharton of 28 Nov. 1759 mentions 'a nonsensical speech of Beckford's' (*Gray*, ii. 651).

[5] *Eunuchus*, 732: 'Without Ceres (food) and Bacchus (wine), Venus (love) is cold.' Beckford should have said *Cerere* rather than *Scelere.*

are Features common to both Faces. Again, these Causes have begun to produce the same Effects now as they did in the Reign of that unhappy Monarch. It is long since I saw Lord Clarendon's Account of it,[6] but unless my Memory fails me much, I think you will find (and indeed it could hardly be otherwise) that the Leaders of the discontented Party, and the several Counties in their Interest, had a good Understanding with each other and devised Means for the Communication of Intelligence, much like our modern Committees of Correspondence.[7]—You ask my Opinion of the Tendency of such Associations—No, I mistake—You do not ask mine, but you give your own, which is exactly according to my own Sentiments. Indeed they are Explicit enough, and if one was inclined to suppose their Intentions peaceable, they have taken care that the Supposition shall be groundless. A year ago they expressed their Wishes that the People would Rise, and their Astonishment that they did not. Now they tell Government plainly that the Spirit of Resistance is gone forth, that the Nation is at last Roused, that they will fly to Arms upon the next Provocation, and bid 'em slight the Yorkshire Petition at their Peril. Sir George Savile's Speech reminded me of that Line in which is described the Opening of the Temple of Janus, a Ceremony that obtain'd as the established Prelude to a War.[8]

Discordia tetra
Belli ferratos Postes Portasque refregit.[9]

[6] C may be referring to a passage such as the following in the Earl of Clarendon's *History of the Rebellion and Civil Wars in England* (1702). Clarendon is describing the declaration made by a Committee of the House of Commons outlawing a Royal Proclamation as a breach of privilege: 'This strange Declaration, so contrary to the known rules and judgments of Law, was no sooner framed and agreed upon in the Committee, than it was printed, and published throughout the City, and Kingdom, before it was Confirmed by, or Reported to the House; which is against the Custom of Parliament. For, by that Custom, no Act done at any Committee should be divulged before the same be Reported to the House.' (vol. i, Book iv, 295).

[7] The original Committees of Correspondence were set up in Massachusetts and Virginia in opposition to the British Crown's influence in those colonies. These committees ultimately extended throughout the colonies. The context of the letter suggests that William Unwin belonged to an English offshoot of these Committees of Correspondence which was working against some of George III's home policies.

[8] Sir George Savile (1726–84) presented his Yorkshire petition to the Commons on 8 Feb. (see *London Magazine*, xlix, 1780, 45, 122–3 for the petition and Savile's speech). The reference to Burke's 'Cause' suggests that the verses were directed against the Opposition, seen as hotheads of Savile's stamp; Burke's speech was that delivered on 11 Feb., when he presented his 'Plan for the Better Security of the Independence of Parliament' (*Works*, 1803, iii. 229–352).

[9] These lines are from the *Annals* of Ennius (239–169 B.C.), but C probably knew them

It seems clear then that Hostilities are intended as the last Resource. As to the Time they chuse for the Purpose, it is in my Mind the worst they could have chosen. So many Gentlemen of the first Rank & Property in the Kingdom, resolutely bent upon their Purpose, their Design professedly so laudable, & their Means of compassing it so formidable, would command attention at any time. A Quarrel of this Kind, even if it proceeded to the last Extremity, might possibly be settled without the Ruin of the Country, while there was Peace with the neighbouring Kingdoms, but while there is War abroad & such an Extensive War as the present, I fear it cannot.

I add to what your Mother says about Indian Ink, a few Brushes, & a Pencil or two, with anything else that may be convenient for the Use of a Beginner, as far as five Shillings. I don't think my Talent in the Art worth more.

She desires me to remind you of your promised Vote & Interest for a Place in Christ's Hospital, of which she understands you are now a Governor,[10] & that the Parcel may come by the Waggon, which it will do if it is sent on a Wednesday to the Windmill in St. John Street
Feb. 13. 1780.

Any Money that remains may be sent with it.

WILLIAM UNWIN — Sunday, 27 February 1780

British Library

My dear Friend,

As you are pleased to Desire my Letters, I am the more pleased with Writing them. Though at the same time I must needs testify my Surprize that you should think them worth receiving, as I

from Horace's quotation of them in *Satires*, I. iv. 60–1: 'After ugly discord had broken open the bronze gates and posts of war.'

10 Unwin was elected a Governor of Christ's Hospital on 28 Oct. 1779 (Guildhall Library, MS. 12806/12, p. 291). As such, he had the right to present children between 1780 and 1786, but he did not exercise the right until 1781 (Governors' Presentation Registers, MS. 12857/1, unfoliated).

Children were nominated (i.e. presented) each year to fill the available vacancies. The right of nomination at this time was restricted to the Lord Mayor, Recorder, and Aldermen of London, the Governors, the benefactors, and certain specially appointed persons or bodies of distinction. Mrs. Unwin wanted her son to act on behalf of a nephew of Newton's. See C to Unwin, 28 Mar. 1780.

seldom send one that I think favorably of myself. This is not to be understood as an Imputation upon your Taste or Judgment, but as an Encomium upon my own Modesty & Humility, which I desire you to remark well. It is a just Observation of Sir Joshua Reynolds, that though Men of ordinary Talents may be highly satisfied with their own Productions, Men of true Genius never are.[1] Whatever be their Subject, they always seem to themselves to fall short of it, even when they seem to others most to Excell, and for this Reason—because they have a certain Sublime Sense of Perfection, which other men are Strangers to, and which they themselves in their Performances are not able to Exemplify.—Your Servant Sir Joshua, I little thought of seeing you when I began, but as you have popp'd in you are welcome.

When I wrote last I was a little inclined to send you a Copy of Verses entitled the Modern Patriot,[2] but was not quite pleased with a Line or two which I found it difficult to mend, therefore did not. At Night I read Mr Burke's Speech in the Newspaper, and was so well pleased with his Proposals for a Reformation,[3] & with the Temper in which he made them, that I began to think better of his Cause and burnt my Verses. Such is the Lot of the Man who writes upon the Subject of the Day; the Aspect of Affairs changes in an Hour or two, & his Opinion with it.—What was just and well deserved Satyr in the Morning, in the Evening becomes a Libel. The Author commences his own Judge, and while he condemns with unrelenting Severity what he so lately approved, is sorry to find that he has laid his Leaf Gold upon Touchwood which crumbled away under his Fingers. Alas! what can I do with my Wit? I have not enough to do great things with, and these little things are so fugitive, that while a man catches at the Subject, he is only filling his Hand with Smoke. I must do with it as I do with my Linnet, I keep him for the most part in a Cage, but now & then set open the Door that he may whisk about the Room a little, & then shut him up again. My

[1] C may be paraphrasing this passage from Reynolds's first discourse (1769): 'But whatever may be our proportion of success, of this we may be sure, that the present Institution, will at least contribute to advance our knowledge of the Arts, and bring us nearer to that ideal excellence, which it is the lot of Genius always to contemplate, and never to attain.': *Seven Discourses Delivered in the Royal Academy by the President* (1778), p. 9. We are grateful to the late Frederick W. Hilles for assistance in preparing this note.

[2] C seems to have reconstructed his original poem to apply to the Gordon Riots of June 1780. As such, 'The Modern Patriot' appeared in *1782*.

[3] See n. 2, C to Unwin, 13 Feb. 1780.

Whisking Wit has produced the following, the subject of which is more important than the manner in which I have treated it seems to imply.[4] But a Fable may speak Truth, & all Truth is Sterling. I only premise that in a Philosophical Tract in the Register, I found it asserted that the Glow:worm is the Nightingale's proper Food.[5]

Have you heard? Who has not? For a recommendatory Advertisement of it is already Published, that a certain Kinsman of your humble Servant's has written a Tract, now in the Press, to prove Polygamy a Divine Institution. A plurality of Wives is intended, but not of Husbands. The End proposed by the Author is to remedy the prevailing Practise of Adultery, by making the Female Delinquent ipso facto, the lawfull Wife of the Male.—An Officer of a Regiment, Part of which is Quarter'd here, gave one of the Soldiers leave to be Drunk Six Weeks, in Hopes of curing him by Satiety. He *was* Drunk Six Weeks, & is so still as often as he can find an Opportunity. One Vice may swallow up another, but no Coroner in the State of Ethics, ever brought in his Verdict when a Vice died, that it was Felo de se.[6] They who Value the Man are sorry for his Book, the rest say—

Solvuntur Risu Tabulæ, tu Missus abibis.[7]

Thanks for all you have done, & all you intend; the Biography[8] will be particularly welcome.

My truly affectionate Respects attend you All.

Yours Wm Cowper.

Feb. 27. 80.

When you feel Postage a Burden send me some Franks.

[4] 'The Nightingale and Glow-worm' (published in *1782*), but the copy of the poem enclosed was separated from this letter.

[5] Such a reference has not been located in *The Poetical Register* or *The Annual Register*, but the juxtaposition of a nightingale and glow-worm may be found in Edward Moore's *Fables* (1744).

[6] Suicide.

[7] Horace, *Satires*, II. i. 86: 'The case will be dismissed with scorn. You will be let off.'

[8] See n. 3, C to Unwin, [March?] 1780.

WILLIAM UNWIN [March? 1780][1]

Victoria and Albert

My dear Friend—

How apt we are to deceive ourselves where Self Interest is in question! You say I am in your Debt, and I accounted you in mine: A mistake to which you must attribute my Arrears, if indeed I owe you any, for I am not backward to write where the uppermost Thought is welcome.

I am obliged to you for all the Books you have occasionally furnish'd me with. I did not indeed Read many of Johnson's Classics. Those of establish'd Reputation are so fresh in my Memory tho' many Years have intervened since I made them my Companions, that it was like Reading what I read yesterday, over again: and as to the Minor Classics, I did not think them worth Reading at all. I tasted most of them, & did not like them.[2] It is a great thing to be indeed a Poet, & does not happen to more than One Man in a Century. Churchill, the great Churchill, deserved the Name of Poet. Such natural unforced Effusions of Genius, the World I beleive has never seen since the Days of Shakespear. I have read him twice, and some of his Pieces three times over, and the last time with more Pleasure than the first. The pitifull Scribbler of his Life, seems to have undertaken that Task, for which he was entirely unqualified, merely because it afforded him an Opportunity to traduce him. He has inserted in it but one Anecdote of Consequence, for which he refers you to a Novel, & introduces the Story with Doubts about the Truth of it.[3] But his Barrenness as a Biographer I could forgive, if the Simpleton had not thought himself a Judge of his Writings, & under

[1] This letter obviously follows C's to Unwin of 27 Feb. since the biography mentioned there has now arrived. C's next letter to Unwin is of 28 Mar. 1780.

[2] In his letter to Unwin of 26 May 1779, C indicates that he was not pleased with Johnson's inclusion of minor poets and selections from their work in the 1779 *Prefaces.*

[3] Charles Churchill (1731–64) was a contemporary of C's at Westminster School. The biography referred to is probably the anonymous *Genuine Memoirs of Mr. Charles Churchill, with an Account of, and Observations on His Writings: Together with Some Original Letters That Passed Between Him and the Author* (1765). Although the *Memoirs* does not conform exactly to C's description, it follows it in many particulars. Well into the narrative, the reader is informed that he will be surprised to discover that Churchill became a 'cyder-dealer'. 'Indeed, reader, be not surprised, such metamorphoses are not uncommon in Wales. Parsons are there horse-jockeys, shop-keepers, bakers, barbers, butchers, ale-sellers, and pig-dealers. You have read Joseph Andrews, I suppose; if you have not, I would not give a farthing for

the erroneous Influence of that Thought, inform'd his Reader that Gotham, Independence, & the Times, were Catchpennies.[4] Gotham, unless I am a greater Blockhead than He, which I am far from beleiving, is a Noble and a beautifull Poem, & a Poem with which I make no doubt, the Author took as much Pains, as with any he ever wrote. Making Allowance, (& Dryden perhaps in his Absalom & Ahithophel stands in need of the same Indulgence) for an unwarrantable Use of Scripture, & it appears to me to be a Masterly Performance. Independence is a most animated Piece, full of Strength & Spirit, & marked with that bold Masculine Character, which I think is the great Peculiarity of this Writer: And the Times, except that the Subject is disgusting to the last Degree, stands equally high in my Opinion. He is indeed a careless Writer for the most part, but where shall we find in any of those Authors who finish their Works with the Exactness of a Flemish Pencil, those Bold & daring Strokes of Fancy, those Numbers so hazardously ventured upon & so happily finished, the Matter so compress'd and yet so clear, & the Colouring so sparingly laid on, and yet with such a beautifull Effect? In short, it is not his least Praise, that he is never guilty of those Faults as a Writer, which he lays to the Charge of others. A Proof that he did not Judge by a borrow'd Standard or from Rules laid down by Critics, but that he was qualified to do it by his own Native Powers and his great Superiority of Genius. For He that wrote so much & so fast, would through Inadvertence and Hurry, unavoidably have departed from Rules, which he might have found in Books, but his own truly Poetical Talent was a Guide which could not suffer him to Err. A Race Horse is gracefull in his swiftest Pace, & never makes an awkward Motion though he is push'd to his utmost Speed. A Carthorse might perhaps be taught to Play Tricks in the Riding School, & might Prance & Curvet like his Betters, but at some unlucky time would be sure to betray the Baseness of his Original. It is an affair of very little Consequence perhaps to the Wellbeing of Mankind, but I cannot help regretting that he died so soon. Those Words of Virgil upon the immature Death of Marcellus might serve for his Epitaph.

you. You may be there acquainted with parson Trulliber, of pig-selling memory' (p. 96). We are grateful to Professor W. F. Cunningham, Jr., of Le Moyne College for his assistance in solving this problem.

[4] All three poems were published in 1764.

Ostendent Terris hunc tantum̀ Fata, neque ultrá
Esse Sinent. ——— ——— ———— ————.[5]

Yours affectionately W C.

Your Mother sends her Love, & begs that when you write next you will send another Frank, & then she will Write too.

MRS. NEWTON Saturday, 4 March 1780

Address: Mrs. Newton.
Princeton

Dear Madam,

To communicate Surprize is almost, perhaps quite, as agreeable as to receive it. This is my present Motive for Writing to you rather than to Mr. Newton. He would be pleased with hearing from me, but he would not be surprized at it; you see therefore I am selfish upon the present Occasion, and principally consult my own Gratification. Indeed if I consulted yours I should be silent, for I have no such Budget as the Ministers, furnished & stuff'd with Ways & Means for every Emergency, & shall find it difficult perhaps to raise Supplies even for a short Epistle.

You have observed in common Conversation, that the man who Coughs & Blows his Nose the oftenest, (I mean if he has not a Cold) does it because he has Nothing to say. Even so it is in Letter Writing, a long Preface, such as mine, is an ugly Symptom, & always forebodes great Sterility in the following Pages.

The Vicarage became a Melancholy Object, as soon as Mr. Newton had left it: When You left it, it became more melancholy: now it is actually occupied by another Family. Even I cannot look at it without being shocked. As I walked in the Garden this Evening I saw the Smoke issue from the Study Chimney, and said to myself, that used to be a Sign that Mr. Newton was there, but it is so no longer. The Walls of the House know nothing of the Change that has taken Place, the Bolt of the Chamber Door sounds just as it used to do, and when Mr. Page goes up Stairs, for aught I know or ever shall know, the Fall of his Foot could hardly perhaps be distinguished from that of Mr. Newton: But Mr. Newton's Foot will never be heard upon that

[5] *Aeneid*, vi. 869–70: 'Him the fates but show to earth, nor longer allow him to stay.'

Stair case again.[1]—These Reflections, and such as these, occurred to me upon the Occasion, and though in many respects I have no more Sensibility left than there is in Brick and Mortar, yet I am not permitted to be quite unfeeling upon this Subject. If I were in a Condition to leave Olney too, I certainly would not stay in it; it is no Attachment to the Place that binds me here, but an Unfitness for every other. I lived in it once, but now I am buried in it, and have no Business with the World on the Outside of my Sepulchre; my Appearance would Startle them, and theirs would be shocking to me.

Such are my Thoughts about the Matter—Others are more deeply affected, & by more weighty Considerations. They have been many Years the Objects of a Ministry which they had reason to account themselves happy in the Possession of. They fear they shall find themselves great Suffirers by the alteration that has taken Place; they would have had reason to fear it in any Case, but Mr. Newton's Successor does not bring with him the happiest Presages, so that in the present State of things they have double Reason for their Fears. Tho' I can never be the better for Mr. Page, Mr. Page shall never be the worse for me. If his Conduct should even Justify the worst Apprehensions that have been formed of his Character, it is no personal Concern of mine; but this I can venture to say, that if he is not Spotless, his Spots will be seen, & the plainer, because he comes after Mr. Newton.

We were concerned at your Account of Robert, and have little Doubt but he will shuffle himself out of his Place. Where he will find another, is a Question not to be resolved by those who recommended him to This. I wrote him a long Letter a day or two after the Receipt of yours, but I am afraid it was only clapping a Blister upon the Crown of a Wig Block.

My Respects attend Mr. Newton & yourself accompanied with as much Affection as I am permitted to feel for you both.

Yours Dear Madam

Wm Cowper.

Mar 4. 80.

[1] Benjamin Page had just been appointed curate at Olney.

JOSEPH HILL Thursday, 16 March 1780

Address: Mr. Joseph Hill / Chancery Office / London.
Postmark: OULNEY
Cowper Johnson

My dear Friend,

If I had had the Horns of a Snail I should have drawn them in, the Moment I saw the reason of your Epistolary Brevity, because I felt it too. May your Seven Reams be multiplied into 14, 'till your Letters become truly Lacedæmonian,[1] & are reduced to a single Syllable—tho' I shall be a Sufferer by the Effect, I shall rejoice in the Cause. You are naturally formed for Business, and such a Head as yours can never have too much of it. Though my Predictions have been fulfilled in two Instances, I do not plume myself much upon my Sagacity, because it required but little to foresee that Thurlow would be Chancellor, & that you would have a crowded Office. As to the rest of my Connections, there too I have given Proof of equal Foresight, with not a Jot more reason for Vanity. Any body might see that they were too much like myself to be good for any thing; disqualified by Temper, & unfurnish'd with Abilities, to be usefull either to themselves or others.

To use the Phrase of all who ever wrote upon the State of Europe, the Political Horizon is dark indeed. The Cloud has been thickening, & the Thunder advancing many Years. The Storm now seems to be Vertical, & threatens to burst upon the Land as if with the next Clap it would shake all in pieces. I did not know, (for I know nothing but what I learn from the General Evening) that there was a deliberate Purpose on the part of Government to set up the Throne of Despotism.[2] If that is the Case, no doubt but the Standard of Opposition will flame against it, till it has consumed to Ashes the Devisers of a Project that in this Country, is sure to terminate in the Ruin of them that form it. Alas! Of what Use is History, & why should Kings be

[1] Laconic (*O.E.D.*).

[2] According to *The General Evening Post* of 8 Mar. 1780 (No. 7179), Richard Rigby (see n. 3, C to Unwin, 13 Feb. 1780) 'drew up a resolution he hoped to present to Parliament: "Resolved, that it is unjust to deprive the Crown of its property, rights, and prerogatives, before due proofs are exhibited, that by flagrant abuses the measure be rendered necessary." . . . Mr. *Fox* said, that if such a resolution should pass the House, there would be an absolute end of English liberty.' At this time, C was very interested in the proposals by Burke and Fox to regulate government spending.

taught to Read, if they Read to so little Purpose. As for me, I am no Quaker except where Military Matters are in Question, & there I am much of the same Mind with an honest Man, who when he was forced into the Service declared he would not fight, & gave this reason, because he saw nothing worth fighting for. You will say perhaps, is not Liberty worth a Struggle? True—but will Success insure it to me? Might I not like the Americans emancipate myself from one Master, only to serve a Score, and with Laurels upon my Brow, Sigh for my former Chains again.

Many Thanks for your kind Invitation—Ditto to Mrs. Hill for the Seeds—unexpected, & therefore the more welcome. I have not a Leg that is not tied to Olney, & if they were all at Liberty not one of them all would Hop to London. The Thought of it distresses me, the Sight of it would Craze me.

You gave me great Pleasure by what you say of my Uncle. His Motto shall be

Hic Ver perpetuum atque alienis Mensibus Æstas.[3]

I remember the time when I have been kept waking by the Fear that he would Die before me, but now I think I shall grow Old first.

Yours my dear Friend Affectionately

Wm Cowper.

Mar 16. 1780.

JOHN NEWTON — Saturday, 18 March 1780

Princeton (*copy*)

Mar: 18th 1780.

Dear Sir—

I am obliged to you for the Communication of your Correspondence with Mr. Madan. It was impossible for any Man of any temper whatever, & however wedded to his purpose, to resent so gentle & friendly an Expostulation as you sent him. Men of lively imaginations are not often remarkable for solidity of judgment. They have generally strong passions to bias it, & are led far away from their

[3] Virgil, *Georgics*, ii. 149: 'Here is spring everlasting, and summer in months not accorded to her.'

proper Road in pursuit of pretty Phantoms of their own creating. If his readers should find in his Book such arguments & assertions as he has hazarded in his Letter to you, they will hardly think the writer of it in earnest. If Adultery was unknown among the Jews in the early periods of their state, there was but little occasion for the heavy penalty affixt to it in the Law. But the Scripture will not suffer any Man to doubt the existence of a crime, instances of which are so frequently recorded in it. No Law ever did or can effect what he has ascribed to that of Moses; It is reserved for Mercy to subdue the corrupt inclinations of Mankind, which threatenings & penalties, through the depravity of the Heart, have always had a tendency rather to inflame. But at any rate, to suppose that appetites are to be quelled by indulgence, is supposing what every Man living may disprove by his own experience. If Luther had treated the doctrine of fidelity to one Wife as a Popish invention, & scouted[1] it as he did that of the celibacy of the Priests, if he had immediately built himself a Seraglio & furnished it with the handsomest Women he could find, with what face could he have censured the Incontinence of the Romish Clergy? I doubt not but he would have frowned upon this new discovery with more severity than upon any of the errors he renounced.

I am sorry to learn, not from the Newspaper, but by a Letter from a very intelligent Person[2] in London, that arbitrary power is the aim of the Court, & Rebellion upon the point of breaking out against it. The love of Power seems as natural to Kings, as the desire of Liberty to their Subjects; the excess of either is vicious, & tends to the ruin of both. But when excess is found on both sides, & nothing but despotism will content the one & anarchy the other, it needs no great political discernment to foresee the consequence. There are many I believe who wish the present corrupt state of things dissolved, in hope that the pure primitive Constitution will spring up from the ruins, but it is not for Man by himself Man, to bring Order out of Confusion. The progress from one to the other is not natural, much less necessary, & without the intervention of Divine aid, they who are for making the dangerous experiment would certainly find themselves disappointed. In the mean time I believe, this tempestuous

[1] To scorn (*O.E.D.*).

[2] C's letter to Hill of 16 Mar. makes it clear that Hill is the 'very intelligent Person' who has written to C concerning 'arbitrary power'.

stir among the People tends to something which the greatest Politicians either in Office or out of it are little aware of. I know not what but this I know, They intend one thing & HE who governs them, intends, & will surely execute another. Time will make us all wiser in this respect than we are, & nothing but Time can do it.

I have written an Essay for a Newspaper, & if I was to sign myself your constant Reader & Admirer, it would be much of a piece with what has gone before it. It serves however to shew that I am in one sense (the meanest indeed) alive, & that I do not forget that we once lived within a hundred yards of each other. I did not mean to draw Tears by my last either from your eyes or Mrs. Newton's, but when a mind in distress speaks its natural Language to the ears of Friendship & Compassion, it is always so.

Believe me affectionately Yours & Hers

Wm Cowper

My Love to Sally Johnston & Peggy.

WILLIAM UNWIN — Tuesday, 28 March 1780

British Library

My dear Friend,

I have heard nothing more from Mr. Newton upon the Subject you mention, but I dare say that having been given to expect the Benefit of your Nomination in behalf of his Nephew, he still depends upon it.[1] His Obligations to Mr. T—n[2] have been so numerous & so weighty, that tho' he has in a few Instances prevailed with himself to recommend an Object now & then to his Patronage, he has very sparingly if at all exerted his Interest with him in behalf of his own

[1] Unwin ultimately nominated Benjamin Nind (b. 1773), who was admitted to the Foundation on 30 Mar. 1781. He was from the parish of St. Leonard Shoreditch, and was described as the son of Benjamin Nind. The boy was later discharged by his father on 8 Jan. 1787 (Guildhall Library, MS. 12818/11, fo. 240).

Newton must have wished to have the nomination made this year. Through C and Mrs. Unwin, Newton kept pressuring Unwin for the nomination. See C to Newton, 25 Apr. 1781, and C to Unwin, 1 May 1781.

[2] John Thornton (1720–90) was a director of the Russia Company and had extensive interests in foreign investments and affairs. In 1779 Thornton had presented Newton to the rectory of St. Mary Woolnoth. He was a generous supporter of many evangelical causes, and he was a loyal and devoted friend to C.

Relations. The best way to reconcile yourself to this Application of your Bounty, will be to consider that your principal & main Intention in it is to oblige your Mother. As to the Boy—

'To whom related, or by whom begot'[3]

Is a very unimportant part of the Subject.

With respect to the Advice you are required to give to a young Lady, that she may be properly instructed in the manner of keeping the Sabbath, you are so well qualified for the Task yourself that it is impossible you should need any Assistance, at least it is hardly possible that I should afford you any, who consider myself as no longer interested in the Question. As you desire it however, & I am not willing to refuse you the little that is in my Power, I just subjoin a few Hints that have occurred to me upon the Occasion, not because I think you want them, but because it would seem unkind to withold them. The Sabbath then I think may be consider'd.

1st. As a Commandment, no less binding upon modern Christians than upon ancient Jews. Because the spiritual People amongst *them*, did not think it enough to abstain from manual Occupations upon that Day, but entering more deeply into the meaning of the Precept, allotted those Hours they took from the World, to the Cultivation of Holiness in their own Souls. Which ever was & ever will be a Duty incumbent upon all who ever heard of a Sabbath, & is of perpetual Obligation, both upon Jews & Christians. The Commandment therefore injoins it, the Prophets have also inforced it, & in many Instances both Scriptural & modern, the Breach of it has been punish'd with a Providential & Judicial Severity that may make By: standers tremble.

2. As a Privilege, which you will know how to dilate upon better than I can tell you.

3. As a Sign of that Covenant by which Believers are entitled to a Rest that yet remaineth.

4. As the Sine quâ non of the Christian Character. & upon this Head I should guard against being misunderstood to mean no more than two Attendances upon Public Worship, which is a Form complied with by Thousands, who never kept a Sabbath in their Lives. Consistency is necessary to give Substance & Solidity to the whole.

[3] Pope, 'Elegy to the Memory of an Unfortunate Lady', l. 72.

To Sanctify the Day at church, & to trifle it away out of church, is Profanation & vitiates all.

After all, I could ask my Catecheuman one short Question, do you Love the Day, or do you not? If you Love it, you will never enquire how far you may safely deprive yourself of the Enjoyment of it. If you do not Love it, & you find yourself obliged in Conscience to acknowledge it, that is an alarming Symptom, & ought to make you tremble. If you do not Love it, then it is a Weariness to you & you wish it was over. The Ideas of Labor & Rest are not more opposite to each other, than the Idea of a Sabbath, & that Dislike and Disgust with which it fills the Soul of thousands to be obliged to keep it. It is worse than bodily Labor, more fatiguing than the Drudgery of an Ass.

I thank you for the intended Salmon &c. We are Sorry for Mrs. Unwin's Tooth—I had a troublesome Stump myself, which I killed with Oil of Thyme, & now it is easy. We are Sorry too for Miss Shuttleworth's Complaint, but it is a Symptom of a Good Constitution, & in some sort a Pledge of good Health tho' a painfull one. We rejoice in the Well being of your little Ones & I am in haste to Save the Post.

Yours affectionately Wm Cowper.

Mar 28. 80.

WILLIAM UNWIN — Thursday, 6 April 1780

Address: Revd. William Unwin at Stock / near Ingatestone / Essex.
Postmarks: 7/AP *and* OULNEY
British Library

My dear Friend,

I never was, any more than yourself, a Friend to Pluralities, they are generally found in the Hands of the Avaricious, whose insatiable Hunger after Preferment, proves them unworthy of any at all. They attend much to the regular Payment of their Dues, but not at all to the Spiritual Interests of their Parishioners. Having forgot their Duty, or never known it, they differ in nothing from the Laity, except their outward Garb, & their exclusive Right to the Desk and Pulpit. But when Pluralities seek the Man, instead of being sought

by him, and when the Man is honest, conscientious, & Pious, carefull to employ a Substitute in those respects like himself, and not contented with this, will see with his own Eyes, that the Concerns of his Parishes are decently & diligently administer'd, in that Case, considering the present Dearth of such Characters in the Ministry, I think it an Event advantageous to the People, & much to be desired by all who regret the great & apparent Want of Sobriety and Earnestness among the Clergy. A man who does not seek a Living merely as a Pecuniary Emolument, has no need, in my Judgment, to refuse one because it is so. He means to do his Duty, and by doing it, he earns his Wages. The two Ramsdens being contiguous to each other, & falling easily under the Care of one Pastor, and both so near to Stock, that you can Visit them without Difficulty, as often as you please—I see no reasonable Objection, nor does your Mother.[1] As to the wry:mouthed Sneers and illiberal Misconstructions of the Censorious, I know no better Shield to guard you against them, than what you are already furnished with, a clear and an unoffended Conscience.

The Salmon came safe & punctual to its Assignation. It served us for two Dinners and Six Suppers, was remarkably fresh and fine; item the Lobster.

I am obliged to you for what you said upon the Subject of Book: buying, and am very fond of availing myself of another man's Pocket, when I can do it creditably to myself & without Injury to Him. Amusements are necessary in a Retirement like mine, & especially in such a State of Mind as I Labour under. The Necessity of Amusement makes me sometimes write Verses—it made me a Carpenter, a Bird Cage maker, a Gardener, and has lately taught me to draw, and to draw too with such surprizing Proficiency in the Art, considering my total Ignorance of it two months ago, that when I shew your Mother my Productions, she is all Admiration & Applause.[2]

You need never fear the Communication of what you entrust to us in Confidence.[3] You know your Mother's Delicacy in this Point

[1] In 1781, Unwin became rector of Ramsden Crayes. He had been appointed rector of Stock and Ramsden Bellhouse in 1769.

[2] An engraving after a drawing by C appeared in *G.M.* lxxiv, pt. 1 (June 1804), facing 505. See *Russell*, p. 138.

[3] This may be a reference to the nomination of Benjamin Nind to Christ's Hospital. See C to Unwin of 13 Feb. and 28 Mar. 1780.

sufficiently, and as for me, I once wrote a Connoisseur[4] upon the Subject of Secret keeping, and from that day to this I believe I have never divulged one.

We were much pleased with Mr. Newton's Application to You for the Charity Sermon, and with what he said upon that Subject in his last Letter, that he was glad of an Opportunity to give you that Proof of his Regard.[5]

Beleive me yours, with the customary but not therefore unmeaning Addition, of Love to all under your Roof. Your Mother sends hers, which being Maternal, is put up in a seperate Parcel.

Wm Cowper.

April 6. 80.

JOHN NEWTON — Sunday, 9 April 1780

Princeton (*copy*)

April 9th 80

My dear Sir

It seems absurd, considering the interest you take in whatever passes at Olney to write to you from thence without transmitting the news of the place. Nothing indeed has passed that would make a figure in any of the daily Papers, but what the public would deem insipid is often agreeable to a private ear. Mr. Page & his Ministry are no doubt the chief objects of your Concern. You may imagine I know but little of either & perhaps others may have anticipated me in the relation of that little. He is a great Gardener like myself. This is all I have heard of him as a man. As a Preacher, he is much liked by some and as much disliked by others. The more judicious seem to be among the latter. What fault they find I can hardly tell you, except that they observe a deficiency in his Capacity rather than in his Views; frequent repetitions of the same thing, references to what he said on a former occasion, which bring the old over again,

[4] Number 119, Thursday, 6 May 1756, 715–20.

[5] In a letter to Mrs. Unwin of 22 Apr. 1780 (Princeton), Newton writes that her son's sermon before the Lord Mayor 'from James I. 27 was in general well received, and he was perhaps the finest person I could have pitch'd upon . . . Something perhaps might have been added, but it was very well. He pleaded strenuously for the Charity, & the collection exceeded £18, which had not been known to exceed £15 in past years.'

and a great proneness to quarrel with the translation, without giving sufficient or indeed any reason to suppose that he understands the original. Exempli gratiâ—I *go a fishing*[1] is not properly rendered. It should have been thus—I go to seek Fish &c. Now I apprehend that unless when a man goes to tickle trout, or to grope in holes of the bank for Cray fish, neither of which was Peter's intention at that time, the former expression has most propriety, & needs no alteration. As to the rest, he does not visit the people, but behaves, I believe, kindly to them when they come in his way; and when they visit *him*, we have been informed that he is not apt to give the Conversation a religious Turn.

We were concerned for what you told us of a certain Author's pertinacious adherence to his purpose of publishing.[2] The zeal of new discoveries has carried some men round the globe, & would push others through the very body of it, if such an attempt were feasible. Had the zeal of this writer taken as innocent a turn, it would have been better for himself, & perhaps for many of his readers. The old adage, Qui vult decipi, decipiatur,[3] would be equally true if the tense were altered, & we should say, Qui vult decipi, deci*pietur*.[4] With respect to Mr. S—r S—y,[5] though he is a good man, & a match for almost any man in point of wit & discernment, I think him a little mistaken in what he supposes to be his duty upon this occasion. I cannot bring myself to believe that any cause whatever, can justify, much less demand the violation of confidential secresy between Friend & Friend. It seems to me to be doing evil that good may come. The book must after all stand or fall by its own merits, & ought to do so, without any reference to the conduct of its Author. Truth is Truth, though the discovery of it were made in a Brothel, & a Lye would be a Lye though all the Bishops upon the Bench should endeavour to establish it. A man indeed cannot conceal his knowledge of a murder, & be guiltless, even though it were committed by his Father—but in the present case there is no such obligation, neither as I said before, if the book is erroneous, as it needs must be, is that the way to refute it. But he would say perhaps that his design was to alarm the reader, & put him upon his guard—.

[1] John 21 : 3.
[2] Martin Madan.
[3] 'He who wishes to be deceived, let him be deceived.'
[4] 'He who wishes to be deceived will be deceived.'
[5] Probably Thomas Haweis. See C to Newton, 19 Nov. 1781 and n.1.

In my judgment the Author does it himself; his very purpose cries with a loud voice, Beware of me, I am going to prove that lawful & right, which all the religious & even the moral part of the civilized world, have universally accounted wrong—This is warning enough to those who are willing to take warning, & no information would be sufficient perhaps to guard others against delusion.

Mrs. Weber[6] has been most obliging indeed. She has made me so rich in seeds that unless she can likewise send me an acre of land from Russia, I shall hardly know where to bestow them. The great Squire at Gayhurst however has room enough, & shall even in our small premises, crowd as many together as I can. I wish I knew how to convince Mr. Lacey[7] of the sense I have of his kindness, but I have no means of doing it. Mrs. Unwin joins me in affectionate respects to yourself and Mrs. Newton. I should have answered yours sooner, but waited for Molly Johnson's[8] journey. We send three pigeons, and two brace of cucumbers, and would have sent more of each but had them not. The latter are small. I was deceived in the seed. To avoid confusion Mrs. Unwin has sent Mr. Teedon's bill . . .

I am dear Sir,
your affectionate
W.C.

JOHN NEWTON Sunday, 16 April 1780[1]

Princeton (*copy*)

Dear Sir,

We were much concerned at the account of your terrible fall, but glad to receive it from your own hand, and at the same time obliged to you for securing us from the uneasiness which the misrepresentations of report might have cost us, by sending us the earliest Intelligence of it. Neither did we forget what Mrs. N. must have suffered upon the occasion. Though her shoulder bone and yours do not move in the same socket, yet your persons together by are bound

[6] Elizabeth Weber, née Foster.

[7] Unidentified.

[8] Probably a relative of the Newtons' maid, Sally.

[1] Dated, in an unknown hand: 'Apr: 16. 1780'.

a bond of sympathy that subjects her to a share of all your troubles. We hope however you will soon be rid of your respective uneasinesses upon the present occasion and rejoice that the Word uneasiness is sufficient to express the consequences of a fall that might have been attended with much worse.

I communicated to Mr. Wilson[2] your apprehensions lest he should take a trip to the river and we both delivered to him very freely our sentiments upon the subject. By his answer he does not seem to be much bent upon such an excursion at present. He is aware of the narrowness and bigotry of that persuasion and much more anxious about the Substance than the sign. His reason for hearing at that meeting is, that he cannot hear Mr. P. to any advantage. But he thinks that for the future he shall attend Mr. Scott[3] at Weston.

Our thanks are due for a piece of very fine fresh salmon & for a ditto Lobster. Our joint love attends yourself and Mrs. Newton.

Yours affectionately Wm. Cowper.

JOHN NEWTON — Sunday, 16 April 1780

Southey, iv. 5

Olney, April 16, 1780.

Since I wrote my last we have had a visit from ——.[1] I did not feel myself vehemently disposed to receive him with that complaisance, from which a stranger generally infers that he is welcome. By his

[2] William Wilson, C's barber. Wilson became a Baptist after the summer of 1781 (see Wright, *Life*, p. 290). 'A trip to the river' in all likelihood refers to the public baptism Wilson would have in joining that sect. From this letter, it would seem that Mrs. Unwin and C had, at this time, convinced Wilson of the 'narrowness and bigotry' of such a move.

[3] The Revd. Thomas Scott (1747–1821), curate of Olney (1781–5). The son of a grazier, John Scott (d. 1777), Thomas left home in 1772 and was ordained deacon at Buckden on 20 Sept. in the same year. On 13 Mar. 1773 he was ordained priest and was appointed to the curacies of Stoke Goldington and Weston Underwood, Bucks at £50 per annum. In May 1775 he had made the acquaintance of Newton, and in 1781 he succeeded the unpopular Revd. B. Page as curate of Olney. At Christmas 1785 Scott left Olney to take up residence in London as chaplain to the Lock Hospital, where he remained until 1803. He spent his last years at Aston Sandford in Buckinghamshire. Scott is known primarily as the author of the voluminous *Commentary on the Bible* (1788–92) and of the spiritual autobiography *The Force of Truth* (1779) which C revised.

[1] Perhaps Samuel Teedon. See n. 1, C to Newton, 25 Feb. 1781.

manner, which was rather bold than easy, I judged that there was no occasion for it, and that it was a trifle which, if he did not meet with, neither would he feel the want of. He has the air of a travelled man, but not of a travelled gentleman; is quite delivered from that reserve which is so common an ingredient in the English character, yet does not open himself gently and gradually, as men of polite behaviour do, but bursts upon you all at once. He talks very loud, and when our poor little robins hear a great noise, they are immediately seized with an ambition to surpass it; the increase of their vociferation occasioned an increase of his, and his in return acted as a stimulus upon theirs; neither side entertained a thought of giving up the contest, which became continually more interesting to our ears, during the whole visit. The birds, however, survived it, and so did we. They perhaps flatter themselves they gained a complete victory, but I believe Mr.—— could have killed them both in another hour.

W.C.

JOHN NEWTON — Wednesday, 3 May 1780

Princeton (*copy*)

Dear Sir

You indulge me in such a variety of Subjects and allow me such a latitude of excursion in the scribbling way that I have no excuse for silence. I am much obliged to you for swallowing such bolusses[1] as I send you for the sake of my gilding and verily believe I am the only man alive from whom they would be welcome to a palate like yours. I wish I could make them more splendid than they are, more alluring to the eye at least, if not more pleasing to the taste, but my leaf gold is tarnished, and has received such a tinge from the Vapours that are ever brooding over my mind, that I think it no small proof of your partiality to me, that for my sake you will read my letters. I am not fond of long winded metaphors, I have always observed they halt at the latter end of their progress, and so does mine. I deal much in ink indeed but not in such ink as is employed by poets, and writers

[1] A large pill (*O.E.D.*).

of essays;[2] mine is a harmless fluid and guilty of no deceptions but such as may prevail without the least injury to the person imposed upon. I draw mountains, valleys, woods and streams & ducks & dabchicks. I admire them myself and Mrs. Unwin admires Them, and her praise & my praise put together are fame enough for me. (The man that expects hereafter to be imprisoned in a dungeon where nothing but misery & deformity are to be found, has a peculiar pleasure in contemplating the beauties of nature and sees a thousand charms in meadows and the flowers that adorn them, in blue skies and skies overhung with tempests in trees and rocks and in every circumstance of rural life that are lost upon a mind in security and are invisible to him that has a peaceful conscience.) O I could spend whole days and moonlight nights in feeding upon a lovely Prospect, my eye drinks the rivers as they flow (& I say to myself how sadly I shall thirst hereafter.) If every human being upon Earth could think for one quarter of an hour as I have done for many years, there might perhaps be many unconverted miserable men among them, but not an unawakened one would be found from the Arctic to the Antarctic Circle. At present the difference between them & me is greatly to their advantage. I delight in baubles, and know them to be so, for rested in & viewed without a reference to their Author, what is the Earth, what are the planets, what is the sun itself but a bauble? Better for man never to have seen them, or to see them with the Eyes of a brute, stupid & unconscious of what he beholds than not to be able to say, the Maker of all these wonders is my friend. I cannot say this, neither can they. But their Eyes have never been opened to see that they are trifles in themselves; and mine have been, and will be till they are closed for ever. They think a fine estate, a large conservatory, a hothouse rich as a West Indian Garden, things of consequence, visit them with pleasure and muse upon them with ten times more. I am pleased with a frame of four lights, doubtful whether the few pines it contains will ever be worth a farthing, amuse myself with a Green house which Lord Bute's[3] Gardener could take upon his back and run away with; and when I have paid it the accustomed visit, and watered it and given it air, I say to myself,

[2] Although C claimed in his letter to Newton of 10 May that he had written 'ink' in two instances, both words read 'Jube' in the Princeton copy, and did so to Newton in the MS. he received. Newton wrote to C to complain about the strange word. See C's rebuttal in his of 10 May.

[3] John Stuart, 3rd Earl of Bute (1713–92), was passionately interested in gardening.

this is not mine, 'tis a plaything lent me for the present. I must leave it soon, (and with it perhaps the very idea of vegetable nature, or if I retain the picture, it will only be that I may regret the loss of the Original. Happy they that sleep in comparison with those who wake to no purpose. Both are in reality miserable, but he is most Emphatically so who knows & feels his misery.)

I have written as above while Mrs. Unwin & Hannah[4] are gone to sleep together. If they come down before I have finished I must conclude for Cæsar himself who could dictate to so many, would have been obliged to wait 'till another post, if Hannah's tongue had been within his hearing. I have heard that Curiosity in a Child is a prognostic of future wisdom, if that be true she is likely to be wise indeed, for she asks more Questions in one hour than could be discreetly answered in two.

We both rejoice at your speedy recovery, and that Mrs. Newton suffered nothing worse from your fall than the present shock. Our love attends her. Olney is as usual newsless, for it is hardly worth while to tell you that Tom Freeman is returned from the Army and turned Baker, that he makes very light English rolls and still lighter French ones, that all the world is astonished at his indefatigable industry and forsee and foretell that if he perseveres in it he will be a great man. This to a man who seldom sees the Newspaper, may be perhaps worth knowing possibly it may be as important as the most of what he would find there if he saw them all.

Yours dear Sir

affectionately—W. Cowper.

Tho' I have little Curiosity to read Mr. M's book I have much to know your sentiments.

3d. May 1780.

[4] Hannah Wilson was the daughter of Dick Coleman's wife, Patty Wilson, who had previously been married to a Mr. Wilson. Patty Wilson was the natural daughter of Mr. Cawthorne, Mrs. Unwin's father. As a young girl, in the 1780s, Hannah acted as a servant at Orchard Side. She moved with the household to Weston Underwood in 1786.

JOSEPH HILL Saturday, 6 May 1780

Address: Mr. Joseph Hill / Chancery Office / London
Postmarks: 8/MA *and* OULNEY
Cowper Johnson

My dear Friend,

I am much obliged to you for your speedy Answer to my Queries, and for the Forty agreeable Surprises that accompanied it. I know less of the Law than a Country Attorney, yet sometimes I think I have almost as much Business. My former Connexion with the Profession has got Wind, and though I earnestly Profess & Protest & Proclame it abroad that I know nothing of the Matter, they cannot be persuaded to beleive that a Head once endued with a Legal Periwig, can ever be deficient in those internal Endowments it is supposed to cover. I have had the good Fortune to be once or twice in the right, which added to the Cheapness of Gratuitous Counsel, has advanced my Credit to a Degree I never expected to attain to in the Capacity of a Lawyer. Indeed if two of the Wisest in the Science of Jurisprudence may give Opposite Opinions upon the same Point, which does not unfrequently happen, it seems to be a Matter of Indifference whether a Man answers by Rule or at a Venture. He that Stumbles upon the right Side of the Question, is just as usefull to his Client as he that arrives at the same End by regular Approaches, and is conducted to the Mark he Aims at by the greatest Authorities.

If you were as idle a man as myself I would ask you what Consequences are likely to follow the Rejection of all Mr. Burke's Œconomical Proposals.[1] Whether the Disappointment has exasperated the Spirits of the Patriots, or whether they will quietly recede from their Undertaking. This perhaps would be the wisest & most Patriotic Course they could persue, for tho' the End they Aim at is desireable & highly reasonable, yet if they kindle the Flames of Civil War in the Pursuit of it, no Success would be Sufficient to countervail the dreadfull Consequences of their Perseverance.

These violent Attacks of a Distemper so often fatal, are very alarming to all who Esteem & Respect the Chancellor as he deserves.[2]

[1] Burke's proposals were defeated on 28 Apr.

[2] Thurlow was suffering from a severe gall bladder disturbance at this time, and he spent a great deal of the spring of 1780 in Bath convalescing from his illness. See Robert Gore-Brown, *Chancellor Thurlow* (1953), pp. 133, 155.

A Life of Confinement and of anxious Attention to important Objects, where the Habit is Bilious to such a terrible Degree, threatens to be but a short one. And I wish he may not be made a Text for Men of Reflection to Moralize upon, affording a conspicuous Instance of the transient & fading Nature of all Human Accomplishments & Attainments.

My Respects wait on Mrs. Hill. The Receipt is on the other Side.

Yours Affectionately

Wm Cowper.

Olney May 6. 1780.

Received of Mr. Hill the Sum of Forty Pounds by a Draft on Child & Co. £40.0.0.

Wm Cowper.

WILLIAM UNWIN — Monday, 8 May 1780

British Library

My dear Friend,

I would advise you by all means to deal frankly with your Competitor, if he should pay you the Visit you expect. It will infallibly obviate all Possibility of Misconstruction, and is the only Course you can take that will do so.[1] You have a very good Story to tell, & nothing to be ashamed of, and as for the awkwardness of the Occasion, that will be no longer felt than just while you are making your Exordium. Your Behavior will please him if he has a Taste for Propriety, and he cannot but forgive you the Crime of having an Uncle that Loves you too well to overlook or Neglect so fair an Opportunity to promote your Interest.[2]

My Scribbling Humor has of late been entirely absorbed in the Passion of Landsckape drawing. It is a most Amusing Art, and like every other Art, requires much Practise & Attention.

[1] A reference to Unwin's interest in obtaining the rectorship of Ramsden Crayes. See C to Unwin, 6 Apr. 1780.

[2] According to the provisions of his will (P.R.O., PROB 11/931 CAPS/7463), Morley Unwin authorized his brother to act as his son's agent in making the necessary financial arrangements to purchase livings for his son. John Unwin (see C to Hill, 25 Sept. 1770) served as patron of William's livings, and he was to serve in a similar capacity at Ramsden Crayes.

Nil sine multo
Vita, Labore, dedit Mortalibus.[3]

Excellence is providentially placed beyond the Reach of Indolence, that Success may be the Reward of Industry, and that Idleness may be punish'd with Obscurity and Disgrace. So long as I am pleased with an Employment, I am capable of unwearied Application, because my Feelings are all of the intense kind. I never received a *little* Pleasure from any thing in my Life; if I am Delighted, it is in the Extreme—the unhappy Consequence of this Temperature is, that my Attachment to any Occupation seldom outlives the Novelty of it. That Nerve of my Imagination that feels the Touch of any particular Amusement, twangs under the Energy of the Pressure with so much Vehemence, that it soon becomes sensible of Weariness & Fatigue. Hence I draw an unfavorable Prognostic, and expect that I shall shortly be constrained to look out for Something else. Then perhaps I may String the Lyre again, and be able to comply with your Demand.

Now for the Visit you Propose to pay us, and propose *not* to Pay us. The Hope of which Plays about upon your Paper, like a Jack o' Lantern upon the cieling. This is no mean Simile, for Virgil, you remember, uses it.[4] 'Tis Here, 'tis there, it vanishes, it returns, it dazzles you, a cloud interposes, and it is gone. However Just the Comparison, I hope you will contrive to Spoil it, and that your final Determination will be to Come. As to the Masons you expect, bring them with you—Bring Brick, bring Mortar, bring every thing that would oppose itself to your Journey—all shall be welcome. I have a green House that is too small, come and enlarge it; build me a Pinery; repair the Garden Wall that has great Need of your Assistance; do any thing; you cannot do too much; so far from thinking You and your Train troublesome, we shall rejoice to see you upon these or upon any Terms you can Propose. But to be Serious—You will do well to consider that a long Summer is before you, that the Party will not have such another Opportunity to meet this great while, that you may finish your Masonry long enough before Winter, tho' you should not begin this Month, but that you cannot always find

[3] Horace, *Satires*, I. ix. 60–1: 'Life gives nothing to men without much labour.' C has used 'multo' in his quotation whereas it should read 'magno'.

[4] C is probably referring to *Aeneid*, vii. 22–5, which compares Turnus' troubled dream to a light which casts various shadows on a ceiling.

your Brother and Sister Powley[5] at Olney. These and some other Considerations, such as the Desire we have to see you, & the Pleasure we expect from Seeing you all together, may, & I think ought to overcome your Scruples. We are only Sorry Miss Shuttleworth cannot come with you, which seems to be set down as a Postulation not to be disputed.

From a General Recollection of Lord Clarendon's History of the Rebellion, I thought & I remember I told you so, that there was a Striking Resemblance between that Period & the present.[6] But I am now reading, & have read 3 volumes of Hume's History, one of which is engrossed entirely by that Subject.[7] There I see reason to alter my Opinion, & the seeming Resemblance has disappeared upon a more particular Information. Charles succeeded to a long Train of Arbitrary Princes, whose Subjects had tamely acquiesced in the Despotism of their Masters, 'till their Privileges were all forgot. He did but tread in their Steps, & exemplify the Principles in which he had been brought up, when he oppressed his People. But just at that time, unhappily for the Monarch, the Subject began to see, & to see that he had a Right to Property & Freedom.—This marks a Sufficient Difference between the Disputes of that Day & the present. But there was another Main Cause of that Rebellion, which at this time does not Operate at all. The King was devoted to the Hierarchy, his Subjects were Puritans, & would not bear it. Every Circumstance of Ecclesiastical Order & Discipline, was an Abomination to Them, & in his Esteem an indispensible Duty. & tho' at last, he was obliged to give up many things, he would not abolish Episcopacy, & 'till that were done, his Concessions could have no conciliatory Effect. These 2 concurring Causes were indeed sufficient to set 3 Kingdoms in a Flame. But they subsist not Now, nor any other I hope, notwithstanding the Bustle made by the Patriots, equal to the Production of such terrible Events—Yours my Dear Friend, Wm Cowper.
May 8. 80.

[5] Susanna Unwin had married the Revd. Matthew Powley (1740–1806) of Slaithwaite, Huddersfield on 15 May 1774. In 1777 Mr. Powley was appointed vicar of Dewsbury.

[6] C's letter of 13 Feb. 1780.

[7] Volume i of Hume's *History of Great Britain* 'containing the Reigns of James I and Charles I', the section of the work which most interested C, was originally published at Edinburgh in 1754. There were various editions of this history from Julius Caesar to 1688, as well as printings of selected parts of it.

JOHN NEWTON — Wednesday, 10 May 1780

Princeton (*copy*)

May. 10. 1780

My dear friend,

If authors could have lived to adjust and authenticate their own text, a Commentator would have been a useless creature.[1] If Dr. Bentley[2] had found, or opined that he had found the word *Jube* where it seemed to present itself to you, and had judged the Subject worthy of his Critical Acumen, he would either have justified the corrupt reading, or have substituted some invention of his own, in defence of which he would have Exerted all his polemical abilities to have quarrelled with half the Literati in Europe; Then suppose the Writer himself, as in the present Case, to interpose with a Gentle Whisper thus—If you look again Good Doctor, you will perceive that what appears to you to be Jube, is neither more nor less than the simple Monysyllable, Ink. But I wrote it in Great haste, and the want of sufficient precision in the Characters has occasioned Your mistake. You will be satisfied when you see the sense Elucidated by the Explanation. But I question whether the Doctor would quit his ground, or allow an Author to be a Competent judge in his own Cause. The world however would acquiesce immediately & Vote the Critic useless.

All that is Ænigmatical in my Case would Vanish, if you and Mrs. U. were able to avail Yourselves of the Solution I have so often given You. That a Calvinist in principle, should know himself to have been Elected, and yet believe that he is lost, is indeed a Riddle, and so obscure that it Sounds like a Solecism in terms, and may well bring the assertor of it under the Suspicion of Insanity. But it is not so, and it will not be found so.

I am trusted with the terrible Secret Myself but not with the power to Communicate it to any purpose. In order to gain credit to such a Relation, it would be necessary that I should be able to produce proof that I received it from above, but that power will never be given Me. In what Manner or by whom the denoüement will be made hereafter, I know not. But that it will be made is

[1] See C to Newton, 3 May 1780.

[2] Richard Bentley (1662–1742), the critic and philologist.

certain. In the mean time I carry a load no Shoulders Could Sustain, unless underpropped as mine are, by a heart Singularly & preternaturally hardened.

James Andrews,[3] who is my Michael Angelo, pays me many Compliments upon my Success in the art of Drawing, but I have not Yet the Vanity to think myself qualified to furnish Your apartment. If I should ever attain to that degree of Self opinion requisite to such an undertaking, I shall labor at it with pleasure, at present I can only say, tho' I hope not with the affected modesty of the above Mentioned Dr. Bentley, Who said the same thing

Me quoque Vatem
Dicunt pastores, Sed non Ego credulus illis.[4]

A Crow, Rook, or Raven, has built a nest in one of the young Elm trees at the side of Mrs. Aspray's Orchard.[5] In the Violent Storm that blew Yesterday Morning I saw it agitated to a degree that Seemed to threaten its immediate destruction & Versified the following thoughts on the occasion.[6]

A raven while with glossy breast,
Her new-laid eggs she fondly press'd,
And on her wicker-work high mounted
Her chickens prematurely counted,
(A fault philosophers might blame
If quite exempted from the same)
Enjoy'd at ease the genial day.
'Twas April as the bumkins say,
The legislature call'd it May.
But suddenly a wind as high
As ever swept a winter sky,
Shook the young leaves about her ears,
And fill'd her with a thousand fears,
Lest the rude blast should snap the bough,
And spread her golden hopes below.

[3] James Andrews (1734–1817) of Olney was a self-taught engraver and painter.

[4] This quotation is from Virgil, *Eclogues*, ix. 34–5: 'The shepherds call me a poet, but I do not believe them.'

[5] The orchard separated the Vicarage garden from C's.

[6] The poem was presumably transcribed by C in his letter, but the copyist simply wrote: A Raven while &c—The Reader is referred for this fable to Wm. Cowper's Poems.' 'A Fable' was first published in *1782*. We have used *1782* as our copy-text in supplying the poem.

But just at eve the blowing weather,
And all her fears were hush'd together:
And now, quoth poor unthinking Raph,
'Tis over, and the brood is safe;
(For ravens though as birds of omen,
They teach both conj'rers and old women
To tell us what is to befall,
Can't prophecy, themselves, at all.)
The morning came, when neighbour Hodge,
Who long had mark'd her airy lodge,
And destin'd all the treasure there
A gift to his expecting fair,
Climb'd like a squirrel to his dray,
And bore the worthless prize away.

MORAL

'Tis providence alone secures
In every change, both mine and your's.
Safety consists not in escape
From dangers of a frightful shape,
An earthquake may be bid to spare
The man that's strangled by a hair.
Fate steals along with silent tread,
Found oft'nest in what least we dread,
Frowns in the storm with angry brow,
But in the sunshine strikes the blow.

Mrs. Unwin would have written by this opportunity but preparation for Visitors prevented.

Our joint love attends your Joint Self—

Yours my dear Sir affectionately
William Cowper.

MRS. COWPER Wednesday, 10 May 1780

Address: Mrs. Cowper / Park Street / Grosvenor Square / London.
Postmarks: 12/MA *and* OULNEY
Panshanger Collection

My dear Cousin,

I do not Write to Comfort you; that Office is not likely to be well performed by One who has no Comfort for Himself. Nor to comply with an impertinent Ceremony, which in general, might well be spared upon such Occasions. But because I would not seem indifferent to the Concerns of those I have so much reason to Esteem and Love. If I did not Sorrow for your Brother's Death,[1] I should expect that nobody would for mine. When I knew him, he was much Beloved, and I doubt not, continued to be so. To Live and Die together is the Lot of a few happy Families, who hardly know what a Seperation means, and one Sepulchre serves them all; but the Ashes of our Kindred are dispersed indeed. Whether the American Gulph has swallowed up any other of my Relations, I know not. It has made many Mourners in England, and probably will many more, 'till the Name of a Congress becomes as Hatefull to Thousands as the Breath of a Pestilence. I beg you will present my Affectionate Regards to all your own Family, and that you will assure my Aunt of the Part I take in her Sorrow upon this Occasion.

Beleive me, my dear Cousin, though after long Silence which perhaps nothing less than the present Concern could have prevailed with me to interrupt, as much as Ever,

Your Affectionate Kinsman
Wm Cowper.

May 10. 1780.

[1] Frederick Madan (see n. 1, C to Mrs. Cowper, 31 Aug. 1769) was a lieutenant-colonel in the Guards and Paymaster to the British Forces in America at the time of his death.

The news of Frederick's death was conveyed at Mrs. Cowper's request to Newton: '. . . the late dispatches from America mention ye. decease of Mr. Frederic Madan on ye. 4th. December last. I suppose at New York, but the place or any particular circumstances are not specified in my account. But I am desired to communicate this news to dear Mr. Cowper' (Newton to Mrs. Unwin, 2 May 1780; Princeton).

MRS. NEWTON [Monday, 5 June 1780][1]

Princeton

Dear Madam,

When I write to Mr. Newton he Answers me by Letter. When I Write to you, You Answer me in Fish. I return you many Thanks for the Mackarell and Lobster. They assured me in Terms as intelligible as Pen and Ink could have spoken, that you still remember Orchard Side, and though they never spoke in their Lives, and it was still less to be Expected from them, that they should speak being Dead, they gave us an Assurance of your Affection that corresponds exactly with that which Mr. Newton expresses towards us in all his Letters.—For my own part, I never in my Life begun a Letter more at a Venture than the present. It is possible that I may Finish it, but perhaps more than probable that I shall not. I have had several indifferent Nights, and the Wind is Easterly—two Circumstances so unfavorable to me in all my Occupations, but especially in that of Writing, that it was with the greatest Difficulty I could even bring my self to attempt it. You have never yet perhaps been made acquainted with the unfortunate Tom Freeman's Misadventure. He and his Wife returning from Hanslip Fair,[2] were coming down Weston Lane, to wit, themselves, their Horse, and their great Wooden Panniers at Ten o'clock at Night. The Horse having a lively Imagination and very weak Nerves, fancied he either Saw or heard Something, but has never been able to Say what. A sudden Fright will impart Activity and a Momentary Vigour even to Lameness itself. Accordingly he Started, and Sprung from the Middle of the Road to the Side of it, with such Surprising Alacrity, that he dismounted the Gingerbread Baker and his Gingerbread Wife in a Moment. Not contented with this Effort, nor thinking himself yet out of Danger, he proceeded as fast as he could to a full Gallop: Rushed against the Gate at the Bottom of the Lane, and Opened it for himself without perceiving that there was any Gate there, still he Gallop'd, and with a Velocity & Momentum continually encreasing till he arrived in Olney. I had been in Bed about 10 Minutes

[1] The left-hand margin of the first page of the letter is inscribed in a hand not C's: 'June 80 5'.

[2] Hanslope is a village in Buckinghamshire, six miles south-west of Olney.

when I heard the most uncommon and unaccountable Noise that can be imagined. It was in fact occasioned by the Clattering of Tin Pattypans and a Dutch Oven against the Sides of the Panniers—Much Gingerbread was picked up in the Street, & Mr. Lucy's Windows were broke all to pieces.[3] Had this been all, it would have been a Comedy, but we learn'd the next Morning that the poor Woman's Collar Bone was broken, & she has hardly been able to resume her Occupation since.

The Small Pox still Rages here, and many children die of it. Mr. Raban's[4] Boy Daniel has had them very full, but a fine Sort, and is thought to be out of Danger. Hannah has yet Escaped, though two of Mrs. Clarke's Children have had them, and Nanny[5] has been extremely ill. As soon as she began to recover, it was feared she would lose her Sight. Her Eyes were terribly inflamed, and the Sight of one of them almost cover'd by a thick Film. But a few Applications of Elliot's Ointment and Eye water[6] have cured her.

The Soldiers leave us to:morrow, when it is expected that the Rags of Silver End will be wet with many a Tear. The mere Rumour of their Departure, about a Month since, though premature, made many Damsels inconsolable.

What is added on the other Side, if I could have persuaded myself to write Sooner would have reached you sooner, 'tis about 10 Days' Old. The first Stanza will make you acquainted with the Occasion of it. I have been astonished to learn from good Authority, that some Persons of respectable Name, have honor'd the Author's Argument with their Approbation.

Antithelyphthora[7]

Muse, Mark the much lamented Day,
  When like a Tempest fear'd
Forth issuing on the last of May,
  Thelyphthora appear'd.

[3] C's letter to Newton of 19 July 1784 describes a similar catastrophe which befell the Lucys.

[4] Daniel Raban was christened on 25 May 1771 (*O.P.R.*, p. 363), and he probably died in 1824 (*O.P.R.*, p. 484).

[5] Perhaps Anne Puttenham, who is mentioned in C to Newton of 27 Nov. 1781.

[6] A patent medicine devised by the well-known physician, Sir John Elliott (1736–86), whose *Medical Pocket-Book* appeared in 1781. C mentions his death in a letter to Mrs. Cowper of 24 Sept. 1792.

[7] This poem was first published in *1782*; it was entitled 'The Doves', and the reference to *Thelyphthora* was omitted from the completely re-worked first stanza.

5 June 1780

That fatal Eve I wander'd late
  And heard the Voice of Love,
The Turtle thus address'd her Mate,
  And Sooth'd the list'ning Dove.

Our mutual Bond of Faith & Truth
  No Time shall disengage,
Those Blessings of our Early Youth,
  Shall cheer our latest Age.

While Innocence without Disguise,
  And constancy Sincere
Shall fill the Circles of those Eyes,
  And Mine can Read them there,

Those Ills that wait on all Below
  Shall ne'er be felt by Me,
Or gently felt, and Only so
  As being shared with Thee.

When Lightnings Flash among the Trees,
  Or Kites are Hov'ring near,
I fear lest Thee alone they Seize,
  And know no other Fear.

'Tis then I feel myself a Wife,
  And Press thy Wedded Side,
Resolv'd an Union form'd for Life,
  Death never shall Divide.

But Oh if fickle and Unchaste
  (Forgive a transient Thought)
Thou couldst become unkind at last,
  And Scorn thy present Lot,

No need of Lightnings from on high,
  Or Kites with cruel Beak,
Denied th'Endearments of thine Eye,
  This Widow'd Heart would Break—

Thus Sang the Sweet Sequester'd Bird,
Soft as the passing Wind,
And I Recorded what I heard,
A Lesson for Mankind.

The Male Dove was Smoking a Pipe, and the Female Dove was Sewing while she deliver'd herself as above. This little Circumstance may lead you perhaps to Guess what Pair I had in my Eye. —

Yours Dear Madam
Wm Cowper.

Sally & Peggy both remember'd.

WILLIAM UNWIN — Thursday, 8 June 1780

British Library

My dear Friend—

It is possible I might have indulged myself in the Pleasure of Writing to you, without waiting for a Letter from *You*, but for a reason which you will not easily Guess. Your Mother communicated to me the Satisfaction you expressed in my Correspondence, that you thought me Entertaining and Clever and so forth. Now you must know I Love Praise dearly, especially from the Judicious, and those who have so much Delicacy themselves as not to Offend mine in giving it. But then I found this consequence attending, or likely to attend the Eulogium you bestowed. If my Friend thought me Witty before, he shall think me ten times more Witty hereafter, where I Joked Once, I will Joke 5 times, and for One Sensible Remark, I will send him a Dozen. Now this foolish Vanity would have spoiled me quite, and would have made me as disgusting a Letter:Writer as Pope, who seems to have thought that unless a Sentence was well turned, and every Period pointed with some Conceit, it was not worth the Carriage. Accordingly he is to me, except in very few Instances, the most disagreeable Maker of Epistles that ever I met with. I was willing therefore to wait 'till the Impression your commendation had made upon the foolish Part of me, was worn off, that I might scribble away as usual, and write my uppermost Thoughts and those only.

You are better skilled in Ecclesiastical Law than I am. Mrs.

Powley desires me to inform her whether a Parson can be obliged to take an apprentice, for some of her Husband's Opposers at Duesbery threaten to clap one upon him. Now I think it would be rather hard, if clergymen who are not allowed to Exercise any Handicraft whatever, should be subject to such an Imposition. If Mr. Powley was a Cordwainer, or a Breeches: maker all the Week, & a Preacher only on Sundays, it would seem reasonable enough in that Case, that he should take an Apprentice if he chose it, but even then, in my poor Judgment, he ought to be left to his Option. If they mean by an Apprentice, a Pupil, whom they will oblige him to Hew into a Parson, and after chipping away the Block that hides the Minister within, to qualify him to stand Erect in a Pulpit—That indeed is another consideration. But still we Live in a free Country, & I cannot bring myself ever to Suspect that an English Divine can possibly be liable to such Compulsion. Ask your Uncle[1] however, for he is Wiser in these things than either of us.

I thank you for your two Inscriptions, and like the last the best—the Thought is Just and Fine, but the two last Lines are sadly damaged by the Monkish Jingle of Peperit and Reperit. I have not yet Translated them, nor do I Promise to do it, tho' at some Idle Hour perhaps I may. In return I send you a Translation of a Simile in the Paradise lost; not having that Poem at hand, I cannot refer you to the Book and Page, but you may Hunt for it if you think it worth your while. It begins

> So when from Mountain Tops the dusky clouds
> Ascending &c.—

> Quales aerii Montis de Vertice, Nubes
> Cum Surgunt, & jam Bouæ tumida Ora quierunt,
> Cælum hilares abdit spissâ Caligine Vultûs,
> Nimbosumque Nives aut Imbres cogitat Æther:
> Tum si Incundo tandem Sol prodeat Ore,
> Et croceo Montes et Pascua Lumine tingat,
> Gaudent Omnia, Aves mulcent Concentibus Agros,
> Balatûque Ovium Colles Vallesque resultant.[2]

[1] John Unwin.

[2] ii. 488–95: As when from mountain tops the dusky clouds
Ascending, while the north wind sleeps, o'erspread
Heaven's cheerful face, the louring element
Scowls o'er the darkened landscape snow, or shower;

If you Spie any Faults in my Latin, tell me, for I am sometimes in doubt, but as I told you when you was here, I have not a Latin Book in the world to consult, or to correct a Mistake by, and some years have passed since I was a Schoolboy.

An English Versification of a Thought that popp'd into my Head about 2 Months since.[3]

Sweet Stream! that Winds thro' yonder Glade,
Apt Emblem of a Virtuous Maid—
Silent & chaste she Steals along
Far from the World's Gay, Busy Throng:
With gentle yet prevailing Force
Intent upon her destin'd Course:
Gracefull & Usefull All she does,
Blessing and Blest where'er she goes:
Pure:bosom'd as that Wat'ry Glass,
And Heav'n reflected in her Face.

Now this is not so exclusively applicable to a Maiden, as to be the Sole Property of your Sister Shuttleworth, if you look at Mrs. Unwin you will see that she has not lost her Right to this Just Praise by marrying you.

Your Mother sends her Love to All, & mine comes Jogging along by the Side of it—Yours Wm Cowper.
June 8th.
—80.—

If chance the radiant sun with farewell sweet
Extend his evening beam, the fields revive,
The birds their notes renew, and bleating herds
Attest their joy, that hill and valley rings.

C's translation was first published in *Hayley*.

Published in *1782*.

JOHN NEWTON Monday, 12 June 1780

Princeton (*copy*)

June 12. 1780.

Dear Sir,

We accept it as an Effort of your friendship that You could prevail with yourself in a time of such terror and distress to send us repeated accounts of yours and Mrs. N.'s welfare. You supposed and with reason enough that we should be apprehensive for your safety, situated as you were, apparently within the reach of so much danger.[1] We rejoice that you have escaped it all, and that except the Anxiety you must have felt, both for yourselves and Others, You have suffered nothing upon this dreadful Occasion. A Metropolis in flames, and a Nation in Ruins, are subjects of contemplation for such a mind as Yours, that will leave a lasting impression behind them. It is well that the design died in the execution, and will be buried, I hope, never to revive again in the ashes of its own Combustion. There is a melancholy pleasure in looking back upon such a Scene arising from the Comparison of possibilities with facts, the enormous bulk of the intended mischief with the abortive and partial accomplishment of it. Much was done, more indeed than Could have been supposed practicable in a Well regulated City not unfurnished with a military force for its protection. As if the freedom of debate might not have subsisted without the least Violation in the midst of an ungovernable Mob, and nothing but the Soldiery could interrupt it. It is natural after such an event, that the public should suspect a deep laid plot, and that their Suspicions should involve in the guilt of it Men of Consequence and figure. Our paper accordingly more than Surmises that several such Characters are Chargeable with this

[1] The Gordon Riots. The riots began in response to Protestant demonstrations opposing the removal of civil restrictions from Catholics. The leader of these activities was Lord George Gordon (1751–93), who was presenting a petition on behalf of the Protestant Association, a group specifically formed for preserving the Protestant religion.

Newton's letter of 10 June (Princeton) begins by assuring C that any account in the papers of 'the burning of a house in Charles' Square [where the Newtons lived] . . . was a false report'. Newton's letter continues with a long description of the ecclesiastical background of the Riots. 'The Original & first members of the Protestant Association such as Mr. Foster & Dr. Ford, are not only much grieved at the unhappy turn things have taken, but have some apprehension of being called to account. For tho' the appointment to meet in St. George's field was solely the act of Lord G— G . . . yet it is likely the acts of the President, will be considered as the act of all. . . .'

horrid Contrivance. If that be the Case, and the Delinquents Can be brought to Justice, Government itself and the nation at large may possibly derive a peace and unanimity from these troubles that they have long wished for, but despaired of attaining. I congratulate you upon the wisdom that witheld you from entering yourself a member of the Protestant association. Your friends who did so, have reason enough to regret their doing it, & even tho' they should never be called upon. Innocent as they are and those who know them cannot doubt their being perfectly so, it is likely enough to bring an odium upon their Profession that will not soon be forgotten. Neither is it possible for a harmless inoffensive Man to discover on a sudden that his Zeal has carried him into such Company, without being to the last degree shocked at his imprudence. Their religion was an honorable mantle like that of Elijah, but the majority wore Cloaks of Guy Vaux's trim, and meant Nothing so little as what they pretended.

Mrs. Unwin desires me to add her love to mine and to say that she sent Miss Catlett[2] a plum Cake, but that never having had any intimation of her having received it, she is afraid it never Reached her—Yours dear Sir,

William Cowper

WILLIAM UNWIN Sunday, 18 June 1780

British Library

Revd. and Dear William,

The affairs of Kingdoms, and the Concerns of Individuals are variegated alike with the Checquer Work of Joy and Sorrow. The News of a great Acquisition in America[1] has succeeded to a terrible Tumult in London, and the Beams of Prosperity are now playing upon the Smoke of that Conflagration which so lately terrified the whole Land. These sudden changes, which are matter of every Man's Observation, and may therefore always be reasonably ex-

[2] Betsy Catlett (*fl.* 1770–1807), the daughter of Mrs. Newton's brother George and his late wife, was adopted by the Newtons when she was about five years old.

[1] After having been successfully defended on several occasions, Charleston was surrendered on 21 May 1780 to the British under Sir Henry Clinton (1738?–95).

pected, serve to hold up the chin of Despondency above Water, and preserve Mankind in general from the Sin and Misery of accounting Existence a Burthen not to be endured; an Evil we should be sure to Encounter, if we were not warranted to Look for a bright Reverse of our most afflictive Experiences. We are obliged to you for your early Communication of the Surrender of Charles Town, and Rejoice with you in an Event, which if my Political Spectacles do not deceive me, is likely to bring the Rebellion in America to a speedy End. The Spaniards were Sick of the War at the very commencement of it, and I hope that by this time the French themselves begin to find themselves a little indisposed, if not desirous of Peace, which that restless and Meddling Temper of theirs is incapable of Desiring for its own sake, yet at least convinced of the Necessity of it. But is it true that this detestable Plot was an Egg laid in France, and Hatched in London under the Influence of French Corruption?[2]—Nam Te Scire, Deos quoniam propius contingis, Oportet.[3] The Offspring has the Features of such a Parent, and yet without the clearest Proof of the Fact, I would not willingly charge upon a civilized Nation, what perhaps the most Barbarous would abhor the Thought of. I no sooner saw the Surmise however in the Paper, than I immediately began to write Latin Verses upon the Occasion. An odd Effect you will say of such a Circumstance, but an Effect nevertheless that whatever has at any time moved my Passions, whether pleasantly or otherwise, has always had upon me. Were I to express what I feel upon such Occasions in Prose, it would be Verbose, inflated, and disgusting, I therefore have recourse to Verse, as a suitable Vehicle for the most vehement Expressions my Thoughts suggest to me. What I have written, I did not Write so much for the comfort of the English, as for the Mortification of the French; you will immediately perceive therefore that I have been

[2] *The General Evening Post* of Thursday–Saturday, 15–17 June 1780 (No. 7223) contains the following notice: 'It is an indisputable fact, that an extraordinary number of French bills were transmitted by the foreign mails to London, previous to the late outrages.' The stimulus to the notice in *The General Evening Post* and to C's concerns on the subject is probably a handbill which was distributed in London on 8 June: 'NO FRENCH RIOTERS. This is to give notice that it now appears, that the horrible riots which have been committed in this city, have been promoted by French money, and to call upon all honest men to stand forth against rioters, who, under the cloak of religion, are wantonly destroying our property . . .' (*Political Magazine*, i (1780), 443).

[3] Horace, *Satires*, II. vi. 51–2: 'You must know—you are much closer to the powers that be.'

Laboring in vain, and that this Bouncing Explosion is likely to spend itself in the Air; for I have no means of Circulating what follows through all the French Territories, and unless that, or something like it can be done, my Indignation will be entirely fruitless. Tell me how I can convey it into Sartine's[4] Pocket, or who will lay it upon his Desk for me. But Read it first, and unless you think it Pointed enough to Sting the Gaul to the Quick, Burn it.

In Seditionem horrendam, Corruptelis Gallicis
(ut fertur) Londini nuper exortam.[5]

Perfida, crudelis, Victa et Lymphata Furore,
  Non Armis Laurum Gallia, Fraude Petit.
Venalem Pretio Plebem conducit, et Urit
  Undique Privatas Patriciasque Domos.
Necquicquam conata Suâ, fœdissima Sperat
  Posse tamen Nostrâ Nos Superare Manû.
Gallia, Vana Struis—Precibus nunc Utere, Vinces,
  Nam mites Timidis Supplicibusque Sumus.

I have lately Exercised my Ingenuity in contriving an Exercise for yours, and have composed a Riddle, which if it does not make you Laugh before you have Solved it, will probably do it afterward. I would Transcribe it now, but am really so fatigued with Writing, that unless I knew you had a Quinsey,[6] and that a Fit of Laughter might possibly save your Life, I could not prevail with myself to do it.—What could you possibly mean, Slender as you are, by Sallying out upon your two Walking Sticks at two in the Morning, into the Midst of such a Tumult? We admire your Prowess, but cannot commend your Prudence.

Our Joint Love attends you all, Collectively and Individually

Yours Wm Cowper.

June 18. 1780.

[4] Antoine-Raymond-Jean-Gualbert-Gabriel de Sartine (1729–1801), ministre de la marine (1774–80).

[5] These verses were printed in *Hayley*. A translation appears in C's letter to Unwin of 11 July 1780.

[6] Tonsillitis.

WILLIAM UNWIN Thursday, 22 June 1780

Address: Revd. William Unwin at / Stock near / Ingatestone / Essex.
Postmarks: 23/IV *and* NEWPORT PAGNEL
British Library

My dear Friend.

A Word or two in Answer to 2 or 3 Questions of yours which I have hitherto taken no Notice of. I am not in a Scribbling Mood, & shall therefore make no Excursions to Amuse either myself or you; the Needfull will be as much as I can manage at present, the Playfull must wait for another Opportunity.

Your Sister is possessed as you suspect, both of the Price and the Purchase, and has left no Salt of Lemons[1] behind her. This will Distress her not a little when she recollects it; but I can tell you One·thing for your Comfort; that the Salt in Question will most certainly be forthcoming when she sees you next, even if that Event should not take place till you are Both Grey:headed.

I thank you for your Offer of Robertson,[2] but I have more Reading upon my Hands at this present Writing, than I shall get rid of in a Twelvemonth, and this Moment recollect that I have seen it already. He is an Author that I admire much, with one Exception, that I think his Stile too Labour'd. Hume, as an Historian, pleases me more.[3]

I have read just enough of the Biographia Britannica to say that I have Tasted it, and have no Doubt that I shall like it.[4] I am pretty much in the Garden at this Season of the year, so Read but little. In Summer time I am as Giddy:headed as a Boy, and can Settle to nothing. Winter condenses me, and makes me Lumpish and Sober, and then I can read all day long.

For the same Reason I have no need of the Landsckapes at present.

1 'This SALT is infinitely preferable to any other thing whatever for discharging of Iron Moulds, Ink Spots, Red Wine, and Stains of every kind out of Lace, Muslin, Lawn, Cambrick . . . Its [*sic*] also excellent for all the purposes which the Lemon itself is used for, being nothing more than the pure acid part of that fruit . . .': *The London Chronicle*, liv (28–30 Aug. 1783), 211.

2 C had read Robertson's *America* two years earlier (see C to Hill, 1 Mar. 1778).

3 For C's original reaction to Hume's *History*, see his letter to Unwin of 8 May.

4 *Biographia Britannica; or, The Lives of the Most Eminent Persons Who Have Flourished in Great Britain and Ireland from the Earliest Ages, Down to the Present Times* originally appeared from 1747 to 1766. A second edition, which went from 'A' to 'Fastolff' only, edited by Andrew Kippis (1725–95), was published from 1778 to 1793.

When I want them, I will renew my Application and repeat the Description, but it will hardly be before October.

I congratulate you upon a Duplicate of Ramsdens. As your Charge is become Twofold, may your Satisfaction be so too. Mine is sure to be Doubled, because you have Promised me a Twin Present of Salmon.

Before I rose this Morning I composed the 3 following Stanzas; I send them because I like them pretty well myself, and if you should not, you must accept this handsome compliment as an Amends for their Deficiencies.

On the Burning of Lord Mansfield's
Library together with his own MSS.[5]

So then—the Vandals of our Isle
  Sworn Foes of Sense and Law,
Have Burnt to Dust, a Nobler Pile,
  Than ever Roman saw.
And Murray Sighs o'er Pope & Swift,
  And many a Treasure more,
The well Judged Purchase or the Gift
  That graced his Letter'd Store.
Their Pages Mangled, Burnt & Torn,
  The Loss was *His alone*,
But Ages yet to come shall Mourn,
  The Burning of *His Own*.

I have only time to add Love &c & my two Initials

WC.

You may Print the Lines if you Judge them worth it.[6]
June 22. —80.

[5] The house and library (at the north end of the east side of Bloomsbury Square) of William Murray, Lord Mansfield (1705–93), were destroyed in June during the midst of the Gordon Riots. 'The destruction of Lord Mansfield's papers may be considered as a public loss: a great number of manuscript volumes of notes, and other professional papers, collected with unremitted assiduity, and written with his own hand, being burnt. One of them was a large quarto, on the distinct Privileges of both Houses of Parliament.' (*London Magazine*, xlix (June 1780), 287.)

[6] They were not published until *1782*.

JOHN NEWTON Friday, 23 June 1780

Hayley, iii. 35–8

June 23, 1780.

My dear Friend,

Your reflections upon the state of London, the sins and enormities of that great city, while you had a distant view of it from Greenwich, seem to have been prophetic of the heavy stroke that fell upon it just after. Man often prophecies without knowing it—a spirit speaks by him, which is not his own, though he does not at the time suspect, that he is under the influence of any other. Did he foresee what is always foreseen, by him who dictates, what he supposes to be his own, he would suffer by anticipation, as well as by consequence; and wish perhaps as ardently for the happy ignorance, to which he is at present so much indebted, as some have foolishly, and inconsiderately done, for a knowledge that would be but another name for misery.

And why have I said all this? Especially to you, who have hitherto said it to me—Not because I had the least desire of informing a wiser man than myself, but because the observation was naturally suggested by the recollection of your Letter, and that Letter, though not the last, happened to be uppermost in my mind. I can compare this mind of mine to nothing that resembles it more, than to a board that is under the carpenter's plane (I mean while I am writing to you); the shavings are my uppermost thoughts; after a few strokes of the tool, it requires a new surface, this again upon a repetition of his task, he takes off, and a new surface still succeeds—whether the shavings of the present day, will be worth your acceptance, I know not, I am unfortunately made neither of cedar, nor of mahogany, but *Truncus ficulnus, inutile lignum*[1]—consequently, though I should be planed 'till I am as thin as a wafer, it will be but rubbish to the last.

It is not strange that you should be the subject of a false report, for the sword of slander, like that of war, devours one as well as another; and a blameless character is particularly delicious to its unsparing appetite. But that you should be the object of such a report, you who meddle less with the designs of government than almost any man that lives under it, this is strange indeed. It is well however, when they who account it good sport to traduce the

[1] Horace, *Satires*, I. viii. I: 'a fig-wood stem, a useless log'.

reputation of another, invent a story that refutes itself. I wonder they do not always endeavour to accommodate their fiction to the real character of the person; their tale would then at least have an air of probability, and it might cost a peaceable good man much more trouble to disprove it. But perhaps it would not be easy to discern, what part of your conduct lies more open to such an attempt, than another, or what it is that you either say or do, at any time, that presents a fair opportunity to the most ingenious slanderer, to slip in a falsehood between your words, or actions, that shall seem to be of a piece with either. You hate compliment I know, but by your leave, this is not one—it is a truth—worse and worse—now I have praised you indeed—well you must thank yourself for it, it was absolutely done without the least intention on my part, and proceeded from a pen that as far as I can remember, was never guilty of flattery since I knew how to hold it.—He that slanders me, paints me blacker than I am, and he that flatters me, whiter—they both daub me, and when I look in the glass of conscience, I see myself disguised by both—I had as lief my taylor should sew gingerbread-nuts on my coat instead of buttons, as that any man should call my Bristol stone[2] a diamond. The taylor's trick would not at all embellish my suit, nor the flatterer's make me at all the richer. I never make a present to my friend, of what I dislike myself. Ergo, (I have reached the conclusion at last) I did not mean to flatter you.

We have sent a petition to Lord Dartmouth, by this post, praying him to interfere in parliament in behalf of the poor lace-makers.[3] I say we, because I have signed it—Mr. G. drew it up.[4] Mr.—— did not think it grammatical, therefore he would not sign it. Yet I think Priscian[5] himself would have pardoned the manner for the sake of the matter. I dare say if his Lordship does not comply with the prayer of it, it will not be because he thinks it of more consequence to write grammatically, than that the poor should eat, but for some better reason.

My love to all under your roof.

Yours,
W.C.

[2] Sham diamonds made of transparent rock-crystal found in the limestone at Clifton outside Bristol.

[3] See n. 2, C to Hill, 8 July 1780.

[4] Perhaps Nat Gee.

[5] Priscian (*fl.* 500), the Latin grammarian. Samuel Teedon (d. 1798), the Olney schoolmaster, may be the person who objected to the grammar.

WILLIAM UNWIN Sunday, 2 July 1780

Hayley, iii. 38–40

July 2, 1780.

Carissime, I am glad of your confidence, and have reason to hope I shall never abuse it. If you trust me with a secret,[1] I am hermetically sealed; and if you call for the exercise of my judgment, such as it is, I am never freakish and wanton, in the use of it, much less mischievous and malignant. Critics (I believe) do not often stand so clear of these vices as I do. I like your Epitaph, except that I doubt the propriety of the word *immaturus*; which (I think) is rather applicable to fruits than flowers, and except the last pentameter, the assertion it contains being rather too obvious a thought to finish with; not that I think an epitaph should be pointed, like an epigram. But still there is a closeness of thought and expression, necessary in the conclusion of all these little things, that they may leave an agreeable flavour upon the palate. Whatever is short should be nervous, masculine, and compact. Little men are so; and little poems should be so; because, where the work is short, the author has no right to the plea of weariness, and laziness is never admitted as an available excuse in any thing. Now you know my opinion, you will very likely improve upon my improvement, and alter my alterations for the better. To touch and retouch is, though some writers boast of negligence, and others would be ashamed to show their foul copies, the secret of almost all good writing, especially in verse. I am never weary of it myself, and if you would take as much pains as I do, you would have no need to ask for my corrections.

Hic sepultus est
Inter suorum lacrymas
GULIELMUS NORTHCOT,[2]
GULIELMI et MARIÆ filius
Unicus, unicè dilectus,
Qui floris ritu succisus est semihiantis,
Aprilis die septimo,
1780, Æt. 10.

[1] Unwin's secret is that he writes poetry.

[2] According to the inscription, William Northcot died aged 10 on 7 April 1780; he was the only son of William and Mary Northcot, presumably parishioners of Unwin's.

Care, vale! Sed non æternùm, care, valeto!
Namque iterùm tecum, sim modò dignus, ero.
Tum nihil amplexus poterit divellere nostros,
Nec tu marcesces, nec lacrymabor ego.

Having an English translation of it by me, I send it, though it may be of no use.

Farewel! 'But not for ever,' Hope replies,
Trace but his steps and meet him in the skies!
There nothing shall renew our parting pain,
Thou shalt not wither, nor I weep again.

The Stanzas that I sent you are maiden ones, having never been seen by any eye but your Mother's and your own.

If you send me franks, I shall write longer Letters—*Valete, sicut et nos valemus! Amate, sicut et nos amamus!*[3]

W.C.

JOHN NEWTON Tuesday, 4 July 1780

Yale[1]

Cardiphonia
or the
Utterance of the Heart
In a Collection of Letters written in the Course of
a Real Correspondence
On a Variety of Religious Subjects
by Omicron

Haec Res et jungit, junctos et servat Amicos.

[3] 'Say farewell, and we leave; love, and we love in turn.'

[1] C's only writing on the address side reads, 'O my Crony'.

Hor. Sat 6. Lib 1.[2]

My dear Friend—

It is difficult to find a Motto for a Book containing almost as many Subjects as Pages, and those Subjects, of the Religious kind. Horace and my Memory are the only Motto:mongers I am possessed of. The former could furnish me with nothing suitable to the Occasion, but the latter, after a deal of Persuasion & Enquiry, has at last supplied me with one that I hope will please you. I think my Greek Word as Characteristic of the Book as need be; I am sure it is a very legitimate Combination, and both my Ears inform me that it is more Musical than Thelyphthora. Thus having Puffed my Performance sufficiently, I leave it to your Admiration, and from yours, (if it so please you) recommend it to that of the Public.

Horace will furnish me with a Motto for the ensuing Paragraph as Pat as Heart can wish.

– nec meus audet
Rem tentare Pudor, quam Vires ferre recusent.[3]

If I had Strength of Mind, I have not Strength of Body for the Task, which you say, some would impose upon me. I cannot bear much thinking. The Meshes of that fine Network the Brain, are composed of such mere Spinner's Threads in me, that when a long Thought once finds its way into them, it Buzzes and Twangs and Bustles about at such a rate, as seems to threaten the whole Contexture. Neither would Mr. M—n ever acknowledge himself Answer'd by any man that could not fight him upon Hebrew Ground, for you say he rests much of his Argument upon such Authority. I told Mr. Scot who spent part of last Saturday Morning with us, that it seem'd difficult to me to discover to what Description of men, the Book could with any Propriety be address'd. I mean Thelyphthora. He that has no Wife, seems but little interested in the Question, *How many* he may have if he will. He that is Married, and Loves his Wife, is not likely to wish for another, and He that does not, will probably think he has already One too many. Such Reasoning as this is just of a Size with my Intellects, but then Mr. M——n's Nose which is a very handsome one at present, would be entirely spoiled by the Contortions &

[2] The quotation is from *Satires*, I. iii. 54: 'This is how to make friends and keep them friends.'

[3] *Epistles*, II. i. 258–9: 'My modesty does not allow me to attempt a task which is beyond my strength to bear.'

Distortions it would undergo, while it endeavour'd to express the Contempt he felt for such an Argument. No—I must needs refer it again to You, and to conclude the Subject as I begun it, in the Words of Horace Say—Operum hoc, mihi crede, tuorum est.[4]

Had you continued at Olney your main Employment would have been to Visit the Sick, & Bury the Dead. It is a time of terrible Mortality; a Putrid Small Pox, and other Putrid Fevers Mow down the People. Poor Thomas Old has lost his Wife, she died Yesterday, not indeed by an Epidemic, but in Child Birth.[5]

Our Love attends Yourself & Mrs. Newton—Sally & Peggy—

Yours affectionately Wm Cowper.

July 4. 1780

JOSEPH HILL — Saturday, 8 July 1780

Address: Mr. Joseph Hill / Chancery Office / London.
Postmarks: 10/IY *and* OULNEY
Cowper Johnson

Mon Ami!

By this time I suppose you have ventured to take your Fingers out of your Ears, being deliver'd from the Deafening Shouts of the most Zealous Mob that ever Strain'd their Lungs in the Cause of Religion. I congratulate you upon a gentle Relapse into the customary Sounds of a great City, which, though we Rustics abhorr them as Noisy & dissonant, are a Musical & sweet Murmur compared with what you have lately heard. The Tinkling of a Kennel may be distinguished now, where the Roaring of a Cascade would have been sunk and lost. I never suspected 'till the Newspaper inform'd me of it a few Days since, that the barbarous Uproar had reached Great Queen Street[1]—I hope Mrs. Hill was in the Country—You I know,

[4] *Satires*, I. vii. 35: 'Believe me, this is a task worthy of you.'

[5] Mary Old was buried on 4 July. Anne, her daughter was christened on 24 July. See *O.P.R.*, pp. 390, 392. Thomas Old, a farmer, died in 1803.

---

[1] *The General Evening Post* of Thursday–Saturday, 29 June–1 July 1780 (No. 7229) carried the following report: '*Thomas Hawes* was charged, on the oaths of two thief-takers, with having been concerned in pulling down Mr. Cox's house in Great Queen-street, Lincoln's-inn-fields; but an alibi being clearly and incontestibly proved by four persons, whose characters are unimpeachable, he was necessarily acquitted.'

are more apt to be Angry than terrified but had more Prudence, I trust, than to Oppose your little Person to such a furious Torrent. I shall rejoice to hear you are in Health, and that as I am sure you did not take up the Protestant Cudgels upon this Harebrain'd Occasion, so you have not been pull'd in pieces as a Papist.

If you ever take the Tip of the Chancellor's Ear between your Finger and Thumb, you can hardly improve the Opportunity to better Purpose, than if you should Whisper into it the Voice of Compassion & Lenity to the Lace Makers. I am an Eye Witness of their Poverty, and do know, that Hundreds in this little Town, are upon the Point of Starving, & that the most unremitting Industry is but barely sufficient to keep them from it. I know that the Bill by which they would have been so fatally affected is thrown out, but Lord Stormont threatens them with another, and if another like it should pass, they are undone.[2] We lately sent a Petition from hence to Lord Dartmouth. I signed it, and am sure the Contents are true.—The Purport of it was to inform him that there are very near 1200 Lace Makers in this Beggarly Town, the most of whom had Reason enough while the Bill was in Agitation, to look upon every Loaf they bought as the last they should ever be able to Earn.—I can never think it good Policy to incur the Certain Inconvenience of Ruining 300,000, in order to prevent a remote and possible Damage though to a much greater Number. The Measure is like a Scythe, and the poor Lacemakers are the Sickly Crop that trembles before the Edge of it. The Prospect of Peace with America is like the Streak of Dawn in their Horizon, but this Bill is like a Black Cloud behind it, that threatens their Hope of a comfortable Day with utter Extinction. I did not perceive 'till this Moment that I had tack'd two Similes together, a Practise, which, though warranted by the Example of Homer and allowable in an Epic Poem, is rather Luxuriant & Licentious in a Letter; lest I should add a third, I conclude myself with my best Respects to Mrs. Hill, Your Affectionate

Wm Cowper.

July 8. 1780.

[2] The removal of tariffs on Irish goods and thus the destruction of a market for English lace must have been the concern of the lace-makers of Olney (there was a parliamentary debate on Irish affairs in Apr. 1780). David Murray, Viscount Stormont (1727–96), who became 2nd Earl of Mansfield in 1793, was Secretary of State for the Southern Department from October 1779 until July 1782.

WILLIAM UNWIN Tuesday, 11 July 1780

British Library[1]

I have no Oracular Responses to make you upon the Subject of gardening, while I know that you have both Millar[2] and Mawe[3] in your Possession. To them I refer you, but especially to the latter, because it will be little or no Trouble to consult him. I have heard, that if the first Crop of Roses are cut off as fast as the Buds appear, a second will be produced in Autumn. I do not know it to be true, but the Fact is easily ascertain'd and I recommend it to Miss Shuttleworth to make the Experiment with her Scissars.

I account myself Sufficiently commended for my Latin Exercise by the Number of Translations it has undergone.[4] That which you distinguished in the Margin by the Word Better was the Production of a Friend, and except that for a modest Reason he omitted the third Couplet, is, I think, a good one. To finish the Group, I have Translated it myself, & though I would not wish you to give it to the World, for more Reasons than one, and especially lest some French Hero should call me to an Account for it, I add it on the other Side. An Author ought to be the best Judge of his own Meaning, and whether I have Succeeded or not, I cannot but wish that where a Translator is wanted, the Writer was always to be his own.[5]

False, cruel, disappointed, Stung to th' Heart,
France quits the Warrior's for th' Assassin's Part.
To dirty Hands a dirty Bribe conveys,
Bids the low Street & lofty Palace Blaze.
Her Sons too Weak to Vanquish us alone,
She Hires the worst & basest of our own.—
Kneel France—a Suppliant conquers us with Ease,
We always Spare a Coward on his Knees.

---

[1] Although no salutation is present, this appears to be a complete MS. However, the paragraph beginning, 'I have not one bright thought' is not in C's hand except for the five concluding words: 'whether I will or not'.

[2] See n. 1, C to Hill, 8 Aug. 1779.

[3] Thomas Mawe's *Every Man His Own Gardener. Being a New . . . Gardener's Kalendar* . . . (1767) had reached a sixth edition by 1773.

[4] The verses in Latin were sent to Unwin in C's letter of 18 June.

[5] The verses were printed in *Hayley*.

I have often Wonder'd that Dryden's illustrious Epigram on Milton, (in my Mind the Second best that ever was made) has never been translated into Latin, for the Admiration of the Learned in other Countries. I have at last presumed to Venture upon the Task myself; the great Closeness of the Original, which is equal in that respect to the most compact Latin I ever saw, made it extremely difficult.

Tres, tria, sed longe distantia Sæcula, Vates
  Ostentant, tribus é Gentibus, eximios.
Græcia Sublimem, cum Majestate disertum
  Roma tulit, felix Anglia, Utrisque parem.
Partubus ex binis Natura exhausta, coacta est
  Tertius ut fieret, Consociare Duos.[6]

I have not one bright thought upon the Chancellor's Recovery,[7] nor can I strike off so much as one sparkling Atom from that brilliant subject. It is not when I will, nor upon what I will, but as a thought happens to occur to me, & then I versify whether I will or not.

I never write but for my Amusement, and What I write is sure to Answer that End, if it Answers no other. If besides this Purpose, the more desirable one of Entertaining You be effected, I then receive double Fruit of my Labor, and consider this Produce of it as a Second Crop, the more valuable because less expected. But when I have once remitted a Composition to you, I have done with it; it is pretty certain that I shall never Read it or Think of it again. From that moment I have constituted You, Sole Judge of its Accomplishments, if it has any, and of its Defects, which it is sure to have. For this Reason I decline Answering the Question with which you conclude your last, and cannot persuade myself to Enter into a Critical Examen of the two Pieces upon Lord Mansfield's Loss, either with respect

[6] This is a translation of Dryden's lines (*c.* 1688):

Three *Poets*, in three distant *Ages* born,
Greece, *Italy*, and *England* did adorn.
The *First* in loftiness of thought Surpass'd;
The *Next* in *Majesty*; in both the *Last*.
The force of *Nature* cou'd no farther goe:
To make a *Third* she joynd the former two.
  (*Works*, iii, ed. E. Miner (Berkeley, 1969), 208).

[7] Thurlow's illness is mentioned in C to Hill, 6 May 1780.

to their Intrinsic, or Comparative Merit.[8] And indeed after having rather discouraged that Use of them which you had design'd, there is no Occasion for it.

I understand, tho' I have not seen it, that the Author of Thelyphthora establishes many of his Premisses upon his own peculiar Interpretation of the Original Hebrew. I am therefore absolutely incompetent to decide the Question whether he has Scripture on his Side or not, and have no more Curiosity to see his Book, than I should have, if it were written in that Language. If I had a Wife of whom I was weary, and wish'd to be indulged with the Liberty of taking another, I would certainly Read it, & Study it too. I should be encouraged in this Undertaking, by a Hope that Passion, Prejudice and Appetite combining together with the Author's Ingenuity to impose upon me, might succeed, and release me from the rusty and oldfashion'd Bonds of Fidelity, Friendship and Love. But I have no Interest in the Question, at least no other Interest than that of every man who wishes well to his Country, and would be Sorry to see the Honest & faithfull English Husband converted into a Turkish Stallion, and the Aimable Character of the English Wife, the most aimable in the World, degraded into the Sordid & Base Condition of a Breed Mare.

Your Mother's Love with mine to all the Family.

Wm Cowper.

July 11. 1780.

JOHN NEWTON — Wednesday, 12 July 1780

Southey, xv. 54–6

July 12, 1780.

My dear friend,

Such nights as I frequently spend, are but a miserable prelude to the succeeding day, and indispose me, above all things, to the business of writing. Yet with a pen in my hand, if I am able to write at all, I find myself gradually relieved; and as I am glad of any employment that may serve to engage my attention, so especially I am pleased

[8] 'On the Burning of Lord Mansfield's Library' and 'On the Same', which appeared together in *1782*.

with an opportunity of conversing with you, though it be but upon paper. This occupation above all others assists me in that self-deception to which I am indebted for all the little comfort I enjoy; things seem to be as they were, and I almost forget that they never can be so again.

We are both obliged to you for a sight of Mr. ——'s letter. The friendly and obliging manner of it will much enhance the difficulty of answering it. I think I can see plainly that though he does not hope for your applause, he would gladly escape your censure. He seems to approach you smoothly and softly, and to take you gently by the hand, as if he bespoke your lenity, and entreated you at least to spare him. You have such skill in the management of your pen, that I doubt not you will be able to send him a balmy reproof that shall give him no reason to complain of a broken head.—How delusive is the wildest speculation when pursued with eagerness, and nourished with such arguments as the perverted ingenuity of such a mind as his can easily furnish!—Judgement falls asleep upon the bench, while Imagination, like a smug, pert counsellor, stands chattering at the bar, and with a deal of fine-spun, enchanting sophistry, carries all before him.[1]

My enigma will probably find you out, and you will find out my enigma at some future time. I am not in a humour to transcribe it now. Indeed I wonder that a sportive thought should ever knock at the door of my intellects, and still more that it should gain admittance. It is as if harlequin should intrude himself into the gloomy chamber where a corpse is deposited in state. His antic gesticulations would be unseasonable at any rate, but more especially so if they should distort the features of the mournful attendants into laughter. But the mind long wearied with the sameness of a dull, dreary prospect, will gladly fix its eyes on any thing that may make a little variety in its contemplations, though it were but a kitten playing with her tail.

You would believe, though I did not say it at the end of every letter, that we remember you and Mrs. Newton with the same affection as ever; but I would not therefore excuse myself from writing what it gives you pleasure to read. I have often wished indeed, when writing to an ordinary correspondent, for the revival of the Roman custom—

[1] *Southey* includes the paragraph, 'If I had strength of mind . . . refer it again to you' at this point. This paragraph is from C's letter to Newton of 4 July 1780.

salutem at top, and *vale* at bottom. But as the French have taught all Europe to enter a room and to leave it with a most ceremonious bow, so they have taught us to begin and conclude our letters in the same manner. However I can say to you,

Sans ceremonie,

Adieu, *mon ami*!

Wm. Cowper.

MRS. COWPER Thursday, 20 July 1780

Address: Mrs. Cowper / Park Street / Grosvenor Square / London.
Postmarks: 21/IY *and* OULNEY
Panshanger Collection

My dear Cousin,

Mr. Newton having desired me to be of the Party, I am come to meet him.[1] You see me Sixteen years Older at the least than when I saw You last, but the Effects of Time seem to have taken Place rather on the Outside of my Head, than Within it. What was Brown is become Grey, but what was Foolish remains Foolish still. Green Fruit must Rot before it Ripens, if the Season is such as to afford it nothing but Cold Winds and dark Clouds that intercept every Ray of Sunshine. My Days steal away Silently and March on (as poor Mad King Lear would have made his Soldiers March) as if they were Shod with Felt.[2] Not so Silently but that I hear them, yet were it not that I am always Listening to their Flight, having no Infirmity that I had not when I was much Younger, I should deceive myself with an Imagination that I am still Young.

I am fond of Writing, as an Amusement, but I do not always find it one. Being rather scantily furnished with Subjects that are good for any thing, and Corresponding only with those who have no Relish for such as are good for Nothing, I often find myself reduced to the Necessity, the disagreeable Necessity of Writing about Myself. This does not mend the Matter much, for though in a Description

[1] Newton to C, 14 July 1780 (Princeton): 'We have thoughts of dining with Mrs. Cowper on friday next, if you should be in tolerable writing hue on Thursday, I should be glad to see the Postman bring her a letter from you while we are there. I am sure she would be glad to hear from you.' Newton to C, 29 July 1780 (Princeton) commences: 'I thank you for trying to meet us at Mrs. Cowper's but we did not go there till yesterday.'

[2] *King Lear*, IV. vi. 186–7.

of my own Condition, I discover abundant Materials to Employ my Pen upon, yet as the Task is not very agreeable to *me*, so I am Sufficiently aware that it is likely to prove Irksome to others. A Painter who should confine himself in the Exercise of his Art to the Drawing of his own Picture, must be a Wonderfull Coxcomb if he did not soon grow Sick of his Occupation, and be peculiarly fortunate, if he did not make others as Sick as Himself.

Remote as your Dwelling is from the late Scene of Riot and Confusion, I hope that though you could not but hear the Report of it, you heard no more, and that the Roarings of the mad Multitude did not reach you. That was a Day of Terror to the Innocent, and the Present is a Day of still greater Terror to the Guilty. The Law was for a few Moments like an Arrow in the Quiver, seemed to be of no Use, and did no Execution, now it is an Arrow upon the String, and many who despised it lately, are trembling as they Stand before the Point of it.

I have talked more already than I have formerly done in three Visits. You remember my Taciturnity, never to be forgotten by those who knew me. Not to depart entirely from what might be for aught I know, the most shining Part of my character, I here Shut my Mouth, make my Bow, & return to Olney.

My Love attends your Family—Mrs. Unwin presents her Affectionate Respects, & desires me to add for the Satisfaction of Mr. & Mrs. Newton, who have heard she was Indisposed, that she is better.[3]

Yours my Dear Cousin—

Wm Cowper.

July 20. 1780.

WILLIAM UNWIN — Thursday, 27 July 1780

British Library

My dear Friend,

As two Men sit Silent after having exhausted all their Topics of Conversation, One says, It is very fine Weather, and the other says,

[3] Probably a reference to Newton's letter to Mrs. Unwin of 19 July 1780 (Princeton) which begins: 'The letter . . . from dear Mr. Cowper has given us some painful feelings for you both. He says you are lower in spirits than usual. By this time I hope the Lord has raised your spirits again.' The letter Newton refers to is not known.

Yes. One Blows his Nose, and the other Rubs his Eyebrow, (by the way this is very much in Homer's Manner). Such seems to be the Case between you and me. After a Silence of some Days, I wrote you a long Something that I suppose was nothing to the Purpose, because it has not afforded you Materials for an Answer. Nevertheless, as it often happens in the Case above stated, One of the distressed Parties being deeply sensible of the aukwardness of a dumb Duette, breaks Silence again, and resolves to Speak though he have nothing to Say, so it fares with me—I am with you again in the Form of an Epistle, though considering my present Emptiness, I have reason to fear that your only Joy upon the Occasion will be that it is conveyed to you in a Frank.

When I began I expected no Interruption, but if I had Expected Interruptions without End, I should have been less disappointed. First came the Barber, who after having embellish'd the Outside of my Head, has left the Inside just as unfurnish'd as he found it. Then came Olney Bridge; not into the House, but into the conversation. The Cause relating to it was tried on Tuesday at Buckingham.[1] The Judge directed the Jury to find a Verdict favorable to Olney. The Jury consisted of one Knave and Eleven Fools, the last mention'd followed the aforemention'd as Sheep follow a Bell Wether, & decided in direct Opposition to the said Judge. Then a Flaw was discover'd in the Indictment, the Indictment was Quashed, & an Order made for a new Trial. The new Trial will be in the King's Bench, where said Knave & said Fools will have nothing to do with it, so the Men of Olney fling up their Caps, and assure themselves of a complete Victory. A Victory will save me and your Mother many Shillings, perhaps some Pounds, which (except that it has afforded me a Subject to Write upon) was the only Reason why I have said so much about it. I know you take an Interest in all that concerns us, and will consequently rejoice with us in the Prospect of an Event in which we are concerned so nearly.

Riddle.

I am just Two & Two, I am Warm, I am Cold,
And the Parent of Numbers that cannot be told.

[1] The King versus the Inhabitants of Olney was tried at the Bucks. Summer Assizes of 1780; the indictment against the town charged that the bridge was in a disastrous state of repair and called upon the townspeople to repair it.

I am Lawfull, Unlawfull, a Duty, a Fault,
I am often Sold Dear, good for Nothing when Bought.
An extraordinary Boon, & a Matter of Course,
And yielded with Pleasure when taken by Force.
Alike the Delight of the Poor & the Rich,
Tho' the Vulgar is apt to Present me his Breech.[2]

Love Abused.
The Thought Suggested by Thelyphthora[3]

What is there in the Vale of Life
Half so delightfull as a Wife,
When Friendship, Love, & Peace combine
To stamp the Marriage Bond Divine?
The Stream of pure and genuine Love
Derives its Current from Above,
And Earth a Second Eden Shows
Where'er the Healing Water flows.
But Ah! if from the Dykes & Drains
Of Sensual Nature's fev'rish Veins,
Lust like a lawless headstrong Flood
Impregnated with Ooze and Mud,
Descending fast on ev'ry Side,
Once Mingles with the Sacred Tide,
Farewell the Soul enliv'ning Scene!
The Banks that wore a Smiling Green.
With rank Defilement overspread,
Bewail their Flow'ry Beauties dead,
The Stream polluted, dark and dull,
Diffused into a Stygian Pool,
Thro' Life's last melancholy Years
Is fed with everflowing Tears,
Complaints supply the Zephyr's Part,
And Sighs that Heave a Breaking Heart.

---

2 A kiss. The first six lines of this riddle were published in *Hayley*.
3 This poem was first published in *Hayley*.

I will say of that Book what I never said, and what no man ought to say of any other, that I could Answer it without Reading it: Deriving all my Arguments from Principles of mere Humanity, Fidelity, and Domestic Expediency.—My Respects with your Mother's Love attend Yourself & the Ladies—the Children are never forgot.

Yours

affectionately Wm C.

July 27. 1780.
My Franks are Out.

JOHN NEWTON — Monday, 31 July 1780

Princeton (*copy*)

My dear Sir —

Though I should never think of sending the same Letter to two Correspondants, yet I confess I am not sorry that your communication with Stock is cut off, at least for the present. I have indeed sometimes wish'd that it had never been opened, & for a reason obvious enough. Though I never make one Letter a Copy of another, yet I have sometimes found myself rather at a plunge, & puzzled when I have attempted to find variety for two. I know you have a sight of those I write to Mr. Unwin, which would, if possible, be still less worth your seeing, if you had before read them addressed to yourself. You may think perhaps that I deal more liberally with *Him* in the way of poetical export than I do with You & I believe you have reason. The truth is This—If I walked the Streets with a Fiddle under my Arm, I should never think of performing before the Window of a Privy Counsellor or a chief Justice, but should rather make free with Ears more likely to be open to such amusement. The trifles I produce in this way are indeed such trifles that I cannot think them seasonable Presents for you. Mr. Unwin himself would not be affronted if I was to tell him that there is this difference between him & Mr. Newton: That the latter is already an Apostle while He himself is only undergoing the business of Incubation, with a hope that he may be hatched in time. When my Muse comes forth arrayed in sables, at least in a robe of graver cast, I make no scruple to direct her to my friend at Hoxton. This has been one reason why I have

so long delayed the Riddle, but lest I should seem to set a value upon it that I do not by making it an Object of still further enquiry, here it comes.

I am just Two & Two, I am warm, I am cold
And the Parent of numbers that cannot be told
I am lawfull, unlawfull, a duty, a fault
I am often sold dear, good for nothing when bought.
An extraordinary boon, & a matter of course
And yielded with pleasure when taken by force
Alike the delight of the Poor & the Rich
Tho' the vulgar is apt to present me his breech.

We are much bound to thank You for a sight of your Letter to the *Author*—Nothing was ever more tenderly or more handsomely managed or at the same time more explicitly and faithfully expressed. It was just what I expected it would be. But permit me just to insinuate that his request in Answer to it, annoyed me more, if possible, than any part of his conduct. What confidence, not to say assurance, does it impart! Be so good as to strike me a Blow, that I may beat you soundly. You have a Temper not to be moved by such a speech & it is well for you, though perhaps still better for him that you have.

A Drama has been lately represented in this County, in which the principal part, (the part of Sisyphus) was performed by Mr. Pomfret.[1] His business was to carry the stones of Olney Bridge to the top of a steep Hill, which he accomplished; but just as he was going to turn them over the summit, they rolled back upon him, & carried him with them to the bottom. The Judge directed the Jury to find for Olney, but they would not. Mr. Pomfret jumpt for joy. The Council for Olney found a flaw in the Indictment, & it was quashed; an order made for a new Trial, & the Cause will be heard next in the King's Bench. Mr. Pomfret is mortified, despairs I suppose of success, as he well may, & wishes he had never meddled with it. Alass poor Sisyphus!

Mrs. Unwin is better Today than at any time within the last 3 weeks. She adds her love to mine

Yours my dear Sir

July 31st— Wm. Cowper.
1780.

The Copy shall be returned the first Opportunity.

[1] Robert Pomfret (1729–1804) served as rector of Emberton, the village across the river from Olney, from 1753 until his death.

WILLIAM UNWIN Sunday, 6 August 1780

Address: The Revd. William Unwin / Stock near / Ingatestone / Essex.
Postmark: 7/AV
Yale

My dear Friend,

You like to hear from me—this is a very good Reason why I should Write—but I have nothing to say—this seems equally a good Reason why I should not. Yet if you had alighted from your Horse at our Door this Morning, and at this present Writing, being 5 o'clock in the Afternoon, had found Occasion to say to me, Mr. Cowper you have not Spoke since I came in, have you resolved never to speak again? It would be but a poor Reply, if in Answer to the Summons I should Plead Inability as my best & only Excuse. And this by the way, suggests to me a Seasonable Piece of Instruction, and reminds me of what I am very apt to forget when I have my Epistolary Business in Hand: that a Letter may be written upon any thing or Nothing, just as that any thing or Nothing happens to Occurr. A man that has a Journey before him, 20 Miles in Length, which he is to perform on Foot, will not Hesitate & doubt whether he shall set out or not, because he does not readily conceive how he shall ever reach the End of it; for he knows that by the Simple Operation of moving one Foot forward first, and then the other, he shall be sure to Accomplish it. So it is in the present Case, and so it is in every similar Case. A Letter is Written, as a Conversation is maintained, or a Journey perform'd, not by preconcerted, or premeditated Means, by a New Contrivance, or an Invention never heard of before, but merely by maintaining a Progress, and resolving as a Postillion does, having once Set out, never to Stop 'till we reach the appointed End. If a Man may Talk without thinking, why may he not Write upon the same Terms? A Grave Gentleman of the last Century, a Tie Wig, Square:toes, Steinkirk[1] Figure would say—my good Sir, a man has no right to do either. But it is to be hoped that the present Century has nothing to do with the Mouldy

[1] A neckcloth, worn by both men and women, having long laced ends hanging down or twisted together, and passed through a loop or ring (*O.E.D.*). The name originated from the victory at Steenkerke (Belgium) by the French over the English and their allies on 3 Aug. 1692. According to Voltaire, the original *cravate à la Steinkerke* gave the appearance of negligence, an allusion to the disordered dress of the French when hastily summoned to battle.

Opinions of the last, and so good Sir Launcelot, or Sir Paul or whatever be your Name, Step into your Picture Frame again, and Look as if you Thought for another Century, & leave us Moderns in the mean time, to think when we can, & to Write whether we can or not, else we might as well be as Dead as you are.

When we Look back upon our Forefathers, we seem to Look back upon the People of another Nation, almost upon Creatures of another Species. Their vast rambling Mansions, Spacious Halls, and painted Casements, the Gothic Porch smother'd with Honey Suckles, their little Gardens and high Walls, their Box Edgings, Balls of Holly, and yew Tree Statues, are become so entirely unfashionable now, that we can hardly believe it possible that a People who resembled us so little in their Taste, should Resemble us in any thing else. But in every thing else I Suppose they were our Counterparts exactly, and Time that has Sewed up the Slashed Sleeve, and reduced the large Trunk Hose to a neat Pair of Silk Stockings, has left Human Nature just where it found it. The Inside of the Man at least has undergone no Change, His Passions, Appetites & Aims are just what they ever were: they Wear perhaps a handsomer Disguise than they did in Days of Yore, for Philosophy and Literature will have their Effect upon the Exterior, but in every other Respect, a Modern is only an Ancient in a different Dress.

When you can send me some Franks, I can send you some Verses. And shall be glad of my Translations of Bourne, when you can conveniently restore them, for I am making a Collection, not for the Public, but for Myself.[2]

Our Love attends Yourself & all your Family.

Yours affectionately Wm Cowper.

Augt. 6. 1780.

[2] 'The Glow-Worm', 'The Jack Daw', 'The Cricket', 'The Parrot', and 'The Cantab.' were written in 1777; the first four appeared in *1782*.

Unwin did not comply with this request, but he did return the translations when C asked again in the postscript of his letter of 1 May 1781. C's letter to Newton of 13 May 1781 would seem to indicate that Unwin had returned three poems, 'The Jack Daw', 'The Cricket', and 'The Parrot', and in his letter to Unwin of 10 May 1781, C states that perhaps Unwin had never had copies of 'The Glow-Worm' and 'The Cantab.'.

WILLIAM UNWIN

post Sunday, 6 August–
pre Sunday, 3 September 1780[1]

British Library

As I Promised you Verse if you would send me a Frank, I am not willing to return the Cover without some, though I think I have already wearied you with the Prolixity of my Prose.

The Lily and the Rose.[2]

The Nymph must lose her Female Friend
  If more admir'd than She—
But where will fierce Contention End
  If Flow'rs can disagree?

2.

Within the Garden's peacefull Scene,
  Appear'd two lovely Foes,
Aspiring to the Rank of Queen,
  The Lily and the Rose.

3.

The Rose soon redden'd into Rage,
  And Swelling with Disdain,
Appeal'd to many a Poet's Page
  To Prove Her Right to Reign.

4.

The Lily's Height bespoke Command—
  A fair Imperial Flow'r,
She seem'd design'd for Flora's Hand,
  The Sceptre of her Pow'r.

[1] In his previous letter to Unwin (6 Aug.), C says: 'When you can send me some Franks, I can send you some Verses.' C seems to be referring to this statement in the opening sentence of the portion of this letter which remains.

[2] Published in *1782*.

5.

The Civil Bick'ring and Debate
  The Goddess chanced to Hear,
And flew to Save, e'er yet too late
  The Pride of the Parterre.

6.

Yours is, she said, the Nobler Hue,
  And Yours the Statelier Mien,
And 'till a Third Surpasses you,
  Let each be deem'd a Queen.

7.

Thus sooth'd and reconcil'd, Each seeks
  The fairest British Fair,
The Seat of Empire is her Cheeks,
  They Reign United there.

I must refer you to those unaccountable Gaddings and Caprices of the Human Mind, for the Cause of this Production; for in general, I beleive, there is no Man who has less to do with the Ladies' cheeks than I have. I suppose it would be best to Antedate it, and to imagine that it was written 20 years ago, for my Mind was never more in a trifling Butterfly Trim than when I composed it, even in the earliest Follies of my Life. And what is worse than All this, I have Translated it into Latin—but that, some other time.—

JOSEPH HILL — [Tuesday, 8?] August 1780[1]

Address: Mr. Joseph Hill at / Wargrove near / Twyford / Berks.
Postmarks: 9/AV *and* OULNEY
Cowper Johnson

My dear Sir,

I greet you at your Castle of Buen Retiro,[2] and wish you could Enjoy the unmixt Pleasures of the Country there, but it seems you

[1] There is a discrepancy between the date C assigns to the letter (10 Aug.) and the post-mark (9 Aug.). The letter must have been written on 8 Aug. and incorrectly dated.

[2] Buen Retiro was the name of a castle of the kings of Spain; it is located in the present public park of El Retiro, Madrid.

are obliged to Dash the Cup with a Portion of those Bitters you are always swallowing in Town. Well—you are honorably and usefully employed, and ten times more Beneficially to Society, than if you were Piping to a few Sheep under a Spreading Beech, or Listening to a tinkling Rill. Besides, by the Effect of long Custom and Habitual Practise, you are not only enabled to endure your Occupation, but even find it agreeable. I remember the Time when it would not have suited you so well to have devoted so large a Part of your Vacation to the Objects of your Profession, and You, I daresay, have not forgot, what a Seasonable Relaxation you found, when lying at full Stretch upon the Ruins of an Old Wall by the Sea side, you amused yourself with Tasso's Jerusalem & the Pastor fido.[3] I recollect that we both Pitied Mr. de Grey[4] when we called at his Cottage at Taplow, and found, not the Master indeed, but his Desk with his White-leaved Folio upon it, which bespoke him as much a Man of Business in his Retirement, as in Westminster Hall. But by these Steps he ascended the Bench, and by such Steps as these, I doubt not but you will rise (perhaps are already risen) tho' not to the Bench, yet to a Rank equally respectable in that part of the Profession you have chosen. In time perhaps you may do as he has done; He has retired, and so may you—Now he may Read what he pleases, and Ride where he will if the Gout will give him leave, and You who have no Gout, and probably never will, when your Hour of Dismission comes, will probably for that Reason, if for no other, be a Happier man than He.

I am sorry the Melons proved no better, I beleive they were cut too soon, a Fault our Gardener is very apt to fall into. Else I have found in general that the Old Rock and the Crimson Cantalupe, are not only good Sorts, but the best that are to be met with, but they require a deal of Ripening.

My Respects attend Mrs. Hill with many Thanks for her obliging Intentions. I have the Plants of several Seeds with which she has favor'd me in our own Garden, and our Neighbor at Gayhurst, has several more, which would not prosper with me, for want of those Advantages which He could give them. Every thing Exotic or Rare is welcome, and is sure to turn to Account in my Hands,

[3] *Il Pastor Fido* (1590) by Battista Guarini (1538–1612), a pastoral drama stimulated by Tasso's *Aminta* (1573).

[4] William de Grey had been appointed Lord Chief Justice of the Common Pleas in 1777, but he resigned for reasons of ill health in June 1780. In October he was created Baron Walsingham.

either as an Ornament of our own Garden, or in the way of Barter with Him.

I am, my dear Friend,
Affectionately Yours Wm Cowper.

Augt. 10. 1780.
The Author of Thelyphthora has not thought proper to favor me with his Book, and having no interest in the Subject, I have not thought proper to Purchase it. Indeed I have no Curiosity to Read what I am sure must be Erroneous before I Read it; Truth is worth every thing that can be given for it, but a mere Display of Ingenuity, calculated only to Mislead, is worth Nothing.—

JOHN NEWTON — Thursday, 10 August 1780[1]

Princeton

My dear Friend—

If the Heat of the Weather at London is such as it is here, and you are now employed in Writing, you find it Hard Work; though a Reaper who Stoops with his Nose within an Inch of his Sickle all the day, would Envy both You and Me, & think us but Laborious Triflers at the best.

Mr. Teedon has received your kind & seasonable Donation at two Payments; Two Guineas before your Remittance came, and the Remainder Yesterday Evening in Weston Field. We met him there just after we had with Difficulty dragged ourselves up that Steep and Close Lane, and were not a little fearfull that his Honest but rather verbose Expressions of Gratitude, would cost us both a Sore Throat, our Pores standing wide open for the Reception of an East Wind which blew rather Sharp over the Top of the Hill.

You have seen Mr. Ashburner,[2] & are consequently in Possession of the whole History of the Warrington Pew;[3] it is difficult to say at

[1] Dated '10 Augst./80' in the Miss Gaviller copy in the Barham Johnson collection.

[2] Perhaps the draper who died in May 1785. See C to Newton, May 1785.

[3] Warrington was a hamlet in the parish of Olney. Mr. Page, then curate of Olney, and Maurice Smith, the vicar's warden, had given orders for the pew to be altered without calling a vestry-meeting, and the parish refused to pay the church carpenter, Thomas Raban. But Raban and his associates were the leading critics of Page's ministry, and their opposition to

present, what will be the Contents of the next Chapter, but the Conclusion is likely to prove disastrous to Mr Page, and not more favorable to his Friend Mr. Smith; for by the best Information we can procure, the latter Gentleman having omitted to take the Opinion of a Vestry (deeming it I suppose an idle Ceremony, not worthy the Attention of a Church Warden acting upon his liberal and enlarged Plan) has mortally offended the Principal Parishioners, who are determined that He & his Principal shall pay for the Alteration. A Resolution in which without Doubt they will be Warranted by the Law. A Mind accustomed to Reflection may derive a Lesson from almost every Incident that occurrs, and the Lesson to be derived from This, seems to be, that the Peace of that Parish is sure to be disturbed and not likely to be soon restored, that is burthened with a quarrelsome Curate & a Meddlesome Church warden.

It is natural before the Winter is half over, to Wish for the Return of Spring; but We shall Wish for the next Spring with unusual Ardor, for till then we must despair of seeing you & Mrs. Newton, & then, we may expect you. The present state of Mrs. Unwin's health will not permit her to expose herself to the certain loss of sleep. Every little novelty agitates her spirits to a degree that may best be conceived by Mrs. Newton, who has been a sufferer in the same way. Quiet walks under the same hedges, & the usual routine of circumstances that meet us daily, suit her best; and as for myself, who have sometimes much ado to attain to a good night's rest, tho' in possession of every advantage, I should certainly miss it at an inn, where I never could find it, in my best health & happiest days.—

Page was soon centered on the issue of Warrington Pew. Page retaliated by dispensing with Raban's carpentry at a time when sixteen victims of the smallpox epidemic were waiting to be buried in coffins which he should have made. See C to Newton, 31 Aug., 29 Oct., 11 Nov., 19 Nov., and 21 Dec. 1780.

JOHN NEWTON Monday, 21 August 1780

Address: The Revd. John Newton / Charles Square / Hoxton / London.
Postmarks: 23/AV *and* OULNEY
Olney

My dear Sir,

I am willing to try if Writing to you will charm the Tooth Ach, which has hitherto defied every other Remedy. I should not have been so Formal as to wait for your Answer to my last, [ ][1] other Hindrances prevented my [ ] As often as a cloudy Sky will [ ] we Walk both Morning and [ ] to the Wilderness, but more fr[ ] Spinney, and this Exercise er[ ] Hours that are favorable to [ ] Employment.

The following Occurrence ought not to be passed over in Silence, in a place where so few notable ones are to be met with. Last Wednesday Night, while we were at Supper, between the Hours of 8 and 9, I heard an unusual Noise in the Back Parlour, as if one of the Hares was entangled, & endeavouring to disengage herself. I was just going to Rise from Table, when it ceased. In about 5 Minutes, a Voice on the Outside of the Parlor Door, Enquired if One of my Hares had got away. I immediately rushed into the next Room, and found that my poor Favorite Puss had made her Escape. She had gnawed in sunder the Strings of a Lattice Work, with which I thought I had Sufficiently secured the Window, and which I preferred to any other sort of Blind, because it admitted Plenty of Air. [From t] hence I hastened to the Kitchen, where I [saw the] redoubtable Tom Freeman, who told [me, that] having seen her just after she had [dropped] into the Street, he attempted to Cover [her with] his Hat, but she Screamed out, and [leaped] directly over his Head. I then desired him [to pur]sue as fast as possible, & added Richard Colman to the Chase, as being Nimbler & carrying less Belly than Tom; not expecting to see her again, but desirous, if possible, to Learn what became of her. In somewhat less than an Hour, Richard returned allmost Breathless, with the following Account. That soon after he began to

[1] The manuscript of this letter is badly torn, and the bracketed areas indicate approximately the number of letters missing. Those words supplied in brackets are taken from *Hayley*, iii. 49–51; the first paragraph of this letter is not in *Hayley*.

Run he left Tom behind him, and came in Sight of a most numerous Hunt, consisting of Men, Women, Children, and Dogs; that he did his best to keep back the Dogs, and presently outstripp'd the Crowd, so that the Race was at last disputed between himself and Puss. She ran right through the Town, and down the Lane that leads to Dropshort. A little before she came to the House, he got the Start and turned her. She pushed for the Town again, and soon after she Enter'd it, sought Shelter in Mr. Wagstaff's Tan Yard, adjoining to Old Mr. Drake's. Sturges's Harvest men were at Supper, and saw her from the opposite Side of the way. There she encountered the Tan Pits full of Water, & while she was strug[gling out] of One Pit & Plunging into another, [and almost] drowned, one of the Men drew her [out by the ears,] and secured her. She was then [well washed in a] Bucket, to get the Lime out of her [coat, and] brought home in a Sack at 10 o'c[lock.] This Frolic cost us four Shillings, but you may suppose we did not grudge a Farthing of it. The poor Creature received only a little Hurt in one of her claws, and in one of her Ears, & is now almost as well as ever.

Your Book was cried at the Sunday Evening Meeting, but is not yet to be heard of.[2]

Mrs. Unwin has had a Return of her old Spasmodic Complaint, which makes Writing hurtfull to her; she has no Atrophy with it, & is better.

I do not call this an Answer to your Letter, but such as it is I send it, presuming upon that Interest I know you take in my minutest Concerns, which I cannot express better than in the Words of Terence a little Varied—Nihil Mei a Te Alienum Putas.[3]

Our Love attends you Both with Miss Catlett, & our Affectionate Remembrances [to] all your Houshold—Yours my Dear Friend Wm C. Augt. 21. 1780.

Mrs. Whitney was here yesterday. She came to Ask my Sage Advice in her disturbed and troublesome Affairs. She Spoke of you with great Affection & of Mrs. Newton. Regretted the Loss of that Instruction she should have received from your Conversation had you been at Olney, and expressed the most Earnest Longings for a Letter.

[2] Newton's *Letters, Sermons, and A Review of Ecclesiastical History* (Edinburgh, 1780).

[3] *The Self-Tormentor*, 77: 'Whatever affects me is of concern to you.' Terence's line reads: 'Humani nil a me alienum puto': 'I hold that what affects another man affects me.'

MRS. COWPER Thursday, 31 August 1780

Address: Mrs. Cowper Park Street / Grosvenor Square / London.
Postmarks: 1/SE and OULNEY
Panshanger Collection

My dear Cousin,

I am obliged to you for your long Letter, which did not seem so, and for your short one, which was more than I had any Reason to Expect. Short as it was it convey'd to me two Interesting Articles of Intelligence, an account of your Recovery from a Fever, and of Lady Cowper's Death.[1] The latter was, I suppose, to be expected, for by what Remembrance I have of her Ladyship, who was never much acquainted with her, she had reached those Years that are always found upon the Borders of another World. As for you, your Time of Life is comparatively of a youthfull Date. You may think of Death as much as you please, (you cannot think of it too much) but I hope you will Live to think of it many Years. It costs me not much Difficulty to Suppose that my Friends who were already grown Old, when I saw them last, are Old Still. But it costs me a good deal sometimes to think of those who were at that time Young, as being Older than they were. Not having been an Eye=Witness of the Change that Time has made in them, and my former Idea of them not being corrected by Observation, it remains the same; my Memory presents me with their Image unimpaired, and while it retains the Resemblance of what they were, forgets that by this time the Picture may have lost much of its Likeness, through the Alteration that Succeeding years have made in the Original. I know not what Impressions Time may have made upon your Person, for while his Claws (as our Grann'am called them)[2] strike deep Furrows in some Faces, he seems to Sheath them with much Tenderness as if fearfull of doing Injury to others. But though an Enemy to the Person, he is a Friend to the Mind, and you have found him so. Though even in this Respect his Treatment of us depends upon what he meets with at our Hands; if we Use him well and Listen to his Admonitions & Instructions, he is a Friend indeed, but otherwise the worst of Enemies, who takes from us daily something that we valued, &

[1] Lady Georgiana Carteret Cowper, the widow of William Cowper, 2nd Earl Cowper (1709–64), died on 25 Aug. 1780. Her will was proved on 3 Sept.

[2] Pennington Goodere Cowper (d. 1727).

gives us nothing better in its stead. It is well with them who like you, can stand a' tip:toe on the Mountain:top of Human Life, look down with Pleasure upon the Valley they have passed, and sometimes stretch their Wings in joyfull Hope of a happy Flight into Eternity. Yet a little while and your Hope will be accomplished.

We are obliged to your Mother and your Sister for their kind Remembrances. Mrs. Unwin is still afflicted with a Nervous Malady, to which I beleive this East Wind which has lasted so long, contributes not a little. She begs me to present her Respects. When you see my Aunt,[3] & when you write to Mrs. Maitland,[4] assure them of my Affectionate Regards, & of the Pleasure I have in hearing of their Welfare. When you can favor me with a little Account of your own Family without Inconvenience, I shall be glad to receive it, for though Separated from my Kindred by little more than half a Century of Miles, I know as little of their Concerns as if Oceans & Continents were interposed between us.

Yours my Dear Cousin
Wm Cowper.

Augt. 31. 1780.

JOHN NEWTON — Thursday, 31 August 1780

Princeton[1]

Augt. 31. 1780.

My dear Sir—

The Curate and Church warden,
And eke Exciseman too,
Have treated poor Tom Raban
As if he was a Jew.

For they have sent him packing
No more in Church to work,
Whatever may be lacking,
As if he was a Turk.

[3] Judith Cowper Madan, C's correspondent. [4] Penelope Madan Maitland.

[1] The concluding portion and the signature to this letter are missing. The poem which opens this letter was first published in *Southey*.

Thus carry they the Farce on,
Which is great Cause of Grief,
Untill that *Page* the Parson
Turn over a *New Leaf.*

Thus Sings the Muse, & tho' her fav'rite Cue
Is Fiction, yet her Song is sometimes true.

At least we are much misinformed if the foregoing Tale be not so. Bright Andrews's Son is employed as Church Carpenter instead of Mr. Raban, and another man has been employed to make Sixteen Coffins, though if Mr. Raban had not sold him the Boards, he could not have found Materials to make them with. Besides all this, we have heard a Rumor which at present is so confused and full of Obscurity as not to be quite intelligible, that a Storm is gathering from the D—h quarter, which threatens both Mr. Robinson[2] & Mr. Raban. It is said to have been raised by Maurice Smith, whose Quarrel with Mr. Raban is that Mr. Page can't Preach to please him. It is certain that the said church Warden Smith & Tolson the Exciseman did lately repair to the House of Mr. Raban, and there expostulate with him in very angry & unhandsome Terms upon that Subject, which, being equal in Zeal and Knowledge, they were well qualified to do. Mr. Sample,[3] who happen'd to be there, was Mr. Raban's Second, & had the Courage to address himself to Mr. Smith in these Terms, 'I'll tell you what Mr. Smith, I do really think you are a very Meddlesome Fellow.' What further passed on the Occasion we have not heard, nor perhaps would it be worth relating, only as it serves as a Specimen of that Disorder & Confusion into which every thing has been thrown in this Parish, by Mr. Brown's two unhappy Appointments.[4]

[2] James Robinson (d. Dec. 1781) (*O.P.R.*, p. 396). See C to Newton, 10 Aug. 1780, n. 3 for details on the Warrington Pew controversy.

[3] Nathaniel Sample who was buried on 9 June 1785 (*O.P.R.*, p. 412).

[4] Moses Browne (1704–87) was the absentee rector of Olney. In his answer to C's letter, Newton (2 Sept. 1780, Princeton) reflected upon the situation: 'Mr. Browne is old & probably will not live a great many years, but perhaps long enough to make them heartily weary of their choice [Page]. . . . I am very sorry Mr. Raban is likely to suffer in his temporals—I love him—& he has a large family. . . . He had too much of the Spirit of a Courtier, servile to his superiors, overbearing & harsh to those whom he considered beneath him, careful for himself, but devoid of much compassion to others. But he has known little hitherto of the inconstancy of Court-favor.'

WILLIAM UNWIN Sunday, 3 September 1780

Address: Revd. William Unwin at / Stock near / Ingatestone / Essex.
Postmarks: 4/SE *and* OULNEY
British Library

My dear Friend,

I am glad you are so provident, and that while you are yet young, you have furnished yourself with the Means of Comfort in Old Age. Your Crutch and your Pipe may be of Use to you (and may they be so) should your years be extended to an Antidiluvian Date. And for your present Accommodation, you seem to want nothing but a Clerk called Snuffle, and a Sexton of the Name of Skeleton, to make your Ministerial Equipage complete.

I think I have read as much of the first Volume of the Biographia as I shall ever read. I find it very Amusing; more so perhaps than it would have been, had they Sifted their Characters with more Exactness, and admitted none but those who had in some way or other Entitled themselves to Immortality by deserving well of the Public. Such a Compilation would perhaps have been more Judicious, though I confess it would have afforded less Variety. The Priests and the Monks of earlier, and the Doctors of later Days, who have signalized themselves by nothing but a Controversial Pamphlet, long since thrown by, and never to be perused again, might have been forgot without Injury or Loss to the National character for Learning or Genius. This observation suggested to me the following Lines, which may serve to illustrate my meaning, and at the same time to give my Criticism a Sprightlier Air.

Oh fond Attempt! to give a deathless Lot
To Names ignoble, Born to be forgot.
In vain recorded in Historic Page,
They Court the Notice of a future Age,
Those twinkling tiny Lustres of the Land,
Drop One by One from Fame's neglecting Hand,
Lethæan Gulphs receive them as they fall,
And dark Oblivion soon absorbs them All.
So when a child (as playfull children use)
Has burnt to Tinder a stale last Year's News,
The Flame extinct, he views the Roving Fire,

There goes my Lady, & there goes the Squire,
There goes the Parson, Oh illustrious Spark!
And there—scarce less illustrious—goes the Clerk.[1]

Virgil admitts none but Worthies into the Elysian Fields; I can not recollect the Lines in which he describes them all, but these in particular I well remember.

Quique sui memores Alios fecere Merendo,
Inventas aut qui Vitam excoluêre per Artes.[2]

A chaste and scrupulous Conduct like His, would well become the Writer of National Biography; but enough of This, I am called upon by a different Subject.

Mr. Cawthorne writes Word that there is a small Piece of Land belonging to the Estate in Ely, so bad that it will never pay the Expence of Draining. He advises your Mother therefore to have it Sold, which with your consent, she is willing to do, and to remitt you Half the Price of it.[3]

Our Respects attend Miss Shuttleworth, with many Thanks for her intended Present. Some Purses derive All their Value from their Contents, but These will have an Intrinsic Value of their own, and though mine should be often Empty, which is not an improbable Supposition, I shall still Esteem it highly on its own Account.

I must answer your Questions about Plumbs & Pears in my next.

Our Joint Love & affectionate Remembrances attend all the Family—Yours Wm C.
Sep. 3. 1780

If you could meet with a Second Hand Virgil, Ditto Homer, both Iliad & Odyssey, together with a Clavis, for I have no Lexicon, & all tolerably cheap, I shall be obliged to you if you will make the Purchase.

I Return you Kiss for Kiss.—

1 These lines were first published in *1782*. C is probably referring to the first volume (Aaron and Julius to Ralph Bathurst), published in 1778, of the second, enlarged edition of *Biographia Brittanica.*

2 C has reversed lines 663–4 from *Aeneid*, vi: 'They who have through service become worthy of remembrance / They who have enriched life by discovering truths.'

3 See n. 1, C to Hill, 1 Mar. 1778. It appears that Mrs. Unwin did not sell the property in 1780.

[JOHN NEWTON] Tuesday, 5 September 1780

Barham Johnson (*copy*)

Septbr 5th. 1780

My dear Sir

My Hurdy Gurdy being in exact unison with your Violincello, has drawn music from it that has even excelled its own. The Church is to be shut up for the next fortnight &c.

We are this instant returned from walking, & have wearied ourselves with endeavoring in vain to recover a track which you will remember. Our point in view was that Clump of trees which you used to call your Oratory. But the green Bank walk which led to it is ploughed up, & the way is intersected with hedges which had no existence 10 years ago. Which hedges have neither gap nor stile. We were obliged therefore to sidle away to the left, & after much hobbling & stumbling over Bean Stubble & other rough ground, were so happy as to find a gate thrown off the hinges which let us into the road again almost at the bottom of Weston lane.

Mr Page is gone a journey—Some Carpenter's work is to be done in the Church on this occasion, but not by Mr Raban, & Some Glazier's work, but not by Mr Hull.[1] The Church-warden's plan is to do all he can (to use his own phrase) to torment the good ones. Mr. P—'s companions are Harold, Talbot, Smith, & Tolson. He entertains them with American stories, & they entertain him by hearing them.

WILLIAM UNWIN Thursday, 7 September 1780

Address: The Revd. William Unwin at / Stock near / Ingatestone / Essex.
Postmarks: 8/SE *and* OULNEY
British Library

My dear Friend—

As many Gentlemen as there are in the World, who have Children, and Heads capable of reflecting upon the important Subject of their Education, so many Opinions there are about it; many of them Just

[1] Probably William Hull (christened 23 Mar. 1743, *O.P.R.*, p. 289), whose father William (d. 1771) had been the glazier at Olney.

and Sensible, though almost All differing from each other. With respect to the Education of Boys, I think they are generally made to draw in Latin & Greek Trammels[1] too soon. It is pleasing no doubt to a Parent to see his Child already in some sort, a Proficient in those Languages, at an Age when most others are entirely ignorant of them; but hence it often happens that a Boy who could construe a Fable in Æsop at 5 or 7 Years of Age, having exhausted his little Stock of Attention & Diligence in making that notable Acquisition, grows weary of his Task, conceives a Dislike of Study, & perhaps makes but a very indifferent Progress afterward. The Mind and the Body have in this respect a striking Resemblance of each other. In childhood they are both Nimble, but not Strong; they can Skip and Frisk about with wonderfull Agility, but hard Labor Spoils them both. In maturer years they become less Active, but more vigorous, more capable of a fixt Application, and can make themselves Sport with That which a little earlier would have affected them with intolerable Fatigue. I should recommend it to you therefore, (but after all you must Judge for yourself) to allott the two next years of little John's Scholarship, to Writing and Arithmetic, together with which for Variety's sake and because it is capable of being formed into an Amusement, I would mingle Geography. A Science which if not attended to betimes, is seldom made an Object of much Consideration; essentially necessary to the Accomplishment of a Gentleman, yet (as I know by sad Experience) imperfectly, if at all inculcated in the Schools. Lord Spencer's Son when he was 4 years of Age, knew the Situation of every Kingdom, Country, City, River, & remarkable Mountain in the World. For this Attainment, which I Suppose his Father had never made, he was indebted to a Plaything; having been accustomed to amuse himself with those Maps which are cut into several Compartments, so as to be thrown into a Heap of confusion, that they may be put together again with an exact Coincidence of all their Angles and Bearings so as to form a perfect Whole.[2]

If he begins Latin and Greek at Eight or even at 9 years of Age, it is surely soon enough. Seven years, the usual allowance for those Acquisitions, are more than sufficient for the Purpose, especially with His Readiness in Learning. For you would hardly wish to have him

[1] Anything that confines or restrains (*O.E.D.*).

[2] John, 1st Earl Spencer (1734–83) and his son, George, 2nd Earl Spencer (1758–1834).

qualified for the University before 15, a Period in my Mind much too early for it, & when he could hardly be trusted there without the utmost Dangers to his Morals. Upon the whole you will perceive, that in my Judgment the Difficulty as well as the Wisdom consists more in Bridling in and keeping back a Boy of his Parts, than in pushing him forward. If therefore at the End of the two next years, instead of putting a Grammar into his Hand, you should allow him to amuse himself with some agreeable Writers upon the Subjects of natural Philosophy, for another year, I think it would Answer well. There is a Book called Cosmotheoria Puerilis,[3] there are Derham's Physico and Astrotheology[4] together with several others in the same Manner, very Intelligible even to a child, & full of usefull Instruction.

Plumbs & Pears in my next.

Your Mother's Love & mine attend you All.

Yours affectionately Wm Cowper.

Sepr. 7. 1780

WILLIAM UNWIN — Sunday, 17 September 1780

Address: The Revd. William Unwin at / Stock near / Ingatestone / Essex.
Postmark: 18/SE
British Library

Sepr. 17. /80.

My dear Friend,

You desire my further Thoughts on the Subject of Education. I send you such as had for the most part occurred to me when I wrote last, but could not be Comprized in a single Letter. They are indeed on a different Branch of this interesting Theme, but not less important than the former.

I think it your Happiness, & wish you to think it so yourself, that you are in every respect qualified for the Task of Instructing

[3] [Andrew Baxter (1686–1750)], *Matho; or, the Cosmotheoria Puerilis. A Dialogue, in Which the First Principles of Philosophy and Astronomy are Accomodated to the Capacity of Young Persons, or Such As Have Yet No Tincture of These Sciences. Hence the Principles of Natural Religion are Deduced* was first printed in Latin in 1738; it was afterwards translated by Baxter (editions in 1740, 1745, 1765).

[4] William Derham (1657–1735), *Physico-Theology, or a Demonstration of the Being and Attributes of God from His Works of Creation* (1713); and *Astro-Theology, or a Demonstration of the Being and Attributes of God from a Survey of the Heavens* (1715).

your Son, and preparing him for the University, without committing him to the Care of a Stranger. In my Judgment, a Domestic Education deserves the Preference to a Public one on an Hundred Accounts which I have neither Time nor Room to mention; I shall only Touch upon two or three that I cannot but consider as having a Right to your most Earnest Attention.

In a Public School, or indeed in any School, his Morals are sure to be but little attended to, and his Religion not at all. If he can catch the Love of Virtue from the fine things that are Spoken of it in the classics, and the Love of Holiness from a customary Attendance upon such Preaching as he is likely to Hear, it will be well, but I am sure you have had too many Opportunities to observe the Inefficacy of such Means, to Expect any such Advantage from them. In the mean time the more powerfull Influence of bad Example, and perhaps bad Company, will continually Counterwork these only Preservatives he can meet with, and may possibly send him Home to you at the End of 5 or 6 years, such as you will be sorry to See him. You escaped, indeed, the contagion yourself, but a few Instances of an happy Exemption from a general Malady, are no Sufficient Warrant to conclude that it is therefore not Infectious, or may be encounter'd without Danger.

You have seen too much of the World, and are a Man of too much Reflection not to have observed, that in proportion as the Sons of a Family approach to years of Maturity, they Lose a Sense of Obligation to their Parents, and seem at last almost divested of that Tender Affection which the nearest of All Relations seems to demand from them. I have often Observed it myself, and have always thought I could sufficiently Account for it, without laying all the Blame upon the Children. While they continue in their Parents's House, they are every Day obliged, and every Day reminded how much it is their Interest as well as Duty, to be Obliging and Affectionate in Return. But at 8 or 9 Years of Age, the Boy goes to School. From that Moment he becomes a Stranger in his Father's House; the Course of Parental Kindnesses is intercepted; the Smiles of his Mother, the tender Admonitions and the Solicitous Care of both his Parents are no longer before his Eyes, year after year he feels himself more and more detached from them, 'till at last he is so effectually weaned from the Connection, as to find himself happier any where than in their Company. I should have been glad of a Frank for this Letter, for I

have said but little of what I could say upon the Subject, and perhaps I may not be able to catch it by the End again. If I can I shall add to it hereafter.

The Land in Question consists of 18 Acres, is fit only to be digged up for Turf. Your Mother thanks you for your Readiness to Join in the Sale of it, & will write to Mr. Cawthorne to Enquire whether he thinks it will be worth while to dispose of it, considering the Expence of the Title Deed.

I understood it to be the Practise for the Purchaser to Pay the Lawyer.

The Breda[1] is the best late Apricot, and the Empress (or Imperatrice) Plumb[2] is that which your Mother principally recommends. It turns to a fine dried Sweet meat upon the Tree, but must not be gather'd sooner.

Yours Wm C.

I thank you for the Offer to Lend me the Books I mentioned, but Borrowing will not serve my Purpose.[3]

JOHN NEWTON Sunday, 24 September 1780

Princeton (*copy*)

My dear Sir!

I should have answered your Letter sooner, & have acknowledged Mrs. Newton's Favor by an earlier Opportunity if it had been in my power.[1] But having dismissed our Gardiner[2] for manifold good Causes

[1] 'The *Breda* Apricot (as it is called from its being brought from thence into *England*) was originally brought from *Africa*: This is a large roundish Fruit, changing to a deep yellow when ripe; the Flesh is soft, full of Juice, and within Side; the Stone is rounder and larger than any of the other Sorts: This is the best Apricot we have, and when ripened on a Standard, is preferable to all other Kinds.' Philip Miller, *The Gardener's Dictionary*, 7th edn., 2 vols. (Dublin, 1764), i. N2^{v}.

[2] Imperatrice, *i.e.* the Empress. This is a large, round Fruit, of a violet-red Colour, very much powder'd with a whitish Bloom; the Flesh is yellow, cleaves to the Stone, and is of an agreeable Flavour. This ripens about the Middle of *September*.' Philip Miller, *The Gardener's Dictionary*, 2nd edn. (London, 1733), 6Q2^{v}.

[3] See postscript of C to Unwin, 3 Sept.

---

[1] Probably Newton to C, 2 Sept. (Princeton). Mrs. Newton had sent a vegetable or fruit with her husband's letter.

[2] The gardener Darlin was replaced by William Kitchener prior to 11 Nov. 1780. See C to Newton of that date.

& reasons us thereunto moving, a great deal of additional employment has consequently fallen into my hands, & I am sometimes so weary before my Morning business is finished, that I am not capable of writing.

If I was not disqualified for the Society of good Men, there are few of that description who would be more welcome to me than Mr. Bull.[3] His eminent spirituallity would recommend him to any man desirous of an edifying Companion. But my condition renders me incapable of receiving or imparting a real benefit.

The short remainder of my Life, the beginning of which was spent in Sin, & the latter part of which has been poisoned with Despair, must be trifled away in Amusements which I despise too much to be entertained with; or sacrificed at the foot of a regret which can know neither End or abatement. I am conversible upon any Topic but the only one which He would wish to converse upon, & being condemned to a state which I in vain endeavor to describe, because it is incredible, I am out of the reach of consolation, & am indeed a fit Companion for Nobody. If Mrs. Unwin attempts to encourage me, & tells me there is Hope, I can bear it with some degree of Patience, but I can do no more. From her however I can endure it, either because I have been long accustom'd to such language from her Lips, or because it is impossible for any thing that she speaks to give me pain. But I should be otherwise affected by the same things spoken by Mr. Bull; & all that he would gain by conversing with me would be summed up in the single word, astonishment. He would wonder that a Man whose views of the Scripture are just like his own, who is a Calvinist from experience, & knows his election, should be furnished with a Shield of despair impenetrable to every argument by which he might attempt to comfort him. But so it is, & in the end it will be accounted for.

It is impossible not to approve highly of the plan you mention. You have two encouragements to undertake it, the one, that you will execute it without difficulty because you are Master of the subject, & the other, that it can hardly fail of being singularly usefull. But if you begin, you must resolve not to intermit your labors 'till you have finished the Task. If a Work is interrupted in the middle, every day increases an Author's unwillingness to resume it, &

[3] The Revd. William Bull (1738–1814), Independent minister of Newport Pagnell, with whom C was to be closely associated in the future.

slackens that fervor & earnestness of Spirit which prompted him to undertake it. So that either, he never returns to it at all, or if he does, he finds it difficult, perhaps impossible to rekindle in himself that Zeal & Energy of thought that is necessary to the happy Performance of it.

We beg Mrs. Newton to accept our Thanks for the Fish, they were exceedingly good, & came perfectly sweet. Mrs. Unwin sends her Love. She is better, but not well. It is strange that the Ladies who are said to love talking are generally glad to shuffle off the Business of writing upon the Men. She promises fair however, & is very apt to be as good as her Word.

Yours my dear Sir
Wm. Cowper.

Sepr. 24th—
1780.

With two curious fivetoed Fowls from Lord Northampton's Menagerie, fed by Squire Cowper; & two Persian Melons. (Added by dear Mrs. Unwin.)[4]

[MRS. NEWTON] Thursday, 5 October 1780

Princeton (*copy*)

Dear Madam—

When a Lady speaks it is not civil to make her wait a week for an Answer. I received your Letter within this Hour & foreseeing that the Garden will engross much of my time for some Days to come, have seized the present opportunity to acknowledge it. I congratulate you on Mr. Newton's safe arrival at Ramsgate, making no doubt but that he reached that Place without difficulty or danger, the Road thither from Canterbury being so good as to afford no room for either.[1] He has now a view of the Element with which he was once so familiar, but which I think he has not even seen for many years.

[4] The postscript enumerating the fowl and fruit that accompanied the letter was written by Mrs. Unwin. The words in parentheses calling attention to this are by C. For Lord Northampton, see n. 1, C to Hill, 9 Jan. 1772.

[1] Later in the month, C composed 'To the Reverend Mr Newton On His Return from Ramsgate'. See C to Newton, 13 Oct.

The sight of his old Acquaintance will revive in his Mind a pleasing recollection of past deliverances, & while he looks at him from the Beach, he may say, You have formerly given me trouble enough, but I have cast Anchor now where your Billows can never reach me. Tis happy for him that he can say so—There are some for whom it would be better to be swallowed up in the deeps of the Ocean, than to sit scribbling quietly & at their ease as I do. Yet it is so natural to shrink back from the thoughts of Eternity, that though I know my days are prolonged, not in mercy, but in judgment, I cannot help preferring the calmness of my present situation to a storm that would endanger my life, though a Life that can bring forth nothing but evil to myself, whatever others may think of it. I did not mean to say one Word of all this when I began, but it sprang up suddenly in my Mind, & what does so, is almost sure to be transferred to the Paper, when I am writing to you or Mr. Newton.

Dear Madam, we both love Fish, are obliged to you for what you have sent, & for what you had a design to send, but when we think of the expence you are at in doing it, we really grudge ourselves the treat with which you have favoured us. The Oysters came safe, & were remarkably good. Some people here are likely to pay dear for loving Fish. Mr. Pell, Mr. Lucy, and Johnston of the George,[2] are all under prosecution for poaching in Ravenstone Water.[3]

Mrs. Unwin returns you many thanks for your anxiety upon her account, she has at some times been very ill indeed, & her Experience having in some respects differed from what it used to be her Spirits have Sunk Lower than they did in her former illness. Her health however, is Considerably mended upon the whole, So as to afford us a hope that it will be re-established. She would be Glad if this Subject might be so far a Secret as that the news of it might not reach to Stock, and she herself has taken Care that it shall not be known in the North.

It will be a pleasure to me to Contribute to the Satisfaction of

[2] Messrs. Pell and Johnston are unidentified. Mr. James Lucy is referred to by C in his letter of 19 July 1784, and Mr. Lucy had his windows broken when Tom Freeman's horse ran off. See C to Newton, 5 June 1780.

[3] The parish of Ravenstone lies between the Northamptonshire boundary and the Ouse. The Finch family held the manor of Ravenstone. George Finch was the owner from 1769 to 1826. 'In the 16th c. the prior had a "manor-place" here with a court in which there were fish-ponds. These were apparently filled by the chalybeat spring from which a little stream now flows south into the Ouse. . . .' *The Victoria History of the Counties of England. Bucking hamshire*. 4 vols. (1927), iv. 440.

any friend of yours in the Gardening Way, but especially to your own. The last winter handled Our Carnations So roughly, that our borders are extremely poor in that article. The few layers I have been able to make this Summer I shall secure in Frames where the Frosts that are coming on will not affect them. These I hope will afford me a large increase next Summer, & then I shall be happy to supply you. I have reason given me to expect a parcel of Seeds from the West Indies, if I am not disappointed your friend shall have a share of them.

We did not know till within this week that Miss Catlett was not in London. Hannah, who has escaped the Small Pox, is very well, & does not forget your kindness to her. Since you gave her a Bonnet, she thinks that every Bonnet she sees was your gift to the Wearer.

Our Love attends you.

Yours dear Madam

Wm. Cowper.

Octr. 5th
1780.

WILLIAM UNWIN — Thursday, 5 October 1780

British Library

My dear Friend,

Now for the Sequel—You have Anticipated one of my Arguments in favor of a Private Education, therefore I need say but little about it. The Folly of Supposing that the Mother Tongue, in some respects the most difficult of all Tongues, may be acquired without a Teacher, is predominant in all the Public Schools that I have ever heard of. To Pronounce it well, to Speak and to Write it with Fluency and Elegance, are no Easy Attainments; not One in 50 of those who pass through Westminster & Eaton, arrive at any remarkable Proficiency in these Accomplishments; and they that do, are more indebted to their own Study and Application for it, than to any Instructions received there. In general, there is nothing so Pedantic as the Stile of a Schoolboy, if he Aims at any Stile at all, and if he does not, he is of course inelegant, and perhaps ungrammatical. A Defect no doubt in great Measure owing to the Want of Cultivation; for the same Lad that is often commended for his Latin, frequently would deserve

to be whipped for his English, if the Fault were not more his Master's than his own.

I know not where this Evil is so likely to be prevented as at Home. Supposing always nevertheless, (which is the Case in your Instance) that the Boy's Parents, and their Acquaintance, are Persons of Elegance and Taste themselves. For to Converse with those who Converse with Propriety, and to be directed to such Authors as have refined & improved the Language by their Productions, are Advantages which he cannot elsewhere enjoy in an equal Degree. And though it requires some time to regulate the Taste and fix the Judgment, and these Effects must be gradually wrought even upon the best Understanding, yet I suppose much less Time will be necessary for the Purpose than could at first be imagined, because the Opportunities of Improvement are continual.

I Promised to say Little on this Topic, & I have said so much that if I had not a Frank, I must Burn my Letter & begin again.

A Public Education is often recommended as the most effectual Remedy for that Bashfull and aukward constraint so Epidemical among the Youth of our Country. But I verily beleive that instead of being a Cure, it is often the Cause of it. For 7 or 8 Years of his Life the Boy has hardly seen or conversed with a Man; or a Woman, except the Maids at his Boarding House. A Gentleman or a Lady are consequently such Novelties to him, that he is perfectly at a Loss to know what Sort of Behavior he should preserve before them. He Plays with his Buttons or the Strings of his Hat, he blows his Nose & hangs down his Head, is conscious of his own Deficiency to a Degree that makes him quite unhappy, and Trembles lest any one should speak to him because That would quite Overwhelm him. Is not all this Miserable Shyness evidently the Effect of his Education? To me it appears to be so. If he saw good Company every day, he would never be terrified at the Sight of it, and a Room full of Ladies and Gentlemen would Alarm him no more, than the Chairs they Sit on. Such is the Effect of Custom.

I need add nothing further upon this Subject, because I beleive Little John is as likely to be exempted from this Weakness as most Young Gentlemen we shall meet with. He seems to have his Father's Spirit in this respect, in whom I could never discern the least Trace of Bashfullness, tho' I have often heard him complain of it. Under your Management, and the Influence of your Example, I think he can

hardly fail to Escape it. If he does, he Escapes that which makes many a Man uncomfortable for Life, and has Ruined not a few, by forcing them into mean and dishonorable Company, where only they could be free and cheerfull.

Connexions formed at School are said to be lasting, and often Beneficial. There are two or three Stories of this kind upon Record, which would not be so constantly Cited as they are whenever this Subject happens to be mentioned, if the Chronicle that preserves their Remembrance had many beside to Boast of. For my own part, I found such Friendships, though warm enough in their Commencement, surprisingly liable to Extinction. And of Seven or Eight whom I had Selected for Intimates out of above 300, in 10 Years' time not One was left me. The Truth is, that there may be, and often is, an Attachment of One Boy to Another, that looks very like a Friendship, and while they are in Circumstances that enable them mutually to Oblige and to Assist each other, Promises well and bids fair to be lasting. But they are no sooner separated from each other by Entering into the World at large, than other Connexions and new Employments in which they no longer share together, efface the Remembrance of what passed in earlier Days, and they become Strangers to each other for ever. Add to this, that the Man frequently differs so much from the Boy, his Principles, Manners, Temper and Conduct undergo so great an Alteration, that we no longer Recognize in him our Old Playfellow, but find him utterly unworthy and unfit for the Place he once held in Our Affections. To close this Article as I did the last, by applying myself immediately to the present concern, Little John is happily placed above all Occasion for Dependence upon such precarious Hopes, and need not be sent to School in quest of some Great Man in Embryo who may possibly make his Fortune.

I have just left myself Room to return Miss Shuttleworth our very sincere Thanks for our respective Purses, and to assure her that we shall value as we ought her obliging Present, and wear them to the last Thread.

Your Mother sends her Love & Hopes you will remember the Franks. Mine with Hers to All at Stock.

Yours my Dear Friend
Wm Cowper.

Octr. 5. 1780

JOHN NEWTON Friday, 13 October 1780

Princeton (*copy*)

Octr. 13. 1780.

My dear Friend

I congratulate you on your Safe return, but especially on your recovery from your late illness. This is the second time that the same letter has brought us the news of your indisposition & restoration and thus we have escaped the anxiety we should otherwise have felt upon your account.—

I followed you in fancy to a coast with which I am not unacquainted,[1] and to a Country where I spent some of the unhappiest days of my life. I too have been at Ramsgate, and at the North Foreland, have stood upon the same spot, and contemplated the same Expanse of Waters. But with very different thoughts, and with far other expectations. The recollection of that season is not pleasant to me now, tho' once it was so. While the sun shone I could look with Comfort at the storm that was overblown but since a blacker cloud, of which I can see no end has succeeded it yields me no Consolation, to have escaped one tempest, only to be overtaken by a worse. Such are the reflections your Journey to the Isle of Thanet has awakened in me, so when I have transcribed a few lines into which I cast them,[2] I will take my leave of a subject which teems with nothing but the painful & the melancholic.[3]

That ocean you of late surveyed
  Those Rocks I too have seen
But, I, afflicted, & dismayed,
  You, tranquil and serene.

You from the flood Controulling steep
  Saw stretched before your view

[1] This letter is in response to Newton's of 11 Oct. (Princeton) in which Newton mentions that he was tempted to go to sea again. 'I had one delightful morning at the North Foreland, when I stood on top of the light house & contemplated my old acquaintance the Sea.' However, Newton also recalled the unhappiness of the seafaring years and expressed his sentiments in a poem of which these are the concluding lines: 'Rememb'ring well their perils once were mine, / I fear for them, tho' now secure myself.'

[2] These verses were first published in *Hayley*.

[3] See C to Unwin of [July] and 17 July 1779.

With conscious joy, the threat'ning deep,
  No longer such to you.

To me, the waves that ceaseless broke
  Upon the dang'rous coast,
Hoarsely & ominously spoke
  Of all my treasure lost.

Your sea of troubles you have pass'd,
  And found the peaceful shore,
I, tempest tost, and wrecked at last,
  Come home to port, No more.

JOHN NEWTON Sunday, 29 October 1780

Princeton (*copy*)

My dear Friend.

Though it was my purpose yesterday to write to you by the opportunity Mr. Widford's[1] Journey to town affords me, I waked this morning in a frame of mind so little suited to the occasion that I should certainly have postponed my letter had not that Gentleman's distress overpowered for a few minutes my present sense of my own. He will be the bearer but does not know that he is to be the subject. I do not mean to tell his story for him which he is very able to do for himself, and shall only say therefore that the cause of his uneasiness is to be found in his late unhappy marriage, and in the straitness of his circumstances, from which he apprehends the very worst consequences to his children. You will see him much altered. His spirits are broken, and his bodily strength declines fast. He has no Appetite, says he does not eat an ounce in a day, and hardly sleeps at all. Such are the sad effects of an anxiety he cannot shake

[1] John Whitford was pastor of the Independent Congregation at Olney from 1776 to 1780. Whitford had originally known Newton at Liverpool and had gone to Olney in 1775 to visit him. Shortly after Whitford's visit, the minister of the Independent Congregation died, and it was arranged that Whitford, a former Methodist, should succeed him.

off for a moment; and which continually preys upon him with a vehemence that visibly wears him out. Indeed Mrs. U. and I are both of opinion that unless some remedy can be found, either his concern will prove his death or that if he lives, it will be only to suffer what is incomparably worse than death, the deprivation of his senses. He has at times that flashing wildness in his eyes, and is of a constitution and temperament that give those who wish him well, but too much reason to apprehend the worst.

He had (as men much afflicted and with little hope are apt to do) formed many schemes, but most of them visionary and vain. Accordingly he has relinquished them all, except the only reasonable one, that of communicating his distress to you. I know how difficult it is to provide for a man with such a family as his, and never have encouraged him to expect much from this measure. If the remedy was in your own hand, he would not want it long, but whether you can assist him or not in his temporal affairs at least you will afford him that good counsel and that compassionate attention, which next to a perfect cure, are the most desirable applications to a case like his. He has conversed unreservedly with me upon this melancholy subject more than once, which has engaged me to say thus much, not to plead his cause, or to move your pity of which there is no need, but to discharge my own mind of what I have felt upon his account, and to act the part of a man who knows what sorrow of heart is, towards a man overwhelmed with it.

If this unceasing Rain has not prevented it, the Warrington people had formed a design of coming down in a body this morning to take possession of their pew. A measure that will probably be attended with confusion enough, but the natural consequence of Mr. Page's encroachment.

Mr. Raban was very happy in receiving a testimony of your approbation of his & Mr. Parry's conduct and was observed to pray that evening with uncommon liberty and affection.—By all accounts they were both very acceptable & well attended.—

Many thanks for the Cocoa Nuts. Mrs. Unwin sent Miss Catlett one of them yesterday with a pot of sweetmeats.

I wish you may be able to tell us in your next that Mrs. Newton is recovered from her indisposition. Mrs. U. is so much interested in my recovery that her own waits for it—She is indifferent and that is the best account I can give of her—

Our respects attend Mr. Bull, and our wishes for his better health. Can you give us any tidings of Mr.——.[2] We have an ugly report about him at Olney.

Yours my dear Sir with our joint love to yourself & Mrs. Newton

W.C.—

Oct. 29.

WILLIAM UNWIN Thursday, 9 November 1780

British Library[1]

I wrote the following last Summer. The Tragical Occasion of it really happen'd at the next House to ours.[2] I am glad when I can find a Subject to work upon; a Lapidary I suppose accounts it a Laborious part of his Business to Rub away the Roughness of the Stone, but it is my Amusement; & if after all the Polishing I can give it, it discovers some little Lustre, I think myself well rewarded for my Pains.

On a Goldfinch Starved to Death
in his Cage.

Time was when I was free as Air,
The Thistle's downy Seed my Fare,
My Drink the Morning Dew,
I Perch'd at Will on ev'ry Spray,
My Form genteel, my Plumage gay,
My Strains for ever New.

[2] In his answer to C of *c.* 1 Nov. 1780 (Princeton), Newton comments upon the 'ugly report': 'If you have heard any thing amiss of Mr. Mayer, I am persuaded it is false. He is a thriving excellent young man. His zeal & fidelity rather exceeded his experience, & brought him into a little difficulty at Beckenham, which issued in his leaving it, but even those who thought him indiscreet, & who were most offended could not help admiring his spirit & honesty.' John Mayor (1756–1826) was appointed an assistant curate at Beckenham (St. George's) in 1778; he was appointed vicar at Shawbury near Shrewsbury in 1781.

[1] The first page of this letter is missing.

[2] Published in *1782*. The 'next House to ours' was probably Dick Coleman's.

2

But gaudy Plumage, Sprightly Strain,
And Form genteel were all in vain,
And of a transient Date,
For caught & Caged and Starv'd to Death,
In dying Sighs my little Breath
Soon pass'd the Wiry Grate.

3

Thanks gentle Swain for all my Woes,
And Thanks for this effectual Close
And Cure of ev'ry Ill:
More Cruelty could none Express,
And I, if you had Shew'n me less
Had been your Pris'ner still.

I shall charge you a Halfpenny a piece for ev'ry Copy I send you, the Short as well as the long. This is a sort of after clap you little expected, but I cannot possibly afford them at a cheaper Rate. If this Method of raising Money had occurred to me sooner, I should have made the Bargain sooner; but am glad I have Hit upon it at last. It will be a considerable Encouragement to my Muse, and Act as a powerfull Stimulus to my Industry. If the American War should last much longer, I may be obliged to Raise my Price, but this I shall not do without a real Occasion for it. It depends pretty much upon Lord North's Conduct in the Article of Supplies—if he Imposes an additional Tax on any thing that I deal in, the Necessity of this Measure on my part will be so apparent, that I dare say you will not Dispute it.

Your Mother desires me to Add her Love to mine which waits on you all as usual. She is much pleased with your Desire to hear from her, but having such an Industrious Secretary in me, she thought it the less necessary. She will Use her own Hand however, when her Nerves which are seldom well strung, and which this turbulent Weather particularly discomposes, will give her Leave.

Yours my dear Friend

Wm Cowper.

Novr. 9. 1780.

WILLIAM UNWIN *post* Thursday, 9 November 1780[1]

British Library

My dear Friend,

You are sometimes indebted to bad Weather, but more frequently to a dejected State of Mind, for my Punctuality as a Correspondent. This was the Case when I composed that Tragi:Comical Ditty[2] for which you Thank me; my Spirits were exceedingly Low, and having no Fool or Jester at hand, I resolved to be my own. The End was Answer'd, I Laughed myself, and I made you Laugh. Sometimes I pour out my Thoughts in a mournfull Strain, but these sable Effusions your Mother will not Suffer me to Send you, being resolved that nobody shall Share with me the Burthen of my Melancholy but herself. In general you may suppose that I am remarkably sad, when I seem remarkably Merry; The Effort we make to get rid of a Load, is usually violent in proportion to the Weight of it. I have seen at Sadler's Wells a tight little Fellow Dancing with a Fat Man upon his Shoulders; to those who Looked at him he seem'd insensible of the Incumbrance but if a Physician had felt his Pulse when the Feat was over, I suppose he would have found the Effect of it there. Perhaps you remember the Undertakers' Dance in the Rehearsal, which they perform in Crape Hatbands & Black Cloaks to the Tune of Hob or Nob, one of the Sprightliest Airs in the World.[3] Such is my Fiddling, and such is my Dancing; but they serve a purpose which at some certain times could not be so effectually promoted by any thing else.

I am informed that Thelyphthora is at last Encounter'd by a Writer of Abilities equal to the Task.[4] An Answer to that base:born Book was a grand Desideratum in the World of Literature. I call it so because it is the Spurious Issue of Scripture violated by Misinterpretation. The Mother is ashamed of the Brat, and disowns it in every

[1] This letter, from the comment on the October *Monthly Review* as a recent publication, probably belongs between C's letters of 9 Nov. and 2 Dec. 1780.

[2] The 'Tragi:Comical Ditty' is 'The Yearly Distress, Or, Tything Time at Stock' which is postmarked '30 OC' (British Library).

[3] C is referring to the antics directed by King Usher, and King Physician in Act IV, scene i of Villiers's play.

[4] C had heard of the review by the Revd. Samuel Badcock (1747–88) in the November issue of the *Monthly Review* (321–39) and he looked forward to seeing it and the earlier notice in the October issue (273–87).

Page, but the Father, (a Father is sometimes proud of his Bastard) Dandles it upon his Knee, and holds it up to the Admiration of all Beholders. This Champion for the Rights and Honors of Single Marriage, comes forth in the Monthly Review; I have not yet seen the first Specimen of his Performance which belongs to October, but I have order'd it down from London. The character I have received of it has pleased me much, and if I find it Answer upon the Perusal, I shall connect the detached Parts of it (for it is to be a Work of some continuance) and Bind them up together. It is high time this false Light should be extinguished; it has alarmed many Families, Misled many Readers, and confirmed not a few in Practices which their own Consciences condemn'd, 'till that Syren Song deceived them.—You will think perhaps I talk big for one that has never read it. But I am acquainted with the Principal Hinges on which the whole depends, and am persuaded that one Flash of Truth would melt them. Mr. Riland of Birmingham sent into this Country a String of 27 Printed Queries, unanswerable as he thinks, unless in such a way as must unavoidably induce a Necessity of adopting Mr. Madan's Plan.[5] But being persuaded that even I was a Match for such an Enemy, I ventured upon the formidable Task, and gave them 27 Answers. Indeed a child might have done the same, and I wonder less at the Author's Predilection in favor of his own conceptions, (which is a Partiality natural enough) than that he has found, and among Ministers too, Understandings so scantily enlighten'd, or so easily perverted, as to afford them welcome Entertainment.

I mourn with you over the tender Conscience of your Collector, whose Peace of Mind is so inconsistent with your Interest, that he cannot think he does his Duty unless he wrongs you.[6] You think the Man's Meaning is good; you have a World of Charity; what is it to Him from whose Purse the Tax is taken? It is his Business to gather it, when that is done, he has discharged his Office. You are not quite so much like Falstaff, as He is like Mr. Dombledon of whom Falstaff

[5] Probably the Revd. John Riland (1736–1822), the controversial writer, who was rector of St. Mary's, Birmingham, at this time. C had heard of Riland's queries which appeared in the 2nd edition of *Thelyphthora* which, despite its title-page date of 1781, may have appeared late in 1780. See W. K. R. Bedford, *Three Hundred Years of a Family Living, Being a History of the Rilands of Sutton Coldfield* (Birmingham, 1889), pp. 121–6, and *The Madan Family*, p. 290.

[6] Probably a reference to the tax on the Unwin property at Ely (see C to Unwin of 3 Sept.).

would have Borrowed Money, and when he refused to Lend him any, the Knight called him a Rascally, worsted Stocking, Yea for-sooth Knave.[7] A tender Conscience is always entitled to Respect, but a Scrupulous one, deserves Suspicion. The Man may be very Honest for aught I know; but I am sure you are so, and He ought to know that a Man of your Principles would not endeavour to force him upon a Conduct incompatible with his Oath.

I have endeavour'd to comply with your Request, though I am not good at Writing upon a Given Subject. Your Mother however Comforts me by her Approbation, and I Steer myself in all that I produce by her Judgment. If She don't Understand me at the first Reading, I am sure the Lines are obscure, and always Alter them; if She Laughs, I know it is not without a Reason, and if She says—that's well, it will do—I have no Fear lest any body else should find Fault with it. She is my Lady Chamberlain who Licenses all I Write.

To Miss Crewzé on her
Birthday.[8]

How many between East and West,
Disgrace their Parent Earth,
Whose Deeds constrain us to detest
The Day that gave them Birth!

Not so, when Stella's natal Morn
Revolving Months restore,
We can rejoice that *She* was Born,
And wish her Born once more.

If you like it, use it—if not, you know the Remedy. It is serious yet Epigrammatic, like a Bishop at a Ball.

P. S.

I have read the Review; it is Learned and Wise,
Clear, candid and Witty, Thelyphthora Dies.

[7] See 2 *Henry IV*, I. ii. 41.

[8] Miss Creuzé was probably a daughter of 'Fra. Creuze Esq; Leightonstone, Essex', a subscriber to C's Homer. Unwin was staying with the Creuzés in December (see address of C's letter of 2 Dec.), and may have been with them at the time C wrote this letter. This poem was first published in *Hayley*.

JOHN NEWTON Saturday, 11 November 1780

Princeton (*copy*)

11 Nov. 1780.

My dear Sir,

I seldom Suffer a week to pass without writing: When I do, it is Either because my Spirits will not Serve me, or because my occupations in the garden are too numerous to allow me time for it.—Since we dismissed Darlin I have found an Excellent Substitute for him in one William Kitchener[1]—a Sober, Civil, industrious lad, who knows very little of the matter but is very teachable. And what may seem almost incredible in an Olney pauper, is perfectly neat, and leaves neither weed in the borders nor dirt upon the Walks behind him. He will cost us about one fourth of what we paid to Darlin and will take ten times the Care of what is Committed to him, so I think we are Gainers by the Exchange. This is the humble character of a laborer, for Man Servant in future we are resolved to have none, having found those Gentry in Every Instance Expensive, and for the most part, worse than Useless.

I have this Instant received yours and Mrs. N's letter. How much are we indebted to you both! Newsmongers & Fishmongers are alike Wittnesses of our Obligations. It seems a dinner was wanted for to morrow: We must have bad memories indeed if we Could forget how kindly you took the alarm when my Silence left or seemed to leave you room to suspect, that one or the other of us, or both were worse than Usual. But be not frighted hereafter tho' the weekly tribute from Olney should chance to fail. I do not know that it will, I only intimate a possibility that it may. That oscitancy which you Yourself Complain of, is incident to me also, and of the two desires that which Prompts me to write, and that which persuades me to let it Alone, the latter may Chance to predominate. But if either of us should happen to be very bad indeed, the other would give the Earliest notice of it, and it is not very likely that we should both be disabled at the same time.

Since I wrote last, the Warrington Contest seems to be at a Stand,

[1] 'Kitch', attired in a blue coat that was once C's, was sent to fetch Lady Hesketh when she arrived at Newport in 1786. See C to Lady Hesketh, 12 June 1786. Darlin had been dismissed by 24 Sept. 1780. See C to Newton of that date.

at least I have not heard of any further operations on either Side. But the breach this silly business of the pew has made, is too wide to be healed by any ordinary means, and together with some other Imprudences on the Curate's part, has made pews Cheap at Olney. The threat respecting ours, late yours, was fulfilled last Sunday, when Prince Maurice[2] and his little boy took possession of it. He expected I suppose that we would have Asked him by what authority? —And I fear will not be a little disappointed when he finds this new usurpation which seemed to promise a good Comfortable Quarrel produces none. But we are ill-natured enough not to pity him under this unexpected Mortification and are determined to maintain a most provoking tranquillity on the occasion—

JOHN NEWTON Monday, 19 November 1780

Princeton

My dear Friend,

I really think your Apprehensions for Mr. Madan are but too well founded. I should be more concerned than Surprized to find them verified. Sanguin and Confident as he has been, his Mortification will be extreme, when he finds that what he took for Terra firma, was a mere Vapour hanging in the Horizon, in Pursuit of which he has Run his Vessel upon Shoals that must prove fatal to her. Discoverers of Truth are generally Sober, Modest, and humble, and if their Discoveries are less valued by Mankind than they deserve to be, can bear the Disappointment with Patience and Equality of Temper. But Hasty Reasoners, and confident Assertors are generally wedded to an Hypothesis, and transported with Joy at their fancied Acquisitions, are impatient under Contradiction, and grow Wild at the Thoughts of a Refutation. Never was an Air:built Castle more completely demolished than his is likely to be; I wish with you that he may be able to Sustain the Shock, but am at a Loss to Conceive how he should do it. After awak'ning the Attention of Mankind, and calling the World around him to Listen to his *'Ευρήκα*, after having

[2] Maurice Smith, the vicar's warden. C is probably alluding to the act of piracy engaged in by the royalist Prince Maurice (1620–52). See n. 3, C to Newton, 10 Aug. 1780 for details of the Warrington Pew affair.

distressed the Serious, and Excited the Curiosity, (perhaps the Appetite) of the Giddy & unthinking, to find himself Baffled with so much Ease, and Refuted with such Convincing Perspicuity on the part of his Opponent, must give a terrible Blow to every Passion that Engaged him in the Task, and that was sooth'd and Gratified to the utmost by his fancied Success in it. This may (and every considerate Person will Wish it may) dispose him to a serious Recollection & Examination of his past Conduct, and Work in him a Reform more Valuable to Him than the Possession of all Solomon's Wives would be, or even the Establishment of Polygamy by Law. Surely the poor Lunatic who uses his Blanket for a Robe, and Imagines that a few Straws Stuck whimsically through his Hair, are a Royal Diadem, is not more to be Pitied, perhaps less, than the profound Reasoner who turns over Shelves of Folios with Infinite Industry and Toil, and at the End of all his Labor, finds that he has grasped a Shadow, & made himself a Jest to the Bystander.

I shall be obliged to you if when you have had an Opportunity to Learn, you will let me know how he bears the Brunt, whether he Hardens himself against Conviction, which in this Case is scarcely possible, whether he Repents of what is past, or whether he is quite overwhelm'd by Regret and fruitless Sorrow.

You do me an Honor I little deserve when you Ask my Opinion upon any Occasion, and Speak of being determined by it. Such as it is however it is always at your Service, and would be if it were better worth your having.—The Dictates of Compassion and Humanity Prompt you to Interpose your good Offices in order to prevent the Publication with which this unhappy Man is threat'ned by Mr. Haweis.[1] They are Advisers you may safely Listen to, and deserve the more Attention on the present Occasion, as you are perhaps the only Man in the World to whom such a Design has been Suggested, and who would know how to manage the Execution of it with sufficient Delicacy & Discretion. The Book and the Author are distinct Subjects, and will be for ever accounted such by all reassonable Persons. The Author indeed may Suffer by the Follies of the Book, but the latter ought not to be Judged by the character of the Writer.

[1] *A Scriptural Refutation of the Arguments for Polygamy Advanced in a Treatise Entitled Thelyphthora* (1781). The Revd. Thomas Haweis whom Madan had recommended for the living of Aldwinkle in 1764, characterized his book as 'the reveries of a disordered head or the . . . delusions of a disordered heart'.

If it were otherwise, yet in this Case there can be no Need of Mr. Haweis, the Point in Dispute being already tried, and Mr. Madan's Arguments condemn'd at the Bar of the Public. Mr. Haweis will hurt himself more by One such ungenerous Proceeding, than he can possibly Hurt Mr. M—n by divulging, if he can do it, a thousand Irregularities in his Conduct. Sensual & Lawless Gratifications are odious enough, especially in a Minister, but double Detestation attends the Man who to Gratify a present Enmity, avails himself of Secrets he could never have had Possession of, had he not once professed himself a Friend. If it should happen too that Mr. Madan's Intellects should be Swept away by such a Deluge of Obloquy & Detraction, following close upon his present Disappointment (an Event not at all improbable,) Mr. H—s will have reason to wish that he had taken his Life rather than destroy'd his character. He thinks perhaps the Interest of the Cause demands it of him; but when was the Cause promoted by a Discovery of the Vices or Follies of its Advocates & Professors?—On the whole therefore if I must Advise, I would Advise to Write.—

I beleive I Return'd Mrs. Newton Thanks for the Cocoa Nuts as soon as we received them, but have now a fresh Occasion to Thank her, Mrs. Unwin having received much Benefit from them, and found her Health improved ever since she began to Eat them.[2]

Our Controversies here are at a Stand for the present. Mr. Raban has not yet received the Citation with which Mr. Page threat'ned him, & the Warringtonians are contented not to Push forward in the Business of the Pew 'till they have seen Mr. Wright, who is expected here on Tuesday.—Mr. Page is very thinly attended, Weston & Clifton and the Meetings drink up all his Congregation. There were but 15 to wait upon his last Thursday's Lecture. The bléssed Effect of Quarrelling about Straws, when he might have had Peace with every body if he had not gone out of his way to seek Contention. His Hearers however complain of great Inconsistency in his Preaching, and some of his warmest Partizans, & whose Attachment to him has lasted the longest, begin to be disgusted.

Many Thanks for two Pair of remarkably fine Soals with Shrimps, they were here in 16 Hours after they set out from London, & came very opportunely for me who having a violent Cold, could hardly have Eaten any thing else.

[2] See n. 7, C to Newton, 22 July 1781.

Mrs. Unwin intended to have sent a Couple of Fowls, but being taken out of the Coop, one of them appear'd to be distemper'd, and two others on Examination, in the same Predicament; One so bad that we were obliged to throw it away, and the other we Gave away, not thinking it Eatable except by those whose Stomachs were less nice than our own. It is I suppose an Epipoultrical Malady.

You told me Mrs. Newton intended to have sent me a long Story about the Fish. With both my two Eyes assisted by both my two Glasses I could make neither more nor less of it than a long Song, and so I read the Passage to Mrs. Unwin once & again. I should have felt more than ordinary Concern for the Business that prevented her, and have endeavor'd by all means to persuade her to resume her Intention and to send me this Song immediately, if Mrs. Unwin had not some time after, discover'd with more Sagacity than I happen'd to have in Exercise, that what I took for a Song was only a Story, the insignificant Letter t being omitted, and the ry having assumed the Appearance on this Occasion of their near Relations ng.—[3]

Mrs. Unwin would have attempted to write, but I dissuaded her from it, because even when she is pretty well, she finds it hurtfull.

You will both beleive us both, as ever,

Your Obliged & Affectionate Friends & Servants

Wm. & M——

Nove. 19. —81.[4]

JOSEPH HILL — Sunday, 26 November 1780

Cowper Johnson

My dear Friend,

I thank you much for your Letter, which without obliging me to Travel to Wargrove at a Time of Year when Journeying is not very agreeable, has introduced me in the most commodious manner to a perfect Acquaintance with your neat little Garden, your Old Cottage, and above all with your most prudent and sagacious Landlady. As much as I Admire her, I Admire much more that Philosophical Temper with which you seem to Treat her, for I know few Characters

[3] This letter from Newton has not been found.

[4] Despite C's dating, this letter by its context belongs to 1780.

more provoking to me at least, than the Selfish, who are never Honest; especially if while they determine to Pick your Pocket, they have not Ingenuity enough to conceal their Purpose. But you are perfectly in the right, and Act just as I would endeavor to do on the same Occasion. You Sacrifice every thing to a Retreat you Admire, and if the natural Indolence of my Disposition did not forsake me, so would I.

You might as well Apologize for sending me 40 £ as for Writing about yourself. Of the two Ingredients I hardly know which made your Letter the most agreeable. (Observe, I do not say the most Acceptable.) The Draft indeed was welcome; but though it was so, yet it did not make me Laugh; I Laughed heartily at the Account you give of Yourself & your Landlady Dame Saveall, whose Picture you have drawn tho' not with a flattering Hand, yet I dare say with a strong Resemblance. As to you, I have never seen so much of you since I saw you in London, where you and I have so often made ourselves merry with each other's Humor, yet never gave each other a Moment's Pain by doing so. We are both Humorists, and it is well for your Wife and my Mrs. Unwin, that they have alike found out the way to deal with us.

More Thanks to Mrs. Hill for her Intentions. She has the true Enthusiasm of a Gardener and therefore I can Pity her under her Disappointment, having so large a share of that Commodity myself.

I am informed that Lady C. has left me an Annuity of 20£. I mention it merely because as you do not, I thought you might not have heard it.

Yours my Dear Sir Affectionately
Wm Cowper.

1781 Nove 26.[1]

[1] Despite the dating in C's hand, this must belong to 1780. Lady Cowper's will was proved 3 Sept. 1780. See C to Hill, 10 Dec. 1780, where the legacy is discussed. It was not from Lady Cowper.

JOHN NEWTON Monday, 27 November 1780[1]

Princeton

My dear Friend

A Visit from Mr. Widford shorten'd one of your Letters to me, and now the same Cause has Operated with the same Effect upon one of mine to you. He is just gone, desired me to send his Love, and talks of inclosing a Letter to you in my next Cover.

Literas tuas Irato Sacerdoti scriptas, Legi, Perlegi, et ne Verbum quidem mutandum censeo. Gratias tibi Acturum si Sapiat, Existimo, sin alitér eveniat, amici tamen Officium praestitisti, et Te corám Te, Vindicâsti.[2]

I have not written in Latin to shew my Scholarship, nor to Excite Mrs. Newton's Curiosity, nor for any other Wise Reason whatever, but merely because just that Moment it came into my Head to do so.

Mrs. Unwin having suggested the Hint, I have added just as many Lines to my Poem lately mentioned, as make up the whole Number 200.[3] I had no Intention to write a round Sum, but it has happened so. She thought there was a fair Opportunity to give the Bishops a Slap, and as it would not have been civil to have denied a Lady so reasonable a Request, I have just made the Powder fly out of their Wigs a little.

I never wrote a Copy of Mary & John in my Life, except that which I sent to you. It was one of those Bagatelles which some times spring up like Mushrooms in my Imagination either while I am Writing, or just before I begin. I sent it to you, because to You I send any thing that I think may raise a Smile, but should never have thought of multiplying the Impression. Neither did I ever Repeat them to any one except Mrs. Unwin. The Inference is fair and easy, that you have some Friend who has a good Memory.[4]

[1] This letter is dated '27 Novr.–81', presumably in Newton's hand, but the reference to *Anti-Thelyphthora* makes it certain that it belongs to 1780.

[2] 'I have read and reread what you have written to the angry priest and in my judgement not a word should be altered. It seems to me that he should thank you (for the letter) if he were wise, but if it should prove otherwise, you have nevertheless discharged your duty as a friend and vindicated yourself in your own eyes.'

In his letter to Cowper of 14 July 1780 (Princeton), Newton mentions that he will preserve his letter to Madan and eventually send it to C.

[3] C is referring to *Anti-Thelyphthora*.

[4] In his letter to C of 25 Nov. (Princeton), Newton remarked: 'I saw your—if John

This afternoon, the Maid opened the Parlour Door, & told us there was a Lady in the Kitchen. We desired she might be introduced, & prepar'd for the Reception of Mrs. Jones. But it proved to be a Lady unknown to us, and not Mrs. Jones. She walked directly up to Mrs. Unwin, and never drew back 'till their Noses were almost in Contact; it seem'd as if she meant to Salute her. An uncommon Degree of Familiarity accompanied with an Air of most extraordinary gravity, made me think her a little Crazy. I was alarmed & so was Mrs. Unwin. She had a Bundle in her Hand, a silk Handkerchief tied up at the 4 Corners. When I found she was not Mad, I took her for a Smuggler, and made no doubt but she had brought Samples of Contraband goods. But our Surprize, considering the Ladie's Appearance & Deportment, was tenfold what it had been, when we found that it was Mary Phillips's Daughter, who had brought us a few Apples by way of Specimens of a Quantity she had for Sale.[5]—She drank Tea with us, and behaved herself during the rest of her Stay with much[6]

WILLIAM UNWIN Saturday, 2 December 1780

Address: The Revd. William Unwin at / Mr. Crewze's / Laytonstone / Essex.
Postmarks: 4/DE *and* OULNEY
British Library

My dear Friend—

Poetical Reports of Law Cases are not very common, yet it seems to me desireable that they should be so. Many Advantages would accrue from such a measure. They would in the first Place be more commodiously deposited in the Memory, just as Linen, Grocery or other such matters when neatly Pack'd, are known to occupy less Room and to lie more conveniently in any Trunk, Chest, or Box to which they may be committed. In the next Place, being divested of that infinite Circumlocution, and the endless Embarrass-

marries Mary in one of the News-papers, but I had no hand in sending it them.' The *Gentleman's Magazine* had printed the poem in the December issue.

5 Newton to C, 29 Nov. 1780 (Princeton): 'None of us ever heard that Mary Philipps had a daughter. I think your Apple Lady must be of another family, at least of a different branch.'

6 The remaining portion of this letter is missing.

ment in which they are involved by it, they would become surprisingly intelligible in Comparison with their present Obscurity. And lastly they would by this means be render'd susceptible of Musical Embellishment, and instead of being quoted in the Courts with that dull Monotony which is so wearisome to Bystanders, and frequently Lulls even the Judges themselves to Sleep; might be rehears'd in Recitativo; which would have an Admirable Effect, in keeping the Attention fixt and lively, and could not fail to disperse that heavy Atmosphere of Sadness and Gravity which Hangs over the Jurisprudence of our Country. I remember many Years ago being Informed by a Relation of mine who in his Youth had applied himself to the Study of the Law, that one of his Fellow Students, a Gentleman of sprightly Parts and very respectable Talents of the Poetical kind, did actually engage in the Prosecution of such a Design; for Reasons I suppose somewhat Similar to, if not the same with those I have now Suggested. He began with Coke's Institutes; a Book so rugged in its Stile, that an Attempt to Polish it seem'd an Herculean Labor, and not less arduous and difficult than it would be to give the Smoothness of a Rabbit's Fur to the prickly Back of a Hedge Hog.[1] But he succeeded to Admiration as you will perceive by the following Specimen, which is all that my said Relation could Recollect of the Performance.

Tenant in Fee
Simple, is He,
And need neither quake nor quiver,
Who hath his Lands
Free from all Demands
To Him and his Heirs for Ever.

You have an Ear for Music, and a Taste for Verse, which saves me the Trouble of pointing out with a Critical Nicety the Advantages of such a Version. I proceed therefore to what I at first intended, and to transcribe the Record of an Adjudged Case thus managed, to which indeed what I have premised was intended merely as an Introduction.[2]

[1] *The Institutes* and *The Reports* of Sir Edward Coke (1552–1634) would have been familiar to C from his years at the Middle and Inner Temples. C is referring to a book such as *The Reports of Sir Edward Coke, Kt. in Verse Wherein The Name of Each Case, and the Principal Points, are Contained in Two Lines* (1742).

[2] Published in *1782*.

2 December 1780

Nose Pl Eyes Deft.
Vid:Plowden.[3]
Folio 6000.

Between Nose and Eyes once a Contest arose,
The Spectacles set them Egregiously wrong,
The Point in dispute was, as all the World knows,
To which the said Spectacles ought to belong.

2.

So the Tongue was the Lawyer, & argued the Cause
With a great deal of Skill, & a Wig full of Learning,
While Chief Baron Ear[4] Sat to Balance the Laws,
So famed for his Talent in nicely discerning.

3.

In behalf of the Nose, it will quickly appear,
And your Lordship, he said, will undoubtedly find,
That the Nose has had Spectacles always in Wear,
Which amounts to Possession Time out of Mind.

4.

Then Holding the Spectacles up to the Court,
Your Lordship observes they are made with a Straddle,
As wide as the Ridge of the Nose is, in short,
Design'd to sit close to it, just like a Saddle.

5.

Again—would your Lordship a Moment suppose,
'Tis a Case that has happen'd, and May be again,
That the Visage or Countenance had not a Nose,
Pray, Who *would*, or who *could*, Wear Spectacles Then.

[3] This refers to the celebrated series of law reports, *Les Commentaires ou Reportes de Edmunde Plowden* (1578–9). There was an anonymous English translation published in London in 1779. Plowden (1518–85) covers the period 1550–78 in his work.

[4] The Chief Baron presided over the Court of Exchequer, which was divided into a court of common law and a court of equity.

6.

On the whole it appears, & my Argument shows
With a Reas'ning the Court will never Condemn,
That the Spectacles plainly were made for the Nose,
And the Nose was as plainly, Intended for Them.

7.

Then shifting his Side as a Lawyer knows how,
He Pleaded again in behalf of the Eyes,
But what were his Arguments few People know,
For the Court did not think they were equally Wise.

8.

So his Lordship decreed with a grave, solemn Tone,
Dicisive & clear, without one If or But,
That whenever the Nose put his Spectacles on,
By Daylight or Candlelight, Eyes should be Shut.

Your Mother will be glad to know when you are to be next in Town —If you can meet with any Person who has a little Spare Money, we know where it may be bestowed to the very best Purpose.—

Decr. 2 1780.

JOHN NEWTON — Saturday, 2 December 1780

Address: Revd. John Newton / Hoxton / London / NfreeNewnham[1]
Postmarks: 4/DE, OULNEY, *and* FREE
Olney[2]

Weary of Transcribing, I shall find perhaps some Refreshment in Scribbling a little de Novo. I send you my Tale, which has made a Shoot or two since I wrote last, and had I kept it longer by me, would probably have continued growing to the last. It is long enough

[1] Nathaniel Newnham (*c.* 1741–1809). Newnham had recently become a member of parliament for London, a post he held until 1790. See Namier and Brooke, *The House of Commons, 1754–1790*, iii (1964), 200–1.

[2] The top of this letter has been torn away, but presumably only the salutation is missing. MS. is also torn.

howev[er for a] Tale, and if it serves the saluta[ry] Purpose of making this one Scheme ridiculous as it is odious, will pay me well for my Pains, if indeed it can be said to have cost me any; for from first to last it has served me merely as an Amusement.

I do not know that Mr. Johnson is in any Degree deserving of such a Suspicion, but I have learn'd by Experience that Printers will sometimes take Liberties with a Copy, and mingle with it somewhat of their own. I shall be obliged to you therefore if you will be so kind as to preserve my Muse immaculate, and not s[uffer her] to be injured by a Thelyphthorian Mixture. I am not so Pragmatical (as the Phrase is) as to suppose that Mr. Johnson has less Wit than I. It is possible, very possible, he may have much more. But I once met with a Printer who served me such a Trick, and was at the same time as illiterate a Blockhead as ever presumed to tread upon a poor Poet's Toe.—I am much obliged to you for your Obstetrical Assistance upon this Occasion, and am pleased with the Thought that you will rejoice with me if the Enclosed should be of Service, for of all the Publications that have appear'd since I could Read my own Name, that in Question seems to me the most pernicious, and the most deserving of the Lash of Satyr.[3] I have spared the Author's Person as much as possible, but the Connection between Self and Self's Book is so close, that it is hardly possible to smite One without Touching the other.

Many Thanks for the Oysters which are come by Mr. Sample. The Clook[4] shall be taken care of. Mrs. Unwin has mention'd Mrs. Cardell[5] to her Brother. I acknowledge the Receipt of Mrs. Newton's Letter, & shall do it more at large hereafter. If you think any thing so Local as the Tything time Ditty worth your having, I will send it.[6] Yours my Dear Sir,

Quite weary—Wm Cowper.

Dece. 2. 1780.

[3] Johnson published *Anti-Thelyphthora* as a 4to pamphlet in January 1781.

[4] C's spelling of cloak.

[5] Unidentified.

[6] A reference to 'The Yearly Distress or, Tithing Time at Stock in Essex' which C probably sent to Unwin on 30 Oct. 1780. The 'Ditty', not published until 22 Aug. 1783 in the *Public Advertiser*, expresses sentiments originally written in C to Unwin, 2 Dec. 1779.

JOSEPH HILL Sunday, 10 December 1780

Address: Mr. Joseph Hill / Chancery Office / London
Postmark: OULNEY
Cowper Johnson

My dear Friend,

It is well for me that as my Intelligencer with respect to Lady Cowper's Legacy proved to be mistaken, the Substantial Part of his Information is, however, authenticated, and the Money not lost, though it comes from a different Mine.[1]

I am sorry that the Bookseller shuffles off the Trouble of Package upon any body that belongs to You. I think I could Cast him upon this Point in an Action upon the Case, grounded upon the Terms of his own Undertaking. He Engages to Serve Country Customers. Ergo, as it would be unreasonable to Expect that when a Country Gentleman wants a Book, he should Order his Chaise & bid the Man drive to Exeter Change, and as it is not probable that the Book would find the Way to him of itself, though it were the Wisest that ever was written, I should suppose the Law would compell him. For I recollect that it is a Maxim of good Authority in the Courts, that there is no Right without a Remedy. And if Another or Third Person shall not be suffer'd to interpose between my Right & the Remedy the Law gives me where that Right is invaded, much less I apprehend, shall the Man Himself who of his own mere Motion Gives me that Right, be suffer'd to do it.

I never made so long an Argument upon a Law Case before; I ask your Pardon for doing it now; you have but little need of such Entertainment.

On the other Side I add an Acknowledgment for the 21£ you

1 The 'Intelligencer' was Mrs. Madan, who wrote to Newton on 22 Sept. 1780: 'I take this first opportunity to return *My Gratitude*, by Sending you an acct: of *an Event*, wch. I know, *you will have*, in ye Satisfaction off, *with me*, & wch. I did not know till yester: from *one*, who was present at the read :g *Ldy Cowpers* will, & she was so kind, as to *leave*, 20£ she [intends], My *Dear Nephew*, *an Annuity for his Life*, to be paid by *Lord Spencer*. . . .' Newton wrote a letter to C on the margins of Mrs. Madan's letter and dispatched both letters to C on 23 Sept. (Princeton).

There is no mention of C in Lady Cowper's will (P.R.O. PROB 11/1069 C 7463), but C probably received an annuity of £20 from George Nassau Clavering Cowper, 3rd Earl Cowper (1738–89), Lady Cowper's stepson, and *not* from her son, John Spencer, of Althorp (1734–83), created Viscount Althorp and Earl Spencer 1 Nov. 1765. From C's letter to Unwin of 10 July 1786, it would seem that Lord Cowper gave the money at Lady Hesketh's instigation.

sent me, together with the Numbers of 10 Books, according to Mr. Bell's Directions.

Many thanks for the Draft, and for the Cod & Oysters, perfectly fresh & remarkably fine. My Respects attend Mrs. Hill.

Yours affectionately
Wm Cowper.

Dece. 10.1780.

1747	1770.
1963.	1791.
1799.	1844.
1736.	1912.
1737.	
1713	

Any Two of the Above Numbers.[2]

MRS. NEWTON — Sunday, 17 December 1780

Princeton

Dear Madam,

Taking it for granted (though not yet made certain by Intelligence from yourself) that we are indebted to you for a Present of Skait & Shrimps received last Thursday, I write to Thank you for it on Mrs. Unwin's part & my own and to let you know that it was remarkably good. We Versemakers have particular Reasons to Hold ourselves

[2] C is referring to *A New Catalogue of Bell's Circulating Library, Consisting of Above Fifty Thousand Volumes* . . . [London] John Bell, Bookseller, New Exeter Exchange in the Strand, [1778?]. Subscribers 'to prevent Disappointment, and Delay, [were] to send a List of ten or twelve Numbers, taken from this Catalogue'. Each participant in this scheme was allowed 'to have two Books at a Time and no more, which they may change once a Day, and no oftner'. C wanted two of the following books:

1747 Fielding's Journal of a Voyage to Lisbon
1963 Benvenuto Cellini (a Florentine Artist) his Life
1799 Lithgow's nineteen Years Travels
1736 Drury's Journal of his fifteen Years Captivity
1737 Doubourdieu and his Wife's surprising Adventures
1713 Campbell's Sequel to the Voyage of the Ship Wager
1770 Hennepin's Discovery of a vast Country in America
1791 Ladies Travels into Spain, 2 vol.
1844 Pennant's Tour in Scotland
1912 Wycke's (Sir Peter) Relation of the River Nile.

obliged to those who will furnish our Tables with light & delicate Fare and such as is most easily digested. In this respect, Man consider'd as a Machine is constructed upon Principles the very reverse of those by which a Clock is actuated; the latter is indebted to the Weight below for all the Constancy & Regularity of its Movement; whereas the Head of a Poet instead of being Benefitted by such an Appendage, is sadly hinder'd in its Operations, all his Wits, as Naturalists observe, being called down into the lower Regions, & employ'd there in the Drudgery of Digestion. It is for this Reason no doubt, that the Muses have always kept their Votaries so poor, thinking it better that they should not Eat at all, than that they should Eat at the Expence of their Reputation, and sacrifice their Genius to their Appetite.

In Hopes that Mr. Unwin did not shew you the following when you saw him last, I subjoin a Copy of it for your Perusal, and to Convince you that though many of our Squabbles at Olney are of a Tragical Cast, they are not all so, and that some of our Disputes though conducted with an Air of much Gravity, are Laughable enough. Mrs. Unwin sat Knitting with her Spectacles on, and I sat looking at her, when the Quarrel I am going to Relate to you, arose.

Between Nose and Eyes a strange Contest arose,
The Spectacles set them unhappily wrong,
The Point in Dispute was (as all the World knows)
To which the said Spectacles ought to Belong.

2.

So the Tongue was the Lawyer, & Argued the Cause,
With a great deal of Skill, & a Wig full of Learning,
While chief Baron Ear sat to Balance the Laws,
So fam'd for his Talent at nicely discerning.

3.

In behalf of the Nose, it will quickly appear,
And your Lordship he said will undoubtedly find,
That the Nose has had Spectacles always in Wear,
Which amounts to Possession Time out of Mind.

4.

Then Holding the Spectacles up to the Court,
Your Lordship observes they are made with a Straddle
As wide as the Ridge of the Nose is, in short,
Design'd to sit close to it just like a Saddle.

5.

Again, would your Lordship a Moment suppose,
('Tis a case that has happen'd, & may be again)
That the Visage or Countenance had not a Nose,
Pray who would, or who could, wear Spectacles Then?

6.

On the whole it appears, & my Argument shows
With a Reas'ning the Court will never Condemn,
That the Spectacles plainly were made for the Nose,
And the Nose was as plainly intended for Them.

7.

Then Shifting his Side, as a Lawyer knows how,
He Pleaded again in behalf of the Eyes,
But what were his Arguments, few People know,
For the Court did not think they were equally Wise.

8.

So his Lordship decreed, with a Grave Solemn Tone,
Decisive and clear, without one If or But,
That whenever the Nose put his Spectacles on,
By Daylight or Candlelight, Eyes should be Shut.

When the Point of Law is attended to, and not the Equity of the Case, Decisions like this are sometimes made in a court of Justice, & I think I have myself heard Arguments upon some Occasions equally Solemn, & equally ridiculous.

We return you many Thanks for the Cocoa Nut. Its Defects were so effectually conceal'd that it was impossible you should find them out. But I had no sooner pierced it, than my Nose inform'd me that it was rotten. I take the Liberty to tell you this, that if you bought it you may know how to trust the Seller another time, for I suppose it

must have been a long time in England. Our Joint Love to Yourself & Mr. Newton.

Yours Dear Madam, Wm Cowper.

Dece. 17. 80.

JOHN NEWTON Thursday, 21 December 1780

Princeton (*copy*) *and* Barham Johnson (*copy*)[1]

Decr. 21st. 1780

My dear friend,

We have frequently said to each other, When will Omicron's letters appear! and are glad to learn from your last that the expected publication is at hand. What a variety of literary characters have you, or will you before you take leave of the press appear in? Biographer, Preacher, Historian, Poet, and Epistolary Writer! While you confine yourselves to subjects of a religious kind, I hardly know what title you can assume that you have not worn already. The best Actors are oftenest obliged to change their dress, while an understrapper goes through the five Acts in the same clothes he wore at the beginning. I never studied to pay you a Compliment in my Life, on the contrary, I have often studied not to do it but on some occasions, and on some subjects, a compliment or something like one slips out before I am aware of it.—

I thank you for your Anecdote of Judge Carpenter.[2] If it really

1 The Princeton copy ends at 'deprive them of it' at the close of the sixth paragraph. The remainder of the letter is supplied from 'Miss Gaviller's Copy' in the Barham Johnson collection. The Gaviller copy also supplies the day in the date, but it omits all of the first, fourth, and fifth paragraphs.

2 'A year after the friends were separated, Cowper thanked Newton for a good story. It was about a candidate for the Common Council in London, a man whom Newton described as "a salesman in Rosemary Lane, that is, in vulgar language, an Old Clothes Man in Rag fair". It was thought presumption for such a man to aspire to the Council but he overcame this objection by printing a circular with the following story: "Once upon a time a Carpenter was employed mending the floor of a Barrister's chambers. He looked into a Law book, became interested and thereafter devoted his leisure to reading Law, buying first one book and then another. By dint of application the Carpenter became, in time, a Barrister and, at length, a Judge. In this capacity he one day reproved a Counsellor, telling him he had failed to make his case *plane*, he had not made it quite *smooth*. The Counsellor, to get his own back, answered, 'I cannot help that My Lord; *I* was not bred to a Carpenter,' to which the Judge, with great Composure replied, 'It is very evident; for had *you* been bred a Carpenter, you would have been a Carpenter still.' " ': Bernard Martin, *John Newton* (1950), pp. 287–8.

happened, it is one of the best stories I ever heard, and if not, it has at least the merit of being *ben trovato*.[3] We both very sincerely laughed at it, and think the whole livery of London must have done the same, tho' I have known persons whose faces as if they had been cast in a mould, could never be provoked to the least alteration of a single feature, so that one might as well relate a good story to a Barber's Block.

Non equidem Invideo miror magis.[4]

The parties have had their hearing before the Archdeacon, at Aylesbury. Mr. Heslop[5] behaved in a manner entirely satisfactory to the popular side of the question. Mr. Page perhaps is not so well pleased, tho' he has no just cause to be offended. When a man makes a preposterous and absurd attempt he has no right to be angry if the want of success is his only punishment.——The affair indeed is not finally determined. Mr. Heslop recommended it to them all to enter into an accommodation and be reconciled to each other before the next court which will be held in less than a fortnight. The parish will propose their terms to the Curate in a few days. If he rejects them, they must all repair to the scene of trial again, when Mr. P. is to be obliged to withdraw his indictment.

Some things have passed at home and some at Aylesbury upon this occasion, that would reflect but little honor on this imprudent man, but they are too paltry for recital and best buried in Oblivion.—

Your sentiments with respect to me, are exactly Mrs. Unwin's. She, like you, is perfectly sure of my deliverance and often tells me so. I make but one Answer, and sometimes none at all. That Answer gives *Her* no pleasure, and would give *You* as little. Therefore, at this time, I suppress it. It is better on every account that they who interest themselves so deeply in that event should believe the certainty of it than that they should not. It is a comfort to *them* at least, if it is none to me, and as I could not if I would so neither would I, if I could, deprive them of it.

I annex a long thought in verse for your perusal.[6] It was produced about last Midsummer, but I never could prevail with myself, till

3 'Wittily expressed'.

4 Virgil, *Eclogues*, i. 11: 'I do not begrudge you—I rather marvel.'

5 John Cowper's friend, Luke Heslop. Heslop became archdeacon of Buckingham in 1778. See n. 1, C to Unwin, 31 Mar. 1770.

6 'Heroism'.

now, to transcribe it. You have bestowed some commendations on a certain poem now in the press,[7] & they I suppose have at least animated me to the task. If Human Nature may be compared to a piece of Tapestry, and why not?, then human nature as it subsists in me, tho' it is sadly faded on the right side, retains all its colour on the wrong. I am pleased with commendation, and tho' not passionately desirous of indiscriminate praise, or what is generally called popularity, yet when a judicious friend claps me on the back, I own I find it an encouragement. At this season of the year, & in this gloomy, uncomfortable climate, it is no easy matter for the owner of a mind like mine, to divert it from sad subjects, & fix it upon such as may administer to its amusement. Poetry, above all things, is useful to me in this respect. While I am held in pursuit of pretty images, or a pretty way of expressing them, I forget every thing that is irksome, &, like a boy that plays truant, determine to avail myself of the present opportunity to be amused, & to put by the disagreeable recollection that I must after all, go home & be whipt again.

It will not be long perhaps before you will receive a poem of much greater length than the Knightly one, it is called the *Progress of Error*; that will be succeeded by another in due time, the length of which is not at present determined, called *Truth*. Don't be alarmed. I ride Pegasus in a curb. He will never run away with me again. I have convinced Mrs. Unwin that I can manage him, & make him stop when I please.

If Anti- should live through a second impression, I have 4 lines by me, that I think might be added with some advantage, tho' I have never taken the trouble to mark the place where they might be inserted. That however might be easily found. Having given one Hero a spear, I would give the other a Shield,—as thus—

> His Shield with Hebrew lore was scribbled round,
> But snatching it impatient from the ground,
> And slinging it revers'd upon his Arm,
> He chang'd it to a Cabbalistic charm.[8]

W.C.—

7 *Anti-Thelyphthora.*

8 These lines, evidently meant to follow line 174, were first published in *Bailey*.

WILLIAM UNWIN Sunday, 24 December 1780

British Library

My dear Friend,

I am sensibly mortified at finding myself obliged to disappoint you; but Though I have had many Thoughts upon the Subjects you propose to my Consideration, I have had none that have been favorable to the Undertaking. I applaud your Purpose for the sake of the Principle from which it Springs, but I Look upon the Evils you mean to animadvert upon, as too obstinate and inveterate ever to be expelled by the means you mention. The very Persons to whom you would Address your Remonstrance, are themselves sufficiently aware of their Enormity; Years ago, to my Knowledge, they were frequently the Topics of Conversation at polite Tables; they have been frequently mention'd in Both Houses of Parliament, and I suppose there is hardly a Member of either, who would not immediately Assent to the Necessity of a Reform were it proposed to him in a reasonable Way. But there it Stops; and there it will for Ever Stop, till the Majority are animated with a Zeal in which at present they are deplorably defective. A Religious Man is unfeignedly Shock'd when he reflects upon the Prevalence of such Crimes, a Moral man must needs be so in a Degree, and will Affect to be much more so than he is. But how many do you Suppose there are among our worthy Representatives that come under either of these Descriptions? If all were such, yet to new model the Police of the Country, which must be done in order to make even unavoidable Perjury less frequent, were a Task they would hardly undertake on account of the great Difficulty that would attend it. Government is too much interested in the Consumption of Malt Liquor, to reduce the Number of Venders. Such plausible Pleas may be offer'd in Defence of Travelling on Sundays, especially by the Trading part of the World, as the whole Bench of Bishops would find it difficult to overrule. And with respect to the Violation of Oaths, 'till a certain Name is more generally Respected than it is at present, however such Persons as yourself may be grieved at it, the Legislature are never likely to Lay it to Heart. I do not mean, nor would by any means Attempt to Discourage you in so Laudable an Enterprize, but such is the Light in which it appears to me, that I

do not feel the least Spark of Courage qualifying or prompting me to Embark in it myself. An Exhortation therefore Written by me, by Hopeless, desponding Me, would be flat, insipid and uninteresting, and Disgrace the Cause instead of Serving it. If after what I have said however, you still retain the same Sentiments, Macte esto Virtute tuâ,[1] there is nobody better qualified than yourself, and may your Success prove that I despair'd of it without a Reason.

Your poor Sister!—She has many good Qualities, and upon some Occasions gives Proof of a good Understanding, but as some People have no Ear for Music, so She has none for Humor. Well—if She cannot Laugh at our Jokes, we can however, at Her Mistakes, and in this way she makes us ample Amends for the Disappointment. Mr. Powley is much like Herself. If his Wife overlooks the Joke, He will never be able to find it. They were neither of them Born to write Epigrams or Ballads, and I ought to be the less mortified at the Coldness with which they Entertain my small Sallies in the way of Drollery, when I Reflect that if Swift himself had had no other Judges, he would never have found One Admirer.

It is indeed, as you observe, incumbent upon Mr. Madan to Reply to the Reviewer if he means to Maintain his Point. But unless he means likewise to Expose himself more in a Second Attempt than he did even in his first, it is still more incumbent upon him to be Silent. I reckon myself a competent Judge of the Argument, so far as the Greek Criticisms are in question, and if I am, a Refutation of what his Antagonist has advanced against that Part of his Performance, is Impossible. That Impossibility is follow'd close at the Heels by a Conclusion not to be Avoided. Syllogistically dress'd it stands thus.

The Scripture is the only Ground on which the Doctrine of Polygamy can be proved.

But it cannot be Proved by Scripture.

Ergo—Not at all.

You desired me some time since to send you my 27 Answers to ditto Number of Queries drawn up by the Revd. Mr. Riland of Birmingham.[2] I would have done it, if the Review had not made it entirely unnecessary. The Gentleman for whose Use in particular I design'd them, declined sending them to the Querist, at my

[1] Horace, *Satires*, I. ii. 32: 'Well done.'

[2] See n. 5, C to Unwin, *post* 9 Nov. 1780.

Instance; so that immediately almost after their Production, they became Waste Paper, and I kept no Copy of them myself. The Questions discover'd such Marks of almost Childish Imbecillity, that I could not possibly propose to myself the Acquisition of any Credit, by the Answer. But as some Men, especially Weak ones, are apt to suppose themselves irrefragable and Invincible in Disputation, I Replied to them merely to Guard the poor Gentleman against the pernicious Effects of so sad a Blunder upon an Occasion of such Importance.

My Respects attend the Family, that is to say my Affectionate ones. I heartily wish Mrs. Unwin better Spirits. Never be afraid of the Multiplication of Children. You do not make them yourself, and He that does, knows how to Provide for them. Poor Bare Breech'd Billy, to whom your Alms were yesterday so acceptable, has no desponding Thoughts upon this Subject, tho' he has now 4, & considering his Age and the Age of his Wife, may possibly have 14.

Yours my dear Friend
Wm Cowper.

Dece. 24. 1780.

JOSEPH HILL — Wednesday, 27 December 1780

Address: Mr. Joseph Hill / Great Queen Street / Lincolns Inn Fields / London.
Postmark: OULNEY
Cowper Johnson

My dear Friend—

Weary with rather a long Walk in the Snow, I am not likely to write a very Sprightly Letter, or to produce any thing that may Cheer this gloomy Season, unless I have recourse to my Pocket Book, where perhaps I may find something to transcribe; Something that was written before the Sun had taken Leave of our Hemisphere, and when I was less fatigued than I am at present.

Happy is the Man who knows just so much of the Law, as to make himself a little merry now & then with the Solemnity of Juridical Proceedings. I have heard of Common Law Judgments[1] before now,

[1] 'Is taken for the Law of this Kingdom simply, without any other Laws; as it was generally holden before any Statute was enacted in Parliament to alter the same: And the

indeed have been present at the Delivery of some, that according to my poor Apprehension, while they pay'd the utmost Respect to the Letter of a Statute, have departed widely from the Spirit of it, and being govern'd entirely by the Point of Law, have left Equity, Reason, and Common sense behind them at an infinite Distance. You will Judge whether the following Report of a Case, drawn up by myself, be not a Proof & Illustration of this Satyrical Assertion.

Nose Plt. Eyes Defts.

Between Nose and Eyes a sad Contest arose,
The Spectacles set them unhappily wrong,
The Point in Dispute was, as all the World knows,
To which, the said Spectacles ought to Belong.

2.

So the Tongue was the Lawyer, and Argued the Cause,
With a great deal of Skill, & a Wig full of Learning,
While Chief Baron Ear, sat to Balance the Laws,
So fam'd for his Talent at nicely Discerning.

3.

In behalf of the Nose, it will quickly appear,
And your Lordship, he said, will undoubtedly find,
That the Nose has had Spectacles always in Wear,
Which amounts to Possession, Time out of Mind.

4.

Then holding the Spectacles up to the Court,
Your Lordship Observes, they are made with a Straddle,
As wide as the Ridge of the Nose is, in short,
Design'd to sit close to it just like a Saddle.

King's Courts of Justice are called the Common Law Courts': *A New Law-Dictionary* (8th edn. 1762).

5.

Again would your Lordship a Moment suppose,
('Tis a Case that Has happen'd, & may be again)
That the Visage or Countenance, had Not a Nose,
Pray Who Would, or Who Could, Wear Spectacles Then?

6.

On the whole it Appears, & my Argument Shows
With a Reas'ning the Court will never Condemn,
That the Spectacles plainly were made for the Nose,
And the Nose was As plainly, intended for Them.

7.

Then shifting his Side as a Lawyer knows how,
He Pleaded again in behalf of the Eyes,
But what were his Arguments few People know,
For the Court did not think they were equally Wise.

8.

So his Lordship Decreed, with a Grave Solemn Tone,
Decisive and clear, without one If or But,
That whenever the Nose put his Spectacles on
By Daylight or Candlelight—*Eyes should be Shut.*

I thank you much for a fine Cod with Oysters; If the foregoing should make you Smile it will Pay me well for the Trouble of Transcribing, which I hate above all Occupations in the World. I consider'd a little while what Sort of Return I should make you for your Acceptable Present, having sent you no Acknowledgment but that of Thanks upon several such Occasions; and at last bethought myself of this Argument, which you are Qualified to Relish by a Professional Habit of Attention, to such nice and intricate Litigations. I am, my Dear Sir,

With my Respects to Mrs. Hill,
Your Affectionate
Wm Cowper.

Dece. 27. 1780.

WILLIAM UNWIN Sunday, 14 January 1781

British Library

My dear Friend—

I seldom write what may properly be called an Answer to a Letter, unless to a Letter that requires an Answer. But on the present Occasion, being conscious that I have not Spirits to enable me to make Excursions on the Wings of Invention, I purpose to confine myself pretty much to the Subjects of yours. Which prudent Procedure will serve the double Purpose of releiving *Me* from the Toil of Pumping in vain, and of convincing *you* that you cannot do a worse thing than to deprive me of your Letters, upon an Apprehension that they can afford me neither Profit nor Amusement.

Impressions made upon the Mind in our early days are seldom entirely effaced. This is an old Observation, but I shall graft a new one upon it. Tho' you have a perfect Recollection of John Cross's[1] pious and wise Remark, I am sadly afraid that you have never made a practical Use of it, which I the more wonder at because his unexpected good Fortune in the Instance you allude to, amounts almost to a Proof of the great Utility of such a Custom. How is it possible, were you but properly carefull to keep that Part uppermost at the time of Rising, that you could be plagued as you are with such a Variety of Misadventures? Tythes unpaid, Dilapidations without End, Law suits revived, and your Curate running away from you for the sake of a pleasanter Country. I dare say John Cross was exempted from all these disagreeable Occurrences; He had not half your Understanding, yet knew how to Avoid them all by attending to the main chance in the Article you Hint at. He presented something more substantial than even a sevenfold Shield[2] to the Arrows of Ill Fortune, and receiving them, (if he receiv'd them at all) where they could not possibly reach his Heart, went through the World insensible of the Troubles with which it abounds. He clapp'd his Hand upon you

1 Possibly a reference to John Cross, D.D. (1630–89), who was Provincial of the Franciscan Order in England from 1674–7 and from 1686–9. He was the author of six works on religious themes and, possibly, some religious verse. The 'ill fortune' and the 'buttress' to which C refers may be related to the fact that the house in which the Franciscans lived in London was attacked by anti-Catholic mobs in 1689. The mobs did not succeed in breaking in, but the order was forced to move for its own protection.

2 *Antony and Cleopatra*, IV. xiv. 38.

know what, and said to Misfortune, Now Madam, I defy you. This you Know as well as I, therefore This you should Practise; and though you cannot I suppose Boast of such a Buttress as he was fenced with, yet, pro Modulo,[3] and according to your Ability, you should make that Use of it his Example teaches, and the most of a Little.

From Mr. Madan's renew'd Publication[4] I cannot but infer that he preserves the same Conduct as before he Publish'd at all. Letters of Admonition, Dissuasion and Exhortation he Burn'd unread, and has treated, I suppose, the Review with the same obstinate Indifference and Contempt. I the rather think so because I am firmly persuaded he could not Reply to his Answerer. Though it is possible his Case may resemble that of a certain Disputant I have heard of, who said upon a like Occasion, I am Confuted but not Convinced.

Impregnable however as He may be to the Attacks of sound Reason back'd with all the Authority of sound Learning, his Advocates are not all it seems quite so Stubborn as himself. Mr. Ryland of Birmingham has at last forsaken the Standard of Polygamy, and betaken himself to the Side of Christian Decorum and Decency again.[5] Mr. Powley, we Learn from good Authority has been Instrumental in working this conversion, which does him the more Honor as he had by all Accounts a very weak, though a very good Man, to deal with. Men that have no large Share of Reason themselves, are seldom sensible of the Force of it in the Hands of another.

I am inform'd that the Reviewer is preparing an Answer at large.[6] And that the Bishop of London has likewise undertaken the Task.[7] If this be the Case, Actum est de Thelyphthorâ.[8] I hear likewise that the King having Read a Part of it, threw it down with Indignation & express'd his Regret that there was no Law by which such an Author could be brought to the Punishment he deserves. This is not unlikely, for by all Accounts He is a Moral Man & consequently a chaste Husband, that he should View therefore such a Proposal with abhorrence is natural enough.

[3] 'In small measure'.

[4] An expanded second edition of *Thelyphthora* appeared in Jan. 1781.

[5] Riland's *The Scripture Preservative of Women from Ruin* appeared in 1782; Riland had changed from his pro-Madan stance of 1780 (see n. 5, C to Unwin, *post* 9 Nov. 1780).

[6] Samuel Badcock (see n. 4, C to Unwin, *post* 9 Nov. 1780). The 'Answer' appeared in the March issue of the *Monthly Review* (196–9). In July, Badcock again castigated Madan in reviewing the third volume (57–65, 161–82).

[7] Such a review was not published.

[8] 'It is all over with Thelyphthora.'

Your Mother returns her Thanks to Mrs. Unwin for her Letter. Our Love attends you both with Miss Shuttleworth & the little ones. The two Guineas may be sent with the Salmon, for which we thank you par avance.

If the Lines of your Letter could be push'd together[9] they would not fill three Sides, and if mine could be moved to the distance at which yours Stand from each other, they would fill four. This however is not my Reason for concluding, but because I am weary, therefore I add

only, that I am Yours as ever Wm C.

Jan. 14. 81

JOSEPH JOHNSON c. Monday, 15 January 1781[1]

Hayley, ii 272–3.

I did not write the line, that has been tampered with, hastily, or without due attention to the construction of it, and what appeared to me its only merit is, in its present state, entirely annihilated.

I know that the ears of modern verse-writers are delicate to an excess, and their readers are troubled with the same squeamishness as themselves. So that if a line do not run as smooth as quicksilver, they are offended. A critic of the present day serves a poem as a cook serves a dead turkey, when she fastens the legs of it to a post, and draws out all the sinews. For this we may thank Pope; but unless we could imitate him in the closeness and compactness of his expression, as well as in the smoothness of his numbers, we had better drop the imitation, which serves no other purpose than to emasculate and weaken all we write.—Give me a manly, rough line, with a deal of meaning in it, rather than a whole poem full of musical periods, that have nothing but their oily smoothness to recommend them.—

[9] The rest of the letter from this point on is inserted on the side of the page, thus emphasizing the humour of the passage.

[1] Although Wright dated this letter 1784 (ii. 286), it must be *c.* 15 Jan. 1781. In his letter to Lady Hesketh of 27 Sept. 1801 (Add. MS. 30803A, fo. 163*v*), Hayley says that the letter refers to *Anti-Thelyphthora* and was sent to Johnson without C's name. The date must be about the middle of Jan. 1781 because 'the much longer poem' is evidently 'The Progress of Error', which was sent to 'our common friend', i.e. Newton, shortly before the letter to him of 21 Jan.

I have said thus much, as I hinted in the beginning, because I have just finished a much longer poem than the last, which our common-friend will receive by the same messenger that has charge of this letter. In that poem there are many lines, which an ear, so nice as the gentleman's who made the above-mentioned alteration, would undoubtedly condemn, and yet (if I may be permitted to say it) they cannot be made smoother without being the worse for it. There is a roughness on a plumb, which nobody that understands fruit would rub off, though the plumb would be much more polished without it. But lest I tire you, I will only add, that I wish you to guard me for the future from all such meddling, assuring you, that I always write as smoothly as I can, but that I never did, never will, sacrifice the spirit or sense of a passage to the sound of it.

JOHN NEWTON — Sunday, 21 January 1781

Princeton

My dear Sir,

I am glad that the Progress of Error did not Err in its Progress as I fear'd it had, and that it has reach'd you safe; and still more pleas'd that it has met with your Approbation; for if it had not, I should have wished it had miscarried, and have been sorry that the Bearer's Memory had served him so well upon the Occasion. I knew him to be that sort of Genius which being much busied in making Excursions of the imaginary Kind, is not always present to its own immediate Concerns, much less to those of others, and having reposed the Trust in him, began to Regret that I had done so, when it was too late. But I did it to save a Frank, and as the Affair has turn'd out, that End was very well answer'd. This is committed to the Hands of a less Volatile person, and therefore more to be depended on.

Since I sent you the Copy, I have added some Lines upon a Character, which did not occurr to me at the first Heat, but which I should have been sorry to have omitted 'till it had been too late to insert it. I must beg you to bespeak a Place for it immediately after the address

to the Novellists, where it will be very properly disposed of, and will add Force to what follows upon the Subject of Thelyphthora.[1]

Chesterfield! All the Muses weep for Thee;
But ev'ry Tear shall scald thy Memory.
The Graces too, while Virtue at their Shrine
Lay bleeding under that soft Hand of thine,
Felt each a mortal Stab in her own Breast,
Abhorr'd the Sacrifice, and curs'd the Priest.
Thou polish'd and highfinish'd Foe to Truth,
Graybeard Corrupter of our list'ning youth,
To Simmer and Scum off the Filth of Vice,
That so refin'd, it might the more entice,
Then pour it on the Morals of thy Son
To taint His Heart, was worthy of thine own.[2]
Now, while the Poison all high Life pervades,
Write, if thou canst, one Letter from the Shades,
One, and One only, charg'd with deep Regret
That thy worst part, thy Principles, live yet,
One sad Epistle thence, may Cure Mankind
Of the Plague spread by Bundles left behind.

But then if you please the Word *tainted* in the first Line of the Passage relating to Thelyphthora must be displaced for the word *daring*, the Word *taint* having been necessarily introduced into the Lines you have just read. So much for This.

As to the Poem call'd Truth, which is already longer than its Elder Brother, and is yet to be lengthen'd by the Addition of perhaps 20 Lines, perhaps more, I shrink from the Thought of transcribing it at present. But as there is no Need to be in any Hurry about it, I hope that in some rainy Season which the next Month will probably bring with it, when perhaps I may be glad of Employment, the Undertaking will appear less formidable.[3]

You need not withold from us any Intelligence relating to

[1] These lines from 'The Progress of Error', with 'Petronius' substituted for 'Chesterfield', appeared as lines 335–52 in *1782*. The lines on *Thelyphthora* were omitted, however, from *1782*.

[2] The published letters (1774) of Philip Dormer Stanhope, 4th Earl of Chesterfield (1694–1773), to his illegitimate son.

[3] Probably the 32-line passage on the virtuous pagans (ll. 515–46 of the printed version).

yourselves, upon an Apprehension that Mr. Raban has been beforehand with you upon those Subjects, for he came down as Costive as if you had fed him with nothing but Quinces, and unless we Engineer'd him with Question after Question we could get nothing out of him. I have known such Travellers in my time, and Mrs. Newton is no Stranger to one of them, who keep all their Observations and Discoveries to themselves 'till they are extorted from them by mere dint of Examination and cross examination. He told us indeed that some invisible Agent supplied you every Sunday with a Coach, which we were pleas'd with hearing, and this I think was the Sum Total of his Information.

It is long since Mrs. Unwin sent the Clook to the Clook maker that he might produce a Clook just like it for the Use of Mrs. Newton. He kept our Clook 'till our Clook was stolen out of his Shop window, and then he was forced to make two new Clooks, one for us and one for Her, according to that Idea of a Clook with which the Sight of our Clook had inspir'd him. But the Idea being imperfect, or his Attention to that Idea not so close as it ought to have been, the Clooks he has made are shorter and slenderer than the Clook after which he should have Copied. Such however as the Clook is, it is much at Mrs. Newton's Service, and Mrs. Unwin purposes to charge Mr. Old with the Commission of laying his Clookship at her feet.

I remember that I thank'd Mrs. Newton for the Cocoa Nut, but I could not at that time tell her that it was the best we had ever eaten, because I had not open'd it when I wrote. But we have since eaten it all up except the Shell, and can give it the very best of Characters upon our own Experience.

We are much concern'd for Mr. Barham's Loss.[4] But it is well for that Gentleman that those Aimable Features in his Character which most incline one to Sympathize with him, are the very Graces and Virtues that will strengthen him to bear it with Æquanimity and

[4] A distinguished member of the Bedford Moravian Congregation, John Foster Barham (1721–81), did not suffer the death of any member of his family at this time. The 'loss' is possibly financial: the Bedford Moravian Congregation Diary (Bedford County Record Office, MO 356) for 29 Dec. 1780 records 'In the News came an Account of a tremendous Hurricane in the West Indies' and on 31 Jan. 1781 it mentions 'Brother Barham returned from London and brought us the joyful account that all our dear Brethren and Sisters were preserved alive in Barbadoes'. Both Foster and Barham families had had property in the West Indies and possibly still did at this time, to which the hurricane could have done great damage. We are grateful to Miss Patricia Bell of the Bedford County Record Office for her assistance in preparing this note.

Patience. People that have neither his Light nor Experience, will wonder that a Disaster which would perhaps have broken their Hearts, is not heavy enough to make any Abatement in the Cheerfull-ness of His.

Your Books came yesterday.[5] I shall not Repeat to you what I said to Mrs. Unwin, after having read two or three of the Letters. I admire the Preface, in which you have given an Air of Novelty to a worn out Topic, and have actually engaged the Favor of the Reader by saying those things in a delicate & uncommon way, which in general are disgusting.

I suppose you Know that Mr. Scott will be in Town on Tuesday.[6] He is likely to take Possession of the Vicarage at last, with the best Grace possible, at least if He and Mr. Brown[7] can agree upon the Terms. The Old Gentleman I find would be glad to Let the House & Abridge the Stipend, in other Words to make a good Bargain for himself, and Starve his Curate.

Our affectionate Respects attend yourself & Mrs. Newton.

Yours my dear Friend
Wm Cowper.

Jan 21. 1781.

JOHN NEWTON — Sunday, 4 February 1781

Address: The Revd. John Newton Charles Square / Hoxton / London[1]
Postmark: 5/FE
Princeton

My dear Friend—

We have waited I suppose with equal Impatience for a Letter. Our last Dispatches cross'd each other, so that each of us has claim'd the Posteriority, the Epistolary Race being always won by him that comes

5 Copies of Newton's *Cardiphonia*.
6 See n. 3, C to Newton, 16 Apr. 1780.
7 See n. 4, C to Newton, 31 Aug. 1780.

1 There is a small design in ink next to the address on the outside of the letter, and C has written at the top of the letter: 'The Outside is of Hannah's Embellishment.' Hannah Wilson was Dick Coleman's stepdaughter.

in, last.[2] This however has not been the only Reason of my Silence. I have been very busy in my way, and e'er long you will see the fruit of my Labor.[3] I shall say nothing of it at present except that *Truth* though long since finish'd must be postponed to this last Production, and that the Progress of Error itself must not take the Lead of it. Truth will be seasonable at any time, and though the Progress of Error has some Connexion with the present day, it is not so closely related to the Occurrences of it as the new one, which has the name of Table Talk. I have almost finish'd the copy of it which I intend for You, but cannot send it 'till from that I have transcrib'd another for myself, the Original being written on so many Scrips and Scraps that it would be very troublesome to range them, and indeed I have no perfect Copy of it but the fair one. I have not number'd the Lines but I suspect that it is longer than either of the others. Now I beleive I shall hang up my Harp for the Remainder of the Year and

Since Eighty one has had so much to do,
Postpone what yet is left, 'till Eighty two.

We were much pleas'd with your Extracts, they were so faithfull to the Truth, that unless Mr. Madan has much of that Candor he will not allow to others, they will put his Friendship for you, to a strong Trial; and yet so affectionate, that he cannot be displeas'd without the Violation of every thing that deserves the Name of Friendship. We both Long to be inform'd of the Reception they have met with, and take it for granted you will indulge our Curiosity when you can. We have been told that the Bishop of London intends an Answer to Thelyphthora, but I think his Lordship would hardly have put off the Publication to so late a day.[4] We have been told likewise that Mr. Riland is a Convert to Monogamy, but from some things we have heard since, are obliged to doubt it.[5]

Mr. Scot call'd on us the very day of his Return from London. We are glad of his Appointment to the Curacy, and so I suppose are all, at least all but a very few, whose Joy or Sorrow on the Occasion

[2] C's letter to Newton of 21 Jan. crossed with Newton's to C of 22 Jan. The present letter must have crossed with Newton's to C of 3 Feb.

[3] A reference to 'Table Talk', which he placed first in *1782* because of its topicality.

[4] We have not been able to locate any such publication.

[5] See n. 5, C to Unwin, 14 Jan. 1781.

is of small Consequence to any but themselves. And yet I think he will meet with troubles, and if my Sagacity does not fail me much, I can see from what quarter they are likely to arise. Instrumentality is generally taken up with some Reluctance, and laid down with a great deal more. But where such a Man, so well qualified in ev'ry respect for the charge assign'd him, has the care of a People, there can be no Occasion for subordinate Assistance. It is not his design to accept of it, and his Refusal I am rather apprehensive, will occasion a Murmur somewhere. Even upon *your* Account we are pleas'd with Mr. Page's Departure, as some disagreeables and awkwardnesses would probably have attended your Interview. He could not have refus'd you his pulpit, and yet there is reason to beleive that you are the last man in the Kingdom he would have wish'd to see in it. He has applied, or rather Mr. Warden Smith in his behalf, for the Curacy at Ravenstone, but Mr. Chapman[6] has given no definitive Answer. Mr. Scot, I should suppose would be sorry to see himself so succeeded. Mr. Dowbiggin's[7] Curate, (if I have spelt the strange Name aright) pays addresses to the same Lady, and Mr. Jones has been Ogling her not a little. But who will be the happy man, Conjecture has not yet ventur'd to surmise.

We wait with some Impatience for the Issue of Lord George's Trial. Somebody late from London, has brought hither the News that fresh Disturbances are expected on the Occasion, especially if he should be condemn'd.[8] But what sort of Patriotism is it, or what sort of Zeal, that is offended when the Laws of the Country take their course?

We are both pretty well. Mrs. Unwin joins with me in Love to yourself and Mrs. Newton.

Yours my dear Sir, Wm Cowper.

Feb. 4. 1781.

[6] The Revd. Robert Chapman was vicar of Ravenstone with Weston Underwood from 1764 to 1785.

[7] The Revd. Robert Dowbiggen was rector of Stoke Goldington with Gayhurst from 1766 to 1795.

[8] See C to Newton, 12 June 1780. Eight months after the Riots, Lord George Gordon's trial began at 8 a.m. on Monday, 5 Feb. and concluded with an acquittal at 4.45 on Tuesday, 6 Feb.

WILLIAM UNWIN Tuesday, 6 February 1781

British Library

My dear friend——

It is high time you should consult your own peace of mind, and not suffer the insatiable Demands and unreasonable Expectations of other men, to be a Source of unhappiness to yourself. You have lived long enough in the world to know that it swarms with people who are always ready to take advantage of the Generosity of such men as yourself, who say in their hearts when they meet with such disinterested treatment as every one receives from your hands: 'Now is the time—the man has a gentlemanly regard for his Character, he loves peace more than money, and will make any Concessions so that he may but approve himself to his own Conscience. Let us Squeeze him; he will yield well. The more he complys the more we will insist, and make him pay dear for the Character he wishes to deserve.' I cannot doubt but your Predecessor's Curate[1] is of this Stamp, his Demand wants nothing but a cock'd pistol to make it Felony without Benefit of Clergy.

As to your proposal to the Executors, if it does not give Contentment, it must be for the Reasons abovemention'd. In which case I would recommend it to you by all means to pay them exactly what they can lawfully demand for Glebe and Tythe and not a farthing more, and in return to insist upon ev'ry Penny you lay out in necessary Repairs, and not a farthing less. It is wrong not to deal liberally with persons who themselves Act upon liberal and honest Principles, but it is weakness to be the willing Dupe of Artifice, and to sacrifice one's own Interest for the sake of satisfying the insatiable or unjust.[2]

[1] Unwin's predecessor was the Revd. Philip Chetwode (1713–69), a graduate of Clare College, Cambridge, who was inducted to the livings of Harvard Stock and Ramsden Bellhouse in 1763. We do not know who the curate was.

[2] Many of the difficulties Unwin experienced with his congregation in 1780 and 1781 must have been related to tithing, although the contexts of C's letters do not always make this clear. The Revd. James Woodforde of Weston Longueville in Norfolk describes a tithing in his diary entry for 2 Dec. 1783: 'This being my Tithe Audit Day, the following People attended, and paid me everything that was due . . . They all dined, spent the Afternoon and Evening till 10. o'clock, and then they all went to their respective homes . . . We had this Year a very agreeable meeting here, and were very agreeable—no grumbling whatever.' (*The Diary of a Country Parson*, ed. J. Beresford (1924–31), ii. 107–8.) 'The Book of the

We are obliged to you for the Rugs, a Commodity that can never come to such a place as this at an unseasonable time. We have given one to an industrious poor Widow with 4 Children, whose Sister overheard her shiv'ring in the Night, and with some difficulty brought her to confess the next morning that she was half perish'd for want of sufficient covering. Her said Sister borrow'd a Rug for her at a Neighbor's immediately, which she had used but one Night when yours arrived. And I doubt not but we shall meet with others equally indigent and deserving of your Bounty.

I hear this Morning (Viâ tonsoris) that Lord George is acquitted. I take it for granted you was at the trial for three reasons. First because you was in town so lately—Secondly because you have a laudable Curiosity that acts as a Spur upon your Spirits on all such Occasions, and thirdly, because you are slender and slim and take up so little room that you are sure of a place when men of ampler Dimensions are necessarily excluded. Tell us all that pass'd, and if he is indeed acquitted, let us know upon what point his Acquittal turn'd, for at present I am rather at a Loss to conceive how he could Escape if the Law was allowed to take its course, uninterrupted by fear and uncontroll'd by a Spirit of Party.

Much good may your Humanity do you as it does so much good to others. You can nowhere find Objects more entitled to your Pity than where your Pity seeks them. A man whose Vices and Irregularities have brought his Liberty and Life into Danger, will always be view'd with an Eye of Compassion by those who understand what Human Nature is made of. And while we acknowledge that the Severity of the Law to be founded upon principles of Necessity and Justice, and are glad that there is such a Barrier provided for the peace of Society, if we consider that the difference between ourselves and the Culprit is not of our own making, we shall be as you are, tenderly affected with the View of his Misery, and not the less so because he has brought it upon himself. I look upon the worst man in Chelmsford Gaol, with a more favorable Eye, than upon a certain Curate who claims a Servant's wages from one who never was his Master.

What goes before was written in the Morning. This Evening I

Archdeacon of Essex' (Guildhall Library, London) records under 31 May 1781 the names of James Corker, James Burrell, John Blow, and Isaac Wood as 'Defaulters to the Church Rate' for Ramsden Bellhouse.

have read the trial as related in the General Evening and can only add to what I said before, in the Words of Horace

—Miror quo pacto Indicium illud
Fugerit.[3]

I give you Joy of your own hair. No doubt you are considerably a Gainer in your Appearance by being disperiwigg'd. The best Wig is that which most resembles the natural Hair, why then should He that has Hair enough of his own, have recourse to Imitation? I have little doubt but that if an Arm or a Leg could have been taken off with as little pain as attends the Amputation of a curl or a lock of hair, the natural Limb would have been thought less becoming or less convenient by some men than a wooden one, and have been dispos'd of accordingly.

Thanks for the Salmon. It was perfectly good, as were the two Lobsters; and the two Guineas came safe. Having some Verses to transcribe[4] and being rather weary, I add no more except our Love to the whole family jointly and severally.—Having begun my Letter with a miserable Pen, I was not willing to change it for a better lest my Writing should not be all of a piece, but it has worn me and my Patience quite out.

Yours ever Wm Cowper.

Feb. 6. 81

JOSEPH HILL — Thursday, 15 February 1781

Address: Mr. Joseph Hill / Chancery Office / London
Postmark: 16/FE
Cowper Johnson

Olney Feb. 15. 1781.

My dear friend—

I was glad you was pleas'd with my Report of so extraordinary a case. If the thought of versifying the Decisions of our Courts of Justice had struck me while I had the honor to attend them, it would perhaps have been no difficult matter to have compiled a Volume of such amusing and interesting Precedents, which if they wanted the

[3] *Satires*, I. iv. 99–100: 'I still wonder how he managed to get off.'

[4] 'Table Talk'. See C to Newton, 4 Feb. 1781.

Eloquence of the Greek or Roman Oratory, would have amply compensated that Deficiency by the Harmony of Rhime and Metre.[1]

Your Account of my Uncle and your Mother gave me great pleasure. I have long been afraid to enquire after some in whose Welfare I always feel myself interested, lest the Question should produce a painfull Answer. Longævity is the Lot of so few, and is so seldom render'd comfortable by the Association of good health and good Spirits, that I could not very reasonably suppose either your Relation or mine so happy in those respects as it seems they are. May they continue to enjoy those Blessings as long as the Date of Life shall last. I do not think that in these costermonger days, as I have a Notion Falstaff calls them,[2] an Antidiluvian Age is at all a desireable thing, but to Live comfortably while we Live is a great matter, and comprehends in it every thing that can be wish'd for on this side of the Curtain that hangs between Time & Eternity.

It is possible that Mrs. Hill may not be herself a Sufferer by the late terrible Catastrophe in the Islands, But I should suppose by her Correspondence with those parts, she may be connected with some that are. In either case I condole with her.[3] For it is reasonable to imagine that since the first Tour that Columbus made into the Western World, it never before experienced such a Convulsion, perhaps never since the Foundation of the Globe. You say the State grows old, and discovers many Symptoms of a decline. A writer possess'd of a Genius for Hypothesis like that of Burnet, might construct a plausible Argument to prove that the World itself is in a State of Superannuation, if there be such a Word, if not there must be such a one as Superannuity.[4] When that just Æquilibrium that has hitherto supported all things seems to fail, when the Elements burst the Chain that has bound them, the Wind sweeping away the Works of Man and Man himself together with his Works, and the Ocean seeming to overleap the Command, Hitherto shalt thou come and no farther, and here shall thy proud Waves be stay'd, these irregular and prodigious Vagaries seem to bespeak a Decay, and forbode perhaps not a very distant Dissolution. This thought has so run

1 C is referring to the poetical law case in his letter to Hill of 27 Dec. 1780.

2 'Virtue is of so little regard in these costermonger times that true valour is turned bear-herd': 2 *Henry IV*, I. ii. 191.

3 See n. 4, C to Newton, 21 Jan. 1781.

4 A reference to one or both of *History of the Reformation in England* (1679–1714) or *History of My Own Times* (1723–4) by Gilbert Burnet (1643–1715).

away with my Attention that I have left myself no room for the little Politics that have only Great Britain for their Object. Who knows but that while a thousand and ten thousand Tongues are employ'd in adjusting the Scale of our national Concerns, in complaining of new Taxes & Funds loaded with a Debt of accumulating Millions, the Consummation of all things may discharge it in a Moment, and the Scene of all this Bustle disappear as if it had never been? Charles Fox would say perhaps he thought it very unlikely; I question if he could prove even That, I am sure however he could not prove it to be impossible.[5]

My best Respects attend Mrs. Hill, with many thanks for her intended favor—I beg to be remember'd to your Mother, and to your Sisters, and if you [remember][6] to think of me when you see my Uncle, do not forget to tell him [how mu]ch I rejoice in his Well-being.

Feb. 15. 1781.

Received of Mr. Hill the Sum of Twenty pounds by Draft on Child and Co. £20.0.0.

Wm Cowper

JOHN NEWTON Sunday, 18 February 1781

Princeton

My dear Friend

I send you Table Talk. It is a Medley of many things, some that may be usefull, and some that for aught I know may be very divarting. I am merry that I may decoy people into my Company, and grave that they may be the better for it. Now and then I put on the Garb of a philosopher, and take the Opportunity that disguise procures me, to drop a word in favor of Religion. In short there is some froth and here and there a bit of sweetmeat, which seems to entitle it justly to the name of a certain dish the Ladies call a Trifle. I did not chuse to be more facetious, lest I should consult the Taste of my Readers at the Expence of my own Approbation, nor more

[5] A reference to the oratorical skills of Charles James Fox (1749–1806), Burke's friend.
[6] MS. torn.

serious than I have been, lest I should forfeit theirs. A Poet in my Circumstances has a difficult part to act. One minute obliged to bridle his Humor if he has any, and the next, to clap a Spur to the Sides of it. Now ready to weep from a Sense of the Importance of his subject, and on a sudden constrain'd to Laugh lest his gravity should be mistaken for Dullness. If this be not violent Exercise for the mind I know not what is, and if any man doubt it, let him try. Whether all this management and contrivance be necessary I do not know, but am inclined to suspect that if my Muse was to go forth clad in Quaker color, without one bit of Ribband to enliven her Appearance, she might walk from one End of London to the other as little noticed as if she were one of the Sisterhood indeed.

As to the word you mention, I a little suspected that you would object to it. Though I really thought that a Book which cannot be supposed to have been written under a Blessing, and that has certainly carried Mischief with it into many Families, deserved an Epithet as harsh as that which I had given it. It is a bargain however that I have made with my Lady Muse, never to defend or stickle for any thing that you object to. So the Line may stand if you please, thus.

Abhorr'd Thelyphthora, thy daring page—[1]

Not *tainted page* for the reason I give in the Letter which contains the Epitaph on Lord Chesterfield.[2]—You will meet with the obnoxious word again in the Copy I send you now, but coupled with a Substantive of so filthy a Character that I persuade myself you will have no Objection to the use of it in such a Connexion. I am no friend to the Use of words taken from what an Uncle of mine call'd the diabolical Dictionary, but it happens sometimes that a coarse Expression is almost necessary to do Justice to the Indignation excited by an abominable Subject. I am obliged to you however for your Opinion; and though Poetry is apt to betray one into a Warmth that one is not sensible of in writing Prose, shall always desire to be set down by it.

[1] C is referring to lines on *Thelyphthora* which were deleted from 'The Progress of Error'. Newton to C, 10 Feb. 1781 (Princeton): 'You have a line that begins Oh *curs'd* Thelyphthora. I wish you would allow me to erase the Word *Curs'd* & supply me with another to substitute in the room of it. The sound of it rather grates upon my ear. I have long had a dislike to the Word. Perhaps I should say Fatal or Hapless Thelyphthora. But you can say something better.'

[2] See C to Newton, 21 Jan. 1781.

We are glad that so able a Writer as Mr. Hill has taken up the Cudgels.[3] He is old enough to know how to reason with precision, and young enough to do it with fire and spirit. In conflicting with a disputant like Mr. Madan, I should suppose these two qualifications almost equally necessary A Writer like Him who knows how to get the Laugh on his side, would be pretty secure of having the world on his side too, if his Adversary had no Skill in the use of the same weapon. It is such a merry world that Truth herself seems to want one of her principal Recommendations, unless she will now and then condescend to the prevailing Temper of her Hearers. But you say you think it will do, and therefore I have no doubt of it.

Mr. Scott told Mr. Wilson[4] yesterday or the day before that he had again ask'd Mr. Raban whether or not he intended to continue his speaking, and that Mr. Raban would give him no determinate Answer. This I had from Mr. Wilson himself. It will be well if that Business ends peaceably. Nothing could be more tenderly cogent than your Letter to his Colleague, & he for aught I know may be properly influenc'd by it; but it seems plain that either the before-mention'd had not seen it, or that if he had, he had not felt it.

Mr. Page has at last found a House at Weston, late Brightman's who now occupies late Whitney's. Mrs. Page the Mother is to be in Lodgings at Ravenstone. Geary Ball has lost his wife.[5] She was buried on Thursday, having left her friends a comfortable Hope of her Welfare.

You had been married thirty one Years last Monday. When you married I was 18 years of age, and had just left Westminster School. At that time I valued a man according to his proficiency & Taste in classical Literature, & had the meanest opinion of all other Accomplishments unaccompanied by that. I lived to see the Vanity of what

[3] In a letter to C of 3 Feb. 1781 (Princeton), Newton mentions a letter he has received from Martin Madan: 'I have an answer to the letter I mentioned having sent to Mr. Madan —a long one. He begins, *I received your letter of excommunication* . . . His wish for an avowed Antagonist will shortly be gratified, for Mr. Hill (Richard) is writing an answer—I am to see a part of it on Monday when I go to breakfast with him.' The book in question is *The Blessings of Polygamy Displayed, in an Affectionate Address to the Rev. Martin Madan* . . . Richard (later Sir Richard) had attacked Madan in 1771 in *A Conversation between Richard Hill, Esq., The Rev. Mr. Madan, and Father Walsh, Superior of a Convent of English Benedictine Monks at Paris* . . .

[4] William Wilson, the barber.

[5] Geary Ball (1754–85) married Sarah Raban (1753–81) on 20 Oct. 1779 (*O.P.R.*, p. 390). According to *O.P.R.* (p. 394), Sarah was buried on Wednesday, 14 Feb. four days before this letter was written.

I had made my pride, and in a few years found that there were other attainments which would carry a man more handsomely through Life than a mere knowledge of what Homer & Virgil had left behind them. In measure as my Attachment to these Gentry wore off, I found a more welcome reception among those whose acquaintance it was more my Interest to cultivate. But all this time was spent in painting a piece of Wood that had no life in it. At last I begun to think *indeed*; I found myself in possession of many bawbles, but not one grain of Solidity in all my treasures. Then I learn'd the truth, & then I lost it, and there ends my History. I would no more than you wish to live such a life over again, but for one reason. He that is carried to Execution, though through the roughest road, when he arrives at the destin'd spot, would be glad, notwithstanding the many Jolts he met with to repeat his Journey. Yours my dear Sir with our joint Love

Wm Cowper.

Feb. 18. 1781.

P.S. I hope the Myrtles will arrive safe. Mrs. Unwin will soon write to acknowledge and thank you for your Kindness in the Affair of the Money.

MRS. HILL — Monday, 19 February 1781

Address: Mrs. Hill- / Great Queen Street / Lincolns Inn Fields / London.
Postmark: 21/FE
Cowper Johnson

Dear Madam,

When a man, especially a man that lives altogether in the Country, undertakes to write to a Lady he never saw, he is the awkwardest Creature in the world. He begins his Letter under just the same Sensations he would have if he was to accost her in person, only with this difference that he may take as much time as he pleases for consideration, and need not write a single word that he has not well weigh'd and ponder'd beforehand, much less a Sentence that he does not think supereminently clever. In every other respect, whether he be engaged in an Interview or in a Letter, his Behavior is for the

most part equally constrain'd and unnatural. He resolves as they say to set the best Leg foremost, which often proves to be what Hudibras calls

> . . . not that of bone,
> But much its better, th' wooden one.[1]

His extraordinary Effort only serves as in the case of that Hero, to throw him on the other side of his horse, and he owes his want of Success, if not to absolute Stupidity, to his most earnest Endeavor to secure it.

Now I do assure you Madam, that all these sprightly Effusions of mine stand entirely clear of the charge of premeditation, and that I never enter'd upon a business of this kind with more Simplicity in my life. I determin'd before I begun to lay aside all Attempts of the kind I have just mention'd, and being perfectly free from the fetters that self conceit commonly call'd Bashfullness fastens upon the mind, am as you see, surprisingly brilliant.

My principal design is to thank you in the plainest terms, which always afford the best proof of a man's Sincerity, for your obliging present. The Seeds will make a figure hereafter in the Stove of a much greater man than myself, who am a little man with no Stove at all. Some of them however I shall raise for my own Amusement and keep them as long as they can be kept in a Bark heat which I give them all the year, and in Exchange for those I part with, shall receive such Exotics as are not too delicate for a Green house.

I will not omitt to tell you, what no doubt you have heard already, though perhaps you have never made the Experiment, that Leaves gather'd at the Fall are found to hold their Heat much longer than Bark, and are preferable in every respect. Next year I intend to use them myself. I mention it because Mr. Hill told me some time since that he was building a Stove, in which I suppose they will succeed much better than in a Frame.

I am to thank you again Madam for the very fine Salmon you was so kind as to favor me with, which has all the Sweetness of a Hertfordshire Trout, and resembles it so much in the flavor that blindfold I should not have known the difference.

I beg Madam you will accept all these thanks, and beleive them

[1] First Part, Canto II. 915–16. The description is of Crowdero's wooden leg, with which he is about to hit Hudibras.

as sincere as they really are. Mr. Hill knows me well enough to be able to vouch for me that I am not overmuch addicted to Compliments [and][2] fine Speeches, nor do I mean either the one or the other when I assure you that I am Dear Madam, not merely for his sake but your own, your most Obedient & Affectionate [humble servant]

Wm Cowper.

Feb. 19. 1781

JOHN NEWTON Sunday, 25 February 1781

Princeton

My dear friend,

He that tells a long Story should take care that it be not made a long Story by his manner of telling it. His Expression should be natural and his method clear, the Incidents should be interrupted by very few Reflections, and Parentheses should be entirely discarded. I do not know that poor Mr. Teedon[1] guides himself in the Affair of Story telling by any one of these rules, or by any rule indeed that I ever heard of. He has just left us after a long visit, the greatest part of which he spent in the Narration of a certain detail of facts that might have been compress'd into a much smaller compass, and my Attention to which has wearied & worn out all my Spirits. You know how scrupulously nice he is in the choice of his Expression; an Exactness that soon becomes very inconvenient both to Speaker and hearer, where there is not a great Variety to chuse out of.—But Saturday Evening is come, the time I generally devote to my Correspondence with you, and Mrs. Unwin will not allow me to let it pass without writing, though having done it herself, both she and you might well spare me upon the present Occasion.

I have not yet read your Extract from Mr. Scott's Letter to Mr. Raban, though I have had an Opportunity to do it. I thought it might be better to wait a little in hope that there might be no need

[2] MS. torn.

[1] Samuel Teedon (d. June 1798) seems to have come to Olney from Bedford in 1775. He lived in a cottage at the junction of Dagnell Street and High Street, and he supported himself by teaching.

to do it at all. If hereafter it should be necessary to inform him of Mr. Scott's Feelings and Sentiments upon the Subject, I will readily perform the Office, and accompany the performance of it with such Advice of my own and such reasons as may happen to occur. In the mean time I am a little apprehensive that Opposition may provoke Opposition in return, and set a sharper Edge upon Inclination already sufficiently whetted to the business.

We are not the proper persons to give Counsell or Direction to Mr. Scott, our Acquaintance with him is of too short a standing to warrant us in the use of such a Liberty.[2] But it is our joint Opinion that he will not find himself easily and comfortably settled at Olney while he retains the Curacy at Weston. The people of that parish are rather inclined to grumble, and as we are inform'd express some Dissatisfaction on finding that they are to have but single Service on the Sabbath, and the people here are not well pleas'd though they will have the same Number of Ordinances as before, that they are not to have them at the same time. Some perhaps may find the Alteration a real Inconvenience, and others who may not find it so, will be glad of an Occasion to pretend one. His Resignation of Weston would at once annihilate all these Complaints, and would beside place the Sunday Evening Meeting and the whole Management of it entirely in his own hands, which as it would prevent the possibility of any Bickerings on the account of supernumerary Speakers, we should think were a most desirable Object. We are well aware that the Vicinity of Weston to Ra'nstone is Mr. Scott's reason for still continuing to hold the former, but whether when weigh'd in the Ballance against the Mischiefs he may incurr by doing it, it will be found a sufficient one, may be a matter deserving Consideration. It can be no very difficult thing for his former people to reach him at Olney, though one Mile will be added to their Journey; if they really preferr him to their new Minister we think such a difficulty as that may be easily surmounted.—Whether Mr. Scott's Circumstances will afford the Sacrifice we do not know, but Mrs. Unwin thinks, & if you ask me my Opinion I think so too, that if there be no other Objection to the measure, he would do well to committ himself to Providence for a Supply. Mr. Brown's Age[3] and the probability, nearly related I suppose to a Certainty, that Mr. Scott will succeed

[2] See n. 3, C to Newton (Princeton *copy*), 16 Apr. 1780.

[3] Browne was *c.* 77 at this time.

him in the Living, seems of itself to reduce that difficulty almost to nothing.

My Paper is so intolerably bad, as you may perceive by the running of the Ink, that it has quite worn out my patience.

Notwithstanding my purpose to shake hands with the Muse & take my leave of her for the present, we have already had a tête á tête since I sent you the last production. I am as much or rather more pleas'd with my new plan than with any of the foregoing. I mean to give a short Summary of the Jewish Story, the miraculous Interpositions in behalf of that people, their great privileges, their Abuse of them & their consequent destruction, and then by way of Comparison such another Display of the favors vouchsaf'd to this Country, the similar Ingratitude with which they have requited them, and the punishment they have therefore reason to expect, unless Reformation interpose to prevent it. Expostulation is its present title. But I have not yet found in the writing it that facility & readiness without which I shall despair to finish it well or indeed to finish it at all.

Beleive me my dear Sir with my Love to Mrs. N.

Feb. 25. —81 Your ever Affectionate

Wm Cowper.

WILLIAM UNWIN Tuesday, 27 February 1781

British Library

My dear friend,

In the first place my paper is insufferably bad, so that though this is the second Sheet on which I have begun to write and taken from another quire, I can hardly flatter myself that I shall be able to persevere to the End of it.

I thank you for your Relation of Mr. Fytche's dispute with the Bishop.[1] It affords matter for some Reflections not altogether

[1] 'Mr Disney ffytche of the Rectory of Woodham Walter in Essex Presented John Eyre Clerk to that Living, who applied to the Bishop of London for Institution, but his Lordship having heard that Mr. Eyre had given his Patron a Bond in Three Thousand Pounds Penalty to resign whenever in the most general Terms and conceiving the Bond Simoniaecal [*sic*] and therefore illegal and that it was exacted to cover the Patron's Estate (one half of the Parish) from the Payment of Tythes, the Bishop positively refused to institute Mr. Eyre, who acknowledged that he had subjected himself to such a Bond.' ('Short State of Case between the Bishop of London and Mr. ffytche', Box 39, Lambeth Papers: Lambeth Palace Library.)

favorable to the Episcopal Order, as it is easy to see that if his Lordship had the power he does not want the Inclination to use the thunders of the Vatican, and anathematize a poor Gentleman that dares to oppose him, without Mercy. I know not in what part of the Scripture he will find it reveal'd, that a Patron by taking a Bond of Resignation from the person he presents, forfeits all hope of Mercy in this world & that which is to come. Yet he asserts it as gravely as if he knew it to be true; but the Laity at this time of day are wiser than when they gave their Bishops credit for Omnipotence. That Cheat will pass no longer.

What Narrative can I send you in return? A part of the Middlesex Militia are quarter'd at this place and at Newport Pagnel. Yesterday being Sunday[2] was distinguish'd by a Riot raised at the Bull Inn by some of the Officers, whose avowed purpose in doing it was to mortify a Town which they understood was inhabited by Methodists. They roar'd and sung and danced, sometimes in the house, sometimes in the street, and at last quarrel'd with a Shoemaker's Son, and in the fray, one of them lost his Sword, which he had drawn with an Oath that he would cut down poor Crispin.[3] He bluster'd much, declar'd he had rather lose his Life than his sword, but was oblig'd to go home without it. This Evening the Bell man cried it, but with what Success has not yet transpir'd.—Oh Shame to the Name of Soldier!

Alas poor Vestris! What a pitiable Object, how truly French in his Humiliation, when he bow'd his Head down to the stage and held it there, as if he meant never to raise it more. As humble in his Abasement as exalted in his capers, equally French in both.[4] Which is most entitled to Compassion, the Dancer who is obliged at the Expence of all that is call'd Dignity in Man, to stoop to the arbitrary Requisitions of an enraged Assembly, or that Assembly themselves

[2] C must have started this letter on Monday, 26 Feb. 1781, and finished it the following morning before the post set out. Despite C's reference to 'yesterday being Sunday' in the text, 27 Feb. 1781 was a Tuesday.

[3] The brothers, Crispin and Crispinian, shoemakers by trade and the patron saints of those in that profession, were martyred during the reign of Diocletian.

[4] C is referring to the disturbance at the King's Theatre, Haymarket, on 22 Feb., the benefit night of the celebrated dancer, Auguste Vestris (1760–1842). 'When the curtain was drawn up, the stage appeared to be half full of spectators; at which the galleries in particular seemed to be so offended, that they would not suffer the opera to go on . . . it was the resolution of the gallery that the performance should not proceed until the stage was cleared . . . at half past nine the business was compromised, and the opera was suffered to go on.' (*Morning Herald*, Sat., 24 Feb. 1781.)

who think it worth their while to spend hours in bellowing for Satisfaction from the Concessions of a Dancer? Considering that Life does not last for ages and they know it, it is not unreasonable to say that both He and they might set a higher value upon their time, and devote it to a better purpose. It is possible too you may think that the Maker of this wise Reflection might himself have been better employ'd than in writing what follows upon the Subject. I subscribe to the truth of the Animadversion, and can only say in my Excuse that the Composition is short, did not cost me much time, & may perhaps provoke a Laugh which is not always useless. If you please you may send it to the Poets' Corner.[5]

A Card

Poor Vestris, griev'd beyond all measure,
To have incurr'd so much displeasure,
Although a Frenchman, disconcerted,
And though lightheel'd, yet heavy hearted,
Begs humbly to inform his friends
Next first of April he intends
To take a Boat and row right down
To Cuckolds' point from Richmond town,
And as he goes, alert and gay,
Leap all the Bridges in his way,
The Boat borne downward with the tide
Shall catch him safe on t'other side.
He humbly hopes by this Expedient
To prove himself their most obedient,
(Which shall be always his Endeavor)
And Jump into their former Favor.

I have not forgot, though when I wrote last I did not think of answering your kind Invitation. I can only say at present that Stock shall be my first Visit, but that Visiting at this time would be attended with insupportable awkwardnesses to me, and with such as the Visited themselves would assuredly feel the weight of. My Witticisms are only current upon paper now, and that sort of paper

[5] This poem was not published until 1836 in *Southey*.

Currency must serve like the Congress Dollars, for want of the more valuable Coin, myself.[6]

We thank you for the intended Salmon, and beg you would get yourself made Bishop of Chichester as soon as possible, that we may have to thank you for every Kind of eatable fish the British Coast produces.

Our joint Love attends yourself and whole family, together with our respectfull Compliments to your Uncle.

Yours ever
Wm Cowper.

Feb. 27. 1781.

I have hurried to the End as fast as possible, being weary of a Letter that is one continued blot.

JOHN NEWTON — Monday, 5 March 1781

Princeton

My dear friend:

Since Writing is become one of my principal Amusements, and I have already produced so many Verses on Subjects that entitle them to a Hope that they may possibly be usefull, I should be sorry to suppress them entirely, or to publish them to no purpose for want of that cheap Ingredient, the name of the Author. If my Name therefore will serve them in any degree as a passport into the public Notice, they are welcome to it. But in that case, I must desire to have the Progress of Error return'd to me that I may cancel the Passage relating to Thelyphthora; for though in that passage I have neither belied my own Judgment nor slander'd the Author, yet on account of Relationship and for reasons I need not suggest to you, I should not chuse to make a public Attack upon his Performance.[1] I will entreat you to give it once more an attentive perusal, and if you think that the Removal of that passage will clear it from all

[6] The Continental Congress in America had authorized the issue of bills of credit from 1776 onwards. Since the Congress had no source of revenue from taxation, the money had little or no backing.

[1] This is the passage referred to in C to Newton, 18 Feb. 1781.

danger of a personal Application to Mr. Madan, be so kind as to tell me so. Your Opinion in the Affirmative will make me easy upon the Subject, and I shall set my Name to it without fear. It is certain that I had him pretty much in view not there only but in other parts of the production likewise, but it seems to me upon present Recollection, that the rest are of such a kind as to stand fairly acquitted of the charge of Personality. When I have cancell'd the offensive portion of it, I will endeavour to supply the hiatus with something that may make Amends for the Loss, either in the same place or in some other part of the Poem.

If you are of my Mind I think Table talk will be the best to begin with, as the Subjects of it are perhaps more popular; and one would wish at first setting out to catch the public by the Ear and hold them by it as fast as possible that they may be willing to hear one on a second and a third Occasion.

The Passage you object to I inserted merely by way of Catch, and think that it is not unlikely to answer the purpose. My design was to say as many serious things as I could, and yet to be as lively as was compatible with such a purpose. Do not imagine that I mean to stickle for it as a pretty Creature of my own that I am loth to part with—but I am apprehensive that without the sprightliness of that passage to introduce it the following paragraph would not show to advantage.—If the world had been filled with men like yourself I should never have written it, but thinking myself in a measure obliged to tickle if I meant to please, I therefore affected a Jocularity I did not feel.[2]—As to the rest, wherever there is War there is Misery and Outrage, notwithstanding which it is not only lawfull to wish, but even a Duty to pray for the Success of one's Country. And as to the Neutralities,[3] I really think the Russian virago[4] an impertinent Puss for meddling with us, and engaging half a score Kittens of her acquaintance to scratch the poor Old Lion, who if he has been insolent in his day, has probably acted no otherwise than they themselves would have acted in his Circumstances, & with his power to embolden them.

You will be so good as to insist upon it as from me, that when

[2] The new passage in 'Table Talk' (ll. 13–28) was sent to Newton for approval on 18 Mar.

[3] The Armed Neutrality, 1780: an alliance among Russia, Sweden, and Denmark, joined later by Prussia and Holland.

[4] Catherine the Great.

Mr. Johnson is in possession of my Name, he shall not on any Account whatever prefix it to Sir Airy,[5] or by any Means direct or indirect either now or hereafter assert or even insinuate that I wrote it.—I believe I have drawn up this precaution with all the Precision of a Lawyer without intending it. I mean however no more than to desire you to impress him with an Idea of the Seriousness with which I make this Stipulation.

Mr. Johnson will therefore if he pleases announce me to the World by the Stile and title of

William Cowper Esqr.
of the Inner Temple.[6]

I am glad that the Myrtles reach'd you safe, but am persuaded from past Experience that no Management will keep them long alive in London, especially in the City. Our own English Grots,[7] the Natives of the country, are for the most part too delicate to thrive there, much more the nice Italian. To give them however the best chance they can have, the Lady must keep them well water'd, giving them a moderate Quantity in Summer time ev'ry other day, and in Winter about twice a Week; not Spring water for that would kill them. At Michaelmas as much of the Mould as can be taken out without disturbing the roots must be evacuated, and its place supplied with fresh, the lighter the better. And once in two years the plants must be drawn out of their pots with the entire ball of Earth about them, & the matted roots pared off with a sharp knife, when they must be planted again with an Addition of rich light Earth as before. Thus dealt with they will grow luxuriantly in a Green house, where they can have plenty of sweet Air which is absolutely necessary to their health. I used to purchase them at Covent garden almost every year when I lived in the Temple, but even in that airy Situation they were sure to lose their Leaf in winter, and seldom recover'd it again in spring. I wish them a better fate at Hoxton.

Olney has seen this day what it never saw before, and what will serve it to talk of I suppose for years to come. At Eleven o'clock this

[5] C does not wish his name linked with *Anti-Thelyphthora* which Johnson had published in late Dec. 1780 or early Jan. 1781. Martin Madan is Sir Airy.

[6] Johnson amended this to: 'William Cowper of the Inner Temple, Esq'.

[7] A fragment or particle (*O.E.D.*). C is probably using the term colloquially to refer to the tender cutting of myrtle.

Morning a party of Soldiers enter'd the town, driving before them another party, who after obstinately defending the Bridge for some time were obliged to quit it and run. They ran in very good order, frequently faced about and fired, but were at last obliged to surrender prisoners of war. There has been much drumming and shouting, much scampering about in the dirt, but not an Inch of Lace made in the town, at least at the Silver End of it.

It is our joint Request that you will not again leave us unwritten to for a fortnight. We are so like yourselves in this particular, that we cannot help ascribing so long a Silence to the worst Cause. The longer your Letters the better, but a short one is better than none.

If the King was to make it his Request to us, we could not furnish him with a plate of Greens from our Garden.—It was one of our Reasons for dismissing Darlin, that under his Management or no Management at all, it produc'd us nothing.

Mrs. Unwin is pretty well, and adds the Greetings of her Love to mine.

Yours my dear friend
Wm Cowper.

Mar. 5. 1781.

JOHN NEWTON — Sunday, 18 March 1781

Princeton

My dear Friend

A slight Disorder in my Larboard Eye may possibly prevent my writing you a long letter, and would perhaps have prevented my writing at all, if I had not known that you account a Fortnight's silence a week too long.

I am sorry that I gave you the trouble to write twice upon so trivial a Subject as the passage in question. I did not understand by your first Objections to it that you thought it so exceptionable as you do, but being better inform'd I immediately resolv'd to expunge it, and subjoin a few lines which you will oblige me by substituting in its place. I am not very fond of weaving a political thread into any of my pieces, and that for two reasons. First because I do not think myself qualified in point of Intelligence to form a decided Opinion

on any such topics, & secondly, because I think them, though perhaps as popular as any, the most useless of all. The following verses are design'd to succeed immediately after—fights with Justice on his side.

Let Laurels drench'd in pure Parnassian dews,
Reward *his* mem'ry, dear to ev'ry Muse,
Who with a Courage of the noblest root,
In Honor's field advancing his firm foot,
Plants it upon the line that Justice draws,
And will prevail, or perish in her cause.
'Tis to the Virtues of such men, man owes
His portion in the Good that Heav'n bestows,
And when recording History displays
Feats of renown, though wrought in antient days,
Tells of a few stout hearts that fought and died,
Where Duty plac'd them, at their Country's side,
The man that is not mov'd with what he reads,
That takes not fire at their heroic deeds,
Unworthy of the Blessings of the brave,
Is base in Kind, and born to be a Slave[1]
  But let &c

I am obliged to you for your Advice with respect to the manner of Publication, and feel myself inclined to be determin'd by it. So far as I have proceeded on the Subject of Expostulation, I have written with tolerable Ease to myself, and in my own Opinion (for an Opinion I am obliged to have about what I write, whether I will or no) with more Emphasis and Energy than in either of the others. But it seems to open upon me with an Abundance of Matter, that forebodes a considerable Length, and the time of year is come when what with walking and Gardening, I can find but little leisure for the Pen. I mean however as soon as I have ingrafted a new Scyon[2] into the Progress of Error instead of Thelyphthora, and when I have transcribed Truth and sent it you, to apply myself to the Composition last undertaken with as much Industry as I can. If therefore the three

[1] Newton evidently objected to some reference in lines 13–28 of 'Table Talk'. There is a fragment containing these lines in the B.L. Ash MSS.; line 15 reads 'sound both heart and root' instead of 'noblest root'.

[2] A shoot or twig for grafting (*O.E.D.*).

first are put into the Press, while I am spinning and weaving the last, the whole may perhaps be ready for Publication before the proper Season will be past. I mean at present that a few select smaller pieces, about 7 or 8 perhaps, the best I can find in a bookfull that I have by me, shall accompany them. All together they will furnish I should imagine a volume of tolerable bulk, that need not be indebted to an unreasonable breadth of Margin for the importance of its figure.

If a Board of Enquiry were to be establish'd, at which Poets were to undergo an Examination respecting the Motives that induced them to publish, and I were to be summon'd to attend that I might give an account of mine, I think I could truly say, what perhaps few Poets could—that though I have no Objection to lucrative consequences if any such should follow, they are not my Aim; much less is it my Ambition to exhibit myself to the world as a Genius. What then, says Mr. President, can possibly be your Motive? I answer with a Bow—Amusement—there is nothing but this, no Occupation within the Compass of my small Sphere, Poetry excepted, that can do much towards diverting that train of Melancholy thoughts, which when I am not thus employ'd, are for ever pouring themselves in upon me. And if I did not publish what I write, I could not interest myself sufficiently in my own Success to make an Amusement of it.

In my account of the Battle fought at Olney, I laid a snare for your Curiosity, and succeeded. I supposed it would have an Ænigmatical appearance, and so it had but like most other Riddles, when it comes to be solv'd you will find that it was not worth the trouble of Conjecture.—There are Soldiers quarter'd at Newport and at Olney—these met by order of their respective officers, in Emberton Marsh, perform'd all the Manœuvres of a deadly[3] Battle, and the result was, that this Town was taken. Since I wrote they have again Encounter'd with the same Intention, and Mr. Raban kept a room for me & Mrs. Unwin, that we might sit and view them at our Ease.[4] We did so, but it did not answer our Expectation; for before the Contest could be decided, the powder on both sides being expended, the Combatants were obliged to leave it an undecided Contest.—If it were possible that when two great Armies spend the Night in expectation

[3] C's holograph appears to read 'deedy', but it would seem obvious he meant to write 'deadly'.

[4] Tom Raban's house was the last on the left as one approached the bridge, and his windows overlooked the meadows.

of a Battle, a third could silently steal away their ammunition and Arms of every kind, what a Comedy would it make of that which always has such a tragical Conclusion!

We are very sorry that Mrs. Newton has been ill, our Love attends yourself and her. Mrs. Unwin is at present troubled with a violent pain somewhat resembling what is call'd a Lumbago, but it has not prevented her walking this Morning as far as Olney Pasture.—Remember us to Miss Catlett, and tell Sally & Peggy we do not forget them.

Yours my dear friend Wm Cowper.

Mar 18.1781

Mrs. Unwin returns you many thanks for your Letter.

WILLIAM UNWIN — Monday, 2 April 1781

British Library

My dear friend—

Fine Weather and a Variety of extraforaneous[1] Occupations (search Johnson's Dictionary for that Word and if not found there insert it, for it saves a deal of Circumlocution, and is very lawfully compounded) make it difficult (Excuse the length of a Parenthesis which I did not foresee the length of when I began it, and which may perhaps a little perplex the sense of what I am writing, though as I seldom deal in that Figure of Speech I have the less need to make an Apology for doing it at present) make it difficult I say for me to find Opportunities for writing. My Morning is ingrossed by the Garden, and in the Afternoon till I have drunk Tea, I am fit for nothing. At five o'clock we walk, and when the Walk is over, Lassitude recommends Rest, and again I become fit for nothing. The current Hour therefore, which I need not tell you is comprised in the Interval between four and five, is devoted to your Service, as the only one in the 24 that is not otherwise engaged.

I do not wonder that you have felt a great deal upon the Occasions you mention in your last, especially on account of the Asperity you have met with in the Behavior of your friend. Reflect however that as it is natural to you to have very fine feelings, it is equally

[1] C is the source of this word for 'outdoor'.

natural to some other tempers to leave those feelings entirely out of the question, and to Speak to you and to Act towards you just as they do towards the rest of Mankind, without the least Attention to the Irritability of your System. Men of a rough and unsparing Address should take great care that they be always in the right, the Justness and Propriety of their Sentiments and Censures, being the only tolerable Apology that can be made for such a Conduct, especially in a Country where Civility of Behavior is inculcated even from the Cradle. But in the Instance now under our Contemplation I think you a Sufferer under the weight of an Animadversion not founded in truth & which consequently you did not deserve. I account Him faithfull in the Pulpit who dissembles nothing that he beleives, for fear of giving Offence. To accommodate a discourse to the Judgment & Opinion of others for the sake of pleasing them, though by doing so we are obliged to depart widely from our own, is to be unfaithfull to ourselves at least, and cannot be accounted fidelity to Him whom we profess to Serve. But there are few men who do not stand in need of the Exercise of Charity and forbearance, and the Gentleman in question has afforded you an ample Opportunity in this respect, to show how readily, though differing in your Views, you can practise all that he could possibly expect from you if your Persuasion corresponded exactly with his own.

With respect to Monsieur le Curé, I think you not quite excuseable for suffering such a Man to give you any Uneasiness at all. The Grossness and Injustice of his Demand, ought to be its own Antidote. If a Robber should miscall you a pitifull fellow for not carrying a Pursefull of Gold about you, would His Brutality give you any concern? I suppose not—Why then have you been distress'd in the present Instance?

I think you pay dear for an agreeable Companion in the person of your own Curate, when you enlarge his Stipend to a Sum that you say exceeds what you can conveniently afford, especially after having had such pregnant proof that his Motives for staying with you, if he stays, are of the pecuniary Kind. But you know the Man and I do not—If he is worth what you buy him for now, I wish he may improve upon your hands, so that you may hereafter have additional cause to rejoice in your Bargain.

Poor Mrs. Rust[2] is much an Object of Compassion. I should

[2] Unidentified; she is probably one of Unwin's parishioners.

apprehend that when she insists upon an Allowance of 300£ a year as the Condition of a Seperation, she acts under the Influence of somebody better acquainted with the value of Money than the worth of peace. For surely the Sum of 100£ per annum is no Object, at least ought not to be an Object, when it stands in Competition with the inestimable Happiness of getting rid of such a Husband.

I have not room for more except to add our Love to all at Stock, & to Subscribe myself theirs and Yours

Wm Cowper.

Thanks for the Salmon which was very fine.

April 2. 1781.

JOHN NEWTON — Sunday, 8 April 1781

Princeton

My dear friend

Since I commenc'd Author, my Letters are even less worth your acceptance than they were before. I shall soon however lay down the Character, and cease to trouble you with directions to a Printer, at least till the Summer is over. If I live to see the Return of Winter I may perhaps assume it again, but my Appetite for fame is not keen enough to combat with my Love of fine weather, my Love of Indolence, and my Love of gardening Employments.

I send you by Mr. Old,[1] my Works complete, bound in brown paper, and number'd according to the Series in which I would have them publish'd. With respect to the Poem call'd Truth, it is *so* true that it can hardly fail of giving Offence to an unenlighten'd Reader. I think therefore that in Order to obviate in some measure those prejudices that will naturally erect their bristles against it, an explanatory preface, such as You, (and nobody so well as you) can furnish me with, will have ev'ry grace of propriety to recommend it. Or if you are not averse to the task, and your Avocations will allow you to undertake it, and if you think it would be still more proper, I should be glad to be indebted to you for a preface to the whole. I wish you however to consult your own Judgment upon the Occasion, and to engage in either of these works, or neither, just as

[1] See n. 5, C to Newton, 4 July 1780.

your discretion guides you. The Observations contain'd in the Progress of Error, though as you say, of general Application, have yet such an unlucky Squint at the Author of Thelyphthora, that they will be almost as sure to strike him in the sore place, as he will be to read the poem if publish'd with my name. And I would by no means wish to involve you in the resentment that I shall probably incurr by those lines, which must be the consequence of our walking arm in arm into the public notice. For my own part I have my Answer ready, if I should be called upon; but as you have corresponded with him upon the Subject, and have closed that Correspondence in as amicable a way as the Subject of it would permitt, you may perhaps think it would appear like a departure from the friendly Moderation of your Conduct, to give an open countenance & Encouragement to a Work in which he seems to be so freely treated. But after all there is no necessity for your name, though I should chuse by all means to be honor'd with it, if there be no unanswerable Objection.—You will find the Substituted passage in the Progress of Error, just where the Ground was occupied by the reflections upon Mr. Madan's performance.

Mr. Hill's answer seems to have no fault but what it owes to a Virtue.[2] His great Charity and Candor has in my mind excluded from it that Animation and Energy, which even a good man might lawfully show when answering a book which could hardly fail to excite a little indignation. Mildness & meekness are not more plainly recommended in Scripture in some instances, than Sharpness of reproof and Severity in others.

I am very well satisfied with the commendation the Reviewers have bestow'd upon Sir Airy.[3] It is as much as I hoped for, and I question much whether they will speak so favorably of my next publication.

I have written a great deal to day, which must be my Excuse for an abrupt Conclusion. Our Love attends you both—we are in pretty good health, Mrs. Unwin indeed better than usual, and as to me I ail nothing but the incurable Ailment.

Yours my dear friend
Wm Cowper.

[2] See n. 3, C to Newton, 18 Feb. 1781.

[3] The *Critical Review* mentioned *Anti-Thelyphthora* briefly. Badcock, in the *Monthly Review*, was encouraging. See *Russell*, p. 34.

8 April 1781

Thanks for the Cocoa nut. Very good.

April 8. 1781.

I send a Cucumber, not of my own raising, and yet raised by me.

Solve this Ænigma, dark enough
To puzzle any brains
That are not downright puzzle:proof,
And Eat it for your pains.

JOHN NEWTON — Monday, 23 April 1781

Princeton

Monday April 23. 1781

My dear friend—

Having not the least doubt of your Ability to Execute just such a Preface as I should wish to see prefixt to my Publication, and being convinc'd that you have no good foundation for those which you yourself entertain upon the Subject, I neither withdraw my requisition, nor abate one Jot of the Earnestness with which I made it. I admitt the delicacy of the Occasion, but am far from apprehending that you will therefore find it difficult to succeed. You can draw a hair stroke where another man would make a Blot as broad as a Sixpence.

With respect to the Heathen and what I have said about them, the Subject is of that kind which every man must settle for himself, and on which we can proceed no further than Hypothesis and Opinion will carry us. I was willing however to obviate an Objection I foresaw, and to do it in a way not derogatory from the truth of the Gospel, yet at the same time as conciliatory as possible to the prejudices of the Objector. After all indeed I see no Medium, either we must suppose them lost, or if saved, saved by Virtue of the only propitiation. They seem to me on the principles of Equity, to stand in much the same predicament, and to be entitled (at least according to human apprehensions of Justice) to much the same Allowance as Infants. Both partakers of a sinfull nature, and both unavoidably ignorant of the remedy. Infants I suppose universally saved, because

impeccable, and the virtuous Heathen, having had no Opportunity to Sin against Revelation, and having made a conscientious use of the Light of Nature, I should suppose saved too.—But I drop a Subject on which I could say a good deal more, for two reasons, first because I am writing a Letter and not an Essay, and secondly because after all I might write about it, I could come to no certain Conclusion.

I once had thoughts of annexing a few smaller pieces to those I have sent you, but having only very few that I accounted worthy to bear them company, and those for the most part on Subjects less calculated for Utility than Amusement, I changed my mind. If hereafter I should accumulate a sufficient Number of these Minutiæ to make a miscellaneous Volume, which is not impossible, I may perhaps collect and print them.

I am much obliged to you for the Interest you take in the Appearance of my Poems, and much pleased by the Alacrity with which you do it; your favorable Opinion of them affords me a comfortable presage with respect to that of the public; for though I make allowances for your partiality to me and mine, because mine, yet I am sure you would not suffer me unadmonish'd to add myself to the Multitude of insipid Rhimers with whose productions the World is already too much pester'd.

It is worth while to send *You* a Riddle, you make such a Variety of Guesses and turn and tumble it about with such an industrious Curiosity. The Solution of that in question is—let me see. It requires some Consideration to explain it even though I made it. I raised the Seed that produced the plant that produced the fruit, that produced the Seed that produced the fruit I sent you. This latter Seed I gave to the Gardener of Terningham,[1] who brought me the Cucumber you mention. Thus you see I raised it—that is to say I raised it virtually by having raised its Progenitor. And yet I did not raise it, because the identical Seed from which it grew was raised at a distance. You observe I did not speak rashly when I spoke of it as dark enough to poze an Œdipus, and have no need to call your own Sagacity in question for falling short of the Discovery.

A Report has prevail'd at Olney that you are coming in a fortnight; but taking it for granted that you know best when you shall

[1] The manor house at Tyringham, three miles from Olney, was at this time the property of William Mackworth Praed (1747–1833), M.P. for St. Ives from 1781 to 1806.

come, and that you will make us happy in the same Knowledge, as soon as you are possessed of it yourself, I did not venture to build any sanguine Expectations upon it.[2]

Mr. Madan seems to be in the condition of that Gentleman of most candid Memory, who though he might be confuted was resolv'd never to be convinced. I have at last read the second Volume of his Work, and had some hope that I should prevail with myself to read the first likewise—But endless Repetitions, unwarranted Conclusions, and wearisome declamations, conquer'd my perseverance, and obliged me to leave the task unfinished. He boasts in his Introduction that he has attended to an happy Mixture of the Utile dulci. The former I find not, and the latter so sparingly afforded, as to be scarce perceptible.—You told us some time since that his reasons for writing on such a Subject were certainly known to a few. If you judge it not imprudent to communicate them by the Post, we should be glad to know them too. You know that we are hermetically seal'd, and that no Secret is the less a Secret for our participation of it. I began his book at the latter end because the first part of it was engaged when I receiv'd the second, but I had not so good an Appetite as a Soldier in the Guards, who I was inform'd when I lived in London, would for a small matter Eat up a Cat alive, beginning at her Tail and finishing with her Whiskers.

Mrs. Unwin sends her Love, she is tolerably well and will rejoice to hear that her Application in behalf of your Nephew has succeeded.[3] Not having lately heard from Stock, she is ignorant of what has passed.

My Love to Mrs. Newton—Yours ut semper

Wm Cowper.

[2] Newton did not arrive at Olney until June.

[3] The Nind affair. See n. 10, C to Unwin, 13 Feb. 1780, and n. 1, C to Unwin, 28 Mar. 1780.

JOHN NEWTON Wednesday, 25 April 1781

Princeton (*copy*)[1]

My dear Sir—

While I thought of publishing only the 4 pieces already sent,[2] I did not give myself the trouble to peruse with any attention what smaller poems I have by me. But on finding it necessary to make an addition, I have again look'd them over, and am glad to find after an enquiry as critical as an Author can be supposed to make into the Merits of his own productions, that I am in possession of 808 Lines that may safely, I hope, venture to shew themselves in public. To these I would add those copies I translated from Vincent Bourn,[3] but having no transcript of them myself, I must beg you to take the trouble either to send them hither, or to get them written out for me. The whole together will amount nearly to a thousand lines, and as I suppose Mr. Johnson will not allot more than one page to one piece, they will fill more paper than the same number of lines written in continuation & upon the same Subject.—There are times when I cannot write, and the present is such a time; and were it not, I should yet prefer this method of swelling the Volume, to that of filling the Vacuity with one long-winded poem like the preceding.

A variety of Measures on a variety of subjects will relieve both the mind and the ear, and may possibly prevent that weariness of which there might otherwise be no small danger.

I hope that what I said in my last has determined you to undertake the preface, in that case the Gentleman you mention'd (Mr Foster)[4] must upon your walking out of the lines, march in to supply your place.

I have no outline to send you, neither shall I have time for any thing but to transcribe, which I will do as fast as I can to be legible, & remit my labors to you by the first opportunity—Title page and Motto at the same time.

[1] The heading on this copy reads: 'A true Copy. The Original being given to Mr Greaves of Clapham by Elizabeth Smith at the request of Mr. Smith January 26—1815—'.

[2] 'Truth', 'Expostulation', 'The Progress of Error', and 'Table Talk'.

[3] Unwin as well as Newton (see n. 2, C to Unwin, 6 Aug. 1780) had copies of the translations from Bourne.

[4] The Revd. Henry Foster of the Protestant Association. See n. 1, C to Newton, 12 June 1780.

We are sorry that you have not heard from Stock, but hope and have no doubt notwithstanding this silence, that the affair will be settled to your wish.[5]

I write in much haste, & have only to add my thanks for your negociations, and our joint Love to you both, with remembrances to all friends at Hoxton.

Yours my dear Sir
Wm Cowper

April 25.1781.

I am at this time a Member of the Inner Temple.[6]

WILLIAM UNWIN Tuesday, 1 May 1781

British Library

May 1. 1781

My dear friend,

Your Mother says I *must* write, and *must* admitts of no Apology; I might otherwise plead that I have nothing to say, that I am weary, that I am dull, that it would be more convenient therefore for You as well as for myself that I should let it alone. But all these pleas, and whatever pleas besides either Disinclination, Indolence, or Necessity might suggest, are overruled as they ought to be the moment a Lady adduces her irrefragable Argument, You Must. You have still however one Comfort left, that what I must Write, you May or May not read, just as it shall please you, unless Lady Anne[1] at your Elbow should say you must read it, and then like a true Knight you will obey without looking out for a Remedy.

I do not love to harp upon strings that to say the least, are not so musical as one would wish, but You I know have many a time sacrificed your own feelings to those of others, and where an Act of Charity leads you, are not easily put out of your way. This Consideration encourages me just to insinuate that your Silence on the Subject of a certain Nomination is distressfull to more than you would wish.

[5] The Nind affair.

[6] Newton must have questioned C's title in his letter to Newton of 5 Mar. He may have thought that C was still a member of the Middle Temple.

[1] A reference to Unwin's wife, Anne.

In particular to the little Boy whose cloaths are outgrown and worn out; and to his Mother, who is unwilling to furnish him with a new Suit, having reason to Suppose that the long blue peticoat would soon supersede it, if she should.[2]

In the Press and speedily will be published in one Volume Octavo, price three Shillings, Poems by William Cowper of the Inner Temple Esqr. You may Suppose by the Size of the publication that the greatest part of them have been long kept secret, because you yourself have never seen them. But the truth is that they are most of them except what you have in your possession, the produce of the last Winter. Two thirds of the Compilation will be occupied by 4 pieces, the first of which sprung up in the Month of December, and the last of them in the Month of March; they contain I suppose in all, about 2500 lines, are known, or are to be known in due time by the names of

Table talk.	Truth
The Progress of Error	Expostulation.

Mr. Newton writes a preface, and Johnson is the printer. The principal, I may say the only reason why I never mention'd to you till now, an Affair which I am just going to make known to all the World, if *that* Mr. All the World should think it worth his knowing, has been this; that 'till within these few days I had not the honor to know it myself. This may seem strange but it is true. For not knowing where to find underwriters who would chuse to insure them, and not finding it convenient to a purse like mine to run any hazard even upon the Credit of my own Ingenuity, I was very much in doubt for some Weeks whether any Bookseller would be willing to subject himself to an Ambiguity that might prove very expensive in case of a bad Market. But Johnson has heroically set all peradventures at defiance, and takes the whole charge upon himself— so Out I come.

Yours my dear friend with your Mother's Love—
Wm Cowper.

I shall be glad of my translations from V. Bourne in your next

[2] The Nind Affair. Each charity school had its own colour for the habits worn by its children. Blue was the colour for Christ's Hospital.

frank.[3] My Muse will lay herself at your feet immediately on her first public Appearance—

[JOHN NEWTON][1] Tuesday, 1 May 1781

Charles Ryskamp

Wm Cowper.

Mrs. Unwin much as usual, sends her Love, and I two Cucumbers, which without a Riddle[2] I have rais'd myself, together with all the 'Sparagus this Easterly Wind would permitt to grow.
May 1st. 1781.

JOSEPH HILL Wednesday, 9 May 1781

Address: Mr. Joseph Hill / Great Queen Street / Lincolns Inn Fields / London.
Postmark: 11/MA
Cowper Johnson

My dear Sir—

I am in the press, and it is in vain to deny it. But how mysterious is the Conveyance of Intelligence from one End to the other of your great City! Not many days since, except one man, and He but little taller than yourself, all London was ignorant of it; for I do not suppose that the public prints have yet announced the most agreeable tidings, the titlepage which is the basis of the Advertisement, having so lately reach'd the publisher; and now it is known to You, who live at least two Miles distant from my Confidant upon the Occasion.

My Labors are principally the production of the last Winter—all indeed, except a few of the minor pieces. When I can find no other Occupation, I think, and when I think, I am very apt to do it in Rhime. Hence it comes to pass that the Season of the Year which

[3] See n. 2, C to Unwin, 6 Aug. 1780.

[1] This postscript fragment is probably from a letter to John Newton.
[2] See C to Newton, 8 Apr. 1781.

generally pinches off the flowers of poetry, unfolds mine such as they are, and crowns me with a Winter garland. In this respect therefore, I and my cotemporary bards are by no means upon a par. They write when the delightfull Influences of fine weather, fine prospects, and a brisk Motion of the Animal Spirits, make poetry almost the Language of Nature; and I, when Iceicles descend from all the Leaves of the Parnassian Laurel, and when a reasonable man would as little expect to succeed in Verse, as to hear a Blackbird Whistle.—This must be my Apology to You for whatsoever want of fire & Animation you may observe in what you will shortly have the perusal of. As to the public, if they like me not, there is no Remedy. A friend will weight & consider all disadvantages, & make as large Allowances as an Author can wish, & larger perhaps than he has any right to expect; but not so the world at large; what they do not like, they will not by any Apology be persuaded to forgive, and it would be in vain to tell *them* that I wrote my Verses in January, for they would immediately reply, why did not you write them in May? A question that might puzzle a wiser head than we poets are generally bless'd with.

If I had the courage to stand the chance of the Market, and printed at my own Expence, I should circulate the Copy amongst my friends, with the greatest pleasure, and find a peculiar one in laying a Volume of my Writing upon your desk, but the Bookseller is the Adventurer, and has the boldness to risk more upon the Success of what I have written, than I dare to hazard upon it myself.[1]

Your Maccarel were excellent. Many thanks to Mrs. Hill for the Seeds. Mr. Wright loves a Garden dearly, but hates the Expence of furnishing it, which makes my gratuitous contributions singularly welcome.

Yours my dear friend as Ever
Wm Cowper.

May 9. 1781.

Will you be so good as to order for me half a Ream of the best post paper? The Stationer will be paid by the Bookkeeper at the Windmill St. John Street.

[1] It was common practice for the publisher to bear the cost of publication and then to divide the profit with the author. Such an arrangement, as was the case here, meant that the publisher owned the copyright. See *Russell*, p. 39.

May 9. 1781
Receiv'd of Mr. Hill the Sum of thirty Guineas by Draft upon Child and Company— £31.10.0. Wm Cowper.

WILLIAM UNWIN — Friday, 11 May 1781[1]

Address: The Revd. William Unwin / at Stock / near Ingatestone / Essex.
Postmarks: 14/MA *and* OULNEY. Also marked in C's hand: Double Letter/Post pd. to London 6d.
British Library

May 10. 1781

My dear friend—

It is Friday; I have just drank tea, and just perused your Letter; and though this Answer to it cannot set off 'till Sunday, I obey the warm impulse I feel, which will not permitt me to postpone the business 'till the regular time of writing.

I expected you would be griev'd; if you had not been so, those Sensibilities which attend you upon every other Occasion, must have left you upon this. I am sorry that I have given you pain, but not sorry that you have felt it. A concern of that sort would be absurd, because it would be to regret your friendship for me, and to be dissatisfied with the Effects of it. Allow yourself however three Minutes only for Reflection, and your penetration must necessarily dive into the motives of my Conduct. In the first place, and by way of preface, remember that *I* do not, whatever your partiality may incline *you* to do, account it of much Consequence to any friend of mine, whether he is or is not employ'd by me upon such an Occasion. But all affected renunciations of poetical merit apart, and all unaffected Expressions of the Sense I have of my own Littleness in the poetical Character too, the obvious and only reeson why I resorted to Mr. Newton and not to my friend Unwin was this—that the former lived in London, the latter at Stock; the former was upon the Spot, to correct that press, to give Instructions respecting any sudden Alterations, and to settle with the publisher every thing that might possibly occurr in the course of such a business. The latter could not

[1] Although C has dated this letter 'May 10. 1781', his opening statement, 'It is Friday . . . ' suggests that he actually wrote it on Friday, 11 May.

be applied to for these purposes without what I thought would be a manifest Incroachment upon his kindness; because it might happen, that the troublesome Office might cost him now and then a Journey, which it was absolutely impossible for me to endure the thought of.

When I wrote to you for the Copies you have sent me, I told you that I was making a Collection, but not with a design to publish. There is nothing truer than that at that time, I had not the smallest Expectation of sending a Volume of poems to the Press. I had several small pieces that might amuse, but I would not when I publish make the Amusement of the Reader my only Object. When the Winter depriv'd me of other Employments, I began to compose; and seeing 6 or 7 Months before me which would naturally afford me much leisure for such a purpose, I undertook a piece of some length; that finish'd; another; and so on, 'till I had amass'd the Number of lines I mentiond in my last.

I should add more, but your Mother wants to put in a Word.—There are two wanting of my translations of Bourne, of which the Glow:worm is one. Perhaps you never had it.[2]—Yours W C.

Beleive of me what you please, but not that I am indifferent to you, or your friendship for me, on any Occasion.—We have no franks.

My dear Billy, accept my most sincere thanks for your favour done me, by that conferred on Mr. Newton's relation. I am sorry Mr. Newton's manner shocked you; but am rejoiced it had no other Effect. It was not for want of sensibility of the obligation I am certain; but I never in my life knew One that seemed so much at a loss as he is for expressing his feelings by word of mouth.—Last Sunday's post brought Mr. Cowper a letter from him with the following passage. 'Yesterday Mr. Unwin came into the vestry & presented me with a Nomination to the Hospital.[3] He did it very Cordially & handsomely, & I thanked him very heartily & honestly. For though I had no right to expect such a favour from him merely on my own account, I am very willing to consider myself personally obliged to him for it. I know Mrs. Unwin will believe I am duly sensible of her kindness, & I call my best thanks to her but a pepper Corn, because they fall short of what I mean:—I am no loser by this disbursement of thanks to him & to her, for Mr. & Mrs. Nind have paed me in

[2] See n. 2, C to Unwin, 6 Aug. 1780.

[3] Benjamin Nind, aged 8, was admitted to Christ's Hospital on 30 Mar. 1781. See C to Unwin, 13 Feb. 1780 and 28 Mar. 1780.

kind.'—I am my dear Billy your obliged & affectionate Mother: M. U:[4]

WILLIAM UNWIN *c.* Friday, 11 May 1781[1]

British Library

That the fact may speak for itself, and that there may be no room for you to Suspect that the following Stanzas were the fruit of an Afterthought, occasion'd by your gentle Remonstrance, I transcribe and send them to you now. And because I know what sort of a Mind yours is, how feeling, and how restless 'till it is pacified & composed, (in which respect it not a little resembles my own) I anticipate the ordinary opportunity by forwarding the Letter to Newport by a private hand—that it may reach you a day the sooner.[2] The lines are now in Johnson's hands, & will I hope in a few days be in the press.

To the Revd. William Unwin.

Unwin, I should but ill repay
  The kindness of a friend,
Whose worth deserves as warm a lay
  As ever Friendship penn'd,
Thy name omitted in a page
That would reclaim a vicious age.

2.

An Union form'd as mine with thee,
  Not rashly or in sport,
May be as fervent in degree,
  And faithfull in its sort,
And may as rich in comfort prove,
As that of true fraternal Love.

[4] The final paragraph of this letter is in Mrs. Unwin's hand.

---

[1] The context of this fragment which exists as a single sheet lacking address, postmarks, and signature places it at about the same time as the letter to Unwin of 11 May. C is again apologizing to Unwin for not telling him sooner that he had planned to publish a volume. 'Little John' Unwin celebrated his sixth birthday on 9 May.

[2] C is intending to send the letter by hand to Newport Pagnell so that it will catch a diligence (or some other carriage) which does not go through Olney on Saturday.

3.

The Bud inserted in the rind,
  The Bud of Peach or Rose,
Adorns, though diff'ring in its kind,
  The Stock whereon it grows
With flow'r as sweet or fruit as fair
As if produc'd by Nature there.

4.

Not rich, I render what I may,
  I sieze thy Name in haste,
And place it in this first Assay,
  Lest this should prove the last—
'Tis where it should be, in a plan
That holds in view the good of Man.

5.

The poet's lyre, to fix his fame,
  Should be the poet's heart;
Affection lights a brighter flame,
  Than ever blaz'd by Art.
No Muses on these lines attend,
I sink the poet in the friend.[3]

I intended to have surprized you with them, but the present Necessity has deprived me of that pleasure.

I just recollect that my good Intentions of extraordinary dispatch are vain, as no Post goes to town on a Saturday.

We wish little John many happy birth days, & beg that you and yours will accept our Love and Congratulations.

I have order'd 2 Copies down to Stock, one of them at your first convenient Opportunity, for Mr. John Unwin.

---

[3] Published in *1782*.

JOHN NEWTON Sunday, 13 May 1781

Princeton

My dear friend

We thank you for the Anecdote sent us in compliance with our desire.[1] Added at the End of a certain Treatise, it would operate as a powerfull Antidote to the Erroneous Opinion it inculcates, and sufficiently explain the mystery of a sensible man addicting himself to a silly Enterprize, and vainly endeavoring to accomplish it by Reasonings that would disgrace a Boy.

You are not sorry I suppose that your Correspondence with him is at an end; you might perhaps have easily secur'd the Continuance of it, had you been less explicit; but it must have been at the Expence of that point of Honor which a Spiritual Warrior of your Rank and Character, will upon no Consideration abandon. A gentler Reprehension, an Air of pleasantry, or any Disguise of your real Sentiments whatever, would still have left room for what he would have called a friendly Intercourse. But your Friendship for him has now produc'd the strongest proof of its Sincerity; and though he is not able to bear it, the time may come, (it will be unhappy for Him indeed if it never should) when he will know how to value it and to thank you for it.

The Rudeness of his Answer, I was going to give it a harsher Character, exceeds all that I could have thought it possible he could be provoked to treat you with, merely because you cannot see with his Eyes, and have had the boldness to tell him so.

M: quarrels with N:—for M: wrote a book,
And N: did not like it, which M could not brook.
So he call'd him a Bigot, a wrangler, a Monk,
With as many hard names as would line a good trunk,
And set up his back, and claw'd like a Cat,
But N: lik'd it never the better for that.
Now N: had a Wife, and he wanted but One,
Which stuck in M's Stomach as cross as a bone.
  It has always been reckon'd a just cause of Strife
For a Man to make free with another Man's Wife;

[1] C is referring to his request in his letter of 23 Apr. 1781 for information on Martin Madan's motivations in writing *Thelyphthora*.

But the Strife is the strangest that ever was known,
If a Man must be scolded for loving his own.[2]

Mrs. Unwin rejoices that the Nomination affair is at last accomplish'd, she accounts your thanks for it more than a Sufficient Recompense, and is sorry it is not in her power to give you and Mrs. Newton more important proofs of her regard.—I ask'd her what I should say, and she bade me say all This.

I am ready to wish that you may not yet have sent the translations of Bourne to Johnson, because I find it necessary to put forth a new Edition of the two last Stanzas of the Cricket. One of them was disgraced by a false rhime, and the other was too long by two lines.—Thus I would have them appear in public. By the way Mr. Unwin has sent me three of them, but the Glow:worm and the Cantab: he has not put[3]

This last Victory over the Americans[4] will go near to verify my poetical prediction,[5] and Sir Joshua[6] will have nothing to do but to record the Completion of a prophecy which is the more respectable, because when first deliver'd, it seem'd so very improbable. Rebellion it should seem must soon be extinguish'd, crippled by Defeat and destitute of Resources, and the Extinction of the War will in all likelihood soon follow it. I have taken prudent care however to save my credit at all Events, and having foretold both fair weather and foul, the former in the piece just alluded too, and the latter in Expostulation, fall back fall Edge,[7] as they say, like the Newton Shepherd's, my soothsaying is sure to be accomplished.

I have lately begun a Poem,[8] which if ever

[There is, I am] afraid, a perverseness and per[severing spirit of opposition] to Mr. Scot, that will grieve you, though you will not

[2] Published in *Southey*.

[3] Approximately one-third of the second folio (the middle portion) of this letter has been cut away; *Southey* (iv. 90) is the source for the words provided in brackets.

[4] Cornwallis defeated Greene at Guilford Courthouse on 15 Mar. 1781.

[5] 'A Present for the Queen of France.'

[6] 'To Sir Joshua Reynolds.'

[7] 'Whatever may happen'; see *The Oxford English Dictionary of Proverbs*, ed. F. P. Wilson (3rd edn., Oxford, 1970), p. 242.

[8] This is probably a reference to 'Hope', which is mentioned as 'lately enter'd upon' in C's letter to Unwin of 23 May 1781.

suffer it to disturb your temper. Mr. Scot acts wisely, and takes no Notice of it either in Conversation with the people or in the pulpit.

The Ducks could not be pull'd because it was necessary they should be kill'd on a Sunday.

Yours my dear friend & Mrs. Newton's

May 13. 1781. Wm Cowper.

Thanks for 6 fine Ma[ ]'ost an Ironical petition in the Name of the Pro[ ] the Printer of the General Evening Pos[t.]

JOHN NEWTON Monday, 21 May 1781

Princeton

My dear friend,

I am not so impatient to see myself in print, as to be at all disconcerted by the delay. I was sufficiently aware, that with Johnson's utmost dispatch he would be too late, and that the Summer which is just at the door, would tread too close upon the heels of the publication. I had much rather therefore proceed leisurely as he advises (if he will indeed go on to print at his leisure) and so avail myself of the complete Opportunity that Winter will bring with it, than open my Stall just when the Fair is over.

The case standing thus, and this leisurely proceeding being so favorable to my purpose, I have conceiv'd a design to save you the trouble of revising the proof, and that for two reasons. First because your time is precious, and mine is not so, and secondly because having written nothing of late that I do not retain memoritèr, it is impossible for the Alteration of a Word, or the least Inaccuracy to escape me.

I mean therefore to furnish myself with London and Country franks, and to desire Johnson to transmitt the proofs to me.[1]

It would have a strange appearance, and is hardly a supposeable case, but for Amusement sake we will endeavor to suppose it for a Moment. A Man (he must be a confirm'd Stoic) stands incompassed by a dozen others—One tweaks his Nose, One pinches his Sides, one slaps his right Cheek, and one his left; one treads upon his toes, one spits in his face, one thrusts pins into the Calves of his

[1] C wishes country franks to enable him to send letters to Johnson, and he requires the London ones for Johnson's replies.

legs, and one Kicks him on the breech; one raps the knuckles of one hand, one of the other; one sets a fool's cap upon his head, and another, a man of some Wit and with a reasonable share of Humor, sneers, laughs, & makes faces at him, while his Associates are thus employ'd in tormenting him:—The Patient, (for patient he must needs be if he keeps his senses) affects to be all the while perfectly at his Ease, denies that any body touches him, calls them his dear friends, observes that it is a very fine day, and takes Snuff.

Extravagant as this picture may seem, it bears I think some resemblance to Mr. M—. He is, or would seem to be insensible of the many smart Strokes he receives from his Antagonists. They are a parcel of insignificant wretches, some of them indeed his very good friends whose Opposition to his book is rather an Argument of their own bigotry or folly than any Inconvenience to Him, and as to the rest, whether they write or the Wind whistles, is a matter of the most absolute Indifference. And yet as in the case above delineated, the unhappy Gentleman must undoubtedly suffer a great deal, so must the Author of Thelyphthora, if the two Clubs of Learning and Logic and the Stinging Nettles of Wit and Humor can possibly make him feel.—By the way we shall be glad if you can bring Mr. Barton's book with you.[2]

Mrs. Unwin sends her Love. We both wait for the day appointed with a pleasing sort of Impatience, and comfort ourselves with the thought that though we cannot hasten its Approach one Moment, it will come, and must come, and that the Interval, let what will happen, and how long soever it may seem, can be but a fortnight. We mean if you are able to keep your Assignation.

She will be obliged to Mrs. Newton if she will be so good as to bring with her 6 tooth brushes, a quarter of a pound of Oystershell powder,[3] and two pounds of the same Bohea[4] as before. We shall hope to see you at dinner on Saturday, and as much sooner as you please; we always dine at two.

Yours my dear Sir and Mrs. Newton's
con ogni rispetto affettuoso[5]
Wm Cowper.

May 21. 1781.

[2] Perhaps a work by Philip Barton (1719?–87), a well-known writer on religious subjects.

[3] A medicinal preparation for ailments such as chilblains (*O.E.D.*).

[4] A black tea of high quality. See *The Rape of the Lock*, iv. 156.

[5] 'With every affectionate wish.'

WILLIAM UNWIN Wednesday, 23 May 1781

British Library

My dear Friend,

If a Writer's friends have need of patience, how much more the Writer! Your desire to see my Muse in public, and mine to gratify you, must both suffer the Mortification of delay. I expected that my Trumpeter would have inform'd the world by this time of all that it is needfull for them to know upon such an Occasion, and that an advertizing Blast blown through every Newspaper, would have said, the Poet is coming! But Man, especially Man that writes verse, is born to disappointments, as surely as Printers and Booksellers are born to be the most dilatory and tedious of all Creatures.—The plain English of this magnificent preamble is, that the Season for publication is just elapsed, that the Town is going into the Country every day, and that my book cannot appear till they return, that is, to say, not 'till next Winter.

This Misfortune however comes not without its attendant Advantage. I shall now have, what I should not otherwise have had, an Opportunity to correct the press myself; no small Advantage upon any Occasion, but especially important where poetry is concern'd. A single Erratum may knock out the brains of a whole passage, and that perhaps which of all others, the unfortunate poet is the most proud of. Add to this, that now and then there is to be found in a printing house, a presumptuous Intermeddler, who will fancy himself a poet too, and what is still worse, a better than he that employs him. The consequence is, that with cobbling and tinkering and patching on here and there a Shred of his own, he makes such a difference between the Original and the Copy, that an Author cannot know his own work again. Now as I chuse to be responsible for nobody's Dullness but my own, I am a little comforted when I reflect that it will be in my power to prevent all such Impertinence, and yet not without your Assistance. It will be quite necessary that the Correspondence between me and Johnson, should be carried on without the Expence of postage, because proofsheets would make double or treble Letters, which Expence, as in every Instance it must occur twice, first when the pacquet is sent, and again when it is return'd, would be rather inconvenient to me, who you perceive am forced

to live by my Wits, and to Him who hopes to get a little matter no doubt by the same means. Half a dozen franks therefore to me, and totidem to Him, will be singularly acceptable if you can without feeling it in any respect a trouble, procure them for me.—Johnson. Bookseller St. Pauls Church Yard—.

My Neck cloths being all worn out, I intend to wear Stocks, but not unless they are more fashionable than the former. In that case I shall be obliged to you if you will buy me a handsome Stock buckle for a very little money; for 20 or 25 Shillings perhaps, a second hand affair may be purchased that will make a figure at Olney.

I am much obliged to you for your Offer to support me in a translation of Bourne. It is but seldom however, and never except for my Amusement, that I translate, because I find it disagreeable to work by another man's pattern; I should at least be sure to find it so, in a business of any length. Again—*that* is Epigrammatic and witty in Latin, which would be perfectly insipid in English; and a translator of Bourne would frequently find himself obliged to supply what is called the Turn, which is in fact the most difficult and the most expensive part of the whole Composition, and could not perhaps, in many instances, be done with any tolerable Success. If a Latin poem, is neat, elegant, and musical it is enough, but English readers are not so easily satisfied.—To quote myself, you will find on comparing the Jackdaw with the Original, that I was obliged to sharpen a point which though smart enough in the Latin, would in English have appear'd as plain & as blunt as the tag of a Lace. I love the Memory of Vinny Bourne. I think him a better Latin poet than Tibullus, Propertius, Ausonius, or any of the Writers in *his* way, except Ovid, and not at all inferior to *Him*. I love him too with a Love of Partiality, because he was Usher of the 5th form at Westminster when I pass'd through it. He was so good natur'd and so indolent, that I lost more than I got by him, for he made me as idle as himself. He was such a Sloven, as if he had trusted to his Genius as a cloak for every thing that could disgust you in his person; and indeed in his Writings he has almost made amends for all. His humor is entirely original, he can speak of a Magpie or a Cat in terms so exquisitely appropriated to the Character he draws, that one would suppose him animated by the Spirit of the Creatures he describes. And with all this drollery there is a mixture of rational and even religious Reflection at times, and always an air of pleasantry, good nature and Humanity, that makes

him in my Mind one of the most Aimable Writers in the World. It is not common to meet with an Author who can make you smile, and yet at nobody's Expence, who is always entertaining, and yet always harmless, and who though elegant and classical to a degree not always found even in the Classics themselves, charms more by the Simplicity & playfullness of his Ideas, than by the neatness & purity of his Verse. Yet such was poor Vinney. I remember seeing the Duke of Richmond[1] set fire to his greasy Locks, & box his Ears to put it out again.

I am delighted with your project, but not with the View I have of its Success. If the World would form its Opinion of the Clerical Character at large, from yours in particular, I have no doubt but the Event would be as prosperous as you could wish. But I suppose there is not a Member of either House who does not see within the Circle of his own Acquaintance, a Minister, perhaps many Ministers, whose Integrity would contribute but little to the Effect of such a Bill. Here are 7 or 8 in the Neighborhood of Olney who have shaken hands with Sobriety, and who would rather suppress the Church, were it not for the Emoluments annex'd, than discourage the Sale of strong beer in a single instance. Were I myself in Parliament, I am not sure that I could favor your Scheme; are there not to be found within 5 Miles of almost every Neighborhood, Parsons who would purchase well accustom'd public houses, because they could secure them a License, and patronize them when they had done? I think no Penalty would prevent the Abuse, on Account of the difficulty of proof, and that no Ingenuity could guard against all the possible Abuses. To sum up all in few words, the generality of the clergy, especially within these last 20 or 30 years, have worn their Circingles[2] so loose, that I verily believe no measure that proposed an Accession of Privilege to an Order which the Laity retain but little respect for, would meet with the Countenance of the Legislature.—You will do me the Justice to suppose that I do not say these things to gratify a splenetic humor or a censorious turn of mind—far from it—it may add perhaps to the Severity of the foregoing Observations to assert, but if it does, I cannot help asserting, that I verily believe them to be founded upon fact, and that I am sure, partly from my own knowledge, and partly from the Report of those whose Veracity I can depend upon, that

[1] See n. 1, C to Unwin, 13 Feb. 1780.

[2] A variant spelling of 'surcingle', which is a belt to keep a cassock in place (*O.E.D.*).

in this part of the World at least, many of the most profligate Characters are the very men to whom the Morals and even the Souls of others are entrusted. And I cannot suppose that the Diocese of Lincoln,[3] or this part of it in particular, is more unfortunate in that respect than the rest of the Kingdom.

Since I have begun to write long poems, I seem to turn up my Nose at the Idea of a short one. I have lately enter'd upon one, which if ever finished, cannot easily be comprised in much less than a thousand Lines.[4] But this must make part of a second publication, and be accompanied in due time, by others not yet thought of. For it seems, (which I did not know 'till the Bookseller had occasion to tell me so) that single pieces stand no chance, and that nothing less than a Volume will go down. You yourself afford me a proof of the Certainty of this Intelligence, by sending me franks which nothing less than a Volume can fill. I have accordingly sent you one, but am obliged to add, that had the Wind been in any other point of the Compass, or blowing as it does from the East, had it been less boisterous, you must have been contented with a much shorter Letter. But the Abridgment of every other Occupation, is very favorable to that of writing.

Our Love attends all the Family at Stock. I am glad I did not expect to hear from you by this post, for the Boy has lost the Bag in which your Letter must have been inclosed. Another reason for my prolixity.

Yours affectionately
Wm Cowper.

May 23. 1781

JOSEPH HILL — Sunday, 27 May 1781

Address: Mr. Joseph Hill / Great Queen Street / Lincolns Inn Fields / London.
Postmark: 28/MA
Princeton

My dear Friend,

I am to thank you for the finest Maccarel I ever saw or tasted, a singular treat at Olney, to which place the best are never imported,

[3] The archdeanery of Buckingham (virtually the whole of the county with certain minor exceptions) was within the diocese of Lincoln until 30 Nov. 1845.

[4] 'Hope'.

nor the worst 'till they are good for nothing. We live upon the banks of the Ouse, much celebrated in pastoral Song, and a River so beautifull and so beautifully border'd that it may well suggest poetical Ideas to any man that has but a moderate share of Fancy. It may even suggest the Idea of fish, and might for aught I know furnish the Reality were it not most unmercifully poach'd and plunder'd from one End of the year to the other. As it is, it is a much better Subject for a Poet than an Angler, and if I was writing Verses upon it, I could say, Here comes Pike the Tyrant of the Streams, there goes the Tench, and the broad sided Bream, but it would be a mere fiction, and the poet might as well expect to catch Salmon and Trout in Helicon, as anything worth dressing in the Ouse. But I have a River in Great Queen Street, which communicating with the Sea, makes amends for all.

It is possible that I ought to have receiv'd a Letter from you by last Wednesday's post. But the Courier thought proper to lose the Bag which contained it if you sent one, a little on this side Newport. If any other Bag had been missing I should have suspected that it was not honestly lost; but I think no man who knows what Money is, and how little we deal in that Commodity here, would hazard his Neck in such a Cause, especially when he had other Bags at his Command. If you wrote, I thank you, though I shall never see your Letter—if you did not, I can only say, I shall be glad to hear from you when you can.

I had the Mortification to learn last Week, that the Season being so far advanced, my Bookseller thought it would be throwing away the Effusions of my Genius, to publish them at present. I should indeed myself be unwilling to send forth at a time when my Verse would be as little regarded as what the Bellman says at Midnight. In the beginning of the ensuing Winter therefore you may expect to see me in print, and in the meantime perhaps I may employ myself in providing materials for another Volume. I never can answer for myself however upon this Subject, because, sometimes it costs me no trouble to write a great deal, and sometimes after much labor I can produce little or nothing. This difference seems to give some countenance to the old Story of a Muse, and rather flatters me with the Idea of Castalian Inspiration. Perhaps the Critics will undeceive me hereafter, but in the mean time I find my Account in supposing it may be so.

Be pleas'd to present my affectionate respects to Mrs. Hill and all your Kindred.

Yours my dear Friend
Wm Cowper

May 27. 81.
I am oblig'd to you for executing my Commission to your Stationer.

JOHN NEWTON Monday, 28 May 1781

Princeton

My dear friend,

I am much obliged to you for the pains you have taken with my Table talk, and wish that my vivâ voce Table talk could repay you for the trouble you have had with the written one. I am quite surprized at Johnson's diligence, and began to wish while reading your account of it, that I had left the Business of correction in your hands. But presently recollecting that it is a tedious troublesome Employment, and fit only for the Author himself to be burthen'd with, I relapsed into my former Sentiment. My franks are not yet ready, but I shall lose no time in procuring them if they are to be got. I enclose a Line to Johnson, to tell him that if in the mean time, and while you are absent from Town, another parcel of the proof should be ready for revisal, I wish him to send it hither by the Diligence. I am as well convinced of the Accuracy & Exactness with which you would perform the Task as it is possible for me to be of my own, and if I can obtain no franks shall after all have recourse to your Assistance.

The Season is wonderfully improved within this day or two, and if these cloudless Skies are continued to us, or rather if the cold winds do not set in again, promises you a pleasant Excursion, as far at least as the Weather can conduce to make it such. You seldom complain of too much Sunshine, and if you are prepar'd for an Heat somewhat like that of Africa, the South walk in our long garden will exactly suit you. Reflected from the Gravel and from the Walls, and beating upon your head at the same time, it may possibly make you wish you could enjoy for an hour or two that Immensity of Shade afforded by the Gigantic Trees still growing in the Land of your Captivity. If you could spend a day now and then in those Forests, and return with a

Wish to England, it would be no small Addition to the number of your best pleasures. But pennæ non homini datæ.[1] The time will come perhaps (but death must come first) when you will be able to visit them without either danger, trouble or Expence, and when the Contemplation of those well remember'd Scenes will awaken in you Emotions of Gratitude and praise surpassing all you could possibly sustain at present. In this Sense I suppose there is a Heaven upon Earth at all times, and that the disembodied Spirit may find a peculiar Joy arising from the contemplation of those places it was formerly conversant with, and so far at least be reconciled to a world it was once so weary of, as to use it in the delightfull way of thankfull Recollection.

Miss Catlett must not think of any other Lodging than we can without any Inconvenience, as we shall with all possible pleasure, furnish her with. We can each of us say, that is, I can say it in Latin and Mrs. Unwin in English, nihil tui á me alienum puto.[2] She shall have a great Bed and a great Room,[3] and we shall have the chamber we always occupy when we have Company, and should certainly occupy, if she was not of the party. This State of the case leaves no room for the least Objection. We desire therefore that you will give our Love to her, tell her we shall expect her, and that she will be but half as welcome to us if she sleeps any where else.

Having two more Letters to write I find myself obliged to shorten this, so once more wishing you a good Journey, and ourselves the happiness of receiving you in good health & Spirits. I remain

affectionately yours

Wm Cowper.

May 28. 81

Mr. Jones begs the favor of you to supply him with a Set of your last Letters handsomely bound and *Letter'd*, and wishes, if it can be done without Inconvenience, that you would be so good as to bring them with you.[4]

I shall be obliged to you if you will put Johnson's Letter into the penny post.[5]

[1] Horace, *Odes*, I. iii. 35: 'Wings are not given to men.'

[2] *The Self Tormentor*, 77: 'Whatever affects you affects me.' See n. 3, C to Newton, 21 Aug. 1780.

[3] Cowper's own room, the large room on the first floor.

[4] *Cardiphonia*.

[5] The letter to Johnson enclosed with this letter has not survived.

WILLIAM UNWIN *c.* Monday, 28 May 1781[1]

British Library

My dear friend,

I believe I never give trouble without feeling more than I give; so much by way of preface, and Apology.

Thus stands the case. Johnson has begun to print, and Mr. Newton has already corrected the first Sheet. This unexpected dispatch makes it necessary for Me to furnish myself with the means of Communication, viz: the franks, as soon as may be. There are reasons, (I believe I mention'd them in my last) why I chuse to revise the proof myself. Nevertheless if your Delicacy must suffer the puncture of a pin's point in procuring the franks for me, I release you entirely from the Task. You are as free as if I had never mention'd them. But you will oblige me by a speedy Answer upon this Subject, because it is expedient that the Printer should know to whom he is to send his Copy; and when the press is once set, those humble Servants of the poets are rather impatient of delay, because the types are wanted for the works of other Authors who are all equally in haste to be born.

This fine weather I suppose sets you on horseback, and allures the Ladies into the Garden. If I was at Stock, I should be of their party. And while they sat knotting[2] or Netting in the Shade, should comfort myself with the thought that I had not a beast under me, whose walk would seem tedious, whose Trot would Jumble me, and whose gallop might throw me into a Ditch. What Nature expressly design'd me for, I have never been able to conjecture, I seem to myself so universally disqualified for the common and customary Occupations and Amusements of Mankind. When I was a Boy, I excell'd at cricket and Football, but the fame I acquir'd by Atchievements in that way, is long since forgotten, and I do not know that I have made a figure in any thing since. I am sure however that she did not design me for a Horseman, and that if all men were of my Kind, there would be an end of all Jockeyship for ever.

I am rather straiten'd in time, and not very rich in materials, therefore with our joint Love to you all,

conclude myself yours Ever Wm C.

May. 1781

[1] Marked in pencil '28 May 1781', presumably in Unwin's hand.

[2] A form of knitting which involves making knots for fringes (*O.E.D.*).

WILLIAM UNWIN Tuesday, 5 June 1781

British Library

My dear friend,

If the old Adage be true that he gives twice who gives speedily, it is equally true that he who not only uses Expedition in giving, but gives more than was ask'd, gives thrice at least. Such is the Stile in which Mr. Smith conferrs a favor.[1] He has not only sent me franks to Johnson, but under another Cover has added Six to you. These last, for aught that appears by your Letter, he threw in, of his own mere bounty.—I beg that my share of thanks may not be wanting on the Occasion, and that when you write to him next you will assure him of the Sense I have of the obligation, which is the more flattering, as it includes a proof of his predilection in favor of the poems his franks are destin'd to enclose. May they not forfeit his good Opinion hereafter! nor yours, to whom I hold myself indebted in the first place, and who have equally given me credit for their deservings. Your Mother says, that although there are passages in them containing opinions which will not be universally subscribed to, the World will at least allow—what my great Modesty will not permitt me to subjoin. I have the highest Opinion of her Judgment, and know by having experienced the Soundness of them, that her Observations are always worthy of Attention and regard. Yet strange as it may seem, I do not feel the Vanity of an Author when she commends me, but I feel something better, a Spur to my diligence, and a Cordial to my Spirits, both together animating me to deserve, at least not to fall short of her Expectations; for I verily believe if my dullness should earn me the Character of a dunce, the Censure would affect Her more than me. Not that I am insensible of the Value of a good name, either as a Man or an Author; without an Ambition to attain it, it is absolutely unattainable under either of those descriptions. But my Life having been in many respects a Series of Mortifications and Disappointments, I am become less apprehensive and impressible perhaps in some points

[1] The banker, Robert Smith (1752–1838), later 1st Baron Carrington, was M.P. for Nottingham borough from 1779 to 1797. Smith abused the privilege of franking more than almost any other Member of Parliament (see Kenneth Ellis, *The Post Office in the Eighteenth Century* (1938), pp. 156–7). He was a man, however, of extraordinary kindness, and C commemorated his anonymous contribution in 1782 toward the maintenance of the poor in Olney in *The Task* (iv. 427–8).

than I should have otherwise been, and though I should be exquisitely sorry to disgrace my friends, could endure my own share of the Affliction with a reasonable measure of tranquillity.

The Lace pattern is given into the hands of one of the best Artificers in Olney, with orders to proceed upon it immediately.

These seasonable showers have pour'd floods upon all the neighboring parishes, but have pass'd us by. My garden languishes, and what is worse, the fields too languish, and the upland grass is burnt. These discriminations are not fortuitous; but if they are providential what do they import? I can only answer as a friend of mine once answer'd a mathematical question in the Schools, prorsús nescio.[2] Perhaps it is that men who will not believe what they cannot understand, may learn the folly of their conduct, while their very senses are made to witness against them, and themselves in the course of providence become the Subjects of a thousand dispensations they cannot explain. But the end is never answer'd; the Lesson is inculcated indeed frequently enough, but nobody learns it. Well, Instruction vouchsafed in vain is, I suppose, a debt to be accounted for hereafter.—You must understand this to be a Soliloquy, I wrote my thoughts without recollecting that I was writing a Letter, and to You.

Our affectionate respects attend yourself and the Ladies, nor are the little ones forgot.

Yours rather in haste
Wm Cowper.

June 5. 1781.

WILLIAM UNWIN — Sunday, 24 June 1781

British Library

My dear friend—

The Letter you witheld so long, lest it should give me pain, gave me pleasure. Horace says the Poets are a waspish race, and from my own Experience of the temper of two or three with whom I was formerly connected, I can readily Subscribe to the Character he gives

[2] 'I have no idea.'

them.[1] But for my own part, I have never yet felt that excessive irritability which some writers discover, when a friend in the words of Pope—

Just hints a fault or hesitates dislike.[2]

Least of all would I give way to such an unseasonable ebullition,[3] merely because a civil question is proposed to me with much gentleness, and by a Man whose concern for my credit and character I verily believe to be Sincere. I reply therefore, not peevishly but with a Sense of the Kindness of your Intentions that I hope you may make yourself very easy on a Subject that I can perceive has occasion'd you some Sollicitude. When I wrote the Poem called Truth, by which is intended Religious Truth, it was indispensibly necessary that I should set forth that doctrine which I know to be true, and that I should pass what I understand to be a just Censure upon Opinions and persuasions that differ from, or stand in direct Opposition to it. Because though some Errors may be innocent, and even religious Errors are not always pernicious, yet in a case where the Faith and Hope of a Christian are concern'd, they must necessarily be destructive. And because neglecting This, I should have betray'd my Subject; either suppressing what in my Judgment is of the last importance, or giving Countenance by a timid Silence to the very Evils it was my design to combat. That you may understand me better, I will subjoin—that I wrote that Poem on purpose to inculcate the eleemosynary Character of the Gospel, as a dispensation of Mercy in the most absolute Sense of the word, to the Exclusion of all claims of Merit on the part of the Receiver. Consequently to set the brand of Invalidity upon the Plea of Works, and to discover upon Scriptural ground the absurdity of that Notion which includes a Solecism in the very terms of it, that Man by Repentance and good works may deserve the Mercy of his Maker. I call it a Solecism, because Mercy deserved, ceases to be Mercy, and must take the name of Justice. This is the Opinion which I said in my last the World would not acquiesce in, but except this I do not recollect that I have introduced a syllable into any of my pieces that they can possibly object to. And even this, I have endeavor'd to deliver from doctrinal dryness, by as many pretty things in the way of trinket and play thing, as I could muster upon the Subject. So that if I have rubb'd their Gums, I have

[1] See *Epistles*, II. i. 214–28.

[2] *Epistle to Dr. Arbuthnot*, 204.

[3] State of agitation (*O.E.D.*).

taken care to do it with a Coral, and even that Coral embellish'd by the Ribbon to which it is tied, and recommended by the tinkling of all the bells I could contrive to annex to it.[4]

You need not trouble yourself to call on Johnson; being perfectly acquainted with the progress of the business, I am able to satisfy your curiosity myself. The post before the last, I return'd to him the second sheet of Table:talk, which he had sent me for correction, and which stands foremost in the Volume. The delay has enabled me to add a piece of considerable length which but for the delay would not have made its appearance upon this Occasion. It answers to the name of Hope.

Your Independent Gardiner's Excuses for his breach of the Sabbath, are in my mind paultry, and all put together amount to no more than this, that I chuse to turn a penny when I can, and am determin'd that the Sanctity of the day shall never interfere with a concern of so much greater Importance. The Barber and Hair dresser who officiates for me, would not wait upon the King himself on a Sunday, though he could easily make Apologies more plausible than any adduced by the old man you mention, were he disposed to trespass against his duty and his Conscience.

I remember a Line in the Odyssey which literally translated imports that there is nothing in the world more impudent than the Belly.[5] But had Homer met with an instance of Modesty like yours, he would either have suppressed that Observation, or at least have qualified it with an Exception. I hope that for the future Mrs. Unwin will never Suffer you to go to London without putting some victuals in your pocket, for what a strange Article would it make in a Newspaper, that a tall well dress'd Gentleman, by his appearance a Clergyman, and with a purse of Gold in his pocket, was found starved to death in the Street? How would it puzzle Conjecture to account for such a phænomenon. Some would suppose that you had been Kidnapt like Betty Canning[6] of hungry memory. Others would say, the Gentleman was a Methodist, and had practised a rigorous Self:denial

[4] C is referring to the toys made of polished coral, decorated with bells, which were given to children to assist them in cutting teeth.

[5] See *Odyssey*, xvii. 286.

[6] A reference to the celebrated disappearance of Elizabeth Canning (1734–73) in Jan. 1753. When she returned home on 29 Jan. of that year, she was half-starved, and she claimed that she had been abducted by a Mrs. Wells. There was a subsequent controversy as to whether Betty Canning had told the truth concerning her disappearance.

which had unhappily proved too hard for his Constitution. But I will venture to say that nobody would divine the real cause, or suspect for a Moment that your Modesty had occasion'd the Tragedy in question. By the way, is it not possible that the spareness and slenderness of your person may be owing to the same cause? For surely it is reasonable to suspect that the bashfullness which could prevail against you on so trying an occasion, may be equally prevalent on others. I remember having been told by Colman that when he once dined with Garrick, he repeatedly press'd him to eat more of a certain dish that he was known to be particularly fond of. Colman as often refused, and at last declared he could not. But could not you, says Garrick, if you was in a dark Closet by yourself? The same question might perhaps be put to you with as much or more propriety, and therefore I recommend it to you either to furnish yourself with a little more Assurance, or always to eat in the dark.

We Sympathize with Mrs. Unwin, and if it will be any comfort to her to know it, can assure her, that a Lady in our Neighborhood, is always on such Occasions the most miserable of all things, and yet escapes with great facility through all the dangers of her State.

Our Love attends yourself, the Ladies, and the children, with congratulations on the Amendment of John's health, which we hope by this time is perfectly restored.

Yours ut Semper,
Wm Cowper.

June 24. 1781.

WILLIAM UNWIN — *c.* Sunday, 1 July 1781[1]

British Library

My dear William for the sound-sake,

I thought it a tribute due to my old friend, who well deserved that what has been learnedly spoken of him in Latin, should be spoken of him in plain English also, to translate the pretty and elegant Exercise

[1] This letter, which is difficult to date precisely, has traditionally been assigned to *c.* 1 July 1781. As such, it does adhere to many sentiments expressed by C to Unwin in letters of this time, i.e. on matters of poetry, requests for advice, and gratitude for franks to facilitate the transmission of proofs to Johnson.

you sent me.[2] If you chuse to do so, you may send my Attempt to the printer, for though the Scissars have passed through the line, I can spell out his request for a Version. I am very busy writing what will probably be yet added to my Volume now in the press. It is an Affair of some length, called Charity. I have been transcribing a good deal this Morning, and should indeed have preferred the finishing to the beginning of a Letter just at the present moment, being rather weary, and not in the best Spirits.

We were truly concern'd at your Relation of the danger you have escaped, and consequently felt a proportionable pleasure at the Account of your Recovery.—I suppose your Uncle's[3] delicacy revolted at the thought of a Chop house, but except one Coffeehouse called Chapman's in May fair,[4] I never knew a House of that denomination, that was fit for a Gentleman to dine in. I do not wonder that he was peevish, and that being so he became more so; it is a temper that provides fuel for itself, either by disconcerting the temper of others, or provoking Neglect and a contemptuous Indifference in return. Had my poor School master abovementioned been as irascible as somebody, his Memory must have wanted the garland that Gratitude has tied around it, and if that somebody had been a pædagogue at St. Peter's[5] he would have had three hundred Wasps about his ears, that in spite of his Authority, would have contriv'd to teize him out of his Senses. Where there is but little Religion, Philosophy may have its use, but where there is neither, and the bilious humor predominates, woe to the unhappy man, who knows no end of what he Suffers in himself, or what he inflicts upon others.

I shall be much obliged by Six more franks, and by the very first

[2] The 'old friend' is Pierson Lloyd (1704?–5 Jan. 1781), who was educated at Westminster and Trinity College, Cambridge. He was an Usher at Westminster for over twenty years, and Under Master from 1749 until 1771. He was the father of C's close friend, Robert Lloyd. The Latin verses were written by his successor as Usher and Under Master, William Vincent (1739–1815). They were recited in Hall at the annual election of scholars to Christ Church, Oxford, and Trinity College, Cambridge (in 1781, 21–3 May). It would seem from the context of this letter that Unwin sent C a newspaper clipping containing Vincent's Latin verses, but the periodical in question has not been traced, nor is this version known to have been printed in any periodical. C's manuscript (now at the British Library) of 'Latin Verses in Memory of the late Dr. Lloyd' accompanied this letter.

[3] John Unwin. For Unwin's involvement in his nephew's affairs, see C to Hill, 25 Sept. 1770, and n. 2, C to Unwin, 8 May 1780.

[4] Chapman's was located on Sackville Street. See Bryant Littlewhite, *London Coffee Houses* (1963), p. 151.

[5] St. Peter's College is usually known as Westminster School.

Opportunity. Johnson is printing away and I am writing away as if it was a race between us. The Volume will be larger in consequence than was at first proposed by near a third of its dimensions. And whether the Six I now request expended, my Occasions will be completely satisfied is doubtfull. I rather imagine not.

So far from thinking Egotisms tedious; I think a Letter good for nothing without them. To hear *from* a friend is little, unless I hear *of* him at the same time. His Sentiments may be just, but his feelings & his welfare are most to the purpose.

I will not trouble you for the poets at present, though I thank you for the offer. Perhaps next Winter I may be glad of them.

Our joint Love to you all is all that I can add

except that I am Yours

Wm Cowper.

N.B.

I mean Six to me and Six to Johnson *as before.*

This is our last frank to You.

JOHN NEWTON — Saturday, 7 July 1781

Princeton

My dear friend—

Mr. Old brought us the acceptable news of your safe Arrival. My Sensations at your departure were far from pleasant, and Mrs. Unwin suffer'd more upon the Occasion than when you first took leave of Olney. When we shall meet again, and in what Circumstances, or whether we shall meet or no, is an Article to be found nowhere but in that Volume of Providence which belongs to the current year, and will not be understood till it is accomplished. This I know, that your Visit was most agreeable here. It was so even to Me, who though I live in the midst of many agreeables am but little Sensible of their charms. But when you came, I determined as much as possible to be deaf to the suggestions of despair, that if I could contribute but little to the pleasure of the Opportunity, I might not dash it with unseasonable melancholy, and like an Instrument with a broken string interrupt the Harmony of the Concert.

Lady Austen waiving all forms has paid us the first Visit, and not

content with showing us that proof of her Respect, made handsome Apologies for her Intrusion. We return'd the Visit yesterday. She is a lively agreeable Woman, has seen much of the World and accounts it a great Simpleton as it is, she laughs and makes laugh, and keeps up a Conversation without seeming to labor at it.

I had rather submitt to Chastisement now, than be obliged to undergo it hereafter. If Johnson therefore will mark with a marginal Q, those Lines that He or His, object to, as not Sufficiently finished, I will willingly retouch them, or give a reason for my refusal. I shall moreover think myself obliged by any hints of that sort, as I do already to somebody who by running here and there two or three paragraphs into one, has very much improved the Arrangement of my matter. I am apt I know to fritter it into too many pieces, and by doing so to disturb that Order to which all Writings must owe their perspicuity, at least in a considerable measure. With all that carefullness of revisal I have exercised upon the Sheets as they have been transmitted to me, I have been guilty of an Oversight, and have suffer'd a great fault to escape me which I shall be glad to correct if not too late.

In the progress of Error, a part of the young Squire's Apparatus before he yet enters upon his travels is said to be

—Memorandum book to minute down
The several posts, and where the Chaise broke down.

Here, the Reviewers would say, is not only down but down derry down into the bargain, the word being made to rhime to itself. This never occurred to me 'till last night just as I was stepping into bed. I should be glad however to alter it thus.—

With Memorandum-book for ev'ry town
And ev'ry Inn, and where the Chaise broke down.[1]

I have advanced so far in Charity, that I have ventured to give Johnson Notice of it, and his Option whether he will print it now or hereafter. I rather wish he may chuse the present time, because it will be a proper Sequel to Hope, and because I am willing to think it will embellish the Collection. Mrs. Unwin purposes to send a couple of Ducks by next Friday's diligence, when I imagine this last production will have a place in the basket.

Whoever means to take my phiz, will find himself sorely perplex'd

[1] Lines 373–4.

in seeking for a fit Occasion. That I shall not give him one is certain, and if he steals one he must be as cunning and quicksighted a thief as Autolycus[2] himself. His best course will be to draw a face and call it mine at a venture. They who have not seen me these 20 years will say, it may possibly be a striking likeness now, though it bears no resemblance to what he was. Time makes great alterations. They who know me better will say perhaps, though it is not perfectly the thing, yet there is somewhat of the cast of his Countenance. If the Nose was a little longer and the Chin a little shorter, the Eyes a little smaller, and the forehead a little more protuberant, it would be just the Man. And thus without seeing me at all the Artist may represent me to the public Eye with as much Exactness as yours has bestow'd upon you, though I suppose the Original was full in his view when he made the Attempt.[3]

We are both as well as when you left us. Our hearty Affections wait upon yourself and Mrs. Newton, not forgetting Euphrosyne the laughing lady.[4]

Yours my dear Sir
Wm Cowper.

No Letters were left
July 7. 1781

Nat Gee's 40 Guineas will be at the Windmill in St. John Street next Saturday Morning, where Mr. Crawford if he is so kind as to enquire after them, will find them.[5]

JOHN NEWTON — Thursday, 12 July 1781

Princeton (*facsimile*)

My very dear friend

I am going to send, what when you have read, you may scratch your head, and say, I suppose, there's nobody knows, whether what

[2] Autolycus, the son of Hermes, from whom he received special powers in thieving and trickery. According to one legend, Autolycus stole from Sisyphus, who revenged himself by seducing Autolycus' daughter, Anticlea.

[3] There was no portrait in *1782*.

[4] Miss Catlett.

[5] Lowndes's *London Directory* (1796) lists an Alexander Crawford, Merchant on Berkeley Street.

I have got, be Verse or not—by the tune and the time, it ought to be rhime, but if it be, did you ever see, of late or of yore, such a ditty before? The thought did occurr, to me and to her, as Madam and I, did walk not fly, over hills and dales, with spreading sails, before it was dark to Weston Park.

The News at Oney, is little or noney, but such as it is, I send it—viz. Poor Mr. Peace,[1] cannot yet cease, addling his head, with what you said, and has left parish church, quite in the lurch, having almost swore, to go there no more.

Page and his Wife, that made such a Strife, we met them twain, in Dag lane, we gave them the Wall, and that was all. For Mr. Scot, we have seen him not, except as he pass'd, in a wonderfull haste, to see a friend, in Silver End. Mrs. Jones proposes e'er July closes, that She and her Sister, and her Jones Mister, and we that are here, our course shall steer, to dine in the spinney, but for a guinea, if the weather should hold, so hot and so cold, we had better by far, stay where we are, for the grass there grows, while nobody mows, (which is very wrong) so rank and long, that so to speak, 'tis at least a week, if it happen to rain, e'er it dries again.

I have writ Charity, not for popularity, but as well as I could, in hopes to do good. And if the Review'r, should say to be sure, the Gentleman's Muse, wears Methodist shoes, you may know by her pace, and talk about grace, that she and her bard, have little regard, for the tastes and fashions, and ruling passions, and hoyd'ning play, of the modern day, and though She assume, a borrow'd plume, and now and then wear, a tittering air, 'tis only her plan, to catch if She can, the giddy and gay, as they go that way, by a production, on a new construction, and has baited her trap, in hopes to snap, all that may come, with a Sugar plumb, his Opinion in this, will not be amiss, 'tis what I intend, my principal End, and if it Succeed, and folks should read, 'till a few are brought, to a serious thought, I shall think I am paid, for all I have said, and all I have done, though I have run, many a time, after a rhime, as far as from hence, to the end of my Sense, and by hook or crook, write another book, if I live and am here, another year.

[1] In his letter to Newton of 24 Dec. 1784 (Princeton), C provides news of this person. 'For more than half a year a report has been current in this place in the way of whisper, but lately with much noise and clamour, that will make William Peace alias Pearce, unless he can clear himself from the aspersion, a most infamous character. It amounts to nothing less than a charge of Pæderastia.'

I have heard before, of a room with a floor, laid upon springs, and such like things, with so much art, in every part, that when you went in, you was forced to begin, a minuet pace, with an air and a grace, swimming about, now in now out, with a deal of state, in a figure of Eight, without pipe or string, or any such thing. And now I have writ, in a rhiming fit, what will make you dance, and as you advance, will keep you still, though against your will, dancing away, alert and gay, 'till you come to an end, of what I have penn'd. Which that you may do, e'er Madam and you, are quite worn out, with Jigging about, I take my leave, and here you receive, a bow profound, down to the ground, from your humble me.

W:C.

P.S.

When I concluded, doubtless you did: think me right, as well you might, in saying what, I said of Scot, and then it was true, but now it is due, to Him to note, that since I wrote, Himself and He, has visited We.

July 12. 1781

Wm Cowper.

JOHN NEWTON — Sunday, 22 July 1781

Princeton

My dear friend,

I am sensible of your difficulties in finding opportunities to write, and therefore though always desirous and sometimes impatient to hear from you, am never peevish when I am disappointed. We thank you for the Letters. The noble Divine is sensible though angry, and the Divine Captain always consistent with himself. What you relate of the unhappy Epsomite is truely shocking, when men cannot find the true Remedy they often have recourse to one that is worse than the disease, and a worse than He has found, if the fact be such, it is not in the power of Quackery to recommend. How wonderfull! that a man can suppose himself employ'd under God's blessing as a discoverer of truth, while he himself is entangled in the worst of Errors, a practical Departure from it. If a traveller were lost in a labyrinth and in the course of his wanderings should stumble upon a vessel of

intoxicating liquor, he could hardly do worse than drink it, or more effectually insure his own destruction.

Johnson having begun to print, has given me some sort of Security for his perseverance, else the tardiness of his Operations would almost tempt me to despair of the End. He has indeed time enough before him, but that very Circumstance is sometimes a Snare, and gives Occasion to delays that cannot be remedied. Witness the Hare in the fable, who fell asleep in the midst of the race, and waked not till the tortoise had won the prize. Taking it for granted that the new marriage bill would pass, I took occasion in the address to liberty to celebrate the joyfull Æra, but in doing so afforded another proof that poets are not always prophets, for the House of Lords have thrown it out.[1] I am however provided with four lines to fill up the gap, which I suppose it will be time enough to insert, when the Copy is sent down.[2] I am in the middle of an Affair called Conversation, which as Table-talk serves in the present Volume by way of Introductory fiddle to the band that follows, I design shall perform the same Office in a second.

Sic brevi fortes jaculamur ævo.[3]

Our Excursion to the Spinney, which I mention'd in the hop o' my thumb lines I sent you, took place yesterday. The weather was just such as it would have been if we had had the choice of it; perhaps better; for of all things in the world we find it sometimes most difficult to please ourselves. We dined in the root:house. Our great wheel-barrow which may be called a first rate in its kind, conveyed all our stores, and afterwards with the Assistance of a board laid over it, made us a very good table. We set off at One and were at home again soon after Eight. I never made one, in a party of pleasure, that answer'd so well. We seperated before we grew weary of each other,

[1] The following event in Parliament on 28 May is recorded in *G.M.*, li (May 1781), 241: 'Ld Beauchamp moved the House of Commons bring in a bill to remedy certain inconveniences arising from the Marriage Act.—This was moved in consequence of a late decision in the Court of King's Bench, on the following occasion: A pauper having been sent, with his wife and children, from one parish to another, was refused by the latter, because the marriage of the paupers had been celebrated in a chapel that was *not in being at the time the Marriage Act was made*, consequently it was not a legal marriage, and the children were bastardized. This verdict, severe as it was, and affecting thousands, the Judges were obliged to confirm, not having it in their power to depart from the express words of the statute. Leave was given, the bill brought in, and will be passed with all expedition.'

[2] C is probably referring to 'Charity', 254 ff.

[3] See Horace, *Odes*, II. xvi. 17: 'We strive for the great in our brief lives.'

which is a happiness seldom enjoyed upon such Occasions; we were 7 in company including Hannah,[4] who though highly delighted with her jaunt, was not at all more pleased than her Elders. She is as much delighted to day with the acquisition of a Sister born last night,[5] but whether the rest of that noble family will have equal cause to rejoice in the Event, is uncertain. Should she be followed by a troop, unless they practise Dean Swift's recommended method for the maintenance of the poor,[6] it is not easy to say where they will find victuals. Certainly not at Olney. You cannot always find time to write, and I cannot always write a great deal; not for want of time, but for want of something equally requisite; perhaps materials, perhaps Spirits, or perhaps more frequently for want of ability to overcome an Indolence that I have sometimes heard even you complain of.

I beg you will remember me to Mrs. Cowper. We are very sorry to hear of Mrs. Newton's Indisposition. Mr. Wright, who called here three times before he could find me at home, informed me the day before yesterday, that poor Lord D. grows worse. His account of him is indeed a most unfavorable one.

Thanks for the Cocoa nuts[7] and the slide.[8] Mrs. Unwin joins love to both—the Summer being so far advanced

She and her Sublimity
Will do without Dimity.

Yours my dear Sir and Mrs. Newton's
Wm Cowper.

July 22. 1781.
Mr Symonds's Letters cannot be found here.[9]

[4] The members of the party were C, Mrs. Unwin, Lady Austen, the Revd. Thomas Jones (curate of Clifton Reynes), Mrs. Martha Jones (wife of Thomas and sister of Lady Austen), Miss Greene, her daughter, and Hannah Wilson (Richard Coleman's stepdaughter).

[5] *O.P.R.* (p. 398) records the baptism on 13 Aug. of Richard and Martha Coleman's daughter, Maria. Martha Coleman was known as Patty Wilson before her marriage to Coleman. See n. 4, C to Newton, 3 May 1780.

[6] *A Modest Proposal.*

[7] 'The Liquor contained in the Kernel is proper for extinguishing Thirst and Fevers, for curing and cleansing the Eyes, and for washing the Skins of Women. It, also, purifies the Blood, cleanses the Stomach, and Urinary Passages, and removes Disorders of the Breast. It is of a grateful Taste, affords much Nourishment, and is an excellent Drink in Biliary Fevers.': R. James, *Pharmacopœia Universalis* (2nd edn. 1752), p. 256.

[8] 'A kind of tongueless buckle or ring used as a fastener, clasp, or brooch' (*O.E.D.*).

[9] The Revd. Joshua Symonds was minister of Bunyan Meeting, Bedford. Many letters of Newton to him are now in the Cowper and Newton Museum, Olney. C and Mrs. Unwin eventually found the missing letters (see C to Newton, 25 Aug.).

WILLIAM UNWIN Sunday, 29 July 1781

British Library

My dear friend—
Having given the case you laid before me in your last all due consideration, I proceed to answer it, and in order to clear my way, shall in the first place set down my sense of those passages in scripture which on an hasty perusal seem to clash with the Opinion I am going to give. If a man smite one cheek, turn the other—if he take thy cloak, let him take thy coat also[1]—that is I suppose—rather than on a vindictive principle avail yourself of that remedy the law allows you in the way of retaliation, for that was the subject immediately under the discussion of the speaker. Nothing is so contrary to the genius of the gospel as the gratification of resentment and revenge, but I cannot easily persuade myself to think that the Author of that dispensation could possibly advise his followers to consult their own peace at the expence of the peace of Society, or inculcate an universal abstinence from the use of lawfull remedies to the encouragement of Injury and oppression.

St Paul again seems to condemn the practise of going to law. Why do ye not rather suffer wrong &c[2]—but if we look again we shall find that a litigious temper had obtained and was prevalent among the professors of the day. This he condemned and with good reason, it was unseemly to the last degree that the disciples of the prince of peace should worry and vex each other with injurious treatment and unnecessary disputes to the scandal of their religion in the eyes of the heathen. But surely he did not mean any more than his Master in the place above alluded to, that the most harmless members of Society should receive no advantage of its laws, or should be the only persons in the world who should derive no benefit from those Institutions without which Society cannot subsist. Neither of them could mean to throw down the pale of property, and to lay the Christian part of the world open throughout all ages to the incursions of unlimited Violence and wrong.

By this time you are sufficiently aware that I think you have an indisputable right to recover at law what is so dishonestly witheld from you. The fellow I suppose has discernment enough to see a

[1] Matthew 5: 39–40.   [2] 1 Corinthians 6: 7.

difference between you and the generality of the clergy, and cunning enough to conceive the purpose of turning your meekness and forbearance to a good account, and of coining them into hard cash which he means to put in his pocket. But I would disappoint the rascal and show him that though a Christian is not to be quarrelsome, he is not to be crushed, and that though he is but a worm before God, he is not such a worm as every selfish unprincipled wretch like himself may tread upon at his pleasure. You will find otherwise that he will soon cease to be singular in his vilainy, and that here and there another will take the liberty to follow his example, 'till at last your Living will be worth no more than your parishioners out of their great goodness will be pleased to allow you.

I lately heard a story from a lady who has spent many years of her life in France, somewhat to the present purpose. An Abbé universally esteemed for his piety, and especially for the meekness of his manners, had yet undesignedly given some offence to a shabby fellow in his parish. The man concluding he might do as he pleased with so forgiving and gentle a Character, struck him on one cheek, and bade him turn the other. The good man did so, and when he had received the two slaps which he thought himself obliged to submitt to, turned again and beat him soundly. I do not wish to see you follow the French Gentleman's example, but I believe nobody that has heard the story condemns him much for the Spirit he showed upon the occasion.

I had the Relation from Lady Austen, Sister to Mrs. Jones, the Wife of the Minister of Clifton. She is a most agreeable woman, and has fallen in love with your mother and me, insomuch that I do not know but she may settle at Olney. Yesterday sev'night we all dined together in the Spinney, a most delightfull retirement belonging to Mrs. Throgmorton of Weston.[3] Lady Austen's lacquey and a lad that waits on me in the garden, drove a wheel-barrow full of eatables and drinkables to the scene of our fête champêtre. A board laid over the top of the barrow served us for a table, our dining room was a root:house lined with moss and Ivy. At Six o'clock the Servants who had dined under a great Elm upon the ground at a little distance, boiled the Kettle, and the said wheel:barrow served us again for a tea-table. We then took a walk from thence to the wilderness about half a mile

[3] Anna Maria Throckmorton (d. 1791) of Weston Hall, the mother of John and George, C's friends.

off, and were at home again soon after eight, having spent the day together from noon 'till Evening, without one cross occurrence, or the least weariness of each other. An happiness few parties of pleasure can boast of.

Yours with our joint love to the family

Wm Cowper.

The Lace is making, and the parties concerned are desired to take notice that it costs but three pence three farthings per yard.

July 29. 1781.

Mr. Smith with the same obliging readiness as before, has furnished me with the franks I wanted. When I publish, my book shall wait on him in acknowledgment of his kindness.

JOSEPH JOHNSON Monday, 6 August 1781

Yale

Sir,

I am obliged to you for your Queries. The poems will be the better for them. I wish you always to read me with the closest Attention, and to give my lines as strict a Scrutiny as you can find time for. Some things always escape a Writer, which yet strike a judicious Reader perhaps at the first view. And while you allow me a right of decision in the last instance, if I go into public with any uncorrected faults upon my head, the blame and the disgrace will be all my own.

You will perceive that I have made some use of the liberty I stipulated for beforehand, and though I have followed your Advice in several passages, yet not in all. I proceed, according to previous engagement to give my reasons.

No man living abhorrs a louse more than I do, but Hermits are notoriously infested with those vermin; it is even a part of their supposed meritorious mortification to encourage the breed. The fact being true becomes an important feature in the face of that folly I mean to expose, and having occasion to mention the loathsome Animal I cannot, I think, do better than call him by his loathsome name.[1] It is a false delicacy that is offended by the mention of any

[1] Apparently a reference to 'Truth', 79 ff. The change Johnson wanted was adopted.

thing that God has seen fit to create, where the laws of modesty are not violated, and therefore we will not mind it.

Die *then*—[2]

The word Italicised to direct the Emphasis, the objection to that line I suppose must vanish. At least I can see none. The Sentiment I take to be unquestionably true.

I confess the two lines that close the period are two of my favorites. They may possibly at first sight, seem chargeable with some harshness of Expression, but that harshness is rather to be ascribed to the truth they convey, than to the terms in which it is conceived.[3] Every body knows that a final rejection of the Gospel, must terminate in destruction. The words *damnable* and *damned* may be vehement indeed, but they are no more than adequate to the case, nor would any other words that I can think of do justice to the Idea they intend. That Vehemence is indeed the very circumstance that gives them a peculiar propriety in the place they occupy, they bring up the rear of a whole clause of admonitions and cautions, and therefore cannot make too forcible an Impression. They are the lead at the end of the bludgeon.

You may draw on me when you please for about 800 lines. I have just finished a poem of that length, which I intended should take the Lead in a second volume, upon proper encouragement to print again. But if you chuse to begin with Table-talk and end with Conversation, (for that is the title of it,) I have no Objection. The last bears no affinity to the first except in the name of it.

I am Sir

Your most humble Servant

Wm Cowper.

Olney
Augt. 6. 1781.

[2] 'The Progress of Error', 589: 'Die then, if pow'r Almighty save you not.'

[3] Lines 597–8: 'If clemency revolted by abuse/Be damnable, then damn'd without excuse.'

MRS. NEWTON *c.* Monday, 6 August 1781[1]

Princeton

Dear Madam,

Though much obliged to you for the favor of your last, and ready enough to acknowledge the debt, the present however is not a day in which I should have chosen to pay it. A Dejection of mind which perhaps may be removed by to:morrow, rather disqualifies me for writing, a business I would always perform in good spirits, because Melancholy is catching, especially where there is much Sympathy to assist the contagion. But certain poultry which I understand are about to pay their respects to you, have advertized for an agreeable companion, and I find myself obliged to embrace the Opportunity of going to town with them in that Capacity.

I thank you for your little abridgment of my family's history.[2] Like every thing that relates to the present world, in which there seems to be nearly an equal Mixture of the lamentable and ridiculous, it affords both Occasion to laugh and to cry. In the single instance of my Uncle[3] I can see cause for both. He trembles upon the verge of fourscore. A white hat with a yellow lining is no Indication of Wisdom suitable to so great an Age. He can go but one step farther in the road of Impropriety, and direct his Executor to bury him in it. He is a very little man, and had he lined his Hat with pink instead of yellow, might have been gathered by a natural mistake for a Mushroom, and sent off in a basket.

While the world lasts Fashion will continue to lead it by the nose. And after all what can fashion do for its most obsequious followers? It can ring the changes upon the same things and it can do no more. Whether our Hats be white or black, our Caps high or low, whether we wear two watches or one, is of little consequence. There is indeed an appearance of Variety, but the folly and Vanity that dictates and adopts the change, are invariably the same. When the fashions of a particular period appear more reasonable than those of the preceding, it is not because the world is grown more reasonable than it was, but because in a course of perpetual changes, some of them

[1] The date of this letter is 6 Aug. or shortly afterwards. In the course of this letter, C refers to the letter of 6 Aug. to Johnson which is said to be a reply to 'a note I received from Johnson last week'.

[2] This account has not survived.

[3] Ashley Cowper, who was born in 1701.

must sometimes happen to be for the better. Neither do I suppose the preposterous customs that prevail at present a proof of its greater folly. In a few years, perhaps next year, the fine gentleman will shut up his Umbrella and give it to his Sister, filling his hand with a crab-tree cudgel instead of it. And when he has done so, will he be wiser than now? By no means. The love of change will have betrayed him into a propriety which in reality he has no taste for, all his Merit on the occasion amounting to no more than this, that being weary of one play thing he has taken up another.

In a note I received from Johnson last week, he expresses a wish that my pen may be still employed. Supposing it possible that he would yet be glad to swell the volume, I have given him an order to draw upon me for 800 lines if he chuses it, Conversation, a piece which I think I mentioned in my last to Sir Newton, being finished. If Johnson sends for it, I shall transcribe it as soon as I can and transmitt it to Charles-Square; Mr. Newton will take the trouble to forward it to the press. It is not a dialogue as the title would lead you to surmise, nor does it bear the least resemblance to Table-talk, except that it is serio-comic like all the Rest. My design in it is to convince the world that they make but an indifferent use of their tongues, considering the Intention of Providence when he endued them with the faculty of Speech; to point out the Abuses, which is the jocular part of the Business, and to prescribe the Remedy, which is the grave and sober.

We felt ourselves not the less obliged to you for the Cocoa nuts, though they were good for nothing. They contained nothing but a putrid liquor with a round white lump which in taste and substance much resembled tallow, and was of the size of a small Walnut. Nor am I the less indebted to your kindness for the fish, though none is yet come.—Mrs Unwin does not forget the Eggs, but while the Harvest continues, Puddings are in such request, that the farmers will not part with them.

Our joint Love to both and to Miss Catlett if at home. Sir's Letter, for which I thank him, shall have an Answer as soon as possible.[4]

Yours dear Madam most affectionately

Wm Cowper.

Poor Nat Gee humbly begs, and hopes no Offence, that in due time

[4] Perhaps C's to Newton of 16 Aug.

he shall be informed in what Stock his Money is laid out, and be favor'd with some Receipt or Security for it.[5]

JOHN NEWTON Thursday, 16 August 1781

Princeton

My dear friend—

I might date my letter from the Green-house, which we have converted into a summer parlour. The Walls hung with garden mats, and the floor covered with a carpet, the Sun too in a great measure excluded by an awning of mats which forbids him to shine any where except upon the carpet, it affords us by far the pleasantest retreat in Olney. We eat, drink and sleep where we always did, but here we spend all the rest of our time, and find that the sound of the wind in the trees, and the singing of birds, are much more agreeable to our Ears, than the incessant barking of dogs and screaming of children, not to mention the exchange of a sweet-smelling garden for the putrid exhalations of Silver End. It is an Observation that naturally occurrs upon the Occasion, and which many other Occasions furnish an Opportunity to make, that people long for what they have not, and overlook the good in their possession. This is so true in the present instance, that for years past I should have thought myself happy to enjoy a retirement even less flattering to my natural taste than this in which I am now writing, and have often looked wistfully at a snug cottage, which on account of its situation at a distance from noise and disagreeable objects, seemed to promise me all I could wish or expect, so far as happiness may be said to be local, never once adverting to this comfortable nook, which affords me all that could be found in the most sequester'd hermitage, with the advantage of having all those accommodations near at hand, which no hermitage could possibly afford me. People imagine they should be happy in circumstances which they would find insupportably burthensome in less than a week. A man that has been cloathed in fine linen and fared sumptuously ev'ry day, envies the peasant under a thatched hovel, who in return envies Him as much his palace and his pleasure-ground. Could they change situations the fine gentleman would find his

[5] See C to Newton, 7 July.

ceilings were too low, and that his casements admitted too much wind, that he had no cellar for his wine, and no wine to put in his cellar. These with a thousand other mortifying deficiencies, would shatter his romantic project into innumerable fragments in a moment. The Clown at the same time would find the accession of so much unwieldy treasure an incumbrance quite incompatible with an hour's ease. His choice would be puzzled by variety, he would drink to excess because he would foresee no end of his abundance, and he would eat himself sick for the same reason. He would have no idea of any other happiness than sensual gratification, would make himself a beast, and die of his good fortune. The rich gentleman had perhaps, or might have had if he pleased, at the shortest notice, just such a recess as this, but if he had it he overlooked it, or if he had it not, forgot that he might command it whenever he would. The rustic too was actually in possession of some blessings which he was a fool to relinquish, but which he could neither see nor feel because he had the daily and constant use of them; such as good health, bodily strength, a head and a heart that never ached, and temperance, to the practise of which he was bound by necessity, that humanly speaking, was a pledge and a Security for the continuance of them all.

Thus I have sent you a School-boy's theme. When I write to you, I do not write without thinking, but always without premeditation, the consequence is that such thoughts as pass through my head when I am not writing, make the Subject of my letters to you.

Johnson sent me lately a sort of Apology for his printer's negligence, with his promise of greater diligence for the future. There was need enough of both. I have received but one sheet since you left us. Still indeed I see that there is time enough before us, but I see like wise that no length of time can be sufficient for the accomplishment of a work that does not go forward. I know not yet whether he will add Conversation to those poems already in his hands, nor do I care much. No man ever wrote such quantities of Verse as I have written this last year, with so much indifference about the Event, or rather with so little ambition of public praise. My pieces are such as may possibly be made usefull. The more they are approved, the more likely they are to spread, and consequently the more likely to attain the end of usefullness, which as I said once before, except my present amusement, is the only end I propose. And even in the pursuit of this

purpose, commendable as it is in itself, I have not the spur I should once have had, my labor must go unrewarded, and as Mr. Raban once said, I am raising a scaffold before a house that others are to live in, and not I.

I have left myself no room for politics, which I thought when I began would have been my principal theme.

Mr. Symonds's letters certainly are not here. Our servants never touch a paper without leave, and are so observant of our Injunction, in this particular, that unless I burn the covers of the News, they accumulate till they make a litter in the parlour. They cannot therefore have been destroyed through carelessness, and consequently if they were with us we should be able to find them.

Our love to you both.

Yours my dear Sir Wm Cowper.

Augt. 16. 1781.

JOHN NEWTON — Tuesday, 21 August 1781

Princeton

My dear friend—

Natt: is very happy in having his hoard so well secured, and so advantageously disposed of. The eighteen pence shall be accounted for by some future opportunity. If Mr. Crawford will be so kind as to receive the Interest for him, he is well content to let it stand in his name.

You wish you could employ your time to better purpose, yet are never idle. In All that you say or do, whether you are alone, or pay Visits or receive them, whether you think or write, or walk or sit still, the state of your mind is such, as discovers even to yourself in spite of all its wanderings, that there is a principle at bottom whose determined tendency is toward the best things. I do not at all doubt the truth of what you say, when you complain of that crowd of trifling thoughts that pesters you without ceasing, but then you always have a serious thought standing at the door of your imagination, like a Justice of peace with the Riot act in his hand, ready to read it and disperse the Mob. Here lies the difference between you and me. My thoughts are clad in a sober livery, for the most part as grave as that

of a Bishop's Servants. They turn too upon spiritual subjects, but the tallest fellow and the loudest amongst them all, is he who is continually crying with a loud voice, Actum est de te, periisti.[1] You wish for more Attention, I for less. Dissipation itself would be welcome to me, so it were not a vicious one, but however earnestly invited, is coy and keeps at a distance. Yet with all this distressing gloom upon my mind, I experience as you do the Slipperiness of the present hour, and the rapidity with which time escapes me. Every thing around us, and every thing that befalls us, constitutes a Variety which whether agreeable or otherwise, has still a thievish propensity, and steals from us days, months and years with such unparalelled address, that even while we say they are here, they are gone. From Infancy to Manhood is rather a tedious period, chiefly I suppose because at that time we act under the controll of others, and are not suffered to have a Will of our own. But thence downward into the vale of years is such a declivity, that we have just an Opportunity to reflect upon the steepness of it, and then find ourselves at the bottom.

Here is a new scene opening, which whether it perform what it promises or not, will add fresh plumes to the wings of time, at least while it continues to be a Subject of contemplation. If the project take effect, a thousand varieties will attend the change it will make in our situation at Olney. If not, it will serve however to speculate and converse upon, and steal away many hours by engaging our Attention, before it be entirely dropped. Lady Austen, very desirous of Retirement, especially of a Retirement near her Sister, an Admirer of Mr. Scott as a preacher, and of your two humble Servants now in the Green house as the most agreeable creatures in the world, is at present determined to settle here. That part of our great building which is at present occupied by Dick Coleman, his Wife, child and a thousand rats, is the corner of the world she chuses above all others as the place of her future Residence.[2] Next spring twelvemonth she begins to repair and beautify, and the following winter, (by which time the Lease of her house in town will determine) she intends to take possession. I am highly pleased with the plan upon Mrs. Unwin's account, who since Mrs. Newton's departure, is destitute of all female connection, and has not in any Emergency a woman to speak to. Mrs. Scott is indeed in the neighborhood, and an excellent person, but always engaged by a close attention to her family, and no more than

[1] 'It is all over for you—you have perished.'

[2] The eastern part of the house.

ourselves a Lover of Visiting. But these things are all at present in the clouds, two years must intervene, and in two years not only this project, but all the projects in Europe may be disconcerted.

Cocoa nut naught,[3]
Fish too dear,
None must be bought
For us that are here.

No Lobster on Earth,
That ever I saw,
To me would be worth
Sixpence a claw.

So dear Madam wait
Till fish can be got,
At a reas'nable rate,
Whether Lobster or not

Till the French and the Dutch
Have quitted the Seas,
And then send as much
And as oft' as you please.

Mrs. Andrews[4] took charge of a couple of fowls and a Duck, and promised to convey them to our friends at Hoxton. Not being mentioned in your last, Mrs. Unwin fears they miscarried.

Yours my dear Sir
Wm Cowper.

Augt. 21. 1781

JOHN NEWTON — Saturday, 25 August 1781

Princeton

My dear friend,

The Letters so long sought in vain are at last found, and found when they were not looked for, wrapt up and ready for package just

[3] Published in *Private Correspondence of William Cowper*, ed. John Johnson (1824).

[4] Perhaps a relation of the Brightman Andrews mentioned earlier in the correspondence. See C to Newton, 31 Aug. 1780.

as Mrs. Newton left them.[1] The fact is that not having the appearance of what they were, they had been frequently seen but never noticed, and had not Mrs. Un— been looking for something else would not have been found at last. They shall be sent by the first Opportunity.

By Johnson's last Note (for I have receiv'd a packet from him since I wrote last to you) I am ready to suspect that you have seen him and endeavor'd to quicken his proceedings. His Assurance of greater Expedition leads me to think so. I know little of Booksellers and Printers, but have heard from others that they are the most dilatory of all people. Otherwise I am not in a hurry, nor would be troublesome; but am obliged to you nevertheless for your Interference if his promised alacrity be owing to any Spur that you have given him. He chuses to add Conversation to the rest, and says he will give me notice when he is ready for it, but I shall send it to *You* by the first opportune conveyance, and beg you to deliver it over to Him. He wishes me not to be afraid of making the volume too large; by which Expression I suppose he means that if I had still another piece, there would be room for it. At present I have not, but am in the way to produce another, faveat modo Musa[2]—I have already begun and proceeded a little way in a poem call *Retirement*. My view in chusing that Subject is to direct to the proper use of the opportunities it affords for the cultivation of a Man's best Interests; to censure the Vices and the follies which people carry with them into their Retreats, where they make no other use of their leisure than to gratify themselves with the Indulgence of their favorite appetites, and to pay themselves by a life of pleasure for a life of Business. In conclusion I would enlarge upon the happiness of that State when discreetly enjoyed and religiously improved. But all this is at present in Embryo. I generally despair of my progress when I begin, but if like my travelling Squire, I should kindle as I go, this likewise may make a part of the Volume, for I have time enough before me.

Mrs. Unwin of Stock has brought forth another Son and calls his name William.[3] Susan Roberts has been supposed dying for some time, was speechless for a Week, then grew better, was siezed with violent Convulsions, and is again grown better. Mr. Scot is recovered, though when we paid him our last Morning Visit, we found him a little disconcerted by the Brutality and profaneness of a drunken

[1] The letters to Symonds mentioned in C to Newton, 22 July and 16 Aug.

[2] 'If the Muse be favourably inclined.'

[3] William Unwin (d. *c.* 1800).

fellow whom he had just been Yoking with a pregnant Lady. The Church was filled with idle folks upon the Occasion who could not be persuaded to behave with any degree of decency or decorum, and the Wretch himself was as insolent as Ignorance and strong drink could make him.

I forgot to mention that Johnson uses the discretion my poetship has allowed him with much discernment. He has suggested several alterations, or rather marked several defective passages which I have corrected much to the advantage of the poems. In the last sheet he sent me, he noted three such, all which I have reduced into better Order. In the foregoing sheet I assented to his Criticisms in some instances, and chose to abide by the original Expression in others. Thus we Jog on together comfortably enough, and perhaps it would be as well for Authors in general, if their Booksellers when men of some taste, were allowed though not to tinker the work themselves, yet to point out the flaws, and humbly to recommend an improvement.

The Embargo I would have laid upon the present of fish, reached you I find too late, and we are now to return our thanks for three pair of fine Soals on which we feasted noon and night. But I beg that said Embargo may have its Effect in future, and that Mrs. Newton will not think of sending more 'till the price is fallen. Once more Love, Thanks and Adieu! —Yours Wm Cowper.

Augt. 25. 1781.

WILLIAM UNWIN — Saturday, 25 August 1781

British Library

My dear friend,

We rejoice with you sincerely in the birth of another Son, and in the prospect you have of Mrs. Unwin's perfect recovery. May your three Children, and the next three when they shall make their appearance, prove so many blessings to their parents, and make you wish that you had twice the number.—But what made you expect daily that you should hear from me? Letter for Letter is the law of all

correspondence whatsoever, and because I wrote the last,[1] I have indulged myself for some time in expectations of a Sheet from You. Not that I govern myself entirely by the punctilio of reciprocation, but having been pretty much occupied of late, I was not sorry to find myself at liberty to exercise my discretion, and furnished with a good Excuse if I chose to be silent.

I expected, as you remember, to have been published last spring and was disappointed. The delay has afforded me an Opportunity to encrease the quantity of my publication by about a third; and if my Muse has not forsaken me, which I rather suspect to be the case, may possibly yet add to it. I have a Subject in hand which promises me a great abundance of poetical matter, but which for want of a something I am not able to describe, I cannot at present proceed with. The name of it is Retirement, and my purpose, to recommend the proper improvement of it, to set forth the requisites for that end, and to enlarge upon the happiness of that state of life when managed as it ought to be. In the course of my journey through this ample theme, I should wish to touch upon the Characters, the deficiencies and the Mistakes of thousands who enter on a Scene of Retirement, unqualified for it in every respect, and with such designs as have no tendency to promote either their own happiness or that of others. But as I have told you before, there are times when I am no more a Poet than I am a Mathematician, and when such a time occurrs, I always think it better to give up the point than to labour it in vain. I shall yet again be obliged to trouble you for franks—the addition of three thousand lines, or near that number, having occasioned a demand which I did not always foresee. But your obliging friend and your obliging self, having allowed me free liberty of application, I make it without apology.

The Solitude, or rather the Duality of our Condition at Olney, seems drawing to a Conclusion. You have not forgot perhaps that the building we inhabit, consists of two mansions. And because you have only seen the inside of that part of it which is in our Occupation, I therefore inform you that the other end of it is by far the most superb as well as the most commodious. Lady Austen has seen it, has set her heart upon it, is going to fit it up and furnish it, and if she can get rid of the remaining two years of the lease of her London house, will probably enter upon it in a twelve-month. You will be

[1] Probably C's letter of 29 July.

pleased with this Intelligence, because I have already told you that she is a woman perfectly well bred, sensible, and in every respect agreeable; and above all because she loves your Mother dearly. It has in my Eyes (and I doubt not it will have the same in yours) strong marks of a providential interposition. A female friend and one who bids fair to prove herself worthy of the appellation, comes recommended by a variety of considerations to such a place as Olney. Since Mr. Newton went, and till this Lady came, there was not in the Kingdom a retirement more absolutely such than ours. We did not want company, but when it came, we found it agreeable; a person that has seen much of the world and understands it well, has high spirits, a lively fancy and great readiness of Conversation, introduces a sprightliness into such a Scene as this, which if it was peacefull before, is not the worse for being a little enlivened. In case of Illness too to which all are liable, it was rather a gloomy prospect if we allowed ourselves to advert to it, that there was hardly a woman in the place from whom it would have been reasonable to have expected either comfort or Assistance. The present Curate's Wife is a valuable person, but has a family of her own, and though a neighbor not a very near one. But if this plan is effected, we shall be in a manner one family, and I suppose never pass a day without some intercourse with each other.

Your Mother sends her warm Affections and congratulations, and welcomes into the world the new-born William.

Yours my dear friend Wm Cowper.

Augt. 25. 1781

No Stock-buckle is wanted at present. But you are desired to order the Shopman to send the handkerchiefs to Mr. Newton's—they having frequent opportunities to send to Olney.

JOSEPH JOHNSON Monday, 3 September 1781[1]

Princeton (*copy*)

Sir

I return the copy always by the first opportunity, though sometimes I may seem to detain it longer than necessary. We have the

[1] This copy was dated '3 Sept. 1781' by its former owner, Thomas Wright.

post but three times a Week.—Mr. Newton writes me word he has recieved *Conversation*, which therefore I suppose will soon pay its respects to You. I am now writing, but whether what I write will be ready for the present volume should you chuse to insert it, I know not. I never write except when I can do it with facility, and am rather apprehensive that the Muse is about to forsake me for the present; ever since I could use a pen I have been subject to such Vicissitudes.

I am Sir

Your most obedient Servant

Wm Cowper

I have corrected no mistakes but my own.[2]

JOHN NEWTON — Sunday, 9 September 1781

Princeton

My dear friend

I am not willing to let the post set off without me, though I have nothing material to put into his bag. I am writing in the green-house, where my Myrtles ranged before the windows make the most agreeable Blind imaginable, where I am undisturbed by noise, and where I see none but pleasing objects. The situation is as favorable to my purpose as I could wish, but the state of mind is not so, and the deficiencies I feel there, are not to be remedied by the stillness of my retirement, or the beauty of the scene before me. I beleive it is in part owing to the excessive heat of the weather that I find myself so much at a loss when I attempt either verse or prose, my animal Spirits are depressed, and dullness is the Consequence. That dullness however is all at your service, and the portion of it that is necessary to fill up the present Epistle I send you without the least reluctance.

I am sorry to find that the censure I have passed upon Occiduus[1] is even better founded than I supposed. Lady Austen has been at his Sabbatical concerts, which it seems are composed of song tunes and psalm tunes indiscriminately, music without words, and I suppose one may say, consequently without devotion. On a certain occasion,

[2] C had not checked the page proofs for errors introduced by the compositor.

[1] Frederick C. Gill in *Charles Wesley, The First Methodist* (1964), pp. 189–91, identifies Occiduus (Western) as Martin Madan, but does not give any evidence.

when her Niece was sitting at her side, she asked his opinion concerning the lawfullness of such amusements as are to be found at Vaux-hall or Ranelagh, meaning only to draw from him a sentence of disapprobation, that Miss Green might be the better reconciled to the restraint under which she was held, when she found it warranted by the Judgment of so famous a divine. But she was disappointed—he accounted them innocent, and recommended them as usefull. Curiosity, he said, was natural to young persons, and it was wrong to deny them a gratification which they might be indulged in with the greatest safety, because the denial being unreasonable, the desire of it would still subsist. It was but a Walk, and a Walk was as harmless in one place as another; with other Arguments of a similar import, which might have proceeded with more grace, at least with less offence, from the lips of a sensual layman. He seems, together with others of our acquaintance, to have suffered considerably in his spiritual character by his attachment to Music. The lawfullness of it, when used with moderation, and in its proper place, is unquestionable; but I beleive that Wine itself, though a man be guilty of habitual intoxication, does not more debauch and befool the natural understanding, than Music, always Music, Music in season and out of season, weakens and destroys the spiritual discernment. If it is not used with an unfeigned reference to the worship of God, and with a design to assist the Soul in the performance of it, which cannot be the case when it is the only Occupation, it degenerates into a sensual delight, and becomes a most powerfull advocate for the admission of other pleasures, grosser perhaps in degree, but in their kind the same.

Mr. Unwin having a little money of ours in hand, has been desired to lay it out in the purchase of silk handkerchiefs; they will probably be sent to your house. Mrs. Unwin will be obliged to Mrs. Newton if she will pack them off for Olney together with the knitting needles she hopes she has received a Commission for.

Mr. Monk though a simple honest good man, such at least he appears to us, is not likely to give general satisfaction.[2] He preaches the truth it seems, but not the whole truth, and a certain member of that church who signed the Letter of Invitation, which was conceived in terms sufficiently encouraging, is likely to prove one of his most strenuous opposers. The little man however has an independent

[2] Thomas Monk was minister of the Congregational Church, Olney, from 1780 to 1782.

fortune, and has nothing to do but to trundle himself away to some other place where he may find hearers neither so nice nor so wise as we are at Olney.

Yours my dear Sir with our united Love

Wm Cowper.

Sepr. 9. 1781.

JOSEPH JOHNSON Sunday, 16 September 1781

Address: Mr. Johnson / Booksr. / St. Pauls Ch. Yard / London / RobfreeSmith
Postmarks: 17/SE, OULNEY, *and* FREE
Berkhamsted Historical Society

Sir

By your not mentioning it, I suppose you have not yet received *Conversation.* Shall be glad to know it when you have. Retirement is grown to about 500 lines, so that I begin to hope that I shall reach the End of it.

Cry aloud &c.[1]

Though the Verse has rather an unusual run, I chose to begin it in that manner for the sake of Animation, and am not able to alter it without flattening its Energy quite away.

Providence adverse &c.[2]

The reduplication of those words was a point I rather labor'd for the sake of Emphasis, and the transposition of them strikes me as artfull and as having an agreeable Effect upon the Ear.

Cured of the golden calves—[3]

The Expression has a figurative boldness in it which appears to me poetical.

All your other marks have been attended to, and I thank you for them.

I am Sir

Your most Obedient

Wm Cowper.

Sepr. 16. 1781

[1] 'Expostulation', 267: 'Cry aloud, thou that sittest in the dust.'

[2] Ibid. 313: 'Providence adverse in events like these?' Line 310 reads: 'In adverse providence, when ponder'd well.'

[3] Ibid. 215–16: 'Cur'd of the golden calves, their fathers' sin,/They set up self, that idol god within.'

MRS. NEWTON Sunday, 16 September 1781

Princeton

A noble theme demands a noble Verse,
In such I thank you for your fine Oy*sters.*
The barrel was magnificently large,
But being sent to Olney at free charge,
Was not inserted in the driver's list,
And therefore overlooked, forgot, or miss'd.
For when the Messenger whom we dispatched,
Enquired for Oysters, Hob his noddle scratch'd,
Denying that his Waggon or his wain,
Did any such Commodity contain.
In consequence of which your welcome boon,
Did not arrive 'till yesterday at noon,
In consequence of which, some chanced to die,
And some though very sweet, were very dry.
Now Madam says, (and what she says must still
Deserve Attention, say she what she will)
That what we call the Diligence, be-case
It goes to London with a swifter pace,
Would better suit the Carriage of your gift,
Returning downward with a pace as swift,
And therefore recommends it with this aim
To save at least three days, the price the same.
For though it will not carry or convey
For less than twelve pence, send whate'er you may,
For Oysters bred upon the salt sea shore
Packed in a barrel, they will charge no more.
 News have I none that I can deign to write
Save that it rained prodigiously last night,
And that ourselves were at the 7th hour,
Caught in the first beginning of the show'r,
But walking, running and with much ado,
Got home just time enough to be wet through.
Yet both are well, and wondrous to be told,
Soused as we were, we yet have caught no cold,

And wishing just the same good hap to you,
We say good Madam, and good Sir, Adieu![1]

Sepr. 16. 1781.

JOHN NEWTON Tuesday, 18 September 1781

Princeton

My dear friend,

I return your preface, with many thanks for so affectionate an Introduction to the public. I have observed nothing that in my judgment required alteration, except a single sentence in the first paragraph, which I have not obliterated, that you may restore it if you please by obliterating my interlineation. My reason for proposing an Amendment of it was that your meaning did not immediately strike me, which therefore I have endeavor'd to make more obvious. The rest is what I would wish it to be—you say indeed more in my commendation than I can modestly say of myself, but something will be allowed to the partiality of friendship on so interesting an Occasion.

I have no objection in the world to your conveying a Copy to Dr. Johnson,[1] though I well know that one of his pointed Sarcasms, if he should happen to be displeased, would soon find its way into all companies, and spoil the Sale. He writes indeed like a man that thinks a great deal, and that sometimes thinks religiously; but report informs me that he has been severe enough in his animadversions upon Doctor Watts, who was nevertheless, if I am in any degree a judge of Verse, a man of true poetical ability.[2] Careless indeed for the most part, and inattentive too often to those niceties which

[1] Published in *Private Correspondence of William Cowper*, ed. John Johnson (1824).

[1] C to Newton, 22 May 1784: 'I am glad to have received at last an account of Dr. Johnson's favourable opinion of my book. I thought it wanting, and had long since concluded that not having had the happiness to please him, I owed my ignorance of his sentiments to the tenderness of my friends at Hoxton, who would not mortify me with an account of his disapprobation.' It appears likely that Benjamin Latrobe, the distinguished Moravian pastor, served as the intermediary who told Newton—and therefore C—that Samuel Johnson had read C's poems. See Maurice J. Quinlan, 'An Intermediary between Cowper and Johnson', *R.E.S.*, xxiv (1948), 141–7.

[2] Newton corrected C's views of Watts. See C to Newton, 4 Oct. 1781.

constitute Elegance of expression, but frequently sublime in his conceptions and masterly in his Execution. Pope, I have heard, had placed him once in the Dunciad, but on being advised to read before he judged him, was convinced that he deserved other treatment, and thrust somebody's blockhead into the gap whose name consisting of a monosyllable happened to fit it.[3] Whatever faults however I may be chargeable with as a poet, I cannot accuse myself of negligence—I never suffer a line to pass 'till I have made it as good as I can; and though my doctrines may offend this King of Critics, he will not I flatter myself, be disgusted by slovenly inaccuracy either in the numbers, rhimes, or language. Let the rest take its chance. It is possible he may be pleased, and if he should, I shall have engaged on my side one of the best trumpeters in the Kingdom. Let him only speak as favorably of me, as he has spoken of Sir Richard Blackmore, who though he shines in his poem called Creation, has written more absurdities in Verse than any Writer of our Country, and my success will be secured.[4]

I have often promised myself a laugh with you about your pipe, but have always forgotten it when I have been writing, and at present I am not much in a laughing humor. You will observe however for your comfort, and the honor of that same pipe, that it hardly falls within the line of my censure. You never fumigate the Ladies, or force them out of company, nor do you use it as an Incentive to hard drinking. Your friends indeed have reason to complain that it frequently deprives them of the pleasure of your own Conversation, while it leads you either into your Study or your garden, but in all

[3] There were references to Watts in Book I, line 126 ('Well-purg'd, and worthy W—y, W—s, and Bl—') and Book III, line 188 ('W—s, B—r, M—n, all the poring kind') in some of the editions of the *Dunciad* in 1728. See the variants in the Twickenham edition of *The Dunciad* (ed. James Sutherland, 1965), which uses the quarto edition of 1729 as copy-text, by which time the references to Watts had been expunged.

Sutherland (p. 79) speculates that it was Watts's popularity with 'humble readers' that caused Pope to place him in the *Dunciad*. 'According to one account, Watts's name was removed on his own "serious, though gentle, remonstrance" (J. Nichols, *Literary Anecdotes of the Eighteenth Century* [1812–16], V, 218); according to another, at the request of Jonathan Richardson, a friend of both Watts and Pope (*Letters by Several Eminent Persons Deceased*, 1772, I 87).'

The 'blockhead' thrust into the gap at line 126 in Book I was Francis Quarles (1592–1644). Pope apologizes for his use of Watts in his note to line 126 in the 1729 quarto. Line 188 in Book III was rewritten without proper names.

[4] *The Creation, a Philosophical Poem Demonstrating the Existence and Providence of God* (1712) by Sir Richard Blackmore (d. 1729), physician to Queen Anne.

other respects it is as innocent a pipe as can be. Smoke away therefore, and remember that if one poet has condemned the practise,[5] a better than he (the witty and elegant Hawkins Brown)[6] has been warm in the praise of it.

We are sorry for poor Peggy, and for your sakes as well as her own shall be glad to hear of her recovery. You will be so kind as to give our Love to her and to Sally, and to Miss Catlett if at home.

Retirement grows, but more slowly than any of its predecessors. Time was when I could with ease produce 50, 60, or 70 lines in a Morning, now I generally fall short of 30, and am sometimes forced to be content with a dozen. It consists at present I suppose of between 6 and 700, so that there are hopes of an end, and I dare say Johnson will give me time enough to finish it.

I nothing add but this, that *still I am*,
Your most affectionate & humble *William.*

The Greenhouse
Sepr. 18. 1781.

Our joint Love attends Mrs. Newton.

WILLIAM UNWIN   Wednesday, 26 September 1781

British Library

Sepr. 26. 1781

My dear friend,

I may, I suppose, congratulate you on your safe arrival at Brighthelmstone, and am the better pleased with your design to close the summer there, because I am acquainted with the place, and by the assistance of Fancy can without much difficulty join myself to the party, and partake with you in your amusements and Excursions. It happened singularly enough, that just before I received your last, in which you apprize me of your intended journey, I had been writing upon the Subject, having found occasion towards the close of my last poem, called Retirement, to take some notice of the modern passion for sea-side entertainments, and to direct to the means by which they

[5] C is playfully referring to lines 245–68 from 'Conversation'.

[6] *Of Smoking: Four Poems in Praise of Tobacco* by Isaac Hawkins Browne the Elder (1705–60) appeared in 1736.

might be made usefull as well as agreeable.[1] I think with you, that the most magnificent object under heaven is the great deep; and cannot but feel an unpolite species of astonishment, when I consider the multitudes that view it without Emotion, and even without reflection. In all its various forms it is an object of all others the most suited to affect us with lasting impressions of the awfull power that created and controuls it. I am the less inclined to think this negligence excuseable, because at a time of life when I gave as little attention to religious subjects as almost any man, I yet remember that the waves would preach to me, and that in the midst of dissipation I had an ear to hear them. One of Shakespear's characters says—I am never merry when I hear sweet Music.[2] The same effect that harmony seems to have had upon him, I have experienced from the Sight and Sound of the Ocean, which have often composed my thoughts into a Melancholy not unpleasing, nor without its use. So much for Signor Nettuno.[3]

Lady Austen goes to London this day sev'night. We have told her that you shall visit her, which is an Enterprize you may engage in with the more alacrity, because as she loves every thing that has any connection with your Mother, she is sure to feel a sufficient partiality for her Son. Add to this, that your own personal recommendations are by no means small, or such as a woman of her fine taste and discernment can possibly overlook.[4] She has many features in her character which you will admire, but one in particular on account of the rarity of it, will engage your Attention and esteem. She has a degree of gratitude in her composition, so quick a sense of obligation, as is hardly to be found in any rank of life, and if report say true, is scarce indeed in the Superior. Discover but a wish to please her, and she never forgets it; not only thanks you, but the tears will start into her Eyes at the recollection of the smallest Service. With these fine feelings, she has the most, and the most harmless vivacity you can imagine, in short she is—what you will find her to be upon half an hour's Conversation with her, and when I hear you have a journey to Town in contemplation I will send you her address.

Your Mother is well, and joins with me in wishing that you may spend your time agreeably upon the Coast of Sussex. I beg you will

[1] 'Retirement', 515–58.

[2] Jessica in *The Merchant of Venice* (v. i. 69).

[3] Neptune.

[4] C tells Unwin of Lady Austen's praise for him in his letter of 27 Aug. 1782.

trouble Mr. Smith with my respectfull Compliments, not because I have any right to intrude them upon him, but because he has done me favors of which I am sensible, and wish to appear so.

Yours Wm C.

JOSEPH JOHNSON Monday, 1 October 1781

Southey, xv. 94[1]

Oct. 1, 1781.

Sir,

I expect to finish *Retirement* in a day or two, and as soon as transcribed I shall forward it to Mr. Newton. This addition, I think, will swell the volume to a respectable size, consisting, as I guess, of between seven and eight hundred lines. I may now grant myself a respite, and watch the success of the present undertaking, determining myself by the event, whether to resume my occupation as an author or drop it for ever.

I am, Sir,
Your most obedient Servant,
Wm. Cowper.

JOSEPH HILL Wednesday, 3 October 1781

Cowper Johnson

My dear friend—

Your draught is worded for twenty pounds and figured for twenty one—I thought it more likely the mistake should be made in the figures than in the words, and have sent you a Receipt accordingly. I am obliged to you for it, and no less bound to acknowledge your kindness in thinking for a man so little accustomed to think for himself. The result of my deliberations on the Subject proposed is that it will be better on many accounts to sell the Chambers, and to

[1] This letter is listed in the Sotheby catalogue of 5 June 1944 (lot 254G); it was purchased by Earles for £14. It was subsequently owned by Mrs. D. Hicks, Cedartop, Stadhampton, Oxford, but it cannot now be traced.

deposit the money in the funds. Public Credit wants a lift, and I would willingly show my readiness to afford it one, at so critical a juncture. If you can sell Morgan at the same time, so as to turn him to any account, you have my free leave to do it; it has been a dry Summer, and frogs may possibly be scarce and fetch a good price, though how his frogship has attained to the honor of that appellation, at this distance from the scene of his activity, I am not able to conjecture.[1]

I hope you have had a pleasant Vacation, and have laid in a fresh stock of health and spirits for the business of the approaching winter. As for me, I have just finished my last piece called Retirement, which as soon as it is fit to appear in public, shall together with the rest of its fraternity lay itself at your feet.

My affectionate respects attend Mrs. Hill and yourself

Yours truely
Wm Cowper.
Olney Octr. 3. 1781

Received of Mr. Hill and Sum of Twenty pounds
By Me Wm Cowper.

JOHN NEWTON — Thursday, 4 October 1781

Princeton

My dear friend,

I generally write the day before the Post, but yesterday had no Opportunity, being obliged to employ myself in settling my Green-house for the Winter. I am now writing before breakfast, that I may avail myself of every Inch of time for the purpose. N.B. an Expression a Critic would quarrel with, and call it by some hard name signifying a Jumble of Ideas, and an unnatural Match between time & space.

I am glad to be undeceived respecting the Opinion I had been erroneously led into on the Subject of Johnson's Criticism on Watts.[1]

[1] The chambers were not sold. See n. 1, C to Hill, 27 May 1777.

---

[1] Johnson's comment that Watts's 'devotional poetry, is, like that of others, unsatisfactory' had offended C, but Newton is right in calling C's attention to Johnson's reverence for Watts's character: '. . . happy will be that reader whose mind is disposed by his verses, or

Nothing can be more judicious or more characteristic of a distinguishing taste than his observations upon that Writer, though I think him a little mistaken in his notion that divine Subjects have never been poetically treated with Success. A little more Christian knowledge and Experience would perhaps enable him to discover excellent poetry upon spiritual themes in the aforesaid little Doctor. —I perfectly acquiesce in the propriety of sending Johnson a Copy of my productions, and I think it would be well to send it in our joint names, accompanied with a handsome card, such an one as you will know how to fabricate, and such as may predispose him to a favorable perusal of the book, by coaxing him into a good temper, for he is a great bear with all his Learning and penetration.

I forgot to tell you in my last that I was well pleased with your proposed appearance in the title page under the name of The Editor,[2] I do not care under how many names you appear in a book that calls me its author. In my last piece which I finished the day before yesterday, I have told the public that I live upon the banks of the Ouse;[3] that public is a great Simpleton if it does not know that you live in London; it will consequently know that I had need of the assistance of some friend in town, and that I could have recourse to nobody with more propriety than yourself. I shall transcribe and submitt to your approbation as fast as possible.—I have now, I think, finished my volume; indeed I am almost weary of composing, having spent a year in doing nothing else. About this time twelvemonth I began with Antithelyphthora and have never allowed myself more than a fortnight's respite since. I reckon my volume will consist of about 8000—lines. The season of dispatch which Johnson has so often promised, is not yet arrived, a fortnight and sometimes three weeks elapse, before I am supplied with a new sheet; the next brings us into the middle of Hope, which I account the middle of the Volume, consequently unless he proceeds with more Celerity the publishing moment will escape us this year as it did the last. For his own sake however I should suppose he will catch it if he can, and be ready to exhibit by the meeting of Parliament after the Christmas recess.

Mrs. Unwin is well and sends her Love. Our thanks are due for a

his prose, to imitate him in all but his non-conformity, to copy his benevolence to man, and his reverence to God.' *Lives of the Most Eminent English Poets* (1781), iv. 292.

[2] Newton's name did not appear on the title-page.

[3] 'Retirement', 804.

fine piece of Skait and some prawns, both as fresh as when they took leave of their native Element. We heartily wish Mrs. Newton better than *pretty* well, and the recovery of all the invalids in your family.

Yours my dear friend

Wm Cowper

Octr. 4. 1781.

WILLIAM UNWIN Saturday, 6 October 1781

British Library

My dear friend,

What a world are you daily conversant with, which I have not seen these twenty Years and shall never see again. The arts of dissipation I suppose are nowhere practised with more refinement or success than at the place of your present residence; by your account of it, it seems to be just what it was when I visited it, a scene of Idleness and Luxury, music, dancing, cards, walking, riding, bathing, eating, drinking, coffee, tea, scandal, dressing, yawning, sleeping. The rooms perhaps more magnificent, because the proprietors are grown richer, but the manners and occupations of the company just the same. Though my life has long been like that of a Recluse, I have not the temper of one, nor am I in the least an Enemy to cheerfullness and good humor; but I cannot envy you your situation; I even feel myself constrained to prefer the Silence of this nook, and the snug fire-side in our diminutive parlour to all the splendor and gaiety of Brighthelmstone.

You ask me how I feel on the occasion of my approaching publication—perfectly at my ease; if I had not been pretty well assured beforehand that my tranquillity would be but little endanger'd by such a measure, I would never have engaged in it, for I cannot bear disturbance. I have had in view two principal objects, first, to amuse myself, and secondly to compass that point in such a manner as that others might possibly be the better for my amusement. If I have succeeded, it will give me pleasure, but if I have failed, I shall not be mortified to the degree that might perhaps be expected. I remember an old adage (though not where it is to be found) bene vixit qui bene

latuit[1]—and if I had recollected it at the right time, it should have been the motto to my Book.[2] By the way it will make an excellent one for Retirement[3] if you can but tell me whom to quote for it. The Critics cannot deprive me of the pleasure I have in reflecting that so far as my leisure has been employed in writing for the public, it has been conscientiously employed, and with a view to their advantage. There is nothing agreeable to be sure in being chronicled for a dunce, but I beleive there lives not a man upon earth who would be less affected by it than myself. With all this Indifference to Fame, which you know me too well to suppose me capable of affecting, I have taken the utmost pains to deserve it. This may appear a mystery or a paradox in practise, but it is true. I consider'd that the taste of the day is refined and delicate to excess, and that to disgust that delicacy of taste by a slovenly inattention to it, would be to forfiet at once all hope of being usefull; and for this reason, though I have written more verse this last year than perhaps any man in England, have finished and polished and touched and retouched with the utmost care. If after all I should be converted into waste paper, it may be my misfortune, but it will not be my fault, & I shall bear it with the most perfect Serenity.

I do not mean to give Quarme[4] a Copy. He is a good natured little man, and crows exactly like a Cock, but knows no more of verse than the Cock he imitates.

Whoever supposes that Lady Austen's fortune is precarious, is mistaken. I can assure you upon the ground of the most circumstantial and authentic Information, that it is both genteel and perfectly safe.

Your Mother adds her Love, mine accompanies hers, and our united wishes for your prosperity in every respect desire to be of the party.

Yours Wm Cowper.

Octr. 6. 1781.

1 Ovid, *Tristia*, III. iv. 25: 'He who hides well, lives well.'

2 For the mottoes actually used by C, see notes 2 and 3, C to Newton, 7 Nov. 1781.

3 C used a motto from Virgil's *Georgics* (iv. 564) for this poem: '— studiis florens ignobilis oti.' ('Rejoicing in the arts of inglorious ease.')

4 Perhaps Robert Quarme who was a subscriber to C's *Homer* (1791). He was probably related to George Quarme (1716?–75) of Padstow, Cornwall; at Westminster School (*c.* 1729–35); Commissioner of Taxes (1762–3) and of Excise (1766–75). C had known George Quarme, a friend of Ashley's, in the 1740s. See *Ryskamp*, p. 131.

JOHN NEWTON Sunday, 14 October 1781

Address: Revd. John Newton
Princeton

My dear friend,

I would not willingly deprive you of any comfort, and therefore would wish you to comfort yourself as much as you can with a notion that you are a more bountifull correspondent than I. You will give me leave in the mean time however, to assert to myself a share in the same species of consolation, and to enjoy the flattering recollection that I have sometimes written three letters to your one. I never knew a Poet except myself who was punctual in any thing, or to be depended on for the due discharge of any duty except what he thought he owed to the Muses. The moment a man takes it into his foolish head, that he has what the world calls Genius, he gives himself a discharge from the servile drudgery of all friendly offices, and becomes good for nothing except in the pursuit of his favorite employment. But I am not yet vain enough to think myself entitled to such self-conferred honors, and though I have sent much poetry to the press, or at least what I hope my readers will account such, am still as desirous as ever of a place in your heart, and to take all opportunities to convince you that you have still the same in mine. My attention to my poetical function has I confess a little interfered of late with my other employments, and occasioned my writing less frequently than I should have otherwise done. But it is over—at least for the present, and I think for some time to come. I have transcribed Retirement, and send it. You will be so good as to forward it to Johnson, who will forward it I suppose to the Public in his own time, but not very speedily, moving as he does. The post brought me a sheet this afternoon, but we have not yet reached the end of Hope.

Mr. Scott I perceive by yours to him, has mentioned one of his troubles, but I beleive not the principal one. The question whether he shall have an Assistant at the great house in Mr. T: R—n[1] is still a question, or at least a subject of discontent between Mr. Scott and the people. In a tête á tête I had with this candidate for the chair in the course of the last week, I told him my thoughts upon the subject

[1] See n. 3, C to Newton, 10 Aug. 1780 for Tom Raban.

plainly. Advised him to change places, by the help of fancy, with Mr. Scott for a moment, and to ask himself how *he* would like a self-intruded deputy, advised him likewise by no means to address Mr. Scott any more upon the matter, for that he might be sure he would never consent to it. And concluded with telling him that if he persisted in his purpose of speaking to the people, the probable consequence would be that sooner or later Mr. Scott would be forced out of the parish, and the blame of his Expulsion would all light upon Him. He heard, approved, and I think the very next day, put all my good counsel to shame, at least a considerable part of it, by applying to Mr. Scott in company with Mr. Perry,[2] for his permission to speak at the Sunday Evening meeting. Mr. Scott as I had foretold was immoveable, but offered for the satisfaction of his hearers to preach three times to them on the Sabbath (which he could have done, Mr. Jones having kindly offered though without their knowledge, to officiate for him at Weston). Mr. R—n answered, that will not do Sir, it is not what the people wish, they want variety—Mr. Scott replied very wisely, if they do they must be content without it, it is not my duty to indulge that Humor.—This is the last Intelligence I have had upon the subject, I received it not from Mr. Scott, but from an Ear-witness.

Poor Mrs. Unwin has been exceedingly ill this last week, with a most violent sore throat attended with a fever. Her throat swelled inwardly on both sides, and broke in both places, since which she has been recovering, but has been much weakened.—I did not suspect 'till the Reviewers told me so, that you are made up of artifice and design, and that your ambition is, to delude your hearers.[3] Well—I suppose they please themselves with the thought of having mortified you, but how much are they mistaken! They shot at you, and their arrow struck the bible, recoiling of course upon themselves.—My turn will come, for I think I shall hardly escape a threshing.

Mrs. Unwin sends her Love and two fowls. We heartily wish Miss Catlett happy in her new Situation—and are glad that Peggy grows

[2] William Perry was buried 9 Oct. 1783 (*O.P.R.*, p. 400).

[3] The *Monthly Review* for Sept. 1781 (lxv. 203) contains an extremely hostile review of *Cardiphonia*: 'We are disgusted with vanity in any form; but when it assumes the dress of religion, we are more than disgusted:—we are really shocked . . . We are not at all surprized to hear men of such principles, as this Writer espouses, exclaim so bitterly against reason. They are conscious of an irreconcilable hatred between the common sense of mankind, and a faith that sets all reason and nature at defiance.'

better. Pray remember us to Sally—Yours my dear Sir and Mrs. Newton's

Wm Cowper.

Sund. Eve. Octr. 14. 1781.

MRS. COWPER — Friday, 19 October 1781

Address: Mrs. Cowper / Park Street / Grosvenor Square / London.
Postmarks: 22/OC *and* OULNEY
Princeton

My dear Cousin,

Your fears lest I should think you unworthy of my correspondence on account of your delay to answer, may change sides now and more properly belong to me. It is long since I received your last, and yet I beleive I can say truly that not a post has gone by me since the receipt of it, that has not reminded me of the debt I owe you for your obliging and unreserved communications both in prose and Verse.[1] Especially for the latter, because I consider them as marks of your peculiar confidence. The truth is, I have been such a Verse-maker myself, and so busy in preparing a Volume for the press, which I imagine will make its appearance in the course of the Winter, that I have hardly had leisure to listen to the calls of any other Engagement. It is however finished and gone to the printers, and I have nothing now to do with it, but to correct the Sheets as they are sent me, and consign it over to the Judgment of the public. It is a bold undertaking at this time of day, when so many writers of the greatest Abilities have gone before, who seem to have anticipated every valuable Subject, as well as all the graces of poetical Embellishment, to step forth into the world in the Character of a Bard. Especially when it is considered that Luxury and Idleness and Vice have debauched the public taste, and that nothing hardly is welcome, but childish fiction, or what has at least a tendency to excite a laugh. I thought however that I had stumbled upon some Subjects that had never before been poetically treated, and upon some others, to which I imagined it would not be difficult to give an air of novelty, by the

[1] C's previous surviving letter to Mrs. Cowper was written on 31 Aug. 1780.

manner of treating them. My sole drift is to be usefull, a point which however, I knew, I should in vain aim at, unless I could be likewise entertaining. I have therefore fixed these two strings upon my Bow, and by the help of both have done my best to send my Arrow to the mark. My Readers will hardly have begun to laugh, before they will find themselves called upon to correct that levity, and peruse me with a more serious air. As to the Effect, I leave it in his hands who can alone produce it; neither prose nor Verse, can reform the manners of a dissolute age, much less can they inspire a Sense of religious obligation, unless assisted and made efficacious by the power who superintends the truth he has vouchsafed to impart.

You made my heart ach with a sympathetic sorrow, when you described the state of your mind on occasion of your late visit into Hartfordshire.[2] Had I been previously informed of your Journey before you made it, I should have been able to have foretold all your feelings with the most unerring certainty of prediction. You will never cease to feel upon that Subject, but with your principles of Resignation and acquiescence in the divine Will, you will always feel as becomes a Christian. We are forbidden to murmur, but we are not forbidden to regret; and whom we loved tenderly while living, we may still pursue with an affectionate remembrance, without having any occasion to charge ourselves with Rebellion against the Sov'reignty that appointed a Seperation. A day is coming, when I am confident, you will see and know that Mercy to both parties was the principal agent in a Scene the recollection of which is still painfull.

Beleive me my dear Cousin
Your ever affectionate Wm Cowper.

Octr. 19.
1781.

Mrs. Unwin presents her respects—She is well.

I beg to be affectionately remember'd to my Aunt.

[2] Mrs. Cowper's trip to Hertfordshire may have called to mind her late husband, the Major, who had died in 1769.

JOSEPH JOHNSON Saturday, 20 October 1781

Address: Mr. Johnson / No. 72. St. Pauls Ch. Yd. / London / RobfreeSmith
Postmarks: 22/OC, OULNEY, *and* FREE
Olney

Sir—

I acknowledge with pleasure the accuracy of your remark on the two lines you have scored in the first page of the inclosed sheet.[1] But though the word *there* in its critical and proper use is undoubtedly an adverb denoting locality, yet I cannot but think that in the familiar strain of poetical colloquy, (especially if the gay careless air of the speaker in the present instance be considered) a less exact application of it may be allowed.—We say in common speech—you was scrupulous on that Occasion; *there* I think you was wrong—meaning, in that part of your conduct. I do not know indeed that I should hesitate to give it that sense if I were writing prose for the press instead of Verse, or on any other occasion whatsoever.

The unexpected arrival of the inclosed so soon after the foregoing sheet, has inspired me with hopes that your printer is about to proceed with the Alacrity he promised so long since. It proves however that he is capable of great dispatch when he is pleased to use it.

I am Sir

Your most Obedient Servant

Wm Cowper.

Olney.

Octr. 20. 1781.

JOHN NEWTON Monday, 22 October 1781

Princeton

My dear friend,

Mr. Bates,[1] without intending it, has passed a severer censure upon the modern world of Readers, than any that can be found in my

[1] Perhaps 'Hope', 402: 'Honesty shines with great advantage there.'

[1] Eli Bates was a member of the Eclectic Society. See Josiah Bull, *John Newton* (*c.* 1868), p. 263, and C to Newton, 26 Jan. 1783.

volume. If they are so merrily disposed in the midst of a thousand calamities, that they will not deign to read a preface of three or four pages, because the purport of it is serious, they are far gone indeed, and in the last stage of a frenzy such as I suppose has prevailed in all nations that have been exemplarily punished, just before the infliction of the Sentence. But though he lives in the world he has so ill an Opinion of, and ought therefore to know it better than I who have no intercourse with it at all, I am willing to hope that he may be mistaken. Curiosity is an universal passion. There are few people who think a book worth their reading, but feel a desire to know something about the writer of it. This desire will naturally lead them to peep into the preface, where they will soon find that a little perseverance will furnish them with some information upon the Subject. If therefore your preface finds no readers, I shall take it for granted that it is because the Book itself is accounted not worth their notice. Be that as it may—it is quite sufficient that I have played the Antic myself for their diversion, and that in a state of dejection such as they are absolute strangers to, I have sometimes put on an air of cheerfullness and vivacity to which I myself am in reality a stranger, for the sake of winning their attention to more usefull matter. I cannot endure the thought for a moment that You should descend to my Level on the occasion, and court their favour in a stile not more unsuitable to your function, than to the constant and consistent strain of your whole character and conduct. No—let the preface stand; I cannot mend it. I could easily make a Jest of it, but it is better as it is.[2]

By the way—will it not be proper, as you have taken some notice of the modish dress I wear in Table-talk,[3] to include Conversation in the same description, which is (the first half of it at least) the most airy of the two? They will otherwise think perhaps that the Observation might as well have been spared entirely; though I should have been sorry if it had, for when I am jocular I do violence to myself, and am therefore pleased with your telling them in a civil way, that I

[2] Joseph Johnson objected to the very serious tone of Newton's Preface and persuaded C to allow it to be suppressed until the fifth edition of 1793. The Preface was included in 'a few special copies' of the first edition. See *Russell*, pp. 42–3.

[3] Newton's Preface: 'His favourite topics are least insisted on in the piece entitled Table Talk: which therefore, with some regard to the prevailing taste, and that those who are governed by it may not be discouraged at the very threshold from proceeding farther, is placed first.'

play the fool to amuse them, not because I am one myself, but because I have a foolish world to deal with.

I am inclined to think that Mr. Scott will no more be troubled by Mr. Raban with applications of the sort I mentioned in my last. Mr. Scott, since I wrote that account, has related to us himself what passed in the course of their Interview; and it seems the discourse ended with his positive assurance that he never would consent to the measure, though at the same time he declared he would never interrupt or attempt to suppress it. To which Mr. Raban replied, that unless he had his free consent he should never engage in the Office. It is to be hoped therefore that in time that part of the people, who may at present be displeased with Mr. Scott for witholding his consent, will grow cool upon the subject, and be satisfied with receiving their instruction from their proper Minister.

Mrs. Unwin has recovered from the immediate effects of her Cold, such as the sore throat and fever, but it has had remoter consequences from which she has not yet recovered. She still complains of weakness and rheumatic affections.

I beg you will on no future occasion leave a blank for Mrs. Newton, unless you have first engaged her promise to fill it, for thus we lose the pleasure of your company without being indemnified for the loss by the acquisition of hers.

Johnson sent me two sheets in the course of the last ten days, to my great astonishment. I complimented him upon his alacrity in hopes that encouragement might insure the continuance of it. The next sheet will bring the beginning of Charity.

Our Love to you both
Yours my dear friend
Wm Cowper.

Olney
Octr. 22. 1781
Tuesday Morning.
Susan Davies died last night between 10 and 11.[4]

[4] Susanna Davis, who had married William Hinde on 7 Nov. 1760, was buried on 24 Oct. 1781 (*O.P.R.*, pp. 334, 396).

WILLIAM UNWIN Monday, 5 November 1781

British Library

My dear William,

I give you joy of your safe return from the lips of the great deep. You did not indeed discern many signs of sobriety or true wisdom among the people at Brighthelmstone, but it is not possible to observe the manners of a multitude of whatever rank, without learning something; I mean if a man has a mind like yours, capable of Reflection. If he sees nothing to imitate, he is sure to see something to avoid; if nothing to congratulate his fellow-creatures upon, at least much to excite his compassion. There is not, I think, so melancholy a sight in the world (an hospital is not to be compared with it) as that of a thousand persons distinguished by the name of gentry, who gentle perhaps by nature and made more gentle by Education, have the appearance of being innocent and inoffensive, yet being destitute of all religion, or not at all governed by the religion they profess, are none of them at any great distance from an eternal state, where self-deception will be impossible, and where Amusements cannot enter. Some of them, we may say, will be reclaimed—it is most probable indeed that some of them will, because Mercy, if one may be allowed the expression, is fond of distinguishing itself by seeking its objects among the most desperate cases; but the Scripture gives no Encouragement to the warmest charity to Hope for deliverance for them all. When I see an afflicted and an unhappy man, I say to myself, there is perhaps a Man whom the world would envy if they knew the value of his sorrows, which are possibly intended only to soften his heart, and to turn his affections towards their proper center. But when I see or hear of a crowd of voluptuaries, who have no ears but for Music, no eyes but for splendor, and no tongue but for impertinence and folly, I say, or at least I see occasion to say, this is madness, this persisted in must have a tragical conclusion; it will condemn you not only as Christians unworthy of the name, but as intelligent creatures. You know by the light of nature, if you have not quenched it, that there is a God, and that a life like yours cannot be according to his will.—I ask no pardon of You, for the gravity and gloominess of these reflections, which I stumbled on when I least expected it; though to say the truth, these or others of a like complexion are sure

to occur to me, when I think of a scene of public diversion like that you have lately left.

I remember Mr. Mitchel well.[1] A man famous for nothing but idling away his time at the coffee-house, and bathing upon the open beach without the decent use of a machine. I may say upon the surest ground, that the world to which he conforms, despises him for doing so, because I remember well that I and my party who had not a grain of religion amongst us, always mentioned him with disdain. His charitable profanation of the Sabbath will never earn him any other wages.

I am inclined to hope that Johnson told you the truth, when he said he should publish me soon after Christmas. His press has been rather more punctual in its remittances than it used to be; we have now but little more than two of the longest pieces and the small ones that are to follow by way of Epilogue, to print off and then the affair is finished. But once more I am obliged to gape for more franks, only these, which I hope will be the last I shall want, at your and Mr. Smith's convenient leisure.

We rejoice that you have so much reason to be satisfied with John's proficiency. The more spirit he has the better, if his spirit be but manageable and put under such management as your prudence and Mrs. Unwin's will Suggest. I need not guard you against Severity, of which I conclude there is no need and which I am sure you are not at all inclined to practise without it. But perhaps if I was to whisper, Beware of too much indulgence, I should only give a hint that the fondness of a father for a fine boy, might seem to justify. I have no particular reason for the caution, at this distance it is not possible that I should, but in a case like yours an admonition of that sort, seldom wants propriety.

Your Mother has been considerably indisposed with a sore throat and feverish complaint, but is well again, except that her strength which is never that of an Amazon, is not quite restored. Her Love attends you and your family, and mine goes with it.

Yours, my dear friend,
Wm Cowper.

[1] Henry Michell (1714–89), a graduate of Cambridge, a classical antiquarian of some distinction, and vicar of Brighton. Mrs. Piozzi shared C's opinion of Michell: 'We were saying every body was like some Animal & we put down ... Old Michell for the Hog' (7 Dec. 1779). See *Thraliana*, ed. K. C. Balderstone (2nd edn. 1951), i. 414.

Lady Austen No. 8

Queen Ann street—East—near Cavendish Square.

You had better send a Card to announce your Visit, as she is a Lady of many Engagements, always dines at 4.[2]

Nove. 5. 1781.

JOHN NEWTON Wednesday, 7 November 1781

Princeton

My dear friend,

So far as Johnson is to be depended on, and I begin to hope that he is now in earnest, I think myself warranted to furnish you with an answer to the question which you say so often meets you. Mr. Unwin made the same enquiry at his shop in his way to Stock from Brighthelmstone, when he assured him that the Book would be printed off in a Month, and ready for publication after the holidays. For some time past the business has proceeded glibly, and if he perseveres at the same rate, it is probable his answer will prove a true one.—Having discontinued the practise of Verse-making for some weeks, I now feel quite incapable of resuming it, and can only wonder at it as one of the most extraordinary Incidents in my life that I should have composed a volume. Had it been suggested to me as a practicable thing in better days, though I should have been glad to have found it so, many hindrances would have conspired to withold me from such an Enterprize. I should not have dared at that time of day to have committed my name to the public, and my reputation to the hazard of their Opinion. But it is otherwise with me now, I am more indifferent about what may touch me in that point than ever I was in my life. The stake that would Then have seemed important, now seems trivial, and it is of little consequence to me who no longer feel myself possessed of what I accounted infinitely more valuable, whether the world's verdict shall pronounce me a Poet, or an empty Pretender to the title. This happy coldness towards a matter so generally interesting to all Rhimers, left me quite at liberty for the undertaking, unfetter'd by fear, and under no restraints

[2] As he promised in his letter of 26 Sept., C is providing Unwin with Lady Austen's London address. Unwin had visited Lady Austen by Feb. 1782.

of that diffidence which is my natural temper, and which would either have made it impossible for me to commence an Author by name, or would have insured my miscarriage if I had.—In my last dispatches to Johnson, I sent him a new Edition of the title-page, having discarded the Latin paradox[1] which stood at the head of the former, and added a French motto[2] to that from Virgil.[3] It is taken from a Volume of the excellent Caraccioli, called Jouissance de soi même, and strikes me as peculiarly apposite to my purpose.

Mr. Bull is an honest man. We have seen him twice since he received your Orders to march hither, and faithfully told us it was in consequence of those Orders that he came. He dined with us yesterday, we were all in pretty good spirits, and the day passed very agreeably. It is not long since he called on Mr. Scott; Mr. Raban came in. Mr. Bull began—addressing himself to the former—my friend you are in trouble; you are unhappy; I read it in your countenance. Mr. Scott replied he had been so, but he was better. Come then, says Mr. Bull, I will expound to you the cause of all your anxiety. You are too common; you make yourself cheap. Visit your people less, and converse more with your own heart. How often do you speak to them in the Week? twice—Ay, there it is—your Sermons

[1] 'Bene vixit qui bene latuit' (see n. 1, C to Unwin, 6 Oct. 1781).

[2] This is from *La Jouissance de Soi-Même* (Chapter XI, 'De la Vérité') by Louis Antoine de Caraccioli (1721–1803). The work was first published in 1759. The motto appeared thus on C's title-page in 1782.

> Nous sommes nés pour la vérité, et nous ne pouvons souffrir son abord. les figures, les paraboles, les emblémes, sont toujours des ornements nécessaires pour qu'elle puisse s'annoncer. et soit quon craigne qu'elle ne découvre trop brusquement le défaut qu'on voudroit cacher, ou qu'enfin elle n'instruise avec trop peu de ménagement, ou veut, en la recevant, qu'elle soit déguisée.

We are born to face the truth and yet we cannot bear to face it. Symbols, parables, and emblems are necessary adornments in which to present it. We are afraid that the truth will blatantly show up the fault we wish to hide. Or, we feel that the truth to be told is readily available to anyone with common sense. Or, we want the truth to be presented in an elaborate guise.

[3] *Aeneid*, viii. 22–5:

> Sicut aquæ tremulum labris ubi lumen ahenis
> Sole repercussum, aut radiantis imagine lunæ
> Omnia pervolitat laté loca, jamque sub auras
> Erigitur, summique ferit laquearia tecti.
>
> So water trembling in a polish'd vase,
> Reflects the beam that plays upon its face,
> The sportive light, uncertain where it falls,
> Now strikes the roof, now flashes on the walls.

are an Old Ballad, your prayers are an Old ballad, and you are an Old ballad too.—I would wish to tread in the steps of Mr. Newton—you do well to follow his steps in all other instances, but in this instance you are wrong, and so was he. Mr. Newton trod a path which no man but himself could have used so long as he did, and he wore it out long before he went from Olney. Too much familiarity and condescension cost him the estimation of his people. He thought he should insure their Love to which he had the best possible title, and by those very means he lost it. Be wise my friend, take warning, make yourself scarce, if you wish that persons of little understanding should know how to prize you.

When he related to us this harrangue so nicely adjusted to the case of the third person present, it did us both good, and as Jaques says

It made my lungs to crow like chanticleer.[4]

Mrs. Unwin wishes me to inform you, that the Character of Thomas Old is no longer a doubtfull one at Olney. He is much addicted to public houses, and every body knows it. Geary Ball led him home drunk from one of them not long since, where he had been playing at quoits, and regaling himself with drink 'till he was unable to stand unsupported. She thought it the part of a friend to communicate to you this piece of intelligence, that you may not lend him money and lose it. He used frequently to borrow of us, but we intend henceforth to discontinue our aids of that sort.

I have only seen Mr. Jones since I received you last, and have had no opportunity to mention to him your enquiry. He was alive yesterday however, and not long since spoke of an intended journey to London.

We wish your letter to your parishioners, may have the best effects, and shall be glad to read it.[5] Many thanks for 3 couple of maccarel, perfectly fresh. Our Love of you both though often sent to London is still with us, if it is not an inexhaustible well, (there is but one Love that can with propriety be called so) 'tis however a very deep one and not likely to fail while we are living.

Yours my dear Sir,
Wm Cowper.

Novr. 7. 81.
Mr. Henley was buried last night.[6]

[4] *As You Like It*, II. vii. 30.

[5] See n. 4, C to Newton, 27 Nov. 1781.

[6] John Henley was buried on 6 Nov. (*O.P.R.*, p. 396).

WILLIAM UNWIN Saturday, 24 November 1781

British Library

My dear friend,

News is always acceptable, especially from another world. I cannot tell you what has been done in the Chesapeak,[1] but I can tell you what has passed at West Wycomb in this County. Do you feel yourself disposed to give credit to a Story of an apparition? No, say you—I am of your mind—I do not beleive more than one in a hundred of those tales with which old Women frighten children, and teach children to frighten each other. But you are not such a Philosopher I suppose, as to have persuaded yourself that an Apparition is an impossible thing, you can attend to a Story of that sort if well authenticated? Yes—then I can tell you one. You have heard no doubt of the romantic friendship that subsisted once between Paul Whitehead and Lord le dispenser, the late Sir Francis Dashwood.[2] When Paul died, he left his Lordship a Legacy. It was his Heart—which was taken out of his body, and sent as directed. His friend having built a Church,[3] and at that time just finished it, used it as a Mausoleum upon this occasion, and having (as I think the newspapers told us at the time) erected an elegant pillar in the center of it, on the summit of this pillar, inclosed in a golden urn, he placed the heart in question. But not as a Lady places a china figure upon her mantle tree or on the top of her cabinet, but with much respectfull ceremony and all the forms of funereal solemnity. He hired the best singers and the best performers, he composed an Anthem for the purpose, he invited all the nobility and Gentry in the country to assist at the celebration of these obsequies, and having formed them all into an august procession, marched to the place appointed at their head, and consigned the posthumous treasure with his own hands to its state of honorable elevation. Having thus as he thought and as he might

[1] The English under Admiral Thomas Graves (1725?–1802) lost a significant naval encounter to the French at Chesapeake Capes on 5 Sept. 1781.

[2] Francis Dashwood, Baron le Despenseur (1708–81), and Paul Whitehead (1710–74) were members of the notorious Hell Fire Club. Dashwood, who died on 11 Dec., had two close connections with Lady Austen. Her husband's cousin, Sir Robert Austen (d. 1743), had married Rachel, Dashwood's sister. Mrs. Barry, one of Lady Austen's sisters, was reputed to have lived at West Wycombe 'on the most friendly and affectionate terms' with Dashwood: see R. F. A. Lee, *Vindication of Mrs. Lee's Conduct* (1807).

[3] The Church of St. Laurence, West Wycombe.

well think (for it seems they were both renowned for their Infidelity, and if they had any religion at all, were pagans) appeased the manes of the deceased, he rested satisfied with what he had done, and supposed his friend would rest. But not so—about a week since I received a Letter from a person who cannot have been misinformed, telling me that Paul has appeared so frequently of late to his Lordship, who labours under a complication of distempers, that it is supposed the Shock he has suffered from such unexpected visits, will make his recovery which was before improbable, impossible. Nor is this all; to ascertain the fact, and to put it out of the power of Scepticism to argue away the reality of it, there are few if any of his numerous household, who have not likewise seen him, sometimes in the park, sometimes in the garden, as well as in the house, by day and by night indifferently. I make no reflections upon this incident having other things to write about and but little room.

I am much indebted to Mr. Smith for more franks, and still more obliged by the handsome note with which he accompanied them. He has furnished me sufficiently for the present occasion, and by his readiness and obliging manner of doing it, encouraged me to have recourse to him in case another exigence of the same kind should offer. A French Author I was reading last night—says, he that has written, will write again.[4] If the Critics do not set their foot upon this first Egg that I have laid, and crush it, I shall probably verify his observation, and when I feel my spirits rise, and that I am armed with Industry sufficient for the purpose, undertake the production of another volume. At present however I do not feel myself so disposed, and indeed He that would write should read, not that he may retail the observations of other men, but that being thus refreshed and replenished, he may find himself in a condition to make and to produce his own. I reckon it among my principal advantages as a composer of verses, that I have not read an English poet these thirteen years, and but One these twenty years. Imitation even of the best models is my Aversion. It is servile and mechanical, a trick that has enabled many to usurp the name of Author, who could not have written at all, if they had not written upon the pattern of some body indeed original. But when the Ear and the taste have been much

[4] C is paraphrasing the following passage from Chapter xxx ('Des Auteurs') of *La Jouissance de Soi-Même* (Lyons, 1762), p. 147: 'Le plaisir de composer a quelque chose de si attrayant, que lorsqu'on le goûte, on ne veut plus en sentir d'autre. Qui a écrit, écrira.'

accustomed to the manner of others, it is almost impossible to avoid it, and we imitate in spite of ourselves, just in proportion as we admire.—But enough of this.

Your mother, who is as well as the Season of the year will permitt, desires me to add her love, and in particular, her enquiries after Mrs. Unwin, who, she hopes, does not find her health injured or her strength greatly impaired by her continual remittances to her new-born William. You will be pleased to mention us affectionately to her and to Miss Shuttleworth.—The Salmon you sent us arrived safe, and was remarkably fresh. What a comfort it is to have a friend who knows that we love Salmon, and who cannot pass by a fish-monger's shop without finding his desire to send us some, a temptation too strong to be resisted!

Yours my dear friend
Wm Cowper.

Nove. 24. 1781.

WILLIAM UNWIN — Monday, 26 November 1781

British Library

My dear friend,

I wrote to you by the last post, supposing you at Stock. But lest that letter should not follow you to Laytonstone,[1] and you should suspect me of unreasonable delay, and lest the frank you have sent me should degenerate into waste paper, and perish upon my hands, I write again. The former letter however containing all my present stock of intelligence, it is more than possible that this may prove a blank, or but little worthy of your acceptance. You will do me the justice to suppose that if I could be very entertaining, I would be so, because by giving me credit for such a willingness to please, you only allow me a share of that universal vanity, which inclines every man upon all occasions to exhibit himself to the best advantage. To say the truth however, when I write as I do to you, not about business nor on any subject that approaches to that description, I mean much less my correspondent's amusement, which my modesty will not always permitt me to hope for, than my own. There is a pleasure

[1] A residential town in the municipal borough of Leyton in north-east Essex.

annex'd to the communication of one's ideas, whether by word of mouth or by letter, which nothing earthly can supply the place of, and it is the delight we find in this mutual intercourse, that not only proves us to be creatures intended for social life, but more than any thing else perhaps, fits us for it. I have no patience with Philosophers—they one and all suppose (at least I understand it to be a prevailing Opinion among them) that Man's weakness, his necessities, his inability to stand alone, have furnished the prevailing motive under the influence of which he renounced at first a life of solitude, and became a gregarious creature. It seems to me more reasonable, as well as more honorable to my species to suppose, that generosity of Soul, and a brotherly attachment to our own kind, drew us as it were to one common center, taught us to build cities and inhabit them, and welcome every stranger that would cast in his lot amongst us, that we might enjoy fellowship with each other, and the luxury of reciprocal endearments, without which a paradise could afford no comfort. There are indeed all sorts of characters in the world, there are some whose understandings are so sluggish, and whose hearts are such mere clods, that they live in society without either contributing to the sweets of it, or having any relish for them. A man of this stamp passes by our window continually.[2] He draws patterns for the lace-makers. I never saw him conversing with a neighbor but once in my life, though I have known him by sight these 12 years. He is of a very sturdy make, has a round belly extremely protuberant, which he evidently considers as his best friend because it is his only companion, and it is the labour of his life to fill it. I can easily conceive that it is merely the love of good eating and drinking, and now and then the want of a new pair of shoes, that attaches this man so much to the neighbourhood of his fellow mortals. For suppose these exigences and others of a like kind to subsist no longer, and what is there that could possibly give Society the preference in his esteem? He might strut about with his two thumbs upon his hips in a wilderness, he could hardly be more silent there than he is at Olney, and for any advantages or comforts of friendship or brotherly affection, he could not be more destitute of such blessings there than in his present situation. But other men have something more than guts to satisfy; there are the yearnings of the heart, which let Philosophers say what they will, are more importunate than all

[2] Unidentified.

the necessities of the body, that will not suffer a creature worthy to be called human to be content with an insulated life, or to look for his friends among the beasts of the forest. Yourself for instance.—It is not because there are no taylors or pastry cooks to be found upon Salisbury plain that you do not chuse it for your abode, but because you are a philanthropist, because you are susceptible of social impressions, and have a pleasure in doing a kindness when you can. Witness the Salmon you sent, and the Salmon you still mean to send, to which your mother wishes you to add an handfull of prawns, not only because she likes them, but because they agree with her so well that she even finds them medicinal.

Now upon the word of a poor creature, I have said all that I have said, without the least intention to say one word of it when I began. But thus it is with my thoughts. When you shake a crab-tree the fruit falls; good for nothing indeed when you have got it, but still the best that is to be expected from a crab-tree. You are welcome to them such as they are, and if you approve my sentiments, tell the philosophers of the day that I have outshot them all, and have discover'd the true origin of Society when I least looked for it.

Except a pain in her face, violent at times, your mother is tolerably well, and sends her Love.

Yours ever Wm Cowper.

Nove. 26 1781.

We should be glad to receive this fresh proof of your regard, viz the additional piece of Salmon, at any time before Christmas.

JOSEPH JOHNSON Tuesday, 27 November 1781

Address: Mr. Johnson / Booksr. / St. Pauls Churchyard / London / RobfreeSmith
Postmarks: 2[undecipherable] *and* FREE
Princeton

Sir

You will oblige me by telling me in your next whether if I should find it proper to displace a paragraph in Expostulation,[1] and

[1] The withdrawal of twenty-four lines (390–413) in which C had denounced the Pope and Roman Catholicism in violent terms. C evidently asked Newton's advice on this matter (see the following letter), and in accord with Newton's reply and his own conscience, C

Substitute another in its stead, there is yet time for the purpose. I have doubts about the expedience of mentioning the Subject on which that paragraph is written.

Many thanks for your judicious remarks.

I am Sir

Your most humble Servant

Wm Cowper.

Olney Nove. 27. 1781.

JOHN NEWTON Tuesday, 27 November 1781

Princeton

My dear friend,

First Mr. Wilson, then Mr. Teedon, and lastly Mr. Whitford, each with a cloud of melancholy on his brow, and with a mouth wide open, has just announced to us this unwelcome intelligence from America.[1] We are sorry to hear it, and should be more cast down than we are, if we did not know that this catastrophé was ordained beforehand, and that therefore neither conduct nor courage, nor any means that can possibly be mentioned, could have prevented it. If the King and his Ministry can be contented to close the business here, and taking poor Dean Tucker's advice, resign the Americans into the hands of their new masters, it may be well for Old England.[2] But if they will still persevere, they will find it I doubt, an hopeless contest to the last; domestic murmurs will grow louder, and the hands of Faction being strengthen'd by this late miscarriage, will find it easy to set fire to the pile of combustibles they have been so long employed in building. These are my politics, and for aught I can see, you and we by our respective firesides, though neither connected with men in power, nor professing to possess any share of that sagacity which thinks itself qualified to wield the affairs of kingdoms, can make as probable

wrote this letter to Johnson. On 4 Dec. C sent the requisite twenty-four lines of fresh material to Newton. A cancel was required; some copies were published with the cancellandum leaf I6 (see *Russell*, pp. 42, 50–2).

[1] The incident referred to is Cornwallis's surrender at Yorktown on 19 Oct. 1781.

[2] Josiah Tucker (1712–99), Dean of Gloucester, maintained the desirability of separation from the colonies in America.

conjectures, and look forward into futurity with as clear a sight, as the greatest man in the Cabinet.

Though when I wrote the passage in question, I was not at all aware of any impropriety in it, and though I have frequently since that time both read and recollected it with the same approbation, I lately became uneasy upon the subject, and had no rest in my mind for three days 'till I resolved to submitt it to a trial at your tribunal, and to dispose of it ultimately according to your sentence. I am glad you have condemned it, and though I do not feel as if I could presently supply its place, shall be willing to attempt the task whatever labour it may cost me, and rejoice that it will not be in the power of the Critics whatever else they may charge me with, to accuse me of Bigotry, or a design to make a certain denomination of Christians odious, at the hazard of the public peace. I had rather my book were burnt than that a single line guilty of such a tendency, should escape me.[3]

We thank you for two copies of your address to your parishioners; the first I lent to Mr. Scott, whom I have not seen since I put it into his hands. You have managed your Subject well, have applied yourself to Despisers and Absentees of every description, in terms so expressive of the interest you take in their welfare, that the most wrongheaded person cannot be offended.[4] We both wish it may have the effect you intend, and that prejudices and groundless apprehensions being removed, the immediate objects of your ministry may make a more considerable part of your Congregation.

I return Mr. Madan's letter, with thanks for a Sight of it. Having forfeited all the rest of his most valuable attachments without regret, and sacrificed I suppose many of his dearest connections to his beloved Hypothesis, he still recollects that he had once a warm place in your affections, and seems still unwilling to resign it. It is easy to see that I and my book were mentioned, merely because we afforded him an opportunity to renew a correspondence, which blind as he is and

[3] See n. 1, C to Johnson, of this date.

[4] *The Guilt and Danger of such a Nation as this!*, a sermon which Newton preached on 21 Feb. 1781, was published about this time. 'He [God] draws with infallible certainty the line of separation. He knows who are truly on his side, whose hearts are tender, and are mourning for their own sins, and the sins of the nation. And he knows and sees that too many here, have neither his fear nor his love abiding in them. You may comply with an outward form, and abstain from a meal, but you neither abstain from sin, nor desire to do so. . . . Do not think that the lip-service of a single-day will make any alteration either in your state or in your guilt' (pp. 35–6).

intoxicated with error, he still catches at with eagerness, and cannot prevail with himself to renounce. But yet how obstinate, and in appearance, how perfectly a Stranger to the convincing arguments by which his whole Edifice of Sophistry and misinterpretation has been so completely demolished. Has he never seen his Opponent in the Review? If he has, he ought at least to attempt to answer him. To treat so able and so learned a writer with neglect, is but a paultry subterfuge, and no reasonable man will ever give him credit for the sincerity of the contempt he may affect for a critic so deserving of his attention. If he has not, his behaviour is disingenuous to the last degree, and will I suppose as little serve his purpose. A champion has no right to despise his Enemy till he has faced and vanquished him. But henceforth I suppose this noisy subject will be Silent; may it rest in peace, and may none be hardy enough hereafter to disturb its Ashes.

Many thanks for a Barrel of Oysters which we are still eating—Nanny Puttenham desires me to send her duty, she is brought to bed, and enjoys a more comfortable frame of mind.[5] The Letter from Mr. Old ought to have waited on you with my last, but was forgot. Our best Love attends yourself and Mrs. Newton.

Yours my dear Sir, as Ever,
Wm Cowper.

Nove. 27. 1781.

JOSEPH HILL — Friday, 30 November 1781

Cowper Johnson

My dear Friend,

Though I have a deal of Wit and Mrs. Unwin has much more, it would require more than our Joint Stock amounts to, to Answer all the Demands of these gloomy Days and long Evenings. Books are the only Remedy I can think of, but Books are a Commodity we deal but little in at Olney. If therefore it may consist with your other Various

[5] The difficulties which Nanny Puttenham experienced were probably associated with the birth of a child. William, the son of Richard and Ann Puttenham, was baptized on 7 Dec. 1781 (*O.P.R.*, p. 398). Anne Gough married Richard Putmam [*sic*] on 17 Oct. 1771 (*O.P.R.*, p. 364).

Multifarious Concerns, I shall be obliged to you if you will be so good as to Subscribe for me to some well furnished Circulating Library, to leave my Address upon the Counter, written in a Legible Hand, and Order them to send me down a Catalogue.[1] Their Address you will be so good as to transmitt to me, and then you shall have no further Trouble.

This being merely a Letter of Business I add no more but that I am Yours

Wm Cowper.

Nove. 30. 1781.

JOSEPH HILL — Sunday, 2 December 1781

Cowper Johnson

My dear friend,

I thank you for the note. There is some advantage in having a tenant who is irregular in his payments. The longer the Rent is witheld, the more considerable the Sum when it arrives, to which we may add, that its arrival being unexpected, a circumstance that obtains always in a degree exactly proportioned to the badness of the Tenant, is always sure to be the occasion of an agreeable surprize, a sensation that deserves to be rank'd among the pleasantest that belong to us.[1]—I gave 250 for the Chambers. Mr. Ashurst's receipt, and the receipt of the person of whom he purchased, are both among my papers, and when wanted, as I suppose they will be in case of a Sale, shall be forthcoming at your order.[2]—The conquest of America seems to go on but slowly; our ill success in that quarter will oblige me to suppress two pieces that I was rather proud of.[3] They were written 2 or 3 years ago, not long after the double repulse sustained

[1] C had earlier been a subscriber to Bell's circulating library through Hill. See C to Hill, 10 Dec. 1780.

---

[1] Probably the Mr. Morgan mentioned in C's letters to Hill of 27 May 1777 (see n. 1) and 3 Oct. 1781.

[2] C purchased the chambers of William Henry Ashurst (1725–1807) for £250 on 17 June 1757. Ashurst, later Sir William, was Judge of the King's Bench.

[3] The two pieces C suppressed are 'A Present for the Queen of France' (see *Ryskamp*, pp. 238–9) and 'To Sir Joshua Reynolds' (see the opening paragraph of C to Newton, 4 Dec.).

by Mr. d'Estaing at Lucia and at Savannah, and when our operations in the Western world wore a more promising aspect.[4] Presuming upon such premisses that I might venture to prophecy an illustrious consummation of the war, I did so; but my predictions proving false, the verse in which they were expressed must perish with them.

I am truely sorry that you are an invalid. I have formerly been a sufferer in the same way; you may remember that when we were at Weymouth a fit of that sort sunk me into the decrepitude of old age at once without the least ceremony or warning. But since I have lived altogether in the country I have been seldom visited with that burthensome disorder. Half an Ounce of Syrup of marsh mallows[5] in a glass of Madeira, if you have no fever, taken just before you go to bed, is one of the best remedies for it in the world.

Since I began to write I have searched all the papers I have, and cannot find the Receipts abovementioned—I hope however they are not essential to the validity of the transaction.

Yours my dear Sir Wm Cowper.

My best respects to Mrs. Hill.

Olney Decr. 2. 1781

Received of Mr. Hill the Sum of fifty pounds by Draft on Child and Co.

50.0.0 Wm Cowper.

JOHN NEWTON Tuesday, 4 December 1781

Princeton

My dear friend,

The present to the Queen of France, and the piece addressed to Sir Joshua Reynolds, my only two political efforts, being of the predictive kind, and both falsified or likely to be so, by the Miscarriage of the royal cause in America, were already condemned when

[4] A reference to the two defeats suffered at St. Lucia (Dec. 1778) and Savannah (Oct. 1779) by the French admiral, Charles Hector, Comte d'Estaing (1729–94).

[5] Marshmallow root is a 'demulcent, and is used in decoction, syrup, pill, and lozenge, in inflammation and irritation of the bronchial and other mucous membranes': *The New Sydenham Society's Lexicon of Medicine and the Allied Sciences* (1881).

I received your last.[1] I have a poetical Epistle which I wrote last Summer, and another poem not yet finished, in Stanzas,[2] with which I mean to supply their places. Henceforth I have done with Politics; the stage of national affairs is such a fluctuating scene that an event which appears probable to day, becomes impossible to morrow, and unless a man were indeed a prophet, he cannot but with the greatest hazard of losing his labour, bestow his rhimes upon future contingencies which perhaps are never to take place but in his own wishes and in the reveries of his own fancy. I learn'd when I was a Boy, being the Son of a staunch Whig and a man that loved his country, to glow with that patriotic Enthusiasm which is apt to break forth into poetry, or at least to prompt a person if he has any inclination that way, to poetical endeavors. Prior's pieces of that sort were recommended to my particular notice, and as that part of the present Century was a season when Clubs of a political character and consequently political songs were much in fashion, the best in that stile, some written by Rowe and I think some by Congreve, and many by other wits of the day, were proposed to my admiration.[3] Being grown up, I became desirous of imitating such bright examples, and while I lived in the Temple, produced several halfpenny ballads, 2 or three of which had the honor to be popular.[4] What we learn in childhood we retain long, and the successes we met with about three years ago when d'Estaing was twice repulsed, once in America and once in the West Indies, having set fire to my patriotic Zeal once more, it discovered itself by the same symptoms, and produced effects much like those it had produced before. But unhappily, the ardor I felt upon the occasion disdaining to be confined within the bounds of fact, pushed me upon uniting the prophetical with the poetical character, and defeated its own purpose.—I am glad it did. The less there is of that sort in my book the better. It will be more consonant to your character who patronize the volume, and indeed to the constant tenour of my own thoughts upon public matters, that I should exhort

[1] See C to Hill, 2 Dec. 1781.

[2] Perhaps 'The Poet, The Oyster, and the Sensitive Plant' and 'Friendship'.

[3] Among the poems to which C is referring would be Prior's *To the Right Honorable Mr. Harley, Wounded by Guiscard* (1711) and *A Memorial against the Fortifying of the Ports of Dunkirk and Mardike* (1715); Rowe's *A Poem upon the Late Glorious Successes of Her Majesty's Arms* (1707, 1719, 1726); Congreve's *A Pindarique Ode on the Victorious Progress of Her Majesties Arms* (1706).

[4] These poems have not been found.

my country-men to repentance, than that I should flatter their pride, that vice for which perhaps they are even now so severely punished.—I subjoin the lines with which I mean to supersede the obnoxious ones in Expostulation. If it should lie fairly in your way to do it, I will beg of you to deliver them to Johnson, and at the same time to strike your pen through the offensive passage.[5] I ask it merely because it will save a frank, but not unless you can do it without inconvenience to yourself. The new paragraph consists exactly of the same number of lines with the old one, for upon this occasion I worked like a taylor when he sews a patch upon a hole in your coat, supposing it might be necessary to do so.—Upon second thoughts I will enclose the lines instead of adding them ad calcem,[6] that I may save you the trouble of a transcript.

We are glad for Mr. Barham's sake that he has been so happily disappointed. How little does the world suspect what passes in it every day! That true Religion is working the same wonders now as in the first ages of the church, that parents surrender up their children into the hands of God, to die at his own appointed moment, and by what death he pleases, without a murmur, and receive them again as if by a resurrection from the dead. The world however would be more justly chargeable with willfull blindness than it is, if all professors of the Truth exemplified its power in their conduct as conspicuously as Mr. Barham.[7]

Easterly winds and a state of confinement within our own walls, suit neither me nor Mrs. Unwin, though we are both, to use the Irish term, rather unwell than ill. The Cocoa nut though it had not a drop of liquor in it, and though the kernel came out whole, entirely detached from the shell, was an exceeding good one. Our hearts are with you—

Yours my dear friend
Wm Cowper.

Decr. 4. 1781.

Mrs. Madan is happy—she will be found ripe, fall when she may.[8] We are sorry you speak doubtfully about a spring Visit to Olney. Those doubts must not outlive the Winter.

[5] See n. 1, C. to Johnson, 27 Nov.

[6] At the foot of the page.

[7] For Barham, see n. 4, C to Newton, 21 Jan. 1781.

[8] Mrs. Madan died three days later, on 7 Dec.

JOSEPH JOHNSON between Tuesday, 4 December and Monday, 17 December 1781[1]

Southey, xv. 110

Sir,

I always ascribe your silence to the cause you assign for it yourself. I enclose *Friendship*, in hopes that it may arrive in time to stand the foremost of the smaller pieces, instead of *Ætna*, which, perhaps, had better be placed at the end. Such a length of the *penseroso* will make the *allegro* doubly welcome; but if the press has gone forward and begun *Ætna*, it is of no great importance: otherwise I should prefer this arrangement, as we shall then begin and end with a compliment to the King—who (poor man) may at this time be glad of such a tribute.[2]

Instead of the fifth line in the supplemental passage you have received, in which the word *disgrace* is inadvertently repeated, being mentioned in the first, I would wish you to insert the following—

'When sin has shed dishonour on thy brow.'[3]

But if the passage is already printed I can make the alteration myself when the sheet comes down for the last revisal.

P. 288.—'because they must.'[4]

I suppose you scored these words as of an import too similar to the word *convenience*, I have therefore relieved the objection by the word *self-impoverished*; otherwise it does not appear to me that the expression is objectionable: it is plain, indeed, but not bald.

I am Sir,
Your most obedient servant,
Wm. Cowper.

[1] The date must be after 4 Dec. when 'Friendship' is first mentioned, and before 17 Dec. because on that day C was expecting the proof of 'Friendship' by the next post (see C to Newton, 17 Dec.).

[2] 'Friendship' ultimately appeared in *Poems . . . of Madame de la Mothe Guion* (Newport Pagnell, 1801). 'Heroism' ('There was a time when Ætna's silent fire') appeared in *1782* on page 357, the third to last poem in the volume.

[3] Line 390 of 'Expostulation' reads, 'Hast thou, when heav'n has cloath'd thee with disgrace', and line 394 ('When sin had shed dishonour on thy brow') must have originally read 'disgrace' rather than dishonour'.

[4] 'Retirement,' 608.

JOSEPH HILL — Sunday, 9 December 1781

Address: Mr. Joseph Hill / Chancery Office / London.
Postmarks: 10/DE *and* OULNEY
Cowper Johnson

My dear friend,

Having returned you many thanks for the fine Cod and oysters you favour'd me with, though it is now morning, I will suppose it afternoon, that you and I dined together, are comfortably situated by a good fire, and just entering on a sociable conversation.—You speak first, because I am a man of few words.

Well Cowper—what do you think of this American war?

I—To say the truth I am not very fond of thinking about it; when I do, I think of it unpleasantly enough. I think it bids fair to be the ruin of this Country.

You—That's very unpleasant indeed—if that should be the consequence, it will be the fault of those who might put a stop to it if they would.

I—But do you really think that practicable?

You—Why not? If people leave off fighting, peace follows of course. I wish they would withdraw the forces and put an end to the squabble.

Now I am going to make a long speech.

I—You know the complexion of my sentiments upon some subjects well enough, and that I do not look upon public events either as fortuitous, or absolutely derivable either from the Wisdom or Folly of man. These indeed operate as second causes, but we must look for the cause of the decline or the prosperity of an Empire elsewhere. I have long since done with complaining of men and measures; having learn'd to consider them merely as the instruments of a higher power, by which he either bestows wealth, peace and dignity upon a nation when he favours it, or by which he strips it of all those honours, when public enormities long persisted in provoke him to inflict a public punishment. The Counsels of great men become as foolish and preposterous, when he is pleased to make them so, as those of two frantic creatures in Bedlam when they lay their distracted heads together to consider of the state of the nation. But I go still farther.—The Wisdom or the want of Wisdom that we observe, or think we observe in those that rule us, entirely out of the question, I cannot

look upon the circumstances of this country, without being persuaded that I discern in them an embranglement and perplexity that I have never met with in the History of any other, which I think preternatural if I may use the word on such a subject, prodigious in its kind, and such as human sagacity can never remedy. I have a good Opinion of the understanding and Integrity of some in power, yet I see plainly that they are unequal to the task—I think as favorably of some that are not in power—yet I am sure they have never yet in any of their speeches recommended the plan that would effect the salutary purpose. If we pursue the war, it is because we are desperate; it is plunging and sinking year after year into still greater depths of calamity. If we relinquish it, the remedy is equally desperate, and would prove, I beleive, in the end no remedy at all. Either way we are undone—perseverance will only enfeeble us more, we cannot recover the Colonies by arms. If we discontinue the attempt, in that case we fling away voluntarily, what in the other we strive ineffectually to regain, and whether we adopt the one measure or the other, are equally undone. For I consider the loss of America as the ruin of England; were we less incumber'd than we are, at home, we could but ill afford it, but being crushed as we are under an enormous debt that the public credit can at no rate carry much longer, the consequence is sure. Thus it appears to me that we are squeezed to death between the two sides of that sort of alternative, which is commonly called a cleft stick, the most threat'ning and portentous condition in which the interests of any country can possibly be found.—I think I have done pretty well for a man of few words, and have contrived to have all the talk to myself.—I thank you for not interrupting me.

Yours my dear friend
Wm Cowper.

Decr. 9. 1781.

WILLIAM UNWIN Saturday, 15 December 1781

British Library

My dear William,

The Salmon and Lobsters arrived safe and were remarkably fine. We knew the reason why you sent no prawns before you mentioned it. Accept our thanks for the welcome present.

I dare say I do not enter exactly into your Idea of a present Theocracy, because mine amounts to no more than the common one; that all mankind, though few are really aware of it, act under a providential direction, and that a gracious superintendence in particular, is the lot of those who trust in God. Thus I think respecting individuals. And with respect to the Kingdoms of the earth, that perhaps by his own immediate operation, though more probably by the intervention of angels, (vide Daniel)[1] the great Governor manages and rules them, assigns them their origin, duration, and end, appoints them prosperity or adversity, glory or disgrace, as their virtues or their vices, their regard to the dictates of conscience and his word, or their prevailing neglect of both, may indicate and require. But in this persuasion, as I said, I do not at all deviate from the general Opinion of those who beleive a Providence, at least who have a scriptural belief of it. I suppose therefore you mean something more, and shall be glad to be more particularly informed.

I am glad (we are both so) that you are not afraid of seeing your own image multiplied too fast. It is not necessarily a disadvantage. It is sometimes easier to manage and provide for half a dozen children, than to regulate the passions and satisfy the extravagant demands of one. I remember hearing Moses Brown say that when he had only 2 or 3 children he thought he should have been distracted, but when he had 10 or a dozen he was perfectly easy, and thought no more about the matter.—Mrs. Unwin is not singular in her distress, but we do not sympathize the less with her for that reason. A Lady in our neighborhood, whom I beleive I have mentioned before upon a like occasion is tormented with apprehensions upon the same account, sometimes almost to a frenzy. She is lately brought to bed however,and has had a very favourable passage through the scene she so much dreaded.[2]

I see but one feature in the face of our national concerns that

[1] Daniel 6: 22.

[2] Probably Nanny Puttenham. See n. 5, C to Newton, 27 Nov. 1781.

pleases me—the war with America it seems is to be conducted on a different plan.[3] This is something. When a long series of measures of a certain description has proved unsuccessfull, the adoption of others is at least pleasing, as it encourages a hope that they may possibly prove wiser and more effectual. But indeed without discipline, all is lost; Pitt himself could have done nothing with such tools. But he would not have been so betrayed—he would have made the traytors answer with their heads for their cowardice or supineness, and their punishment would have made survivors active.

I send you on the other side some lines I addressed last Summer to a Lady in France, a particular friend of Lady Austen, a person much afflicted, but of great piety, and patience—a Protestant.—They are not for publication and therefore I send them.[4]

Madam—
   A stranger's purpose in these lays
Is to congratulate, and not to praise.
To give the creature her creator's due,
Were Sin in me, and an offence to you;
By Man to Man, or ev'n to Woman paid,
Praise is the medium of a knavish trade,
A coin by craft for folly's use design'd,
Spurious, and only current with the blind.
   The path of sorrow, and that path alone,
Leads to the land where sorrow is unknown.
No trav'ler ever reach'd that blest abode,
That found not thorns and briars in his road.
The world may dance along the flow'ry plain,
Cheered as they go, by many a sprightly strain,
Where Nature has her mossy velvet spread,
With unshod feet they yet securely tread,

[3] *The London Chronicle*, Saturday–Tuesday, 8–11 Dec. 1781 (No. 3905): 'The arrival of Lord Cornwallis, and the field officers of his unfortunate army, is hourly expected. . . . The American war, it is said, will be pursued on our part with the utmost vigour, and to facilitate this system, it is reported, overtures have been sent to Russia for 40,000 troops and a naval reinforcement. . . .'

[4] The poem was ultimately published in *The Theological Miscellany; and Review of Books on Religious Subjects*, edited by the Revd. C. de Coetlogon, vi (July 1789), 332–4, as part of a correspondence between *Aspasia* (Lady Austen) and *Clara* (Mme Jane Billacoys), edited by the Revd. Samuel Greatheed. Madame Billacoys, formerly Lady Austen's waiting-woman Jane Saunders, practised Evangelicalism in secret after her marriage to an inhabitant of Sancerre. See K. Povey, 'Cowper and Lady Austen', *R.E.S.* x (1934), 412–27.

Admonish'd, scorn the caution and the friend,
Bent upon pleasure, heedless of its end.
But He who knew what human hearts would prove,
How slow to learn the dictates of his love,
That hard by nature and of stubborn will,
A life of ease would make them harder still,
In pity to the sinners he design'd
To rescue from the ruins of mankind,
Call'd for a cloud to darken all their years,
And said, go spend them in the vale of tears.
Oh balmy gales of soul-reviving air,
Oh salutary streams that murmur there!
These flowing from the fount of grace above,
Those breathed from lips of everlasting Love,—
The flinty soil indeed their feet annoys,
And sudden sorrow nips their springing joys,
An envious world will interpose its frown
To mar delights superior to its own,
And many a pang experienced still within,
Reminds them of their hated Inmate, Sin,
But Ills of ev'ry shape and ev'ry name,
Transformed to blessings miss their cruel aim,
And ev'ry moment's calm that sooths the breast,
Is giv'n in earnest of Eternal Rest.
  Ah be not sad! although thy lot be cast
Far from the flock and in a distant waste;
No shepherds' tents within thy view appear,
But the chief shepherd is for ever near,
Thy tender sorrows and thy plaintive strain
Flow in a foreign land, but not in vain,
Thy tears all issue from a source divine,
And ev'ry drop bespeaks a Saviour thine—
'Twas thus in Gideon's fleece the dews were found,
And drought on all the drooping herbs around.[5]

Pray remember the poor this Winter.

Your humble Bellman
Wm Cowper.

Decr. 15. 1781.

[5] Judges 6: 37–40.

LADY AUSTEN Monday, 17 December 1781

Hayley, i. 116–20

Dear Anna—Between friend and friend,
Prose answers every common end;
Serves, in a plain, and homely way,
T' express th' occurrence of the day;
Our health, the weather, and the news;
What walks we take, what books we chuse;
And all the floating thoughts, we find
Upon the surface of the mind.
  But when a Poet takes the pen,
Far more alive than other men,
He feels a gentle tingling come
Down to his finger and his thumb,
Deriv'd from nature's noblest part,
The centre of a glowing heart!
And this is what the world, who knows
No flights, above the pitch of prose,
His more sublime vagaries slighting,
Denominates an itch for writing.
No wonder I, who scribble rhyme,
To catch the triflers of the time,
And tell them truths divine, and clear,
Which couch'd in prose, they will not hear;
Who labour hard to allure, and draw
The loiterers I never saw,
Should feel that itching, and that tingling,
With all my purpose intermingling,
To your intrinsic merit true,
When call'd to address myself to you.
  Mysterious are his ways, whose power
Brings forth that unexpected hour,
When minds that never met before,
Shall meet, unite, and part no more:
It is th' allotment of the skies,
The Hand of the Supremely Wise,
That guides, and governs our affections,

And plans, and orders our connexions,
Directs us in our distant road,
And marks the bounds of our abode.
Thus we were settled when you found us,
Peasants and children all around us,
Not dreaming of so dear a friend,
Deep in the abyss of Silver-End.
Thus Martha, even against her will,
Perch'd on the top of yonder hill;
And you, though you must needs prefer
The fairer scenes of sweet Sancerre,
Are come from distant Loire, to chuse
A cottage on the Banks of Ouse.
This page of Providence, quite new,
And now just opening to our view,
Employs our present thoughts and pains,
To guess, and spell, what it contains:
But day by day, and year by year,
Will make the dark ænigma clear;
And furnish us perhaps at last,
Like other scenes already past,
With proof, that we, and our affairs
Are part of a Jehovah's cares:
For God unfolds, by slow degrees,
The purport of his deep decrees;
Sheds every hour a clearer light
In aid of our defective sight;
And spreads at length, before the soul,
A beautiful, and perfect whole,
Which busy man's inventive brain
Toils to anticipate in vain.
  Say Anna, had you never known
The beauties of a Rose full blown,
Could you, tho' luminous your eye,
By looking on the bud, descry,
Or guess, with a prophetic power,
The future splendor of the flower?
Just so th' Omnipotent who turns
The system of a world's concerns,

From mere minutiæ can educe
Events of most important use;
And bid a dawning sky display
The blaze of a meridian day.
The works of man tend, one and all,
As needs they must, from great to small;
And vanity absorbs at length
The monuments of human strength.
But who can tell how vast the plan,
Which this day's incident began?
Too small perhaps the slight occasion
For our dim-sighted observation;
It pass'd unnotic'd, as the bird
That cleaves the yielding air unheard,
And yet may prove, when understood,
An harbinger of endless good.
  Not that I deem, or mean to call
Friendship a blessing cheap, or small;
But merely to remark, that ours,
Like some of nature's sweetest flowers,
Rose from a seed of tiny size,
That seem'd to promise no such prize:
A transient visit intervening,
And made almost without a meaning,
(Hardly the effect of inclination,
Much less of pleasing expectation!)
Produc'd a friendship, then begun,
That has cemented us in one;
And plac'd it in our power to prove,
By long fidelity and love,
That Solomon has wisely spoken:
'A three-fold cord is not soon broken.'[1]

[1] Ecclesiastes 4: 12.

JOHN NEWTON Monday, 17 December 1781

Princeton

My dear friend,

The poem I had in hand when I wrote last, is on the subject of Friendship. By the following post I Received a pacquet from Johnson; the proof sheet it contained brought our business down to the latter part of Retirement, the next will consequently introduce the first of the smaller pieces. The volume consisting, at least four fifths of it, of heroic verse as it is called and graver matter, I was desirous to displace the burning mountain from the post it held in the van of the light Infantry, and throw it into the rear. Having finished Friendship and fearing that if I delayed to send it, the press would get the start of my intention, and knowing perfectly that with respect to the Subject and the subject matter of it, it contained nothing that you would think exceptionable, I took the liberty to transmitt it to Johnson, and hope that the next post will return it to me printed. It consists of between 30 and 40 stanzas, a length that qualifies it to supply the place of the two cancelled pieces, without the aid of the Epistle I mentioned. According to the present arrangement therefore, Friendship which is rather of a lively cast though quite sober, will follow next after Retirement, and Ætna will close the volume. Modern Naturalists, I think, tell us that the Volcano forms the mountain; I shall be charged therefore perhaps with an unphilosophical error in supposing that Ætna was once unconscious of intestine fires and as lofty as at present, before the commencement of the eruptions. It is possible however that the rule, though just in some instances, may not be of universal application, and if it be, I do not know that a poet is obliged to write with a philosopher at his elbow, prepared always to bind down his imagination to mere matters of fact. You will oblige me by your opinion, and tell me if you please whether you think an apologetical note may be necessary, for I would not appear a dunce in matters that every Review-reader must needs be apprized of. I say a note, because an alteration of the piece is impracticable, at least without cutting off its head and setting on a new one, a task I should not readily undertake, because the lines which must in that case be thrown out, are some of the most poetical in the performance.[1]

[1] The poem was not altered. See C to Newton, 13 Jan. 1782. After more than three

Possessing greater advantages, and being equally dissolute with the most abandoned of the neighbouring nations, we are certainly more criminal than they. They *cannot* see, and we *will* not. It is to be expected therefore that when Judgment is walking through the earth, it will come commission'd with the heaviest tidings, to the people chargeable with the most perverseness. In the latter part of the Duke of Newcastle's administration, all faces gather'd blackness.[2] The people as they walked the streets, had, every one of them a countenance like what we may suppose to have been the prophet Jonah's, when he cried, yet 40 days and Nineveh shall be destroyed.[3] But our Nineveh too repented. That is to say, she was affected in a manner somewhat suitable to her condition. She was dejected; she learn'd an humbler language, and seemed, if she did not trust in God, at least to have renounced her confidence in herself. A respite ensued; the expected ruin was averted; and her prosperity became greater than ever. Again she became self-conceited and proud as at the first. And how stands it with our Nineveh now? Even as you say. Her distress is infinite, her destruction appears inevitable, and her heart as hard as the nether millstone. Thus I suppose it was when antient Nineveh found herself agreeably disappointed; she turned the grace of God into lasciviousness, and that flagrant abuse of Mercy exposed her at the expiration of 40 years to the complete execution of a sentence she had only been threat'ned with before. A similarity of events accompanied by a strong similarity of conduct, seems to justify our expectations that the catastrophe will not be very different. But after all the designs of Providence are inscrutable, and as in the case of individuals, so in that of nations, the same causes do not always produce the same effects. The Country indeed cannot be saved in its present state of profligacy and profanenness, but may nevertheless be led to Repentance by means we are little aware of, and at a time when we least expect it.

months of rumblings and earthquakes, Mount Etna had erupted violently on 18 May 1780; it should be noted that volcanoes were a matter of some interest in 1780, after Sir William Hamilton's account was published in the *Philosophical Transactions of the Royal Society*, lxx, pt. 1, 42–84.

[2] Thomas Pelham-Holles, 1st Duke of Newcastle (1693–1768), was prime minister from 1754 to 1756 and from 1757 to 1762. Newcastle resigned on 7 May 1762 because of a general lack of support of his foreign policy in the Americas. See Basil Williams, *The Whig Supremacy* (1965), p. 371.

[3] Jonah 3: 4.

In the mislaid letter I took notice of certain disagreeable doubts you had expressed in one inclosed to us and unsealed, concerning your Visit next Spring to Olney.[4] You will be so good as to send those doubts packing, and convince them that they are unreasonable intruders, by coming down as soon as your famous festival is over. We have to thank you for a barrel of Oysters, exceeding good.

Poor Mr. Whitford! We are sorry for him.[5] It is melancholy indeed at his time of life and with such a family to be obliged to seek a Settlement, with so little probability of finding one. While his spirits are supported he may make shift, but if they should fail him, as they have done once already, his condition will be deplorable indeed, and the consequences much to be dreaded by those that value him.

Our best love attends yourself and Mrs. Newton, and we rejoice that you feel no burthens but those you bear in common with the liveliest and most favor'd Christians. It is a happiness in poor Peggy's case that she can swallow five shillings worth of physick in a day, but a person must be in her case to be duely sensible of it. We hope Sally is well—pray remember us to Miss Catlett, whose holidays I suppose are begun or near at hand.

Yours my dear Sir
Wm Cowper.

Decr. 17. 81

Mrs. Unwin begs Mrs. Newton's acceptance of a couple of chickens. She would have sent a goose, but none have come our way.

James Robinson was buried on Sunday.[6] The Opinion of the well-inform'd is that his Drams cost him a guinea a week to the last.

We shall be obiged to Mrs. N. if she will get the inclosed piece of Silk Knitting dyed black.

[4] C is referring to the postscript of his letter to Newton of 4 Dec.

[5] For Whitford, see n. 1, C to Newton, 29 Oct. 1780.

[6] James Robinson of the Warrington Pew affair was buried on 16 Dec. 1781 (*O.P.R.*, p. 396).

JOHN NEWTON Friday, 21 December 1781

Princeton

My dear friend,

I might easily make this letter a continuation of my last, another national miscarriage having furnish'd me with a fresh illustration of the remarks we have both been making. Mr. Smith, who has most obligingly supplied me with franks throughout my whole concern with Johnson, accompanied the last parcel he sent me with a note dated from the House of Commons, in which he seemed happy to give me the earliest intelligence of the capture of the French transports by Admiral Kempenfelt, and of a close engagement between the two fleets so much to be expected.[1] This note was written on Monday, and reached me by Wednesday's post, but alas! the same post brought us the newspaper that informed us of his being forced to fly before a much superior enemy, and glad to take shelter in the port he had left so lately. This event I suppose will have worse consequences than the mere disappointment, will furnish Opposition as all our ill-success has done, with the fuel of dissention, and with the means of thwarting and perplexing Administration. Thus all we purchase with the many millions expended yearly, is Distress to ourselves instead of our enemies, and domestic quarrels instead of victories abroad. It takes a great many blows to knock down a great nation, and in the case of poor England a great many heavy ones have not been wanting. They make us reel and stagger indeed, but the blow is not yet struck that is to make us fall upon our knees. That fall would save us, but if we fall upon our side at last, we are undone. So much for Politics—next comes News from the North of a different complexion, which it is possible may be News to you.

Mr. Fletcher on his recovery from his late dangerous illness, has started up a Perfectionist.[2] He preached Perfection not long since at Dewsbury where Mr. Powley and his Curate heard him. He told the

[1] Richard Kempenfelt (1718–82), Rear-Admiral, who went down with the *Royal George* in 1782. C is referring to Kempenfelt's victory over the French on 12 Dec. near Ushant, and his return with captured French ships to Plymouth.

[2] John William Fletcher or De La Flechere (1729–85), the evangelical preacher and friend of the Wesleys, was vicar of Madeley, near Wellington, Shropshire (1760) and superintendent of Lady Huntingdon's College at Trevecca House in Talgarth, south-east Wales (1768–71). Fletcher resigned the latter post because of his Arminian views, which he defended in *Checks to Antinomianism* (1771).

people that He that Sinned was no Christian, that he himself did not Sin, Ergo had a right to the Appellation. Mr. Powley was so shock'd by his violent distortion of the scriptures by which he attempted to prove his doctrine, that he thought it necessary to preach expressly against him the ensuing Sabbath. And when he was desired to admitt the perfect man into his pulpit, of course refused it. I have heard that he is remarkably spiritual. Can this be? Is it possible that a person of that description can be left to indulge himself in such a proud conceit, is it possible he should be so defective in Self-knowledge, and so little acquainted with his own heart? If I had not heard you yourself speak favorably of him, I should little scruple to say, that having spent much of his Life and exerted all his talents in the defence of Arminian errors, he is at last left to fall into an error more pernicious than Arminius is to be charged with, or the most ignorant of his disciples.[3] When I hear that you are engaged in the propagation of Error, I shall beleive that an humble and dependent mind is not yet secured from it, and that the Promises which annex the blessing of Instruction to a temper teachable and truely child-like, are to be received cum grano salis, and understood with a limitation. Mr. Wesley[4] has also been very troublesome in the same place, and asserted in perfect harmony of sentiment with his brother Fletcher, that Mr. Whitfield[5] disseminated more false doctrine in the nation, than he should ever be able to eradicate. Methinks they do not see through a glass darkly[6] but for want of a glass, they see not at all.

I inclose a few lines on a thought which struck me yesterday, if you approve of them, you know what to do with them. I should think they might occupy the place of an Introduction, and shall call them by that name, if I did not judge the name I have given them necessary for the information of the reader. A flatting Mill is not met with in every street, and my book will perhaps fall into the hands of many, who do not know that such a Mill was ever invented.[7] It happen'd to me however to spend much of my time in one when I was

[3] Jacobus Arminius (1560–1609), the Dutch Reformed theologian, who denied Calvin's doctrine of irresistible grace and thus modified the strict conception of predestination.

[4] John Wesley (1703–91), the evangelist and Methodist leader.

[5] George Whitefield (1714–70), the Methodist divine. Whitefield held very rigid Calvinistic views whereas Fletcher and Wesley were Arminians.

[6] See 1 Corinthians 13: 12.

[7] C's poem 'The Flatting Mill', finally published by John Johnson in 1815, provides a description of the machine which flattens pieces of gold and silver.

a boy, when I frequently amused myself with watching the operation I describe.

Mrs. Unwin sends her love, and will be much obliged to Mrs. Newton if she will order her down a loaf of sugar from 9d to 10d the pound, for the use of my sweet self at breakfast. The sugar merchant if she will be so kind as to give him the necessary instruction will be paid by the Book keeper at the Inn.

Yours my dear Sir
Wm Cowper.

the shortest day
1781.

WILLIAM UNWIN — Saturday 22–Monday 24 December 1781[1]

Address: Revd. William Unwin[2]
British Library

My dear Friend—

I write under the Impression of a Difficulty not easily Surmounted, the Want of Something to Say. Letter:Spinning is generally more Entertaining to the Writer than the Reader, for your sake therefore I would avoid it; but a Dearth of Materials is very apt to betray one into a Trifling Strain, in spite of all one's Endeavours to be Serious.

What have you done with your perverse Parishioner? Perhaps when he has put a Lock upon his Pew, he may shut up himself in it oftener than he used to do; you remember a certain Story about the Boy & his Trunk.[3] The Consciousness that the Seat is become his own so Emphatically that he can Exclude every body else, may make him fond of it. I beleive many a Man that keeps a Carriage, Rides in it because he keeps one, tho' sometimes he would otherwise prefer a Walk.

I lay by my Paper for the Present—I really can go on no further.

[1] C had written to Unwin on Saturday, 15 Dec. He must have begun this letter on 22 Dec., and he probably posted it on 24 Dec. The allusion to the American war ('The present awfull Crisis') indicates that the letter belongs to the last part of 1781.

[2] This letter was sealed and sent; there is no further address, however, and there are no postmarks.

[3] Unidentified.

I left off Saturday, this present being Monday Morning, I renew the Attempt, in hopes that I may possibly Catch some Subject by the End, and be more Successfull.

> So have I seen the Maids in vain
> Tumble & teaze a tangled Skein,
> They Bite the Lip, they Scratch the Head,
> And cry—the deuce is in the Thread,
> They torture it & Jerk it round,
> 'Till the right End at last is found,
> Then Wind & Wind & Wind away,
> And what was Work, is changed to Play.[4]

When I wrote the 2 first Lines, I thought I had engaged in a hazardous Enterprize. For thought I, should my Poetical Vein be as dry as my Prosaic, I shall spoil the Sheet, & send Nothing at all, for I could upon no Account endure the Thought of beginning again. But I think I have succeeded to Admiration, & am willing to flatter myself that I have even seen a Worse Impromptû in the Newspaper.

Though we Live in a Nook, and the World is quite unconscious that there are any such Beings in it as ourselves, yet we are not unconcern'd about what passes in it. The present awfull Crisis, Big with the Fate of England, engages much of our Attention. The Action is probably over by this time, and tho' *We* know it not, the grand Question is decided, whether the War shall Roar in our own once peacefull Fields, or whether we shall still only hear of it at a Distance. I can compare the Nation to no Similitude more apt, than that of an Ancient Castle that had been for Days assaulted by the Battering Ram. It was long before the Stroke of that Engine made any sensible Impression, but the continual Repetition at length communicated a slight Tremor to the Wall, the next and the next & the next Blow encreased it. Another Shock puts the whole Mass in Motion, from the Top to the Foundation it bends forward, & is every Moment driven farther from the Perpendicular; 'till at last the decisive Blow is given, & down it comes. Every Million that has been raised with the last Century, has had an Effect upon the Constitution like that of a Blow from the aforesaid Ram upon the aforesaid Wall. The Impulse becomes more & more important, & the Impression it makes is continually augmented; unless therefore something Extraordinary Intervenes to

[4] First published in *Hayley*.

prevent it, you will find the Consequence, at the End of my Simile. Yours & Theirs. W.C.

JOHN NEWTON — Monday, 31 December 1781

Princeton

My dear friend,

Yesterday's post which brought me yours, brought me a pacquet from Johnson. We have reached the middle of the Mahometan Hog.[1] By the way, your lines which when we had the pleasure of seeing you here, you said you would furnish him with, are not inserted in it.[2] I did not recollect 'till after I had finished the flatting mill, that it bore any affinity to the motto taken from Caraccioli; the resemblance however did not appear to me to give any impropriety to the verses, as the thought is much enlarged upon, and enlivened by the addition of a new comparison. But if it is not wanted, it is superfluous, and if superfluous, better omitted.—I shall not bumble Johnson for finding fault with Friendship, though I have a better opinion of it myself; but a Poet is of all men the most unfit to be Judge in his own cause.[3] Partial to all his productions, he is always most partial to the youngest. But as there is a Sufficient quantity without it, let that sleep too. If I should live to write again, I may possibly take up that subject a second time, and cloath it in a different dress. It abounds with excellent matter, and much more than I could find room for in 2 or 3 pages.

I consider England and America as once one country. They were so in respect of interest, intercourse, and affinity. A great earthquake has made a partition, and now the Atlantic Ocean flows between them. He that can drain that Ocean, and shove the two shores together so as to make them aptly coincide and meet each other in

[1] 'The Love of the World Reproved; or, Hypocrisy Detected' had been published in the *Leeds Mercury* of 9 Nov. 1779 as 'The Tale of the Mohometan Hog, Evincing the manifest Deception of the modern Christian World' and in the Sept. 1780 *G.M.* before its appearance in *1782*.

[2] Lines 9–14 by Newton, which had appeared in the *Leeds Mercury* and *G.M.*, were inserted in proof in *1782*.

[3] See n. 2, C to Johnson, *c.* 4–17 Dec. 1781.

every part, can unite them again; but this is a work for Omnipotence, and nothing less than Omnipotence can heal the breach between us. This dispensation is evidently a scourge to England. But is it a blessing to America? Time may prove it one, but at present it does not seem to wear an aspect favorable to their privileges either civil or religious. I cannot doubt the truth of Dr. W.'s[4] assertion; but the French who pay but little regard to treaties that clash with their convenience, without a treaty, and even in direct contradiction to verbal engagements, can easily pretend a claim to a country which they have both bled and paid for; and if the validity of that claim be disputed, behold an army ready-landed and well appointed, and in possession of some of the most fruitfull provinces, prepared to prove it. A scourge is a scourge at one end only. A bundle of thunderbolts such as you have seen in the talons of Jupiter's Eagle, is at both ends equally tremendous, and can inflict a judgment upon the West, at the same moment that it seems to intend only the chastisement of the East.

In my last letter, in which I desired your Opinion of Ætna, whether its poetical merits might not atone for its philosophical defects, I begg'd the favour of Mrs. Newton to get the silk knitting dyed black.[5] Mrs. Unwin will take care of the Hams, but the Pig is not likely to bequeath them yet. She is sorry that Mrs. N— has bespoke them, having one in cure for her at this time. Is very much disappointed that she cannot procure a Goose, but has a couple of very fine fowls, which wait your orders, and will be sent at whatever time you shall appoint. She will be glad of a loaf of Sugar, the Grocer to be paid at the Inn.

I should have sent you a longer letter, but a Visitor who is more tedious than entertaining has rather disconcerted me and exhausted my spirits.[6] 'Your humble Servant Sir—I hope I see you well—I thank you Madam, but indifferent. I have had a violent cholic, which providentially took a turn downwards, or I think I must have died. 7 or 8 times in a night Madam. My neighbor Banister has the same disorder, and is remarkably costive, so that I verily fear for his life.[7] Yes truely, I think the poor man cannot get over it.' This is a small

[4] Unidentified.

[5] The letter referred to is C's of 17 Dec., not 21 Dec.

[6] Samuel Teedon.

[7] Probably William Bannister who was buried on 2 Mar. 1782 (*O.P.R.*, p. 397).

specimen—how should you like the whole? I can send you a sheet full of the like whenever you please, taken faithfully from his lips.

Our joint love attends you both. We rejoice to hear that Mrs. Newton is better. Yours my dear Sir

Wm Cowper.

the last day of 81.

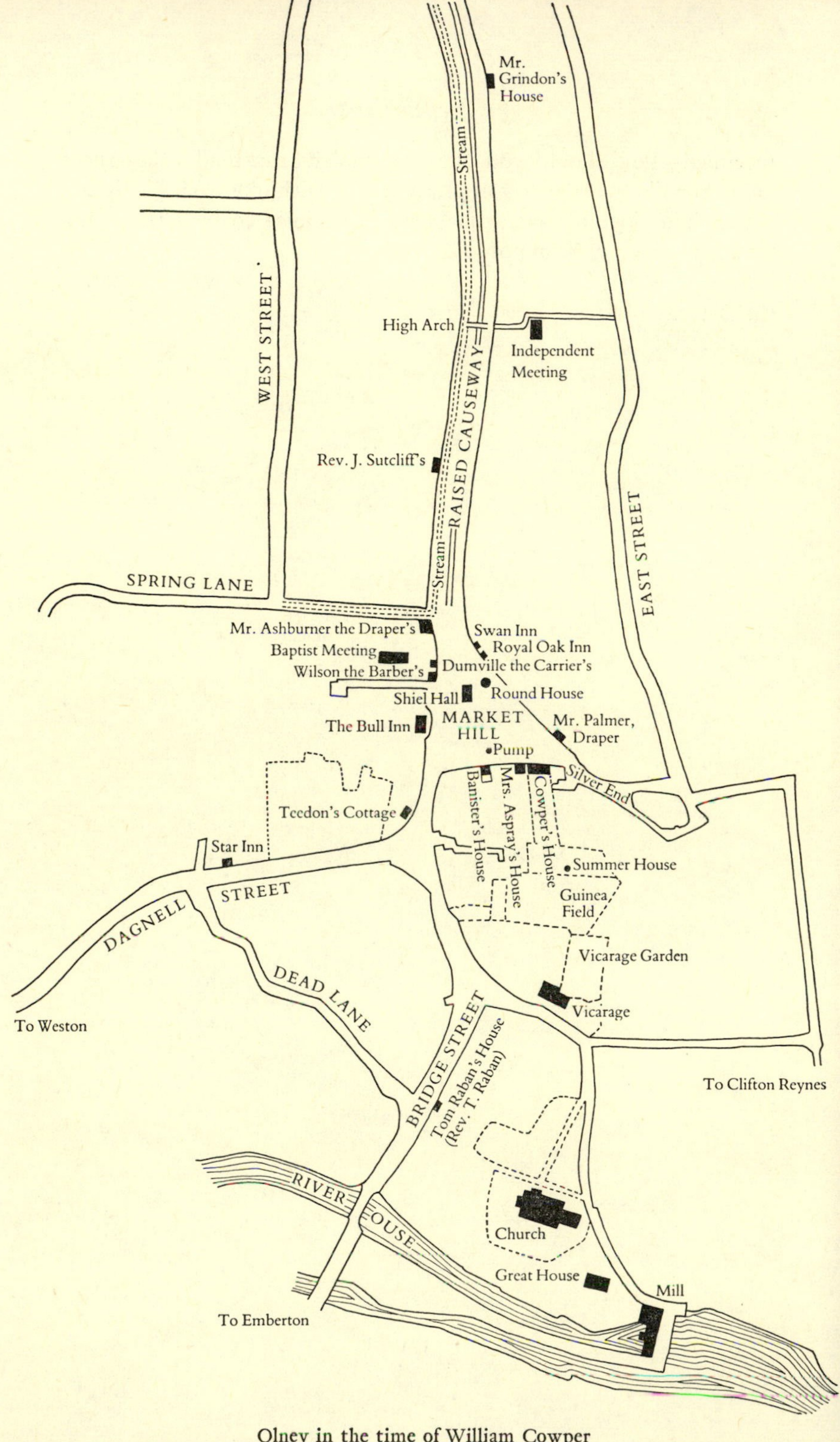

Olney in the time of William Cowper

Map of environs of Olney

MISSING LETTERS

In this list, we have provided details of missing letters which Cowper mentions having written and transmitted or whose existence we know of from external evidence. It is likely that Cowper had an extensive correspondence with his brother, John, although not one letter to him survives. It is also likely that Cowper wrote to Theadora Cowper. At this point, we can provide information on the following.

Date	*Recipient*

c. December 1763 — John Cowper

Adelphi: 'At this time [after the suicide attempt in 1763] I wrote to my brother at Cambridge to inform him of the distress I had been in ...'

c. August 1764 — John Cowper

Adelphi: 'As soon as it pleased God... to visit me with the consolations of His Grace, it became one of my chief concerns that my relations might be partakers of the same mercy. In the first letter I wrote to my brother ...'

pre 25 October 1765 — Eamonson

Cowper to Hill, 25 October 1765: 'I have wrote to Eamonson ...'

c. April 1766 — Nathaniel Cotton

Cowper to Hill, 3 April 1766: 'I Correspond with the little Man [Cotton] because I Love him... I should be glad if my Uncle can find Leisure, and it be not contrary to Act of Parliament, if he will be so good as to furnish me with half a Dozen Franks to Dr. Cotton ...'

post 1767 — Elizabeth Charlotte Cowper, afterwards Lady Croft

Lady Hesketh to William Hayley, 8 October 1803 (Add. MS.30803B, f. 144r): 'She [Lady Croft] had not however any letters from him in his youthful days, nor *any* 'till after his retirement at Olney; and they were (I have reason to think) on *Serious* Subjects ...'

Date	*Recipient*

c. 1768 Lady Hesketh

Cowper to Mrs. Madan, 18 June [1768]: 'I know not by what means Lady Hesketh heard that there was such a thing in the World as my Narrative; but the News of it having reached her, she wrote to me to beg a Sight of it. At first I was very unwilling to shew it to her, but having consulted with Mr. Newton about the Propriety of doing so ... I consented; but restrained it absolutely to her own Perusal ...'

February 1770 Ashley Cowper

Cowper to Hill, 4 March 1770: 'I wish I could tell you that my Brother is better... he is much in the same State as when I wrote to my Uncle ...' There are probably a substantial number of missing letters to Ashley.

21 February 1771 John Newton

A letter of this date is mentioned in Newton's letter to Cowper of 27 February 1771 (Princeton).

28 February 1771 John Newton

A letter of this date is mentioned in Newton's letter to Cowper of 2 March 1771 (Princeton).

24 December 1778 Joseph Hill

This letter, described as an A.L.S. with a perfect seal, was offered for sale in the Puttick and Simpson catalogue, 29 July–2 August 1861 (lot 379). This catalogue, which is devoted to the manuscripts and autograph letters belonging to Robert Cole, describes the letter thus: 'Thanks Mrs. Hill for the garden seeds, but has nothing of the sort in his garden worth her notice, or that she is not already furnished with.'

c. March 1780 Robert (?)

In his letter to Mrs. Newton of 4 March, Cowper mentions that he has written Robert a 'long Letter a day or two after the Receipt of yours' (presumably the letter he is in the process of answering). The context of the letter to Mrs. Newton would seem to indicate that Robert is a servant in the Newton household.

Date	*Recipient*

6 May 1780 John Newton

C. E. Lamb list. This is a list made by C. E. Lamb which was attached to the Ring copies, now at Princeton. In his list, Lamb enumerates some Cowper to Newton letters whose existence is now known only through his compilation.

18 May 1780 John Newton

C. E. Lamb list.

25 June 1780 John Newton

C. E. Lamb list.

c. 18 July 1780 John Newton

There is a 'Letter . . . from dear Mr. Cowper' mentioned in Newton's letter to Mrs. Unwin of 19 July 1780 (Princeton), and from the context of Newton's letter the missing letter to Newton would have been written about the 18th of July.

c. 30 October 1780 William Unwin

A manuscript of 'The Yearly Distress, Or, Tything Time at Stock' (British Library) is postmarked '30 OC', and 1780 is the appropriate year of composition of this poem. A letter from Cowper to Unwin of this date almost surely accompanied the poem.

28 May 1781 Joseph Johnson

This missing letter was enclosed with Cowper's to Newton of this date and is mentioned in the text and postscript to that letter: '. . . I enclose a Line to Johnson, to tell him that if in the mean time, and while you are absent from Town, another parcel of the proof should be ready for revisal, I wish him to send it hither by the Diligence.'

LIST OF LETTERS

List of Letters

List of Letters

INDEX

British nobility are listed under titles with cross-references to family names.

Women are listed under their married names with cross-references to maiden names.

Incidental references in the text to important friends and acquaintances are not cited.